Oxford Studies in Philosophy of Mind

Oxford Studies in Philosophy of Mind

Volume 4

Edited by
URIAH KRIEGEL

OXFORD
UNIVERSITY PRESS

Great Clarendon Street, Oxford, OX2 6DP,
United Kingdom

Oxford University Press is a department of the University of Oxford.
It furthers the University's objective of excellence in research, scholarship,
and education by publishing worldwide. Oxford is a registered trade mark of
Oxford University Press in the UK and in certain other countries

Published in the United States of America by Oxford University Press
198 Madison Avenue, New York, NY 10016, United States of America

British Library Cataloguing in Publication Data
Data available

Library of Congress Control Number: 2022952227

ISBN 978-0-19-892412-8

DOI: 10.1093/9780198924159.001.0001

Printed and bound by
CPI Group (UK) Ltd, Croydon, CR0 4YY

Links to third party websites are provided by Oxford in good faith and
for information only. Oxford disclaims any responsibility for the materials
contained in any third party website referenced in this work.

Contents

Preface   vii
List of Contributors   xi

PART I. TWENTY-FIRST-CENTURY IDEALISM

1. Is Universal Consciousness Fit for Ground?   3
   Miri Albahari

2. Modal Idealism   46
   David Builes

3. Idealism and the Interface Theory   108
   Geoffrey Lee

4. Idealism and the Best of All (Subjectively Indistinguishable)
   Possible Worlds   144
   Helen Yetter-Chappell

PART II. ACQUAINTANCE AND PERCEPTION

5. The Sense-Data Language and External World Skepticism   175
   Jared Warren

6. Naïve Realism, Incorporeal Objects, and the Time-lag
   Argument   231
   William Fish

7. Relationalism, Acquaintance, and Subjectivity: Some
   Metaphysical Implications   251
   Dorothea Debus

8. I Feel Your Pain: Acquaintance and the Limits of Empathy   277
   Emad H. Atiq and Matt Duncan

PART III. ACQUAINTANCE AND CONSCIOUSNESS

9. Inferential Seemings   311
   Elijah Chudnoff

10. Inner Acquaintance Theories of Consciousness 334
Anna Giustina

11. Revelation and the Appearance/Reality Distinction 380
Michelle Liu

12. The Conscious Theory of Higher-Orderness 414
Nicholas Silins

PART IV. BOOK SYMPOSIUM ON DAVID
CHALMERS' *REALITY*+

13. Précis of *Reality*+ 441
David J. Chalmers

14. The Simulation Hypothesis, Social Knowledge,
and a Meaningful Life 447
Grace Helton

15. Why Virtual Worlds Aren't Real: How Phenomenal
Intentionality Constrains Mental Reference 461
Terry Horgan

16. Simulation: Its Metaphysics and Epistemology 483
Christopher Peacocke

17. The Simulation Hypothesis: Metaphysics, Epistemology, Value 498
David J. Chalmers

PART V. HISTORY OF PHILOSOPHY
OF MIND: ARISTOTLE

18. Aristotle on *Thumos* 517
Patricia Marechal

Index 542

Preface

The core of this fourth volume of *Oxford Studies in Philosophy of Mind* is a group of twelve articles surrounding acquaintance, consciousness, perception, and idealism, divided somewhat arbitrarily into three clusters. The volume features also a symposium on David Chalmers' book *Reality+* and a historical paper on Aristotle's philosophy of mind.

Part I is dedicated to "21st-century idealism." It opens with a lengthy article by Miri Albahari defending what she has elsewhere called "perennial idealism": a metaphysical position that recurs in various mystical traditions, according to which observer-independent, theory-independent reality consists in a single "consciousness soup" (not Albahari's term!)—a single, undifferentiated, universal consciousness, from which the appearances of individual material objects, as well as individual conscious selves, emanate or flow. In her article, Albahari identifies what she considers the four main sources of resistance to perennial idealism and defends it against them. Chapter 2, by David Builes, develops a positive case for what Builes calls "modal idealism": the view that it is a *necessary, a priori* truth that all the properties at the fundamental level of reality are phenomenal properties. The case consists in three core arguments plus a battery of plausibility considerations amounting to a "serviceability argument" for modal idealism. The first two arguments are perhaps the most important, and both flow essentially from a single principle, namely, that there are no brute necessities. Builes attempts to show that when this principle is combined with certain other considerations, it generates a case for modal idealism. Chapter 3, by Geoffrey Lee, is a thorough examination of a form of idealism, or at least antirealism, that has seen much discussion among scientists and educated laypersons but has as yet not received a serious treatment in the hands of philosophers. This is the "interface theory" of Donald Hoffman and colleagues, which Lee analyzes as growing out of two ideas: the structural opacity thesis, according to which the structure of the external world as presented by perception does not match its objective structure, and the irreversibility thesis, according to which the cognitive system has no means to "unscramble" the way perceptual experience distorts the objective structure of reality. Chapter 4, by Helen Yetter-Chappell, starts from the fact that many possible metaphysics are consistent with everything that is given to us in experience, each corresponding to a (or *some*) possible world(s) in which that metaphysics is true. It then highlights ways in which worlds where the correct metaphysics is idealist are more attractive than subjectively indistinguishable worlds in which a non-idealist metaphysics is correct—notably insofar as in such worlds our perceptual experience would be "Edenic" in that it would present the intrinsic natures of sensible qualities exactly as they are.

Part II of the volume concerns the role of acquaintance in perception. In modern analytic philosophy, the idea of acquaintance comes to us from Russell's epistemology, with its focus on foundational knowledge-by-acquaintance of sense data, from which empirical propositional knowledge of the external world is abductively inferred. This outlook is widely rejected today, in large part because of ontological scruples about sense data themselves. The first chapter of Part II, by Jared Warren, defends ontological commitment to sense data by using the Putnam-Hirsch idea of quantifier variance: the notion that the existential quantifier is used in different senses within different ontological frameworks. Warren's thought is that we can define an existential quantifier such that traditional claims to the effect that there are sense data we are acquainted with will come out true when framed in terms of it (a crucial rule for the use of this quantifier is that from "there appears to be a green dot" we can derive "there is an appearance of a green dot"). The next two chapters concern the role of acquaintance in naïve realism, which is sometimes framed as the thesis that the perceptual relation between subject and object is an acquaintance rather than representational relation. In Chapter 6, Bill Fish defends naïve realism against the objection that the simultaneity of the subject and object of acquaintance is inconsistent with the existence of a time lag between some perceptual experiences and the objects they're directed at. For instance, we see the sun not as it is now, but as it was eight minutes ago, because that's the time it takes for light to travel from the sun to us. Fish's response involves an ontological distinction between material objects and certain associated objects—the light sources the material objects "sustain" or "give rise to"—such that (i) the light sources are simultaneous with the perceptual experiences and (ii) the light sources are what we *really* perceive in perceptual experience. In Chapter 7, Dorothea Debus argues that naïve realism is committed to a nonreductive account of perception. The reason is that the acquaintance relation it posits between subjects and objects of perception is irreducible to the underlying causal relations that mediate between the two. Chapter 8, the final chapter in Part II, co-authored by Emad H. Atiq and Matt Duncan, develops an account of empathy as a kind of perception-like acquaintance with the mental states of others. They also argue for a variety of epistemic and moral benefits in the practice of empathy so understood.

Part III of the volume focuses on the role of such notions as acquaintance, revelation, and seeming in our understanding of phenomenal consciousness. It opens, in Chapter 9, with an article by Elijah Chudnoff on the phenomenon of "inferential seeming": it phenomenally seeming to one that one is inferring some proposition from others. After arguing against some extant approaches to this phenomenon, Chudnoff presents a model on which an inferential seeming consists in a kind of mental declarative that is indirectly used as an imperative. Just as the declarative "It would be nice if you brought pizza to the party" implies the imperative "Please bring a pizza to the party!," an inferential seeming of q following from p and $p \rightarrow q$ implies the imperative "Adopt the belief that q on the basis of the beliefs that p and that $p \rightarrow q$!." Chapter 10, by Anna Giustina, explores an alternative to higher-order and self-representational theories of consciousness that would be structurally very similar but appeal to acquaintance instead of representation. After pointing out a number of advantages that such higher-order acquaintance and self-acquaintance accounts might have, Giustina explores the main decision points that proponents of such approaches would face, in particular concerning the nature of the two relata of the acquaintance relation and of the relation between them. Chapter 11, by Michelle Liu, digs into the notion that there is "no appearance/reality gap" for consciousness, seeking an explication of this notion that could sustain the antiphysicalist purposes with which it is sometimes advanced. Without pretending to settle the question, Liu identifies a particular reading of the "no appearance/reality gap" thesis, closely associated with a specific notion of revelation, that she thinks does pose a genuine and significant challenge to physicalism. In the final chapter of this part, Chapter 12, Nicholas Silins presents a novel position on the relationship between phenomenal consciousness and our alleged inner awareness of our phenomenally conscious states. Debates in this area have tended to focus on two main views: one claims that even if we sometimes enjoy inner awareness of our conscious states, this is by no means a universal, let alone necessary, feature of our conscious life; the other claims that such inner awareness is not only necessary but constitutive of what makes our conscious states such. Silins argues instead that while phenomenal consciousness and inner awareness do necessarily go together, the order of explanation for this goes from phenomenal consciousness to inner awareness rather than the other way round: it is because a mental state is phenomenal that it is the object of inner awareness, not because it is the object of inner awareness that it is phenomenal.

The volume closes with a book symposium on David Chalmers' recent book *Reality+* (Part IV) and our customary section on the history of philosophy of mind (Part V). Chalmers' book revolves around three main theses. The first is metaphysical: that the objects and events in a virtual reality are just as real as the tables and chairs in ordinary reality, and are simply otherwise constituted or "realized." The second is epistemological: that we don't actually know that we don't live in a virtual reality. The third is ethical: that it is possible to live a good, meaningful life inside a virtual reality. The third of these theses is the topic of Grace Helton's commentary, while Terry Horgan and Christopher Peacocke target mainly the first thesis.

The final chapter in the volume, Chapter 18, by Patricia Marechal, discusses Aristotle's notion of *thumos* (roughly: drive or impulse, something akin to Spinoza's *conatus*). In it, Marechal presents, an interpretation of *thumos* as a kind of second-order motivation: a motivation to act on first-order motivation, so as to transition from mere motivation to actual action.

Volume 5 of *Oxford Studies in Philosophy of Mind* will focus on the philosophical psychology of the reactive attitudes and on points of contact between philosophy of mind and epistemology, as well as philosophy of mind in the history of Asian Philosophy.

List of Contributors

Editor

Uriah Kriegel is Professor of Philosophy, Rice University, USA.

Contributors

Miri Albahari is Senior Lecturer in Philosophy, University of Western Australia, Perth, Australia.

Emad H. Atiq is Professor of Law & Philosophy, Cornell University, Ithaca, NY, USA.

David Builes is Assistant Professor of Philosophy, Princeton University, NJ, USA.

David J. Chalmers is University Professor of Philosophy and Neural Science, New York University, New York, NY, USA.

Elijah Chudnoff is Professor of Philosophy, University of Miami, Coral Gables, FL, USA.

Dorothea Debus is Professor of Philosophy, Department of Philosophy, University of Konstanz, Konstanz, Germany.

Matt Duncan is Professor of Philosophy, Rhode Island College, Providence, RI, USA.

William Fish is Professor of Philosophy, Massey University, New Zealand.

Anna Giustina is Assistant professor (Ramon y Cajal fellow), Philosophy Department, University of Valencia, Spain.

Grace Helton is Assistant Professor, Philosophy Department, Princeton University, Princeton, NJ, USA.

Terry Horgan is Emeritus Professor of Philosophy, University of Arizona, USA.

Geoffrey Lee is Associate Professor of Philosophy, UC Berkeley, Berkeley, CA, USA.

Michelle Liu is Lecturer in Philosophy, School of Philosophical, Historical and International Studies, Monash University, Melbourne, Australia.

Patricia Marechal is Assistant Professor of Philosophy, University of California, San Diego, San Diego, CA, USA.

Christopher Peacocke is Johnsonian Professor of Philosophy, Columbia University in the City of New York, New York, NY, USA.

Nicholas Silins is Professor, Sage School of Philosophy, Cornell University, Ithaca, NY, USA.

Jared Warren is Assistant Professor, Department of Philosophy, Stanford University, Palo Alto, CA, USA.

Helen Yetter-Chappell is Assistant Professor of Philosophy, University of Miami, Miami, USA.

PART I

TWENTY-FIRST-CENTURY IDEALISM

1

Is Universal Consciousness Fit for Ground?

Miri Albahari

1. Introducing Perennial Idealism

In 1946, Aldous Huxley wrote a book called *The Perennial Philosophy*. Coined by Leibniz, the phrase *Philosophia Perennis* speaks of an ultimate mode of being which is:

> the metaphysic that recognises a divine Reality substantial to the world of things and lives and minds; the psychology that finds in the soul something similar to, or even identical with, divine Reality; the ethic that places man's final end in the knowledge of the immanent and transcendent Ground of all being—the thing is immemorial and universal.
>
> (Huxley, 1946, 9)

Huxley draws together sources from twenty-five centuries of different religious and mystical traditions that seem to present, in different idioms, this common theme. According to Huxley, the feature that is 'the most important, the most emphatically insisted upon by all exponents of the Perennial Philosophy' is expressed through the Sanskrit phrase *tat tvam asi*, or 'that thou art' (1946, 14). It signifies that our inherent nature is pure and boundless consciousness which is at one with the ground of all being. While we appear to be a personal self with physical and psychological boundaries—a thinker, owner and agent in the world which *has* consciousness—we are, in reality, the core of that consciousness which is not *had* by anything at all. The consciousness is universal and aperspectival. What we ordinarily take to be the world of separate subjects and objects is all, somehow, grounded in this consciousness. Seeing things as fundamentally separate, as not grounded in this consciousness, locks us in the grip of a deep cognitive illusion. The illusion is sustained by perpetually attaching to the satisfaction of desire, which reinforces the sense of being a separate agent whose happiness depends on the 'world out there'. Such self-identity lies at the root of all mental suffering. With suitable preparation, the mental tendencies can be undone, such that we come to directly experience the inherent nature of *our* being as the nature and ground of *all* being. Known by various terms including 'enlightenment' or 'awakening', this *summum bonum* of human existence is blissful and requires 'annihilation of the self-regarding ego, which is the barrier separating 'thou' from 'that'' (Huxley, 1946, 47). Waking up from the illusion of self to this unconditioned and hyper-real mode of being is often compared, quite literally, to waking up from a dream.

These central ideas of the Perennial Philosophy, which I also refer to as 'Perennialism', can be summarised through the following four tenets:[1]

1. Everything that we take to be the world is somehow grounded in unitary, aperspectival consciousness. This consciousness is supremely real: in essence self-subsistent and unconditioned by parameters such as subject and object, space and time, and the sensory-mental qualities which usually mediate our experience.
2. This pure unitary consciousness is the underlying and abiding nature of our conscious minds.
3. What prevents us from directly recognising our abiding nature *as* the ultimate ground is the illusion of self, which takes the form of a thinker/owner/agent. The illusion manifests principally through the mistaken assumption that our consciousness is intrinsically confined to a private, localised perspective which confronts an external, mind-independent world. It is sustained by desire-driven mental tendencies that make us identify as a subject who attaches to objects.
4. Through various practices, it is psychologically possible to destroy the illusion of self together with its underpinning mental tendencies, thereby unveiling our real and abiding nature as none other than that of unconditioned, grounding consciousness. The psychology of one who

---

[1] Readers should be aware that there are different definitions of the Perennial Philosophy floating around in the literature. Huxley himself didn't emphasise pure consciousness, and he added further elements into the mix. It is sometimes expressed as the purely doctrinal thesis that 'there is…one underlying esoteric set of beliefs embedded in all traditional religions that all mystics share' (Jones, 2022), a definition echoed in Wikipedia. In being centred around 'that thou art' my definition of the Perennial Philosophy makes no universal or doctrinal claim about world religions, and it connects metaphysical insight with direct experience. For an interesting recent discussion that critiques a purely doctrinal and 'universalist' notion of the Perennial Philosophy see Sawyer (2021).

operates from this liberated standpoint, recognised to be that of the ground, is blissfully happy: freed from the capacity to mentally suffer, become attached, or act from a sense of individual agency.

Whether or not one agrees with this Perennial Philosophy, it is depicted as an exalted way of being that is directly discovered, woken up to and lived through experience. We cannot therefore treat tenets 1–4 as a philosophical system, such as that of Kant or Spinoza, which has been arrived at through the usual discursive philosophical methods. So how are we to approach it philosophically? I approach the Perennial Philosophy as an intriguing hypothesis that is based on reports made by mystics from different times and traditions.[2] My ongoing project has been to build a system that extrapolates from the Perennial Philosophy to explain how the world could be configured if the Perennial Philosophy were in fact true.[3] As tenet 1 makes apparent, any such system must be a type of idealism, placing consciousness at the fundamental level. I have accordingly called the edifice 'Perennial Idealism'. While its full elaboration will include dimensions that are epistemological, ethical, phenomenological, psychological, and axiological, my focus to date has been on developing its metaphysical foundation. How do we build our world from a ground of unconditioned and aperspectival consciousness which we could directly discover, through experience, to be our abiding nature? Does the system withstand philosophical scrutiny?

My approach to the construction and defence of Perennial Idealism has come from three main angles which I will call here 'the motivational approach', 'the building approach' and 'the defensive approach'. (There's

---

[2] There is a major debate over whether various mystics from different traditions are in fact uniformly expressing statements that can be summarised around such claims as 'that thou art'. Steven Katz, for instance, thinks that all mystical experience must be indelibly infused with cultural content, allowing for no cross-traditionally convergent experiences that could give rise to such core commonalities as tenets 1–4 (Katz, 1978, 26). My response to this has been to enlist textual evidence in arguing that mystics from different (but not necessarily all) traditions are making claims that are at least consistent with tenets 1–4. Making the case for their actual convergence, I maintain, will involve a multi-stranded argument. The arguments in the current chapter can be seen to contribute to this part of the project.

[3] My most complete attempt to date at this system-building, which includes a survey of mystical literature, is in Albahari (2019). Has the Perennial Philosophy been defended before in the history of Western philosophy? Having extensively researched the matter (as part of an unpublished manuscript for work in progress) I would say that no philosophers in the West have explicitly defended all four tenets which I think define the Perennial Philosophy. The closest I have encountered is Plotinus whose *Enneads* (250 ACE) capture much of tenets 1–4 in an admirably complex neo-Platonic metaphysical system. But as he does not consider the self to be an illusion, his account falls short of exemplifying the Perennial Philosophy as I've spelt it out.

overlap, but these names describe what is predominant in each.) This chapter will focus on the defensive approach, which is concerned with justifying the ground on which the edifice is built. However, I'll first briefly summarise my lines of thinking on the motivational and building approaches. This will provide some necessary background.

1.1 The Motivational Approach

What might draw a philosopher to hold such a position that sounds, to those schooled in standard Western analytical philosophy, a bit nuts? Here, I situate Perennial Idealism in the modern mind-body debate, with its major contenders of dualism, materialism and panpsychism. I have argued that when developed as a novel brand of panpsychism, Perennial Idealism is not only *not* outlandish but has theoretical advantages over its rivals. A typical version of panpsychism will hold that matter has a hidden inner nature of mind and that our mind, whose outer nature is the material brain, is made from the combined minds of various smaller material entities (such as neurons or atoms). These entities will in turn have an inner nature whose minds are comprised from those of yet smaller entities until we reach the fundamental level. Philosophers have in recent years been drawn to panpsychism because they see the endowment of matter with mind as closing the mind-matter gap that is well known to dog its mainstream competitors of materialism and dualism. But panpsychism has its own setbacks. For instance, how can a subject such as myself, as a conscious mind endowed with its own private perspective, be made from a combination of other subjects' minds with their own private perspectives? How can private perspectives breach their boundaries to form a larger perspective?[4] I have argued that if panpsychism is taken in a more robustly idealist direction—as shortly outlined in the building approach section—this kind of 'combination

---

[4] Some thinkers (e.g., Goff (2017, 2020), Shani (2015, 2022), Shani and Keppler (2018), Kastrup (2018)) have recently dealt with this 'combination problem' through proposing a version of panpsychism known as 'cosmopsychism'. Cosmopsychists typically regard the universe as a whole to be a conscious subject in virtue of which simpler subjects, such as ourselves, are conscious. This, however, generates a 'decombination' problem of how a wider conscious subject could coherently share parts of its perspective with simpler subjects (Albahari (2019, 2020, 2022), Shani (2022)). In developing panpsychism in an idealist direction, I allow that subjects may manifest at a micro or cosmic level, the main difference being that a subject's consciousness is owed to a ground of aperspectival consciousness rather than to individual consciousness(es) of other subject(s).

problem' vanishes.[5] Avoiding the problems of its rivals, I have thus argued, provides a strong theoretical motivation to adopt Perennial Idealism.

1.2 The Building Approach

Such theoretical virtues are, however, of little use if Perennial Idealism cannot stand on its own feet as a coherent position. The building approach asks such questions as: How can we construct a lawlike, consciousness-based world with entities that behave in the way they do while cohering with science? How do we prevent the system from collapsing into a solipsistic dream without recourse to a Berkeleyan God-like figure? As I've just hinted, I develop Perennial Idealism as an idealist version of panpsychism.

Its rough outline is this. There is a ground of aperspectival, pure consciousness out of which subjects arise. Such consciousness is intrinsically unconditioned: not dependent upon perspective, space, time, causal laws or any discernible qualities that are known to us through the sensory or cognitive faculties. While comprising a subject's conscious field, the existence of pure consciousness does not rely on any subjects. A subject, at first blush, is what we take ourselves to be: a first-person, conscious perspective to which objects in the world, including our own bodies, appear. The objects include not only external items, such as people and chairs, stars and atoms, our bodies and brains, but also our own thoughts, sensations and emotions. But the objects, at least many of them, are not what we commonly think they are. They are not mind-independent entities in a mind-independent spatial world. Everything that we (as subjects) perceive as an object is also the outer appearance of another subject, or aggregate of subjects, or aspect of a subject, all of which arise from pure unconditioned consciousness. It is easy to infer that some of these objects are indeed also subjects: humans and animals most obviously. But plants, tables, stars, atoms, our thoughts, and the cosmos: these too, on Perennial Idealism, must be the outer appearances of other subjects—in part, whole, or many.

Any object(-like appearance), be it star, atom, table, or thought must be automatically registered by an internal first-person perspective of a subject. The object-like appearances are made from what I call 'cognisensory imagery': ordered constellations of multimodal sensory and cognitive

---

[5] See note 7 for my outline of the solution.

experiences.[6] This constantly shifting imagery, as it presents to a given subject, both frames and maintains that subject's perspective. The conscious awareness that seems enclosed within each subject's perspective is, in essence, the ground itself. Like a honeycomb, what seems to enclose each subject's perspective into a private sphere are literally the outer imagistic appearances, to its viewpoint, of other subjects. Each other subject is in turn a perspectival locus ringed by a set of outer appearances, to its perspective, of yet other subjects.[7] The imagery comprising each set of appearances will usually differ markedly from our own: much simpler if the subject to whom it appears is a neuron or atom, or more complex if the subject is our cosmos. The system will entail a vast, interconnected network of co-dependent subjects, ruling out the possibility of solipsism.

What of the lawlike regularities in the appearances of subjects to one another (as objects), such that each appears to sustain a predictable and causally connected pattern of imagery? I explain this by making subjects dispositional.[8] A subject, as a localised viewpoint, is disposed to have its imagery appear to it in a particular stable way and is in turn disposed to appear to other subjects in a specific stable way (depending on their dispositions). The edifice is being worked out in its details, facing plenty of logistical challenges. But I think it is fair to say that from the perspective of the building approach, Perennial Idealism is in no worse shape than rival

---

[6] As I hold cognisensory imagery to carry representational content, the view is committed to a form of phenomenal intentionality. For a clear outline of this kind of view, see Kriegel (2013).

[7] This, by the way, is how I propose to sidestep the (subject) combination problem for panpsychism. I have argued that most contemporary versions of panpsychism, despite overtly renouncing materialism, are still stuck in a materialist paradigm. Such a paradigm envisages mind-independent spatial objects containing inside themselves a spark of inner conscious life. The combination problem then arises because we envisage our inner conscious life, with an outer spatial aspect of a mind-independent brain, being comprised from the combined inner conscious lives of smaller material spatial entities (e.g., neurons) that are encased inside the spatial brain. The idea of their spatial containment railroads us into thinking that the internal contents of these physical vessels have to mix together in a way that breaches their boundaries. On the idealist version of panpsychism, the problem doesn't occur because we reconceive our cognisensory experience to come not from a merging together of other (spatially contained) subject's inner lives, but simply from the combined outer appearances of other subjects that arise in consciousness and frame our perspective. Our thoughts (also objects, under Perennial idealism) are for instance speculated to be the collective outer appearances of other subjects (arising from consciousness) that are disposed to visually appear to us, in different conditions, as neural networks. As no perspectival boundaries are breached there is no subject combination problem. For further details on this, see Albahari (2022).

[8] In my work to date I have adapted Martin's (2008) view of dispositional/quality identity (also defended by Strawson (2008)) to that of a dispositional/subject identity. I have since become more sympathetic to those views that ground dispositions or powers in qualitative subjects. For modern exemplars of such a view see Builes (2023) and Mørch (2019).

panpsychist positions. If we agree that it avoids the combination problem, then, all other things being equal, it may actually be in better shape.

2. Four Holes in the Ground? The Defensive Approach

I suspect the main sticking points, which could render all things *not* equal, to lurk in the ground. The subjects are stipulated to arise, on Perennial Idealism, from a bedrock of unconditioned and aperspectival consciousness. For brevity I'll sometimes refer to this as 'universal consciousness'. Such bedrock, many will think, is of dubious substance. There are several ground-trembling objections to it. As arguing for the ground turns out to be mainly an exercise of defence, I call this angle the 'defensive approach'. The guiding question here is essentially: Is universal consciousness fit for ground?[9] Is it solid enough to withstand the earthquakes? Or does it perhaps liquify into a quicksand of incoherence that can support no structure? If the ground liquifies, then the other two approaches to its defence will be nullified. It is therefore important, if Perennial Idealism is to be taken seriously, to meet these objections as frankly as possible. I have already, in other work, endeavoured to meet most of them (Albahari, 2019). But never all in one place and not always as clearly as I would like. The purpose of this chapter is to corral the objections together into an ordered sequence, before addressing each in turn. These challenges, I have discovered, can be divided into a set of four telescoped objections, such that if the first is met, the second arises, and if the second is met, the third arises, and so on. I will refer to these challenges as (1) the Thales Objection, (2) The Problem of the One and the Many, (3) the Self-defeating Objection and (4) the Power Challenge. The rest of this section sets them out, with the remaining sections of the chapter devoted to a response.

2.1 The Thales Objection

I owe this objection to Daniel Stoljar, who presented it to me at a conference Q&A, summarised in recent correspondence from which I will be quoting.

---

[9] I use the term 'ground' in a way that is supposed to capture the general spirit of 'x grounds y iff y obtains in virtue of x' where 'x' is universal consciousness and 'y' are the items we take to be the world. It will transpire, however, that the nature of the grounding relation will be unlike what is usually espoused in Western philosophy.

The Greek philosopher Thales was famous for claiming that everything in nature is grounded in water. An initial objection to Thales, says Stoljar, would be that from the standpoint of the universe, water is a local phenomenon. It is present in our bodies, baths and oceans but is hardly ubiquitous. 'Suppose that Thales responds by saying that by 'water' he means not ordinary water but *universal* water, understood as the ground of all being. Now, his thesis is that everything is grounded in the ground of all being.' In such universal application the notion of 'water' has been effectively redefined to fit the desired role, thereby 'ceasing to be the interesting thesis he started out with'. Stoljar says that an analogous charge to Thales can be made to the claim that everything is grounded in (unconditioned, aperspectival) consciousness: from a universal standpoint, consciousness is not observed to be ubiquitous, but a localised phenomenon that is had by individuals such as humans and animals. The defender of Perennial Idealism may then respond by insisting that by 'consciousness' he means not individual consciousness but *universal* consciousness, understood as the ground of all being. But then, just as with Thales, the thesis now becomes the uninteresting claim that everything is grounded in the ground of all being. So, when recast as the ground of all being, 'consciousness' effectively becomes the label for a role whose occupant, if it exists, bears no more connection to real consciousness than universal water does to real water.

2.2 The Problem of the One and the Many

I'll endeavour to meet the Thales Objection by arguing that when the term 'consciousness' is applied universally it bears a meaningful relation to individual consciousness that (say) universal water does not bear to local water. But even if this objection is met, a new and more pernicious problem arises, to do with the relation between the ground and what is grounded. I refer to this as the 'Problem of the One and the Many'. The problem is not confined to Perennial Idealism but has been faced throughout the history of philosophy by such monist thinkers as Parmenides (5 BCE), Plotinus (250 ACE), Spinoza (1677, and as discussed in Wolfson, 1965) and Schelling (as discussed in Beiser, 2002). Targeting any philosophical system that proposes an unconditioned substratum, the objection goes: how can a ground, as a principle of unity that is completely self-subsistent and unconditioned, indivisible and undifferentiated, coherently interface with the many and finitely specified items that it is supposed to ground or yield? The very distinction between the ground and the grounded—the one and the many—imposes a boundary between them, thereby placing a limitation on what is supposed to be unlimited. The problem is present whether the finite items are placed within the ground or outside of it. Commenting for instance on Schelling's numerous attempts to overcome the problem and secure his 'Parmenidean vision' of 'the absolute', Frederick Beiser writes:

> On the one hand it is necessary to exclude the realm of the finite from the absolute, because the finite and the absolute contradict one another; more specifically, the absolute is independent and indivisible while the finite is dependent and divisible.
> On the other hand, however, it is also necessary to include the realm of the finite in the absolute, because, as the whole of all reality, the absolute cannot be limited by something outside itself.... An absolute that excludes the finite becomes, just by that token, a finite absolute, and so not really an absolute at all.
>
> (Beiser, 2002, 567–568)

There is an alternative—to deny that the finite things or their divisions exist, and embrace instead an austere form of monism on which only the ground exists and nothing else. While in earlier works I've referred to this position as a kind of existence monism, it is actually much stronger than standard existence monism which only states that there is exactly one concrete token. Existence monism still permits a plurality of properties, divisions and abstract objects. *Absolute monism*, as I'll refer to it (following Kriegel's suggestion), permits no plurality along any ontological axes whatsoever. While absolute monism entails existence monism, existence monism does not entail absolute monism.[10] Absolute monism faces a serious objection. Not only does it seem to render otiose all the effort that is put into building a system of how the finite world or its manifold appearance comes

---

[10] On existence monism there is exactly one concrete token, while on its close cousin of *priority monism*, a view often adopted by cosmopsychists, there is exactly one *fundamental* concrete token (Schaffer, 2014). Some recent defenders of existence monism include Horgan and Potrč (2008), Della Rocca (2020) and Builes (2021). None of their versions are as austere as that implied by Perennial Idealism, although Builes' version comes closest. Allowing no profusion of objects or properties that could exist as individual entities, his view nevertheless permits divisions in the form of *modes* or *aspects* of the one 'World Quality'. These aspects can be thought of as viable abstractions (second-order properties) that are deduced from the whole in the same way that a particular hue, saturation and brightness can be deduced from a determinate colour such as scarlet (Builes, 2021, 20). Perennial Idealism does not permit these sorts of divisions to be deduced from the ground, so is more austere than Builes' position.

about—because there's no such thing as finite, manifold entities—but it denies some of most obviously true-seeming statements that even a resolute sceptic would be hard-pressed to deny, such as 'thinking exists' or 'there is pain occurring in me right now' or even 'there *appears* to be a pain occurring in me right now'. Appearances cannot exist if there is only the ground.

Perennial Idealism is thus faced with what would appear to be a vicious dilemma: accept the many (imagery-bound subjects), and face negating the One (unconditioned consciousness), or accept only the One and face the absurdities that come with negating the many.

2.3 The Self-defeating Objection

My proposed resolution to the Problem of the One and the Many will recruit a tactic espoused by mystics associated with Advaita Vedānta, a Hindu tradition whose tenets are most explicitly Perennialist.[11] The advaitin tactic originates not as a heuristic that is meant to resolve a philosophical problem, but as the upshot of what they describe as an abidance in unconditioned consciousness. This leads these mystics to reject the authority of the very standpoint—that of subject versus object—from which *any* divisions are made. The subject-object framework and its ensuing divisions are likened to the inhabitants and happenings of a dream that is woken up from and recognised to lack reality. The Problem of the One and the Many, posed from inside this spurious framework, will have no traction from an awakened standpoint that is the ultimate arbiter of truth.[12] The unsavoury implications of absolute monism will nevertheless be averted by allowing objects and their truths to exist in relation to subjects (just as dream-events exist in relation to a dream-subject).

But accepting this resolution yields a further problem that I refer to as the 'Self-defeating Objection'. For if it is granted that subjects, objects and their divisions lack reality, then so too must the conceptual distinctions that are drawn upon in arguing for Perennial Idealism. A bit like Wittgenstein's analogy of climbing the ladder to be kicked away, philosophical method will

---

[11] For an account of Advaita Vedānta from the lived perspective of Sri Ramana Maharshi, who was widely believed to be fully awakened, see Muruganar (2004, 2008). For a philosophical reconstruction of Advaita Vedānta, see Eliot Deutsch (1973). I will be drawing extensively upon Ramana's teachings in this chapter.

[12] I'll also argue that the problem doesn't apply to the 'unawakened' standpoint either. The metaphysics of Perennial Idealism doesn't permit any standpoint from which the Problem of the One and the Many could legitimately take hold.

be harnessed to reach a point where it is argued that while Perennial Idealism has merit, its very supporting arguments rest on a framework that, by its own lights, must ultimately fail.

2.4 The Power Challenge

I will argue that the Self-defeating Objection is less pernicious than it initially sounds. The line I'll take will be that although any truths pertaining to distinctions must be relativised to the standpoint of an object-viewing subject—a standpoint invalidated by awakening—such invalidation doesn't so much contradict the truths of the subject-world as render them inapplicable. I'll offer reasons to suppose that reality may extend well beyond what can be captured in logical, discursive thought. Accepting this much, a new challenge (as relativised to a subject's standpoint) arises, which I'll call the Power Challenge. How can unconditioned consciousness, which lacks any structure, impart order and structure to what we might call the 'great dream network'—an edifice whose items cannot be said to objectively *exist* in relation to the ground? The challenge has two parts. First, how can we understand such a grounding relation which will be, to say the least, unconventional? And second, supposing a feasible model can be found for such grounding, is there anything we can point to about universal structureless consciousness that could help generate the subject-relative appearance of our world as spatial, temporal and lawlike?[13] Is universal consciousness, in this active sense, fit for ground?

3. Filling in the Holes

I'll now attempt to defend Perennial Idealism against these four objections.

3.1 Response to the Thales Objection

Addressing the Thales Objection will involve an exercise of conceivability that meaningfully connects consciousness as we know it with the notion of consciousness as a universal ground that is aperspectival and unconditioned. Is

---

[13] The Power Challenge has been pressed upon me many times by David Chalmers in conversation.

there anything about our consciousness that could allow its essence to conceivably be such a ground of all being—while still remaining *consciousness*? In other words, what could make consciousness, as opposed to (say) water, a meaningful rather than vacuous filler for the role 'ground of all being'?

Immediately setting claims about universal consciousness apart from those about universal water (or suchlike) is that their content is proposed not as a hypothetical philosophical entity, but as the datum of direct experience. Mystics have long reported being established in a standpoint of pure consciousness that is not limited by individual perspective, space, time or cognisensory quality. Regardless of whether such claims are true, a concrete example of such testimony will bring to life the idea that such a mode of consciousness might well be experienceable and thus conceivable. I will outline such a case in 3.1.1. In 3.1.2 I present a thought experiment which goes into more detail about how universal consciousness could conceivably be experienced. While this can be seen to complement and further elucidate the example, accepting this argument is not dependent on conceding that such testimony is or could be true. It stands as a separate argument for the idea that universal consciousness, unlike that of universal water, can be made sense of.

3.1.1 The Case of Sri Ramana Maharshi

One of the most well-known and widely documented mystical figures of recent times is Sri Ramana Maharshi (1879–1950), a South Indian sage in the Advaita Vedānta tradition. At the age of sixteen Ramana (known then as Venkataraman) had an experience that was to irrevocably alter his perception of reality. Gripped with a sudden and inexplicable fear that he was about to die, he enquired if anything in his nature could survive death. In this spontaneous act of what he called 'self-enquiry' his attention entirely withdrew from objects and became absorbed in the source of the 'I-ness' from which all thought and perceptions seemed to arise. This, he said, catalysed an irreversible psychological transformation that destroyed his sense of individual 'I'. In his words:

> [T]he question arose in me, 'What was this "I"? Is it the body? Who called himself the "I"?' So I held my mouth shut, determined not to allow it to pronounce 'I' or any other syllable. Still I felt within myself, the 'I' was there, and the thing calling or feeling itself to be 'I' was there. What was that?
>
> (Godman, 2019, 1)

In another record of this event he wrote:

> When I scrutinised within the mind 'Who is the seer?' the seer became non-existent and I saw that which remained. The mind does not [now] rise to say 'I saw'; how [therefore] can the mind [a bounded perspective] rise to say 'I did not see'?
>
> (Maharshi, 2007, 151)

Commenting on this, leading Ramana scholar David Godman writes:

> This is a sutra-like summary of the experience in which Ramana boiled down the whole [awakening] narrative into its essence. He asked himself 'Who is the one who sees objects?' He focused on that entity, saw it disappear into its source, and from that moment on the individual perceiving 'I' never rose or functioned in him again.
>
> (Godman, 2019, 3)

As Ramana described it, what used to be his frame of reference—that of a separate locus of consciousness belonging to an individual self who perceives a mind-independent spatio-temporal world—permanently vanished. Shattered was the usual, unquestioning mode of perceiving the world through the framework of a duality between subject and object (Tamil: *suṭṭaṟivu*), with the trinity of seer/seeing/seen or knower/knowing/known (Sanskrit: *tripuṭī*). What remained as his abiding frame of reference, as he tells it, was an experience as undecaying Self-awareness (*ahaṁ-sphuraṇa*) not dependent on the body or any other conditions:

> ...In the vision of death, though all the senses were benumbed, the *ahaṁ-sphuraṇa* (Self-awareness) was clearly evident, and so I realised that it was that awareness that we call 'I', and not the body. This Self-awareness never decays. It is unrelated to anything. It is Self-luminous. Even if this body is burnt, it will not be affected. Hence, I realised on that very day so clearly that that was 'I'.
>
> (*Letters from Sri Ramanasramam*, 22 November 1945)

This pure consciousness, which Ramana often referred to as the Self (with an upper-case 'S'), was from that point taken to be his real nature (*svarūpa*). The following excerpts, conveyed through his close disciple Muruganar (whose writings Ramana personally signed off on), provide further evidence that this was indeed Ramana's ongoing experience:

> This world phenomenon, consisting of dualities and trinities, shines because of thoughts. Like the unreal circle traced in the air by a whirling firebrand, it [the world phenomenon] is created by the spinning of the illusory mind. However, from the point of view of *svarūpa*, the fullness of intense consciousness, the illusory mind is non-existent.
>
> (Muruganar, 2008, 20)
>
> What exists is the plenitude of object-free *jñāna* [knowingness] which shines as unconditioned reality. The world appears as an object that is grasped by your *suṭṭaṛivu* [object-directed consciousness]. Like the erroneous perception of a person who sees everything as yellow, this entire world is a deluded view consisting wholly of a mind that has defects such as ego, deceit, desire, and so on.
>
> (Muruganar, 2008, 21)
>
> Consciousness will become replete when the knower enquires within and knows himself.
>
> (Muruganar, 2004, 87)
>
> Knowing consciousness is not different from knowing reality. They are one and the same because reality is not different from consciousness.
>
> (Muruganar, 2004, 86)
>
> To a *mūni* [a sage], all the multifarious scenes that appear before him will shine merely as the ever-present pure consciousness.
>
> (Muruganar, 2004, 94)

While space and time constrain the world of objects perceived through the localised and limited perspective of an embodied subject, Ramana frequently said that these dimensions were not applicable to pure consciousness:

> The idea of time is only in your mind. It is not in the Self. There is no time for the Self. Time arises as an idea after the ego arises. But you are the Self beyond time and space; you exist even in the absence of time and space.
>
> (Muruganar, 2008, 325)

Ramana's testimony provides evidence that universal consciousness can be the datum of direct experience and, as such, be conceivable. But more is needed to dispel the Thales Objection. It can well be replied: With all due respect to Ramana, why trust the veracity of such reports? Might Ramana have been mistaken about the content of his experience—not only in terms of there really *being* a pure consciousness as ground of all being, but also in terms of the experience genuinely *conveying* an ongoing establishment in such consciousness? Is the undergoing of such experience *really* conceivable? This brings us then to the second approach which can help us make better sense of what Ramana is saying, while serving as an independent line of argument as to the conceivability of such a state.

3.1.2 The Cognisensory Deprivation Tank

Can we actively conceive of a scenario that will allow sense to be made of the idea that one could ongoingly experience their life from the standpoint of aperspectival and unconditioned consciousness? If so, then regardless of its actual psychological possibility, it will be enough to demonstrate a meaningful connection between consciousness as we know it and consciousness in its capacity as unconditioned. It will be enough to meet the Thales objection.

To this end I have in other work proposed a thought experiment that seeks to meaningfully connect the notion of consciousness in everyday experience with that of consciousness as universal ground (Albahari, 2019). Before running through this, it helps to clarify some central terms, starting with what I mean by 'consciousness in everyday experience'. Here, consciousness is defined with reference to subject and object.[14] A subject, as I define it, is a localised perspective that is aware of objects via various sensory and cognitive modalities, however complex or simple. Objects are broadly anything discernible that could conceivably appear to a subject as separate from itself: trees, birds, rocks, atoms, sensations, thoughts, ideas, mathematical entities. We are immediately aware of objects through the medium of what I've been calling 'cognisensory imagery'. The notion of 'imagery', in this multimodal capacity, has a wider scope than that typically employed by psychologists or introspectionists. Cognisensory imagery includes not only the visual or the imagined dimensions to lived experience, but all of its cognitive and multi-sensory aspects as well, including their content. Perennial Idealism proposes that all objects are in fact made of cognisensory imagery.

---

[14] Significantly, this usage aligns with how Ramana used the terms.

We will often not be explicitly aware of objects currently impinging on experience: think of a ringing in the ear, or subtle thoughts and feelings subtending the sense of agency. But insofar as objects are experienced, they will appear within the conscious purview of a subject: attentively or inattentively, focally or peripherally, externally or internally. The subject's perspective is the localised and centred point of view *to which* objects are presented; the subject's consciousness is the field of awareness *in which* objects are presented. A perspective, to which objects appear, divides one subject from another insofar as objects experientially apparent to one subject (e.g., a headache or look of a tree) are not directly accessible to another. What unites various contents within a given subject's perspective, such that the objects seem given to the *same* perspective, is the field of consciousness itself.

In its capacity of presenting as the field of an object-witnessing subject, I refer to consciousness as 'witness-consciousness' (Albahari, 2009). Witness-consciousness is mode-neutral knowing with intrinsic phenomenal character. It is that percipient aspect of the mind by which we seem to be aware, attentively or inattentively, of the babble of voices at the same time as the taste of lemonmint ice-juice and the thought 'that's nice'. It is mode-neutral in that it does not depend upon which cognitive or sensory modality is operative but occurs in tandem with them all. Witness-consciousness arguably comes with a basic and elusive sense of its own presence. There is something it is like to experience this presence; yet such phenomenal character pertains not, in and of itself, to any object that consciousness may target but to the percipient medium of the consciousness itself. In philosophical parlance, we can say that witness-consciousness is *intransitive* and *reflexive*. For consciousness to be intransitive is for it to pertain not (merely) to an object but to subjectivity itself. For consciousness to be reflexive is for it to take itself as its own (non-objectual) content such that it is self-revealing, like the sun. Combining all these aspects, we can say that witness-consciousness shines by its own 'light', knowing itself implicitly as it does so. It knows itself by being itself while illuminating objects within its purview.[15]

It can be hard to pinpoint the intrinsic phenomenal character of witness-consciousness, which is why I say that it *arguably* has such a character. But if it does have it, which I'm supposing it does for current purposes of conceivability, then there's a good explanation for its elusive presentation. So long

---

[15] For a detailed description of witness-consciousness that alludes to its knowing, reflexive, luminous and intransitive nature, see Thompson (2015, 13–18).

as one is conscious, be it waking or dreaming, the attention is almost always being pulled away from it and out towards objects, whether via thoughts, perceptions or sensations. Objects are also perpetual residents of one's peripheral, inattentive awareness. I've proposed elsewhere that when the intrinsic phenomenal character of witness-consciousness gets superimposed with the flow of peripheral imagery (such as that pertaining to feelings of agency and ideas about who one is) the witnessing becomes reified into a background, personalised sense of self we call 'me' (Albahari, 2006). Regardless of whether we agree with this theory, it gives us a way of envisaging how, if witness-consciousness *were* to carry its own intrinsic sense of presence, a deep assumption of limitation could impose itself on its nature and scope. If consciousness is always being directed towards objects that simultaneously reinforce the background sense of being a limited, bounded self, then it will be natural to assume, very deeply, that the consciousness is intrinsically confined to the format of *suṭṭaṛivu*: the perspective of a subject or self who confronts objects in the world. This suggests an intriguing question. What if the registration of all objects were to cease? How might witness-consciousness be experienced then?

Before going further, it helps to reflect upon what is it that immediately lends our everyday experience of the world its spatio-temporal, perspectival character. Regardless of any wider theory of origin, we can note that our sense of spatiality, whether waking or dreaming, is directly borne out through multimodal imagery with elements that are visual, tactile, auditory and cognitive, including our implicitly felt perception of depth and so forth. Without such imagery, what would give us our spatial cues? Similarly, our impression of passing time, regardless of wider theory, is immediately borne out through the perpetual flux of imagery in all modalities, enhanced by that which we associate with memory and imagination. Our sense of occupying the centralised perspective of a subject or self also depends plausibly on cognisensory imagery, be it a subtle peripheral flow of thoughts and desires, or the feelings of embodiment that locate us in a wider spatio-temporal setting. The suggestion, then, is that multimodal cognisensory imagery is what immediately cues witness-consciousness into the sense of belonging to an embodied and perspectival subject in a spatio-temporal world.

The engine for the thought-experiment now primed, I introduce the Cognisensory Deprivation Tank. This is the name I give to a fictional machine that aims to simulate the end-result of what Ramana Maharshi and other mystics reportedly experienced. Ramana's method of self-enquiry, *ātma-vicāra*, instructs the seeker to practice what he, in his death experience, spontaneously underwent. The idea of *ātma-vicāra* is to repeatedly turn the attention away from objects and towards the thread of subjectivity or 'I-am'-ness, following it back to its source as pure consciousness. With enough practice the sense of individual self, which relies on an object-bound sense of identity, is supposed to dissolve. In his words:

> …take up the 'thread' or the clue of 'I'-ness or 'I-am'-ness and follow it up to its source.…whatever be the *sādhana* [meditation practice] adopted, the final goal is the realisation of the source of 'I-am'-ness which is the primary datum of your experience. If you, therefore, practise *ātma-vicāra* [self-enquiry] you will reach the Heart which is the Self.
>
> (Anon, 2002, 85)

The Cognisensory Deprivation Tank (CDT) will be an exercise of conceivability rather than practice, and one that imaginatively removes objects rather than withdraws attention from them. While such an exercise won't actually get us into an object-free mode, the CDT is otherwise meant to be somewhat analogous to *ātma-vicāra*. It invites us to extrapolatively imagine what could happen with the systematic removal of all objects from our consciousness (and hence attention to them) until *only* consciousness remains.[16]

So, let us now imagine stepping into a device that sequentially zaps each category of cognisensory imagery from purview: sights, sounds, tastes, smells, tactile and proprioceptive sensations, thoughts, feelings, emotions, desires. At each zap, our witness-consciousness remains. Upon removal of all the perceptual and bodily sensations, consciousness will be alight with thought. But being no ordinary tank, each set of cognitive imagery, including every thought, is now also zapped. Opinion will diverge here as to whether our consciousness disappears with the final zap of imagery. The idea is not to arbitrate on this matter, but to note that the scenario of consciousness remaining present is *minimally conceivable* insofar as there is no obvious contradiction in the idea.[17]

---

[16] With *ātma-vicāra,* emphasis is on the attention being removed from all objects (such that consciousness comes to be known as it is in itself) rather than all objects being removed from consciousness. However, the removal of all objects from consciousness would guarantee the removal of attention from all objects, so it is in this way the thought experiment parallels *ātma-vicāra.*

[17] As Chalmers (2002) puts it, a scenario is minimally or *prima facie* negatively conceivable if no obvious contradictions within it are revealed on first appearances prior to rational reflection.

In the complete absence of objects, what might reflexive and intransitive consciousness, if it does remain, be like? It will conceivably present itself, by sheer default, as a luminous and uninterrupted percipience: a boundless, undifferentiated and unified presence that is unimpeded by limitations of space, passing time, cognisensory imagery, and localised perspective. For if we agree that our spatio-temporal experience is cued in by object-imagery, then without any such imagery there would be nothing to curtail consciousness into a sense of spatio-temporal limitation. Nor would there be anything to hem consciousness into the distinct viewpoint of a subject or self whose defining characteristic is to occupy a centre *to which* objects appear. In the absence of imagery there is nothing to mark centre from periphery, subject from object. Consciousness could thus very well appear as if it were really unconditioned and aperspectival in these central respects.

It is important to be clear on what the CDT thought experiment is and isn't showing. The aim of the CDT is not to demonstrate that consciousness really is unconditioned or aperspectival, or that an experience of pure objectless consciousness is psychologically possible. It isn't even to show that the experience of pure objectless consciousness is required in order to allow the apprehension of consciousness as unconditioned. After all, *ātma-vicāra* doesn't aim to expunge consciousness of all cognisensory imagery but simply seeks to render consciousness salient enough for the alleged insight to occur. The aim of the CDT is rather to make concrete sense of mystical experience such as Ramana's by connecting ordinary with unconditioned consciousness. It is a declaration of this sort: 'Here is what we can arguably say about witness-consciousness, as we reflect on it in ordinary experience. And here is how, with the removal all imagery—upon which plausibly depends our immediate sense of space, passing time, objectual qualities and perspective—this intransitive and reflexive sense of presence, were it to remain, could conceivably and by default make itself known.' A similar thought experiment would not work with water or any other object whose nature is limited by spatio-temporal and qualitative parameters. Any *object* would be a non-starter. In this central respect, consciousness rendered as pure subjectivity is profoundly disanalogous to water or suchlike— thereby making consciousness eminently more fit, on this dimension, for ground. We have met the first stage of the Thales Objection.

What of Ramana's claims about ongoing abidance in a ground of pure consciousness? This can be made sense of by imagining the reappearance of objects after immersion in the Tank. The Tank is entered with a primal assumption that one's consciousness is intrinsically limited to an embodied perspective in a spatio-temporal world. The Tank dissolves away the fabric of this assumption. Having reflexively experienced consciousness in the absence of a limiting framework, it is quite conceivable that the standpoint of a person who emerges from the Tank will be one in which the dissolved assumption does not return, even if their consciousness, once again, appears as perspectival.

To press this point I give a further analogy (Albahari, 2019, 17). Suppose Lucy is confined from birth to a square windowless room. It will be natural for her to assume that space is intrinsically limited to the shape of the room. That is, until the day that Lucy leaves the room and experiences a vast expanse of sky. The space in the room still looks square-shaped upon her return but her perception of it will have greatly altered. She will no longer experience space as being *intrinsically* square-shaped. An analogous story could be told of someone emerging from the CDT. Until immersion in the Tank, a person's consciousness as their central point of reference will seem intrinsically 'perspective-shaped'—the only format ever known up until that point. While emersion from the Tank ushers a nominal return to the subject-object format, their central point of conscious reference will no longer assume the intrinsic confinement that the format suggests. This makes sense of what Ramana and other mystics say when they speak of being 'established in the ground' even while appearing to interact in the world. Having experienced consciousness as wholly independent of worldly parameters, they no longer behave as if consciousness—as their abiding point of reference—were confined to the parameters.

The notion of universal consciousness is not doomed to be an empty role-occupier. The idea of it meaningfully connects with that of ordinary consciousness in such a way that the idea of abidance in universal consciousness, unlike that of universal water, makes initial sense. The Thales Objection has been met.

3.2 Response to the Problem of the One and the Many

In attempting to meaningfully connect the idea of individual with universal consciousness, the Cognisensory Deprivation Tank thought experiment invited us to imagine vanquishing all world-suggesting imagery, leaving only the underlay of pure consciousness. Perennial Idealism further proposes that this world-suggesting imagery is the outward appearance of subjects to one another, arising from the ground of universal consciousness.

But does such a relation between subject, imagery and unconditioned consciousness withstand closer scrutiny? The Problem of the One and Many would suggest it does not. Admitting a profusion of interconnected subjects, with their kaleidoscopic flux of co-dependent imagery, would seem to impose a boundary between the limited subjects and their supposedly boundless ground. In a show of consistency, Ramana and other mystics sometimes eschewed talk of boundaries by declaring the ground of consciousness to be all that there is. But then this suggests the second horn of the dilemma: absolute monism and its problematic drawbacks. Can Perennial Idealism escape this objection which threatens to impale any metaphysical system that admits of an unconditioned ground?

I believe that the first step towards its resolution lies in challenging the framework from which the problem is usually posed. The Problem of the One and the Many arises through trying to reconcile the relation between multiplicitous, limited entities on the one hand and a single limitless ground on the other. This usually presupposes a neutral, observer-independent standpoint—even if idealised—from which the two can be compared. Often associated with a scientific quest to discover the basic structure of physical reality, the implicit endorsement of an objective point of reference is found in many strands of Western philosophical thought.[18] The division between primary and secondary qualities, for instance, arose from philosophers seeking to capture the fundamental and essential properties of matter in a way that abstracted from the sensibilities of human observers. Locke's famous list of primary qualities—shape, size, solidity, number, motion and rest—was intended to describe the intrinsic observer-independent nature of Newtonian atomic fundaments. The secondary qualities—colour, taste, smell, sound, tactile properties—were thought to depend on observers, and so not be true denizens of physical reality. In modern times, the catalogue of primary qualities has altered but the metaphysical quest to discover the world's basic structures remains the same. It is in this intellectual context, which assumes an observer-independent reality, that questions about ultimate metaphysical grounding are usually framed. Facts about the world, sometimes including minds, are thought to depend upon facts that stand clear of how observers perceive things.

One might think that the recent panpsychist turn within the mind-body debate will have altered the trajectory. But this is mostly not so. The positing

---

[18] This tacit philosophical endorsement of an objective standpoint when it comes to understanding physical reality has been discussed at length by Thomas Nagel (1974, 1989).

of a wider-than-usual range of intrinsically minded material entities, such as sub-atomic particles or the cosmos, comes with the pervasive assumption that our scientific measurements are still picking up on their external, observer-independent structures rather than on features that depend for their reality upon the observing scientist. In a recent paper David Chalmers describes this mainstream brand of panpsychism as 'realist':

> ...what it is for physical facts p to obtain is for certain structural roles to obtain [with]...no commitment to 'esse est percipi'....[V]iews like this are naturally understood as versions of realism about the physical world, rather than versions of anti-realism. The physical world really exists out there, independently of our observations; it just has a surprising nature. Indeed, views of this sort are highly congenial to epistemological structural realism, which says roughly that science reveals the structure of the physical world but not its intrinsic nature.
>
> (Chalmers, 2020, 354)

He contrasts this with 'anti-realist' approaches upon which:

> for any nonmental fact p about concrete reality, what it is for p to obtain is for appearances that p (or closely related appearances) to obtain.
>
> (Chalmers, 2020, 354)[19]

Perennial Idealism tilts towards the anti-realist side of the pitch. The system does not permit an outside point of objective comparison from which a relation between the ground (the One) and the structured subjects (the many) could legitimately take hold *sub specie aeternitatis*. The only admissible standpoints, on Perennial Idealism, are those of the *jñāni*—the advaitic term for someone said to be established in the ground—and the *ajñāni* (which is most of us) who assumes the individual perspective of a subject.[20] With respect to neither of these standpoints is there an objective, outside

---

[19] Chalmers (2020) describes both these views as types of *idealism* in virtue of being mind-based. In the current context, I am using the term 'idealism' in a stronger way, to convey a consciousness-based metaphysic whereupon objects and their structures depend on being viewed as such by an observer.

[20] In Sanskrit, placing an 'a' in front of a word can signify its negation. So, the opposite of *jñāni* is *ajñāni*. The related word meaning 'ultimate knowledge' is *jñāna*. *Jñāna* is pronounced 'nyana', (or 'gynana' with a soft 'g') and not, as a Spelling Bee once supposed, 'ja-nana'. Similarly, *jñāni* is pronounced 'nyani'.

point of reference. And the position allows no other point of reference from which the Problem of the One and the Many could take hold.

Take, first, the *jñāni*. His is a standpoint that denies the reality of a subject's individual perspective on which depends, in turn, the impression of individual objects and their divisions. The Problem of the One and the Many presupposes a framework in which there is a division between the ground and what is grounded. But a division between the ground and what is grounded can have no reality from the *jñāni*'s standpoint that rejects the very framework on which such divisions depend. Admitting of only the ground, the *jñāni*'s standpoint allows for no point of comparison, outside or otherwise, between the ground and subjects. I will return to this later in the section.

What about the standpoint of a subject? This also prohibits an outside, observer-independent point of reference from which the relation between the ground and the grounded could be analysed. As any distinction or division only exists from *inside* a given subject's perspective, we cannot permit any abstract, outside, objective point of reference from which any distinctions, including the enumeration of subjects in relation to the ground, could take hold. The unfolding world that I experience—trees, apples, thoughts, ideas, atoms, chairs, people, colours, shapes—exists because other subjects are appearing to me as such from inside my perspective. What we call 'the world', in Perennial Idealism, is always an outer appearance of other subjects *to* a given subject's perspective. Distinctions and qualities, space and time, events, objects and multiple subjects, including those recruited to explain Perennial Idealism—including what I'm saying here—must manifest inside a given subject's perspective and must always be tacitly indexed to it. There exists no subject-independent point of reference from which we could even say that there are facts about how the world appears to a subject.[21] There is no fact of the matter about any subject without a perspective to take it in; no observer-independent point of reference from which we could say that there exists, objectively, a web of numbered and structured, inter-perceiving subjects who could interface problematically with the ground. To talk in such a way is to make a category mistake.

Could a legitimate point of comparison between the ground and the grounded not be made from *within* a given subject's perspective? We have described Perennial Idealism as a position upon which pure consciousness

---

[21] This doesn't entail that the subject must be an epistemic authority on what appears within her perspective. I say more about this soon.

is a subject's abiding nature, out of which arises imagery—the outward appearance of other subjects—to that subject's perspective. This may then seem to involve a problematic interface, as perceived from within the perspective of a single subject, between pure unconditioned consciousness on the one hand and multiplicitous imagery on the other.

Despite appearances, the interface between imagery and unconditioned consciousness is not problematic for the simple reason that such an interface does not exist. Imagery, which is the outer appearance of other subjects, never manifests by itself in pure consciousness, but always to the localised perspective of what we have been calling a subject. It is subjects (perspective to which imagery appears), not simply imagery (the outer appearances of other subjects), that form the basic units of manifestation within Perennial Idealism. If the Problem of the One and the Many is to take hold, then the correct relata will be subjects (or a subject network) and pure consciousness, not imagery and pure consciousness.[22] And we have just seen that subjects cannot be objectively enumerated in relation to the ground.

Whether one considers the standpoint of the *ajñāni* or the *jñāni*, there is therefore no legitimate point of reference from which Problem of the One and the Many can take hold. This is not yet enough, however, to fully dissolve the problem. It is one thing to argue that the system does not permit a standpoint from which the Problem of the One and the Many has traction, and quite another to show how it explains away the very appearance of the problem. (Compare: it is one thing to imply that one's deterministic system prohibits libertarian freewill and quite another to show how it explains away the subjective appearance of freewill). Imagery, objects and their distinctions, along with the subject's perspectives to which they appear, ordinarily present to us as being real—as real, indeed, as anything could be. It seems hard to deny the reality of someone having the experience of a headache. And science, mathematics and philosophy propose all kinds of distinctions that are presumed to be real. These distinctions will all be rendered spurious if consciousness is to maintain its ultimacy in a way that allows no boundary between it and the many. Can this lack of boundary be shown to hold without incurring the unwelcome implications outlined in connection with absolute monism? Addressing the challenge will require further consideration of the *jñāni's* standpoint, but before going there, it will be

---

[22] In the discussion ahead, about the *jñāni's* standpoint, another avenue is offered via a dream analogy that independently argues that the boundary between pure consciousness and the many objects is spurious.

instructive to compare Perennial Idealism with the system of another philosopher whose metaphysic bears a striking affinity with it: Immanuel Kant.

When it comes to the world's divisions and structures, Kant's philosophy, just as with Perennial Idealism, does not endorse an observer-independent standpoint. Although still positing a mind-independent world, Kant insists that we can know nothing about its nature. All knowable principles of division—such as space, time, mathematical principles, qualitative variation, causation, quantity, relational dependency—are imposed on experience by the mind. While data from the world enter our senses as a 'manifold of raw intuition', as he calls it, our minds stamp onto it all the distinctions. The mind's grounding terminus is in unified consciousness:

> There can be in us no modes of knowledge, no connection or unity of one mode of knowledge with another, without that unity of consciousness which precedes all data of intuitions, and by relation to which representation of objects is alone possible.
>
> (Kant, 1929, A107)

A unified consciousness is required for us to be able to behold and recognise multiple objects all together in a single awareness, both at a time and over time. Kant sometimes calls this consciousness the 'transcendental I' as it is a condition for the possibility of our having structured experiences of the kind that we have. This I-consciousness, says Kant, is in itself unconditioned by the parameters and structures imposed by the mind onto experience, including space, time, qualitative variation and relational dependency (1929, A404).

Insofar as the unified consciousness is the unconditioned portal through which conditions are imposed on experience, Kant's philosophy aligns with Perennial Idealism. Both agree that conditioned structures and parameters cannot be imposed onto the consciousness, which is a precondition for the presentation of such parameters. But there is a major difference. Kant insists that all knowledge and experience is object-directed and thereby thoroughly transitive, mediated by structures of the mind. Because of this, he holds that any attempt to know or experience the 'I' as it is in itself, aside from rationally figuring out its purely functional role, will be doomed to failure, illegitimately imposing onto consciousness the very structures that consciousness is meant to impose onto experience (1929, B422). Perennial Idealism, by contrast, rejects the assumption that all experience and knowledge must be object-directed. The possibility of unified and unstructured consciousness intransitively knowing itself fully as it is in itself is a foundational tenet.

I believe that the possibility of consciousness intransitively knowing itself as it is in itself will be needed to adequately resolve the Problem of the One and the Many. To see how this is so, consider first where Kant's system leaves us. As with Perennial Idealism, the Problem of the One and the Many should in principle have trouble taking hold. For Kant does not permit an outside observer-independent point of reference from which unconditioned consciousness could be said to exist in a problematic relation to the numerous individual subjects and the world that appears to them. All structures and divisions, including the category of quantity, are only supposed to have application from *inside* the perspective of any given conscious subject, rather than *between* subjects, considered from an outside standpoint. Subjects and their structures cannot therefore be objectively numerous, such that they stand in a problematic relation of 'many' to the one unconditioned consciousness, imposing a boundary on it. Yet Kant does not consistently follow through on these strictures, leaving us with questions and loose ends. He still talks as if subjects or persons were objectively real and numerous entities, each backed by a transcendental 'I'. It is left a mystery as to how the transcendental I, purportedly unconditioned by quantity and relation, could manifest, or appear to manifest, as one per person or if not this, then how a single unconditioned consciousness could interface with multiple persons, as well as provide diverse structure to their fields of perception.[23] And what of the relation between the transcendental I and the mysterious noumenal world? Is there a boundary here too? This is also left unspecified.

The shortfall demonstrates how it is one thing to imply that a system prohibits the Problem of the One and the Many from arising, and quite another to positively show how it explains away the appearance of the problem. Despite proposing a system that should allow no objective profusion of

---

[23] Schopenhauer, who saw himself as improving on elements of Kant's philosophy, argued that plurality (what Kant called 'quantity') was closely linked to spatio-temporal division such that if the thing in itself were to lack spatio-temporal division then plurality would also be lacking: 'But if *time* and *space* is foreign to the thing in itself, i.e. to the true essence of the world, then necessarily plurality is foreign to it also: consequently in the countless appearances of this world of the senses it can really be only one, and only the one and identical essence can manifest itself in all of these. And conversely, that which presents itself as a *many*, and hence in time and space, cannot be thing in itself, but only *appearance*' (Schopenhauer, 2009, 251). Despite initial similarities, along with a professed admiration for the *Upaniṣads*, the thing in itself that Schopenhauer called the 'will' does not map onto universal consciousness (*Brahman*) as it is alluded to in Upaniṣadic and Advaitic teaching, and which informs Perennialism. The will is characterised as a 'blind striving' (2009, xix), which universal consciousness is most definitely not.

subjects or divisions, Kant still writes as if subjects and divisions are object-ively profuse, which fortifies, rather than explains away, the problem at hand. And it is hard for him to not talk in this way. His system lacks the resources from which to positively account for the status of multiple sub-jects and divisions as actually spurious—as they need to be—while appear-ing to be real.

Does Perennial Idealism have the resources to meet this demand? Return to the *jñāni*'s standpoint. It was mentioned that with the *jñāni*'s establish-ment in the ground, the individual subject, on which the impression of objects depends, is perceived to lack reality. The *jñāni* will commonly declare the only reality to be that of unlimited consciousness. Known as the *ajāta* doctrine, meaning 'not created, not caused', it is a notion that was expounded by a distinguished early proponent of Advaita Vedānta: Gauḍapāda (Nikhilānanada, 1949). The doctrine originated not as a theory but as a putative insight based on direct experience. Gauḍapāda's summary was approvingly paraphrased by Ramana Maharshi:

> The *ajāta* doctrine says, 'Nothing exists except the one reality. There is no birth or death, no projection [of the world] or drawing in [of it]...no *mumukṣú* [seeker of liberation], no *mukta* [liberated one], no bondage, no liberation. The one unity alone exists ever.'
>
> (Muruganar, 2008, 50)

In another account of this interchange, Ramana adds:

> One who is established in the Self [the ground] sees this by his knowledge of reality.
>
> (Godman, 2005, 240)

Is this absolute monism? It could be argued that if no objects or distinctions have validity, then the very condition under which absolute monism is meaningfully asserted, as a position in contrast to other positions, is not met. Be that as it may, we still seem to be left with the same troubles. If there is only the one reality, then how is the system to explain the appearance of division, not only from the limited perspective of the *ajñāni*, but from the standpoint of the *jñāni* himself? Did not Ramana Maharshi, in the fifty years since his awakening experience, engage in the world and attend to its divisions? And is not the very appearance of division still *itself* really divided and multiplicitous in nature, and so, in that capacity, real? More is needed.

It is this further expansion of the *ajāta* doctrine by Ramana that offers the crucial clue to a resolution:

> To such as find it difficult to grasp this truth and who ask, 'How can we ignore this solid world we see all around us?' the dream experience is pointed out and they are told, 'All that you see depends on the seer. Apart from the seer, there is no seen'.
>
> (Muruganar, 2008, 50)

The dream analogy provides a handle on how to conceive of subjects, objects and their divisions as lacking in reality while appearing, from a limited standpoint, as if they were as real as anything could be. To explore the idea further, imagine that Lucy, after her initial escape from the square room, starts dreaming of open spaces: a beach with sand, waves and an expansive blue sky. She dreams of other people with whom she goes swimming and of a crab who nips her toe causing pain, before apologising (this is a dream!). We can agree that this dream phenomenon is somehow in a general way dependent on Lucy's consciousness. But it would be incorrect to say that an inventory of the dream's items, events and qualities—*the beach, the people, the blue of the sky, Lucy's swimming, the pain in the toe* and *the crab's apology*—are grounded in Lucy's consciousness. These items don't exist, and so can neither be grounded nor not grounded in her consciousness. There cannot then be a *boundary* between the dream objects and Lucy's consciousness. It is only in relation to Lucy's dream-perspective that there are dream-objects on which depend facts about what she does or does not dream. The unreality of herself as occupant of the dream-perspective, upon which the dream-objects depend, is something she recognises as soon as she wakes up.

In Perennial Idealism, the situation of the *jñāni* 'waking up' from ordinary life is directly analogous to that of the *ajñāni* waking up from a dream. Realising their abiding nature to be that of pure, non-dual consciousness, the *jñāni* wakes up from the false idea that their consciousness is confined to a limited, psycho-physical perspective. With disidentification from the embodied perspective comes the reciprocal recognition that all the objects and imagery, dependent on this spurious perspective, are also unreal. What we, the *ajñāni*, take to be a self-standing, spatio-temporal world of objects and imagery to a real perspective all appears as non-existent to the *jñāni*, just as the dream-objects and imagery, once we wake up and recognise the dream-perspective to be spurious, appear as non-existent to us. And since the perspective and its items do not exist, they cannot be said to be grounded in universal consciousness such that there would be a problematic boundary between these items and the pure consciousness.

Insofar as the *jñāni* still appears to engage with the world and its objects, they might be described as retaining something of a *notional* perspective, akin to that of someone who fully knows they are in a dream and is keenly aware that its items don't exist beyond the purview of that spurious dream-perspective. That this was Ramana's direct experience finds support in the following passage by Narayana Iyer who frequently visited 'Bhagavan', as he was often known:

> One day I felt puzzled by the teaching that everything in the world is *māyā* or illusion. I asked Bhagavan how with the physical existence before our eyes we can all be unreal and non-existent? Bhagavan laughed and asked me whether I had any dream the previous night. I replied that I saw several people lying asleep. He said 'Suppose now I ask you to go and wake up all those people in the dream and tell them they are not real, how absurd would it be! That is how it is to me. There is nothing but the dreamer, so where does the question of dream people, real or unreal, arise; still more of waking them up and telling them that they are not real. We are all unreal, why do you doubt it? **That** [the ground] alone is real.'
>
> (Narain, 2009, 261–262, emphasis his own)

By all accounts these were not merely words. In the fifty years that followed his awakening experience, Ramana's comportment was invariably described as consistent with one who would regard the world as a dream, neither identifying with his body nor emotionally investing in worldly matters.

The dream analogy allows us to avoid the unwelcome implications of absolute monism. For it can account for the appearances of the many without reifying these appearances into objectively real and multiplicitous items. Objects do exist, but only to the perspective of the subject to whom they appear. Our unquestioning identification with our perspective, as an embodied being in space and time, bestows a reciprocally solid sense of reality to the objects that appear to us. This is so whether we are waking or dreaming.[24]

---

[24] Some may point out that even so, there's still a marked difference between dreaming and waking states, insofar as items in the dream states depend only on the dreamer. For an account of this difference under Perennial Idealism, see Albahari (2019), 23.

Relativising the existence of objects to a subject's standpoint grants Perennial Idealism the enormous advantage of being able to preserve the subject matter of such domains as science, mathematics and philosophy. Working out the semantics (based on appropriate epistemic standards) is the province of the building approach, but it bears noting that the subject-relativity of truths about the world does not entail a mushy anything-goes status such as 'If subject S judges that Q occurs within her perspectival field then Q is the case'. While facts about our world will always be derived from how cognisensory imagery appears to a given subject, that given subject is not the infallible authority on what appears within its perspectival field. With no observer-independent point of reference from which to index statements of fact about the contents of a subject's conscious field, the semantics for Perennial Idealism will develop an intersubjective approach by which standards of relative objectivity can be secured.[25]

In allowing for the possibility of an awakened standpoint, Perennial Idealism thus has the resources to explain both how the Problem of the One and the Many fails to take hold, and how it could nevertheless *appear* to take hold. For it provides an explanation of how apparently real phenomena, such as that of someone having the experience of a headache, could turn out to depend on a perspective that is itself spurious. And by relativising world-based truths to a subject's perspective it avoids the unwelcome implications of absolute monism. Given the long history of the Problem of the One and the Many for any philosophical system positing an unconditioned ground, this solution, if it succeeds, is not a trivial outcome. Not only Kant, but (as mentioned previously) Parmenides, Plotinus, Spinoza and Schelling were among those who did not have similar resources, so the problem always remained a thorn in the side of their metaphysical systems.

But Perennial Idealism is not yet out of the woods. If all distinction-based truths lack ultimate authority, including those within philosophical thought, then is not the philosophical system of Perennial Idealism itself rendered ultimately untrue by its own lights, and hence self-defeating?

---

[25] My suggestion would be to modify Daniel Dennett's (1991) heterophenomenological approach. When seeking to understand a given subject's conscious happenings, the reports which that subject gives about her experiences are included in the data, along with a host of behavioural observations, neurological scans, and so forth. The interpretation of the collated data will retain a degree of objectivity insofar as it does not rely solely upon the judgements of the subject from which it is harvested. Nevertheless, the data will itself be embedded in the cognisensory imagery of whoever is trying to discern the relevant patterns. Its existence and interpretation will in this way remain fallible and subject-dependent.

3.3 Reply to the Self-defeating Objection

When it comes to its expression of ultimate truth, it is hard to deny that Perennial Idealism has a self-defeating air to it. Arguments and assertions in its favour are expressed through discursive thought that relies on divisions rendered inapplicable from the ultimate standpoint. This includes declarations about the nature of ultimate reality by the *jñāni* himself. After expounding on the *ajāta* doctrine, Ramana Maharshi said:

> This [explanation] is all from the point of view of the current conversation. In reality, there is only the *Ātman* [one's real nature as pure consciousness]. Because this is so, there is nothing to know and nothing to be known.
>
> (Godman, 2005, 262)

But why even accept as true such a statement as 'in reality there is only the Atman' when the discursive claim has no application from the standpoint of ultimate reality? And why accept the *jñāni*'s standpoint as ultimate if its very declaration of ultimacy cannot be known or declared? Why indeed argue for a system whose philosophy, enmeshed in distinctions, lacks ultimate legitimacy by its own lights?

It pays first to disentangle, from within Perennial Idealism, the levels on which a logical tension might arise. The standpoint of a *jñāni*, not perceiving distinctions, will admit of no contradictions. Any logical tensions must take hold from the perspective of a perceiving subject—including when talking *about* the *jñāni*'s standpoint. This granted, there is a notable difference between logical tensions that occur from within the world of objects and concepts, including a philosophical system as understood from a subject's standpoint, and those that occur between the subject's and the *jñāni*'s standpoints. The former sort of tension involves straight-out contradictions and paradoxes, such as when a proposition is deemed both true and false. These are the more pernicious cases that can infect the plausibility of a philosophical system. The latter sort of tension—between the articulation of a philosophical system from the subject's standpoint and its declaration as inapplicable from the *jñāni*'s standpoint—is not of this sort. For the *jñāni* is not saying that the statements made from the subject's standpoint are false by the same standards of truth and falsity that would apply from within the subject's perspective. There is no straight-out contradiction. He is, rather, saying that the very framework, from which ordinary and distinction-based notions of truth and falsity have purported ultimacy, lacks validity from the standpoint of the *jñāni*. This takes some of the sting out of the logical tension. The self-defeating air around Perennial Idealism stems more from a tension of the second than the first kind.

When it comes to defending Perennial Idealism, it is impossible to avoid using concepts, logic, and discursive thought. But insofar as such language is a medium through which to express the system's claims about ultimate reality, we must be candid about its limitations. Language and logic should be understood to have either a pragmatic use, such as helping orient the mind to its conscious underlay, or an attenuated epistemic use, such as employing the tools of philosophical method to climb as far up the logical ladder as one reasonably can. But by the system's own admission it can never get us to the top. Descriptions of ultimacy can never be taken to convey absolute truths about pure consciousness that could be understood perfectly through logic and concepts. To use a simile from Zen Buddhism, words are like fingers pointing to the moon. An experience as pure consciousness will always outrank any argument for its existence.

This may not be as radical a departure from ordinary life as might initially be thought. For when it comes to explaining and understanding our world of concrete entities, confidence in discursive thought can be overestimated. Just as with maps, the use of concepts and logic is crucial for navigating the world, but they are not always a substitute for what is being mapped. There is still much that escapes the net. Thomas Nagel's seminal paper 'What is it like to be a bat?' (1974) and Frank Jackson's parable of Mary in the black-and-white room (1986) are both famous modern exemplars of this point. The idea is also behind the push for panpsychism, its advocates drawing upon Russell's (1927) and Eddington's (1928) contention that the language of physics tells us what matter *does* but not what matter *is*. But it is William James, inspired by Bergson, who puts it in a way most pertinent to the current theme:

> When you have broken the reality into concepts you never can reconstruct it in its wholeness. Out of no amount of discreteness can you manufacture the concrete. But place yourself at a bound, or *d'emblée*, as M. Bergson says, inside of the living, moving, active thickness of the real, and all the abstractions and distinctions are given into your hand: you can now make

the intellectualist substitutions to your heart's content. Install yourself in phenomenal movement, for example, and velocity, succession, dates, positions, and innumerable other things are given you in the bargain. But with only an abstract succession of dates and positions you can never patch up movement itself. It slips through their intervals and is lost.

(James, 1909, 261–262)

This propensity to wholeness over discreteness is what we might expect with an underlay of pure, unified consciousness. Even when distinctions are made, they are often fluid and entangled and hard to pin down. James believes that puzzles such as Zeno's paradox arise from the 'intellectualist' assumption that the essence of all things can be captured and understood in static abstract terms. Having described himself as caught in its net for many years, he writes:

Well, what must we do in this tragic predicament? For my own part, I have finally found myself compelled to *give up the logic*, fairly, squarely, and irrevocably. It has an imperishable use in human life, but that use is not to make us theoretically acquainted with the essential nature of reality.... Reality, life, experience, concreteness, immediacy, use what word you will, exceeds our logic, overflows and surrounds it.

(James, 1909, 212)

Logic being the lesser thing, the static incomplete abstraction, must succumb to reality, not reality to logic. Our intelligence cannot wall itself up alive, like a pupa in its chrysalis. It must at any cost keep on speaking terms with the universe that engendered it.

(James, 1909, 207)

To 'keep on speaking terms with the universe' is to 'fall back on raw unverbalized life as more of a revealer', allowing reality to disclose itself through direct experience, as opposed to merely what we think it is (James, 1909, 272). The reality of which James speaks is that of our ordinary empirical world, as viewed from the perspective of a subject. If the necessity of raw non-discursive experience for understanding our world is already apparent within the subject/object framework, then it is less of leap to suppose that an acquaintance with what could be its ultimate underlay, that of pure aperspectival consciousness, will be entirely immersive and beyond all logic and concepts.

3.4 Reply to the Power Challenge

Even if James is right about nature's propensity to unity over division, the divisions must still be accounted for. How might pure undivided consciousness supply its ultimately non-existent and dream-like subjects with inner conscious lives that contain the spatio-temporal, perspectival and lawlike parameters of our structured and diverse world? And how are we to understand a grounding relation where the subjects to be grounded do not literally exist as objective entities in relation to the ground? This, in broad outline, is the Power Challenge.

The difficulty immediately faced is that universal consciousness is supposed to be unstructured by any parameters. Conceiving of it as such was the point of the Cognisensory Deprivation Tank. The experienced dimensions space, time and perspective (with all their causal goings-on) were envisaged to depend proximally upon the presence of cognisensory imagery whose removal would hypothetically leave our experience structureless. How, then, could this unconditioned consciousness meaningfully contribute to these dimensions as they appear within our perspectives? To compound the trouble, mystics have been notoriously elusive on the broader question as to how or why pure consciousness would give rise to the illusion of world-viewing subjects as opposed to, say, nothing at all. To pose the question in metaphysical terms: what explains the fact that we are in a world in which consciousness generates the appearance of world-viewing subjects rather than a world in which it does not? Mystics sometimes account for the origin of manifestation with explanations such as that of divine play (*līlā*), a power to delude (*māyā*), or the universe seeing itself in a mirror, but these explanations are not usually considered to have ultimacy. While Ramana sometimes alluded to manifestation as a kind of desire-driven projection, this description, on closer examination, applied only to the relation between the ultimately non-existent subject (sometimes referred to as 'mind') and the world rather than to a relation between the ground and a world-perceiving subject:

> There is in fact nothing but the *Atman* [Self, our inherent nature as pure consciousness]. The world is only a projection of the mind. The mind originates from the Atman. So Atman alone is the one being.
>
> (Muruganar, 2008, 390)

A modicum of reflection will show that the mystics are not simply copping out. If the metaphysics of Perennial Idealism are correct, the question as to how or why consciousness would generate the illusion of world-viewing subjects, as opposed to nothing at all, is an impossible one to answer. It is impossible for the same reason that the Problem of the One and the Many has no traction. From the standpoint of a *jñāni*, any answer would have to assume the validity of distinctions from within a subject/object framework that they reject as unreal. From the standpoint of an *ajñāni*, questions about the how and why of apparent manifestation could only have a proper answer if posed hypothetically from the *outside* of the subject network which would objectively relate subjects to the ground. For reasons recently discussed, this is a non-starter. Distinctions and divisions exist only from inside a given subject's perspective with no 'outside' to any subject that could interface with the ground. It thus makes no sense to ask: why are we in a world where consciousness generates the appearance of world-viewing subjects rather than a world where it does not? That there *is*—from the standpoint of a putative subject—the manifestation of itself as a subject to which a multifarious world of imagery appears must therefore, from its perspective as a subject, be taken as a *brute fact*.

But now there seems something troublingly uninformative about the grounding story that ensues. It would seem that no aspect of universal consciousness is being recruited to explain *either* the subject's own brute appearance to itself as a subject, *or* the distinctive characters of how other subjects appear to it—which is all being accounted for by the imagery. It puts one in mind of that cheaty-sounding tactic whereupon a novelist, unable to patch up the holes in his plot, finishes the story with 'and then she woke up and it was all a dream!' In grounding the existence and characters of subjects and their experienced world, universal consciousness seems to be doing no heavy lifting at all. While this does not show Perennial Idealism to be false, it is a serious strike against it. This is the heart of the Power Challenge.

Can Perennial Idealism do better? Let us revisit the implications just drawn from the CDT. I had observed that multi-modal cognisensory imagery seems immediately to cue consciousness into assuming the standpoint of a localised perspective in a spatio-temporal world. The problem was raised as to how consciousness, intrinsically lacking such parameters as space, time or perspective, could play any meaningful role in their grounding. But maybe I gave up too quickly in supposing it to have no such role. This may now be seen through posing the question: if we accept that imagery is proximally necessary for the parameters to seem to take hold, is it also completely sufficient? In an obvious sense, the answer must be no: it is after all *consciousness* that is being cued into taking the form of a subject with its various parameters. But could pure consciousness, as it comes through in the subject's experience, also be contributing something more specific to the parameters? Consider perspectivality. Imagery is never free-floating but will automatically appear to a perspective which we are calling a subject. And the *modus operandi* of a subject's perspective is to witness. In the absence of imagery, consciousness is not structured into the *triputī* of witness/witnessing/witnessed, but presents itself, all the same, as a non-directional, intransitive percipience. Upon the arising of imagery, that percipience becomes directed towards the objects in the capacity of *witnessing*. This witnessing, importantly, is none other than directed percipience; it does not suddenly appear out of the blue as a novel feature of subjects. As such, we can see how pure consciousness *qua* percipience could well help to sustain a subject's distinct impression of its perspectival subjecthood.

This opens up the Scrabble board. If pure consciousness could discernibly feed into a subject's impression of perspectivality, then might it not also, when overlaid with imagery, feed discernibly into its impression of other structural parameters such as space, time and causal order? And might this line of thinking suggest a model through which to conceive of the grounding, at least in terms of how pure consciousness could contribute to the structural character of a subject's experience?

I'll start with the grounding story. Because the objects of a subject's experience have an ultimately non-existent, dream-like status, it will fittingly be a model that utilises the dream-mechanism. So let us return, once again, to Lucy's dream, but imagine this time that the pain she feels from the 'crab nipping her toe' is actually from a scorpion stinging her foot as she slumbers. The pain is genuine, but the dream-narrative she weaves around it is not. I suggest that this could be analogous to the way in which pure consciousness may pervade the experiential life of a putative subject, with the structural aspects discernibly traceable, at least in part, to its original form. Just as a genuine feeling of pain or an alarm-sound can puncture a dream-perspective and be woven into its narrative while still retaining, in the dream, its painful or ringing quality, so too—from the standpoint of a subject—might pure and unified consciousness pervade a putative subject's waking life while retaining, in the subject's experience, something of its original form.[26] I have elsewhere referred to this phenomenon as a

---

[26] Kriegel (in conversation) has pointed out that there's a disanalogy in as far as the alarm clock exists independently of the dream and its contents, whereas consciousness is ultimately

'two-tiered illusion' whereupon a tier of genuine, *unified* consciousness seems to become infused with cognisensory imagery to produce the composite illusion of a separate but *unified* self (Albahari, 2006).

We should be reminded that the very posing of such a model would have no validity from the *jñāni*'s standpoint. Conceiving of pure consciousness as a source to which different dimensions of experience (such as unity) can be traced, such that we describe its original form as this way or that way, is an exercise that invokes abstraction. Pure consciousness, in and of itself, is beyond all abstractions and divisions. Yet when it comes to conceiving of the connection between pure consciousness and the character of a subject's experience as it appears from inside their 'waking dream' (as I'll call it) the two-tiered model is as good as any we can hope for.[27] The scope of illusion, with its tier of real consciousness, will extend much further than to just that portion of the world we take to be our unified self. Since the boundaries of a subject's perspective are also built from the world-inducing appearances of other subjects that fill its experiential field, the illusion will encompass the subject's entire perceived world. On the two-tiered model, addressing the Power Challenge—with the proviso that a subject's general appearance be taken as brute fact—amounts to addressing the following question. Posed from the standpoint of a subject, is there anything about how an underlay of pure consciousness could pervade the subject's waking dream such that, together with an overlay of imagery, it may traceably account for what appears to that subject as the world's most salient parameters of space, time and causal power?[28]

---

comprising the dream and all its contents! The crucial part of the analogy, however, rests on the idea that something's original form (alarm sound, pure consciousness) can pervade a subject's dream world such that it bestows to the dreamscape something of its original character while still getting warped by the imagery. The matter of how pure consciousness came to yield non-existent dream subjects with their dream objects is something that we've already established, from the standpoint of a subject, as unassailable brute fact.

[27] There is a masterful music video by Lady Gaga called '911' which aptly illustrates the two-tiered model.

[28] We should be reminded that Kant (1929) sought to explain the organising parameters of our sensory input—space, time, qualitative variation and relational dependence—as originating in a transcendental principle of unified consciousness which could not itself be conditioned by the parameters. Kant's philosophy thereby sets a powerful precedent for a system upon which unconditioned consciousness can impose onto experience structures that explain mathematical and natural order. Some of his arguments can be recruited to strengthen Perennial Idealism, making him is an important ally. However, the reverse is less true. Since Kant allows consciousness no intrinsic phenomenology, it cannot permeate ordinary experience in a way that is analogous to the sound of an alarm permeating a dream. The two-tiered model will not apply to Kant's system as it stands. The reflections to be offered will all assume the two-tiered model.

Answering this question in detail would take us into the building approach. But having seen how an underlay of universal consciousness can feasibly percolate into a putative subject's experience of perspectivality, it will help to close this section by *hinting* at ways through which pure consciousness could similarly play into a subject's experience of space, time and causal power. Even if a complete story cannot be given, discernibly tracing each of these parameters to a possible source in pure consciousness will give us optimism that the Power Challenge can be significantly ameliorated.

Take our experience of space. Be it physical or mental space, this dimension essentially conveys an empty, neutral, unified medium through which a diversity of objects can simultaneously be known to their subject. The CDT allowed us to conceive of consciousness in its original mode as an absolute unity, undifferentiated by any structural dimension. I postulate space to be the extroverted form that the pure unity of consciousness could take when appearing as bifurcated, in the waking dream, into subject and object. Space is the unified and empty medium through which a subject is able to view objects in opposition to itself. I conjecture that when the imagery is visual or auditory, the emptiness takes on the external character of physical space; when the imagery is cognitive, emptiness assumes the internal character of mental space. In either case, the character of unified emptiness that helps to mark our experience as spatial can be discernibly traced to the absolute unity of pure consciousness.

Now consider time. Devoid of objects to mark the passage of time, consciousness in the CDT was described as timelessly present. While an unmoving present doesn't add up to a sense of passage, it may feed into a central component of it. It has often been remarked upon that our experience of passing time is anchored in the present, and that this present moment appears real in a way that past and future do not. Ever-present universal consciousness, when refracted through a lens of subject and object, is naturally placed to serve as this anchor-point. I conjecture that our sense of passage comes from our attention being perpetually pulled out into objects of memory and imagination whose content is imbued with ideas of past and future. The present may then take on the more fleeting and ephemeral characteristic of being a mere moment that is sandwiched in between past and future. But our locus of experience, for all that, is always in the present—naturally traceable to ever-present consciousness.

How about causal laws? Perennial Idealism regards its putative subjects to be inherently dispositional and it is part of the building approach to explain the appearance of causal and lawlike structures in terms of these dispositional powers. Significantly, the powers are not independent of consciousness. They are all about how conscious subjects can be *known* as imagistic objects to one another: as particular modes of *being*. But could such powers be traceable to unconditioned consciousness? Return again to the Cognisensory Deprivation Tank. In stripping our consciousness of its objects, it is tempting to think of our remaining unconditioned awareness as a passive and powerless void. But if descriptions from mystical literature are anything to go by, this notion is utterly mistaken. While consciousness may be empty of objects, it is also frequently depicted as a fullness or plenum: a unity of knowing and being whose reality transcends the illusory *tripuṭī* of knower/knowing/known. Our ordinary capacity to know things, even if based in illusion, is described by Ramana Maharshi as depending on our real nature as the Self, which is the very fountainhead of knowingness:

> Since Self shines without another to know or be known by, it is [true] knowledge. It is not a void. Know thus.... Self, which is clear knowledge, alone is real. Knowledge of multiplicity is ignorance. Even this ignorance, which is unreal, cannot exist apart from the Self, which is knowledge.
>
> (Muruganar, 2004, 58)

> *Knowing* the Self is *being* the Self, and being means existence—one's own existence—which no one denies, any more than one denies one's eyes, although one cannot see them. The trouble lies in your desire to objectify the Self, in the same way that you objectify your eyes when you place a mirror before them. You have become so accustomed to objectivity that you have lost knowledge of yourself, simply because the Self cannot be objectified.
>
> (Muruganar, 2004, 60)

Just as the materialist framework of Big Bang theory posits a singularity of infinite density that explodes forth as the physical universe, so too the idealist framework of Perennial Idealism posits a 'singularity' of knowing-being that will seem to splinter forth, through a subject's waking dream, as the duality of knower and known. I think it not implausible, on our idealist framework, that the subjects' power to *know* and be *known* to one another—through modes of objectified *being* in the form of lawfully ordered imagery-to-a-perspective—could have their precursor in a primal nexus of knowing and being.

The Power Challenge posed a bleak prospect. The metaphysics of Perennial Idealism had rendered the general fact of a subject's appearing to itself, with all its experiences, a brute fact. And it seemed that unconditioned consciousness, lacking structure, could not contribute anything discernible to that putative subject's structured experience of the world, leaving all the heavy lifting to configurations of imagery. But while the *fact* of the world appearing to a subject remains (to its perspective) unavoidably brute, I hope to have shown how the *manner* of the world's appearing may not be brute. The salient patterns and characters of manifestation could well be owed to more than just configurations of imagery happily coalescing in an orderly manner. As understood through the two-tiered model of grounding, there is reason to suppose that each major parameter within our experience—perspectivality, space, time, causal power—bears the traceable imprint of pure consciousness as it pervades all aspects of our waking dream. Pursuing such lines of inquiry may well prove universal consciousness, on this front, to be fit for ground.

4. Conclusion

This chapter offered a novel defence of an ancient view. Four major challenges were launched at the idea that universal consciousness could ground all phenomena. Does Perennial Idealism survive the earthquake of the Thales Objection, the Problem of the One and the Many, the Self-defeating Objection and the Power Challenge? Is universal consciousness fit for ground?

The answer is an optimistic *probably*. I hope to have shown that when relativised to the standpoint of a subject, the system offers a stable enough ground on which to commence building. A fuller test of the ground's stability has to come through the building approach itself, which is needed to properly address such objections as the Power Challenge. But having defended the ground to the extent offered here, I would say that Perennial Idealism, inspired by the vision of mystics, is a serious contender in the mind-body debate.[29]

[29] I am grateful to David Godman, David Builes and Uriah Kriegel for their insightful feedback on this chapter and to Andrew Milne for discussion in relation to the Kant section.

References

Albahari, Miri. 2006. *Analytical Buddhism: The Two-Tiered Illusion of Self.* Basingstoke: Palgrave Macmillan.

Albahari, Miri. 2009. 'Witness-Consciousness: Its Definition, Appearance and Reality', *Journal of Consciousness Studies* 16(1): 62–84.

Albahari, Miri. 2019. 'Perennial Idealism: A Mystical Solution to the Mind-Body Problem', *Philosophers' Imprint* 19(44): 1–37.

Albahari, Miri. 2020. (Written 2015) 'Beyond Cosmopsychism and the Great I Am: How the World Might Be Grounded in Universal (Advaitic) Consciousness', in W.E. Seager, (ed.), *The Routledge Handbook of Panpsychism*, New York: Routledge, 119–130.

Albahari, Miri. 2022. 'Panpsychism and the Inner-Outer Gap Problem', *The Monist* 105(1): 25–42.

Anon. 2002. *Maharshi's Gospel*, Tiruvannamalai: Sri Ramanasramam.

Beiser, Frederick. 2002. *German Idealism: The Struggle against Subjectivism, 1781–1801.* Cambridge, MA: Harvard University Press.

Builes, David. 2021. 'The World Is Just the Way It Is', *The Monist* 104(1): 1–27.

Builes, David. 2023. 'A Humean Non-Humeanism', *Philosophical Studies*, 180(3): 1031–1048.

Chalmers, David J. 2002. 'Does Conceivability Entail Possibility?', in T.S. Gendler and J. Hawthorne (eds), *Conceivability and Possibility*. Oxford: Oxford University Press, 145–200.

Chalmers, David J. 2020. 'Idealism and the Mind-Body Problem', in W.E. Seager (ed.), *The Routledge Handbook of Panpsychism*, New York: Routledge, 353–373.

Della Rocca, Michael. 2020. *The Parmenidean Ascent.* Oxford: Oxford University Press.

Dennett, Daniel. 1991. *Consciousness Explained.* London: Penguin.

Deutsch, Eliot. 1973. *Advaita Vedānta: A Philosophical Reconstruction.* Honolulu: University of Hawaii Press.

Eddington, A. 1928. *The Nature of the Physical World.* Cambridge: Cambridge University Press.

Godman, David. 2005. *The Power of the Presence (Part One).* Colorado: David Godman, Avadhuta Foundation.

Godman, David. 2019. 'Bhavagan's Self-Realisation', https://www.davidgodman.org/bhagavans-self-realisation/2/

Goff, Philip. 2017. *Consciousness and Fundamental Reality*. Oxford: Oxford University Press.

Goff, Philip. 2020. 'Cosmopsychism, Micropsychism and the Grounding Relation', in W.E. Seager (ed.), *The Routledge Handbook of Panpsychism*, New York: Routledge, 144–156.

Horgan, Terence E., and Potrč, Matjaž. 2008. *Austere Realism: Contextual Semantics Meets Minimal Ontology*. Cambridge, MA: MIT Press.

Huxley, Aldous. 1946. *The Perennial Philosophy*. London: Fontana Books.

Jackson, Frank. 1986. 'What Mary Didn't Know', *Journal of Philosophy* 83(5): 291–295

James, William. 1909. *A Pluralistic Universe*. New York: Longmans, Green & Co.

Jones, Richard. 2022. 'Perennial Philosophy and the History of Mysticism', *Sophia* 61: 659–678.

Kant, Immanuel. 1929. *Immanuel Kant's Critique of Pure Reason*. Translated by Norman Kemp Smith. London: Macmillan.

Kastrup, B. 2018. 'The Universe in Consciousness', *Journal of Consciousness Studies* 25(5–6): 125–155.

Katz, Steven T. 1978. 'Language, Epistemology and Mysticism', in S.T. Katz (ed.), *Mysticism and Philosophical Analysis*, New York: Oxford University Press, 22–74.

Kriegel, Uriah. 2013. 'The Phenomenal Intentionality Research Program' in Uriah Kriegel (ed.), *Phenomenal Intentionality*, Oxford: Oxford University Press, 1–26.

Maharshi, Ramana. 1913–1914. *Sri Arunachala Stuti Panchakam*. Translated by Sadhu Om. Tiruvannamalai: Sri Ramana Kshetra, 2007.

Martin, C.B. 2008. *The Mind in Nature*. Oxford: Oxford University Press.

Mørch, Hedda Hassel. 2019. 'The Argument for Panpsychism from Experience of Causation', in W.E. Seager (ed.), *The Routledge Handbook of Panpsychism*.

Muruganar. 2004. *Padamalai*. Translated by T.V. Venkatasubramanian, R. Butler, and D. Godman; edited and annotated by David Godman. Colorado: David Godman, Avadhuta Foundation.

Muruganar. 2008. *Guru Vachaka Kovai*. Translated by T.V. Venkatasubramanian, R. Butler, D. Godman; edited and annotated by David Godman. Colorado: David Godman, Avadhuta Foundation.

Nagel, Thomas. 1974. 'What Is It Like to Be a Bat?', *Philosophical Review* 83(4): 435–450.

Nagel, Thomas. 1989. *The View from Nowhere*. Oxford: Oxford University Press.

Narain, Laxmi (ed.). 2009. *Face to Face with Sri Ramana Maharshi*. Hyderabad: Sri Ramana Kendram.

Nikhilānanada, Swāmi (translator and annotator). 1949. *The Māṇḍūkyopanishad, with Gauḍapāda's Kārikā and Śankara's Commentary*. Mysore: Sri Ramakrishna Ashrama.

Parmenides. *On Nature*. Poem taken from J. Burnet, *Early Greek Philosophy*, 3rd edn. London: A & C Black, 1920.

Plotinus, written 250 ACE. *The Six Enneads*. Translated by Stephen Mackenna and B.S. Page. http://classics.mit.edu/Plotinus/enneads.html

Russell, Bertrand. 1927. *The Analysis of Matter*. London: Kegan Paul.

Sawyer, Dana. 2021. 'Redressing a Straw Man: Correcting Critical Misunderstandings of Aldous Huxley's Perennial Philosophy', *Journal of Humanistic Psychology*, July: 1–29.

Schaffer, Jonathan. 2014. 'Monism', *The Stanford Encyclopedia of Philosophy* (Winter 2016 Edition), Edward N. Zalta (ed.), https://plato.stanford.edu/entries/monism/.

Schopenhauer, Arthur. 2009. *The Two Fundamental Problems of Ethics*. Translated and edited by Christopher Janaway. Cambridge: Cambridge University Press.

Shani, Itay. 2015. 'Cosmopsychism: A Holistic Approach to the Metaphysics of Experience', *Philosophical Papers* 44(3): 389–437.

Shani, Itay. 2022. 'Cosmopsychism, Coherence and World-affirming Monism', *The Monist* 105(1): 6–24.

Shani, Itay., and Joachim Keppler, 2018. 'Beyond Combination: How Cosmic Consciousness Grounds Ordinary Experience', *Journal of the American Philosophical Association* 4(3): 390–410.

Spinoza, Benedictus. 1934[1677]. *Ethics*. Translated by Andrew Boyle. London: Heron Books.

Strawson, Galen. 2008. 'The Identity of the Categorical and Dispositional', *Analysis* 68(4): 271–282.

Thompson, Evan. 2015. *Waking, Dreaming, Being: Self and Consciousness in Neuroscience, Meditation, and Philosophy*. New York: Columbia University Press.

Wolfson, Harry Austryn. 1965. *Philosophy of Spinoza*. Ohio: World Publishing.

Miri Albahari, *Is Universal Consciousness Fit for Ground?* In: *Oxford Studies in Philosophy of Mind Volume 4*. Edited by: Uriah Kriegel, Oxford University Press. © Miri Albahari 2024. DOI: 10.1093/9780198924159.003.0001

2

Modal Idealism

David Builes

1. Introduction

According to some philosophers, consciousness has a fundamental place in nature. Property Dualists hold that there are fundamental properties involving consciousness. Substance Dualists and Panpsychists go further in ascribing such fundamental properties to some fundamental entities (e.g. immaterial souls, particles, or the universe as a whole). Idealists go even further in claiming that *every* fundamental entity is conscious, and moreover every fundamental property is a phenomenal property (i.e. a property that specifies what it's like to be something).[1] My goal will be to argue for a thesis that goes even beyond Idealism: it is *metaphysically necessary* that Idealism is true. Call this view Modal Idealism.

Modal Idealism might seem to be an incredible thesis to most contemporary philosophers, but philosophical fashion was not always this way. Bradley (1893) explicitly endorsed Modal Idealism in his *Appearance and Reality*, and even went so far as to say that is "evident at once":

> We perceive, on reflection, that to be real, or even barely to exist, must be to fall within sentience. Sentient experience, in short, is reality, and what is not this is not real. We may say, in other words, that there is no being or fact outside of that which is commonly called psychical existence. Feeling, thought, and volition (any groups under which we class psychical phenomena) are all the materials of existence, and there is no other material, actual or even possible. This result in its general form seems evident at

---

[1] For a defense of property dualism, see Chalmers (1996). For a defense of substance dualism, see Swinburne (2013). For defenses of panpsychism, see Strawson (2006), Chalmers (2013), and Goff (2017). For defenses of idealism, see Adams (2007), Kastrup (2018), Albahari (2019), Chalmers (2019), and Robinson (2022). The phrase "idealism" has been defined in various different ways: some versions of "panpsychism" will coincide with the present definition of idealism (in particular, see Chalmers' (2019) definition of "pure" panpsychism).

once...[Any] fact that falls elsewhere seems, in my mind, to be a mere word and a failure, or else an attempt at self-contradiction. It is a vicious abstraction whose existence is meaningless nonsense, and is therefore not possible.

(Bradley (1893): 144–145).

While I do not think that Modal Idealism is as obvious as Bradley takes it to be, I do think that it is a plausible view with many attractions. My hope in what follows is to illustrate some of these attractions.[2]

I'll begin by arguing for a claim that is closely related to, but strictly weaker than, Modal Idealism (sections 2–6), after which I'll proceed to give three more arguments for Modal Idealism (sections 7–9) and then conclude (section 10).

2. The First Argument: A Question and an Answer

In order to state the first claim I'll be arguing for, we'll need to draw several distinctions between different kinds of properties. First, we'll be restricting our attention to "one-place" properties that apply to a single thing, rather than more general "n-place" properties (or "relations"), which apply to multiple things. We'll also restrict ourselves to *fundamental* properties, where a property F is fundamental whenever it is necessarily the case that, if [x is F], then [x is F] does not hold in virtue of any other facts.[3,4] Note that

---

[2] Sprigge (1984: 110–140) also defends a view that is close to Modal Idealism, namely that we cannot *conceive* of something that is not in some way conscious.

[3] For more on the "in virtue of" relation, see Rosen (2010) and Audi (2012). One can also take the notion of "fundamentality" to be primitive and not defined in terms of the "in virtue of" relation" (e.g. see Sider (2011) and Wilson (2016)).

[4] One worry about this definition of "fundamental property" is the following. Say that a property F is *weakly fundamental* iff it is *possibly* the case that, if [x is F], then [x is F] does not hold in virtue of any other facts. Might there be properties that are weakly fundamental but not fundamental, and if so, will anything of substance turn on this point? For example, perhaps *being in pain* is weakly fundamental but not fundamental, since *being in pain* could figure in fundamental facts if Dualism is true, but it could also figure in non-fundamental facts if Physicalism is true (supposing that both Physicalism and Dualism are possibly true). In response to this kind of example, one could think that there really are two properties here, namely $pain_{Dualism}$ and $pain_{Physicalism}$, the first of which is a fundamental property and the second of which is a non-fundamental property. Following Correia (2005), Faller (forthcoming), and others, I will be assuming that properties are at least partly individuated by how they are grounded, and so a property is weakly fundamental if and only if it is fundamental. However, if properties are not individuated in this way, much of the following discussion will still hold with suitable modifications.

fundamental (one-place) properties must be *intrinsic* properties, given the definition that a property F is intrinsic to x if and only if [x is F] does not hold partly in virtue of facts involving entities distinct from x and its parts.[5]

I'll be further restricting my attention to (intrinsic) fundamental *non-haecceitistic* properties.[6] Intuitively, a property F is a haecceitistic property just in case [something is F] is about some particular object(s); any property that is not haecceitistic is non-haecceitistic. So, for example, the property of *being Alice* is a haecceitistic property, since [someone is Alice] concerns a particular object (namely Alice), but the property of *being red* is a non-haecceitistic property, since [something is red] is not about any particular object(s).

Within the space of possible fundamental non-haecceitistic properties, some philosophers believe that some such properties are *dispositions* or *powers*. The nature of a disposition or power is exhausted by its causal/nomic relations to other possible properties. For example, perhaps *being massive* is a dispositional or powerful property: to have a certain mass *just is* to resist acceleration in certain ways and interact gravitationally with other massive objects in certain ways. Some philosophers believe that there are fundamental non-haecceitistic properties that are *quiddities*, whose nature is not even partly characterized by their causal/nomic relations to other possible properties.[7, 8]

Following Hildebrand (2016), we can further distinguish between two types of quiddities: *bare quiddities* and *qualitative quiddities*. David Lewis' "Humean" metaphysics was committed to bare quiddities.[9] According to Lewis (1986: 205), "there isn't much to the intrinsic nature of a [quiddity]," and Black (2000: 91) goes further in saying that "just about all there is to a

---

[5] See Rosen (2010) for this definition.

[6] For more on the distinction between haecceitistic and non-haecceitistic properties (sometimes called "non-qualitative" and "qualitative" properties), see Dasgupta (2017) and Plate (2022).

[7] The "nature" of a property is meant to be a hyperintensional notion, so this definition of a quiddity leaves it open whether a quiddity might necessarily have a particular causal/nomic role. Alternatively, one could say that the "essence" of a quiddity is not characterized by its causal/nomic role, or that quiddities are not "individuated" by their causal/nomic role.

[8] Might there be "mixed" properties whose nature is partly characterized by their causal/nomic role and partly characterized independently of their causal/nomic role? Perhaps "conjunctive" properties like *being red and resisting acceleration* are like this, but no such property would be fundamental (since it will be grounded in each of its conjuncts), so we can set such examples aside. Some defenders of "powerful qualities" (e.g. Strawson (2008b), Martin (2008), and Heil (2010)) hold a view where properties are both "powerful" and "qualitative" (yet not merely conjunctive), but following Coates (2020) and Tugby (2022), I think the best way to make sense of such properties are as (qualitative) quiddities that ground (and hence necessitate) their dispositional role.

[9] Although the label is now entrenched, it is not clear which aspects of David Lewis' metaphysics are ones that David Hume himself would have endorsed (e.g. see Strawson 2014).

Humean fundamental [quiddity] is its identity with itself and its distinctness from other [quiddities]." So, let us say that a bare quiddity is a quiddity whose nature is wholly characterized by which other quiddities it is (non-) identical with, and let us say that a qualitative quiddity is any quiddity that is not a bare quiddity. Intuitively, qualitative quiddities have a "substantive" qualitative nature, while bare quiddities lack any substantive nature.

For short, I will use the word "quality" to refer to fundamental qualitative quiddities. The first question that I will be addressing is the following:

Question: What is the space of all metaphysically possible qualities?

Anyone who accepts the coherence of the notions of "metaphysical possibility" and "quality" is faced with this question. However, there is remarkably little that has been said to try to answer this question. The first thesis I want to defend tries to provide an answer:

Answer: The space of all metaphysically possible qualities just is the space of all metaphysically possible fundamental phenomenal properties.

3. The First Argument: Two Initial Objections

Before I begin arguing for this answer, it will be helpful to address two immediate objections one might have about it.

One objection is that phenomenal properties are not even qualities in the first place. There are three reasons why one might think this. First, one might think that there simply are no phenomenal properties. It might seem as if we have phenomenal properties, but this seeming is an illusion.[10] Second, one might think that phenomenal properties are identical with, or reducible to, facts about the spatiotemporal and causal structure of physics.[11] Third, one might think that phenomenal properties both exist and are irreducible to such structural facts, but nevertheless one might think that no phenomenal property is *fundamental*. For example, a "Panprotopsychist" might think that, although phenomenal properties are not identical, or reducible, to such structural facts, they are nevertheless wholly constituted

---

[10] See Frankish (2016) and Kammerer (2022).
[11] Facts about the "spatiotemporal and causal structure of physics" are facts that only use logical/mathematical, causal/nomic, and spatiotemporal notions. See Papineau (2002) and Balog (2012).

by the non-experiential qualities found in matter.[12] Whether one of these three views is correct is a matter of intense debate, and I will not be entering into this debate here. Instead, this first argument will simply be assuming, alongside Dualists, Panpsychists, and Idealists, that phenomenal properties cannot be reduced to, or identified with, wholly non-experiential phenomena. This is certainly a large assumption, but there is still a large gap between the claim that *some* qualities are phenomenal properties and the claim that *all possible* qualities are phenomenal properties. The main goal of this first argument will be to try to bridge this gap.

A second worry one might have is that our proposed answer is incompatible with science, on the grounds that physics has already given us examples of qualities that are non-experiential, such as (say) mass and charge. In response, I will be assuming, alongside "epistemic structural realists," that physics does not tell us about the underlying qualities possessed by fundamental physical entities. Physics only describes the causal role of properties like mass and charge. For example, it only tells us that massive objects resist acceleration and attract other massive objects, but it does not tell us about the underlying quiddity that plays this causal role. This kind of structuralism has been defended by Kant, Russell (1927/1996), Foster (1982), Lewis (2009), and many other contemporary metaphysicians and philosophers of science, and I will be assuming it for this first argument.[13]

In the absence of these two objections, we at least know that (i) some qualities are phenomenal properties, and that (ii) science does not tell us of any non-experiential qualities, so our answer starts to become a live option. In fact, our answer immediately becomes the most conservative and parsimonious response to our Question, since the only examples of qualities we seem to know of are phenomenal properties.[14, 15] But how can we rule out the possibility that there are non-phenomenal qualities that we have not thought of? Addressing this challenge will be the task of the next section.

---

[12] See Stoljar (2006).

[13] See Langton (2004) for an interpretation of Kant along these lines, and see Ladyman (2023) for an overview of structural realism in the philosophy of science.

[14] I will address other potential examples of qualities we might know about in section 5.

[15] Goff (2017: 169–171) argues that parsimony reasons give us good grounds for thinking that the only qualities that are actually instantiated in our world are phenomenal qualities, but it's doubtful whether similar parsimony reasons give us good grounds for thinking that the only *possible* qualities are phenomenal qualities. In general, there is no methodological requirement for thinking that modal space is as simple as possible. Perhaps the simplest modal space is one that only contains the actual world, but, on its own, this doesn't give us good reasons to endorse Spinozism.

4. The First Argument: The Unity of Qualities

My goal is to argue that if *some* possible qualities are phenomenal properties, then *all* possible qualities are phenomenal properties. However, before
I present my official argument, I'll start with an intuition pump.

Suppose physics had ended with classical electromagnetism, so that the
fundamental intrinsic properties of matter seemed to be exhausted by *mass*
and *electric charge*. Furthermore, suppose someone (who was not a structuralist about physics) put forward the following bold hypothesis: the only
qualities that *there could possibly be* are qualities associated with mass and
electric charge.

Of course, given that physics has advanced beyond classical electromagnetism, we know that such a position can't be right. However, it seems to me
that even if physics had never advanced beyond classical electromagnetism,
this answer still would have been problematic (even bracketing worries
about structuralism). It would have been problematic because it seems
unacceptably *arbitrary*. What's so special about mass and charge? Why
couldn't there have been some third kind of quality, which is as different
from mass and charge as mass and charge are from each other? It's very
unclear how there could be satisfying answers to these questions. But, if
there are no satisfying answers to these questions, then the space of possible
qualities would itself be arbitrary. This arbitrariness would then lead to a
corresponding *brute necessity*: it would be necessary that there are at most
two distinct kinds of qualities in the world, but there would be no explanation for why there could only be *those two* kinds of qualities (rather than
some extra third kind).

However, one of the main motivations to be a non-reductionist about
consciousness in the first place is to avoid brute necessities. If experiential
phenomena wholly reduced to non-experiential phenomena, then experiential phenomena would have to be necessitated by non-experiential phenomena.[16] However, there doesn't seem to be any intelligible way for
experiential phenomena to "arise out of" wholly non-experiential phenomena, because experiential phenomena seem so radically different in kind
from non-experiential phenomena. As Strawson (2006) puts it, "The

---

[16] There is some controversy about whether all "grounding" relationships involve necessitation (e.g. Skiles (2015)), but it is widely agreed that reductionism about consciousness requires
some kind of supervenience thesis.

experiential/non-experiential divide, assuming that it exists at all, is the most fundamental divide in nature" (17–18).

With this intuition pump in mind, here is how one might put the argument:

1) Some possible qualities are phenomenal qualities.
2) There are no brute necessities.
3) If some possible qualities are phenomenal qualities and some possible qualities are non-phenomenal qualities, then there are brute necessities.
4) Therefore, all possible qualities are phenomenal qualities.

Premise 1 follows from the assumption that experiential phenomena cannot be reduced to wholly non-experiential phenomena.

Premise 2 is what underlies one of the main motivations for being a non-reductionist about consciousness: if experiential phenomena were reducible to non-experiential phenomena, then such a reduction would involve brute necessitation, but necessitation can't be brute, therefore experiential phenomena cannot be reduced to non-experiential phenomena.[17] Even bracketing issues about consciousness, many other philosophers have independently defended the view that there are no brute necessities.[18] To give an illustrative example, suppose it was a brute contingent fact that there were exactly 823093874138 fundamental particles. That doesn't seem philosophically problematic. But suppose someone further said that it was *absolutely necessary* that there be exactly 823093874138 particles: no possible world contains one fewer or one more. Moreover, there is no reason at all why the number 823093874138 should be special in this way. It is just a brute fact that there is no possible world that contains any other number of particles. Such a view seems bizarre. It seems to be in the nature of metaphysical necessity that metaphysical necessity cannot be brute in this way. Metaphysical necessity is often defined to be the "broadest" objective kind of necessity, but a kind of necessity that was subject to these kinds of

---

[17] Chalmers (2003a) analyzes the "knowledge" argument, the "conceivability" argument, and the "explanatory gap" argument as all involving an assumption that metaphysical necessities cannot be brute. How we should understand the claim that "there are no brute necessities" is controversial, but one popular way is via Chalmers' (2002) thesis of Modal Rationalism. Also see Goff's (2019) "Essentialist" Modal Rationalism.

[18] For an overview of the literature on brute necessities, see Van Cleve (2018).

arbitrary and ad hoc restrictions could not be the broadest objective kind of necessity.[19]

Premise 3 is supposed to be justified by similar kinds of reasons as the mass/charge example above. If the space of possible qualities consisted of phenomenal qualities, together with (say) three other unknown kinds of qualities, qualities of kind X, Y, and Z, then it's not clear how there could be an intelligible explanation for why the space of all possible qualities consisted of *just those four* kinds of qualities, rather than some other extra fifth kind of quality.

On its own, this justification for premise 3 is too quick. One might just despair at the possibility of *ever* explaining why the space of possible qualities has the structure that it has, no matter what one's views are about the space of possible qualities. If so, the hypothesis that the space of all possible qualities is exhausted by phenomenal qualities might be just as inexplicable as any other hypothesis.

In order to provide a helpful contrast, let's consider an example of an *intelligible* space of possible qualities. Consider the quality space in Figure 2.1. It seems like this quality space is the space of all possible greys. Moreover, it seems intelligible why this quality space exhausts all possible greys. The source of the intelligibility seems to be that there is an underlying *unity* to the space of possible greys, where one can intelligibly see how all the possible greys can be generated by continuous variation across a certain dimension.

Here is a speculative hypothesis about the space of all possible qualities: the explanation for why the space of all possible qualities is ultimately intelligible is similar in kind to the explanation for why the space of all possible

Figure 2.1 The space of possible greys.

[19] One modality is "broader" than another just in case the first kind of modality recognizes more possibilities than the second. It is controversial what it takes for a modality to be "objective," but at a minimum it is supposed to be non-epistemic, non-deontic, and not sensitive to the guises under which various objects, properties, and relations are presented. For more on the claim that metaphysical modality is the "broadest objective" modality, see Rosen (2006), Williamson (2016), Clarke-Doane (2019), Balaguer (2021), and Glazier (2021).

greys is ultimately intelligible. Namely, the space of all possible qualities has a certain kind of *unity* to it. The relevant notion of "unity" is hard to pin down, but at a minimum it can be understood in terms of a certain kind of connectedness: for any two possible qualities, there is a path through the space of possible qualities that connects any one quality to any other (just as there is a path through the space of possible greys that connects any grey-quality to any other). Let's call this the *Unity Hypothesis*.

In order to make the Unity Hypothesis more precise, we would need to take a stand on certain controversial structural questions about the space of possible qualities. For example, a natural *sufficient* condition for the Unity Hypothesis is that the relevant space of possible qualities P is "path-connected," in the topological sense that for any two qualities q_1 and q_2 there is a continuous function $f: [0,1] \rightarrow P$ that connects q_1 and q_2 (i.e. $f(0) = q_1$ and $f(0) = q_2$).[20]

However, given minimal assumptions, this would imply that P is in certain ways structurally similar to the real numbers (e.g. the cardinality of P would have to be at least as great as the cardinality of the real numbers).[21] This would be a controversial commitment.[22] An alternative (epistemic) possibility is that P is "discrete" in the sense that the integers are discrete: it is not the case that for any two qualities there is a third quality "between" the first two (just as there is no integer between 1 and 2).[23] If P was discrete in this way, then P could be represented by a *graph*, a mathematical structure consisting of a set of "vertices" together with a set of "edges" between certain vertices. In order to represent P, the vertices in such a graph would represent possible qualities, and an edge between two vertices would represent that the two vertices are qualitatively "adjacent" to one another. For example, 1 and 2 are adjacent in the integers, but 1 and 3 are not adjacent in the integers. If the space of possible greys was discrete, then two grey qualities q_1 and q_2 would be qualitatively adjacent to one another just in case q_1 is either minimally darker or minimally lighter than q_2 (where q_1 is

---

[20] Here, "[0,1]" refers to the set of all real numbers greater than or equal to 0 and less than or equal to 1.

[21] Any path-connected topological space that (i) has more than one element and (ii) is "Hausdorff" has a cardinality at least as large as the continuum. For an introduction to these topological notions, see Munkres (2013).

[22] See Builes and Wilson (2022) for skepticism about the possibility of there being continuum-many things. However, such a view might be able to interpret the space of possible qualities as "indefinitely extensible" (just like it interprets the space of possible real numbers as indefinitely extensible).

[23] See Lee (MS) for further clarification and discussion about whether consciousness is continuous or discrete.

"minimally lighter/darker" than q_2 if and only if q_1 is lighter/darker than q_2, but no other quality q_3 is both (i) lighter/darker than q_2 and (ii) darker/lighter than q_1). If we grant ourselves a notion of qualitative adjacency,[24] then we can say that an alternative sufficient condition for the Unity Hypothesis is that P is representable by a *connected graph*, which is a graph where any two vertices can be connected by a path of edges starting at the first vertex and ending at the second vertex.

In what follows, I will remain neutral on how exactly the Unity Hypothesis should be made precise, since our informal characterization of the Unity Hypothesis will be sufficient for our purposes.[25]

Why believe that the Unity Hypothesis is the only way for the space of possible qualities to be intelligible? I don't have any decisive reason to offer. For all I know, there might be some totally different way in which the space of possible qualities might be rendered intelligible. However, positing this kind of unity in the space of possible qualities, by analogy to the space of possible greys, is the only way I can see how the space of possible qualities might be rendered intelligible. More specifically, if the space of all possible qualities consisted of multiple "disjoint" quality spaces, which were fundamentally different in kind and could not be seen to be connected with one other (like the case of mass and electric charge), then I don't see how there could be an intelligible explanation for why *those exact* disjoint quality spaces would be the only possible ones. The only way for there to be an explanation for this, it seems to me, is if those quality spaces could somehow be "generated" by some underlying mechanism (such as continuous variation across a dimension in the case of the greys), but such an explanation doesn't seem to be applicable if such quality spaces are fundamentally different in kind.[26]

---

[24] One natural way to precisify the notion of qualitative adjacency is that two qualities are qualitatively adjacent if and only if they minimally differ with respect to one dimension of quality space, but they are otherwise identical with respect to every other dimension of quality space.

[25] Another epistemic possibility is that P might be structured similarly to the rational numbers, in the sense that, although it is "infinitely divisible" (for any two qualities q_1 and q_2, there is a quality q_3 "between" q_1 and q_2), it is nevertheless only countably infinite. In such a case, one could impose a slightly different definition of the standard topological notion of path-connectedness. If we let $[0,1]^*$ be the space of *rational* numbers between 0 and 1, then another sufficient condition for the Unity Hypothesis might be that P is path-connected*, in the sense that for any two qualities q_1 and q_2 there is a continuous function $f\colon [0,1]^* \to P$ such that $f(0) = q_1$ and $f(1) = q_2$.

[26] One might instead posit that there are an *infinite* number of disjoint quality spaces, in order to avoid any arbitrariness that comes with specific finite numbers (e.g. seventeen disjoint quality spaces). However, the cardinality of disjoint quality spaces is not the issue. Even if there

Of course, one could easily define spaces of possibility that do not satisfy the Unity Hypothesis. For example, the space of possible properties that are *determinates of either mass or electric charge* is clearly not unified in the relevant sense. In this kind of "disjunctive" case, we can straightforwardly analyze the property of "being a determinate of mass or electric charge" into the properties of "being a determinate of mass" and "being a determinate of electric charge," and we can intelligibly see how there is a unified space of properties corresponding to both disjuncts, which results in a disunified space of properties for the overall disjunctive property. Perhaps the best way to resist the Unity Hypothesis is to try to argue that the notion of a *quality* is also a disjunctive notion that can be analyzed into multiple unified components in this way, but it's difficult to see how one could motivate a (non-arbitrary) disjunctive analysis of the notion of a quality.

If we are willing to grant the Unity Hypothesis, then premise 3 can be supported in a more convincing way. The idea is that, if there *were* fundamentally different kinds of possible non-phenomenal qualities, then the space of possible qualities would be disunified, and if the space of possible qualities were disunified, then it could not be rendered intelligible. For example, if there were exactly seventeen disjoint different kinds of quality spaces, there could be no explanation why there were *exactly those seventeen*, rather than some other number.[27]

---

were infinitely many disjoint quality spaces, we could still ask why there couldn't be an extra disjoint quality space that we were missing, even though such an extra quality space would not affect the overall cardinality of quality spaces. Moreover, there is no "maximal" infinite cardinality: for every infinite cardinality, there is a larger one. So, there would still be arbitrariness in specifying the exact cardinality of the number of disjoint quality spaces. To get around these problems, one might hypothesize that the number of disjoint quality spaces is *indefinitely extensible*, in the sense that, no matter how many fundamentally different kinds of qualities that there could have been, there could always have been more (e.g. see Uzquiano (2015) for different ways to make the notion of "indefinite extensibility" precise). This would avoid the worry that there could always be an additional kind of quality, since there is no definite totality of "all possible qualities" in the first place. However, the only reason for thinking that *sets* are indefinitely extensible is that there is a formal procedure that can be used to generate a new set given any plurality of sets (e.g. one could consider the set of all sets in that plurality), but there doesn't seem to be any kind of formal "procedure" that could generate a fundamentally new kind of quality from a plurality of other kinds of qualities. Moreover, positing that there are indefinitely many kinds of non-phenomenal qualities seems rather exterme when we cannot even concieve of a single example of a non-phenomenal quality.

[27] One might worry that positing seventeen kinds of quality spaces is just as arbitrary as positing one quality space: why one rather than seventeen? But the number of quality spaces isn't what's important. What's important is that the space of possible qualities satisfies the Unity Hypothesis: a space needs to be unified in order to be intelligibly "generated" by some underlying mechanism (such as continuous variation along certain dimensions like the grey case), and a *consequence* (rather than a presupposition) of the Unity Hypothesis is that there aren't multiple disjoint quality spaces that are fundamentally different in kind.

Why accept the assumption that the space of possible qualities would be disunified if it contained both phenomenal and non-phenomenal qualities? Because of the motivations behind our initial assumption that consciousness cannot be reduced. The reason for thinking that experiential phenomena cannot be reduced to wholly non-experiential phenomena is captured by Strawson's (2006) intuition that "[t]he experiential/non-experiential divide, assuming that it exists at all, is the most fundamental divide in nature" (17–18). If one thought that experiential/non-experiential distinction was *not* a fundamental divide, then the motivation for non-reductionism about consciousness would evaporate. If experiential phenomena were fundamentally unified and continuous with wholly non-experiential phenomena, then it would be natural to think that phenomenal experience is reducible for the very same reasons that other kinds of phenomena, such as *life*, are reducible. There is no "fundamental divide" between the living and the non-living (e.g. viruses), so we should not be non-reductionists about life. Similarly, if there is no fundamental divide between the experiential and the non-experiential, then we shouldn't be non-reductionists about consciousness.

So, we now have the argument fully in view. In order for the space of possible qualities to be intelligible (i.e. in order for it not to lead to brute necessities), it must be unified. But adding both phenomenal and non-phenomenal qualities to the space of qualities would be disunified, because there is a "fundamental divide" between the experiential and non-experiential (motivated by the thought that experience cannot be reduced to non-experience).

This kind of argument raises an immediate objection, so I'll close this section by addressing this objection.

The objection is that it is not at all clear whether the space of all possible phenomenal qualities is *itself* unified: visual experiences seem fairly different in kind than (say) auditory experiences. However, if the space of all phenomenal qualities is not unified, then identifying the space of possible qualities with the space of possible phenomenal qualities would not result in a unified space either.

I have four main responses to this worry. My first response is to try to emphasize the continuity of conscious experience by appealing to particular examples. For example, gustatory-experiences seem to seamlessly combine with olfactory-experiences when eating food: eating food without a sense of smell is remarkably different than eating food with a sense of smell. Affective experience can seamlessly combine with various kinds of perceptual experience, such as by experiencing a foul-smelling odor, a screeching loud sound, an extremely spicy taste, or an unpleasantly rough and abrasive texture.[28] Cognitive phenomenology seems at least closely related to various kinds of sensory phenomenology, to the extent that some philosophers believe that cognitive phenomenology can be fully reduced to sensory phenomenology.[29] Furthermore, there are at least sixty different known kinds of "synesthesia," where certain sensory experiences of one modality become associated with sensory experiences of a different modality.[30] Perhaps in some of these cases, sensory experiences of different modalities can be seen to be connected in ways that those of us without synesthesia cannot fully appreciate. More generally, ordinary human experience is very limited, as those who have taken various kinds of mind-altering substances can attest to. So we should be very cautious in making the inference that different kinds of experiences cannot be connected with one another just because we cannot imagine how they might be connected.

My second response is to appeal to certain very general views about conscious experience that suggest that conscious experiences might be more connected than we might initially think. For example, according to "holistic" views about the structure of conscious experience, the most basic kinds of conscious experiences are total experiential states at a given time, so that at any given time, the various visual, auditory, gustatory, olfactory, cognitive, affective, *etc.* kinds of experiences that one is having should be thought of as mere aspects of a total experience that integrates all of these kinds of experiences into a unified whole.[31] On this holistic view, it easier to see how total states of consciousness of various different modalities might be continuously connected to other total states of consciousness of various modalities. For example, on the assumption that our own total conscious states evolve continuously through time, we can continuously connect any total conscious state you have at one time (e.g. dancing at a rock concert) to any other total conscious state you have that same day (e.g. having a relaxing massage) by tracing the continuous trajectory of how your total conscious experience evolves throughout that day. Lastly, one might worry that the space of possible phenomenal qualities does not satisfy the Unity Hypothesis

---

[28] For more on how affective experience combines with various kinds of perceptual experience, see Fulkerson (2020) and De Vignemont (2023).

[29] For a survey of debates about the nature of cognitive phenomenology (including whether cognitive phenomenology might reduce to sensory phenomenology), see Smithies (2013).

[30] For an overview of synesthesia, see Banissy, Jonas, and Cohen Kadosh (2014).

[31] For more on the distinction between "holistic" and "atomistic" approaches to conscious experience, see Bayne and Chalmers (2003), Bayne (2010), and Lee (2014).

on the grounds that radically different kinds of experience have nothing in common, but some philosophers have argued that all experiences *do* have a particular phenomenal aspect in common: namely a distinctive kind of *for-me-ness* that is supposed to capture the essentially subjective or perspectival character of all experience.[32]

My third response is that the Unity Hypothesis only applies to *fundamental* phenomenal qualities, and it is not at all clear that the ordinary phenomenal properties that we are familiar with are fundamental. For example, according to certain "constitutive" versions of panpsychism and idealism, the macroscopic phenomenal properties we are familiar with are non-fundamental properties that are grounded in the phenomenal properties had by fundamental entities (e.g. particles or the universe as a whole). It may be that our ordinary macroscopic phenomenal properties seem to be fairly disunified, even if the fundamental phenomenal properties that ground them are ultimately unified.[33]

My fourth and final response to this worry is simply to *modus tollens*. The space of all possible qualities must be intelligible, and if it is to be intelligible then it must be unified, and so if phenomenal qualities are included in the space of possible qualities, then the space of phenomenal qualities must be unified.[34] It might be *prima facie* difficult to see how the space of phenomenal qualities can be unified, but we all have reason to think that it must somehow be if we are to avoid brute necessities.

5. The First Argument: Potential Counterexamples

I have so far argued that if *some* possible qualities are phenomenal qualities, then we should think that *all* possible qualities are phenomenal qualities, on the grounds that the space of possible qualities must exhibit a certain kind of unity in order to avoid brute necessities. However, in response to this fairly abstract argument, one might simply point to certain alleged

---

[32] See Kriegel and Zahavi (2015). To take another example, it has also been argued that various sensory experiences of different modalities all have a certain spatial character in common (e.g. see Aasen (2018) and Wilson (2023)).

[33] See Lee (2019) for further discussion of the possibility that our introspectable macrophenomenal properties are realized by non-introspectable microphenomenal properties.

[34] Technically speaking, it might be that the space of phenomenal qualities is a disunified subspace of the (unified) space of all possible qualities. But this seems implausible: phenomenal qualities seem more unified to each other than they are to allegedly non-phenomenal qualities.

counterexamples of possible non-phenomenal qualities. The job of this section is to respond to two potential kinds of counterexamples.

The first kind of counterexample appeals to properties found in science. As we have seen earlier, the most obvious kinds of counterexamples—e.g. mass, charge, spin, etc.—can be responded to by a structuralist stance towards physics. Physics only tells us about the causal role that these kinds of properties play, rather than any intrinsic qualities underlying this role. However, one might argue that *geometrical* properties, like *being spherical*, might constitute a different kind of counterexample. On the face of it, properties like *being spherical* seem to be intrinsic properties that have a non-dispositional nature.

There are several things to say about such geometrical examples. First, *being spherical* does not seem to be a *fundamental* property, and by "quality" I mean to only be referring to (intrinsic) fundamental qualitative quiddities. More generally, a standard view is that spatiotemporal structure is grounded in fundamental spatiotemporal *relations*, such as distance relations, that ground shape properties like *being triangular* or *being spherical* (e.g. a macroscopic object is only spherical because of the spatial relations that its parts stand in). Such a view is perfectly compatible with the claim that all possible qualities are phenomenal qualities, since such a view does not posit any fundamental spatiotemporal *qualities*. It should also be noted that the view that there are only fundamental spatiotemporal relations (rather than qualities) is compatible with a substantival view of space-time, according to which there are fundamental space-time points, which are themselves structureless entities that lack any spatiotemporal extension and dimensionality, that stand in various spatiotemporal relations to one another.[35, 36]

A second point to make is that there are strong independent reasons for thinking that, at least in the context of science, spatiotemporal

[35] See Pooley (2013) for an overview of the debate between substantivalism and relationism. One might think that an ontology of space-time in terms of space-time points might still need to posit fundamental intrinsic geometrical properties to space-time points, such as the property of *being point-sized*. But *being point-sized* might be better understood as a "merely negative" property, such as *lacking spatial extension* and *lacking dimensionality*, and merely *lacking* a certain property should not be understood as a fundamental property itself (see note 44 for more discussion). Sider (2006) discusses this point further, writing that "a natural and economic theory of points of spacetime is that each one is a partless, truly bare particular that stands in a network of spatiotemporal relations" (393).

[36] Substantivilist views of space-time need not be committed to a fundamental ontology of space-time points. For example, Schaffer (2009) argues for a monistic conception of space-time, according to which the spatiotemporal manifold as a whole is the only fundamental entity.

concepts pick out *functional* properties rather than intrinsic qualities. For example, one could have a phenomenological analysis of spatiotemporal concepts, where spatiotemporal concepts pick out whatever properties play a role in bringing about certain spatial/temporal experiences, or a non-phenomenological analysis of spatiotemporal concepts, where spatiotemporal concepts pick out whatever properties play a suitable "spatiotemporal role" in fundamental physical theories.[37] Such a functionalist approach is needed to account for a variety of fundamental physical theories, such as certain philosophical interpretations of quantum mechanics and certain speculative theories of Quantum Gravity, where space-time is "emergent" rather than fundamental.[38]

A third and last point to make is that one could just as easily *modus tollens* potential geometric counterexamples to Modal Idealism by means of the argument in the previous section. On the face of it, phenomenal qualities and wholly non-experiential geometric qualities seem radically different in kind. If the space of possible qualities consisted of a space of phenomenal qualities together with a totally disjoint space of geometric qualities, this would cry out for explanation. What could explain why there are only *these two* specific kinds of qualities, rather than some other third kind of quality? In the absence of any kind of unity between the space of phenomenal qualities and geometric qualities, it's unclear how there could be an answer to this question. But if there is no answer to this question, then there would be brute necessary facts about the space of possible qualities.

Let us now turn to a second kind of counterexample, which is inspired by perception rather than physics. Within perception, it is natural to think that our perceptual states represent external objects as having certain primitive non-phenomenal qualities, which Chalmers (2006) calls "Edenic" qualities. For example, color experience seems to represent the surfaces of external objects as being primitively and qualitatively colored, where there is no *a priori* connection between such primitive Edenic colors and (say) the surface-reflectance properties studied by physics. Naïve Realists about perception believe that external physical objects really have such primitive

---

[37] Both such analyses are explored in Chalmers (2021), focusing mostly on the spatial case. Also see Lam and Wüthrich (2018) for more on the relevant functional role of space-time in physical theories. Chalmers also discusses whether we might have a primitive (non-functional) concept of "Edenic shape" properties that are represented in perception. I have two responses to this. First, perhaps Edenic shape properties are also better thought of as non-fundamental properties that are grounded in Edenic spatial relations, and second, I will be further discussing the general class of "Edenic qualities" later in this section.

[38] For more on space-time emergence, see Huggett (2021).

(non-phenomenal) qualities, and they typically appeal to such Edenic qualities to explain the phenomenal character of our (veridical) perceptual experiences.

In my own view, there are good reasons for thinking that external objects don't have Edenic qualities. However, the mere fact that external objects don't *actually* have Edenic qualities doesn't let Modal Idealism off the hook. If it is even *possible* for there to be (non-phenomenal) Edenic qualities, then Modal Idealism would be false. Moreover, Edenic qualities have the interesting feature that they seem to be very closely related to phenomenal properties, so they might serve as a counterexample to Modal Idealism that *also* avoids our argument in the previous section. In particular, perhaps Edenic qualities are sufficiently closely related to phenomenal qualities that they would not render the space of possible qualities "disunified" in the way that other kinds of qualities might. The purpose of the rest of this section will be to address this important potential counterexample to Modal Idealism.

However, before I begin to argue that Edenic qualities are impossible, I want to make a (less important) dialectical point. In section 3, I flagged that I would be making the assumption that experiential phenomena cannot be reduced to non-experiential phenomena, contrary to Physicalists and "Panprotopsychists." However, it is natural to think that, if Edenic qualities are possible, then it *would* be possible to reduce facts about experience to facts about Edenic qualities (together with other (non-phenomenal) psychological facts). After all, one of the main motivations for positing Edenic qualities is precisely to account for our (perceptual) phenomenal experiences in terms of such Edenic qualities.[39] So, technically speaking, the possibility of Edenic qualities might not be relevant to the claim that I wish to defend. The metaphysical possibility of Edenic qualities *does* pose a counterexample to the unconditional claim that "Modal Idealism is true," but it's unclear whether it poses a counterexample to the conditional claim that "*if* phenomenal qualities cannot be reduced, then Modal Idealism is true," because the possibility of Edenic qualities might make the antecedent of that conditional false.

Having made this dialectical point, let us set it to the side and see whether a case can be made that Edenic qualities are impossible. In broad strokes, I think that Edenic qualities only seem to be possible when we narrowly focus on Edenic colors. When we broaden our focus to the *general* category of Edenic qualities, we find that the general concept of an Edenic quality

---

[39] This is one of the main motivations behind "Panqualityism" (see Chalmers (2013) and Coleman (2017)). Although this is one of the main motivations for positing Edenic qualities, see Cutter (2022) and Mihálik (2022) for arguments that this motivation cannot succeed.

starts to unravel, and we find that there are good reasons to reject the general concept as incoherent.

Here is a formal way to state my argument against the possibility of Edenic qualities. If Edenic qualities *were* possible, there would have to be a precise and non-arbitrary answer to the following question:

Question: What is the space of all possible Edenic qualities?

However, there is no precise and non-arbitrary answer to this question. So, we should reject the possibility of Edenic qualities. This way to put the argument is rather formal and unintuitive, but I hope that, as I defend it, it will start to become more intuitive why Edenic qualities are not possible.

Start with the first step: why think that there has to be a precise and non-arbitrary answer to this Question? Because different answers to this Question entail different views about the space of possible fundamental qualities. If the answer to this question was arbitrary, then it would imply that the structure of modal space was arbitrary. However, as we've seen before, one of the main assumptions of this first argument is that modal space is not arbitrary. If the answer to this question was vague rather than precise, then, because I do not think that the concept of a "possible fundamental quality" is *semantically* vague, such an answer would commit to *metaphysical* vagueness. However, following most philosophers, I think that vagueness should be understood only as a feature of how we *represent* reality, rather than as a feature of reality itself.[40]

The next step is the important one: why think that there is no precise and non-arbitrary answer to this Question? Well, to start, the concept of an "Edenic quality" is supposed to pick out a (non-phenomenal) quality that a possible phenomenal experience can represent an object as having. So, in order for there to be answer to our Question, there would have to be answers to the following two questions:

Question-1: Which possible phenomenal experiences represent objects as having a corresponding Edenic quality?
Question-2: Among the Edenic qualities that possible experiences can represent objects as having, which are possible?

The purpose of the first question is to pick out which Edenic qualities are represented by possible experiences, and the purpose of the second

---

[40] For an overview of arguments against metaphysical vagueness, see Barnes (2010).

question is to decide, of the Edenic qualities picked out by the first question, which are genuinely possible. Note that the second question is needed because it is consistent to hold that (say) visual experience *represents* external objects as having Edenic colors, but nevertheless such Edenic colors are not genuinely metaphysically possible. Once we have answers to these two questions, then we immediately have an answer to our main Question. Conversely, it seems like any answer to our main Question will have to presuppose corresponding answers to Question-1 and Question-2.

What is left is to argue is that there are no precise and non-arbitrary answers to Question-1 and Question-2. If neither question has a precise and non-arbitrary answer, then our main Question will not have a precise and non-arbitrary answer either. In fact, I really only need to argue that *one* of these two questions lacks a precise and non-arbitrary answer, but in fact I believe that neither question has a precise and non-arbitrary answer.

Start with Question-1. It is most common to think that paradigm cases of perceptual experiences represent objects as having primitive non-mental qualities, but we can also ask more broadly: which phenomenal experiences in *general* represent objects as having Edenic qualities? When I start reflecting on this question, I find that I quickly start losing my grip on the question. Consider the following experiences: *feeling anxious, feeling happy, feeling sad, feeling dizzy, feeling nauseous, feeling sexually aroused, having cognitive phenomenology* (associated with thought and understanding), *feeling the need to urinate, feeling nostalgia, feeling anger, feeling regret, feeling hot, feeling cold,* etc. All of these experiences have a distinctive phenomenology associated with them, but for which (if any) of these experiences is there a corresponding primitive non-mental Edenic quality that is represented as being instantiated by some object? I'm not at all sure. But when I reflect on experiences of these various kinds, it seems pretty clear to me that there is no (non-arbitrary) *precise* line to be drawn between those experiences that represent objects as having primitive Edenic qualities, and those that do not.

Moreover, my source of puzzlement about which of these experiences have corresponding Edenic qualities is peculiar. For example, when I try attending to an experience of *feeling dizzy*, it seems like I know perfectly well what that experience is like.[41] Still, even given complete knowledge of the phenomenal character of dizzy-experiences, it's still unclear whether the

---

[41] See Lee (forthcoming) for further clarification and discussion concerning the extent of our knowledge of our conscious experiences.

idea of a corresponding "Edenic dizziness" makes any sense (or "Edenic nausea"). This makes me wonder whether the source of my puzzlement is really puzzlement about what it is to be an "Edenic quality" in the first place.

In response to Question-1, one might simply say the following: a phenomenal experience represents a corresponding Edenic quality in some object if and only if that phenomenal experience is a *perceptual* experience. My first response to this suggestion is that it's not clear that it is extensionally adequate, and my second response to this suggestion is that I don't think the distinction between a "perceptual" experience and a "nonperceptual" experience is a precise distinction anyway (and what is needed is a precise and non-arbitrary answer to Question-1).

Consider, for example, experiences like *being in pain, experiencing an orgasm, feeling an itch*, or *feeling the need to urinate*. It is fairly plausible that such experiences represent certain Edenic qualities in different portions of our bodies. For example, a pain in my foot plausibly represents a certain kind of primitive quality in my foot. However, are such bodily experiences supposed to count as "perceptual"? If perceptual experiences are defined as those that are supposed to give us information about the "external world," then this question boils down to the question of whether our bodies count as part of the "external world." This question seems to be a merely verbal question, but the question of which Edenic qualities there could possibly be should not be a merely verbal question. It should be a question of fundamental metaphysics. Sometimes perceptual experiences are thought of as those that we do not have voluntary control over (e.g. visual or auditory experiences), as contrasted with (say) thought or imagination, where we do seem to have more voluntary control. However, *feeling dizzy* and *feeling nauseous* are experiences that we do not have voluntary control over, and it is not at all clear whether such experiences have corresponding Edenic qualities. Lastly, consider the experiences we have while dreaming, or while imagining. Perhaps it is most natural to categorize such experiences as "non-perceptual," but it's not clear whether such experiences lack any corresponding Edenic qualities, contrary to the suggestion that an experience represents a corresponding Edenic quality if and only if it is perceptual.

Having argued that there is no precise and non-arbitrary answer to Question-1, let us now turn to Question-2.

Of the possible Edenic qualities that phenomenal experiences can represent objects as having, which are genuinely possible? It seems to me that at least *some* of them are not genuinely possible. Consider an experience of intense pain in your foot (perhaps you just stubbed your toe). It seems like such an experience represents a certain Edenic painful quality as inhabiting your foot. However, Edenic qualities are supposed to be *non-mental* qualities, and such non-mental qualities should be able to be instantiated by physical objects in the absence of any experiencers (just like Edenic colors). But could there really be an intensely painful quality that is not experienced by anyone? For example, could a rock floating in space instantiate an Edenic quality of intense pain, without being experienced by anyone? It seems like it couldn't. Intense pain seems to have an intrinsically motivating force to it that it doesn't make sense to ascribe to an unexperiencing floating rock. Perhaps in response one could say that, while Edenic pain is possible, it is nevertheless necessary that, whenever it is instantiated, there must be a corresponding experiencer that is "acquainted" with the relevant Edenic pain. There are two worries with this response. First, if it really is necessary that Edenic pain must be experienced whenever it is instantiated, then it is unclear why Edenic pain would still count as a "non-mental" quality in the first place. Second, insofar as we can make sense of a non-mental quality that is necessarily experienced, such a view would seem to be positing a brute necessary connection between wholly distinct existences, and it was an assumption of my original argument that there can't be brute necessities of this kind.

Suppose, then, that at least Edenic pain is impossible. Then so long as *some* Edenic qualities are impossible, the question immediately arises as to *where is the precise line* between those Edenic qualities that are possible and those that are not? Prima facie, it's hard to see where such a precise line should be drawn.

Let us think about some other experiences. Consider the taste experience of something that is really *spicy*. Is Edenic spiciness possible? Well, sufficiently spicy experiences can be, in a way, painful: they can be very unpleasant in a way that quickly makes us try to relieve the spiciness. So, if Edenic pain is impossible, then it seems like intense Edenic spiciness should be too. However, once one says that intense Edenic spiciness is impossible, what should one say for mild Edenic spiciness? Since there doesn't seem to be any non-arbitrary precise line to draw, it seems like we should say that, no matter how mild it is, no Edenic spiciness quality is possible.[42] Similarly, consider *sourness*. Intensely sour things have very different effects on us than intensely spicy things, but in a way, they are also unpleasant, and so for the

---

[42] A structurally similar argument was given by Berkeley in his *Three Dialogues between Hylas and Philonous*.

very same reasons, it seems like Edenic sourness (no matter how mild) should be thought to be impossible. Similar things can be said for sweet and bitter taste experiences (although mildly sweet experiences can be pleasant rather than unpleasant). Once one sees this pattern, it is easy to apply all over the place. For example, consider a *very loud* auditory experience. Such an experience is unpleasant, and so for similar reasons one should think that a corresponding loud Edenic quality is impossible. But, because there is no non-arbitrary dividing line, one should similarly conclude that any auditory Edenic quality, no matter how soft, is impossible. Similar things can be said for (good-smelling or bad-smelling) olfactory Edenic qualities.

One might think that these kinds of examples suggest an interesting response to Question-2: perhaps only phenomenal experiences with *neutral* valence (i.e. ones that are neither pleasant nor unpleasant) have corresponding Edenic qualities that are possible.[43] This is an intriguing suggestion, but it's not clear that it works. For one, consider a holistic taste experience that has both positive and negative aspects to it, but these positive and negative aspects exactly "cancel out" to result in a holistic taste experience that has overall neutral valence (e.g. perhaps something is sweet and spicy, and the pleasantness of the sweetness exactly cancels out the unpleasantness of the spiciness). Is it possible for there to be a corresponding "holistic" Edenic taste quality? Insofar as I have intuitions about this, the answer seems to be "no": so long as there is an aspect to the experience that is not neutrally valenced, then there needs to be a corresponding experiencer who is affected by that valenced-aspect (just like the pain case).

In response, one might suggest that only phenomenal experiences that don't have *any* aspect to them that is positively or negatively valenced have corresponding Edenic qualities that are metaphysically possible. One worry about this view is that it's not clear whether it picks out a precise class of phenomenal experiences, since it is not clear if there are precise facts about "all aspects" of an experience (or even whether there are precise facts about whether a particular aspect is exactly neutrally valenced). It is also unclear whether there are any phenomenal experiences that satisfy this description in the first place (partly because it's unclear how to make sense of "every aspect" of an experience). Lastly, the project of stripping away all possible valence out of an experience doesn't seem to be getting at the heart of the issue. The heart of the issue is that phenomenal experiences have all sorts of

---

[43] The exact nature of valence is contested, but see Carruthers (2018) for two contrasting accounts.

capacities to affect us in various ways. This is most obvious in the case of painful experiences, but it is also clearly the case for bad odors, itches, orgasms, etc. Insofar as experiences have these capacities, then it seems like there needs to be a corresponding subject that is affected by these capacities. Moreover, the ways that experiences affect us are many and varied: the impact that experiences have on us can't be fully captured with a single dimension of "positive" or "negative": experiences can be more or less interesting, or vivid, or surprising, or beautiful, or sublime, or nostalgic, or visceral, or disgusting, etc. What we would need for an Edenic quality to be possible is to have an experience that has no capacity to affect us in any way whatsoever, and it is unclear whether there are any examples of such experiences.

The case of Edenic color is perhaps the best case for such an example, but on reflection, many of the same things that can be said for other sensory modalities could also be said for color. Consider, for example, being shown an intensely bright white light as soon as you wake up from a deep sleep. Such an experience would be unpleasant (just like sourness and spiciness), and it is moreover unclear where to draw a precise line between such an intense visual experience and other more common visual experiences. Or consider how a visual experience of a beautiful sunset affects you, and how greatly it differs from an experience of uniform grey. Or consider a uniformly white visual field with a flashing bright red circle in the center, and how the red seems to be intrinsically "attention grabbing" in a way that its surroundings are not. The ways that colors affect us are clearly not as striking as the way that (say) placing one's hand on a hot stove affects us, but it's unclear whether there is a *sharp* line to be drawn between these experiences, which is what would be needed to delineate metaphysically possible Edenic qualities from metaphysically impossible ones.

In sum, I have argued that *neither* Question-1 nor Question-2 admits of a precise and non-arbitrary answer. But, if at least *one* of them does not admit of a precise and non-arbitrary answer, then our main Question will not admit of a precise and non-arbitrary answer either, which is incompatible with the possibility of Edenic qualities.

6. Interlude: Getting to Modal Idealism

I've finally finished arguing that it is necessary that every quality is a phenomenal quality. But how do we get from this claim to Modal Idealism?

Recall that Modal Idealism is the claim that it is necessary that (i) every fundamental entity is conscious and (ii) every fundamental property is a phenomenal property. However, we can disambiguate the second condition in two ways. According to *Impure* Modal Idealism, every fundamental *one-place* property is phenomenal. Such a view is neutral on whether there might be fundamental relations that are not consciousness-involving. According to *Pure* Modal Realism, every fundamental property *and relation* is consciousness-involving. In order to keep the discussion manageable, I will argue for Impure Modal Idealism in the main text, and I will further argue for Pure Modal Idealism in an appendix.

It turns out that there are three ways to resist (Impure) Modal Idealism while granting that every possible quality is a phenomenal quality. However, all three of these ways are highly controversial. In this section, I'll briefly describe these three ways, and mention why they are controversial.

First, one could reject Modal Idealism by arguing that there could be fundamental entities that are *bare particulars*, which do not possess any (non-haecceitistic) fundamental properties at all.[44] If there could be bare particulars, then it would be false that it is necessary that every fundamental entity is conscious (contrary to Modal Idealism), since bare particulars would not be conscious.

My first response to this worry is that many philosophers, both historically and in contemporary times, have thought that bare particulars are in some way incoherent or unintelligible.[45] For one, it is not clear that we can positively conceive of bare particulars. Try to positively conceive of a world that contains nothing but a single bare particular. Such a world would be completely devoid of colors, shapes, masses, particles, fields, conscious

---

[44] By "bare particular" I mean to refer to what Sider (2006) calls "truly bare particulars" (rather than any "substratum" in the context of the substratum theory of objects and properties). I am also assuming that "merely negative" properties, like *lacking mass* or *lacking electric charge* are not fundamental properties (because otherwise bare particulars would have such non-haecceitistic fundamental properties). If such merely negative properties were fundamental properties, then there might be an infinity of extra fundamental properties that we would have to ascribe to everything: for every fundamental alien property P that is not instantiated in our world, there would seem to be a corresponding fundamental property of *lacking P* that would be instantiated by everything in our world. I am also assuming that "trivial" properties like *being self-identical* are not fundamental properties, since fundamental properties are typically thought of as substantive properties that are contingently instantiated. For more on properties concerning identity and distinctness, see note 48. Even if one does recognize such merely negative or trivial fundamental properties, then bare particulars could be defined as entities that do not possess any (non-haecceitistic) fundamental non-trivial positive properties.

[45] See, e.g., Plato's *Timaeus* (48c–53c), Aristotle's *Metaphysics* (1029a20–33), Locke (1689/1997), Russell (1996), Mertz (2003), Lowe (2003: 86), Bailey (2012), and Giberman (2012).

experiences, etc. Now conceive of a world that contains nothing at all. Did you manage to conceive of two clearly distinct possibilities? To many, the answer will be no. Insofar as one finds bare particulars to be inconceivable, this gives one some (defeasible) reason to think that bare particulars are not genuinely possible. In writing about the "obvious incoherence" of bare particulars, Strawson (2017) writes, "Clearly there can no more be objects without properties than there can be closed plane rectilinear figures that have three angles without having three sides...to be is necessarily to be somehow or other, i.e. to have some nature or other, i.e. to have properties" (69). Armstrong (1997: 109–110) claimed that bare particulars were "vicious abstractions" and was explicit about their impossibility when building his own metaphysics. Although Sider (2006) defends the intelligibility of bare particulars, he aptly summarizes a common attitude towards bare particulars in saying that "bare particulars are widely regarded as the grossest of metaphysical errors" (392).

The second response to make is that there are independently motivated metaphysical views that are incompatible with the existence of bare particulars. For example, according to the "bundle" theory of objects, objects are mere bundles of properties, so if there are no properties to bundle together (as with bare particulars), then there is no corresponding object. The same could be said for a wide variety of other views that reject the existence of an underlying "substratum," whose role it is to "instantiate" various properties.[46] The idea of a bare particular only seems to make sense according to such a theory—a bare particular is simply an underlying substratum that does not instantiate any fundamental properties. For arguments against this kind of substratum theory, see Dasgupta (2017), Builes (2021), and Strawson (2021).

The second way to resist Modal Idealism is by arguing that there could be fundamental entities that possess fundamental dispositions or powers (and such fundamental powers would not be phenomenal properties, contrary to Modal Idealism). Of course, it is common to believe in dispositions or powers, like the fragility of a glass, but the posit of *fundamental* dispositions or powers, which lack any underlying categorical grounding, is a posit that is highly controversial. For example, while it is intuitive to think that a glass is fragile (i.e. disposed to break if struck) in virtue of its microphysical organization, the idea of a *primitively fragile* glass, which isn't fragile in

---

[46] See, e.g., Dasgupta (2009) and Turner (forthcoming).

virtue of any other features that it possesses, seems dubiously coherent. Sider (2001) argues against such brute dispositions on the grounds that
they posit brute "hypothetical properties [that] 'point beyond' their
instances" (41). More generally, anyone who believes that modal facts must
be grounded in non-modal facts will reject the possibility of such brute dispositions. For further criticisms of metaphysical views that posit fundamental powers, see Barker and Smart (2012), Barker (2013), and Jaag (2014).[47]

Lastly, one could resist Modal Idealism by arguing that there could be
fundamental entities that possess *bare quiddities*—that is, quiddities whose
nature is wholly characterized merely by which other quiddities they are
(non-)identical with. Perhaps the primary metaphysical reason to be wary
of bare quiddities is that they seem to imply a proliferation of metaphysical
distinctions that are ultimately illusory. For example, because bare quiddities lack any substantial nature, it is unclear what the difference is supposed to be between a bare particular and an object whose only fundamental
property is a bare quiddity. It is furthermore unclear what the difference is
supposed to be between a world where a single object x instantiates bare
quiddity Q_1, and a world where instead x instantiates a numerically distinct
bare quiddity Q_2. Because bare quiddities do not have any substantive qualitative nature, such possibilities would be qualitatively indiscernible. Lastly,
the main motivation for adopting quiddities (namely, to avoid positing fundamental dispositions or causal powers) is satisfied by adopting qualitative
quiddities, which Modal Idealism already does. As Hildebrand (2016)
argues, the reasons to posit quiddities are perfectly satisfied by qualitative
quiddities, and the many arguments *against* quiddities are only persuasive
against bare quiddities.[48]

---

[47] It should be noted that a popular argument against fundamental powers, namely that
positing fundamental powers involves a certain kind of vicious regress (e.g. see Robinson
(2022: ch. 9)), only applies to views where *all* fundamental properties are powers. However,
what is needed here is the stronger claim that it is impossible for there to be *any* fundamental powers.

[48] There are some other more exotic ways to resist Modal Idealism. For example, one could
think that there are possible fundamental haecceitistic properties, such as the property of *being
identical to p* or the property of *being distinct from q*. However, such properties are not needed
to have fundamental haecceitistic facts. For example, suppose the fundamental facts were of
the form $[p_1$ is F], $[p_2$ is G],…, $[p_1$ bears relation R to $p_2]$,…, etc. where all of the properties and
relations are non-haecceitistic, but $p_1, p_2,$ etc. are primitively distinct individuals. Such a view
would have fundamental haecceitistic facts, but not because of the fundamental properties that
the view recognizes. One could also think that everything has a fundamental non-haecceitistic
property of *being self-identical*, which would also be a counterexample to Modal Idealism.
However, because everything "trivially" has this property, it seems to be better to not posit this
as an additional fundamental property, since fundamental properties are often thought of as

In sum, the case from "all possible qualities are phenomenal qualities" to Modal Idealism is not airtight. One could avoid Modal Idealism by upholding the possibility of bare particulars, fundamental powers, or bare quiddities. Still, all of these posits are highly controversial, and the claim that all possible qualities are phenomenal qualities at least makes Modal Idealism much more plausible than it otherwise might be.

7. The Second Argument: The Eleatic Principle

The second argument for Modal Idealism appeals to the following principle:

> The Eleatic Principle (EP): Necessarily, every concrete object has causal powers.[49]

First, I'll argue that the best way to develop a metaphysics based on EP is to endorse Modal Idealism. Second, I'll argue that several potential counterexamples to Modal Idealism can be resisted by appealing to EP. In sum, I'll be arguing that EP strongly supports Modal Idealism.

Could there be a concrete object that is entirely causally inert? For example, could there be a spatiotemporally located object (hence, a concrete object) that is entirely causally inert? At the very least, it is hard to see how we could ever *know* about the existence of such an entity, since we could never causally interact with it. So perhaps we could never justifiably believe in any counterexamples to EP. However, many philosophers, both historically and in contemporary times, have gone further and defended the metaphysical requirement that having causal powers is a necessary condition for (concretely) existing in the first place. According to Leibniz (1714: 65), "activity...is of the essence of substance," and Schopenhauer (1813/1974: 119) wrote that "matter is throughout pure causality, its essence is action in general."[50] Further contemporary supporters of EP include Armstrong

---

contingently instantiated. Lastly, even if these kinds of counterexamples to Modal Idealism succeed, one could refine the definition of Modal Idealism to be "necessarily, every fundamental entity is conscious, and all non-haecceitistic contingently instantiated fundamental properties are phenomenal properties." Defending such a view would still be of great metaphysical interest. For different accounts of the grounding of identity and distinctness facts, which don't commit to fundamental properties concerning identity and distinctness, see Litland (2022) and Rubenstein (2024).

[49] A popular strengthening of EP is that "to be is to have causal powers." I will appeal to this strengthening of EP towards the end of this section.

[50] Strawson (2016) also attributes something like EP to both Plato and Aristotle.

(1978), Ellis (1990: 22), Field (1989: 68), and Strawson (2016). My goal in this section won't be to further argue for EP. Instead, my goal will be to draw out some of the consequences of EP for those who have some antecedent attraction to the principle.

My overall strategy for arguing that the best way to endorse EP is to endorse Modal Idealism will be to argue that Modal Idealism allows the defender of EP to avoid having to posit all sorts of brute necessities. Since EP is crucially about causation, and since philosophical views about causation are inextricably linked to views about laws of nature, I will be considering how EP might be developed according to different views about the nature of causation and laws.

To start, consider a "Humean" view of causation and laws. According to Humeanism, there is a spatiotemporal mosaic that is filled with local, point-sized qualities, and there are no metaphysically necessary connections between the intrinsic state of one spatiotemporal region and any other non-overlapping spatiotemporal region. According to the most influential development of Humeanism by David Lewis, laws of nature are merely simple and informative summaries of the mosaic, and facts about counterfactuals and causation are determined by reference to such laws.[51] The problem with combining Humeanism with EP is that there are metaphysically possible mosaics that do not exhibit any simple or informative patterns at all, so such possible mosaics would have no laws at all. However, in the absence of any laws, entities in such a mosaic would not stand in any causal relations, violating EP.[52] In response, the Humean could simply reject the metaphysical possibility of such mosaics, but without any independent reason to do so, such a rejection would be committing to brute constraints on modal space. Moreover, as Cowling (2015) has noted, there might be mosaics where it is *indeterminate* whether there are any laws, because it might be indeterminate whether there are any sufficiently simple and informative regularities in such mosaics. In order to comply with EP, the Humean would either have to say that the space of possible mosaics is itself indeterminate, or else they could admit the possibility of things that "indeterminately exist" (since it is indeterminate whether they stand in causal relations). Neither option is particularly attractive.

---

[51] Versions of this "best systems account" of laws are developed and defended by Earman (1986), Lewis (1994), Loewer (2007), Cohen and Callender (2009), and Hall (2015).
[52] There are other versions of Humeanism that do not reduce causation to laws (e.g. see Wilson (2009)), but such views face similar problems.

Among Non-Humean approaches, some account for causation in terms of laws of nature, and others account for laws of nature in terms of causation. Let's start by considering the former.

According to law-based views, laws of nature can either be understood as fundamental entities in one's ontology, or else as relations of "necessitation" between universals.[53] A familiar objection to such views is that the metaphysically necessary connection between their Non-Humean posit ("laws" or "necessitation relations") and corresponding events in the concrete world is mysterious. Why is it absolutely necessary that if a universal F-ness stands in a certain relation to a universal G-ness, then every F must also be G?[54] However, going beyond this standard objection, in order to comply with EP, such views would have to say that *all possible worlds* have primitive laws or necessitation relations, because in the absence of any such laws, nothing would stand in any causal relations.[55] Given that it seems easily conceivable for there to be worlds that lack these Non-Humean posits, this seems to be a problematic brute necessity. In addition, there not only have to be *some* laws in every world, every world has to have laws that govern *every property* in that world. Otherwise, there could be objects with causally inert properties that are not governed by any corresponding law. It would be better if the defender of EP could do without these brute constraints on modal space.

Third, there are Non-Humean approaches that posit fundamental causal powers.[56] The first problem for this view is one we've already seen: while it is familiar to posit causal powers or dispositions that obtain in virtue of underlying categorical facts, fundamental powers are much more controversial. Furthermore, this view faces a similar problem to the previous view: it would have to be combined with the view that it is *impossible* for there to be fundamental properties that are not powers: otherwise, it seems like something could exist that only possesses such non-powerful properties. In the absence of any independent motivation for this modal constraint, this would be a brute necessity that it would be better to avoid.

Let us finally see how Modal Idealism might secure EP. According to EP, everything must have causal powers, but according to Modal Idealism,

---

[53] See Carroll (1994), and Maudlin (2007) for views of the former sort, and see Dretske (1977), Tooley (1977), and Armstrong (1983) for views of the latter sort.

[54] For more on this "inference problem," see van Fraassen (1989), Sider (1992), and Schaffer (2016).

[55] Maybe other views about causation could hold in worlds without laws of nature (e.g. Humeanism). But such a position would then also face the problems faced by other views of causation.

[56] See Mumford (2004), Bird (2007), and Chakravartty (2007).

there are no *fundamental* causal powers. The only fundamental properties are phenomenal properties. So, the combination of EP and Modal Idealism entails that everything must have *non-fundamental* causal powers. This immediately raises a worry about brute modal facts. Facts about the distribution of non-fundamental properties must be necessitated by facts about the distribution of fundamental properties, since non-fundamental facts supervene on fundamental facts. So to avoid brute modal facts, the Modal Idealist must be able to explain why things have the non-fundamental causal powers they do by appealing to facts about the distribution of fundamental phenomenal properties. How could this be done?

The answer is that it can be done by the *Phenomenal Powers* view, which is precisely the view that phenomenal qualities ground corresponding causal powers.[57] The fundamental insight behind the Phenomenal Powers view is that the connection between phenomenal qualities and their corresponding causal powers seems to *make sense*. For example, it is not a mystery why someone who is in pain would try to get rid of that pain: the reason why people try to avoid pain is because of its intrinsically repulsive character. Similarly, it is not a mystery why someone who feels hungry or thirsty would be motivated to try to satisfy their hunger or thirst, or why someone who feels an itch would be motivated to try to scratch the itch, or why someone who entertains an obvious proposition like "$2 + 2 = 4$" would be motivated to endorse it,[58] or why someone who feels exhausted would want to stay in bed, etc. So, the Phenomenal Powers view not only entails that phenomenal qualities ground corresponding causal powers, but it also claims that this grounding relationship is intelligible. In fact, Mørch (2017, 2018, 2019a, 2019b) has argued that it is *inconceivable* that phenomenal properties ground any alternative power to the one that they in fact ground. For example, it is inconceivable that the experience of pain makes someone try to *pursue* further pain in virtue of its phenomenal character.[59]

---

[57] For different defenses of the Phenomenal Powers view, see Langsam (2011), Mørch (2017, 2018, 2019a, 2019b), Builes (2020), and Pallies (2022). The Phenomenal Powers view is an instance of the more general "grounding view of powers," according to which qualities ground corresponding causal powers. Kimpton-Nye (2021), Builes (2022b, 2023, forthcoming), and Tugby (2022) all defend the grounding view of powers in ways that do not presuppose the Phenomenal Powers view.

[58] This kind of view is defended by Brentano (1933/1981: 55–56).

[59] More specifically, Mørch has argued that phenomenal properties ground certain *mental* effects (e.g. pain grounds the power to *try* to avoid it). One might worry that phenomenal powers cannot account for all of the causal powers in the world because phenomenal powers cannot intelligibly ground *physical* (or non-mental) effects. This kind of worry is often raised in the context of the interaction problem for Dualism, where it's not clear how mental causes can

Of course, in all of these cases, the connections between one's experiences and their corresponding dispositional roles is defeasible: for example, you might experience a pain that you don't try to get rid of if you have some other motive for enduring the pain (e.g. being at the dentist). However, in the absence of any interfering motives, phenomenal states seem to have at least a "default" corresponding power.[60]

In sum, by appealing to the Phenomenal Powers view, Modal Idealism directly entails EP in a way that avoids any additional *ad hoc* assumptions, and it avoids all of the kinds of brute necessary facts that other views have to commit to in order to abide by EP. It is also important to note that both the Phenomenal Powers view and Modal Idealism are needed to secure EP. Without the Phenomenal Powers view, Modal Idealism is consistent with phenomenal properties not grounding any powers at all, and without Modal Idealism, the Phenomenal Powers view is consistent with there being non-conscious entities that lack any causal powers.

Finally, not only is Modal Idealism beneficial to EP, but EP is also beneficial to Modal Idealism. By appealing to EP, three potential kinds of counterexamples to Modal Idealism can be avoided.

First, there is the case of Edenic qualities, such as Edenic colors. If there could be concrete objects with fundamental Edenic qualities, then Modal Idealism would be false. Here the crucial question becomes: do Edenic qualities intelligibly ground corresponding intrinsic causal powers in the same way that phenomenal qualities do? If the answer is "no," then the possibility of Edenic qualities is in tension with EP, since an object whose only fundamental properties are Edenic qualities would lack any corresponding intrinsic causal powers.

---

have physical (or non-mental) effects, if the category of the mental is fundamentally different in kind than the category of the physical (or non-mental). However, while this worry might be plausible with a background Dualist metaphysics, it does not have any force given Modal Idealism, since it impossible for there to be anything non-mental given Modal Idealism. One might also worry that phenomenal qualities had by a subject can only produce mental effects for *that very subject*, and so phenomenal qualities cannot explain how distinct subjects causally interact. Partly for this reason, I think Modal Idealists should endorse what Chalmers (2019) calls Cosmic Idealism, according to which the only fundamental entity is a single cosmic mind or "universal consciousness" (see Kastrup (2018) and Albahari (2019, 2020) for different versions of Cosmic Idealism).

[60] Another common objection to the claim that pain has a *ceteris paribus* power to make one try to avoid it is the phenomenon of *pain asymbolia*, since people with the condition of pain asymbolia report that they are in pain but don't feel any motivation to get rid of the pain (e.g. see Grahek (2007)). However, this would only be an objection to the phenomenal powers view if the phenomenal character of normal pain is the very same as the phenomenal character of asymbolic pain, which is highly controversial (e.g. see Rachels (2000), Bain (2014), and Mørch (2019a)).

I think there are good reasons for thinking the answer is no. As we saw in section 5, the plausibility of an Edenic quality possibly existing independent of experience crucially turns on that quality *not* having any intrinsic causal powers. One reason why it is implausible that Edenic pain is possible is because of the intrinsically motivating force that pain seems to have. One reason why it is more plausible that Edenic colors are possible is because it might seem like colors lack any such intrinsically motivating force. For example, insofar as Edenic colors are intelligible, it seems like we can conceive of a primitively red sphere floating in otherwise empty space doing nothing at all, which would violate EP.

In response, perhaps the defender of Edenic colors might say that Edenic colors have the causal power to affect the phenomenal experiences of perceivers who look at them: for example, Edenic redness might have the power to cause phenomenally red experiences when perceived. There are a number of problems for this proposal. For one, even if the actual world was endowed with Edenic colors, it is far from clear that they would causally affect our phenomenal experiences. Our phenomenal experiences are completely causally explained by surface reflectance properties rather than such Edenic properties.[61] Perhaps instead one might say that Edenic colors have the causal power to affect the phenomenal experiences of perceivers *of the right kind*: namely, perceivers who can be "directly acquainted" with the Edenic colors of external objects. There are two major problems with this proposal. First, it is not at all clear that we have an intelligible account of how one could be directly acquainted with external non-mental qualities of physical objects. Naïve realists typically take such an acquaintance relation to be a *sui generis* relation that cannot be understood in any other terms, but one might easily wonder whether such a *sui generis* relation is intelligible.[62] Second, insofar as we can make sense of direct acquaintance with non-mental qualities, it is not clear whether such Edenic qualities would be *causing* our perceptual experiences or whether they would be (partly) *constituting* our perceptual experiences. For example, Chalmers (2006) writes that "perfect perception" of Edenic qualities "requires unmediated acquaintance with the object or the property, and perhaps also requires that the

---

[61] The defender of Edenic properties could in principle identify (or ground) Edenic colors in surface reflectance properties (e.g. see Campbell (1993) and McGinn (1996)), but such a proposal would face the same "explanatory gap" worries that come with identifying (or grounding) phenomenal experiences in brain states.

[62] Yetter-Chappell (forthcoming) argues against the intelligibility of acquaintance with non-mental qualities. For more on the primitive nature of the acquaintance relation, see Brewer (2011), Soteriou (2013), and French and Phillips (2023).

object or the property is itself a constituent of one's perceptual experience" (94). If direct acquaintance is understood in terms of constitution, then Edenic qualities might only constitutively contribute, rather than causally contribute, to the phenomenal character of perceptual experiences in cases of "perfect perception."

In sum, it is at least far from clear that Edenic qualities are capable of intelligibly grounding intrinsic causal powers in the way that phenomenal qualities can, and if they cannot, then EP entails that Edenic qualities are impossible, in conformity with Modal Idealism.

Other potential counterexamples to Modal Idealism can be handled with a popular strengthening of EP, which is also entailed by Modal Idealism and the Phenomenal Powers view:

EP+: Necessarily, *everything* has causal powers.

Consider, for example, the case of bare particulars. If there could be bare particulars, then Modal Idealism would be false. However, the possibility of bare particulars is in tension with EP+, since bare particulars do not have any intrinsic causal powers.[63] There are some views that could give *extrinsic* causal powers to bare particulars, but there are independent reasons for thinking that such views do not square well with EP. For example, on a Humean view, bare particulars could be said to "cause" things if there are suitably many bare particulars that exhibit appropriately simple and informative regularities. However, as we have already seen, (i) Humean views must reject EP insofar as they are committed to the possibility of Humean mosaics without any simple and informative regularities, and (ii) since it can be vague whether a Humean mosaic has any laws, EP commits the Humean to vagueness about existence and/or modality.[64]

Second, there are bare quiddities. If there could be objects whose only fundamental properties are bare quiddities, Modal Idealism would also be false. Again, however, the possibility of objects whose only fundamental

---

[63] Note that it is consistent with EP, but not EP+, that there could be abstract objects that are bare particulars (contrary to Modal Idealism).

[64] Alternatively, one could have a Non-Humean view in which there are external governing laws that give causal powers to bare particulars. However, there is no independent reason for thinking that all possible worlds with bare particulars must also include Non-Humean laws that govern all bare particulars. In the absence of any such independent reason, such Non-Humean views must swallow brute necessary connections between the existence of bare particulars and the existence of corresponding governing laws to comply with EP.

properties are bare quiddities is in tension with EP+ for the very same reason that the possibility of bare particulars is in tension with EP+.

In conclusion, there is a natural harmony between EP (and EP+) and Modal Idealism, together with the Phenomenal Powers view. Anyone who has some sympathy with EP therefore has extra reason to endorse Modal Idealism (together with the Phenomenal Powers view).

8. Third Argument: Our Knowledge of Consciousness

The third argument for Modal Idealism, like the first argument, will assume a background view of non-reductionism about phenomenal consciousness. However, I hope the argument will also be relevant to those who are eliminativists about phenomenal consciousness, since the argument I will be pursuing is closely related to a central motivation for eliminativism.

In broad strokes, the argument is the following. We seem to know that we are phenomenally conscious. But, Chalmers (2018, 2020) has recently developed an argument that attempts to "debunk" our beliefs about our own conscious states.[65] The third argument for Modal Idealism will be that it helps to respond to Chalmers' debunking argument. In other words, Modal Idealism helps us secure our knowledge of our own phenomenally conscious states.

In order to state the debunking argument, let the phrase "phenomenal intuitions" pick out our judgments about our own states of phenomenal consciousness (e.g. "I am conscious" or "I am in pain"), where "judgements" are understood in purely functional terms (e.g. dispositions to report and behave in appropriate ways). Chalmers' presents his debunking argument as follows:

1. There is an explanation of our phenomenal intuitions that is independent of consciousness.
2. If there is an explanation of our phenomenal intuitions that is independent of consciousness, and our phenomenal intuitions are correct, their correctness is a coincidence.

---

[65] Although I will be focusing on Chalmers' development of this debunking argument, similar issues arise in Kirk (2008), as well as in Frankish's (2016) discussion of the "illusion problem" (also see Kammerer (2018)).

3. If our phenomenal intuitions are correct, their correctness is not a coincidence.

4. Therefore, our phenomenal intuitions are not correct.

If this argument is sound, it would imply that none of us is conscious. So, anyone who believes that we *are* phenomenally conscious must reject one of the premises.[66]

The motivation for premise 3 is straightforward: other things being equal, it is better for a theory to avoid coincidences. Moreover, if it is a mere coincidence that our phenomenal intuitions are correct, that might naturally be taken to undermine our justification in our belief that we are phenomenally conscious.

The motivation for premises 1 and 2 crucially turns on what is meant by "independent." One sense of independence is "descriptive independence." On this sense, an explanation of our phenomenal intuitions is independent of consciousness if it never explicitly *mentions* any conscious states. On this reading, premise 1 is plausible: it seems like we can give a complete "structural" explanation of our phenomenal intuitions that never mentions consciousness, but rather only appeals to facts about the structure and dynamics of our brain. However, on this reading of "independence," premise 2 is clearly false. For example, there might be brain-based explanations of our judgements about *cats* that never explicitly mention cats, but that does not make our (correct) judgements about cats a coincidence. This is because cats are still playing a *causal* role in bringing about the relevant brain states. Similarly, there might also be physics-based explanations of our judgements about cats that involve massively complex arrangements of particles-arranged-cat-wise, but so long as those particles *constitute* cats, it again seems like our judgements about cats are not coincidental.

For this reason, Chalmers argues that the best response to this debunking argument involves a strategy he calls "realizationism," according to which the physical structures in our brain that explain our phenomenal intuitions are themselves realized by consciousness, so that "brain-based" explanations of our phenomenal intuitions still allow for consciousness to be

---

[66] One could also run the argument in terms of "beliefs" instead of (functionally construed) "phenomenal intuitions." This would raise subtle issues about whether beliefs are themselves constituted by phenomenal consciousness (e.g. see Chalmers (2003b), Yetter-Chappell (2022), and Duncan (forthcoming)). However, even if our beliefs might be justified by the fact that they are constituted by consciousness itself, one can still ask whether the correctness of our phenomenal intuitions is a mere coincidence.

causally and constitutively involved in explaining our phenomenal intuitions (much like the "cat" case above). For example, according to realizationism, if I were to make a judgement that I am in pain in ordinary circumstances, then the structures in my brain responsible for my judgement would be at least partly realized by the corresponding phenomenology of pain that my judgement is about.

However, one could still worry that realizationism does not completely remove the threat of coincidence. Even if we grant that the physical structures in our brain that explain our phenomenal intuitions are realized by the phenomenal qualities that our phenomenal intuitions are about, isn't it possible that the *very same* physical structures could be (i) realized by totally different phenomenal qualities that do not correspond to the relevant phenomenal intuitions or (ii) realized by something entirely non-phenomenal?

If either (i) or (ii) are possible, then structural explanations for our phenomenal intuitions would still be *modally* independent of the relevant phenomenal states: in the sense that the very same structural explanation could have obtained without the relevant phenomenal states. It could have been realized by totally different phenomenal states, or it could have been realized by something wholly non-phenomenal. Given this modal independence, however, it can still seem to be a coincidence that our phenomenal intuitions are correct. It would just be a matter of luck that we happened to have the right realizers that cause our phenomenal intuitions. In other words, substituting "independent" for "modally independent" in the debunking argument still poses a significant challenge for the realizationist response.

According to Chalmers, the best response to (i) involves commitment to the Phenomenal Powers view developed by Mørch (2020), where phenomenal states necessarily have specific corresponding causal powers. On this view, it is not the case that phenomenal states can be "modally recombined" to play any causal role; rather, phenomenal states necessarily play particular causal roles whenever they are instantiated.[67] For example, following an idea by Langsam (2011), Mørch suggests that perhaps phenomenal states have a *ceteris paribus* power to cause judgements that we are in the relevant states, at least under suitable background conditions of sufficiently attending to our phenomenal states. For example, suppose your visual field is green on the left-half and red on the right-half, and you judge that there is a

---

[67] A weaker view is that it is *nomically*, but not metaphysically, necessary that phenomenal states have specific causal powers. Such a view is developed by Saad (2019).

phenomenological difference between the left-half and right-half of your visual field. On the relevant kind of Phenomenal Powers view, the actual phenomenal contrast in your visual field (partly) causally explains why you made the relevant judgement, and you wouldn't have made the same judgement if you had a uniformly colored visual field, or if you were blind and had no visual field at all, because those different phenomenal states (necessarily) have different powers that would (*ceteris paribus*) causally bring about different phenomenal intuitions. Although I am sympathetic to this response, I won't be pursuing it any further here, since whether it is successful is independent of the viability of Modal Idealism.

Modal Idealism becomes relevant in responding to (ii). Even if the Phenomenal Powers view successfully responds to (i), there's still a worry that the physical structures in our brains that explain our phenomenal intuitions could have existed without being realized by any phenomenal qualities at all. For example, there might be a "zombie world" that is structurally just like ours but where the structure of our brain is realized by wholly non-experiential qualities. In that zombie world, there would be a structural-isomorph of each of us that has the very same phenomenal intuitions, but they would all be massively mistaken. Alternatively, there might be a zombie world that is structurally identical to ours but where the structure of our brain isn't realized by *any qualities at all*. For example, such a "purely structural" world might consist of various bare particulars standing in spatiotemporal relations to one another.

Is it just a coincidence that we inhabit a world where the structure of our brain is realized by *phenomenal* qualities, rather than a world where the structure of our brain is realized by non-phenomenal qualities, or a world devoid of any qualities at all? Not according to Modal Idealism. According to Modal Idealism, the structure of our brain *must* be realized by underlying phenomenal qualities. Modal Idealism therefore removes an important threat to realizationism, and therefore helps secure our justification and knowledge of our own phenomenal states.

9. Fourth Argument: Theoretical Fruitfulness

My final argument for Modal Idealism, unlike the previous three, is amenable to every philosopher, regardless of their background philosophical views. The argument is simply this: Modal Idealism is theoretically fruitful. There is a variety of thorny metaphysical problems that philosophers have wrestled with for a very long time, and Modal Idealism helps us make progress on these problems in illuminating ways. This gives us some reason to take Modal Idealism seriously.

We've already seen some examples of the metaphysical work that Modal Idealism does. For example, the question that we started with is a metaphysical problem that everyone faces:

Question: What is the space of all metaphysically possible qualities?

Modal Idealism gives a simple and elegant solution to this problem. Similarly, insofar as one wants to build a metaphysics on the basis of the Eleatic Principle, Modal Idealism is also theoretically fruitful.

For the remainder of this section, I'll describe four other examples of Modal Idealism at work.

9.1 The Structure of Objects and Properties

Consider the metaphysical dispute about the relationship between "objects" (i.e. things that have or instantiate properties but cannot themselves be "had" or "instantiated") and "properties." According to one popular view, which is sometimes called the "substratum theory," objects and properties both exist and occupy fundamentally different ontological categories. Objects function as the underlying "substratum" that are the bearers of properties. According to a rival view, which is sometimes called the "bundle theory," there really are only properties. What we think of as "objects" are really just properties that are "bundled" together by a primitive relation of "compresence."[68] Lastly, in other work, I have defended a view where there is no real distinction between an object and its corresponding properties.[69] In particular, I've argued that we should start by endorsing a kind of "property monism," where any fundamental entity should be thought of as only having a single fundamental property. However, instead of endorsing a

---

[68] There are eliminativist versions of the bundle theory that do not ontologically commit to the existence of "bundles" as distinct from their constituent properties, and there are reductionist versions where bundles exist but are grounded in the properties that constitute them. For an introduction to debates about the substratum theory and the bundle theory, see Loux and Crisp (2017: 82–117).

[69] See Builes (2021). Strawson (2021) defends the same view, attributing it to Descartes, Spinoza, and Kant as well.

two-category ontology where there is fundamental entity x and a distinct fundamental property F such that "x is F" (where "is" is the is of predication), we should instead collapse the distinction between x and F and say that "x is F-ness" (where "is" is the is of identity rather than predication).

How should we decide between these views? Well, it turns out that there is an exactly similar debate in the philosophy of mind about the structure of conscious experience. What is the relationship between the subject of experience (i.e. the thing that "has" phenomenal properties) and the corresponding phenomenal properties that it has? According to one popular view, which is analogous to the substratum theory, the subject of experience and its corresponding phenomenal properties both exist and occupy different ontological categories. According to a rival view, which is analogous to the bundle theory, there really is no "subject of experience." There really are only phenomenal properties that are "bundled" together by a primitive relation of "co-consciousness." Lastly, Strawson (2003) has defended the view that there is no real distinction between a subject of experience and the corresponding phenomenal properties that it "has." Instead, we should think that the subject of experience is *identical* to the experience that it is having.

According to Modal Idealism, these debates are, as a matter of necessity, collapsed into one. The view that there is an underlying substratum that is ontologically distinct from its properties *just is* the view that there is an underlying subject of experience that is ontologically distinct from its phenomenal properties. The view that there is no underlying substratum, and instead there are only properties that are bundled together, *just is* the view that there is no underlying subject of experience, and instead there are only phenomenal properties that are bundled together. The view that there is no real distinction between an object and its corresponding properties *just is* the view that there is no real distinction between a subject of experience and its corresponding phenomenal properties. By collapsing these debates, Modal Idealism reduces two philosophical problems into one. Furthermore, one can "carry over" all of the arguments in one debate to the other. For example, insofar as one thinks that there is no real distinction between a subject of experience and the corresponding phenomenal properties that it has, then one should also think that there is no real distinction between an object and the corresponding properties that it has.

Lastly, "property monism"—the view that all fundamental entities only have a single fundamental property—also has an analog in the philosophy of mind. In particular, many philosophers have been led to endorse the analog of property monism with respect to consciousness by virtue of the "unity of consciousness." According to Bayne and Chalmers (2003), we should say that experiences are "unified" just in case they are "aspects of a single encompassing state of consciousness." Such a view has many defenders. For example, Searle (2002) argues that we have a "single, unified conscious field containing visual, auditory, and other aspects" and that "there is no such thing as a separate visual consciousness" (54). Tye (2003) also endorses what he calls "the one-experience view." In considering the different aspects of our experience he writes, "There are not five different…experiences somehow combined together to produce a new unified experience." Rather, "there is just one experience here" (27). If one rejects this kind of holistic view with respect to consciousness, one faces the awkward question of saying *exactly how many* basic phenomenal qualities somehow combine to make up one's total experiential state (e.g. is there supposed to be a basic phenomenal quality for every "pixel" of one's visual field?).

As before, Modal Idealism collapses the general metaphysical question of property monism into the question of whether global conscious states are prior to their experiential parts. Any reasons one has for endorsing or rejecting one of these views will carry over to apply to the other view.

9.2 Fundamental Abstract Entities

Should we include abstract entities, like numbers or propositions, into our fundamental ontology? Metaphysicians sharply disagree on this question.[70] Moreover, many have argued that it is difficult to see how we could have a justified opinion on the matter, given that any abstract entities would be causally inert and isolated from us.[71]

Fortunately, Modal Idealism immediately resolves this dispute. There cannot be abstract objects like numbers in our fundamental ontology because there cannot be *any* fundamental entities that are not conscious. Abstract objects are (by definition) non-mental entities, so they cannot exist.

If we were to unpack this kind of argument, we could start by asking: what would abstract objects like numbers be like if they existed? If they aren't "bare particulars" (which there are independent reasons to be skeptical of), then they would have to possess some quality. But what

---

[70] For an introductory survey of debates about abstract entities, see Cowling (2017).
[71] See Warren (2017).

qualities should we think that they possess? An increasingly popular "structuralist" position in the philosophy of mathematics is that mathematics only tells us about the *relations* that abstract objects like numbers stand in, rather than about any qualities that they possess.[72] So, mathematics seems to leave us completely in the dark about what qualities they possess. According to Modal Idealism, however, the only possible qualities are fundamental phenomenal properties. Given that numbers aren't supposed to be conscious, it follows that they can't possess any qualities at all. Instead of believing in a Platonic realm consisting of a plenitude of bare particulars, we should instead conclude that there is no Platonic realm at all.[73]

9.3 Fundamental Concrete Entities

Metaphysicians also disagree about what *concrete* entities to admit into our fundamental ontology. One important choice point is between Monistic theories, according to which the universe as a whole is part of our fundamental ontology, and theories according to which the "smallest" entities—such as particles or space-time points—are fundamental entities.[74]

How are we to decide between these views? Prima facie, it might seem like such views are empirically equivalent to one another, so one might wonder how we can decide between them. Some philosophers have even expressed skepticism about whether there is an objectively correct answer about how the concrete world should be "carved up" into fundamental entities.[75] However, given Modal Idealism, these views have clear differences. For example, Monistic theories imply that the universe as a whole is conscious, whereas theories that posit particles or space-time points as fundamental are committed to thinking that such point-sized entities are conscious. Moreover, many philosophers have argued that the project of grounding our ordinary "macroscopic" conscious states in the conscious

---

[72] For an overview of structuralist approaches to mathematics, see Reck and Schiemer (2020).

[73] I elaborate on this argument, without the help of Modal Idealism, in Builes (2022c). I also give other independent reasons to reject the existence of abstract objects in Builes (2022a). For different philosophies of mathematics that do not rely on the existence of abstract objects, see Hellman (1989), Azzouni (2004), and Balaguer (2009).

[74] For defenses of Monism, see Schaffer (2007, 2010a, 2010b, 2010c, 2013), Horgan and Potrč (2008), Ismael and Schaffer (2020), Perry (2017), Builes (2021), and Builes and Teitel (2022). For arguments against Monism, see Sider (2008) and Baron and Tallant (2016).

[75] See Hirsch (2011) and Balaguer (2018).

states of fundamental point-sized entities is very different than the project of grounding our macroscopic conscious states in the conscious state of the world as a whole. In particular, many philosophers have argued that grounding our ordinary conscious states in the conscious states of the world as a whole is a much more promising approach.[76] If these philosophers are right, then Modal Idealism gives us extra reasons to endorse Monism.

9.4 The Temporal Structure of Reality

Philosophers of mind disagree about the temporal structure of conscious experience. Dainton (2023) describes one popular school of thought as follows:

> [A]ll forms of consciousness, from the most complex to the simplest possible, are essentially temporal: all possess experienced flow. Experienced duration necessarily possesses some temporal depth, and as such cannot exist in a durationless instant. (22)

Views of this kind has been endorsed by William James, Henri Bergson, F. H. Bradley, Edmund Husserl, and more recently by Strawson (2008a: 388–402).[77] If this view is right, then it has important consequences for which fundamental properties could possibly be instantiated. In particular, it implies that no possible fundamental property can be instantiated in a durationless instant.[78] On the other hand, philosophers such as St. Augustine and Thomas Reid, and more recently Chuard (2011) and Builes and Impagnatiello (forthcoming-b), have argued that our most basic conscious experiences are confined to the present moment.

If we look to our best theories in physics, fundamental physical properties seem to be instantiated at durationless instants, rather than over temporally extended intervals. For example, the properties of having a particular mass or electric charge are typically thought of as being instantiated at a particular instant, rather than over an extended temporal

---

[76] See Goff (2017), Shani and Keppler (2018), Kastrup (2018), and Albahari (2020).
[77] For an overview of the views of these philosophers with respect to temporal experience, see Dainton (2022).
[78] It also seems to imply that *Presentism*—the view that only the present moment exists—is false, because no fundamental properties can be instantiated at the present moment. For a recent defense of Presentism, see Builes and Impagnatiello (forthcoming-a).

interval.[79] In our more advanced quantum theories, the wave function of the universe is also supposed to describe the state of the universe at a single moment of time, rather than over an extended temporal interval.

If Modal Idealism is correct, then one's views about the essential temporal structure of phenomenology should correspond to one's views about the temporal structure of fundamental physical properties.[80] By drawing this correspondence, Modal Idealism lets our views about physics inform our views about phenomenology, and vice versa. For example, insofar as our best theories in physics keep positing instantaneous fundamental physical properties, then Modal Idealism should make us more confident that phenomenal properties are not essentially temporally extended.

10. Conclusion

I have argued that Modal Idealism can be supported in at least four ways:

1) It is the best answer to the question of what the space of all possible qualities is like.
2) It is the best way to implement a metaphysics based on the Eleatic Principle.
3) It is the best way to secure our knowledge of our own conscious states.
4) It is theoretically fruitful: it gives us substantial insight into a variety of important and perennial metaphysical questions.

However, none of these four arguments even attempt to show that Modal Idealism is, in Bradley's (1893: 144) words, "evident at once." Might there be some relatively simple *a priori* insight that reveals why Modal Idealism is (allegedly) evident?

---

[79] One might think that *velocity* or *momentum*, or more generally properties that are defined in terms of temporal derivatives of other properties, are examples of properties in physics that cannot be instantiated at durationless instants. However, typically such properties are reduced to the properties that they are temporal derivatives *of*: for example, according to the "at-at" theory of velocity, instantaneous velocity at a time is reduced to positions at nearby times. A reductionist view of this kind implies that such properties are not fundamental properties. Some philosophers have argued for non-reductionist views about quantities like velocity, but such non-reductionist views typically imply that the relevant property *is* instantiated at a durationless instant. For more on this debate, see Tooley (1988), Arntzenius (2000), Lange (2005), and Builes and Teitel (2020).

[80] This is compatible with a structuralist view of physics, where physics is silent on the underlying *qualities* of matter, but nonetheless physics tells us a lot of important information about the *structure* of the physical world.

I'm not sure if there is, but in some moods, I think there might be. Here is a (somewhat silly) syllogism:

1) For x to *be*, x must be *like* something.

The intuitive content of this premise is just that there can't be bare particulars. If something is to exist at all, it must have some positive, intrinsic nature to it. Now consider the following:

2) For x to be like something, there must be something it's like to be x.

This gets us Modal Idealism, more or less:

3) For x to be, there must be something it's like to be x.

In certain moods, reflecting on 2) gives me a feeling of insight. How can x be intrinsically like something if there's nothing it's like to be x? For x to be like something, there must be something it's like *for* x. Sometimes philosophers describe the absence of experience by saying that "all is dark inside."[81] But if "all is dark inside" for x, then it seems like x isn't positively like anything, contrary to 1).

In a way, what these intuitions are trading on is that there seems to be a close connection between *intrinsicality* and *subjectivity*. Talk of what things are like "inside" is often used to characterize both intrinsicality and subjectivity. What something is like "from the outside" are its extrinsic features that do not characterize what it's like to be that thing, and what something is like "from the inside" are its intrinsic features that do characterize what it's like to be that thing.

In asking about something's intrinsic states, we are asking a *what-is-it-like?*-question. In asking about something's subjective states, we are asking a *what-is-it-like-to-be?*-question. Modal Idealists recognize that there's a conceptual distinction we can draw between intrinsicality and subjectivity, but they nevertheless think that these categories are necessarily co-extensive (just as there is a conceptual distinction between *triangularity* and *trilaterality*, even though these categories are necessarily co-extensive).[82]

---

[81] See Chalmers (1996: 96).
[82] See Adams (2007: 46–47) for a similar intuition.

If you want a test for how "intuitive" Modal Idealism strikes you, then ask yourself whether there seems to be a genuine difference between a world in which "all is dark inside," and a completely empty world, which contains nothing at all.[83]

Appendix: Pure Modal Idealism

In the main text, I argued for Impure Modal Idealism, which is the thesis that it is necessary that: (i) every fundamental entity is conscious and (ii) every fundamental (one-place) property is a phenomenal property. The purpose of this appendix is to further argue for Pure Modal Idealism, which supplements Impure Modal Idealism with the claim that every fundamental property *and relation* is a phenomenal property or relation.

Perhaps the most salient counterexamples to Pure Modal Idealism include the possibility of fundamental *spatiotemporal* relations, *causal* relations, and *mathematical* relations (such as the membership relation between sets and the successor relation between natural numbers).

There are two ways to defend Pure Modal Idealism in the face of these kinds of examples. First, one could give general arguments against the possibility of any fundamental (non-phenomenal) relation. Second, one could argue against specific alleged counterexamples to Pure Modal Idealism, by arguing that such alleged non-phenomenal relations are not (or cannot be) fundamental. I'll begin by giving three general arguments of the first kind, after which I'll give three specific arguments of the second kind. Needless to say, there is much more that can be said about the nature of relations than can be covered here.[84] My goal will simply be to give an initial case in favor of Pure Modal Idealism, which complements the discussion in the main text.

The first general argument is that the very same reasons for favoring the Unity Hypothesis for fundamental (one-place) properties generalize to favor the Unity Hypothesis for fundamental relations. Just as it's hard to see how there could be an explanation for why there are (say) exactly seventeen fundamentally different kinds of (one-place) properties, it's hard to see how there could be an explanation for why there are (say) exactly seventeen fundamentally different kinds of relations. For the space of qualities to be intelligible, it must be unified. Similarly, for the space of possible fundamental relations to be intelligible, it must be unified.

---

[83] Thanks to Matt Duncan, Jack Himelright, Uriah Kriegel, Andrew Lee, Hedda Mørch, Adam Pautz, Galen Strawson, and Helen Yetter-Chappell for their helpful feedback.

[84] For a recent introductory survey on the metaphysics of relations, see Heil (2021). Lowe (2016) argues that there are no fundamental relations. For a recent idealist case against fundamental physical spatiotemporal relations, see Robinson (2022: 187–206).

On its own, the Unity Hypothesis does not immediately rule out all potential counterexamples to Pure Modal Idealism. It only implies that there can be at most one fundamental kind of relation, which (for all we've said so far) might be a non-phenomenal kind of relation. One way to bridge this gap is to argue that there is a fundamental kind of *phenomenal* relation, and since phenomenal and non-phenomenal relations would be fundamentally different in kind, the Unity Hypothesis would imply that there cannot also be fundamental non-phenomenal relations. Perhaps the most plausible candidate for a fundamental phenomenal relation is the *co-consciousness* relation, which is the relation that experiences stand in when they are experienced "together." Some philosophers have argued that the co-consciousness relation plays a central role in accounting for the unity of consciousness, and others have argued that it could play the role of the "phenomenal bonding" relation, which accounts for how distinct subjects of experience might combine to form a new subject of experience.[85]

Another way to (partially) bridge the gap from the Unity Hypothesis to Pure Modal Idealism is to argue that certain alleged kinds of fundamental non-phenomenal relations would not satisfy the Unity Hypothesis. For example, it's not clear whether the space of all possible mathematical relations is appropriately unified: prima facie, the membership relation between sets and the successor relation between natural numbers do not seem appropriately unified. So, it is unclear whether the space of all possible fundamental mathematical relations would satisfy the Unity Hypothesis. Furthermore, it is also unclear whether the space of all possible spatiotemporal relations is appropriately unified. Spatiotemporal structure involves many different kinds of structure: including topological, affine, metrical, and differential structure. Moreover, it is unclear what kinds of structural constraints need to be met in order for some relations to count as "spatiotemporal" in the first place. This is most clear when considering various potential candidate theories of Quantum Gravity, which posit fundamental physical structures that are in some ways "approximately" spatiotemporal. Baron and Le Bihan (2022) have recently argued for a version of "quietism" with respect to the status of space-time in Quantum Gravity, according to which there is no precise and non-arbitrary way to delineate which kinds of physical structures are genuinely "spatiotemporal":

> In the context of quantum gravity…we don't need to argue about what space-time is in any deep sense, since it doesn't matter. Nothing much seems to be lost by simply conceding that the term "spacetime" has escaped semantic control, and now picks out a hodgepodge of different things, which don't bear much, if anything, in common.
>
> (Baron and Le Bihan (2022: 173))

---

[85] For more on the co-consciousness relation, see Dainton (2000) and Miller (2017). For more on the phenomenal bonding relation, see Goff (2016).

Such a "hodgepodge" view of space-time is deeply at odds with the Unity Hypothesis.

The final two general arguments against the possibility of fundamental (non-phenomenal) relations both assume that fundamental relations must correspond to fundamental entities in one's ontology (either as tropes or universals). Many of the same reasons for positing fundamental *properties* in one's ontology can be given for positing fundamental relations in one's ontology. For example, one might accept a truthmaking principle, according to which relational truths require relational truthmakers, and relational truthmakers require the existence of relations.[86] To take another example, a popular way to mark the distinction between (perfectly) natural predicates (e.g. green) and other kinds of gerrymandered predicates (e.g. grue) is to posit the existence of corresponding properties for (perfectly) natural predicates (but not for gerrymandered predicates). Similar reasons apply in the case of relations. Not *every* arbitrary set of ordered pairs corresponds to a (perfectly) natural relation. For example, there is no fundamental relation whose extension consists of {(Mars, Earth), (The Statue of Liberty, The Eiffel Tower)}. If one thinks that the distinction between (perfectly) natural and gerrymandered properties should correspond to a distinction in one's ontology, then one should also think that the distinction between (perfectly) natural and gerrymandered relations should correspond to a distinction in one's ontology.

However, given an ontology of fundamental relations, then many have argued that one is faced with Bradley's Regress. Bradley's Regress can be formulated in many ways, but here is one formulation.[87] Suppose there is a fundamental relation R that relates individuals a and b. Well, the mere existence of R, a, and b doesn't seem to adequately account for the fact that R relates a to b. After all, it could be that R exists and relates some other things distinct from a and b. So, in order for R to relate a and b, R must stand in an appropriate relation to a and b. So, there must be some other relation R^* that appropriately relates R to a and b. However, the mere existence of R^* doesn't seem to adequately account for the fact that R is related to a and b by R^*. It must be that R^* is appropriately *related* to R, a, and b. So, there must be some other relation R^{**} that relates R^* to R, a, and b. This kind of reasoning leads to an infinite regress, and many philosophers have argued that this kind of infinite regress shows that there cannot be fundamental relations.[88]

There is also a much quicker general argument against the possibility of fundamental non-phenomenal relations if one believes that fundamental relations should be construed as entities in one's ontology. According to Impure Modal Idealism, every fundamental entity is conscious. So, if fundamental non-phenomenal

---

[86] For an introduction to truthmaker theory, see Cameron (2018, 2021).

[87] The following is a modal formulation of Bradley's Regress, which some philosophers have responded by appealing to certain kinds of relational tropes (e.g. see Maurin (2010)). For a non-modal formulation of Bradley's Regress that is responsive to this objection from relational tropes, see Hakkarainen and Keinänen (2022).

[88] See Maurin (2012) for a survey of different responses to Bradley's Regress.

relations exist, then they would have to be conscious! After all, such entities should not be construed as *bare particulars*: they must have a qualitative nature to them. However, Impure Modal Idealism says that the only qualities there could possibly be are phenomenal qualities, so any fundamental non-phenomenal relations would have to be conscious. However, it is absurd to think that fundamental non-phenomenal relations (e.g. "being seven meters away from") are conscious. There is nothing it is like to be a distance relation (if there *was* something it's like to be a distance relation, then it's unclear why the distance relation would count as a "non-phenomenal" relation in the first place).

Having seen these three general arguments that take us from Impure Modal Idealism to Pure Modal Idealism, let us now turn to specific arguments for thinking that putative counterexamples to Pure Modal Idealism should be resisted.

First, take the case of fundamental mathematical relations, such as the membership relation between sets or the successor relation between numbers. If there were fundamental mathematical relations, then there would have to be mathematical entities that are related by such relations. However, in section 9.2, I argued that Impure Modal Idealism entails the impossibility of mathematical entities. Therefore, Impure Modal Idealism entails that fundamental mathematical relations are impossible.

Second, take the case of fundamental causal relations. There is a variety of metaphysical views that account for causal facts without appeal to fundamental causal relations. For example, Non-Humean views that appeal to fundamental laws, Non-Humean views that appeal to intrinsic causal powers (that explain the causal relations that things stand in), and Humean views that reduce all causal/nomic facts to categorical facts all avoid positing fundamental causal relations. Moreover, certain views in the metaphysics of time are also incompatible with the existence of fundamental causal relations. For example, given the standard view that fundamental causal relations hold between an earlier event (or object) and a later event (or object), then *Presentist* views, according to which only present entities exist, are incompatible with the existence of fundamental causal relations. Lastly, anyone who is wary of fundamental causal powers that do not have any underlying categorical grounding should be similarly skeptical of fundamental causal relations that do not have any underlying categorical grounding. Both kinds of posits involve a kind of primitive necessity that is not explicable in terms of underlying non-modal facts.

Lastly, take the case of fundamental spatiotemporal relations. As we've already seen, according to many theories of Quantum Gravity, and certain interpretations of quantum theories in general, spatiotemporal structure is not fundamental. Moreover, as we've seen earlier in this section, many theories of Quantum Gravity suggest that it is unclear what counts as "spatiotemporal structure" in the first place. This makes the (epistemic) possibility that the space of possible fundamental relations corresponds to the space of possible spatiotemporal relations in tension with the Unity Hypothesis. However, beyond these general points, one might still wonder whether anything specific can be said about why there couldn't be (say) fundamental distance relations in worlds that operate according to classical physical laws in a background space-time. One reason to be skeptical of such a possibility is that our best physical theories define spatiotemporal distance in a way that makes it constitutively depend on the entire spatiotemporal manifold. In particular, it is standard to define the distance between two points as the *minimum path length* of all possible paths throughout the spatiotemporal manifold that begin at the first point and end at the second. To see this definition at work, consider what would happen to the distance between two points if we were to remove some of the space between them (Figure 2.2).

On the right-hand side, there is *no path at all* between the relevant two points, because the two points inhabit entirely disconnected spatial regions, analogous to Lewisian "island universes." So, according to the minimal path conception of distance, the two points on the right-hand side do not stand in any distance relation at all. The only reason that the points might seem to be at some fixed distance apart is due to the artifact that these pictures are themselves drawn on (or embedded within) a unified spatial region that is this page. However, these pictures are meant to represent the universe as a whole, which is *not* embedded in any wider spatial arena.

Schaffer (2009: 135) uses the fact that distance relations (as well as other spatiotemporal notions such as topological connectedness and handedness) make implicit reference to the entire spatiotemporal manifold to motivate a Monistic view of space-time, according to which the spatiotemporal manifold as a whole is fundamental.[89] Such a Monistic view implies that there are no fundamental relations, since there is only a single fundamental entity in the first place. Historically, such a Monistic conception of space-time has also been defended by Descartes, Spinoza, Leibniz, and Kant.[90]

However, putting aside Monism, the way that distance relations (as well as many other spatiotemporal properties and relations) are typically determined is by appealing

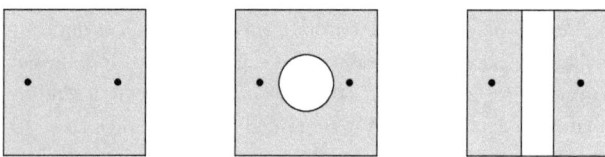

Figure 2.2 Examples of how distance might depend on the ambient space-time.

---

[89] Schaffer also argues that certain views (e.g. metric essentialism and moderate structural realism) that imply that the *parts* of space-time are individuated by their place in the *whole* of space-time support Monism (e.g. see Maudlin (1989) and Esfeld and Lam (2008)). Perry (2017) also argues for a Monistic conception of space-time.

[90] For the case of Descartes, see Carriero (2002: 53). For the case of Spinoza, see Bennett (1984: 86). For the case of Leibniz, see Adams (1994: 232–234). For the case of Kant, see Schaffer (2009: 136).

to the *metric* on space-time, where the metric is represented by a mathematical function that takes different values on every point in space-time. How the metric should be interpreted metaphysically remains an open question in the philosophy of physics. Some have argued that the metric should be construed as an ordinary physical field akin to the electromagnetic field, which assigns intrinsic properties to points (e.g. see Earman and Norton (1987)). On a monistic view, such a field might be thought of as an intrinsic "distributional property" of the universe as a whole (e.g. see Parsons (2004)). Others have argued that the metric should be construed as assigning intrinsic properties to infinitesimal regions rather than to points (e.g. see Bricker (1993)). These interpretational matters are still a matter of debate, but it is at least far from clear that the best analysis of the space-time metric appeals to any kind of fundamental relation, in conformity with Pure Modal Idealism.[91]

In sum, I have given three general arguments against the possibility of fundamental non-phenomenal relations, and I have argued against three specific alleged counterexamples to Pure Modal Idealism. I conclude that Impure Modal Idealists should plausibly go all the way and endorse Pure Modal Idealism.

References

Aasen, Solvieg. 2018. Spatial Aspects of Olfactory Experience. *Canadian Journal of Philosophy*. 49, no. 8: 1041–1061.

Adams, Robert. 1994. *Leibniz: Determinist, Theist, Idealist*. New York: Oxford University Press.

Adams, Robert. 2007. Idealism Vindicated. In *Persons: Human and Divine*, edited by Peter van Inwagen and Dean Zimmerman, 35–54. Oxford: Oxford University Press.

Albahari, Miri. 2019. Perennial Idealism: A Mystical Solution to the Mind-Body Problem. *Philosophers' Imprint* 19, no. 44: 1–37.

Albahari, Miri. 2020. Beyond Cosmopsychism and the Great I Am: How the World Might Be Grounded in Universal "Advaitic" Consciousness. In *The Routledge Handbook of Panpsychism*, edited by William Seager, 119–130. New York: Routledge.

Armstrong, David. 1978. *Universals and Scientific Realism*. Cambridge: Cambridge University Press.

Armstrong, David. 1983. *What Is a Law of Nature?* Cambridge: Cambridge University Press.

---

[91] For a much more throughout treatment of the metaphysics underlying modern space-time theories, see Arntzenius and Dorr (2012).

Armstrong, David. 1997. Against "Ostrich Nominalism": A Reply to Michael Devitt. In *Properties*, edited by D.H. Mellor and Alex Oliver, 101–111. New York: Oxford University Press.

Arntzenius, Frank. 2000. Are There Really Instantaneous Velocities? *The Monist* 83, no. 2: 187–208.

Arntzenius, Frank, and Cian Dorr. 2012. Calculus as Geometry. In *Space, Time, and Stuff*, edited by Frank Arntzenius, 213–278. Oxford: Oxford University Press.

Audi, Paul. 2012. Grounding: Toward a Theory of the In-Virtue-Of Relation. *Journal of Philosophy* 109, no. 12: 685–711.

Azzouni, Jody. 2004. *Deflating Existential Consequence: A Case for Nominalism*. New York: Oxford University Press.

Bailey, Andrew. 2012. No Bare Particulars. *Philosophical Studies* 158: 31–34.

Bain, David. 2014. Pains That Don't Hurt. *Australasian Journal of Philosophy* 92, no. 2: 305–320.

Balaguer, Mark. 2009. Fictionalism, Theft, and the Story of Mathematics. *Philosophia Mathematica* 17, no. 2: 131–162.

Balaguer, Mark. 2018. Why the Debate about Composition is Factually Empty. *Synthese* 195, no. 9: 3975–4008.

Balaguer, Mark. 2021. *Metaphysics, Sophistry, and Illusion: Toward a Widespread Non-Factualism*. Oxford: Oxford University Press.

Balog, Katalin. 2012. In Defense of the Phenomenal Concept Strategy. *Philosophy and Phenomenological Resesarch* 84, no. 1: 1–23.

Banissy, Michael, Clare Jonas, and Roii Cohen Kadosh. 2014. Synesthesia: An introduction. *Frontiers in Psychology* 5: 1414.

Barker, Stephen. 2013. The Emperor's New Metaphysics of Powers. *Mind* 122, no. 487: 605–653.

Barker, Stephen, and Benjamin Smart. 2012. The Ultimate Argument against Dispositional Monist Accounts of Laws. *Analysis* 72, no. 4: 714–722.

Barnes, Elizabeth. 2010. Arguments Against Metaphysical Indeterminacy and Vagueness. *Philosophy Compass* 5, no. 11: 953–964.

Baron, Sam, and Baptiste Le Bihan. 2022. Spacetime Quietism in Quantum Gravity. In *The Foundations of Spacetime Physics: Philosophical Perspectives*, edited by Antonio Vassallo, 155–175. New York: Routledge.

Baron, Sam, and Jonathan Tallant. 2016. Monism: The Islands of Plurality. *Philosophy and Phenomenological Research* 93, no. 3: 583–606.

Bayne, Tim. 2010. *The Unity of Consciousness*. New York: Oxford University Press.

Bayne, Tim and David Chalmers. 2003. What Is the Unity of Consciousness? In *The Unity of Consciousness*, edited by Axel Cleeremans. Oxford: Oxford University Press.

Bennett, Jonathan. 1984. *A Study of Spinoza's Ethics*. Indianapolis: Hackett Publishing Company.

Bird, Alexander. 2007. *Nature's Metaphysics: Laws and Properties*. Oxford: Oxford University Press.

Black, Robert. 2000. Against Quidditism. *Australasian Journal of Philosophy* 78, no. 1: 87–104.

Bradley, Francis. 1893. *Appearance and Reality: A Metaphysical Essay*. London: Oxford University Press.

Brentano, Franz. 1933/1981. *The Theory of Categories*, translated by Roderick Chisholm and Norbert Guterman. The Hague: Martinus Nijhoff.

Brewer, Bill. 2011. *Perception and Its Objects*. Oxford: Oxford University Press.

Bricker, Phillip. 1993. The Fabric of Space: Intrinsic vs. Extrinsic Distance Relations. *Midwest Studies in Philosophy* 18, no. 1: 271–294.

Builes, David. 2020. Derivatives and Consciousness. *Journal of Consciousness Studies* 27, no. 9–10: 87–103.

Builes, David. 2021. The World Just Is The Way It Is. *The Monist* 104, no. 1: 1–27.

Builes, David. 2022a. Ontology and Arbitrariness. *Australasian Journal of Philosophy* 100, no. 3: 485–495.

Builes, David. 2022b. The Ineffability of Induction. *Philosophy and Phenomenological Research* 104, no. 1: 129–149.

Builes, David. 2022c. Why Can't There Be Numbers? *The Philosophical Quarterly* 72, no. 1: 65–76.

Builes, David. 2023. A Humean Non-Humeanism. *Philosophical Studies*. https://doi.org/10.1007/s11098-023-01927-5.

Builes, David. Forthcoming. How to Ground Powers. *Analysis*.

Builes, David, and Michele Odisseas Impagnatiello. Forthcoming-a. An Empirical Argument for Presentism. In *Oxford Studies in Metaphysics Volume 14*, edited by Karen Bennett and Dean Zimmerman. Oxford: Oxford University Press.

Builes, David, and Michele Odisseas Impagnatiello. Forthcoming-b. Experience and Time: A Metaphysical Approach. *Analytic Philosophy*.

Builes, David, and Trevor Teitel. 2020. A Puzzle about Rates of Change. *Philosophical Studies* 177, no. 10: 3155–3169.

Builes, David, and Trevor Teitel. 2022. Lawful Persistence. *Philosophical Perspectives*: 1–26. https://doi.org/10.1111/phpe.12171.

Builes, David, and Jessica Wilson. 2022. In Defense of Countabilism. *Philosophical Studies* 179, no. 7: 2199–2236.

Cameron, Ross. 2018. Truthmakers. In *The Oxford Handbook of Truth*, edited by Michael Glanzberg, 333–354. Oxford: Oxford University Press.

Cameron, Ross. 2021. Truthmaking and Metametaphysics. In *The Routledge Handbook of Metametaphysics*, edited by Ricki Bliss and J. T. M. Miller, 233–244. New York: Routledge.

Campbell, John. 1993. A Simple View of Colour. In *Reality, Representation, and Projection*, edited by John Haldane and Crispin Wright, 257–268. Oxford: Oxford University Press.

Carriero, John. 2002. Monism in Spinoza. In *Spinoza: Metaphysical Themes*, edited by Olli Koistinen and John Biro, 38–59. Oxford: Oxford University Press.

Carroll, John. 1994. *Laws of Nature*. Cambridge: Cambridge University Press.

Carruthers, Peter. 2018. Valence and Value. *Philosophy and Phenomenological Research* 97, no. 3: 658–680.

Chakravartty, Anjan. 2007. *A Metaphysics for Scientific Realism: Knowing the Unobservable*. Cambridge: Cambridge University Press.

Chalmers, David. 1996. *The Conscious Mind: In Search of a Fundamental Theory*. Oxford University Press.

Chalmers, David. 2002. Does Conceivability Entail Possibility? In *Conceivability and Possibility*, edited by Tamar Gendler and John Hawthorne, 145–200. Oxford University Press.

Chalmers, David. 2003a. Consciousness and Its Place in Nature. In *Blackwell Guide to the Philosophy of Mind*, edited by Stephen Stich and Ted Warfield, 102–142. Oxford: Blackwell.

Chalmers, David. 2003b. The Content and Epistemology of Phenomenal Belief. In *Consciousness; New Philosophical Perspectives*, edited by Quentin Smith and Aleksandar Jokic. Oxford: Oxford University Press.

Chalmers, David. 2006. Perception and the Fall from Eden. In *Perceptual Experience*, edited by Tamar S. Gendler and John Hawthorne, 49–125. Oxford: Oxford University Press.

Chalmers, David. 2013. Panpsychism and Panprotopsychism. Amherst Lecture in Philosophy 8: 1–35.

Chalmers, David. 2018. The Meta-Problem of Consciousness. *Journal of Consciousness Studies* 25, no. 9–10: 6–61.

Chalmers, David. 2019. Idealism and the Mind-Body Problem. In The Routledge Handbook of Panpsychism, edited by William Seager, 353–373. New York: Routledge.

Chalmers, David. 2020. Debunking Arguments for Illusionism about Consciousness. *Journal of Consciousness Studies* 27, no. 5–6: 258–281.

Chalmers, David. 2021. Finding Space in a Nonspatial World. In *Philosophy Beyond Spacetime*, edited by Christian Wüthrich, Baptiste Le Bihan, and Nick Huggett, 154–181. Oxford: Oxford University Press.

Chuard, Philippe. 2011. Temporal Experiences and Their Parts. *Philosophers' Imprint* 11, no. 11: 1–28.

Clarke-Doane, Justin. 2019. Metaphysical and Absolute Possibility. *Synthese* 198: 1861–1872.

Coates, Ashley. 2020. Making Sense of Powerful Qualities. *Synthese* 198, no. 9: 8347–8363.

Cohen, Jonathan, and Craig Callender. 2009. A Better Best System Account of Lawhood. *Philosophical Studies* 145: 1–34.

Coleman, Sam. 2017. Panpsychism and Neutral Monism: How to Make Up One's Mind. In *Panpsychism: Contemporary Perspectives*, edited by Godehard Brüntrup and Ludwig Jaskolla, 518–596. New York: Oxford University Press.

Correia, Fabrice. 2005. *Existential Dependence and Cognate Notions*. Munich: Philosophia Verlag.

Cowling, Sam. 2015. Advice for Eleatics. In *The Palgrave Handbook of Philosophical Methods*, edited by Chris Daly, 306–330. London: Palgrave Macmillan.

Cowling, Sam. 2017. *Abstract Entities*. New York: Routledge.

Cutter, Brian. 2022. The Mind-Body Problem and the Color-Body Problem. *Philosophical Studies* 180, no. 3: 725–744.

Dainton, Barry. 2000. *Stream of Consciousness: Unity and Continuity in Conscious Experience*. New York: Routledge.

Dainton, Barry. 2022. Temporal Consciousness. In *The Stanford Encyclopedia of Philosophy* (Summer 2022 Edition), edited by Edward Zalta. https://plato.stanford.edu/archives/sum2022/entries/consciousness-temporal/

Dainton, Barry. 2023. The Silence of Physics. *Erkenntnis* 88: 2207–2241.

Dasgupta, Shamik. 2009. Individuals: An Essay in Revisionary Metaphysics. *Philosophical Studies* 145, no. 1: 35–67.

Dasgupta, Shamik. 2017. Can We Do Without Fundamental Individuals? Yes. In *Current Controversies in Metaphysics*, edited by Elizabeth Barnes, 7–23. New York: Routledge.

De Vignemont, Frederique. 2023. Fifty Shades of Affective Colouring of Perception. *Australasian Journal of Philosophy* 101, no. 1: 1–15.

Dretske, Fred. 1977. Laws of Nature. *Philosophy of Science* 44, no. 2: 248–268.

Duncan, Matt. Forthcoming. How You Know You're Conscious: Illusionism and Knowledge of Things. *Review of Philosophy and Psychology*: 1–21.

Earman, John. 1986. *A Primer on Determinism*. Dordrecht: Reidel.

Earman, John, and John Norton. 1987. What Price Spacetime Substantivalism? The Hole Story. *British Journal for the Philosophy of Science* 38, no. 4: 515–525.

Ellis, Brian. 1990. *Truth and Objectivity*. Oxford: Blackwell.

Esfeld, Michael, and Vincent Lam. 2008. Moderate Structural Realism about Space-time. *Synthese* 160, no. 1: 27–46.

Faller, August. Forthcoming. Grounding and Properties. *Inquiry*.

Field, Hartry. 1989. *Realism, Mathematics, and Modality*. Oxford: Blackwell.

Foster, John. 1982. *The Case for Idealism*. London: Routledge.

Frankish, Keith. 2016. Illusionism as a Theory of Consciousness. *Journal of Consciousness Studies* 23, no. 11–12 11–39.

French, Craig, and Ian Phillips. 2023. In *Contemporary Debates in the Philosophy of Mind* (2nd edition), edited by Brian McLaughlin and Jonathan Cohen, 363–383. Oxford: Wiley-Blackwell.

Fulkerson, Matthew. 2020. Emotional Perception. *Australasian Journal of Philosophy* 98, no. 1: 16–30.

Giberman, Daniel. 2012. Against Zero-Dimensional Material Objects (and Other Bare Particulars). *Philosophical Studies* 160: 305–321.

Glazier, Martin. 2021. The Difference between Epistemic and Metaphysical Necessity. *Synthese* 198: 1409–1424.

Goff, Philip. 2016. The Phenomenal Bonding Solution to the Combination Problem. In *Panpsychism: Contemporary Perspectives*, edited by Godehard Bruntrup and Ludwig Jaskolla, 283–302. Oxford: Oxford University Press.

Goff, Philip. 2017. *Consciousness and Fundamental Reality*. New York: Oxford University Press.

Goff, Philip. 2019. Essentialist Modal Rationalism. *Synthese* 198: 2019–2027.

Grahek, Nikola. 2007. *Feeling Pain and Being in Pain*. Cambridge, MA: MIT Press.

Hakkarainen, Jani, and Markku Keinänen. 2022. Bradley's Relation Regress and the Inadequacy of the Relata-Specific Answer. *Acta Analytica*. https://doi.org/10.1007/s12136-022-00516-1.

Hall, Ned. 2015. Humean Reductionism about Laws of Nature. In *The Blackwell Companion to David Lewis*, edited by Barry Loewer and Jonathan Schaffer, 262–277. Oxford: Blackwell.

Heil, John. 2010. Powerful Qualities. In *The Metaphysics of Powers: Their Grounding and Their Manifestations*, edited by Anna Marmodoro, 58–72. New York: Routledge.

Heil, John. 2021. *Relations*. New York: Cambridge University Press.

Hellman, Geoffrey. 1989. *Mathematics without Numbers: Towards a Modal-Structural Interpretation*. Oxford: Clarendon Press.

Hildebrand, Tyler. 2016. Two Types of Quidditism. *Australasian Journal of Philosophy* 94, no. 3: 516–532.

Hirsch, Eli. 2011. *Quantifier Variance and Realism: Essays in Metaontology*. Oxford: Oxford University Press.

Horgan, Terence, and Matjaž Potrč. 2008. *Austere Realism: Contextual Semantics Meets Minimal Ontology*. MIT Press.

Huggett, Nick. 2021. Spacetime "Emergence." In *The Routledge Companion to Philosophy of Physics*, edited by Eleanor Knox and Alistair Wilson, 374–385. New York: Routledge.

Ismael, Jenann, and Jonathan Schaffer. 2020. Quantum Holism: Nonseparability as Common Ground. *Synthese* 197, no. 10: 4131–4160.

Jaag, Siegfried. 2014. Dispositional Essentialism and the Grounding of Natural Modality. *Philosophers' Imprint* 14, no. 34: 1–21.

Kammerer, François. 2018. Can You Believe It? Illusionism and the Illusion Meta-problem. *Philosophical Psychology* 31, no. 1: 44–67.

Kammerer, François. 2022. How Can You Be So Sure? Illusionism and the Obviousness of Phenomenal Consciousness. *Philosophical Studies* 179, no. 9: 2845–2867.

Kastrup, Bernardo. 2018. The Universe in Consciousness. *Journal of Consciousness Studies* 25, no. 5–6: 125–155.

Kimpton-Nye, Samuel. 2021. Reconsidering the Dispositional Essentialist Canon. *Philosophical Studies* 178, no. 10: 3421–3441.

Kirk, Robert. 2008. The Inconceivability of Zombies. *Philosophical Studies* 139, no. 1: 73–89.

Kriegel, Uriah, and Dan Zahavi. 2015. For-me-ness: What It Is and What It Is Not. In *Philosophy of Mind and Phenomenology: Conceptual and Empirical Approaches*, edited by Daniel Dahlstorm, Andreas Elpidorou, and Walter Hopp, 36–53. New York: Routledge.

Ladyman, James. 2023. Structural Realism. In *The Stanford Encyclopedia of Philosophy* (Summer 2023 Edition), edited by Edward N. Zalta and Uri Nodelman. https://plato.stanford.edu/archives/sum2023/entries/structural-realism/.

Lam, Vincent, and Christian Wüthrich. 2018. Spacetime Is as Spacetime Does. *Studies in History and Philosophy of Modern Physics* 64: 39–51.

Langton, Rae. 2004. Elusive Knowledge of Things in Themselves. *Australasian Journal of Philosophy* 82, no. 1: 129–136.

Lange, Marc. 2005. How Can Instantaneous Velocity Fulfill Its Causal Role? *Philosophical Review* 114, no. 4: 433–468.

Langsam, Harold. 2011. *The Wonder of Consciousness: Understanding the Mind Through Philosophical Reflection*. MIT Press.

Lee, Andrew. 2019. The Microstructure of Experience. *Journal of the American Philosophical Association* 5, no. 3: 286–305.

Lee, Andrew. Forthcoming. Knowing What It's Like. *Philosophical Perspectives*.

Lee, Andrew. MS. Consciousness and Continuity.

Lee, Geoffrey. 2014. Experiences and their Parts. In *Sensory Integration and the Unity of Consciousness*, edited by David Bennett and Christopher Hill, 287–322. MIT Press.

Leibniz, Gottfried. 1714/1965. *Monadology: And Other Philosophical Essays*. Translated by Paul Schrecker and Anne Martin Schreker. Indianapolis: Bobbs-Merrill.

Lewis, David. 1986. *On the Plurality of Worlds*. Basil: Blackwell.

Lewis, David. 1994. Humean Supervenience Debugged. *Mind* 103, no. 412: 473–490.

Lewis, David. 2009. Ramseyan Humility. In *Conceptual Analysis and Philosophical Naturalism*, edited by David Braddon-Mitchell and Robert Nola, 203-222. MIT Press.

Litland, John. 2022. Grounding and Defining Identity. Noûs: 1–27. https://doi.org/10.1111/nous.12430.

Locke, John. 1689/1997. *An Essay Concerning Human Understanding*, edited by Roger Woolhouse. London: Penguin Books.

Loewer, Barry. 2007. Laws and Natural Properties. *Philosophical Topics* 35: 313–328.

Loux, Michael, and Thomas Crisp. 2017. *Metaphysics: A Contemporary Introduction 4th Edition*. New York: Routledge.

Lowe, Edward. 2003. Individuation. In *The Oxford Handbook of Metaphysics*, edited by Michael Loux and Dean Zimmerman, 75–95. New York: Oxford University Press.

Lowe, Edward. 2016. There Are (Probably) No Relations. In *The Metaphysics of Relations*, edited by Anna Marmodoro and David Yates, 100–112. Oxford: Oxford University Press.

Martin, Charles. 2008. *The Mind in Nature*. Oxford: Oxford University Press.

Maudlin, Tim. 1989. The Essence of Space-time. In *Proceedings of the 1988 Biennial Meeting of the Philosophy of Science Association*: 82–91.

Maudlin, Tim. 2007. *The Metaphysics within Physics*. Oxford: Oxford University Press.

Maurin, Anna-Sofia. 2010. Trope Theory and the Bradley Regress. *Synthese* 175, no. 3: 311–326.

Maurin, Anna-Sofia. 2012. Bradley's Regress. *Philosophy Compass* 7, no. 11: 794–807.

McGinn, Colin. 1996. Another Look at Color. *Journal of Philosophy* 93: 537–553.

Mertz, Donald. 2003. Against Bare Particulars: A Response to Moreland and Pickavance. *Australasian Journal of Philosophy* 81: 14–20.

Mihálik, Jakub. 2022. Panqualityism, Awareness and the Explanatory Gap. *Erkenntnis* 87: 1423–1445.

Miller, Gregory. 2017. Forming a Positive Concept of the Phenomenal Bonding Relation for Constitutive Panpsychism. *Dialectica* 71, no. 4: 541–562.

Mørch, Hedda. 2020. The Phenomenal Powers View and the Meta-problem of Consciousness. *Journal of Consciousness Studies* 27, no. 5–6: 131–142.

Mørch, Hedda Hassel. 2017. The Evolutionary Argument for Phenomenal Powers. *Philosophical Perspectives* 31: 293–316.

Mørch, Hedda Hassel. 2018. Does Dispositionalism Entail Panpsychism? *Topoi* 39, no. 5: 1073–1088.

Mørch, Hedda Hassel. 2019a. Phenomenal Knowledge Why: The Explanatory Knowledge Argument against Physicalism. In *The Knowledge Argument*, edited by Sam Coleman, 233–253. Cambridge University Press.

Mørch, Hedda Hassel. 2019b. The Argument for Panpsychism From Experience of Causation. In *The Routledge Handbook of Panpsychism*, edited by William Seager. Routledge.

Mumford, Stephen. 2004. *Laws in Nature*. New York: Routledge.

Munkres, James. 2013. *Topology: Pearson New International Edition*. Englewood Cliffs, NJ: Pearson.

Pallies, Daniel. 2022. The Pleasure Problem and the Spriggean Solution. *Journal of the American Philosophical Association* 8, no. 4: 665–684.

Papineau. David. 2002. *Thinking about Consciousness*. Oxford: Oxford University Press.

Parsons, Josh. 2004. Distributional Properties. In *Lewisian Themes: The Philosophy of David K. Lewis*, edited by Frank Jackson and Graham Priest, 173–180. Oxford: Clarendon Press.

Perry, Zee R. 2017. How to Be a Substantivalist without Getting Shifty about It. *Philosophical Issues* 27, no. 1: 223–249.

Plate, Jan. 2022. Qualitative Properties and Relations. *Philosophical Studies* 179, no. 4: 1297–1322.

Pooley, Oliver. 2013. Substantivalist and Relationist Approaches to Spacetime. In *The Oxford Handbook of Philosophy of Physics*, edited by Robert Batterman, 522–586. Oxford University Press.

Rachels, Stuart. 2000. Is Unpleasantness Intrinsic to Unpleasant Experiences? *Philosophical Studies* 99, no. 2: 187–210.

Reck, Erich., and Schiemer, Georg. 2020. Structuralism in the Philosophy of Mathematics. In *The Stanford Encyclopedia of Philosophy* (Spring 2020 Edition), edited by Edward Zalta and Uri Nodelman. https://plato.stanford.edu/archives/spr2023/entries/structuralism-mathematics/

Robinson, Howard. 2022. *Perception and Idealism: An Essay on How the World Manifests Itself to Us, and How It (Probably) Is in Itself.* Oxford: Oxford University Press.

Rosen, Gideon. 2006. The Limits of Contingency. In *Identity and Modality*, edited by Fraser MacBride, 13–39. Oxford: Oxford University Press.

Rosen, Gideon. 2010. Metaphysical Dependence: Grounding and Reduction. In *Modality: Metaphysics, Logic, and Epistemology*, edited by Bob Hale and Aviv Hoffman, 109–136. Oxford: Oxford University Press.

Rubenstein, Ezra. 2024. Grounding Identity in Existence. *Philosophy and Phenomenological Research* 108, no. 1: 21–41.

Russell, Bertrand. 1927/1996. *An Inquiry into Meaning and Truth*, 2nd edition. London: Routledge.

Saad, Brad. 2019. A Teleological Strategy for Solving the Meta-Problem of Consciousness. *Journal of Consciousness Studies* 26, no. 9–10: 205–216.

Schaffer, Jonathan. 2007. From Nihilism to Monism. *Australasian Journal of Philosophy* 85, no. 2: 175–191.

Schaffer, Jonathan. 2009. Spacetime the One Substance. *Philosophical Studies* 145, no. 1: 131–148.

Schaffer, Jonathan. 2010a. Monism: The Priority of the Whole. *Philosophical Review* 119, no. 1: 31–76.

Schaffer, Jonathan. 2010b. The Internal Relatedness of All Things. *Mind* 119, no. 474: 341–376.

Schaffer, Jonathan. 2010c. The Least Discerning and Most Promiscuous Truthmaker. *Philosophical Quarterly* 60: 307–324.

Schaffer, Jonathan. 2013. The Action of the Whole. *Aristotelian Society Supplementary* Volume 87, no. 1: 67–87.

Schaffer, Jonathan. 2016. It is the Business of Laws to Govern. *Dialectica* 70: 577–588.

Schopenhauer. Arthur. 1813/1974. *On the Fourfold Root of the Principle of Sufficient Reason*. Translated by E. F. J. Payne. LaSalle: Open Court.

Searle, John R. 2002. *Consciousness and Language*. Cambridge: Cambridge University Press.

Shani, Itay, and Joachim Keppler. 2018. Beyond Combination: How Cosmic Consciousness Grounds Ordinary Experience. *Journal of the American Philosophical Association* 4, no. 3: 390–410.

Sider, Theodore. 1992. Tooley's Solution to the Inference Problem. *Philosophical Studies* 67: 261–275.

Sider, Theodore. 2001. *Four-Dimensionalism: An Ontology of Persistence and Time*. Oxford University Press.

Sider, Theodore. 2006. "Bare Particulars". *Philosophical Perspectives* 20: 387–397.

Sider, Theodore. 2008. Monism and Statespace Structure. *Royal Institute of Philosophy Supplement* 62: 129–150.

Sider, Theodore. 2011. *Writing the Book of the World*. Oxford: Oxford University Press.

Skiles, Alexander. 2015. Against Grounding Necessitarianism. *Erkenntnis* 80, no. 4: 717–751.

Smithies, Declan. 2013. The Nature of Cognitive Phenomenology. *Philosophy Compass* 8, no. 8: 744–754.

Soteriou, Matthew. 2013. *The Mind's Construction: The Ontology of Mind and Mental Action*. Oxford: Oxford University Press.

Sprigge, Timothy. 1984. *The Vindication of Absolute Idealism*. Edinburgh: Edinburgh University Press.

Stoljar, Daniel. 2006. *Ignorance and Imagination: The Epistemic Origin of the Problem of Consciousness*. Oxford: Oxford University Press.

Strawson, Galen. 2003. What is the Relation Between an Experience, the Subject of the Experience, and the Content of the Experience? *Philosophical Issues* 13, no. 1: 279–315.

Strawson, Galen. 2006. Realistic Monism: Why Physicalism Entails Panpsychism. *Journal of Consciousness Studies* 13, no. 10–11: 3–31.

Strawson Galen. 2008a. *Selves: An Essay in Revisionary Metaphysics*. Oxford: Oxford University Press.

Strawson, Galen. 2008b. The Identity of the Categorical and the Dispositional. *Analysis* 68, no. 4: 271–282.

Strawson, Galen. 2014. *The Secret Connexion: Causation, Realism, and David Hume: Revised Edition.* Oxford: Oxford University Press UK.

Strawson, Galen. 2016. Mind and Being: The Primacy of Panpsychism. In *Panpsychism: Contemporary Perspectives,* edited by Godehard Brüntrup and Ludwig Jaskolla, 75–112. Oxford: Oxford University Press.

Strawson, Galen. 2017. *The Subject of Experience.* New York: Oxford University Press.

Strawson, Galen. 2021. Identity Metaphysics. *The Monist* 104: 60–90

Swinburne, Richard. 2013. *Mind, Brain, and Free Will.* Oxford: Oxford University Press.

Tooley, Michael. 1977. The Nature of Laws. *Canadian Journal of Philosophy* 7, no. 4: 667–698.

Tooley, Michael. 1988. In Defense of the Existence of States of Motion. *Philosophical topics* 16: 225–254.

Tugby, Matthew. 2022. *Putting Properties First.* Oxford: Oxford University Press.

Turner, Jason. Forthcoming. On Doing without Ontology: Feature-Placing on a Global Scale. In *The Question of Ontology,* edited by Javier Cumpa. Oxford: Oxford University Press.

Tye, Michael. 2003. *Consciousness and Persons: Unity and Identity.* MIT Press.

Uzquiano, Gabriel. 2015. Varieties of Indefinite Extensibility. *Notre Dame Journal of Formal Logic* 56, no. 1: 147–166.

Van Cleve, James. 2018. Brute necessity. *Philosophy Compass* 13, no. 9: e12516.

Van Fraassen, Bas. 1989. *Laws and Symmetry.* Oxford: Clarendon Press.

Warren, Jared. 2017. Epistemology Versus Non-Causal Realism. *Synthese* 194: 1643–1662.

Williamson, Timothy. 2016. Modal Science. *Canadian Journal of Philosophy* 46, no. 4–5: 453–492.

Wilson, Jessica. 2009. Resemblance-based Resources for Reductive Singularism (or: How to Be a Humean Singularist about Causation). *The Monist* 92, no. 1: 153–190.

Wilson, Jessica. 2016. The Unity and Priority Arguments for Grounding. In *Scientific Composition and Metaphysical Ground,* edited by Ken Aizawa and Carl Gillett, 171–204. Basingstoke: Palgrave Macmillan.

Wilson, Keith. 2023. The Auditory Field: The Spatial Character of Auditory Experience. *Ergo* 9, no. 40: 1080–1106.

Yetter-Chappell, Helen. 2022. Dualism All the Way Down: Why There Is No Paradox of Phenomenal Judgement. *Synthese* 200, no. 2: 1–24.

Yetter-Chappell, Helen. Forthcoming. Get Acquainted with Naïve Idealism. In *The Roles of Representations in Visual Perception*, edited by Robert French and Berit Brogaard. Synthese Book Series.

David Builes, *Modal Idealism* In: *Oxford Studies in Philosophy of Mind Volume 4*. Edited by: Uriah Kriegel, Oxford University Press. © David Builes 2024. DOI: 10.1093/9780198924159.003.0002

3

Idealism and the Interface Theory

Geoffrey Lee

1. Introduction

Metaphysical idealists in the Berkeleyian tradition advocate for the global metaphysical priority of the mental over the physical. This kind of idealism is widely regarded as highly revisionary and difficult to develop in a coherent and plausible way, although occasionally theorists take on the challenge.[1] Kantian Metaphysical Idealists, on the other hand, hold that there is a mind-independent "noumenal" world, but that it is unknowable to observers such as ourselves. Moreover, what is accessible is the "phenomenal world," a kind of mental construction that does not reflect the true nature of the noumenal world, but rather reflects the nature of the perceiving mind itself (for Kant, the a priori organizational constraints on perceptual experience).

Views with a Kantian-idealist flavor often pop up in contemporary philosophy.[2] For example, recently some analytic metaphysicians (Langton (1998), Lewis (2001)), have developed a Kantian view on which it is the intrinsic nature of fundamental physical properties that constitutes the inaccessible noumena. Views of this kind have proliferated among so-called Russellian Monists (including Panpsychists), who hold that the hidden intrinsic nature of the fundamental world could be the ingredient we are missing in understanding how conscious experience could be grounded in physical events.[3] On these views, we can access the abstract structure of the physical world—both at the fundamental level and macroscopically—through

---

[1] See Pelczar (2015) for a recent version and Lee (2016) for a response. For a more detailed taxonomy of idealist views see Chalmers (2022).

[2] In addition to Langton and Lewis style "Kantian Humility," views that are skeptical of stronger forms of "metaphysical realism" (whatever that amounts to), such as the internal realism of Putnam (1981, 1983), and the pragmatist views of thinkers like Dewey, Carnap, Rorty, or Brandom can be seen as at least having a Kantian-idealist flavor to them.

[3] Chalmers (2015), Goff (2017), Mørch (2014), Roelofs (2019) and Strawson (2009) are some recent examples.

mathematical modelling. But such abstract structural descriptions do not tell us which properties and relations actually fill out this structure.[4]

Here I'm also interested in a kind of Kantian view, but one that instead focuses precisely on the kind of structural knowledge that is *not* challenged on Russellian Monist views. On the *Structural Idealist* view, it is the structure of the noumenal world that is inaccessible to us. For the purposes of this chapter, I will give this a *perceptual* reading in terms of two theses. First, according to *Structural Opacity* (as opposed to *Structural Transparency*), the structure of the external world as presented in perceptual experience does not reflect its objective physical structure. Perception is not a transparent window onto the world, but more like a highly distorting filter that changes the appearance of the physical world beyond all recognition. Second, according to a thesis I'll call *Irreversibility*, we lack the epistemic means to undo the distorting filter and recover the true structure of the world. Our attempts to "get behind appearances" and model the structure of the physical world at best enable us to understand features of the physical to phenomenal transforming function (for example, certain kinds of invariances in it), but not to actually reverse it and know what the world is really like (structurally) in itself. We are forever "stuck inside the headset."

A version of Structural Opacity has been defended recently under the guise "The Interface Theory," by Hoffman, Singh and Prakash (henceforth "HSP") (Hoffman et al. (2015a, 2015b), Hoffman (2019), Prakash et al. (2020), Prakash et al. (2021)). Theirs is a Darwinian spin on the idea. They offer an evolutionary debunking argument against Structural Transparency. Our perceptual systems are not tuned (or *primarily* tuned) to present to us the objective physical structure of the environment around us, but rather, qua results of natural selection, are tuned to present the *fitness payoff structure* of the environment. Moreover, there is no happy alignment between these structures. They are *uncorrelated,* and this means that in an important sense, perception is not a "veridical" presentation of the environment, but rather a pragmatically motivated *interface*, akin to a desktop environment on a computer—a metaphor familiar from Dennett's work on consciousness (e.g. Dennett (1993)). Moreover, the physical-to-phenomenal function is

---

[4] To put it another way, two universes could be structurally identical, and appear to function the same way to observers mathematically modelling these universes, but differ in the properties and relations that actually fill out the structural models. Observers have no way of distinguishing these situations, beyond conceiving of them indexically as the one that *actually obtains* (the exception being the qualitative character of their own minds, of which they do have non-structural knowledge).

non-monotonic (i.e. not order-preserving) in a way that gives us a version of Irreversibility. Evolution has not given us a perspective on the world that allows knowledge of its noumenal structure, even in principle. The following quote makes very clear the Kantian flavor of the view:

> When we compare psychophysical measurements of shape to spatial measurements in the physical (or a simulated) environment, we are simply evaluating the degree of coherence between two different levels of description within our perceptual interface. This can indeed be an informative evaluation. But we are not somehow getting outside of our own interface in order to compare perceptual experience with objective reality.
>
> (HSP 2015b: 1573)

It's true that Hoffman himself has developed a decidedly non-Kantian version of the interface theory, supplementing it with a view of noumenal world he calls "conscious realism" (Hoffman 2019, ch.10). On that view conscious subjects are the fundamental entities whose properties and relations constitute the objective world (the view is similar in spirit to Millian phenomenalism). But the interface theory (as I will read it) is not committed to conscious realism, and here I do not engage with that aspect of Hoffman's view.[5] For example, it is consistent with the interface theory that the realizer of unknowable noumenal structure is wholly non-mental.

My goal in this chapter is to explain and evaluate the interface theory *qua structural idealist view*. In section 2, I argue that it is clearly intended as a structural idealist view, and that this is what makes it interesting—a point that I think has been lost in translation in the (limited) critical reaction it has received from philosophers. In section 3, I unpack and partially evaluate HSP's case for the view. In section 4, I further develop the view and explain how I see the shape of the debate with realist opponents. My overall goal is to make a tentative case for structural transparency: our perceptual experience does provide access to the objective physical structure of the environment. Despite realism itself involving some ambitious and questionable commitments, the objections to structural idealism and the weakness of the positive case for it make realism the more attractive position.

---

[5] Since the interface theory (at least as I understand it) is committed to unknowable noumenal structure that grounds the phenomenal world, it's not even totally clear how conscious realism, which grounds everything in the (knowable?) states of conscious agents, is *compatible* with the interface theory.

2. Three Notions of Veridicality

The interface theorists make the claim that *perception is typically non-veridical* the centerpiece of their view. They sell this as an iconoclastic debunking of the standard views of both philosophers and cognitive scientists, liberally quoting figures in both camps they see themselves as at odds with, even going so far as to claim opposition to the correspondence theory of truth (!) (e.g. Prakash et al. (2020) p. 3). Although I think their view is interesting, I see this as a mistake that invites misunderstanding. What they should have said is: "There is an important notion of veridicality that has been missed by recent cognitive scientists and philosophers. Even if perception is typically veridical in the sense that recent theorists have claimed, it could be non-veridical in an important (and disturbing) further sense; moreover, it *is* non-veridical in this further sense."

In fact I think there are three important notions of veridicality that are in play here: the content-based notion, the relational notion, and the structural-transparency notion.

On the content-based notion, perceptual experience has a content: a proposition that specifies how the environment is arranged around the subject. Perception is veridical provided the proposition is true. For example, my experience might represent that an orange sphere is in front of me, and is veridical provided an orange sphere is in fact in front of me. This is the standard notion of veridicality in the literature, although for reasons I'll get to, it doesn't really figure in the interface theory.

To say that experience is veridical in the *relational* sense presupposes a relational view of the phenomenal character of experience. On that view, having an experience with a certain phenomenal character consists in standing in a special sensory relation (e.g. awareness or acquaintance) to the *objects* of experience (facts/events/objects/properties/propositions).[6] Perception is *relationally-veridical* provided the phenomenal character of experience relates the subject to an actually-obtaining mind-independent arrangement of entities in their environment. The classic version of a relational view is naïve realism, where the character of experience is constituted by acquaintance with mind-independent items in the physical environment

---

[6] On some relational views, these are not "objects of experience" in the ordinary sense, such as tables and trees, and the relevant sensory relation is not "awareness" or "perception" in any ordinary sense. For example, on representationist views, the object is a proposition or property, and the sensory relation is a special representational relation (see e.g. Pautz (2020) ch. 3).

around the subject: experience is something like a "transparent window" onto the external world. A sense-datum view would also be a kind of relational view, but it doesn't give us veridical experience in the relevant sense, because the relata are mind-dependent sense-data which merely stand in for external items.

Although HSP don't give the kind of theoretical formulation that would please philosophers, it is fairly clear they do not think experience has relational veridicality. For them, the mind-independent world is (in some sense) hidden from us behind a veil of appearance.[7] However, I don't think this is the big fish they have to fry, so I set it aside here.

Their big fish is the idea that experience is not veridical in a *structure-preserving* sense. The intuition that matters here, I think, is that the manifest image does not distort or scramble the fundamental physical image beyond all recognition. In some sense, the manifest features we perceive are reasonably "natural" in the way they derive from the fundamental, and as a result the project of reverse engineering the world and trying to infer what fundamental image looks like, is not hopelessly misguided. A loose comparison might be with a photograph of a detailed scene. The photograph will inevitably have limited resolution, and as a result much detail will be lost. Still, some of the broad overall features of the original scene are straightforwardly available in the photo, in a way that they wouldn't be if the camera totally scrambled the image. Similarly, although perception is not a direct window onto the fundamental physical world, we think that it gives us a summary that is not completely unrelated to the fundamental layout, but rather tells us some interesting broad features of how fundamental reality around us is arranged. This means that "filling in the details" theoretically is not a misguided project.

This intuitive formulation stands in need of much clarification, and I will say more later about how I think we should develop it. But I hope this is enough to make it intuitive that there might be an important notion of veridicality in this ballpark that we should pay attention to. This is the primary sense in which I am in complete agreement with the interface theorists

---

[7] In an attempt to clarify their position, McLaughlin and Green (2015) understandably read them as holding a sense-datum theory. In response, they vigorously deny this and seem to adopt a representationalist view on which the phenomenal character of experienced is to be understood intentionally—it is constituted by the sensory representation of a proposition concerning the layout of the external world—but on which this proposition is typically *false*—it represents objects and property instantiations that *don't exist* (see HSP 2015b: 1569–1572). That discussion suggests their view is similar to the Chalmers/Pautz "Edenic" view of perceptual experience (Chalmers (2006), Pautz (2020)).

(the difference is in our attitude to whether experience *is* veridical (i.e. structurally transparent)).

I will also immediately note that "representation through resemblance" has, of course, always been a central idea in approaches to representation;[8] so there is nothing new in suggesting an approach in that category. What I think is interesting is a specific *version* of that idea ("veridicality as non-scrambling"), which I see embodied in HSP's approach. As I will explain below, notions of representation-by-resemblance in play in current debates in the philosophy of cognitive science typically do *not* capture the kind of "non-scrambling" I am interested in here.

The way the idea is developed by the interface theorists themselves requires a little set up. Following the classic psychophysics tradition, they believe in what I will call the *psychometric mapping thesis*: for a given organism, there is a relevant,[9] well-defined psychometric mapping from objective physical structure to phenomenal structure (it could be probabilistic rather than deterministic). So for example, a component of this mapping function could be a map from spatial distances into an internal experiential quality space that we would intuitively describe as "experiences of distance (or length)." The map tells us (something like) the typical experience (or experien*ces* if the map is non-deterministic) that the subject would have in response to an item with a certain length impinging on their retina.

Now, as this example may immediately make vivid, our experiences of features like spatial distance can be quite context-sensitive (even under optimal, ecologically valid conditions, etc.), which could make trouble for an overly simplistic mapping thesis that does not contain contextual parameters as variables. I ignore this important complication for now, however (we can perhaps imagine these variables to be absorbed by an appropriate choice of what the physical stimulus parameter is). One might also wonder: what determines the choice of physical stimulus parameters? Are there specific "optimal" conditions where the functioning of perceptual systems is

---

[8] For example, the idea plays an important role in early modern debates about mental representation, for example in the debate about realism between Locke and Berkeley. Shepard's notion of second-order isomorphism is foundational to modern accounts of representation-by-resemblance—see Shepard and Chipman (1970) (Shea (2018) and Neander (2017) are examples of recent accounts along these lines).

[9] By which I mean: the function captures a theoretically important relationship between experience and reality—the kind of relationship we have in mind when we talk about what the experience is *of*, what it *represents*, or what it has as a *content*. How exactly to understand this relationship is of course a central problem in philosophy of perception.

particularly relevant to the determination of the function? I briefly return to these issues below.

Assuming we have these functions in hand, HSP (2015: 1482) define a *perceptual strategy* as the psychometric mapping that an organism in fact uses. They then distinguish various different kinds of strategy. For current purposes, two are particularly relevant: a *hybrid realist* strategy and an *interface* strategy. The issue here is the extent to which the psychometric map is structure-preserving (if it is, they call it "realist" or "critical realist"[10]). HSP typically understand structure-preservation specifically in terms of whether the function is *monotonic* (i.e. order-preserving), although I think it should be an open question what kinds of structure-preservation are theoretically important here (more on this below).

The "hybrid realist" view is that perception is realist with respect to "primary" qualities like duration, spatial distance, and mass, and is non-realist (i.e. scrambling) with respect to "secondary" qualities like color or smell (I think it's fair to say that this is both a non-standard but also theoretically attractive and intuitive way to draw this distinction). Whereas on an "interface strategy" the mapping is non-monotonic with respect to *every* stimulus parameter—that is, distance, duration etc. are not really different from color and smell after all! The *Interface Theory* is the view that we humans use an interface strategy.[11]

Some clarifications. First, to preserve order (monotonicity) is to preserve structure only in a fairly weak sense. In particular, the class of order-preserving mappings between metric spaces includes maps that distort distances in strange ways, warping the world in a way that (intuitively) gives us a kind of non-veridicality which we might want a notion of "structural transparency" to capture. But this is no real objection. Considering monotonicity is motivated in part by a desire not to make strong assumptions about the structures of physical and phenomenal variables (e.g. that they have a well-defined metric), but also (I assume) because monotonicity is

---

[10] They distinguish two kinds of realism, *naïve realism* and *critical realism*. They are hard to interpret here, but on my reading critical realism is intended as an umbrella category that includes naïve realist views in the philosopher's "phenomenology as acquaintance with the world" sense, but also includes views like sense-datum views, qualia views and representationalist views. That is, the critical realist only requires a structure-preserving psycho-physical mapping, and does not further require that phenomenal properties are individuated in terms of relations to mind-independent stimulus properties, whereas the "naïve realist" does include this requirement (in addition to the structure-preservation requirement).

[11] Cf. Berkeley's argument in his *Three Dialogues* for assimilating allegedly primary qualities like shape and size with mind-dependent secondary qualities like taste and color (Berkeley (1713/1979)).

typically *necessary* for structure-preservation in other senses we might be interested in (e.g. preserving metric structure). Attacking the monotonicity of perception is therefore strong dialectically for HSP, and is consistent with considering stronger kinds of structure-preservation in other contexts.

Second, we can distinguish between strongly and weakly monotonic functions. The difference is that a weakly monotonic function need not be strictly increasing or decreasing, but can map points in an interval onto the same point. HSP are arguing that our perceptual functions are not even weakly monotonic. One way in which this is significant is that dimensionality reducing mappings (e.g. a 3D to 2D linear projection), which are often characteristic of human perception, are only weakly monotonic: but that is consistent with them being structure-preserving in the relevant sense.

Third, in real life when we are presented with some kinds of non-monotonic maps (e.g. a jigsaw puzzle), we *can* figure out how to undo them. But that's because we have priors about the true structure of things. For example, imagine taking a picture of a face and cutting it into horizontal strips and scrambling their order—most of us can solve this kind of puzzle. But imagine you had only ever seen faces scrambled in a certain systematic way or, more saliently, the *whole world* scrambled in a certain systematic way!! Then (perhaps) you would not have priors that would enable you to "solve" for the true structure. In fact, the world might not even seem incongruous or surprising or in need of solving or rearranging in the way that a jigsaw puzzle does. So the mere fact that "the world looks normal" is not in itself evidence against perception being non-monotonic (although there may be more sophisticated objections in this ballpark that are telling (more later)).

Fourth, how we should understand the "structure-preservation" in structural transparency of course depends on the theoretical role we want it to play. From my point of view (which I believe is similar to HSP's on this point), there are (at least) three important roles to consider. First, I think veridical experience can reasonably be understood as an *epistemic end-in-itself*,[12] and that structural-transparency gives one reasonable gloss on this. We want experience to "tell us what the world is like," and if structural transparency fails, then there is one way in which it does not live up to

---

[12] For example, creating photos that allow us to view previously unseen objects in deep space (e.g. the 2022 images of a black hole from the event horizon telescope), enables what feels to us like an epistemic achievement with respect to these objects, even if we already knew they exist and what features they have.

this epistemic aspiration.[13] Second, veridical experience (understood in any of the three ways discussed here) potentially helps explain the functioning and success of the organism; that is, the notion has a (potential) high-level *causal-explanatory role*. When it comes to structural transparency, we can ask whether veridical experience (in that sense) might help explain how an organism succeeds in surviving and reproducing, or otherwise functions psychologically and behaviorally (wouldn't scrambled perception be useless and lead the organism to quickly die?). Third, there is an *epistemic-theoretical role* for the notion, with respect to the scientific project of *downwards inference:* inferring the deeper structure of the world from the manifest appearances. Is perception structure-preserving in a sense that would make the project of downwards inference epistemically tractable?

HSP's Darwinian debunking argument (discussed below in section 3) can be seen as an argument that the causal-explanatory role of experience (surprisingly) supports the view that experience is *not* structurally transparent in the ways that matter for the two epistemic roles just mentioned. In the case of downwards inference/reversibility (which I will be particularly focused on), they might therefore be read as saying that, in general, monotonic perception is necessary for the underlying structure of the world to be knowable. But examples like jigsaws already show that this isn't quite right. We might also mention cases like color and smell which may violate monotonicity in their relationship to underlying physical properties, but in a way that we can figure out, because it is merely local. What HSP have in mind is that a *global* kind of non-monotonicity might make for unknowable noumenal structure. But how exactly do we characterize this epistemically problematic kind of scrambling? On reflection, it's a tricky substantive problem to figure out what kinds of structure-preservation we implicitly assume in making downwards inferences. I'll return to this issue in section 4, discussing monotonicity for now as a place-holder for the kinds of "non-scrambling" we might ultimately be interested in if downwards inference is our focus.

Fifth, the notion of structural transparency presupposes we have some grip on the idea of the "objective structure" of the environment—an idea that of course can be challenged. As I discuss in section 4, a crucial idea here is that the world has *fundamental* physical (or non-physical) structure. I think of this in terms of a commitment to fundamentality or naturalness

---

[13] Although it may live up to this in other ways, e.g. by having an accurate representational content (see below).

as a basic piece of metaphysical ideology (Lewis 1983, Sider 2013), although the discussion here is probably compatible with other approaches. Further, in section 4 I discuss one way of developing the idea of "real patterns" or "objective structure" in the grounded non-fundamental world. In the end (section 4), I think perceptual transparency is best understood as the view that we perceive such real patterns.

Sixth, I think it's crucial to understand that non-veridicality in the structural-transparency sense is perfectly compatible with veridicality in the standard content-theoretic sense.[14] I think HSP are rather illicitly side-stepping the debates about experiential content by granting themselves a *relevant* psychometric function. In particular, we might think that part of what makes a function "relevant" is that the stimulus parameter is *represented* (in some theoretically relevant sense) by the experience it maps to. I suspect that the spadework that would go into spelling out what determines the psychometric function as relevant would be fairly similar to the spadework that goes into theorizing the notion of experiential content or representation. Regardless, the important point here is that non-monotonic perceptual mappings are prima facie consistent with experience veridically representing real features of the environment. For example, it is common-place to hold that color experiences represent *spectral reflectance profiles*, even if the psychometric color map is massively dimensionality reducing and non-monotonic. On this framework, a color experience is veridical provided the surface has the kind of reflectance profile the experience represents where, for example, this might be cashed out as the kind of profile the experience is designed (by evolution or learning) to detect. So we have veridicality *plus* non-monotonicity.

It's also important to note here that we can take the form of the psychometric mapping function, and use it to define a mind-independent high-level property of surfaces, such that we can think of *this* property as the stimulus property, and think of the psychometric map as completely structure-preserving. For example, if experienced brightness is a power function of luminance, we can apply this function to luminance to get a

---

[14] It's also consistent with veridicality in the *relational* sense, assuming I can be perceptually related to macroscopic properties that are grounded in a structurally opaque way. I note also that because on my reading HSP are not offering a debunking argument against content-theoretic veridicality, their argument has a different target from Plantinga's "evolutionary argument against naturalism" (see Plantinga (2002)), whose goal is to show that by naturalism's own lights, our belief forming processes are *not reliable*. A more detailed comparison of HSP's argument with Plantinga's would be a useful supplement to the current discussion.

mind-independent quantity defined in terms of luminance ("physical brightness"). Call this the *induced* stimulus property. Even if perception scrambles the world, we can legitimately think of it as veridically presenting the subject with these induced worldly features (although typically it's more theoretically illuminating to take the underlying physical parameter like luminance to be what's represented). Again, this is perfectly consistent with it being *non*-veridical in the important structural-transparency sense.

When theorists in philosophy and cognitive science say that unless an organism's perceptual experience is typically veridical they would quickly die, they are talking about this content-theoretic sense of veridicality. For example, if the function of experiencing the color red is to distinguish fruit from foliage, then if an organism's perceptual system started misfiring and randomly assigning red to non-fruit parts of trees instead, then the organism might quickly die because it could not find fruit to eat. All of this is perfectly compatible with color experience being non-monotonic. (Cohen (2015) makes a similar point in his critique of HSP, but I think he fails to pick up on the fact that HSP are really interested in veridicality in a different sense).

Finally, the difference with notions of structural/imagistic/iconic/analog representation that have been theorized in the recent literature is this.[15] Those notions typically allow that the mapping from lower-level physical structure onto representational structure could be fairly complex and gruesome (think of how color experience can be a structural representation of surface reflectance). One way to put this is that on these views, we could happily construe the external structure being represented as the *induced* structure, which can be veridically represented even under "scrambling" conditions. Of course, if the function of internal structural representations is to mirror external structure inside the organism in a way that is computationally and behaviorally useful, we will want to know *why* a structure that is only gruesomely related to physical structure *is* useful to structurally represent. But that is conceivably answerable (e.g. it might be fitness payoff structure (see below)!).

In section 4 I will discuss in more detail the definition and theoretical importance of structural transparency. First, I want to briefly consider HSP's arguments for the interface theory.

---

[15] See again Shea (2018), Neander (2017); also Beck (2018) on analog representation.

3. The Case for the Interface Theory
(aka "The Case Against Reality")

On my reading, HSP's argument is structured in the following way (I'll call this "the master argument"):

(1) **Fitness perception thesis**: Perception presents us (only) with the structure of fitness payoffs.

(2) **Payoff distribution thesis**: Fitness payoff structure is non-monotonically related to physical structure

Therefore:

(3) **Perceptual Non-monotonicity**: Our perceptual strategy is globally non-monotonic

Therefore:

(4) **Non-veridicality**: Perception is non-veridical

As we will see, although HSP sell their argument as a Darwinian debunking of perceptual veridicality, one of their strategies for motivating the premises of the argument ("the indifference argument") gives us an argument that in fact has nothing to do with Darwinian considerations.

On my reading, the move from (3) to (4) is trivial once we get clear on what "veridical" is supposed to mean (I'm assuming for now that monotonicity is an adequate way to theorize "non-scrambling"). So the main issue is the motivation of the premises. Let's consider them in turn. ·

3.1 The Fitness Perception Thesis

A fitness payoff is the expected change in fitness from performing an action. So we might also call the thesis "strong perceptual pragmatism" : we only perceive the expected payoffs/costs of possible actions we could perform. This is quite prima facie counterintuitive, and can be usefully contrasted with a realist view on which we perceive action-independent features of how the world is arranged, which, *together with an independent sense of goals and priorities*, we use to *compute* an optimal course of action.

That said, there are cases such as *tastiness* and *attractiveness* where something like perceptual pragmatism is fairly plausible. For example, it might be that the function of tastiness is to make a recommendation to eat or not eat the food, so there is (at least) an immediate *connection* between the perceived property and a pragmatic implication. So we can read the fitness perception thesis as saying that all perceived features are like tastiness and attractiveness in this way. When we think about properties like spatial distance and duration this might seem a surprising view (what in general is the expected cost of an item (*any* item) having a certain size, or being a certain distance away?), but perhaps there is a good argument for it.

HSP's argument for the view is that in toy evolutionary models, perceptual strategies that are monotonic in fitness outcompete those that are not.

In these toy models (Figures 3.1 and 3.2), there is an environment consisting of a grid with resources distributed in different quantities across grid squares. Fitness payoff is taken to be a normal (and therefore non-monotonic) distribution of resource quantity—both taking too little and taking too much is non-optimal. Creatures grab resources from squares based on their perceptual state. In one kind of model, populations with different perceptual strategies engage in an evolutionary competition. The result is that an interface strategy (i.e. a non-monotonic psychometric

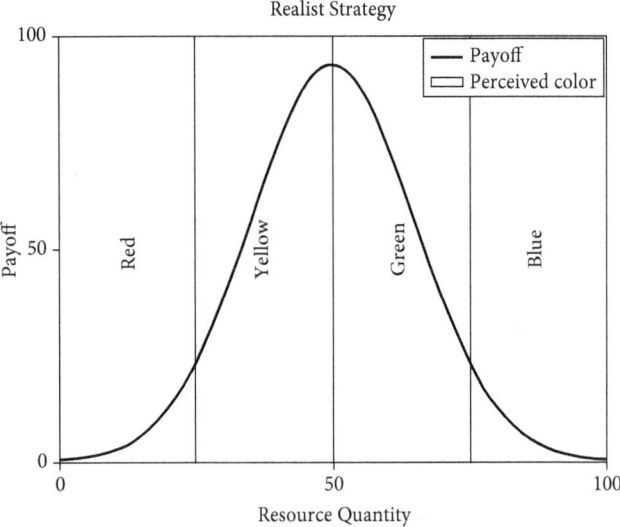

Figure 3.1 (based on HSP (2015a fig 2)). Realist psychometric function mapping resource quantities to perceived colors, with payoff also shown. This discrete mapping is (weakly) order preserving (note: colors are assumed to be ordered in hue circle in standard way).

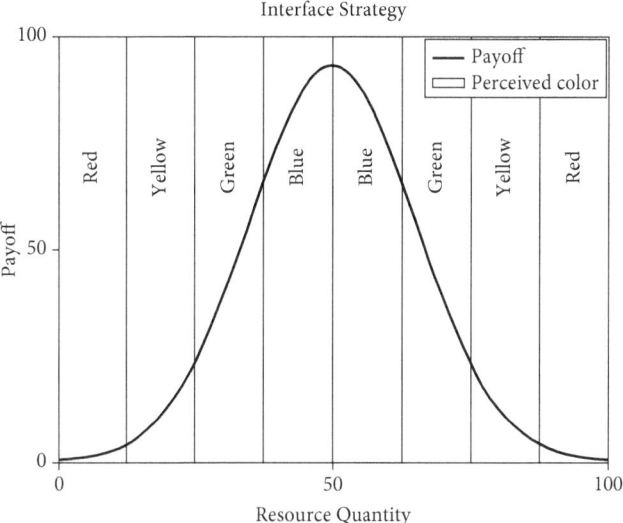

Figure 3.2 (based on HSP (2015a fig 3)). Interface psychometric function, mapping resource quantity to perceived colors, with payoff also shown. This discrete mapping is not order-preserving.

function) for resource quantity (Figure 3.2) dominates a critical realist strategy (Figure 3.1). That is, it is advantageous to perceptually group together resource quantities with similar payoffs, even though they do not form a contiguous grouping (consider e.g. the yellow grouping in Figure 3.2). In another kind of model, the strategy itself is allowed to evolve through combining strategies of mates in a quasi-genetic way. This genetic algorithm ends up optimizing toward an interface strategy for resource quantity.[16]

Does this support perceptual pragmatism for *all* perceived properties? Note that the argument just assumes the payoff distribution thesis—that payoffs are non-monotonic with respect to physical stimulus properties. If they were for example linearly related, then there would be no competition between payoff and physical quantity to be perceptually represented. It may seem unsurprising that if we assume payoff non-monotonicity, the interface strategy ends up dominating: we'll come back to this momentarily. But actually there is another problem here, which is that real systems are subject to computational constraints that (arguably) aren't adequately modelled

---

[16] Prakash et al. (2021) provide a proof that "fitness beats truth" in a class of such toy models.

here. The optimal course of action for an organism is a very complicated function of stimulus parameters, and to even approximate it requires a complex multi-stage computational process. Perceptual transducers typically only modestly and monotonically transform a perceptual parameter—for example, representing a power function. This inputs into a complex multi-layered computational system that outputs a motor instruction only after many layers of processing, layers which may represent stimulus features at increasing levels of abstraction from the transduced properties. This means that even if a complex non-monotonic transformation of the stimulus property occurs to determine action, there may also be, in earlier layers, properties represented which are fairly simple monotonic functions of stimulus quantities. These earlier layers might correspond to conscious experiences. For example, it could be that a creature experiences resource quantity in a monotonic way, and then this is transformed non-monotonically *post-perceptually*, to determine optimal course of action. So critical realist vs interface could be a false contrast: we might need both.

Relatedly, there may be stimulus features that are useful to (monotonically) represent as an input to a broad variety of these action-oriented computations, across different contexts. Surely it is plausible to speculate that spatial structure is like this. For example, it is useful both for computing the energy cost of movement and for object identification. Moreover, such flexible-use representations are plausibly evolutionarily accessible (they don't require a designer with foresight), because the broad use could be an exaptation from a more simple use. For example, spatial distance perception might evolve first because it is useful for simple computations of cost of motion; but then it is exapted for a host of other useful purposes.

A natural speculation would then be that if we study toy models that are subject to more realistic computational constraints and where a more realistic range of physical parameters is relevant to the organism's fitness, we would get results that instead support the hybrid realist view. I would note in this regard that (ironically) the perceptual strategies that dominate in HSP's models are actually, contrary to advertising, only interface with respect to resource quantity, and are *overall* critical realist, because the organisms "veridically" (i.e. structurally veridically) perceive layout properties of their environment such as where environmental boundaries are. Future work that investigates the properties of these models might be illuminating.[17]

---

[17] In this direction, some preliminary joint work with Amalie Trewartha suggested that if we include these layout properties as features whose perceptual strategy can vary between organisms, a veridical *layout* perception tends to dominate, even if an interface strategy dominates for resource quantity.

So the argument for the fitness perception thesis is questionable. Let's turn to the payoff distribution thesis: non-monotonicity of payoff with respect to physical parameters.

3.2 The Payoff Distribution Thesis

Again, this is the thesis that fitness payoff structure is non-monotonically related to underlying physical structure (however that is understood). HSP have two arguments for this thesis, an empirical argument, and a philosophical argument which I will call the "indifference argument."

The empirical argument is that organisms are homeostatic systems that are trying to maintain parameters in their internal state (e.g. temperature) within a livable range. So fitness functions vis-á-vis physical parameters will often be normal distributions (and therefore non-monotonic) that represent this "not too little, not too much" mode of interaction with the physical world (HSP 2015: 1486).

One problem here is that there seem to be obvious counterexamples. Again, spatial distance is a good case. The energy cost of motion along a path through physical space is a monotonic function of distance along the path. Cost of motion is obviously very useful to compute, and so it's not surprising that organisms have this capacity (admittedly overall computation of optimal path in an environment with hills and obstacles etc. is rather more complicated, but cost comparisons along a single path could be a component of that computation, and could be evolutionarily more ancient). Similar points could be made about duration.

Now, rather than further developing this objection, I want to immediately note that there is an attractive escape route here for the interface theorist, which would also help with the earlier objections. They could jettison the fitness perception thesis, and instead focus on the consciously perceived features of the environment that are at least the immediate *inputs* to computations of fitness payoffs (or at least, to action choices). Call these *intermediate features*. Unlike strongly pragmatic features (like, say, tastiness), these features might lead to quite different behaviors combined with different utilities and background information—that is, they might have the kind of pragmatic flexibility I just suggested is characteristic of spatial distance. Still, we might ask: given that these intermediate features are adapted to computation of optimal action choice, and optimal action choice is often only very indirectly and non-monotonically related to physical stimulus features, why think that what is in conscious perception hasn't already been transformed beyond recognition? Why think that anything like structural transparency obtains for intermediate features?

Call the view that perception of intermediate features is structurally opaque *weak perceptual pragmatism*. To my mind, it is a more compelling challenge to perceptual transparency, because it doesn't require the strong, and rather implausible commitments of the strong pragmatist discussed in the previous section. For example, although it is surprising as a view of duration or spatial distance, weak pragmatism at least avoids implausibly treating them as directly tied to particular kinds of action payoff. This makes it at least somewhat more viable to maintain that these are intermediate features for which structural transparency does not obtain, and which therefore are *not physical input parameters in the relevant sense*. Thus, even if it is true that cost of motion is a monotonic function of spatial distance, that wouldn't show that the payoff distribution thesis is false, because spatial distance itself could be non-monotonically related to the true physical structure of the world (more on this momentarily).

Still, there are two important objections to weak perceptual pragmatism that I want to consider. These will also helpfully motivate HSP's other argument for Payoff Non-monotonicity, the indifference argument.

First, one might object that the appeals to Darwinian evolution, homeostasis, etc. in the argument assume that we know that we are organisms of a certain kind with a certain history. But if perception is globally non-veridical, doesn't that call this into question, and therefore call into question some of the premises of the argument? Is the argument self-undermining?

Interestingly, this is a point where, in one way, HSP's position is actually rather stronger than they allow for. They think that we can know we are products of Darwinian selection even conditional on doubting the existence of biological entities like animals and plants that perception presents us with (because perception is "non-veridical"). They also speculate that even if perception isn't reliable, other aspects of our cognition (e.g. mathematical reasoning and other kinds of abstract reasoning) could be reliable, allowing us to know that Darwinism is true (HSP 2015a: 1500, 2019: ch. 4). This suggests a kind of transcendental argument for Darwinism: a priori, it is the best explanation for the existence of complex structure in *any* situation prior to investigation. So we don't need to make any substantial empirical claims about the world to believe that we are the products of Darwinian natural selection. But actually I don't think they need this kind of speculative defense. We noted earlier that perception being non-veridical in the *structural* sense is perfectly compatible with it being veridical in the *content-involving* sense; and it's the latter sense that it is relevant to whether our beliefs based on experience are *true*. So there's no reason why HSP can't hold that there really exist such things as populations of organisms, their prey and predators, environmental resources etc. etc., and that the best explanation of their features and distribution is that they were created by Darwinian natural selection. True enough, our entire scheme for describing the biological world might be only non-transparently related to physics (or whatever exists fundamentally), but that's no reason for saying it isn't a roughly *correct* description of a real mind-independent system.

So far so good: however, there's still trouble here. The problem is that by the interface theorist's own lights, empirical evidence can only ever tell us about the form of the mapping function from properties *at different levels of the interface*. For example, on their view, a property like resource quantity or spatial distance is an *output* of the scrambling function. So even if there's an empirical argument that the mapping from resource quantity to perceptual space is non-monotonic, that doesn't show that the map from the underlying physical space to the perceptual space is *also* non-monotonic. It leaves it completely open what that is. I think this is a serious objection: it suggests that any empirical argument for the interface view really will be self-undermining! This motivates their more a priori argument: the indifference argument (see below).

Second, there is a point made by Bertrand Russell in *The Problems of Philosophy* (and noted by HSP) which might seem to support perceptual transparency.

> If a regiment of men are marching along a road, the shape of the regiment will look different from different points of view, but the men will appear arranged in the same order from all points of view. Hence, we regard the order as true also in physical space, whereas the shape is only supposed to correspond to the physical space so far as is required for the preservation of the order.
>
> (Russell 2001: 51)

In other words: perceptual invariance (across changes in the position of the perceiving subject) is evidence for structural transparency (e.g. perception is structurally transparent with respect to *order* of perceived objects).

Now, HSP have an interesting response to this objection, which exploits what they call the "invention of symmetry" theorem (2015: 1498). What the theorem shows is that invariance of the psychometric function across symmetry translations like rotation and change of position is *consistent* with the function being non-transparent. So there is no necessary implication from invariance to structural transparency. For example, we might suppose that the physical world just consists in a completely unstructured set of points!! One can consistently have a psychometric function on this unstructured set that gives a phenomenal world where, e.g. from various different viewing points, it looks like there is a group of ten squirrels standing in a line.

That's an important point, but it is limited in the following way. It may be objected that even if non-transparency is *consistent* with perceptual invariance, in many cases (but not all), the *best explanation* for perceptual invariance is that we are perceiving structure that is an objective physical structure. Presumably that is what we would say for Russell's regiment, for example; and presumably that is the reason that the hypothesis of a completely unstructured fundamental world is highly unattractive.

The interface theorist may respond as follows. Such an explanation is a *downwards inference*—an inference from manifest perceptual structure to the underlying physical structure. But the form of this relationship is exactly what is at stake in the debate between the realist and the interface theorist. Indeed, it is surely true that if we are not allowed to assume any prior constraints on the form of the connection between manifest properties and underlying physical properties (call this the *grounding function*) then we can't legitimately rule out, for example, an unstructured fundamental world. Now, this is precisely HSP's second argument against structural transparency (on my reading of them). They say: if we consider the space of all possible grounding functions, the functions that that give us perceptual transparency occupy a vanishingly small region of the space of all such functions. So by a principle of indifference, we should not assume that the kinds of principles which (presumably) are implicitly operative in ordinary downwards inferences (e.g. those performed by scientists) are revealing of objective structure. Rather, they are just ways of nicely systematizing invariances and connections in the psychometric function—we are forever stuck in the headset![18]

They will also wheel out the indifference argument in response to another obvious objection. We might say: haven't we learned that spatio-temporal structure and causal structure is transparently related to fundamental physical structure? True enough, these days we take seriously fundamental

---

[18] see HSP (2015) and Prakash et al. (2020). I should also note here the resemblance to epistemic arguments against realist views of fundamentality/naturalness (see e.g. Cohen and Callender (2009)).

theories on which space and time are non-fundamental and emergent (e.g. Wüthrich (2019)). But still, the connecting function is not a non-monotonic scrambler; otherwise we could not have made the downwards inference to the physical deeper structure. In response, HSP can say that the assumption that such downwards inferences reveal objective fundamental structure is question-begging against the interface theorist. If we are initially indifferent among possible grounding functions, the chance of this is effectively zero.

Now of course, whether this is convincing depends on how much force the indifference argument has. The problems with it are both technical and philosophical. On the more technical (but still philosophical!) end, we should ask: what exactly is the space of grounding functions? What kind of mathematical objects are we talking about here, and how are they measured? What is the argument that structural maps are a measure zero subset? The way I will proceed is to grant (quite charitably) that we are operating with a reasonable answer to this question, on which by a natural mathematical measure, structural functions really are a vanishingly small subset.[19] My objection will be more philosophical: why should the realist concede from this that they should have low prior probability? This will be the subject of the final section of this chapter, where I also develop in more detail the realist's view.

4. Realism vs the Interface Theory

I now consider in more detail what non-structural grounding *is* and why rejecting it really is an interesting form of idealism.

Now, I suspect some will object that the interface theory is *not* actually saying anything very radical or interesting. Recall that the theory claims perception has evolved to track the *payoff structure* of the environment, and that this is non-monotonically related to the physical structure of the environment. The objector claims that this simply amounts to the banal claim that we perceive features of the environment that are useful to know about given our adaptive needs, and that these are distinct from, and only indirectly related to whatever physical features the Interface theorists is including in

---

[19] Prakash et al. (2020) considers four classes of structures which could be used in psycho-metric modelling and argues that only a vanishingly small subclass are homomorphisms. Of course, other kinds of structures could be relevant (as they are well aware), and one could question the underlying indifference principle.

W (= the input to the psychometric function). What are these? On one important reading, states of W are supposed to be *fundamental physical states of affairs* (this is certainly suggested by HSPs' discussion). So the interface theory can start sounding like the combination of the following two positions:

Non-fundamental Perception: The environmental features that we perceive are not fundamental physical features

Non-structural grounding: The mapping from fundamental physics to the high-level features that perceptual experience presents to us is not a structure-preserving mapping

The problem with non-fundamental perception (considered alone) is it's not at all a surprising claim. Granted, it has been historically tempting to think that at least space and time as perceived by us might be fundamental features of the universe. Indeed, HSP emphasize in support of their view that space-time may well turn out to be non-fundamental (note that this supports interpreting them as limiting W to fundamental states of affairs). But still, it's not a radical or surprising claim that we only perceive high-level features of the world, and not fundamental features. Pretty much everyone thinks of the project of fundamental physics as getting behind the appearances that constitute the "manifest world," and inferring the detailed physical structure that is behind these appearances. Also, when philosophers or cognitive scientists have claimed that evolution has given us perceptual systems that typically present the world in an "accurate" or "veridical" way, they clearly did not mean to claim that it provides a direct window onto the fundamental physical world.

Furthermore, if we allow non-fundamental states of affairs into W, this raises the question "which ones"? Among the high-level states of affairs will be precisely the states of affairs that we have evolved to perceive (whatever these are!)! If we include these in W, then perception *will* be "veridical" by HSP's own lights! Furthermore, if W is deliberately limited to some set of non-fundamental states of affairs that are *not* those we have evolved to perceive, but for which a psychometric function F still exists, why is it interesting to be told that the mapping from W states to the states we *are* evolved to perceive, is a somewhat indirect and non-structural one? (more on this momentarily).

Relatedly, it is reasonable to wonder why supplementing non-fundamental perception with non-structural grounding is such a bold move. It is commonly believed that the story one would have to tell to get from a fundamental physical description of the world to the kind of description that mentions that manifest phenomena we know and love, could involve a very complex series of abstractions and inferences. Why think that the mapping implicit in this story would be a nice, simple, structure-preserving one? And who exactly has claimed otherwise?

Although I think HSP are at fault for not addressing this kind of objection, I also think that there is a compelling answer here. Consider again the problem of downwards inference: what are the correct epistemic principles to use to infer the lower-level grounds of the observable manifest world? A good answer to this question needs to explain how we can rule out what I call *micro-skeptical scenarios*. These are scenarios where the fundamental world is nothing like what we have come to believe, but nonetheless grounds our manifest world through a counterintuitively complex and gruesome grounding function. For example, consider *Game of Thrones world*. This is a world which, given knowledge of its fundamental layout, we would intuitively describe as a world where something like the world of the *Game of Thrones* novels is playing out. Now, consider the hypothesis that this is in fact the world that we (locally) live in; furthermore, the reason why we don't see any of the game of thrones participants is that we and all the objects we observe are *metaphysical junk*: our manifest world is related to the fundamental level in a complex and gruesome way. If informed of our existence, philosophers in the game of thrones world would think of us as fanciful and purely notional constructions, rather than solid concrete beings. Or for another example, consider *the dust world hypothesis*: the fundamental world is random swirling dust; nonetheless the manifest world exists in a way that is derived in a complex gruesome way from the dust.[20]

What is "metaphysical junk"? I am assuming here a plenitudinous view of objects and properties. On this view, there is an object for every function from possible worlds to sets of space-time points (it's actual and possible space-time trajectories). Also, there is a property or relation for every function from worlds to sets of objects (or sets of n-tuples of objects for n-place relations; for quantities we can consider functions from objects to real numbers). I assume that a subset of these objects and properties are privileged as fundamental—for example, these could be individual space-time points, or particles, and the features ascribed to them by fundamental physics.

---

[20] Chalmers (2022) also discusses this skeptical scenario, which he attributes to sci-fi writer Greg Egan.

The rest includes the objects we know and love like mountains and trees, but also so much else! Although we typically ignore most of the metaphysical junk, it at least exists. A well-known challenge is—what exactly distinguishes the junk from the entities we know and love? Here the issue is: how do we know that we aren't junk?

In an important discussion which I consider in detail elsewhere (Lee (manuscript)), Shoemaker (1988) gives a method of constructing systems of junk objects ("ghosts") in such a way that the correlations across modal space between events in these junk systems mimic the correlations we find in real functional systems, and the objects are spatiotemporally like real objects.[21] This raises the question—why, if at all, do these ghosts not count as genuine functional systems? Admitting that they are would seem to be catastrophic—for example, we would have to admit that the world is densely populated with "ghost brains" that functionally replicate all manner of different consciously perceiving brains. But as Shoemaker notes, it's not actually clear what the relevant difference is between the thin correlational causation that ties together ghost systems and the causation that we observe and theorize in the world. This is the *ghost world puzzle*. It asks what rules out ghosts existing that are functionally like us. The micro-skeptical puzzler on the other hand asks: how do we know that *we* aren't ghosts? (Obviously, there is a close relationship here with triviality arguments against functionalism,[22] although I find that Shoemaker's set up gets us into the issues from a different angle in an illuminating way).

The connection here with the interface theory is that it is precisely in the business of challenging whether our downwards inferences are reliable in the sense that they might reveal the objective physical structure of the world. Arguably, ordinary scientific practice assumes that there is an epistemically tractable, structure-preserving map from the fundamental physical world to the manifest world (it might be complex and multi-stage, but it is not totally scrambling). The interface theorist, both with the empirical argument and the indifference argument, aims to show that this is almost certainly *not* the case. To my mind, this amounts to saying that we are almost certainly *are* in a micro-skeptical scenario. (If anything then, the interface

---

[21] Shoemaker implicitly assumes a flat space-time, and then takes ghost objects to be regions of space-time whose trajectories have the same shape as regions occupied by ordinary objects in a source world (e.g. a world where a completely different distribution of "ordinary" macro-objects exists).

[22] See Sprevak (2018) for a helpful review.

challenge is stronger than a mere skeptical challenge that asks: how do you know that you're not in the skeptical situation?).[23]

One way in which this is (arguably) a clearer framing of the interface theory that HSP's own is this. It's very natural to read the interface theory as treating us as non-junk ordinary material objects, with non-junk ordinary brains, and then picturing the non-monotonic scrambling as occurring in our brains—the perceptual system acts as a kind of distorting lens. But of course, as HSP themselves make clear, objects like human bodies and brains are all part of the manifest phenomenal interface, and so are the *results* of the scrambling function. So in fact the "scrambling brain" seems to fall out of the picture when we think things through. As mentioned, this is a place where it's reasonable to suspect that there's a kind of inconsistency in the empirical argument from evolution (which very much seems to be directed at *establishing* a scrambling brain)—but I won't press this further here. I will note that the indifference argument does not depend on the scrambling brain idea, nor on considerations of evolution, and in this way is very much akin to the kind of philosophical challenge we get from micro-skepticism and the possibility of ghost-systems.

This is why I think that the interface theory is not at all a banal idea, but rather is interesting and challenging. Let's now consider how a realist (understood as someone who thinks that downwards inference to the objective structural of the world is tractable) might respond. The first thing is to briefly consider what our downwards inference principles typically actually are.

I won't be able to get into much detail on this, but I think it's helpful here to distinguish *formal principles* and *causal principles*. Formal principles might include HSPs favored monotonicity principle, but might also include stronger kinds of structure-preservation, such as linearity.[24] Another kind of formal principle (not unrelated to these others), is *derivational complexity minimization*. There are different ways of measuring complexity. A salient measure here might be *Kolmogorov complexity*—the minimum length of program needed to generate a derivation. I think it would not be surprising if it turns out we implicitly strive to minimize this kind of computational

---

[23] In this way the interface theorist's challenge is similar to arguments for the Boltzmann brain hypothesis (e.g. Dogramaci (2019)) and the simulation hypothesis (Bostrom (2003)).

[24] For example, chemical properties like shell-numbers in atoms might be linearly related to features of the quantum-mechanical wave function describing the atom.

complexity in postulating grounds for higher-level states of affairs, although I offer this only as an empirical speculation.

Causal principles tell us how to relate causal structure at higher and lower levels. Two related ideas seem very important here. The first is spatio-temporal locality. We start with the assumption (which has very much turned out to be defeasible), that causal processes operate in a spatio-temporally local way. The second is a principle of causal-mechanism. A causal process occurring in a certain region of space-time is undergirded by a lower-level causal process occurring in the same region. One way to make vivid these principles is precisely to consider how they might break down if we are Shoemakerian ghosts. Intuitively, that would mean that when we trace the causal processes going on, say, locally inside the ghost, we would find a mismatch at the fundamental level whereby "ghost processes" are not mechanistically underpinned in the way our causal principles lead us to believe (e.g. the ghost might exist in a completely empty region of space-time!).

Now, there are many interesting questions (unfortunately not addressed here) about how exactly to formulate these principles and how they are related. One thing to flag immediately is whatever view we end up taking of them will translate into a certain understanding of the "structural preservation" at stake in this discussion, which might therefore not *just* include monotonicity as a condition (as already suggested above). For example, theories of the world that violate our causal principles might be said to *not* be structure-preserving in an important sense.[25] And as I argued above, the monotonicity condition itself is in need of refinement, because some non-monotonic maps *are* epistemically reversible.

Once we have completed the *descriptive* task of figuring out how downwards inference works in practice, how might we justify or unify these principles? Although I don't have space to pursue it detail here, I do want to briefly discuss what I see as an intriguing and potentially powerful strategy for addressing this issue. The idea is that we should *start* with the fundamental world, and then consider the question "*what are the real patterns here?*," with the goal of building *upwards* from physical *to* natural high-level objects and properties. One might hope that this would reveal our downwards inferences to involve exactly those principles that would construct a

---

[25] If we are trying to triangulate multiple kinds of "structure-preservation" this also makes it more plausible that we could leverage a subset of principles to argue that preservation of one kind or other is violated.

fundamental world from which our manifest world can be recovered as "natural structure."

The way for the realist to approach this, I think, is to ask "what patterns in the fundamental evolution would be of interest to a being who is *purely* interested in the fundamental evolution?" (e.g. they do not from the outset have any of our parochial interests in medium-sized objects like food and mates). Let us further suppose that such a being is interested in finding convenient compact ways of *summarizing* the fundamental evolution. Famously, Humeans about dynamical laws believe that the laws can be recovered from the fundamental distribution as a compact summary of how the world evolves.[26] To my mind, an attractive speculation (ambitious but not totally implausible) is that this approach (broadly understood) can be successfully generalized beyond laws to many other worldly patterns.[27] A nice example is the notion of a material object and the notion of center of mass, as applied in a well-known component of Newton's theory. A set of particles rigidly stuck together will behave like a particle of the same mass located at the object's center of mass. One way of thinking of this is that because the particles are stuck together, there will be great redundancy in a complete description of their trajectories, because they are highly correlated. So if we are concerned with knowing approximately for each particle where it will end up, treating the system as an object is a highly efficient way to summarize these particle trajectories.[28]

Let's say that a notion that features in such an efficient summary has "Humean objective significance" or just is "Humean" or "objectively significant" for short. If the notion of a material object is Humean, then notice that, plausibly, any property that helps efficiently predict/explain its trajectory will *also* be Humean. So for example, folk psychology could be of interest to a being only concerned with efficiently describing physics, because it is useful for predicting how the correlated particles that make up human bodies will move around. I also think it's plausible that thermodynamic properties like temperature can be given the Humean treatment: for example, if I want to know roughly where a particle will end up, knowing the

---

[26] Lewis argued that the laws are axioms in a theory of the world that optimally trades off strength and simplicity (see e.g. Lewis (1994)). For further discussion see Loewer (1996), Cohen and Callender (2009), Ismael (2015), Hall (2015), Callendar (2023) and Jaag and Loew (2020).

[27] The idea here is *not* that the ordinary macro-world falls out from the details of a best-system account like Lewis's. It's that Humean reasoning in the spirit of best-systems accounts can recover the macro-world.

[28] It's no coincidence that Dennett (1991) also uses this example in his discussion of "real patterns."

thermodynamic properties of the parts of the system that it is embedded in will often be very useful.[29] In this way, the kind of time-directed causal structure that depends on the thermodynamic arrow of time could emerge naturally through Humean reasoning from the fundamental level.

These ideas obviously stand in need of much further development, but let's suppose we have recovered a world of high-level patterns as objectively significant in this way.[30] Then I would make two further, closely connected proposals in a realist spirit. One is that much of our manifest ontology (e.g. the idea of a material object) is objectively significant.[31] A Humean super-being would care about mountains and trees and animals and planets, and the features of them that we use to explain and predict their behavior. The second proposal is that our downwards inference principles lead us to construct theories of underlying physical structure (including fundamental structure) in just such a way that our manifest ontology (chairs, mountains, etc.) turns out to be objectively significant. That is: we construct our physics *so as* to make our manifest world come out as a Humean real pattern.

Now, this latter idea, if correct, does invite a line of objection very much in the spirit of the interface theory. Given that our perceptual systems were defined with survival and mating in mind, why think that they would deliver categories with objective significance? Why would it be useful for us Darwinian beings to perceive and think about categories that also would be of interest to a disinterested Humean super-being? Wouldn't that be to illicitly assume that our parochial human perspective offers a direct window onto how the world really is (where now that is understood as the vision of a Humean super-being)? Call this the *modified Darwinian debunking argument*.

There is also a version of the indifference argument here. The interface theorist is likely to accuse the realist indulging in these Humean speculations as massively begging the question. Of course, if we make downwards inferences that reverse engineer the manifest world as objectively significant, realism will seem to have been vindicated. But if we start off uncertain

---

[29] For example, consider a particle that is part of a gas that cools or dissipates, or a particle that is part of a moving piece of machinery in an engine whose functioning can be modelled in thermodynamic terms. Thanks to Amalie Trewartha for helpful discussion on this point.

[30] One pressing issue here is this: famously Humean accounts of laws risk making laws anthropocentric because "best system" could mean *best for us* given our cognitive limitations and place in the world (Lewis called this "ratbag idealism"). I assume my super-being has an interest in efficiently summarizing the fundamental facts—is that really a parochial human interest that undermines the claim that the revealed patterns are "objective" in an interesting sense?

[31] There is an intriguing resemblance here with "natural scene statistics" approaches to explaining perceptual and cognitive categories in cognitive science (e.g. Geisler (2008)).

about the form of the grounding function—in particular, if we are completely indifferent over the space of possible grounding functions (however that be modelled and measured), then the chance that this kind of reasoning is successful is effectively zero.

At this point, the issue of burden of proof in the end-game very much rears its head. In addressing these challenges, I think it's helpful to distinguish two different types of debunking arguments: what I'll call *by-your-lights* and *by-my-lights* debunking arguments. The difference is this. The by-your-lights debunker presents a challenge that is easier to meet, because they are willing to provisionally grant the world-view of their opponent. They challenge a particular assumption of the opponent by asking them to explain, *given the resources of their world-view*, how it is that the assumption is reliably held (or has whatever other epistemically important feature that is at issue). Take, for example, our belief in the presence of medium-sized perceptible objects like humans, trees, chairs, etc. A by-your-lights debunking challenge against these beliefs can be successfully met by pointing out that given that these items exist, and given that knowing about them would be important for the survival of an organism like us (appealing to our overall scientific world-view), there is every reason why we would have a perceptual system that reliably informed us about them. To meet this challenge then, there is nothing wrong with simply appealing to the assumption in question, as part of a world-view that explains why our making that assumption is reliable (the challenge is therefore in the spirit of the *epistemological naturalism* of Quine (1969). Notice that this doesn't mean it is trivial to meet the challenge. Consider, for example, the intuition that a dualist view of conscious experience is true. One can imagine a theorist, who by their own lights, has this intuition because of the way their brain works, not because non-physical experiential properties exist and have caused the intuition; so the epistemic challenge is effective even if we grant provisionally that dualism is true.

The by-my-lights challenger, by contrast, is an individual who is *not* willing to provisionally grant the assumption in question, and wants an *independent* argument for thinking that it is correct. Famously, this kind of challenge is very hard to meet—to establish anything we need to make assumptions, but those assumptions themselves can be attacked with a by-my-lights challenge. So it's not particularly disturbing if in the end our belief-system can't be given this very demanding kind of vindication. This, famously, is the moral many draw from considering traditional skeptical attacks on human knowledge. On the other hand, if we can't provide the holistic kind of vindication demanded by the by-your-lights challenger, that is more epistemically disturbing.

Now, the way I see it, if the interface theorist's debunking challenges are understood in the weaker by-your-lights sense, they are still non-trivial challenges, but ones that can potentially be met. As the interface theorist's own empirical argument from homeostasis etc. illustrates, one could envisage investigating how our perceptual systems actually evolutionarily developed, and finding that we have the rug pulled out from under our feet, because our best theory tells us that perception is likely to be structurally opaque. However, I do not believe that this is what we will actually find. In particular, if we start by assuming that ourselves, our food, mates, predators and other behaviorally significant objects and features are objectively significant (i.e. that these objects are all Humean objects), then it would be adaptive to perceive Humean objects, and it would be adaptive to perceive the Humean features that explain their behaviors (consider what we said earlier about spatial distance). Furthermore, in so far as it's useful to be able to mentally model the causal mechanisms underpinning manifest causal interactions, it would be adaptive to be disposed to engage in downwards inferences that uncover the Humean causal structure underpinning these interactions; and so our reasoning would be revealed (by our lights) to be reliable.

It's true that there can turn out to be local exceptions to this. For example, color and smell could turn out to be quite gruesome and therefore non-Humean. In this way, a kind of evolutionary debunking argument against the Humean significance of these properties can succeed. It can also turn out that our epistemic principles are unreliable in various ways and need to be locally revised. But presumably we could not bootstrap our way to extremely radical revisions. More generally, if all we face is a by-your-lights challenge, a broadly realist view seems to be structurally built in as an upshot.[32]

Of course, there is something unsatisfying about this. It would be great to be able to assume nothing and build our world-view from a completely a priori starting point. But of course this is overambitious. Arguably, the proponent

---

[32] It must be acknowledged here that the history of physics shows that we are capable of empirically establishing a surprising degree of "mismatch" between manifest structure and the fundamental structure (quantum mechanics being one famous example). I still think there are surely limits built in here given the priors reflected in our downwards inference principles, but it's an interesting question what the extent is to which they limit the space of viable physical theories (relatedly, are there limits to what we could *observe* as data for our theories?).

of a by-my-lights version of the interface challenge is guilty of this kind of unreasonable demand. To say we should be indifferent between different downwards inference principles is to say that we should start with no assumptions whatsoever about how the manifest world is generated. But of course if we start there, there is no hope of knowing anything about that generative base. Similarly, if I start with no assumptions about how my perceptual experience is causally generated, there is no hope of recovering the manifest perceptual world. Philosophers have long learned to live with this kind of result, and learned to only expect the more holistic "internal" kind of vindication, not a full-blooded refutation of the radical skeptic. If the interface theorist is only an old-fashioned radical skeptic, then theory loses some of its interest, or at least fails to be a compelling threat to the realist.

Now, this doesn't mean that progress can't be made within the realist holistic project. We can figure out the relationship between our principles, including trying to recover as much as we can from as few principles as possible, or modifying or clarifying principles when they clash with each other or otherwise result in unattractive consequences. The Humean program that I sketched above is supposed to be an example of this kind of theorizing. It doesn't start from nowhere, because the Humean super-being *must themselves be operating with some principles*—for example, they want an "efficient summary" of the fundamental world in some substantive sense. What if they had a different interest?

Is this the end of the story? Actually no. At this point the interface theorist regains composure and launches into the following defense. They can ask why, even if their view is structurally akin to, say, radical skepticism about the existence of the external world, it should be considered objectionable in the same way. In particular, they may point to the fact that structural non-veridicality is perfectly consistent with content-based veridicality. So the "skepticism" they are serving up is completely consistent with our having a largely correct view of the world!! They might say: the idea that we should expect or strive for a model of the world that mirrors or structurally corresponds to the objective fundamental structure of nature is an overambitious or hubristic metaphysical gloss on our theorizing that is a philosopher's fantasy and not part of our ordinary theoretical understanding; moreover, it is completely dispensable, pragmatically speaking. In this way, it is quite unlike the idea that our beliefs are more or less true, or that our belief-forming methods are at least somewhat reliable—that's an assumption without which enquiry into the world, and in fact just human life in general, cannot go on. Why not settle for a more "internal" Kantian kind of realism, rather than the "external" realism that structural correspondence demands?

Along these lines, one can make an interesting comparison here to the debate about moral realism (i.e. that mind-independent moral norms are part of the fundamental furniture of the world). It is common to offer evolutionary debunking arguments against moral realism,[33] and it has also been common for moral realists to respond by saying that they can at least meet a by-your-lights debunking challenge,[34] and that by-my-lights challenge really amounts to an unworrying form of moral skepticism. In this case though, I would be inclined to side with the debunkers! Moreover, it is quite plausible to make the same kind of appeal to modesty and pragmatism—moral realism just doesn't seem to achieve much theoretically or pragmatically in the way that a belief in the reliability of our epistemic norms probably does.

To my mind, this is the most interesting line of defense that an interface theorist can make. But note that it is spiritually far-removed from HSP's interface theory. They see themselves as iconoclasts smashing up common sense with their radical lessons from evolution. This interface theorist is offering their view in the spirit of theoretical restraint and pragmatism.

Now, although I think this is a better way to think about the theory, I'm not ultimately convinced that it is an attractive resting place. There's a more minor and a more major defense the structural realist has up their sleeve. The minor defense is this: they could potentially make the case that the comparison between structural transparency and moral realism is unconvincing, because the moral realist can't even in the end meet the by-your-lights challenge. Even if we take for granted what the moral facts are (construed realistically), do they really explain our moral intuitions in a way that makes it clear that these intuitions are a reliable form of moral perception into a mind-independent moral realm, in the way that visual perception can be argued (in a by-my-lights spirit) to be a reliable perception of medium-sized objects? That actually does not seem plausible (to me at least!), although of course much more needs to be said (maybe the comparison with perception is unfair). On the other hand, the by-my-lights defense of

---

[33] e.g. Street (2006) is a classic example.

[34] If we are allowed to take for granted what the moral facts *are*, then it's at least *less* challenging to explain how our physical evolution lead to us having reliable moral beliefs. For example, if murdering people in your community is objectively wrong, and evolution predictably leads us to think that it is wrong (because e.g. it was adaptive for us to live in peaceful communities), then there is a sense in which this moral belief is reliably formed.

structural transparency looks to be quite solid (modulo the inevitable sense of question-beggingness).

This defense is more minor, because it doesn't tackle head-on the accusation that structural transparency is theoretically otiose and hubristic; it just shows there's a kind of internal coherence to it. The more major response does tackle this head-on though. Here's the thing: one way to put the "modest" view we are contemplating is as saying that there's nothing problematic about the idea that the manifest world, and the rest of the known universe (i.e. the world we think we know through theoretical inference), is really a system of junk objects and properties/relations, only remotely and gruesomely related to the true noumenal structure of the world. But that leads to an acute version of Shoemaker's ghost world puzzle. For if the functional structure that we are familiar with (e.g. the structure involved in our brain's functioning), can exist consistently with our being junk objects, then why doesn't that lead to a massive explosion of equally robust functional structure densely populating the universe? Specifically, if we assume a plenitudinous ontology,[35] then although we may then have to admit systems of ghost objects and properties whose interactions *mimic* real causal interaction in a modal-correlational sense, we might have hoped that ultimately these interactions are not underpinned mechanistically at the fundamental level in such a way to count as *robustly causal* (e.g. imagine, again, reading a system of ghosts into a completely empty space-time). But if we ourselves are junk, this way of distinguishing ourselves from junk is (arguably) doomed, and we risk having to think of other systems of junk objects and properties as not just existing, but also *not differing in a metaphysically significant way from the world we know and love* (e.g. being robustly functional in just the same way). But that's a wild view: for example, it would seem to entail that every possible functional structure that could characterize every possible brain of the same complexity as the human brain, actually is instantiated in our universe.[36] So the problem is this: metaphysical modesty about who we are, and how our manifest world relates to the fundamental world, might lead to extreme *liberality* about what other beings with genuine functional

---

[35] An important lacuna in this chapter is (admittedly) the consideration of sparse ontologies that simply deny that junk objects and property instantiations really exist. In other work I consider the viability of these kinds of views and their potential to solve the ghost world puzzle in a different way (Lee (2023), Lee (manuscript)).

[36] And of course it's not a big step from this to the view that there exist an infinite variety of consciously experiencing subjects! In my view, even if we reject functionalism about consciousness, the problem is serious because we will still have an infinite variety of "quasi-conscious" subjects (see Lee (2019) for elaboration).

structure inhabit the universe. That's not a modest view at all—in fact it's extremely theoretically crazy!!!!

In my current thinking, this is why, in the end, I lean in the direction of structural-transparency realism. To believe that we are alone in the world (qua robustly functional beings), we have to think of the mind as a mirror of nature. I must admit though that a principle that says "avoid functional explosion" is an odd kind of foundation stone. So even if we like this realist picture, there is surely interesting work to be done taxonomizing and theorizing its foundational assumptions; once we have done this, perhaps there is a way of justifying the resistance to functional explosion in a way shows how it follows from, or at least coheres nicely with, other basic tenets. It's also natural to wonder whether the interface theorist can avoid the excesses of explosion without embracing structural transparency. Denying plenitude and holding that unlike our manifest world, the alleged junk-systems do not really exist, is one tempting path along these lines—a path that I skeptically discuss in detail elsewhere (Lee (2023), Lee (manuscript)). One can also consider views that deny the existence of any objective fundamental structure that would constitute the unknowable noumenon, thereby sidestepping the issue of structural transparency. One interesting (but rather obscure) view along these lines also metaphysically privileges the manifest world *above* the underlying structure (it is not a mere "construction," even if the so-called "fundamental" world is) so that there is no possibility of experience failing to present "the world as it really is" (the manifest world is the world at its most real!!). Whether such views can be developed in a compelling way is a question I will have to leave for another time.[37]

References

Beck, J. (2018). Analog Mental Representation. *Wiley Interdisciplinary Reviews: Cognitive Science*, 9(6), e1479.

Berkeley, G. (1713/1979). *Three Dialogues between Hylas and Philonous*. Hackett.

Bostrom, N. (2003). Are We Living in a Computer Simulation? *Philosophical Quarterly*, 53(211), 243–255.

---

[37] Many thanks to Uriah Kriegel, Robert Prentner, Jonathan Simon, Galen Strawson and Amalie Trewartha for helpful comments on an earlier draft, and to participants in the 2023 workshop at Rice university for helpful discussion and feedback.

Callendar, C. (2023). Humean Laws of Nature: The End of the Good Old Days. In M. Hicks, S. Jaag and C. Loews, eds. *Humean Laws for Humean Agents* (16–42). Oxford University Press.

Chalmers, D. (2006). Perception and the Fall from Eden. In T. Gendler and J. Hawthorne, eds. *Perceptual Experience* (49–126). Oxford University Press.

Chalmers, D. (2015). Panpsychism and Panprotopsychism. In T. Alter and Y. Nagasawa, eds. *Consciousness in the Physical World: Perspectives on Russellian Monism* (246–276). Oxford University Press.

Chalmers, D. (2022). Idealism and the Mind-Body Problem. In J. Farris and B. P. Göcke, eds. *The Routledge Handbook of Idealism and Immaterialism* (591–614). Routledge.

Chalmers, D. (2022). *Reality+: Virtual Worlds and the Problems of Philosophy.* Norton.

Cohen, J. (2015). Perceptual Representation, Veridicality, and the Interface Theory of Perception. *Psychonomic Bulletin & Review, 22,* 1512–1518.

Cohen, J., and Callender, C. (2009). A Better Best System Account of Lawhood. *Philosophical Studies,* 145(1), 1–34.

Dennett, D. C. (1991). Real Patterns. *Journal of Philosophy,* 88(1), 27–51.

Dennett, D. C. (1993). *Consciousness Explained.* Penguin UK.

Dogramaci, S. (2019). Does My Total Evidence Support That I'm a Boltzmann Brain? *Philosophical Studies,* 177(12), 3717–3723.

Geisler, W. S. (2008). Visual Perception and the Statistical Properties of Natural Scenes. *Annual Review of Psychology, 59,* 167–192.

Goff, P. (2017). *Consciousness and Fundamental Reality.* Oxford: Oxford University Press.

Hall, N. (2015). Humean Reductionism about Laws of Nature. In B. Loewer and J. Schaffer (eds.), *The Blackwell Companion to David Lewis* (262–277). Oxford: Blackwell.

Hoffman, D. (2019). *The Case against Reality: Why Evolution Hid the Truth from Our Eyes.* W. W. Norton.

Hoffman, D. D., Singh, M., and Prakash, C. (2015a). The Interface Theory of Perception. *Psychonomic Bulletin & Review,* 22(6), 1480–1506. http://doi.org/10.3758/s13423-015-0890-8

Hoffman, D. D., Singh, M., and Prakash, C. (2015b). Probing the Interface Theory of Perception: Reply to Commentaries, *Psychonomic Bulletin & Review,* 22(6), 1551–1576.

Ismael, J. (2015). How to Be Humean. In B. Loewer and J. Schaffer (eds), *The Blackwell Companion to David Lewis* (188–205). Oxford (Wiley-Blackwell).

Jaag, S., & Loew, C. (2020). Making Best Systems Best for Us. *Synthese, 197,* 2525–2550.

Langton, R. (1998). *Kantian Humility: Our Ignorance of Things in Themselves.* Oxford University Press.

Lee, G. (2016). Worlds, Voyages and Experiences: Commentary on Pelczar's Sensorama. *Analysis, 76*(4), 453–461.

Lee, G. (2019). Alien Subjectivity and the Importance of Consciousness. In A. Pautz and D. Stoljar, eds. *Blockheads! Essays on Ned Block's Philosophy of Mind and Consciousness.* MIT Press.

Lee, G. (2023). Against Magnitude Realism. *Crítica. Revista Hispanoamericana De Filosofía, 55*(163), 13–44.

Lee, G. (manuscript). Getting out of Ghost World: Grounding and High-level Structure.

Lewis, D. (1983). New Work for a Theory of Universals. *Australasian Journal of Philosophy, 61*(4), 343–377.

Lewis, D. (1994). Humean Supervenience Debugged. *Mind*, 103, 473–490.

Lewis, D. (2001) Ramseyan Humility. In David Braddon-Mitchell and Robert Nola, eds. *Conceptual Analysis and Philosophical Naturalism* (203–222). MIT Press.

Loewer, B. (1996). Humean Supervenience. *Philosophical Topics, 24*(1), 101–127.

Mclaughlin, B. P., and Green, E. J. (2015). Are Icons Sense Data?, *Psychonomic Bulletin & Review, 22*(6), 1541–1545.

Mørch, H. H. (2014). Panpsychism and Causation: A New Argument and a Solution to the Combination Problem. PhD Thesis, University of Oslo.

Neander, K. (2017). *A Mark of the Mental: In Defense of Informational Teleosemantics.* MIT Press.

Pautz, A. (2020). *Perception.* Routledge.

Pelczar, M. (2015). *Sensorama: A Phenomenalist Analysis of Spacetime and Its Contents.* Oxford University Press.

Plantinga, A. (2002) Introduction: The Evolutionary Argument against Naturalism. In J. Beilby, ed. *Naturalism Defeated? Essays on Plantinga's Evolutionary Argument against Naturalism* (1–12). Cornell University Press.

Prakash, C., Fields, C., Hoffman, D. D., Prentner, R., and Singh, M. (2020). Fact, Fiction, and Fitness. *Entropy, 22*(5), 514.

Prakash, C., Stephens, K. D., Hoffman, D. D., Singh, M., and Fields, C. (2021). Fitness Beats Truth in the Evolution of Perception. *Acta Biotheoretica*, 69, 319–341.

Putnam, H. (1981). *Reason, Truth and History.* Cambridge University Press.

Putnam, H. (1983). *Realism and Reason: Philosophical Papers, Volume 3.* Cambridge University Press.

Quine, W. (1969). Epistemology Naturalized. In *Ontological Relativity and Other Essays* (114–138). Columbia University Press.

Roelofs, L. (2019). *Combining Minds: How to Think about Composite Subjectivity.* Oxford University Press.

Russell, B. (2001). *The Problems of Philosophy.* Oxford University Press.

Shea, N. (2018). *Representation in Cognitive Science.* Oxford University Press.

Shepard, R. N., and Chipman, S. (1970). Second-order Isomorphism of Internal Representations: Shapes of States. *Cognitive Psychology,* *1*(1), 1–17.

Shoemaker, S. (1988). On What There Are. *Philosophical Topics,* *16*(1), 201–223.

Sider, T. (2013). *Writing the Book of the World.* Oxford University Press.

Sprevak, M. (2018). Triviality Arguments about Computational Implementation. In M. Sprevak and M. Colombo (eds), *The Routledge Companion to the Computational Mind* (175–192). Routledge.

Strawson, G. (2009). Realistic Monism: Why Physicalism Entails Panpsychism. *Journal of Consciousness Studies* (3–31). *13*(10–11).

Street, S. (2006). A Darwinian Dilemma for Realist Theories of Value. *Philosophical Studies* 127: 109–166.

Wüthrich, C. (2019). The Emergence of Space and Time. In S. Gibb, R. F. Hendry and T. Lancaster (eds), *The Routledge Handbook of Emergence* (315–326). Routledge.

Geoffrey Lee, *Idealism and the Interface Theory* In: *Oxford Studies in Philosophy of Mind Volume 4.*
Edited by: Uriah Kriegel, Oxford University Press. © Geoffrey Lee 2024.
DOI: 10.1093/9780198924159.003.0003

4

Idealism and the Best of All (Subjectively Indistinguishable) Possible Worlds

Helen Yetter-Chappell

Let's begin with what is beyond dispute. We live in a world filled with stars, planets, rocks, trees, rivers, animals, brains...and other physical objects. These objects do not depend for their existence on my perceiving them or on my existence. They do not depend on your mind or Sally's mind or the minds of any other organisms.

Materialists hold that this is because phenomenology is irrelevant to physical objects.[1] The river is made of flowing water; the water of H_2O molecules; the molecules of hydrogen and oxygen; these of protons, electrons, and (for oxygen) neutrons; protons and neutrons of quarks, and these...well, they're not fundamentally experiential, that's for sure! Perhaps structure is all that these physical objects are. Or perhaps there is a further "something" that has this structure, but which is beyond our grasp. Whatever the account, it's difficult to see how the materialist's world could be anything like the world we take ourselves to inhabit. The world we take ourselves to live in is one of dark green avocados, blue sky, and warm kittens; a world of solidity, colors, and smells. But science doesn't reveal properties like these. Instead of color, it gives us surface reflectance properties and wavelengths. Instead of heat, it gives us molecular kinetic energy. Instead of solidity, it gives us closely packed molecules. As David Chalmers (2006) puts it, "[s]cience does not reveal any primitive properties in the object, and furthermore, the hypothesis that objects have the relevant primitive properties seems quite unnecessary in order to explain color

---

[1] Note that dualists are materialists about the *physical world*. But they think that there is more to *reality as a whole* than merely the physical. While dualists deny that our experiences are wholly grounded in the physical, they think that physical objects exist independently of phenomenology.

perception." Likewise for the other primitive properties that seem to populate our world.[2]

For the materialist, there is the world of appearances: the world of *bittersweet* chocolate, *hot* tea, and *red* strawberries. And then there is the world as it truly is: colorless, tasteless, without odor or warmth. What do we know of this *real* world? Its structure. Its effects. And nothing more.

The materialist picture is perfectly coherent. For any way the world seems, materialists can account for why it seems that way, offering an account of (i) the structure of the physical world and (ii) how this affects our experiences. The microphysical structure of the strawberry explains why it reflects certain wavelengths of light. Light hitting the retina triggers a cascade of brain activity. The brain activity is (or grounds or causes) an experience of a primitively red strawberry. The picture is perfectly intelligible; perfectly coherent.

If materialism offers an intelligible account of the physical world and the way it appears to us, why look any further? Why upset the received wisdom if we don't have to? In short: Because idealism can offer us something better. Because we can embrace all the structural truths that our empirical investigation reveals…and have common-sense, too. Because holding that the world is nothing like it seems is a *cost*. It's a cost that we might have to accept, but it's not one that we should accept unless we *must*. Common-sense is not something to throw out just for the hell of it.

This chapter proceeds as follows:

§1 *Nontheistic Realist Idealism*: I develop the version of idealism that strikes me as most plausibly capturing the world we live in. This is a form of nontheistic realist idealism (Yetter-Chappell 2018). And I'll lay out a theory of perception that fits naturally with this idealist theory (Yetter-Chappell 2024).

§2 *Living in Eden*: I show how this combined account of reality and perception offers a picture of reality and our place within it according to which (a) the world we inhabit genuinely is as it appears—trees are *green*, fire is *warm*—and (b) we are in literal contact with reality, since perception involves extending our minds to literally overlap with aspects of the physical world. Against naïve realism about

---

[2] It is not universally agreed that materialism is at odds with (e.g.) primitive color properties. Color primitivists dispute this. We'll return to color primitivism in §2.2, where I'll argue that naïve realist color primitivism is not a viable option.

perception and qualities, I argue that idealism is uniquely able to capture (a) and (b), and hence offers a uniquely optimistic view of the world and out place within it.

§3 *Theoretical Virtues or Wishful Thinking?*: I argue that worldviews which intelligibly capture (a) and (b) have an advantage over those that don't. Insofar as direct contact with an intelligible world is possible, such worlds should be taken seriously as contenders for actuality.

1. Nontheistic Realist Idealism

I am looking at a daffodil. The bright yellow flower is unmistakable. We could dismiss this as a mere construction of my brain. But let's suspend disbelief and take seriously the idea that the world is as it seems. The *yellow* of the daffodil is part of reality. But there's far more to the daffodil than this. Let's suppose that my color inverted twin is also looking at the daffodil. She sees it as a bright purple. There's no reason to ontologically privilege my experiences over hers. So the *purple* of the daffodil is also part of reality. A bee is buzzing about the daffodil. It sees a striking pattern of ultraviolet stripes all over the daffodil. Once again, there's no reason to privilege my experiences (or human experiences more generally). The *ultraviolet* of the daffodil is part of reality.

Plausibly, there aren't any actual color inverts. We might suppose that there's no bee looking at the flower. We can imagine that I walk on, to look at the hyacinths blooming further down the garden, and there is now no one perceiving the daffodil at all. Even so, *insofar as it's implausible that objects and their properties pop in and out of existence as different perceivers observe them*, the yellow, purple, and ultraviolet of the daffodil persist as aspects of reality. (And since I find this a plausible assumption to make, and I'm in the business of constructing the form of idealism that most plausibly captures our world, I'll assume this.) How can this be? When I look at the daffodil, I have an *experience of yellow*. How can the experience of yellow persist when I am no longer having it?

Berkeley answered this question with an appeal to God. The exact manner in which God pulls this off is up for debate. Perhaps, as the famous limerick would have it, God is always about (perceiving all aspects of the daffodil) in the quad, and that's why the daffodil continues to be: "since observed by, Yours faithfully, God."[3] Perhaps God sustains the daffodil not

---

[3] The limerick is attributed to Ronald Knox, and cited in Downing (2004) among others.

through his perceptions, but through his thoughts—"i.e. by having ideas of them in His understanding" (Pitcher 1977, 175). Perhaps it's God's dispositions that sustain reality by ensuring that should a human/color invert/bee come along, they *would* perceive yellow/purple/ultraviolet. Or perhaps some combination of these (Winkler 1985).

Berkeley's God is an *agent*. He has doxastic attitudes. He is all-powerful, all-knowing, and all-loving. There may be excellent reasons for believing in such a God. But he is *not* essential to sustaining the daffodil in all its colorful glory. Take the interpretation of Berkeley from the famous limerick: The daffodil exists (and is yellow/purple/ultraviolet) when no one's about in the quad because God is experiencing the daffodil, and God experiences the daffodil in its entirety (as yellow, purple, and ultraviolet). What's essential here to sustaining reality isn't God's beliefs, desires, love, knowledge, or agency. What's essential is simply his sensory experiences.[4]

We can construct a more minimal, ontologically neutral form of idealism by peeling away the attributes of Berkeley's God that aren't essential to sustaining the daffodil. God experiences the daffodil in all its yellow/purple/ultraviolet glory. God does not simply experience the world from a single vantage point, as limited agents like us do, but from *all* vantage points. Thus, even when no finite agent is in the garden, the phenomenal yellow, purple, and ultraviolet (as well as all the other features of the daffodil) persist. The yellow of the daffodil is not a merely possible experience. And it does not pop in and out of existence as humans perceive it. It is an *actual experience* existing independently of all ordinary minds. When we peel away divine attributes from Berkeley's God, we retain these actual experiences. But this is not all. We retain the phenomenal *structure*.[5]

Walking through a garden, I don't simply have a barrage of disjoint phenomenology: yellow, green, lavender, sweet, cool, soft, rough, blue, pressure, long, brown, trumpet-shape, and so on. The phenomenology is structured by a number of different relations, including: the unity of consciousness relation, property binding relations, spatial relations, and temporal relations. As I walk

---

[4] Something similar is true for other interpretations of Berkeley. Insofar as it's God's *dispositions* that sustain reality for Berkeley, we simply need the relevant dispositions. This would give us a nontheistic phenomenalism, á la Mill (1865) and Pelczar (2019, 2022). Although in this case, getting rid of God leaves the dispositions brute. And this is something one might be skeptical of (Yetter-Chappell forthcoming).

[5] If God simply had a disjoint set of experiences, with no structure, there's nothing that would make his experiences qualify as *a* world. Without structure binding together the rectangularity of my table, its brownness, and its solidity, there wouldn't be *an object*. Without structure, we could not make sense of space. While Berkeley does not describe the structure of God's experiences, I take it God's experiences must have such structure if they are to form a world.

through the garden, I see the yellow daffodils blowing in the breeze, feel the wind against my skin, and hear birds tweeting overhead. I experience this as part of a single over-arching multimodal experience. This is quite different from a case where three different people observe different aspects of the scene: Marcia seeing the daffodils, Jan feeling the breeze, and Cindy hearing the birds. For me, there is a *single, unified* experience combining all these features. The features are related by the *unity of consciousness relation*. But some aspects of my experience are related more intimately than this. The yellow, the softness, and the trumpet-shape of the daffodil seem *bound together*, while the *brownness* of the tree's bark seems bound up with its *roughness* and the *shape* of the trunk and branches. There is a *property binding* relation that fuses certain bits of my experience together such that they behave and present as single objects. My experiences appear to belong to a single shared space. And this shared experiential space has structure: The trumpet-shaped yellow daffodil seems to be *above* the long, green stem; the tree seems to be *behind* the daffodils; its green leaves, *above* its rough brown trunk. Finally, there are temporal relations. The notes of the bird's call aren't merely different pitches; they are arranged temporally, with some appearing *before* others, some enduring *longer* than others.

Thus far, I've simply described the structure of *my* experiences. But the structure of my experiences plausibly reflects the structure of the world I'm experiencing.[6] The yellow of the daffodil really is bound together with the trumpet-shape (as opposed to floating free or being bound up with the tree shape). The yellow head of the daffodil really is above the green stem. The proposal is that the same relations that structure our own experiences of reality—for the idealist—structure reality itself. Property binding provides (some of) the internal structure of objects. Phenomenal spatial and temporal relations are the spatial and temporal relations of our world. And the unity of consciousness binds together all these phenomenal aspects into a single *world*. For the idealist, reality is fundamentally phenomenal, and the relations that structure reality are phenomenal relations.

But while we can largely appeal to the familiar relations that structure our own experiences to structure reality, the idealist cannot leave it at that. The idealist's reality is far richer than our own experiences reflect. While I simply experience the daffodil as yellow, in reality, the daffodil includes purple, ultraviolet, and a myriad other phenomenal properties. I have only a

---

[6] We could obviously follow Kant in denying this. But my aim is to sketch the world of common-sense.

single perspective on the world. But the world contains all perspectives.[7] There is no basis for privileging my experience of the daffodil (with my human perceptual system) over that of the bee or the color invert. Insofar as we find it plausible that the world is as it appears, there isn't just *one* way the world is, but *many*. This raises a challenge: It means that the head of the daffodil is both yellow all over and purple all over. This sounds quite absurd! Note that the same challenge can equally well be raised against the limerick interpretation of Berkeley. If God perceives everything from all possible perspectives, God will perceive the daffodil as both yellow all over and purple all over.

This is far from an insurmountable challenge. But it does show the idealist's world needs an additional layer of structure to account for the multitude of perspectives. Think about Berkeley's God. One interpretation has it that God sustains the reality not through his perceptions, but through his *thoughts*. It's obvious how this interpretation should respond to the challenge. God doesn't have the thought: *Daffodil yellow-all-over and purple-all-over*. Rather, he has the thought: *Daffodil yellow-all-over from perspective 1 and purple-all-over from perspective 2*. And there's nothing contradictory in that!

The nontheistic idealist can offer an analogous response. Rather than constructing reality directly out of experiences, we simply need to construct it out of experiences *indexed to perspectives*. I think of the nontheistic idealist's world as akin to a tapestry. In an ordinary tapestry, fiber threads (typically wool) are woven via over-under relations into a two-dimensional image. A thread is not a single strand of fiber. Rather, multiple individual strands are twisted together to form the thread. The thread is not simple; it has structure! This offers a compelling analogy for understanding a multiperspective phenomenal unity. Reality is not woven directly out of bits of phenomenology. Rather, bits of phenomenology *indexed to a perspective* are bound into the "threads" out of which reality is woven. The yellow phenomenology I have as I look at the daffodil is indexed to a perspective: $yellow_{[perspective1]}$. The purple phenomenology my inverted twin has as she looks at the flower is indexed to another perspective: $purple_{[perspective2]}$. These two bits of indexed phenomenology (along with phenomenology indexed to all other possible perspectives) are bonded into the thread out of which the daffodil is woven: $yellow_{[perspective1]} + purple_{[perspective2]} + \ldots$ Thus, it is not

---

[7] Or, at least, the phenomenology as-though from all perspectives.

true to say that the daffodil is yellow all over and purple all over *simpliciter*. Rather, the daffodil is yellow all over from *perspective 1*, and purple all over from *perspective 2*. And there's nothing problematic about that.

So here is the picture of the world we've arrived at: Reality is a phenomenal tapestry, comprised out of *actual experiences qualitatively identical to all possible veridical perceptual experiences*.[8] These experiences are akin to the fibers that make up a thread of wool in an ordinary tapestry. Threads are bundles of such phenomenal fibers, *indexed to perspectives*. These threads of indexed phenomenology are woven into a world via the same relations that structure our own experiences of the world. The unity of consciousness explains why we have *an* experience at a moment (rather than a disjoint collection of experiences). For the nontheistic idealist, it explains why the tapestry is *a* tapestry—*a* world—rather than a heap of disconnected phenomenal threads. Property binding explains why we perceive the yellowness of the daffodil as bound up with the trumpet shape. And for the nontheistic idealist, it explains why the yellow (and purple and ultraviolet) *really are* bound up with the daffodil's trumpet shape. The phenomenal spatial and temporal relations that structure our experiences of the world also provide the spatial and temporal structure *of the physical world itself*. The reality of the world is not disconnected from the appearance. It is comprised of threads of such experience.

1.1 The Physical Structure of Reality

Thus far, I've discussed the way the world is at a macroscopic level. We are well on our way to seeing how idealism vindicates common-sense. But I claimed

---

[8] Two complications: (1) This does not mean that all possible experiences are part of the daffodil. It seems plausible that far more experiences than just yellow, purple, and ultraviolet are part of the daffodil. But these need not go on endlessly. There may simply be some possible experiences (e.g. vertigo or the alien phenomenal property ugabav) that are simply *not* part of the daffodil. One having vertigo experience when in the presence of a daffodil would simply not be having a *veridical* experience, given the plausible assumption that no such phenomenology is part of the daffodil of the tapestry.

(2) It's important that we are not defining *possible veridical experiences* by reference to those experiences present within the tapestry. This would be circular. Rather, when I describe the tapestry as "comprised out of **actual experiences qualitatively identical to** all possible veridical perceptual experiences," I am presuming an *independent* intuitive grasp on what sorts of possible experiences are veridical. The idea is to show that there are idealist worlds that are precisely the way we take our world to be. As such, I am taking our sense of how the world seems to be as a guide. Your milage may vary on what you take the world to be like qualitatively. But plug in whatever you take the world to be like, and the idealist can capture it.

that idealism could do this while embracing the structural truths that are revealed by empirical investigation. How can the idealist make good on this claim?

While a detailed account is outside of the scope of this chapter,[9] the basic idea is straightforward. The world contains not only yellow daffodils, but molecules, atoms, electrons, protons, and quarks. Just as the daffodil is a structure of indexed phenomenology, so too (assuming entity realism) are the molecules, atoms, and so on that comprise it.[10]

By shooting beams of electrons at materials from different angles, physicists are able to construct images of atoms and molecular bonds. While we may not be able to do this without the aid of imaging technology, this is immaterial. The idealist should take there to be such experiences bound up as part of the phenomenal tapestry. God, presumably, would have phenomenology of molecules, atoms . . . and quarks within his purview. Likewise, the nontheistic idealist should take such experiences to be part of the tapestry.

But this alone does not give us the physical structure of our world. The physical world doesn't merely *have* daffodils, molecules, atoms, and so on. We take the daffodil to be *made up out of* molecules; these to be *made out of* atoms, these out of electrons, protons, and neutrons; and so on. Now, for the idealist, the *yellow* of the daffodil is not made out of molecules (even if molecules are bits of phenomenology).[11] But if we pull out our electron microscopes, we will find that when we zoom in on the daffodil, there's nothing but cells. When we zoom in on these, there are molecules, when we zoom in on these: atoms. In this sense, we can say that daffodils are made out of atoms. Furthermore, the idealist can accept that macroscopic entities have the appropriate counterfactual dependency relations on microscopic entities. There is a daffodil *because* there are the right sorts of molecules, arranged in the right sorts of ways. These exist *because* there are the right sorts of atoms, arranged in the right sorts of ways. And so on. Were there not atoms, there would not be molecules. Were there not molecules, there would not be cells.

---

[9] Such an account is developed in ch. 5 of *The View From Everywhere* (forthcoming).

[10] It is also open to the idealist to reject entity realism. At the most extreme end of this, we could take the entities posited by science (but not directly observed by us) to be mere theoretical posits that are useful for predicting and systematizing observable phenomena, and nothing more. But I'll set this aside, as entity antirealism obviously compatible with idealism, since it doesn't require accounting for any entities beyond those that are directly observed.

[11] Those with constitutive panpsychist leanings may take this to be a viable option, but I find it deeply obscure how yellow phenomenology could be constructed out of non-color phenomenology (which it presumably must be if the same small set of microphysical particles compose the totality of the physical world).

Were there not cells, there would not be a yellow daffodil. Appropriate changes at the micro-level bring about corresponding changes at the macro-level.

Why do these dependency relations exist? Much as dualists take the brain to give rise to conscious experience, the idealist (who wishes to accommodate these counterfactual dependencies) should take the micro-level to give rise to the macro-level. In both cases, "giving rise to" is accounted for by phenomenal laws of generation. Just as for the dualist, the micro-level does not metaphysically necessitate the macro. The necessitation is merely nomological. This might seem inelegant, but it should also strike us as natural and empirically unavoidable. Science simply doesn't reveal properties like *greenness* and *warmth*. So of course we should *expect* these to be metaphysically separable from what's revealed by science.

1.2 Naïve Idealism

We now have an idealistic account of the physical world we inhabit. This gives us a world that is as it appears: a world of color, solidity, and warmth. But there's more to our intuitive worldview than this. If we are to have a good basis for thinking that the world is as it appears, we must perceive the world directly—not as it is reflected by carnival mirrors that may distort its character in unknowable ways. Intuitively, we don't stand at a distance from reality, but grasp it directly. To determine whether this sort of direct contact with physical reality is intelligible, we must have more than an account of physical reality: We must have an account of us and our relation to the physical world.

A full discussion of the mind-body problem within the context of idealism is far too large for this chapter. So let me make a stipulation of what I think is the most natural way for idealists to understand the mind-body problem, so that we can turn to the nature of perception.

Idealism itself is a position about the nature of *physical reality*; not a position on the relationship between minds and aspects of physical reality. I argue in Yetter-Chappell (forthcoming) that analogues of all the familiar positions on the mind-body problem can exist within an idealistic framework. But I argue that it is most natural for idealists to embrace a non-reductive account of conscious subjects like us, akin to dualism. On this account, our phenomenal experiences do not reduce to our brains. Our experiences are causally related to the tapestry by way of psycho-physical bridging laws akin to those posited by dualists. But instead of linking immaterial phenomenology to the workings of a material world, they link the workings of the immaterial phenomenal tapestry to further phenomenology. Thus far, there is nothing novel here. The only departure from traditional dualism is the dispute over the nature of brains (and the rest of the physical world). Where the difference comes is in the structure of the bridging laws.

Traditional property dualism presumes that bridging laws are "local": that the intrinsic features of our brain states alone determine our phenomenal experiences. Whether I'm feeling pain, hallucinating a daffodil, or having a veridical perception of a daffodil, my brain is the sole physical entity of relevance to the existence of the phenomenology I'm now experiencing. These local bridging laws function to *generate* phenomenology which, in some sense, reflects the world. Idealists could likewise embrace local bridging laws, by simply tweaking the account of the nature of brains to understand them as fundamentally phenomenal. Once again, the laws are essentially *generative*. Given that the brain is doing thus-and-so, *generate* daffodil phenomenology. But it's also open to idealists to embrace a different, "externalist" account of the bridging laws. Externalist bridging laws concern not only the intrinsic features of the agent's brain, but their circumstances more broadly. I'll argue that externalist bridging laws bring important epistemic benefits. They can put us in a very literal and direct epistemic contact with reality by ensuring that—in perception—the external world literally overlaps with and is a part of our minds.

For local bridging laws, the physical relatum is the physical state of the agent's brain (i.e. the brain-bits of the tapestry). It makes no difference whether there's a daffodil causally related to the agent or not. So long as the same thing is happening in the agent's brain, the bridging laws will function in the same way: to generate daffodil-y phenomenology. (See Figure 4.1.)

By contrast, on the externalist account of bridging laws, the physical relatum includes not just the physical state of the agent's brain, but the agent's physical environment more broadly. As for the local bridging laws, if no daffodil is appropriately causally connected to the agent (as in hallucination), externalist laws are generative: generating new phenomenology that is phenomenally unified with the agent's mind, but not with the tapestry. But when there is a daffodil standing an appropriate causal relation to the agent (as in perception), the laws function differently. Rather than generating new phenomenology, the laws *unify existing bits of the tapestry with the agent's mind*. We might think of this as "expanding" the agent's mind, so that it

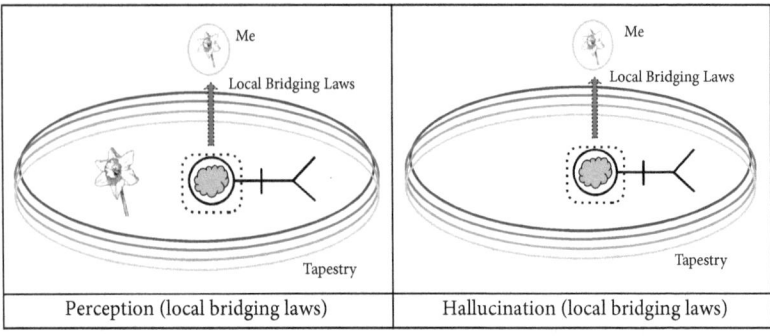

Figure 4.1 Perception and hallucination with local bridging laws.

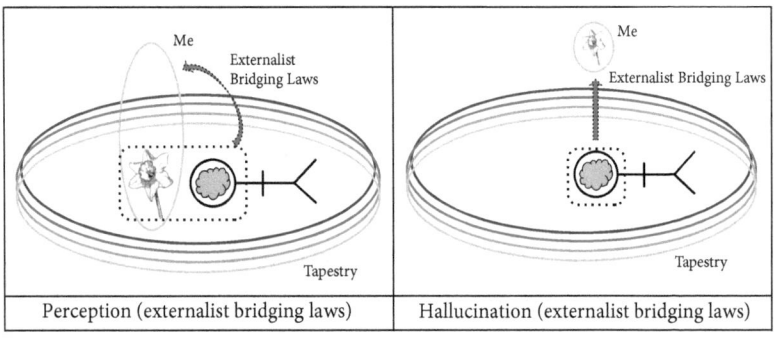

Figure 4.2 Perception and hallucination with externalist bridging laws.

overlaps with facets of the existing tapestry.[12] The result is that some of the bits of phenomenology that make up the daffodil's body are simultaneously parts of two phenomenal unities: the tapestry of physical reality and the perceiver's mind. In these contexts, the bridging laws might be described as "laws of phenomenal unification." (See Figure 4.2.)

So externalist bridging laws play very different roles in cases of hallucination and perception. Although the daffodil phenomenology I'm acquainted with in both cases is *qualitatively* identical, it's numerically distinct. In cases of hallucination, the bridging laws are generative: generating new phenomenology that is not part of the tapestry of reality. In cases of perception,

---

[12] For this to be possible, the phenomenal unity relation cannot be transitive. This is controversial. Roelofs (2016) argues that the relation is not transitive. Dainton (2000) and Bayne (2013) argue that it is transitive. In (forthcoming), I find the pro-transitivity arguments wanting.

the bridging laws are unificatory: phenomenally unifying the perceived facets of reality with my mind.[13]

Whether I'm perceiving or hallucinating, I'm directly acquainted with my phenomenal experiences (since these are parts of my mind). But perception is special. In perception, the phenomenal experiences that partially constitute my mind aren't merely aspects of me, but *are themselves aspects of the physical world*. When I perceive the yellowness of the daffodil, the yellowness is part of my mind. But that very yellowish sensation is also a literal part of the daffodil. My mind, quite literally, touches reality. We might dub this view "naïve idealism."

2. Living in Eden

David Chalmers (2006, 49–50) evocatively describes our pretheoretic view of the world and our relation to it as a perceptual garden of Eden:

> In the Garden of Eden, we had unmediated contact with the world. We were directly acquainted with objects in the world and with their properties. Objects were simply presented to us without causal mediation, and properties were revealed to us in their true intrinsic glory.
>
> When an apple in Eden looked red to us, the apple was gloriously, perfectly, and primitively *red*. There was no need for a long causal chain from the microphysics of the surface through air and brain to a contingently connected visual experience. Rather, the perfect redness of the apple was simply revealed to us. The qualitative redness in our experience derived entirely from the presentation of perfect redness in the world.
>
> Eden was a world of perfect color. But then there was a Fall.

We ate from the Tree of Science.[14] We came to realize that color perception can be explained in terms of the microphysical structure of objects, the way these microphysical structures reflect light, and the effect this light has on our brain. The world doesn't *need* to be colored to explain why we perceive it as such. Further, scientific investigation failed to reveal primitive colors of

---

[13] I don't overlap with the daffodil in its entirety, since I don't perceive all properties of the daffodil. While the color-invert's perspective and the bee's are present within the tapestry and make up part of the daffodil, *I* am not acquainted with these features of the daffodil.

[14] And the Tree of Illusion. There is not space to discuss illusions in this chapter. But see Yetter-Chappell (forthcoming) for an account of this.

the sort we take objects to have. So we abandon Eden. We abandon primitive color and a world that is as our world seems.

> We no longer live in Eden. Perhaps Eden never existed, and perhaps it could not have existed.
>
> (Chalmers 2006, 50)

And yet... And yet, the science by itself doesn't require us to abandon Eden. And yet, if our world is an idealist world, we *do* live in Eden. The idealist world I've described is a world of glorious, perfect, primitive *reds, yellows, warmth, solidity,* and *softness.* The world does not eschew these appearances, but is constructed out of them. Further, the idealist world I've described is a world in which we have unmediated contact with the world. When I perceive the apple as red, I *literally overlap with* the redness of the apple. The redness of the apple is a part of the physical world (phenomenally unified with the tapestry of reality). But the perceived facets of it are also a part of *me* (phenomenally unified with the rest of my mind). As a result, I have precisely the same sort of direct access to the redness of the apple as I do to my own thoughts and bodily sensations. The qualitative redness in my experience of the apple is derived entirely from the apple's perfect redness in the world, for the redness of the apple in the world *is numerically one and the same as* the redness that I experience.

There are some respects in which Chalmers's characterization of Eden does not match the idealist world I've characterized. First, for the nontheistic idealist, there *is* a long causal chain from the microphysics of the surface of the apple, through air, to my brain. (This is what separates perception from hallucination, such that the bridging laws function as laws of unification.) It's just that the end result of this causal story is that I gain knowledge of the primitive redness of the apple, by coming to literally overlap with the apple's redness. If representationalism involves a long causal chain, at the end of which is a *reflection of an apple,* naïve idealism involves a long causal chain, at the end of which is an open door, and *the apple.* The causal chain explains how we come to perceive objects. It doesn't explain what perception consists in.

Second, the experience that I have at the end of this causal chain is one that I have only contingently, for the bridging laws that put me in contact with reality—opening the door on the apple—are contingent. Had the bridging laws been different, I might have been put in contact with the greenness of the apple (which my inverted twin perceives). Had they been absent, I might not have overlapped with reality at all. Nothing would have been presented to me. But *given that the bridging laws are as they are*, it turns out that I am in direct contact with the apple's primitive, perfect redness.[15]

So we have seen how idealism gives us a world that is as it appears, whose character can be grasped directly. And we've seen that idealists can do this without giving up science. But one might wonder whether we have to engage in such a radical revision of our metaphysics to have direct acquaintance with reality or a world that is as it seems. Idealism offers the promise of making good on Eden. But this is only a reason to embrace idealism if it is *uniquely* able to offer this. If we can coherently embrace direct contact with a world that is as it seems *without* embracing idealism, there is no distinctive benefit to idealism, though there may be distinctive costs.[16] In short, wouldn't it be a whole lot easier to just be naïve realists?

Easier, perhaps. The only problem is that it's unintelligible.

2.1 Against Perceptual Naïve Realism

Perceptual naïve realism is the conjunction of (i) a naïve account of perception, and (ii) a materialistic account of the world-perceived. Perception fundamentally consists in our standing in a certain sort of disclosing relationship (an acquaintance relation) to mind-independent objects of perception. Our perceptions—or at least the phenomenal characters of our perceptions[17]—are constituted by the mind-independent objects that we perceive. As Michael Martin puts it,

> the actual objects of perception, the external [mind-independent] things such as trees, tables and rainbows, which one can perceive, and the properties which they can manifest to one when perceived, *partly constitute one's conscious experience*, and hence determine the phenomenal character of one's experience.
>
> (Martin 1997, 83–84, emphasis added)

---

[15] Thus, idealism does not give us a response to skepticism. At least, it doesn't give us a response that goes beyond what a Moorean representationalist could offer.

[16] Potential costs are discussed in ch. 5 of Yetter-Chappell (forthcoming), the most pressing of which is the challenge of profligacy.

[17] Different naïve realists describe this idea slightly differently. Martin (1997) writes that these objects partially constitute *the experience*. Campbell (2002) writes that they constitute the *phenomenal character* of the experience. Nudds (2009) writes that they constitute experiential *episodes*.

Naïve idealists agree with (i). They disagree with (ii). I'll argue that it's only by rejecting (ii) that we can have an intelligible account of (i): In particular, it's only by rejecting materialism that acquaintance with physical objects becomes intelligible. I argue for this conclusion in detail elsewhere (Yetter-Chappell 2024, forthcoming). What follows in this section is a brief account of these arguments.

Naïve theories of perception are predicated on the possibility of our standing in a relation of direct acquaintance with the physical objects that we perceive. The acquaintance relation is not just any old relation. It's a relation that affords us special epistemic contact with objects, by putting us in direct contact with the truth-makers of our perceptual judgments.

For the naïve view of perception to be intelligible, it must be intelligible how we can stand in a relation of acquaintance to physical objects. Is it?

For the idealist, acquaintance with physical objects poses no more challenge than acquaintance with our own thoughts or bodily sensations. I stand in precisely the same relation to the yellow of the daffodil as I do to the itchiness of my nose: both are intrinsically phenomenal, and both are aspects of my mind (phenomenally unified with my other conscious mental states). While the yellow of the daffodil is *also* a part of the phenomenal tapestry, this does not affect the relationship that *I* stand in to it.

Thus, familiar accounts of acquaintance with our own minds can be co-opted by naïve idealists to offer accounts of acquaintance with the physical world. Acquaintance with the world is just more of the same: just more acquaintance with phenomenal aspects of my mind. The interesting action for the naïve idealist comes from the externalist bridging laws that unify bits of the phenomenal tapestry with my mind.[18]

What account of acquaintance can the naïve realist offer? Curiously, despite the centrality of the acquaintance relation to naïve realism, naïve realists have, by and large, been silent on the nature of this relation. This strikes me as especially odd given that there is a strong prima facie case for thinking that we cannot be directly acquainted with material objects. Recall the Martin quote above: "external things such as trees, tables and rainbows ... partly constitute one's conscious experience" (1997, 83–84). The idea is evocative. And for the naïve idealist, it's easy to see how it could be literally true. But how could an experience literally contain a *mind-independent* object as a constituent? Experiences are paradigmatically mental. Minds can

---

[18] For further details fleshing out the naïve idealist's account of acquaintance, see Yetter-Chappell (2024, forthcoming).

contain sensations, thoughts, desires. But a mind cannot have free-floating numbers or beauty as constituents. Likewise, a mind cannot have a (non-mental) material flower as a constituent. Only the right sorts of things can be bound together by phenomenal unity relations. Only the right kinds of things can be components of minds. And a material flower cannot form a constituent of my mind any more than a material flower can be a constituent of a computer simulation.

It's hard to see how a naïve realist could hold a non-materialistic account of subjects. If subjects are not material, it's difficult to see how material objects could form parts of their experiences. While a naïve realist could embrace externalist bridging laws, analogous to those of the naïve idealist, these bridging laws would essentially have to function as laws of *generation*. And this puts us in contact with generated phenomenology—not (directly) with the physical objects we perceive.

I take it that naïve realists have a very different conception of experience from the one that implicitly underwrites the prima facie challenge. Experiences are not qualia. (Flowers are not constituents of qualia.) Experiences are not brain states. (Flowers are not constituents of brain states.) As Keith Allen puts it, perceptual experiences "*consist in* the obtaining of a conscious relation of awareness or acquaintance between perceiving subjects and mind-independent objects and properties in their environment" (Allen 2021, 43, emphasis added). If this is our analysis of experience, flowers can be constituents of experiences, insofar as they are constituents of a subject-acquaintance-flower completion.[19]

We can characterize experience in this way. But it does not dispel the sense of mystery or the need to say more about what the acquaintance relation is such that subjects can be so-acquainted with material objects. The acquaintance relation is not just any old relation. It's one that has a special epistemic significance. It's one that renders us directly *aware* of the object, *disclosing* the object of our awareness to us. How can it do this? Why is it that I can be related to objects in this way, whereas my car (with its pedestrian-detecting back-up camera) can't? What is it that distinguishes me from my perfect blind-sight twin, such that I am acquainted with the daffodil while she is not? As Mark Johnston (2011) might put it, the blind-sighter lacks the attentive *sensory* episodes that I have. But how is it that the material daffodil comes to be a constituent of an attentive sensory episode?

---

[19] Where, following Kit Fine's (2000, 4) terminology, "[t]he completion of a relation R by the objects a1, a2,... is the state of the objects a...standing in the relation R."

Allen's conception of perceptual experience does not address this. The fundamental challenge remains.[20]

Alva Noë has (to my knowledge) offered the most detailed explication of a naïve-realist-friendly notion of acquaintance. As Noë (2001, 51) puts it, "[p]erceptual awareness…is a state of interactive engagement with the world, not a state of picture-making." He suggests we think of perceptual awareness as

> a form of active engagement with the environment. In the case [of our tactile experience of a] bottle, it is not our possession of an internal model of the bottle that is the basis of our contact. Rather, it is the fact that we are so related to the bottle that we are, as it were, ready and able to acquire information as need arises. And so in the visual case: the ready availability of environmental detail, and…the skill-based confidence on the part of the perceiver that he or she is able to acquire that detail through movement, is the basis of our feeling of the presence of the environment as a whole.
>
> (Noë 2001, 50–51)

This suggests that the acquaintance relation is one of being "ready and able to acquire information as need arises." That may be all that need be said to explain the richness of our conception of the world (where we seem to be confronted by a world with bottles, as opposed to a world of momentary snapshots of bottles[21]), but it does not answer the central question that I've argued the naïve realist must address. It does not tell us how we can *acquire information*—the sort of direct information that puts us in immediate contact with reality—*in the first place*. Insofar as we have such a direct grasp of reality, we can rest secure in our knowledge that the world will continue to present itself to us. As Noë notes, I needn't grasp the bottle in its entirety at any given moment, as I can continue to scan my eyes over new parts of the

---

[20] One might respond: "Who knows? But it's manifest that it does. This is something that we can simply take for granted." As Allen (2020, 56) proposes, the naïve realist theory might be taken to be "the transcendental project of explaining *how it is possible* that perceptual experience has the distinctive characteristics that it does" and, as such, might be "immune to falsification." But while there's a case to be made for granting the truth of the phenomenological datum that our experiences reach out to objects and put us in contact with the world, naïve *realism* includes more than this. It includes that the world we're put in contact with is material. I have no idea why this would be taken to be a starting point immune from question, particularly when the world-disclosing nature of experience is *intelligible* assuming idealism, but mysterious given materialism.

[21] This is the central question that Noë himself is concerned to address.

bottle as time goes on. But all of this is predicated on the background assumption that I am in direct contact with the bottle at all!

Another proposal would be for the naïve realist to embrace a version of the Extended Conscious Mind Hypothesis (Clark 2009), according to which (i) experiences are material, and (ii) they extend into the world such that they include the distal objects of experience. Unlike a local materialist, who holds that the experience of the daffodil is grounded in a brain state (perhaps of daffodil-fibers-firing (DFF)), an externalist might hold that the daffodil experience is grounded in DFF + material daffodil. The relation between my experience and the daffodil is, thus, one of constitution.

But while this proposal allows us to *say* that the daffodil and its properties are constituents of my experience, it doesn't account for the distinctive epistemic benefits that naïve realism is supposed to yield. Compare this view to an indirect view on which the experience of the daffodil is grounded in DFF (where these are merely caused by the daffodil). Why does the former, but not the latter, *disclose* the daffodil to the subject? It seems we've done no more than engage in some word-play, carving off "experience" in a different way. On one view, DFF is the experience, and is caused by daffodils. On the other, DFF + causally-related-daffodil is the experience. But it's hard to see why individuating experiences in one way or the other should come with the epistemic differences naïve realists take there to be between naïve views and indirect ones. We still are left with no explanation of the central mystery: If subjects are not material, how can a material world be directly related to them? If subjects are material, how can we relate a material world to them in a way that goes beyond the material relations that fail to be world-disclosing for the representationalist?

One might object that I am asking for too much. Naïve realists often describe acquaintance as a *primitive relation* (e.g. Crane and French 2021). The naïve realist might hold that, as such, it is a relationship about which nothing substantial can be said. Fumerton (1995, 76–77) writes of acquaintance that

> Because the relations of acquaintance and correspondence…are sui generis, there is precious little one can say by way of trying to explain the concept to one who claims not to understand it. Because acquaintance is not like any other relation, there is no useful genus under which to subsume it.

Some relations can be helpfully elucidated (e.g. being a sibling), while others are simply bedrock. This is certainly true. We can point out the identity relation. But nothing illuminating can be said to explain it to one who doesn't understand. If the naïve realist maintains that we've hit bedrock, is it reasonable to demand further elucidation to render the relation intelligible?

But even if we grant that the acquaintance relation is like the identity relation in this respect, we have not dissolved the mystery. For the puzzle is not simply what acquaintance is, but what it is *such that we can be directly acquainted with material objects.*

By way of analogy, suppose a theorist tells us that electrons are identical to the number four:

You: That makes no sense. How could that possibly be?

Interlocutor: Ah, well, identity is sui generis. There's precious little that can be said to explain it to you if you claim not to understand it.

You: But I'm not denying that I understand! I understand it well enough. That's precisely *why* it seems incoherent that electrons could possibly be identical to a number.

Similarly, the naïve realist doesn't just tell us that there's a relation of acquaintance, but that *we (conscious subjects) are so related to a mind-independent world.* And, like the claim that electrons are identical to the number four, there is (at least a prima facie) reason to find this unintelligible. (How could a material apple be a part of an experience?[22]) The naïve realist must say more, if not about the acquaintance relation itself, then about how it is that we can be so-acquainted with a material world.

Where does this leave us? The naïve idealist doesn't merely assert that we are in direct contact with the physical world: She has an intelligible account of how this is possible, of how it is that we can literally grasp the phenomenal character of the world around us. The world, for the idealist, is precisely the right sort of thing to be part of our minds. And, in perception, it is. The naïve realist, by contrast, asserts that we are in direct contact with the world. They assert that there is a relation that acquaints us with a mind-independent reality. But what this relation is and *how* it accomplishes this is a mystery. This is not to say that one cannot be a naïve realist. One might simply embrace the mystery. But it is a *cost* to embrace a view that is

---

[22] Or, likewise, how could a material apple be a part of *the phenomenal character* of an experience?

premised on a mystery. And it is a cost that we should think twice about incurring if there are alternative options that do not have this cost.

2.2 Against Property Naïve Realism

We take ourselves to know a lot about the world we live in: The river is a dark, cloudy green. The rain falling from the sky is cold. The tree's leaves are yellow, its bark is rough. The common-sense view is that these are things we know about *the world*: that the world we live in is not disconnected—alienated—from the world of acquaintance.

As Berkeley writes in the Third Dialogue (1996),

> I cannot for my life help thinking that snow is white, and fire hot. You indeed, who by SNOW and fire mean certain external, unperceived, unperceiving substances, are in the right to deny whiteness or heat to be affections inherent in THEM. But I, who understand by those words the things I see and feel, am obliged to think like other folks.

If ours is a world of experience, there is no problem with the color and heat that we perceive existing *in the world*. By contrast, it's difficult to see how the materialist's world could be anything like the world we take ourselves to inhabit. Third-personal investigation doesn't reveal properties like color and warmth. Instead of color, it gives us surface reflectance properties and wavelengths. Instead of heat, it gives us molecular kinetic energy. While some materialists take there to be material properties that are simply unknowable to us, this does not help. The properties of interest (e.g. color and heat) are precisely the properties that *are* known to us. The problem is not that the properties we naïvely take to populate the world are *unknowable*, but that they're only knowable through *first-personal* means. And that is arguably at odds with their being material.

Still, some philosophers take materialism to be compatible with the existence of the sorts of properties that we naïvely take to populate our world. Call this Property Naïve Realism (PNR). While I'll focus on color properties, as this is what has received the most attention in the literature, I see no reason why the arguments shouldn't extend to other appearance properties.

According to color PNR, colors are mind-independent primitive properties possessed by physical objects. These primitive color properties supervene on microphysical properties, but are not themselves revealed by scientific investigation. Naïve realism about color is often paired with perceptual naïve realism (Allen 2016, Campbell 1993)—the resulting view being one on which perception directly acquaints us with these primitive color properties.

I've argued that idealism gives us a world that is as it appears. If idealism is not necessary to deliver on this promise, this would undercut the motivation for embracing idealism. This is just what PNR threatens. But PNR faces significant challenges. Here, we'll just consider one challenge: the question of *which* color properties PNR attributes to objects.[23]

The very same daffodil may appear yellow7 to me, yellow12 to you, and purple to my inverted twin. Which primitive color property(s) does the flower have? The naïve realist about color has two options. They can privilege one of these appearances as the true one, or they can try to embrace the idea that objects can have many color properties at once. The first option seems arbitrary. For the same reason that we should not privilege human experiences or HYC experiences in constructing an idealist reality, there's no basis for including any one perceiver's color experiences in our ontology, to the exclusion of all others. The second option—color pluralism—is intriguing, but faces serious difficulties. Color pluralism entails that the flower is simultaneously yellow all over and purple all over. This is not a problem per se. (Nontheistic idealism holds the same.) The challenge lies in whether a *materialist* can successfully account for this.

For an idealist, there was no problem in holding that multiple conflicting color properties can be simultaneously instantiated, as these can be intelligibly indexed to different *perspectives*. But perspectives essentially require minds. Mind-independent properties can't be essentially tied to perspectives. To say that these properties are inherently perspectival is tantamount to admitting that they're not mind-independent.[24]

This is not to say that materialist color PNR is incoherent. PNR could reject color pluralism, while denying that *real* primitive colors are anything like the colors that agents perceive. This would avoid the challenges of arbitrariness and of inherent perspectivality. But it entails that the world is not (with respect to color) anything like we think it is, undermining the

---

[23] See Yetter-Chappell (forthcoming), ch. 6 for further challenges.

[24] Admittedly, this is too quick. Mark Johnston (2007) embraces perspectivality as a fundamental, objective feature of reality, but denies that this requires *minds*. Due to space constraints, I cannot do justice to his view here. But see Yetter-Chappell (forthcoming) for discussion of the relation between Johnston's view and naïve idealism. There I argue that while the challenges faced by standard naïve realists do not apply to Johnston, this is because Johnston's view has a fundamental commonality with naïve idealism, in taking reality itself to be irreducibly qualitative as well as irreducibly perspectival.

motivation for color PNR. By contrast, naïve idealism has no difficulty coherently embrace color pluralism and a world that is (in part) precisely as it seems to us. Idealism is uniquely able to give us a world that is as it seems.

3. Theoretical Virtues or Wishful Thinking?

Thus far, I've outlined an idealistic account of reality. It's an account on which reality is not dependent on our minds or on the minds of any other organisms. It's an account on which there is an external world that is real and independent of our perceptions and thoughts. And it's an account that renders the naïve view of perception *intelligible* in a way that (I've argued) materialism cannot.

What I haven't done is to offer an argument that idealism is true. Perhaps, if you're a philosopher of perception and you put high credence in the naïve view, you'll take the arguments offered thus far as reason to take idealism seriously. But what about the rest of us? What should we make of idealism? Is it just a curious account of a way some world could be, and nothing more? Or is there reason to take seriously the proposition that *our world* may be an idealist world?

Mind-body physicalism is often taken to be a contingent thesis. Physicalism is taken to be true *at a possible world* iff … every property instantiated at that world is (or supervenes on or is grounded in …) a physical property. Physicalists do not generally argue that no possible world could contain nonphysical elements. Rather, they argue that there is no good reason to think that *our world* contains such elements: We can account entirely for the way we take our world to be—including tricky things like conscious experiences—without anything nonphysical.

I think the idealist should take a page from the physicalist's book. Idealism, as I mean to defend it, is a contingent thesis. Idealism is true *at a possible world* iff that world is fundamentally experiential. It should be unsurprising that there are possible worlds where idealism is true: Imagine a world with ghosts, then get rid of everything but the ghosts. More surprising is the idea that there could be *idealistic worlds that appear to their inhabitants precisely as our world appears to us*. That is what the first section of this chapter demonstrated.

I began by sketching a novel idealistic account of reality—an account of reality, on which it is a phenomenal tapestry. The world is not free-floating phenomenology, but is structured via phenomenal unity relations of the same sort that structure our own experiences. This is like a *recipe for constructing an idealist world*. Put together the right experiences, structured in the right ways, and you can get a world containing a hunk of quartz (and nothing else). You can get a world that contains all the macro- objects and properties that our world has, but with none of the micro-structure. You can get a world that has micro-structure like our world, but lacks the familiar macro-properties. You can get a world that contains only properties that are observable by humans.... Or you can include all and only the phenomenology for constructing a world of the sort that we take our world to be.

The second task for the defender of idealism as a contingent truth is to argue that there is good reason to think that *our world* is such a world. The reason should not be that only idealist worlds can appear to their inhabitants as our world appears to us. It seems preposterous to deny that there are materialistic worlds that are structurally akin to ours, where complex causal chains relate the inhabitants to their world, giving rise to experiences just like our experiences.[25] (But see Builes, this volume for ingenious arguments to the contrary.) If there are both materialistic and idealistic worlds that appear to their inhabitants precisely as our world appears to us, the question is: What reason do we have for taking our world to be among the idealist ones, versus the materialist ones? What should our credence be that—from among the vastness of modal space—our world is among the idealistic ones rather than the materialistic ones?

A thorough comparison of idealistic and materialistic worlds is far too large a task for a single chapter.[26] But we can gesture at respects in which idealism seems at an advantage. I've argued that the idealist's world is one on which (a) the world we inhabit genuinely is as it appears—trees are *green*, fire is *warm*—and (b) we are in direct and literal contact with reality. We are not cut off from reality, but are directly acquainted with the truthmakers for our judgments about the world. If (and only if) our world is among the idealist worlds, our intuitions about perception and the transparency of reality are vindicated. Idealism offers a uniquely optimistic view of reality and our place within it. This is the appeal of idealism.

But while optimism may make us feel all warm and fuzzy inside, does it really offer a reason to embrace idealism? Does capturing these intuitions really justify us in putting more credence in our world being among the

---

[25] I think such experiences require fundamental phenomenology. But that's not to say the phenomenology must be part of the physical objects.

[26] But see Yetter-Chappell (forthcoming).

idealist worlds? Or is the idealist's worldview simply better at capturing wishful thinking? While an intelligible world that is manifest to us *sounds nice*, so does cosmic justice. And we don't take this to be a reason for thinking that there *is* cosmic justice. Why should we give more credence to (e.g.) our world being as it appears than to its being an alienating materialistic world?

In fact, while the claims of idealism may sound nice, they may also strike one as *less likely* to capture the way our world truly is. It may seem downright *counterintuitive* to think that reality is as it appears. It may seem that we really know nothing of the thing in itself. Likewise, readers who embrace representationalism might find the idea that we *directly* grasp the world around us completely baffling. We all know that vision comes about by light bouncing off of objects in our surroundings, and carrying information about those objects to our retinas and brains. In light of this, the suggestion that we can literally grasp or overlap with reality might seem to get our world *wrong*.

There is a sense in which I find these points quite compelling. When presuming materialism, I don't presume that the world-in-itself is anything like my experience of it. (And I don't take this to be problematic or counterintuitive.) When presuming materialism, I don't take perception to involve direct acquaintance with reality. (And I don't take this to be problematic or counterintuitive.) So why is it that when confronted with idealism, we should take these features to tell in idealism's favor?

Consider an analogy. My son has a puzzle with pieces made out of hexagons conjoined in different configurations. There are countless ways the puzzle can be put together. But each piece you put down constrains the remaining pieces. Trying to make sense of the world around us, and our place in it, is a vast task, with many separate pieces and considerations. Like the hexagon puzzle, there are many different ways the physical world and conscious minds could be and fit together. And like the hexagon puzzle, each explicit position you take and each implicit background assumption you leave in place, functions to constrain where the other pieces of the Cosmic Puzzle can go.

Once we put down the puzzle piece of materialism, that constrains where the other pieces go. Once we lay down materialism, it follows that the world is not as it appears. Given that we have laid down the materialism piece, this doesn't seem bizarre: it strikes us as how the world *must be*. But it would be a mistake to conclude from this that the world's being as it appears is something that we should reject as implausible *independently of materialism*. It would be a mistake to conclude that there is nothing intuitively more plausible about the world being how it appears *if there is another way of putting together the Cosmic Puzzle that renders this intelligible.*

Thus, rather than considering the upshots of idealism against our background presuppositions, we should look at the complete worldview on offer (the completed Cosmic Puzzle) and compare this to the completed Cosmic Puzzle on offer by materialists. These are package-views, with pieces that cannot necessarily be mixed and matched, and we should compare them as such. Further, we should begin by suspending judgment about where individual pieces go, as these judgments may be implicitly based on presumptions that make sense within our original worldview but which should not necessarily be universally presumed. My claim is that when we do this—when we hold up the completed puzzles on offer from the idealist and the materialist, and assess from a truly neutral starting point—we find significant advantages to the idealist's worldview. We find things that, from a neutral starting point, we would take to be theoretical advantages.

Suppose (setting aside preconceptions about what the world is like) that there are two coherent accounts of reality: according to one, reality is just as it seems; according to the other, reality is nothing like it seems. Which seems more plausible? Obviously, that the world is as it seems. Why would one take the world to be other than it seems, unless required to do so by the placement of some other piece of the Cosmic Puzzle? *A win for idealism.*

What of direct perceptual contact with the world? Imagine first coming to philosophy from a naïve starting point and finding that there are two coherent theories of perception that you could embrace. On the first view, perception is like an open window on the world. The world is there and we can simply reach out and grasp it. On the second view, perception is more like a mirror, reflecting a world beyond our reach. Which theory would seem more plausible; more likely to be true? The consensus view is that pretheoretical intuition favors the former (e.g. Broad 1952, Hellie 2007, Logue 2012, Levine 2018, Allen 2019). If this consensus view is right, idealism puts us in the unique position to intelligibly capture another feature of how the world pretheoretically appears: the way we intuitively relate to our surroundings. *A win for idealism.*

Unless forced to hold otherwise by other commitments, we should expect the world to be as it appears; we should expect reality to be directly grasped in perception. Giving up on each of these is a cost. It's a cost we might have felt that there was no possibility of avoiding. You might have thought you simply had to resign yourself to death, taxes, and the veil of perception. But idealism, it turns out, can free us from the last.

Idealism shows us that the world *can be* just as it appears, and that the world *can be* comprehended more thoroughly than merely understanding its structure. Once we see that it is possible to grant each of these intuitive claims, the failure to do so becomes apparent as a cost. Looking out at the space of possible worlds from a theoretically neutral starting point, it looks less plausible that our world is among the materialist worlds—ungraspable, unintelligible, nothing like anything that we're aware of—and far more plausible that ours is among the idealist worlds: worlds of color, heat, and flow, worlds that we can grasp and comprehend.

Of course, there may also be drawbacks to idealism when compared neutrally to materialism. A thorough evaluation of the nature of our world would need to weigh these, too. What is clear is this: (1) It is epistemically possible that our world is an idealist world. There are possible worlds that appear (from the inside) just like our own, where idealism is the correct account of the metaphysics. (2) There are genuine virtues that idealist theories have over their materialist competitors. When we set aside our background commitments regarding the positions of individual pieces and compare the idealist's way of fitting together the Cosmic Puzzle with the materialist's, there are important respects in which the idealist has the upper hand. Hence, (3) your credence that our world is an idealist world should not be insignificant—and should probably be much higher than it was prior to reading this chapter.

If the world is an idealist world, we live in a perceptual Eden. We did not fall from Eden. Rather, we deluded ourselves into believing that we couldn't possibly live in Eden when we committed to the materialism piece in the cosmic puzzle. With this in mind, it's time to reset our commitments. It's time to re-evaluate our solution to the cosmic puzzle.

References

Allen, K. (2016). *A Naïve Realist Theory of Colour*. New York, NY: Oxford University Press UK.

Allen, K. (2019). Merleau-Ponty and Naïve Realism. *Philosopher's Imprint*, *19*(2), 1–25.

Allen, K. (2020). The Value of Perception. *Philosophy and Phenomenological Research*, *100*(3), 633–656.

Allen, K. (2021). Bridging the Gap? Naïve Realism and the Problem of Consciousness. In H. Logue and L. Richardson (eds), *Purpose and Procedure in Philosophy of Perception* (43–62). Oxford University Press.

Bayne, T. (2013). *The Unity of Consciousness*. Oxford University Press.

Berkeley, G. (1996). *Principles of Human Knowledge and Three Dialogues* (H. Robinson, ed.). Oxford University Press.

Broad, C. D. (1952). Some Elementary Reflexions on Sense-Perception. *Philosophy*, *27*(January), 3–17.

Builes, D. (this volume). Modal Idealism. In U. Kriegel (ed.), *Oxford Studies in Philosophy of Mind*, volume 4.

Campbell, J. (1993). A Simple View of Colour. In J. J. Haldane and C. Wright (eds), *Reality: Representation and Projection* (257–268). Oxford University Press.

Campbell, J. (2002). *Reference and Consciousness*. Oxford University Press.

Chalmers, D. (2006). Perception and the Fall from Eden. In E. Gendler and Hawthorne (eds), *Perceptual Experience* (49–125). Oxford University Press.

Clark, A. (2009). Spreading the Joy? Why the Machinery of Consciousness is (Probably) Still in the Head. *Mind*, *118*(472), 963–993.

Crane, T., and French, C. (2021). The Problem of Perception. In *Stanford Encyclopedia of Philosophy*.

Dainton, B. (2000). *Stream of Consciousness: Unity and Continuity in Conscious Experience*. Routledge.

Downing, L. (2011). George Berkeley. *Stanford Encyclopedia of Philosophy*.

Fine, K. (2000). Neutral Relations. *Philosophical Review*, *109*(1), 1–33.

Fumerton, R. A. (1995). *Metaepistemology and Skepticism*. Rowman & Littlefield.

Hellie, B. (2007). Factive Phenomenal Characters. *Philosophical Perspectives*, *21*, 259–306.

Johnston, M. (2007). Objective Mind and the Objectivity of Our Minds. *Philosophy and Phenomenological Research*, *75*(2), 233–268.

Johnston, M. (2011). *On a Neglected Epistemic Virtue. Philosophical Issues*, 21 (1), 165–218.

Levine, J. (2018). Conscious Awareness and (Self-)Representation. In *Quality and Content*. Oxford University Press.

Logue, H. (2012). Why Naive Realism? *Proceedings of the Aristotelian Society*, 112 (2pt2), 21–237.

Martin, M. G. F. (1997). The Reality of Appearances. In M. Sainsbury (ed.), *Thought and Ontology* (81–106). Franco Angeli.

Mill, J. S. (1865). *An Examination of Sir William Hamilton's Philosophy, and of the Principal Philosophical Questions Discussed in His Writings*. Longman, Green, Longman, Roberts & Green.

Noë, A. (2001). Experience and the Active Mind. *Synthese*, *129*(1), 41–60.

Nudds, M. (2009). Recent Work in Perception: Naïve Realism and Its Opponents. *Analysis*, *69*(2), 334–346.

Pelczar, M. (2019). Defending Phenomenalism. *Philosophical Quarterly*, *69*(276), 574–597.

Pelczar, M. (2022). *Phenomenalism: A Metaphysics of Chance and Experience*. Oxford: Oxford University Press, Oxford.

Pitcher, G. (1977). *Berkeley*. Routledge.

Roelofs, L. (2016). The Unity of Consciousness, Within Subjects and Between Subjects. *Philosophical Studies*, *173*(12), 3199–3221.

Winkler, K. (1985). Unperceived Objects and Berkeley's Denial of Blind Agency. *Hermathena*, *139*, 81–100.

Yetter-Chappell, H. (2018). Idealism Without God. In *Idealism: New Essays in Metaphysics*. Eds. Tyron Goldschmidt and Kenneth L. Pearce (66–81). Oxford University Press.

Yetter-Chappell, H. (2024). Get Acquainted With Naïve Idealism. In *The Roles of Representations in Visual Perception*. Eds. French and Brogaard. Synthese Library, Springer.

Yetter-Chappell, H. (forthcoming). *The View from Everywhere: Realist Idealism Without God*. Oxford University Press.

Helen Yetter-Chappell, *Idealism and the Best of All (Subjectively Indistinguishable) Possible Worlds*
In: *Oxford Studies in Philosophy of Mind Volume 4*. Edited by: Uriah Kriegel, Oxford University Press.
© Helen Yetter-Chappell 2024. DOI: 10.1093/9780198924159.003.0004

PART II
ACQUAINTANCE AND PERCEPTION

5

The Sense-Data Language and External World Skepticism

Jared Warren

1. The Early Modern Project

Philosophy starts with the data of consciousness and builds outwards. At least, that's what the early modern philosophers did, starting with Descartes. This starting point allows us only what is directly accessible to consciousness. The real problem of external world skepticism is a problem raised from this starting point. Because of this, modern skepticism goes beyond the skepticism of the ancients.[1] This goes for every school of ancient skepticism—the Pyrrhonians, the Academic Skeptics, and the Cārvāka.

The early modern project, inaugurated by Descartes, was to build a complete theory of the world outward from this starting point. In many ways, the story of contemporary philosophy is the story of a flight from Descartes. It is only slightly misleading to say that both analytic and continental philosophy were created by this flight. The founders of these traditions are often credited with reorienting philosophy. Reorienting it, that is, away from the first-person starting point.

Depending on what you're interested in, reorientation might be advisable, but is it *required*? Nearly everyone seems to think so. There is a very— *very*!—widespread feeling that the early modern project is broken, cracked to its core. I disagree. The first-person starting point remains viable. What is more, the project is, in a real sense, forced upon us. What is even more, there is yet hope that we can complete the project without cheating. All of this I will argue for here. To say that I have my work cut out for me is an understatement.

---

[1] See Burnyeat 1982 and Williams 2010.

2. From Ideas to Sense-Data

The central crack in the early modern project is supposed to be in its characterization of the *data* of consciousness. For Descartes, Locke, Berkeley, and others this data was said to consist of "ideas". Hume departed from this in terminology but not in doctrine by using "ideas" only for the less vivid mental particulars and "impressions" for the others.

This "idea" terminology was extended to cover all mental particulars. Not just mental images, not just data from other senses, but even emotional states. This already stretched the terminology too far, but the early moderns stretched it further still. They also tried to understand *beliefs* and *concepts* and *meanings* using ideas.[2] This is a hopeless approach to cognition and we should have no part of it. To free ourselves from it, both terminology and theory need updating.

The early moderns themselves might have gone along with this—we already find Berkeley writing:

> As for our senses, by them we have the knowledge only of our sensations, ideas, or those things that are immediately perceived by sense, call them what you will.[3]

Call them what you will; I will call them *sense-data* (plurally) or *sense-datum* (singularly). This terminology was popularized by Moore and Russell in the early twentieth century.[4] Subsequently the notion of sense-data, if not always the terminology of "sense-data", was widely accepted by British philosophers.[5]

Sense-data are supposed to be what we are directly *aware of* or *conscious of* during perception. The mere existence of hallucinations and illusions shows that conscious, perceptual experiences do not require the existence of external objects.[6] As the terminology suggests, *sense-data* covers less ground than *ideas*. It includes only the data of sensory experience. Sense-data are private objects accessible to consciousness and usually associated

---

[2] For discussion, see section 17 of Bennett 1966.
[3] From Section 18, Part I of *A Treatise Concerning the Principles of Human Knowledge*—see Berkeley 2008: 89.
[4] Perhaps the first published use of the term is in Moore 1909–10, it was popularized by Russell 1912. See also Moore 1913–14 and Russell 1914*a, b*.
[5] For prominent examples from the period, see Broad 1923, Price 1932, and Ayer 1940.
[6] Arguments of this kind are offered in, for example, Broad 1923 and Price 1932.

with a single sense.[7] They are not *inherently* intentional or representational, but are instead phenomenal or qualitative.[8] With sense-data there is no significant gap between appearance and reality. Some proponents also stipulate up-front that sense-data are non-physical, but I think their metaphysical nature should initially be left open.[9]

In some ways, the "sense-data" terminology is also less than ideal. It might suggest *raw data* from the senses, but that isn't right. Sense-data are instead the sensory data *accessible to first-person conscious experience*. For this reason, Ayer later switched to "sense-qualia" instead of "sense-data".[10] The reasoning behind this terminological change is sound, but, unfortunately, the "qualia" terminology has even more baggage. Russell also later adopted a different terminology, in his case moving to "percepts". He also characterized this move as a *rejection* of sense-data, but this is misleading.[11] I agree with Ayer's assessment:

. . . [Russell's] rejection of sense-data turns out only to be a rejection of the subject-object analysis of sensation.[12]

So, despite their respective moves away from "sense-data" terminology, both Ayer and Russell remained sense-data theorists until the end.[13] Despite some minor misgivings, I'm going to stick with the "sense-data" terminology that they (and Moore) popularized.

Sense-data enjoyed a brief heyday from the early to mid-twentieth century. But by mid-century the very idea of sense-data was under heavy fire. The most damaging assaults were launched by the towering ordinary language philosophers, Ryle and Austin.[14] A consensus *against* sense-data started to build, a consensus that the battle against sense-data had been well-fought and fairly won. By the late 1970s Charles Taylor could open a critical article on sense-data by saying:

---

[7] But see the final chapter of Ayer 1968 for a useful discussion of whether privacy should be stipulated, up-front.

[8] As I will discuss in section 6, these lines start to blur at a few points.

[9] Robinson (1994) stipulates that sense-data are non-physical.

[10] See Ayer 1973, for example.   [11] See the discussion in Russell 1959.

[12] Ayer 1969: 174.

[13] Many other sense-data theorists also used different terminology—for example, Broad 1923, Price 1932, and Mackie 1976.

[14] See Ryle 1954 and Austin 1962.

> I want in this paper to return to a subject which has been out of fashion
> now for about two decades, the subject of sense data.[15]

So over forty years ago sense-data had already been "out of fashion" for
twenty years. Today the subject is covered with more than *sixty years* of dust
and cobwebs.

Even under this debris, the sense-data theory is not totally dead, but it
is now extremely unpopular. In the 2020 philpapers.org survey just over
1 percent of surveyed philosophers accepted sense-data, and only 4 percent "leaned toward" accepting sense-data. In this environment, sense-
data cannot simply be assumed the way the early moderns assumed the
existence of ideas. For them, the idea framework was the starting point.
They didn't think it required a significant defense. But after criticisms by
Reid and Kant, ideas could never again be assumed without comment.
Likewise now, for sense-data. Accordingly, contemporary defenders treat
sense-data theories as *substantive* positions.[16] They think we can only
adopt sense-data talk at the *end* of the trail, not at the *start*. With many
intricate arguments and rebuttals and constructions required to get us to
that point.

I think that this is a mistake. The move to sense-data is the move to a
sense-data *language*.[17] It is a way of approaching experience, not a substantive theory about the nature of experience. The sense-data language is
extremely useful. It is useful for talking about experience, for posing philosophical questions, and for offering theories that demystify the apparently
mystical. Only within this sense-data language can substantive sense-data-
based theories of perception be given. Yet the existence of sense-data does
not hinge on the success of such theories. As Descartes and Locke and
Berkeley and Hume all assumed, we can talk about sensory experience on
the cheap, for the sense-data language is their idea language shorn of over-
reach and muddles. To defend these claims, I'll draw from contemporary
metaontology. As a lead-in to that, let me introduce sense-data talk in
more detail.

---

[15]   Taylor 1979: 99.

[16]   In particular, I'm thinking of the major defenses in Jackson 1977 and Robinson 1994.

[17]   Grammatical purists might prefer calling it "the sense-datum language", but to my
twenty-first-century English ears, "the sense-data language" now sounds more natural.

3. A Framework for Sense-Data

I see a red apple on the counter in front of me. Given this, a red apple exists. Red apples aren't in my mind, so it follows that *something*—something outside of my mind—exists. This reasoning won't satisfy the skeptic, because sometimes we *seem* to see things without *actually* seeing them.

We can't always tell the difference, from the inside, between seeing an *F* and seeming to see an *F*.[18] This cannot be reasonably denied.[19] Let's carefully go over how sense-data talk is introduced on this basis.[20] Start with a standard natural language report about visual experience:

(1) I see a red apple on the counter in front of me

This entails that there is a red apple on the counter in front of me. Yet, as just noted and as stressed by historical sense-data theorists, we sometimes think we see something in the world when we actually do not. Much more secure than (1) is the related claim about how things seem to me:

(2) It seems to me that I see a red apple on the counter in front of me

On one reading, (1) does not entail (2)—I might see a red apple that looks brown because of the lighting. And obviously (2) does not entail (1) either—I might be hallucinating a red apple.

The distinction between (1) and (2) is uncontroversial. Yet it provides the foundation on which the sense-data language is built. To start talking about sense-data explicitly we add a transition from (2) to:

(3) I see a seeming-red-apple-on-the-counter-in-front-of-me

Where (3) is used in an ontologically committing way. Given a standard, Quinean account of ontological commitment, this means that from (3) we infer:[21]

---

[18] A sentence like "I seem to see an apple" is here equivalent to: I am currently having a visual experience that is as if I'm seeing an apple.

[19] Cases of change blindness show that we sometimes judge that scenes look the same without them actually looking the same. On reflection, the scenes can be distinguished. This isn't relevant to the claim here.

[20] A similar approach to the introduction of sense-data talk is taken in Ayer 1956.

[21] From Quine 1948.

(4) There is something that I see

Of course, the witness to (4) can't be an ordinary object since, as already noted, (2) can be true even when no external object is being seen. (2) is supposed to entail (3) which is supposed to entail (4). Given these entailments, (4) can be true when no external object is seen.

The ordinary language critics of sense-data seized on this point. They argued that by talking like this we sin against the ordinary usage of "see".[22] My example concerns vision, but similar points also go for the other canonical senses. As a point of descriptive linguistics there might be something to this objection. Speaking with the vulgar, I *see* a red apple. Speaking with the learned, I *see* a seeming-red-apple. The red apple is not the seeming-red-apple. Therefore, speaking with everyone, there are at least two distinct things that I see, in this very moment, in this very act of perceiving. That sounds extremely strange.[23]

We could live with the strangeness if we had to, but it's more comfortable to introduce special terminology for the way in which we "see" a sense-datum.[24] We could unimaginatively call this "see*", but it's slightly more artful to instead replace (3) and (4) with the following principles:[25]

(3*) I am directly visually aware of a seeming-red-apple-on-the-counter-in-front-of-me

(4*) There is something that I am directly visually aware of

The sense of "direct visual awareness" here is purely *phenomenal*. It applies only to sense-data, so there is no double counting. We *see* ordinary objects but are only *directly aware* of sense-data.

Versions of this terminological move have a long history. I already quoted Berkeley introducing the terminology of "immediately perceiving" to the same purpose. Others have said that we "directly" see only sense-data.[26]

---

[22] The criticism is most associated with Austin 1962, but a similar point had already been made about "perceives" in Reid's 1785 *Essays on the Intellectual Powers*—see Reid 1983. But Reid was more subtle (or more fair-minded) than Austin, since he also admitted that we are "conscious of" ideas (sense-data). For a contemporary endorsement of Reid's criticisms, see Maddy 2017.

[23] Mates (1981) makes a similar point.

[24] This also side-steps objections from the premise that *in English* "see" is not always ontologically committing.

[25] Paul 1936 replaces "looks" with "looks¹" for roughly the same purpose.

[26] Jackson 1977 says this.

Still others that we are "acquainted" or "directly acquainted" only with sense-data.[27] Whatever we call it, this notion of *direct acquaintance* is crucial. It will be spelled out further below.

This terminological change seems cosmetic, but even by itself it goes a long way toward side-stepping ordinary language complaints about sense-data.[28] With this change made sense-data theorists no longer need to say—implausibly—that we do not ever *see* trees, travelers, and trebuchets. We do see ordinary objects, often and happily. The sense-data theorist instead says that while we see trees, we are never directly visually aware of them. We are never directly acquainted with them. This is the only conclusion that is established by the infamous arguments from illusion and hallucination, not any stronger conclusions about "seeing" in the ordinary sense.[29] We can accept that sense-data is all we are ever "acquainted with" or "directly visually aware of" in this *special* sense, but not that we only ever "see" sense-data.[30] If you also want to say that there is some way we "directly" see trees, feel free. Just take care to distinguish *that* sense of direct perception from *this one*.

When we reason in this way to (3*) and (4*) we have already introduced a sense-data extension of natural language. The extension involves "direct awareness" relations for each of our senses and a new family of terms, ⌜seeming-F⌝, for any natural language noun phrase F. To this we also add an explicit sortal predicate, "sense-datum", governed by the following principles:

If something is a seeming-F, then it is a sense-datum

And:

Someone is directly aware of α if and only if α is a sense-datum

---

[27] Fumerton 1985 and Russell 1912 say something like this.

[28] It also side-steps worries about the causal relationship between *us* and *our sense-data*. We can think of direct acquaintance as constituted, in part, by sense-data without requiring a causal connection *between* sense-data and an independent self. This is related to Ayer's claim quoted above, against Russell, that rejecting a subject-object analysis of sensation is not tantamount to rejecting sense-data.

[29] Searle (2015) calls the stronger version of the argument from illusion "the bad argument" and he blames it for many horrors that philosophy has delivered over the ages. Robinson (1994) contends that the role of the argument from illusion and related arguments in the history of philosophy has been overblown. Hirsch (2002) notes that, if you argue yourself into accepting "we never see trees", you will have unwittingly altered English and are speaking an alternative language.

[30] For some relevant empirical information concerning whether English speakers would *say* that we "see" or "perceive" hallucinations, see D'Ambrosio 2022.

This biconditional principle can be understood tenselessly. In adopting its right-to-left direction, I am ruling out—as *existing*—objects of the same metaphysical status as sense-data that are unsensed over all of history, what Russell called "sensibilia".[31] I am also implicitly ruling out the identification of sense-data with aspects of ordinary objects, such as their surfaces.[32] Neither of these exclusions is based in *metaphysics*. I am merely specifying what *I* mean by "sense-data", while keeping my usage firmly within the mainstream among historical sense-data theorists.

In introducing these adjuncts to English I have characterized what Carnap called a "linguistic framework" for talking about sense-data.[33] A few of the second-wave sense-data theorists explicitly recognized that the sense-data-framework had to be distinguished *linguistically* from the ordinary-object-framework.[34] This contrasts with the procedure of the most prominent recent sense-data theorists, who think the introduction of sense-data is both philosophically and empirically substantive.[35]

To fully flesh out and defend this linguistic approach and its philosophical relevance, we need to reflect carefully on the metaontology of the sense-data framework.

4. The Metaontology of Sense-Data Talk

Suppose we start with English and then add sense-data vocabulary governed by the inferences from (2) to (3*) and from (3*) to (4*). We thereby start speaking a new extended language, SD-English—English augmented with the ability to talk about sense-data. I claim that SD-English is a coherent language.

I mean this in a strong sense. Everyone agrees that we could start speaking SD-English, in that we could reason using the inferential transitions from (2) to (3*) and the like. My claim goes beyond this near platitude. I additionally claim that *if* we started to speak SD-English in this benign sense, *then* the inferential transitions from (2) to (3*) and from (3*) to (4*)

---

[31] See Russell 1914a. Note however, that we can still talk about merely possible sensory experiences. See sections 7 and 11 for relevant discussion.

[32] See Ayer 1945 for defense of similar stipulations against Moore 1918–19.

[33] In Carnap 1950.

[34] Paul 1936 and Ayer 1940, 1945 are particularly clear examples of this recognition. Also, see chapter 3 of Mates 1981 and the brief discussion in Hirsch 2002: 60–61.

[35] As mentioned above, here I have in mind the major defenses in Jackson 1977 and Robinson 1994.

would be *valid in our new language*. If it is true that I seem to see a red apple, this means the following sentence will also be true:

There is a seeming-red-apple

And since a seeming-red-apple is a sense-datum, this means it will also be true that sense-data exist. True *in SD-English*, that is, not in English. These aren't sentences of (pre-philosophical) English, so the question of their truth in English does not even arise.[36]

Your spider senses are probably tingling right now. It *sounds* like I'm claiming that merely by *talking* in a certain way, we *create* objects. But that's silly. We can only create sound-waves and word-tokens and the like by talking. Whatever sense-data are, they aren't created just by speaking a language. So, if I were making this claim, you would be right to worry. But I am not. Clarity on this point has been hard-won, and only worked out carefully over the last twenty-five years of developments in metaontology. Let's go over it in detail.

In full generality, the step from (2) to (3*) looks like this:

I seem to see an F

Therefore:

I am directly visually aware of a seeming-F

We can allow this to apply even when F isn't obviously sensible—"I seem to see some kosher food"—but doing so will introduce a more than moderate amount of indeterminacy (see the discussion in sections 6–8).[37] This transition is an example of what Schiffer called a "something-from-nothing transformation".[38] Such transitions move from a sentence that seems ontologically neutral with respect to some objects to one that is ontologically committed to those objects. But despite the ontological commitment, the transformation itself also *seems* completely unobjectionable. It even seems to—in a coarse-grained sense—preserve meaning.

---

[36] English talks about some particular types of sense-data—"I saw a red afterimage"—and may even talk about sense-data generally with terms like "appearances". I am not denying this, of course, and it will be relevant in sections 7 and 11 below.
[37] Thanks to Eli Hirsch here.   [38] In Schiffer 1996, 2003.

Something-from-nothing transformations are all over the place. Schiffer focused on the following three kinds:

(PROPERTIES) the ball is red, therefore: the ball has the property of redness

(NUMBERS) there are four moons, therefore: the number of moons is four

(PROPOSITIONS) Lassie is a dog, therefore: the proposition that Lassie is a dog is true

The idea that something-from-nothing transformations or the like can settle ontological debates has been dubbed "easy ontology", by Sider.[39] The most fully worked-out version of easy ontology is probably Neo-Fregeanism in the philosophy of mathematics.[40]

The central idea behind easy ontology is that the crucial something-from-nothing transformations are analytic or conceptual truths. This invites controversy. Not only because the very existence of analytic and conceptual truths has been prominently denied.[41] But also because the idea that *existence claims* could be analytic, *even conditionally*, seems especially hard to fathom.[42]

Making sense of it requires a metaontology—a meta-theory for ontology—showing how existence claims can be cheap. Sider, Hirsch, and I have all argued that easy ontologists must be implicitly assuming *quantifier variance*.[43] The name, "quantifier variance", comes from Hirsch, who has done more than anyone else to develop, defend, and apply the view.[44] But the doctrine is older than the name. Quantifier variance was previously advocated by Putnam and perhaps also by Carnap and others.[45]

According to quantifier variance there are different possible ontological languages. These are languages in which the respective unrestricted existential quantifiers, as individuated by syntactic inferential role, *mean different*

---

[39] In Sider 2011.

[40] See Dummett 1956, Wright 1983, Hale 1987, and Hale and Wright 2001. Easy ontology is also endorsed in Thomasson 2009 and Fine 2005.

[41] See Quine 1951 and Williamson 2006 for the denials, and Grice and Strawson 1956 and Warren 2021b for rebuttals.

[42] A nice statement of this point of view is found at the start of Field 1984. See also the discussion in chapter 8 of Warren 2020.

[43] See the discussions in chapter 9 of Sider 2011, the introduction to Hirsch 2011, and chapter 9 of Warren 2020. There has been opposition to this—see Hale 2007, Hawley 2007, and Eklund 2006—but taking up this debate here would be a distraction.

[44] See especially the essays in Hirsch 2011.

[45] See Putnam 1987, 2004, and Carnap 1950.

things. The classic illustrating example involves mereology. In a world with two mereological atoms, *a* and *b*, located at different places in an otherwise empty space, how many *objects* are there? How many *things* exist in this world? In English, we say that only two things—*a* and *b* themselves—exist in that world. Yet it is easy to imagine a language just like English save for including the principles of classical mereology. Among these principles is a universal composition axiom holding that for any two distinct objects there is another object with each original object as a proper part. In this alternative language it is then correct to say that there are three things in the imagined world—*a*, *b*, and also their mereological fusion, $a + b$.

This is an apparent disagreement about *how many* objects exist. Therefore, it cannot come down to a disagreement about how predicates are distributed over given objects.[46] We have two distinct and seemingly incompatible answers to a straightforward ontological question about a simple toy case. Which answer is correct? Metaphysical realists assimilate this ontological disagreement to standard factual disagreements. There is supposedly a matter of objective fact here that the two parties in the dispute differ over. Many of us find this assimilation strange. What possible matter of fact is hidden here? In our toy case all of the facts are in. I completely described everything about the possible world in question. Nothing about the case was hidden. Nothing about the case could be hidden. Rather than a factual difference, it is more plausible to see this dispute as owing to a difference of *language*. The mereologist speaks a language that differs from ours. In particular, their language differs from ours over the meanings of "there is", "exists", "objects", "things", and related expressions.

The background argument for this appeals to charity in metasemantics. Following certain rules and using language in certain ways, with a clear head, guarantees that the meanings of your sentences vindicate said uses. This is the basic claim of constitutive metasemantic charity.[47] Essentially the same point can also be made by appeal to the slogan that "meaning is use", or in terms of conceptual or inferential role semantics (inferentialism).[48] On all of these approaches, because of how the mereologist is disposed to use expressions like "there are" and "exists", he speaks *truly* when he describes the *a-b* world as a world where there are "exactly three objects".

---

[46] It also can't come down to only the identity predicate; see the appendix to Warren 2022*a*.

[47] Charity was introduced in Wilson 1959 and was influentially advocated by Quine (1960*a*), Davidson (1973), and Lewis (1974), among others.

[48] The slogan is associated with Wittgenstein (1953).

And because of how we are disposed to use language, we speak truly when we describe the *a-b* world as a world where there are "exactly two objects".

The two languages are quite similar, but they differ in the precise use of quantifier expressions. Even still, the structural features of the use of these quantifier expressions are common to both languages. In particular, in both mereological and non-mereological English, the expressions "exists" or "there are" play the exact same structural inferential role. That is: in both languages, these expressions play the inferential role of the unrestricted existential quantifier familiar from the elementary logic classroom. According to the standard, Quinean, account of existence and ontological commitment, both languages have a concept of existence that is expressed by their unrestricted existential quantifier. Using their own existential quantifier, they can make existence claims. Yet because of subtle differences in use, the two languages have *distinct* concepts of existence. The meanings of the quantifiers and related expressions *vary* across the two languages.

This is the crucial point. In neither language are any objects being "created" by mere talk. The linguistic activities of language users instead only determine what is meant, which concepts are expressed. The best way to describe the situation is by saying that the languages both have concepts of existence, but that the two concepts of existence differ. Despite the differences, they both still count as concepts of *existence*, or as existence-like concepts, because of their relevant inferential similarity. They are similar, they are both unrestricted quantifiers, yet they are distinct. Sentences containing these expressions can differ in their truth values across the two languages. This example shows that our familiar English concept of the existence of an object is not built into all possible languages.

This is roughly the claim of modest quantifier variance. Strong quantifier variance adds to the pluralism of modest variance the claim that some pairs of distinct quantifier languages are expressively equivalent and therefore of equal metaphysical merit.[49] So for the on-record quantifier variantists— Putnam, Hirsch, myself—metaphysical merit is understood in terms of expressive power.[50] Expressive equivalence is plausible in the mereological case—any world you can describe in English can just as well be described in mereological English, and vice-versa. Hirsch has argued that many—though not all—of the ontological debates of philosophers satisfy the conditions of strong quantifier variance. That is: the ontological languages associated with

---

[49] For both modest and strong variance, see Hirsch and Warren 2019*a*.
[50] See Putnam 1983, Hirsch 2011, and Warren 2015.

the opposing sides in the debate are expressively equivalent and therefore (according to variantists) of equal metaphysical merit.

Ontologists reject this account of metaphysical merit. The best alternative theory, from Sider, accepts modest variance but understands metaphysical merit using a distinctive metaphysical primitive—*metaphysical structure*.[51] This way of rejecting strong variance allows the coherence of the sense-data language. But it enables critics to deny the existence of sense-data in the metaphysically special sense of "existence". For my part, I don't think that metaphysical structure is coherent; and even if it were coherent, I don't think it could have a reasonable epistemology.[52] For both of those reasons, I reject the concept of metaphysical structure and all related concepts.

Quantifier variance has, of course, faced many related and further objections from metaphysicians.[53] I think that it can be defended from these objections. In fact, I think it *has been* defended from these objections.[54] I won't recapitulate all of the back-and-forth here. My goal right now is to apply quantifier variance, not defend it. My point is that the application of quantifier variance vindicates the sense-data language.

Turning back to sense-data, note that the same charity argument that applied to the imagined mereological language also applies to SD-English. Speakers of SD-English clear-headedly accept the inferential transitions from (2) to (3*) and from (3*) to (4*). In so doing they follow general rules of inference for the newly introduced sense-data terminology. Given that they clearheadedly use language in this fashion, charity requires us to interpret them as speaking a language in which these inferential transitions are valid. So, since it is true that we seem to see things, true as a matter of empirical fact, then it also must be true that sense-data exist—true in SD-English, that is.

Well-known issues of social externalism might block English speakers from transitioning to SD-English, but those issues can be side-stepped.[55] I hereby stipulate that our imagined SD-speakers do not explicitly or implicitly defer to English speakers in their relevant uses of language. If SD-English extends English, then its expressions, "there is", "exists", "object", and "thing" differ slightly in meaning from their English counterparts while retaining the same structural-inferential roles. SD-English speakers have a

---

[51] See Sider 2009, 2011.   [52] See Warren 2016*a,b*.
[53] For examples, see Dorr 2005, 2014, Eklund 2009, and Hawthorne 2006, 2009.
[54] See Hirsch 2011, Hirsch and Warren 2019*a,b*, and Warren 2015, 2022*a*.
[55] See Burge 1979.

slightly different concept of *existence* than standard English speakers do.[56] English and SD-English are an example of modest quantifier variance. Below (section 7) I will argue that they aren't an example of strong quantifier variance, since SD-English has more expressive power than English (at least if English is stripped of its existing sense-data talk).

The quantifier variance metaontology vindicates SD-English's something-from-nothing transformations and—given the facts of sensory experience—the truth of the sentence "there are sense-data". A few earlier sense-data theorists approached matters from a similar perspective, but without the supporting metaontological details.[57] And the canonical early moderns took the "idea" language in a similar spirit, seeing it as a background framework that did not require substantive defense. Quantifier variance frees these approaches from every blemish. It is not that sense-data are created by language. Rather, the sense-data language talks about experience in an ontologically committing way, using its distinct concept of existence. If you speak the sense-data language, the standard claims about sense-data and their existence are *true*, unproblematically so, without sense-data being creations out of language.

From this perspective, objections to the existence of sense-data begin to seem a bit silly. They seem as silly as objections to the existence of tables seem to many of us. And the complex alternative schemes for talking about the data of sensory experience in a non-ontologically committing way start to seem, not silly, but unmotivated.[58] Both metaphysical

---

[56] I haven't said anything about the other famous Quinean metaontological slogan—"no entity without identity" from Quine 1957–58. But a criterion of identity for sense-data poses no special problems, for we can simply appeal to Leibniz's law. It is true that different sense-data theorists may differ over the properties of sense-data, but most of these are best seen as questions of *decision*, not *discovery*. Paul (1936) nicely advocated for a similar point of view. See the relevant discussion in sections 5 and 7 below.

[57] In particular, again see Ayer 1940, Paul 1936, and Mates 1981.

[58] I have in mind the adverbial theory, advocated in Chisholm 1957. Adverbial theories analyze experience claims like, "I see an orange circle", using adverbs that modify the perceptual verb—for example, "I see orange-circle-ly". This approach is sometimes endorsed over sense-data on grounds of parsimony, but the gain in ontological parsimony here is paid for in the coin of ideological profligacy—compare: nihilists who reject chairs but talk of simples arranged chairwise, following van Inwagen 1990. There is a famous problem for the adverbial theory, the so-called "many properties" problem—Jackson 1975, Casullo 1987, and Dinges 2015. Here is the problem: suppose I see an orange patch and circular shape. To simply say, as before, that I see orange-circle-ly is wrong. There is a difference between seeing something orange and seeing something circular at the same time when they are distinct, versus seeing something that is both orange and circular. Object talk is our standard way of making exactly these distinctions, so the sense-data alternative faces no analogous problem. Adverbialists have attempted to solve the problem (see Sellars 1975, Tye 1984, and D'Ambrosio 2019). Perhaps the easiest solution is to appeal to results from Quine 1960*b* concerning predicate-functor

and epistemological questions about sense-data are illuminated by this language-based way of looking at things. Let me demonstrate this.

5. The Metaphysics of Sense-Data

The obvious metaphysical question about sense-data concerns the *properties* of sense-data. Is a seeming-red-apple actually red? Most historical sense-data theorists said "yes". In fact, most sense-data theorists accepted the inference from:

(2**) It seems to me that I see a red thing

To:

(3**) I am directly visually aware of something that is red

This move is widely associated with sense-data and nearly as widely decried. Chisholm even called this sort of thing the "sense-datum fallacy".[59]

This inference differs from the inference between (2) and (3*) above. Plugging into the earlier schema, (2**) would only lead to:

(3***) I am directly visually aware of a seeming-red-thing

The question then is whether (3***) entails (3**). More generally: does seeming-*F* entail being *F*, at least for sensible properties like colors and shapes? For a hardcore metaphysician, things get interesting at precisely this point. This certainly seems like a deep metaphysical puzzle about the nature of these important new objects. But a metaphysical approach to this question is unfruitful.

We have here not a deep metaphysical puzzle, but instead a practical question of language engineering—in constructing a sense-data language,

---

languages like those in Strawson 1959. But talking in terms of complex predicate functors or quantifying over events or the like either smuggles in object talk through the back door or else assumes a strange kind of metaphysical holism—see Turner 2011 and Filcheva 2023. And even if all of these difficulties can be handled, they can't be handled in a simple and natural way. So even if adverbialists can gain expressive parity, we should prefer the sense-data language on practical grounds.

[59] In Chisholm 1957.

should we build in this inference or not? If we do, we might end up saying that a seeming-red-apple sense-datum is red *and* that a red apple is also red. But this sounds a bit odd. To avoid the oddity, we might instead prefer to say that apples are never red, but the sense-data that are caused by some apples sometimes are.[60] Or we might say that there is only one color property here, but that sense-data instantiate properties in a different way than do ordinary things.[61] Or perhaps we could say that while some apples are really red, sense-data are only red* or phenomenally red or p-red.[62]

As this shows, there are a number of options for sense-data theorists. Here I will adopt a version of the final option. I think this is the clearest way of talking, at least in this context.[63] Accordingly, let's distinguish color predicates as applied to sense-data from color predicates as applied to ordinary objects. As far as possible, we can do this while remaining neutral about whether these are two distinct properties. The move I make here for color I also make for the other sensible properties of sense-data.[64] This approach to the properties of sense-data helps to defend sense-data against one of the most powerful arguments against them—Huemer's location argument.[65]

In brief, the argument goes like this. If sense-data have spatial properties like sizes and shapes, it seems that they must also have spatial *locations*. So where are the sense-data located? Where is the seeming-red-apple I'm directly visually aware of? Huemer argues that there is no satisfying answer to this question and so we should reject the existence of sense-data. For example, suppose we try saying that sense-data are located inside our heads. Then there is a red, apple-shaped object *inside of my skull* whenever I am directly visually aware of a seeming-red-apple. That's absurd. But there are also problems with locating sense-data where they appear to us to be.[66] And with locating sense-data where the distal objects are located.[67] Both of these

---

[60] Jackson 1977 and Robinson 1994 accept this kind of view.

[61] Mally said similar things about abstract objects; see Linsky 2014.

[62] Even some supposed direct realists, like Searle (2015), appeal to something like p-red in their accounts of color experience.

[63] As already noted in passing, natural language does talk of some kinds of sense-data, for example, after-images. We say things like "the after-image is red", but nothing in my approach is incompatible with this.

[64] This isn't forced—we might allow that shape properties are shared by sense-data and ordinary objects but not color or size properties. If this option is pursued, the location argument might still be avoided by pointing out that some mathematical objects also have shapes without having spatial locations (see below).

[65] Developed in chapter VII of Huemer 2001.   [66] This is Jackson's (1977) view.

[67] Moore (1918–19) flirted with this approach.

options have sense-data out in the physical world overlapping and co-locating with ordinary physical objects. What is in the room? Not just a chair, but also a seeming-chair sense-datum. All of these options for locating sense-data in space are awkward.

There is nothing like a refutation here; the bullet can be bitten. Still, the awkwardness should be avoided. A response that does so leans on the metaphysical strategy from above (though it is also the best option for sense-data theorists who do not distinguish red* from red). If we deny that sense-data have shapes and sizes and colors in the *same sense* that physical objects do, the pressure to provide sense-data with locations dissipates. The obvious thing to say instead is that (most) sense-data do not have spatial locations. In this, they are similar to numbers and to fictional characters and—unsurprisingly—to experiences. That is: we typically don't think that subjective experiences have spatial locations, except in a derivative sense.[68] As it is with experiences, so it is with sense-data.[69] Sense-data do not have spatial locations. We should be no more flummoxed by the question of *where* sense-data are than we are by the question of *how much they weigh*.

Huemer objects that many sense-data have sizes and shapes, and that this requires them to have spatial locations too. But I have already suggested that sense-data might only have sizes* and shapes*, so the premise of this counter-argument can be denied by sense-data theorists. Further, even if some sense-data have (for example) shapes, so do triangles and other abstract mathematical objects, yet these also lack spatial locations. Huemer also argues that in perception we seem to see things with locations, so if we see sense-data, we should ascribe them locations. But sense-data theorists can say that we do see things with locations—ordinary objects. They have locations, they seem to have locations, but the sense-data we are directly

---

[68] Huemer himself admits that experiences don't have locations, but he thinks that saying this requires dualism (I disagree). Somewhat related thoughts are expressed in chapter 4 of McGinn 1999.

[69] Another option that Huemer discusses is locating sense-data in a private, phenomenal space. Something like this is endorsed in Broad 1925, Russell 1927, and Price 1932. But this is not actually an answer to the original question, so I don't think it should be treated as a distinct option. Instead, this idea can be combined with one of the other options. It best coheres with the view that sense-data have no spatial locations. The p-space option might be especially helpful in assigning motion properties to sense-data. There are visual illusions where it seems like there is movement in an objectively static image, and the illusion persists even after you learn that the image is actually static.

visually aware of do not. The sense-data language as I have developed it here avoids the problems that Huemer raises for the "no location" option.[70]

All of this is well and good for visual sense-data that, while not representational themselves, are necessary for any visual representation of the external world (see section 8). And the same thing also goes for the sense-data associated with the other canonical five senses. Yet today we also recognize additional *internal* senses—of pain, hunger, bodily position, and more. When I have a stomach ache, I am directly aware of a sense-datum. But isn't the ache *in my stomach*? And isn't *that* a location in the world at any given time? If so then these sense-data, at least, must have spatial locations.

I take these as spoils for the victorious army. We may well want to argue that these internal senses generate bodily sensations but not sense-data. But as an answer to the challenge, that seems a bit arbitrary. Personally, I would be happy enough to say that the stomach ache sense-datum isn't located anywhere. But I also think that for internal senses we can unproblematically locate their sense-data in the relevant bodily location, thus providing them with egocentric spatial locations. Unlike with a visual sense-datum, in this kind of case, when we locate the sense-datum somewhere in the world, we don't face a problem of overpopulation. It is strange to think the seeming-red-apple sense-datum is located in the same place in the world as the actually red, actual apple. But double-counting oddities don't arise with anything like the same force when I locate my stomach ache *in my stomach*. Some remaining cases might give us pause—is the amputee's pain in their (currently non-existent) left leg?—but hard cases make bad law.

A related metaphysical question is: what are sense-data made out of? Is there some kind of phenomenal *stuff* out of which they are composed? I think this is analogous to asking what the number 3 is made out of. If these questions have any answer at all, the answer is *nothing*. Sense-data are not made out of any stuff, any more than numbers are. As I will discuss below (section 8) a sense-datum can be *composed* out of other sense-data, but that is different than being *made* out of stuff. The oddity is that sense-data, unlike numbers, are not supposed to be abstract objects. Yet if they have no locations, and aren't made out of anything, how could they be anything but

---

[70] A potential problem Huemer doesn't raise concerns temporal properties—it is natural to say that sense-data have temporal locations, but then physical reality seems to require that they have *space*time locations. I think this move can be resisted in a few different ways, but I also think the premise can be reasonably denied. Any event of directly accessing a sense-datum might have (or be) a spacetime location, but that doesn't mean that the sense-data so accessed have locations.

abstract objects? The answer is that there isn't a simple, one-dimensional binary division between abstract and concrete objects. Sense-data should not be classified with ordinary physical objects, but they shouldn't be classified with pure abstract objects either.

More could be said about the metaphysics of sense-data. But let's now turn to the epistemology of sense-data, which is the more historically important issue.

6. The Epistemology of Sense-Data

The natural epistemological questions about sense-data concern our *access* to sense-data and the *epistemic status* of our beliefs about sense-data. How do we know that sense-data have the properties they have?

The traditional view is that it is literally impossible to be wrong about the properties of your own sense-data. Yet without some nuance added, this is probably too strong. Even prominent sense-data epistemologists like Ayer admitted that merely *verbal* mistakes about sense-data are possible.[71] The real question is whether *factual* mistakes are also possible. The seeming-red-apple seems red, to me. Following the discussion in the previous section, we can say that it is red*. This is a matter of fact. Can I be mistaken about it? Some opponents of sense-data made much of this possibility.[72] Ayer himself later clarified that his position requires only that in matters of sense-data the subject is the ultimate authority.[73]

This is very easy to misunderstand. The claim is *not* that whenever you are directly accessing a sense-datum, you are thereby making an explicit judgement that the sense-datum is F.[74] Animals and children (for example) have direct access to sense-data without making any explicit judgements about the properties of sense-data. The point is not about judgement at all, even implicit or tacit judgement, but instead about our non-linguistic *acquaintance* with sense-data.

This is related to an important background issue: the connection between sense-data and dualism in the philosophy of mind. The sense-data theory is sometimes associated with mind/body dualism. This is because sense-data were sometimes stipulated to be non-physical. This association between

---

[71] In Ayer 1940.   [72] See Austin 1962.
[73] See the discussion of Austin's 14th argument in Ayer 1967.
[74] See the clarifying discussion in Ayer 1945.

sense-data and, if not dualism, at least a mysterious concept of conscious-ness sometimes derives from sense-data theorists themselves.[75] Given this tight association, direct arguments against dualism or p-consciousness have sometimes been taken as indirect arguments against sense-data. This is a mistake. Far from being at odds with sense-data, alternative, access-based approaches to consciousness cohere neatly with reasonable views about both the metaphysics and epistemology of sense-data.[76]

Despite what is sometimes claimed by opponents, sense-data theorists don't need to make "the given" metaphysically basic, determinate, and mys-terious.[77] In fact, as I have already been stressing, sense-data is *not* such a given *and was never thought to be*. Sense-data theorists can and do admit that cognitive processing of all sorts goes into generating sensory experi-ence. This point is most naturally made using an access-based approach to consciousness, but even dualist sense-data theorists always take care to make room for it. Witness Robinson:

> It seems to be a phenomenological fact that attitudes, beliefs and anticipa-tions can enter into the structure and tone of the basic phenomenal field, without being fundamentally phenomenal themselves.[78]

Similar points were even made by Locke, in his idea framework.[79] The sense-data framework is independent of our metaphysical theory of con-scious experience. The sense-data language begins from the facts of con-scious awareness, whatever they may be. And sense-data are not, and were never thought to be, the pure unprocessed input taken in by your senses. Put metaphorically, sense-data is what you get at the sensory finish line, not the sensory starting gate.

This perspective helps to flesh out Ayer's claim that the subject is the ultimate authority about their own sense-data. Here access-based theories of consciousness are particularly well-placed, since they already make the access of a subject metaphysically constitutive of conscious experience. A metaphysical role for access easily gives way to an epistemological role for access. The properties of a sense-datum may well be *partly* or even, in some

---

[75] See Robinson 1994, for example.

[76] See Block 1995 for the distinction between access and phenomenal consciousness.

[77] The derisive term "the given" is from Sellars 1997. Taylor 1979 mistakenly criticizes sense-data theories for requiring an unconceptualized given.

[78] Robinson 1994: 207.   [79] See Mackie 1976 for some discussion of this.

cases, *fully* determined by the access of the subject. What is crucial, meta-physically, is that a lot goes on *behind* our access, so we need not think of the sense-data as an entirely unprocessed given. What is crucial epistemo-logically is that our access to the properties of a sense-datum is often much more direct and secure than our access to the properties of ordinary objects. This point, *in some form*, is all that is required for sense-data to play their special role in the early modern project.[80]

Doubts about the existence of the seeming-red patch I am directly visu-ally aware of, in this exact moment, are otiose. Likewise for doubts that the seeming-red patch is actually red*. Such doubts simply cannot gain a foot-hold. Unlike other skeptical doubts, no plausible possibility of error has here been described. No cogent possibility of error about these matters *can be* described. This contrasts starkly with doubts about the existence and properties of the red apple I currently seem to be seeing. There are many coherent ways for me to fall into error about apples. Not so with sense-data.

A nice illustration of this difference leans on idealization. If we idealize our ordinary computational and cognitive powers to their limits, all of the errors about sense-data go away, but many errors about ordinary objects remain. If you had no limits of memory, concepts, attention, or computing power, you would be a first-person sense-data oracle. If this idealized ver-sion of you had no answer about whether a given sense-datum was F, then it could only be because there is no fact of the matter about whether the given sense-datum is F. In other words, all of our errors about sense-data fall on the performance side of Chomsky's famous performance/competence div-ision.[81] This illuminates Ayer's claim that, concerning sense-data, the sub-ject is the ultimate authority. And it does so in a way that starkly distinguishes the epistemology of sense-data from the epistemology of ordinary objects.

Even leaving idealizations aside, our direct acquaintance with sense-data gives us epistemological security with respect to their existence and basic qualitative properties. But this epistemological security does not rule out indeterminacy or insecurity concerning more complex properties of sense-data.

---

[80] This might be called into question by Wittgenstein's (1953) notorious "private language" argument. I won't discuss this directly, since I doubt there is a serious challenge to sense-data along these lines. For direct replies to the private language argument by sense-data theorists see Ayer 1954 and chapter IV of Robinson 1994.

[81] From Chomsky 1965.

To illustrate, let's consider the famous problem of the speckled hen.[82] I seem to see a hen with many speckles. So, I see a seeming-many-speckled-hen. How many speckles does it have? I am unable to give a precise answer. This apparently undermines the claim that we have direct access to all properties of our sense-data. In response, Ayer suggested that there is no determinate answer to the question of how many speckles are on the seeming-many-speckled-hen, no fact of the matter. This made his critics uncomfortable, but I think it's the right thing to say in *some* cases. It also dovetails nicely with the indeterminacies standardly posited by access-theories of consciousness.[83]

This is not to deny that sometimes a sense-datum has a non-basic or non-qualitative property and because our access to the datum is fleeting and memory is fallible, our beliefs about whether said sense-datum had said property can be in error. This *can* happen. It *does* happen. It usually happens when the properties are holistic and require changes of attention over a given sense-datum. Similar issues arise with mixed properties that have a computational element—does this speckled-hen sense-datum have a prime number of speckles? With non-qualitative properties, or computationally complex qualitative properties, errors are possible. The sense-data language approach is flexible enough to accommodate all of these cases.

A related challenge concerns the intransitivity of relations like "looks the same as". As vagueness and other well-known phenomena demonstrate, α might look the same as β, and β might look the same as γ, while α does *not* look the same as γ.[84] The natural sense-data account of this posits ambiguity.[85] The crucial background point is that it is impossible to directly access all of α, β, and γ at the very same time while still making these same judgements. Given this, it is best to see the tokens of "β" above as picking out two distinct sense-data—β_1 and β_2.

A similar move is also natural to make when considering duck-rabbits and necker cubes.[86] Likewise for some visual illusions. In the checker shadow illusion, one checker square looks darker than another checker square even though the squares are, objectively speaking, the very same shade. Are we

---

[82] From Ayer 1940, where it is attributed to Gilbert Ryle; see Chisholm 1942.

[83] Both Dennett 1991 and Warren 2021a defend the idea that conscious experience can be *indeterminate* in several ways.

[84] This has been raised as a problem for sense-data by Armstrong (1968).

[85] See chapter VIII of Robinson 1994.

[86] The duck-rabbit is from Wittgenstein 1953. Ayer makes the move I suggest in Ayer 1985: 86.

here mistaken about the qualitative features of a sense-datum? No. Instead, the sense-data *are* different, but the actual squares in the image are not. There is no contradiction. The same stimulus at or over time can result in distinct sense-data. Once again: sense-data come at the end of a long process of unconscious processing, they should not be identified with either the object-ive stimulus, nor with an unprocessed sensory given.

When properly understood, the special directness of our cognitive access to sense-data is not undermined by the traditional challenge cases. The same also goes for change blindness and all other related cases discovered and explored by scientists long after the heyday of sense-data. In some of these cases the properties of a sense-datum are indeterminate. In others, the properties are determinate but are not directly qualitative, so that attribut-ing them places additional cognitive demands on a subject beyond their direct access to the sense-datum. This opens up room for mistakes. In still others, what was initially thought of as a single sense-datum was actually two distinct sense-data. None of this undermines the special epistemo-logical role of sense-data. Doubts about the existence and basic sensory properties of sense-data have a different status than doubts about the exist-ence and basic properties of ordinary objects.

7. Basic Sense-Data

Above I set up "the" sense-data language using terms for sense-data that are parasitic on natural language terms for ordinary objects. But in actual fact, we obviously learn the expression "red apple" long before learning anything like "seeming-red-apple". Nothing I have said is in tension with this.

I introduced the sense-data language in the way I did because it makes it very easy to understand. However, a complex sense-datum like a seeming-red-apple is actually *composed*, in some fashion, out of more fundamental sense-data. This applies across all sensory modalities, not just vision. I can be directly aurally aware of a Brahm's-4th-symphony sense-datum. Yet this sense-datum is extremely complex, being itself composed of an arrange-ment of more basic aural sense-data.

Some philosophers have introduced frameworks for *basic* sense-data. Most famously and influentially, both Carnap and Goodman did this.[87]

---

[87] See Carnap 1928 and Goodman 1951. See also Peacocke 1983.

I won't do the same thing here, but I do think that a basic sense-data language is *possible*. Possible for each individual sensory modality, and also possible for all of them at once. An adequate basic sense-data language would need to include enough basic sense-data properties to ensure that any non-basic sense-datum could be composed out of instances and co-instances of said properties.

If you consider again the Brahm's-4th-symphony sense-datum, you'll get a sense of how complex this might end up being. We would need names for all of the fundamental sounds that together, in a specific arrangement, constitute this complex sense-datum. However, the difficulties about this do not seem to be "in principle" difficulties. They are instead *practical* difficulties of tedium and unnaturalness. Aiming for basic sense-data, in any modality, is not natural to us in our thinking, talking, or philosophizing. The task involves only the sounds themselves, without care for meaning, emotional shading, context, or anything else. The final output of this painful and tedious process is likely to be quite ugly—a sound of type-C, form-(*iv*) is happening now!—yet ugliness is not impossibility.

I don't think that the in-principle possibility of a basic sense-data language really requires an argument. Nevertheless, here is (a sketch of) an argument. Our sensory system involves several distinct and non-overlapping modalities. These modalities correspond to sub-systems that can each be in various distinct states, all accessible to consciousness. Our experience informs us that these states are structured into local and repeatable qualitative features.[88] That is, our own experiences make this apparent to us, from the first-person. And from the third-person, our hard-won empirical understanding of images, sounds, tastes, smells, and more, reinforces this. Any language that is able to talk about all of these basic sensory property occurrences—red* and circular* or the like—along with all collections and combinations of the same, would be sufficient as a basic sense-data language.

The easiest way to understand composition here is by allowing that any mereological fusion of basic sense-data is itself another sense-datum in the same modality.[89] But appealing to mereology isn't our only option, of course. In fact, our options for individuating sense-data directly parallel our

---

[88] Uriah Kriegel has noted to me that some gestalt psychologists have argued that while atomic elements can be distinguished in thought as abstractions, that the *reality* of conscious experience is holistic. I think that this position ultimately requires a Sider-style (2011) rejection of strong quantifier variance, but I won't go into the issue in detail here.

[89] Mates (1981) suggests something like this.

options for individuating ordinary objects, though as discussed in section 5, sense-data are not made of *stuff*. And I stress again that my language-oriented approach does *not* imply that sense-data are created by language. They are not. What I am discussing now is the possible construction of a basic sense-data language, and this too is about how to talk. Different ways of talking will give rise to similar but distinct *concepts* of basic sense-data, just as different ways of talking can give rise to similar but distinct *concepts* of ordinary objects. All of this is again backed up by quantifier variance (section 4).

It is useful to talk about "sensory runs" consisting of all of your sense-data, from every sense-modality, over a given stretch of time. A sensory run usually includes various types of sense-data. The sensory features of any sensory run are themselves factual features of reality. They are not created or generated by language. An adequate language for talking about experience should be able to describe *any possible* sensory run. Any adequate basic sense-data language will give us this ability. If there are two or more distinct languages adequate for all sensory runs, they will be fully intertranslateable.

In this, an adequate basic sense-data language expressively advances over standard English. Many—*many*—possible sensory runs cannot be described in standard English unaugmented by sense-data talk. You can say that it seems to you that there is a red apple on the table, but it is much harder to describe the sensory experience with any precision. And describing disordered experiences, even in coarse-grained terms, may be impossible.[90] When having an experience that has no order at the level of ordinary object talk, there is no way to talk about the experience by saying it is "as if" you are in some coherent perceptual situation. All such disordered experiences can, in contrast, be referred to and generalized over and talked about in an adequate basic sense-data language. This means that such a language—call it SD-English+—has more expressive power than standard English.

We don't often feel this lack in English, because in reality, *English is already a sense-data language*. When we speak, in English, about the red afterimage, we are talking about a sense-datum. Likewise for many cases where we talk about sounds, smells, tactile sensations, tastes, and images.

---

[90] I think that most direct realist theories, whether intentionalist (Huemer 2001, Searle 2015) or disjunctivist (McDowell 1982, Martin 2002), eschew the project of characterizing qualitative experience. From the current perspective, this means they have opted for an expressively impoverished language.

Ordinary English doesn't include the term "sense-data", but it includes many *ad hoc* terms and expressions for talking about sense-data. And the same is true of every other natural language too. This, together with the open-endedness of actual languages, means that actual English probably isn't expressively impoverished relative to SD-English+. Yet this is no comfort to opponents of sense-data, since expressive equivalence comes only because English and other natural languages already include sense-data under different names.

Given all of this, SD-English+ and "English"—English minus its devices for talking about sense-data—provide an example of modest but not strong quantifier variance. Though the ultimate correctness of this claim depends on the exact equivalence conditions that suffice for languages to be of equal metaphysical merit. On every approach to equivalence aligned with quantifier variance, it will be agreed that many sensory runs can be described in SD-English+ that cannot be described in "English", and so the languages are inequivalent. SD-English+ is simply a more expressive language.

The general fundamentality of sense-data talk was a commonly held view among early sense-data theorists. One reading of this is modal. When you see a table, you must be directly accessing some sense-data. The opposite is certainly not the case, and this asymmetry is important. Witness Ayer's comments from the mid-1940s:

> For whereas in every case in which it is possible to apply the physical-object language, it is also possible, at least in principle, to apply the sense-datum language, one can conceive an order of experience to which the sense-datum language would have application, but the physical-object language would not. Thus, while it is convenient, for purposes of exposition, to introduce people to the sense-datum terminology by setting forth sentences which refer to sense-data as translations of sentences which refer to physical objects, it would be a mistake to conclude from this that the sense-datum language was nothing more than a technical substitute for the other. There is, on the contrary, an asymmetry between the two languages which may be described by saying that the sense-datum language is logically prior; and this is shown by the fact that, while referring to sense-data is not necessarily a way of referring to physical objects, referring to physical objects is necessarily a way of referring to sense-data.[91]

---

[91] Ayer 1945: 312. In the context, Ayer was responding to and agreeing with claims from Price 1941 about Ayer 1940.

I agree with almost all of this. My only disagreement is with the last sentence. When the paper from which this quote was drawn was written, Ayer still accepted phenomenalism. In later work, like virtually every other historical phenomenalist, Ayer rejected phenomenalism as unworkable.[92]

Certain central sentences, expressible in the sense-data language, are epistemologically special. They do not go beyond what is directly accessible to consciousness in a moment of awareness. We might call these "basic experience claims".[93] Many of them can be made in SD-English, and *all of them* can be made in SD-English+. This is not a merely formal claim, since it is not about *labels*.[94] The flux of experience is real, it is the empirical data available to consciousness. And the sense-data language is the best way of talking and thinking about the data of experience.

This is a way in which the sense-data language is "logically prior" to the ordinary object language. Another way, discussed in the next section, concerns the role that sense-data plays in our philosophical theorizing. Yet another, discussed thereafter, concerns the epistemological role of sense-data in facing down the unavoidable challenge of skepticism.

8. Sense-Data Theories of Perception and Color

Consider again the three illustrative claims from section 3:

(1) I see a red apple on the counter in front of me

(2) It seems to me that I see a red apple on the counter in front of me

(3*) I am directly visually aware of a seeming-red-apple-on-the-counter-in-front-of-me

There is a natural explanatory order on these claims: (2) is at least partly explained by (3*) and (1) is partly explained by (2) and partly explained by the fact that there is a red apple on the counter in front of me that I stand in a relevant causal relationship to.

Why didn't I say that (2) is "fully" explained by (3*)? Because there is an important ambiguity already touched on: when I say it seems like *F* to me, often, though not always, some conceptual ability is imputed to me with

---

[92] Ayer became a realist of a sort; see the extended discussions in Ayer 1968, 1973.

[93] Similar terminology is used in (for example) Russell 1940 and Ayer 1968.

[94] See Ayer 1940 on the errors of formalism for important clarity about this.

respect to *F*. But as also stressed throughout, sense-data themselves are not inherently intentional or representational. So I sometimes prefer to say that (2) is *partly* explained by (3*) and *partly* explained by some fact about my concepts and how I am exercising them in this given situation. If we instead build this conceptual understanding into the truth conditions of (3*), then we can say that (3*) itself fully explains (2). Likewise if (2) is used without ascribing conceptual understanding to the subject (which it often is).

Don't be misled by any of this. Direct realists make much of the intentionality of perceptual experience.[95] Sense-data theorists can agree with them, at least at the level of (2). Yet, when so understood, (2) is not metaphysically or epistemologically fundamental. However, a sophisticated representational theory of perception can be combined with a sense-data theory. This is because sense-data are the data of conscious sensory experience, but this data is itself built out of information taken in by the senses and processed and altered in various ways on its way to the global workspace. The representational role is, in an externalist sense, a generalization of the cognitive role played by the deliverances of perception.[96]

Sense-data theorists have flexibility in offering theories of both perception and perceptual properties. To illustrate this, focus on color.[97] Above, in section 5, I distinguished between red as a property of ordinary objects and red* as a property of sense-data. Even supposing that these are two distinct properties, they are obviously very closely related. In fact, the ordinary object property of red can be explained in terms of the sense-data property of red*.

An appealing approach for this is a sense-data version of color dispositionalism. The key observation is that when I see a red object, in normal conditions, I am directly visually acquainted with a red* sense-datum:

SD Color Dispositionalism. An ordinary object is red just in case the object would cause ordinary human observers in normal conditions to be directly visually aware of a red* sense-datum appropriately associated with the object

This is an explanatory principle where the right-hand-side explains the left-hand-side.

---

[95] Both Huemer 2001 and Searle 2015 stress this.
[96] See Cao and Warren forthcoming.
[97] For an overview of color for philosophers, see Hardin 1988.

This simple color dispositionalism would need to be elaborated and refined in various ways for a full account. This would require explaining the relevant notions of "ordinary observer" and "normal conditions", though I don't think that either task poses significant problems. The final bit, about the red* sense-datum being "appropriately associated with the object" is meant to rule out a few lingering non-standard cases. An object that produces a blinding flash of light might cause observers to see a red afterimage. An object that sends out nanobots to tinker with the red*-producing center of an observer's brain might cause the observer to imagine red rockets. Intuitively, neither of these objects is red, despite these dispositional features.

Color dispositionalism of this kind goes back, at least, to Locke. Modern forms of color dispositionalism have also been defended in the contemporary literature.[98] But the modern forms typically eschew sense-data. This omission threatens dispositionalism with circularity. Put baldly then, suppose that *being red* is explained in terms of *looking red*. But what is looking red? Don't we need some independent account of redness to avoid circularity? There may be other ways out, but the circularity challenge doesn't even arise for sense-data versions of color dispositionalism. The sense-data approach doesn't explain red-facts in terms of other red-facts, it instead explains red-facts in terms of red*-facts. What goes for color can also go for all of the other so-called "secondary" qualities of objects. Locke smiles down on us from philosophical heaven.

I won't go into further detail here. Obviously, these remarks don't amount to a worked-out theory. My goal was only to suggest that the sense-data language can be leveraged to give plausible theories of perception and secondary properties. Given this, sense-data theorists are not boxed in when it comes to theorizing about perception, the mind, and the relationship between the mind and the world. However, the *ultimate* question about this relationship is the problem of external world skepticism. Echoing Reid's similar claims about the idea theory, *many* philosophers have claimed that if you accept the sense-data theory you are forced into skepticism. Since we shouldn't be skeptics, by *modus tollens*, we shouldn't be sense-data theorists either. This challenge is the final boss for sense-data proponents. It's time to face it.

---

[98] For examples and discussion see Bennett 1971, Dummett 1979, Hardin 1988, and Johnston 1992.

9. Facing up to the Problem of Skepticism

The challenge of early modern skepticism was to vindicate our beliefs about the external world on the basis of our ideas alone. The modern version of this challenge is to vindicate our beliefs about the external world on the basis of our sense-data alone. Even posing this challenge properly requires something like the sense-data language. If this challenge is, once posed, unanswerable, that is not itself a reason for rejecting sense-data. The sense-data language isn't *creating* the skeptical problem, it is merely *enabling* its clear statement. Avoiding the sense-data language because you fear an unanswerable challenge is the intellectual equivalent of sticking your fingers into your ears and humming.

Many contemporary discussions of skepticism leave the traditional problem completely untouched. They aim instead to show how we can know that the cat is on the mat despite not knowing that we're not dreaming.[99] Or that the burden of proof is on the skeptic, so we can wave our hands, one at a time, and be done.[100] Or that in most contexts, the skeptical scenarios can be appropriately ignored.[101] Or that because of semantic externalism we can't even think the thought that we might be in a skeptical scenario.[102] Or that ordinary knowledge is possible because, given that the external world is as we think it is, our beliefs about cats and hands couldn't easily be mistaken.[103] Or that the nature of belief itself makes accepting a global skeptical position impossible.[104] Or that it seems like an external world exists and this seeming can be taken at face-value.[105] Or... well, you get the point.

With these labors has philosophy at last solved the great skeptical problem? Let's perform a small thought experiment. Suppose we resurrect Descartes and the other early modern giants. Suppose also that we teach them today's English and allow them to study contemporary works on skepticism.

> *Question*: Would they be impressed by the progress we've made on this most difficult of philosophical problems?
> *Answer*: No. *Not at all.*

At least, this is what I think would happen if Descartes and Locke and Berkeley and Hume and friends were faced with the array of options just listed off. It's also what happens to many undergraduate students every year.

---

[99] See Dretske 1970.   [100] See Moore 1939.   [101] See Lewis 1996.
[102] See Putnam 1981.   [103] See Williamson 2000.   [104] See Greco 2012.
[105] See Pryor 2000.

Having been gripped by the skeptical problem, the student is invariably disappointed at the responses. Many of these students are eventually browbeaten into holding their tongues when faced with various types of externalism and a shifting burden of proof, but they never shake the feeling that all of this misses the point. This is a rational response on their part.

I am not saying that all contemporary work on skepticism is worthless. I am not even saying that any of the work mentioned above is worthless. I am merely saying that, even if these works succeed perfectly at their aims, they are not relevant to the traditional problem of skepticism posed by Descartes.[106]

My point isn't merely that the skeptical challenge should be understood in an *internalist* sense rather than an *externalist* sense. There is more to it than that. Most contemporary internalist responses to skepticism don't resolve the real problem either. Let me illustrate this by considering the last view mentioned in the litany above.

Many so-called "internalists" accept something like the following principle about *prima facie* (internalist) justification:[107]

Seeming-to-Justification. If it seems to you that *p*, then you are *prima facie* justified in believing that *p*

This principle is accepted by many direct realists about perception, but sense-data theorists don't need to deny it. The principle has been mooted as a reply to skepticism—it seems to me that there is an external world, so I am *prima facie* justified, even justified in an internalist sense, in believing that there is an external world. Voila.

Fair enough, but this doesn't address the real problem. Our *prima facie* justification can be defeated, and whatever *prima facie* justification "seeming" provides surely *is* defeated when we consider skeptical scenarios. You look out to the world and it seems to you that there is a barn in the field. By the above principle, you are *prima facie* justified in believing that there is a barn in the field. Yet this is actually the famous field of fake barns, built by a

---

[106] We might compare Chalmers's (1995) contrast between the "easy" and "hard" problems of consciousness. I originally used parallel terminology here, but ended up thinking it was more distracting than helpful, though I have kept the Chalmers-inspired section title.

[107] For relevant discussion see (for example) Pryor 2000 and Huemer 2001. There are differences between the positions of Pryor and Huemer, and my discussion here uses Huemer's framing. See Kriegel forthcoming for some relevant critical discussion of Pryor's distinctive approach.

family of philosophers for the epistemological edification of the public. When I tell you this, your epistemic situation changes. Whatever *prima facie* justification you had for your barn-belief is over-ridden. If you continue to form barn-beliefs here on the basis of perceptual seemings, you are making a serious mistake. The same is true even if I lied to you, or if I was wrong about our location. Either way, a possibility of error has been made salient and it must be addressed. Addressing these possibilities of error *is* the problem.

When external world skeptical scenarios are presented we find ourselves in an analogous situation. There are many coherently describable scenarios where I have the very same sensory run I just had but without any external world. Given these possibilities of error, how can my external world beliefs possibly be rational? Without an answer to this sort of question, the real skeptical problem is untouched. This is true even if my *prima facie* justification remains. The skeptical questions highlight the gap between *prima facie* and all-things-considered justification.

When I talk about *external world skepticism* or *the real skeptical problem*, I am talking about the traditional, early modern version of the problem. An acceptable resolution to this problem cannot go beyond the first-person starting point. We have our sense-data and whatever processing and reasoning can be launched from it, *a priori*, virtually nothing else. This isn't meant as a controversial philosophical claim, but instead as something that is obvious once it is pointed out. We face the world looking out from our eyes, not from God's point of view. If someone asks you to back-up your fundamental beliefs in the external world without assuming anything about said external world up-front, you owe them an answer. Descartes has asked us, so we owe him an answer.

At least, you owe an answer *if* the first-person perspective is coherent. If it is not, then the challenge itself is incoherent. The famous ordinary language criticisms of sense-data would have shown this, if successful. My defense of the sense-data language in the first eight sections of the chapter is my reply to their attempt. Yet, the failure of the ordinary language challenge was already obvious even without a detailed defense of sense-data. Mates provides a lovely statement of this point:

> To the complaint that the epistemologists who have introduced the term "sense data" and its various associates have not succeeded in making us aware of what they are talking about, the response is a simple denial. In fact, to complain that a typical sense-datum epistemologist like

G.E. Moore, with his endless explanations…is careless about the use of language is nothing short of preposterous.…Often [the critics of sense-data] tell us authoritatively that "You *can't* say this" and "You *can't* say that," when the this and the that are precisely what large numbers of native speakers *do* say, managing without any difficulty to communicate with one another thereby. Thus, "I can perceive only my own perceptions" may sound linguistically odd at first hearing, and one might be inclined to retort "No, you perceive books and chairs and trees and the sky, but you don't perceive *perceptions*." But after the epistemologist gives all his explanations of the word "perception," the proposition appears as a truism. It's too late then for the Ordinary Language philosopher to tell us, "But you *can't say* 'I am perceiving a perception.'" We *can* say it; we *do* say it; and it seems obviously true.[108]

Indeed. And the quantifier variance analysis of the sense-data language theoretically vindicates this intuitive reply.

The sense-data language is coherent. You understand exactly what is meant when Descartes, Locke, Berkeley, Hume, Russell, Ayer, and I say things like, "You are not ever directly acquainted with ordinary objects, only with sense-data". You understand it and you know that it's true. Trivially and obviously and blamelessly true. From here, we stare into the mouth of the dragon. The problem—the *real* problem—of external world skepticism is now upon us. It is one of the deepest and most disturbing of all philosophical problems. You are free to avoid answering, but don't dare pretend that by ignoring the problem you have *thereby* answered it.

10. Patterns in Experience

A sensory run consists of all of your sense-data over an unbroken temporal interval. All of the sense-data from all of your senses over that interval. You are directly acquainted with this data. Yet there is more going on in your head than just this. The first-person perspective must also allow acquaintance with (at least) emotions and the activities of the will.

It is also important to recognize that direct awareness takes time. We shouldn't think of acts of awareness as being instantaneous. Instead, we should recognize what William James called, following some precursors,

---

[108] Mates 1981: 152–153. See also Mates 1967.

"the specious present".[109] Some early sense-data theorists already recognized the importance of this.[110] It secures the passage of time as something we have direct awareness of, from the inside. Whenever I talk about direct awareness "in a moment" or "at a time", it should be understood in this way.

There is room for debate about exactly what is first-person accessible to consciousness.[111] As an illustrative model, I will limit our first-person access in a moment to the following:

sense-data from all sensory modalities (in full generality this includes data from interior senses too)

emotional states (understood broadly)

activities of the will (including internal willings and inclinations)

temporal awareness (of the specious present and local temporal change)

I tentatively think we can understand imagining, remembering, and all other cognitive phenomenology using only these components in various combinations. Others might prefer to understand willing itself in a sensory or emotional way. Still other variations are possible. Most ways of cutting up this pie would serve for my purposes, provided that *sui generis* states of rational insight or intellectual intuition are *not* included.

I will say that these accessible states of the sensory system, the affective system, and the will (the first three) at a moment of time (the fourth) constitute one's *accessible (or first-person) mental state* at that time. An accessible mental state over an extended interval consists of one's accessible mental states over the moments in the interval. Since the "moments" are not literally instantaneous, we should think of them as overlapping and approximately continuous.

This is all that we have to work with. This and whatever we can get *a priori* from this basis. Nothing else. Of course, when discussing the skeptical problem we usually allow as data your accessible mental state over your entire existence up to the present. This is a simplification. Ultimately, this full history is also something that must be secured *in each moment* on the basis of what you are directly acquainted with in that moment.[112]

---

[109]   In James 1893.
[110]   For example, see Russell 1914b and Broad 1923.
[111]   Thanks to Uriah Kriegel here.
[112]   This point is made in, for example, Rinard 2017. Traditional sense-data epistemologists were well aware of it.

Your accessible mental state, even over your entire life, does not deductively entail the existence of the external world. This was illustrated forcefully by Descartes. Ever since his discussion, nobody has thought otherwise. But in his *Meditations* Descartes himself tried to solve the problem deductively in a more circuitous way, by first proving the existence of God, *a priori*, and then using God to vouchsafe the evidence of the senses. Today, this strategy is unlikely to appeal even to theologians. The problem is simply that, with apologies to Saint Anselm, God's existence cannot be proven *a priori*. The *a priori* cannot turn water into wine; there is no epistemic magic in the world.[113]

In the previous section I galloped over a broad landscape, claiming that much contemporary philosophical work on skepticism is powerless against the real problem. Much, but not all. There is one plausible strategy for solving the real skeptical problem. One and only one. The strategy is to argue that we are *rational* to posit the external world as the *best explanation* of the patterns and regularities in our Cartesian mental states. This broad strategy is known as *abductivism* or the *IBE-strategy*. The phrase "inference to the best explanation" was only invented in the 1960s, but the type of reasoning is much older.[114] The IBE-reply to skepticism, or something like it, was offered, at least implicitly, by many canonical sense-data theorists—Russell, Broad, Ayer, and Jackson, for example.[115]

The IBE-strategy has more recently been both widely advocated and widely criticized.[116] The strategy is often presented in a somewhat confused form, even by proponents. For example, perhaps the most prominent version of the strategy, from Vogel, isn't fully explicit about what is being explained or how. Vogel also appeals to (in my view) implausible principles concerning explanation and necessary truth. A proper version of the IBE-strategy must initially appeal only to facts stated in the sense-data language or some equivalent.

The IBE-strategy refines the simple causal strategy implicit in Locke's *Essay Concerning Human Understanding*. That simple causal approach claims that external objects are the cause of (many of) our ideas. It develops

---

[113] For a theory of the *a priori* without magic, see Warren 2022*b*.

[114] The phrase derives from Harman 1965.

[115] See Russell 1912, Broad 1925, Ayer 1973, and Jackson 1977. Russell and Ayer also endorsed phenomenalism at various respective points, though both later flirted with a broadly IBE-style defense of scientific realism. Ayer later disavowed this understanding of his approach in favor of a more pragmatic interpretation, see Ayer 1992.

[116] See Slote 1970, Mackie 1976, 1982, Cornman 1980, Vogel 1990, Fumerton 1992, BonJour 1999, Neta 2004, Beebe 2009, Gifford 2013, and Rinard 2017.

this thought by holding that our ideas of objects "resemble" the things in the world that they are ideas *of*. But it is unclear how to justify this claim from the first-person on empiricist grounds. If we can only ever perceive our ideas, then we can never break through the "veil of perception".[117] Thus, we might be justified in claiming that two ideas resemble each other, but never in claiming that an idea resembles something in the world. Both Berkeley and Hume savaged Locke's approach, and Hume infamously put causation itself under the empiricist microscope. It also didn't help that Locke never set up his explanatory target carefully or properly.[118]

Probably the best early discussion of this kind of approach is from Hume, though he adopted it only as a descriptive story of *why* we believe in an external world—there is no normative element in his account. Like Locke, Hume often contaminated his discussion of the patterns we are trying to explain by building in information about the external world. Even so, his discussion is impressive and historically important. Here is Bennett commenting on this section of Hume's *Treatise*:

> It is extremely difficult, full of mistakes, and—taken as a whole—a total failure; yet its depth and scope and disciplined complexity make it one of the most instructive arguments in modern philosophy. One philosopher might be judged superior to another because he achieved something of which the other was altogether intellectually incapable. By that criterion Hume surpasses Locke and Berkeley—because, and only because, of this one section.[119]

Hume's treatment was also nicely discussed in a now little-remembered book by Price.[120] I might be the only person to have read this book in the twenty-first century, but it remains worth reading.

Hume focused on the constancy and coherence of our impressions (remember that, for him, "ideas" were fainter copies of impressions). Price cleaned up this approach. Sometimes a sensory run consists of a sequence of sense-data—or, to use Hume's term, *impressions*—over time:

$$E_1, E_2, E_3, E_4, E_5$$

---

[117] This famous phrase was introduced in Bennett 1971: 69.
[118] See the discussion in Bennett 1979.   [119] Bennett 1971: 313.
[120] See Price 1940.

A series like this exhibits constancy just in case each member of the series is qualitatively identical to the next member of the series. Coherence is then defined as a relation between two different series, one with a "gap" and one without:

$A, -, -, -, E$

A, B, C, D, E

The first and last terms of each series are qualitatively identical, and this is what coherence consists in. The sense-data in the first and last positions of two distinct sensory runs can be indistinguishable, even if the middle parts are very different. The Humean idea is that we posit stable "impressions" to account for both constancy and coherence. In this way the imagination projects itself *into* perceptual gaps.

Hume seemed to think it was "impressions" *themselves* that were assumed stable and independent. He even sometimes talks as if the very idea of external, mind-independent objects is a bit of nonsense that philosophers invented to gloss the talk of the vulgar. In this, he—and Berkeley before him—might have been overly focused on mistakes by Locke. Mistakes that they also overstated. Later, Reid savagely mocked this strand in empiricist thought and rightly exposed it as an absurdity. The vulgar themselves posit external, physical objects. The only invention of philosophers is the claim that they don't.

This is one problem with Hume's account, another is that—as already noted—the patterns he spells out are often mischaracterized in his discussion. His examples repeatedly build in or implicitly assume the existence of external objects and so aren't actually patterns *in impressions* at all. As both Bennett and Price note, greater care must be taken for a proper treatment.

The sense-data language allows us to take this greater care. Our accessible mental states exhibit many different patterns and regularities. Using the sense-data language we can talk about these patterns in a very *general* way, over our overall accessible mental states, or in *particular* ways, over a single sense-datum at or over time. Here is a non-exhaustive and schematic list of patterns in our first-person mental states:[121]

---

[121] Two clarificatory points: (*i*) synchronic patterns still have a small amount of temporal structure, due to the specious present being the temporal unit of psychological awareness; (*ii*) if our data consists only of the specious present, then the diachronic patterns will not be directly given, but rather inferred in the same way as the external world.

(1) synchronic structure in the sense-data of each sensory modality—visual experience (for example) is not a random flux or even a kaleidoscope, as I look at the room right now there are clusters and regularities even in the moment

(2) synchronic regularities connecting the sense-data of different sensory modalities—when I have the visual sense-datum of seeing-fingers-snapping, I also have the tactile sense-datum of feeling-fingers-snapping, and the aural sense-datum of hearing-fingers-snapping

(3) diachronic structure in the sense-data of each sensory modality—examples include but aren't limited to Hume's constancy and coherence

(4) diachronic regularities connecting the sense-data of different sensory modalities—when playing the piano over an interval, visual, tactile, and auditory sense-data co-occur in regular and repeated ways

(5) correlations between willing and sense-data in each sensory modality—I can imagine a pink elephant, I can also, less directly, make a sensory run repeat but in reverse order, by walking back into the room, turning my head from side to side, or the like

(6) correlations between sense-data and emotional states—when I have a sense-datum of a seeming-hammer-hitting-my-thumb, an emotional state of extreme pain and distress immediately follows

This list is neither exhaustive nor extremely detailed, but even at this level of description the point is powerful. There are *striking* patterns *over* sense-data both synchronically and diachronically, as well as *striking* patterns *across* the different components of our accessible mental states. Our subjective experience of the world is extremely structured and well-patterned.

The sense-data language enables us to describe and theorize about all of these patterns in the most general way. If you don't have the sense-data language, or something expressively equivalent, you might be able to talk about some of the patterns, but not all of them. Merely saying that you seem to see a brown chair suggests that there is a type-(1) pattern. If you seem to see a brown chair over an interval of time, you can even capture some type-(3) patterns. Yet I would also seem to see a brown chair over an interval of time if my vision was cycling between distinct brown chairs at one-second intervals. The actual patterns to be explained are difficult to capture at this level of description, perhaps impossible.

It is also difficult to capture type-(5) patterns with this way of talking. I seem to see a brown chair, I close my eyes, I seem to see a brown chair again. I seem to see a brown chair, I walk out of the room, and I seem to see a brown chair again, with an experience that is roughly reversed. The general difficulty is that seeing to see an F is too coarse-grained. Seeming to see an F is compatible with a great many distinct subjective experiences. Many of these are not similar to each other in a qualitative sense. In order to pick out the crucial patterns, you will need to introduce more and more complex descriptions—seeing a brown chair from the side at twenty paces in neon lighting with a head angle of twenty degrees. Complexities of this kind can be added almost without end, but at a high price. If this approach can reach expressive parity with the sense-data language at all, it does so at the cost of extreme unnaturalness.

In stark contrast, the sense-data language makes the statement and description of these patterns both natural and easy at every level of granularity. There is no better or more flexible way to talk about experience than with the sense-data language. But, of course, the patterns are there whether we use the sense-data language or not. We did not make them with language, *we* did not make them at all. The sense-data language allows us to talk and reason and refer to and generalize about these empirical patterns.

Once we have identified these patterns, we see that they call out for an explanation. The best explanation of them is that there is an independent external world that causally impacts upon us in regular ways. This is the answer to external world skepticism. I have stated it baldly, but still, it is the answer. Let me explain.

11. Explaining the Patterns

There are patterns in our first-person mental states, patterns we can access and identify from the inside. I have said that these patterns call out for an explanation, but why is that?

We could simply take it as an *a priori* principle that certain striking facts need to be explained. Yet something more systematic can also be said. Think of all of the possible qualitative experiences you could be having in a moment or over an interval. To limit the scope of things, let's focus just on vision. Most of the possible arrays of visual sense-data that you could be experiencing at any given moment are utterly incoherent to you. They don't even have the structure of a kaleidoscope experience, let alone the structure of ordinary visual experiences.

The number of possibilities here is—*at least*—finite but astonishingly large, even in a single interval of awareness.[122] This is most obvious for vision, but something similar holds for the array of sense-data that could potentially be delivered by *any* of our senses. Mixing and matching these possibilities gives the number of possible overall sensory states, both at a time and over time. The numbers are truly astronomical. Now add in the states of the will and the emotions, and you have a staggeringly, extra-astronomically large finite number of possible states of conscious experience.

The number of such states is certainly much larger than one billion. But to cleanly illustrate the point, suppose there are a mere one billion distinct overall experiences you could be having in a single second. Let's also suppose that your accessible states develop discretely over time. In reality, development over time is much messier, likely leading to even more possibilities. Since these states are *logically* independent of each other, the number of possible experiential runs over ten seconds of time is:

$$1,000,000,000^{10}$$

If written out in full decimal notation this would be a one followed by *ninety* zeroes. It's almost a googol (not really, but you know what I mean). Remember that this is over only *ten seconds*, and remember too that this estimate drastically understates the actual number of possible experiences even over this brief interval.

Out of this vast number of possible experiences only a very small fraction exhibit any of the regularities mentioned in the previous section. If sensory runs of 10 seconds in duration were chosen at random out of all possible experiences, it would be very, very unlikely that the chosen runs would exhibit any regularities of the kinds mentioned in section 10, let alone all of them. This combinatorial point gives bite to the idea that regularities in experience are unexpected—they have a very, very low *a priori* prior probability.[123]

---

[122] The sense of "possibility" at issue here is largely *a priori*, nothing about the physical workings of the sensory system is being assumed. In fact, nothing about *physics* is being assumed, at all.

[123] My discussion here largely dovetails with the Huemer's (2016) discussion of the brain-in a vat case. Huemer isn't advocating an abductivist reply, but his appeal to *a priori* probability is, I think, in line with abductivism.

This reasoning assumes that each *a priori* possibility should be treated on a par. This can be supported by some kind of general symmetry principle for *a priori* probability. The most famous of these is the infamous principle of indifference. According to indifference, absent any evidence to act as a symmetry breaker, it is rational to assign equal probability over the cells in a partition of possible outcomes, even *a priori*. Incautious formulations of indifference risk inconsistency, but there are many proposals for avoiding these troubles.

The very idea of *a priori* rationality constraints on belief and degrees of belief *sounds* controversial. As a matter of descriptive fact, it *is* controversial. Yet it shouldn't be. If *a priori* rationality constraints are not accepted, then there is no difference between rationality and irrationality.[124]

Of course, to fully vindicate either IBE or *a priori* probability principles from the first-person starting point requires solving Hume's problem of induction. I hope readers will forgive me for not trying to do that here. Instead, I will briefly explain one shape that Hume's challenge takes in this particular context, and why I think it can be answered.[125]

Suppose that I win the lottery by playing my birthday numbers. I might think that the connection between my birthdate and the winning number requires some special explanation. I might think that, but I'd be wrong. There is no explanatory hole left if we take this alignment as a brute coincidence. The feeling to the contrary is an illusion. We all agree about this. The inductive skeptic thinks the idea that the patterns in experience are unlikely and so need to be explained is also an illusion.

Some proportion out of all possible sensory runs are patterned. And any other collection of experiences of the same size is just as probable, *a priori*.[126] But then *whatever* particular experiences we have, patterned or not, we can engage in analogous reasoning. Suppose we have apparently random experiences over a time, where a multicolored quasi-patch forms and instantly vanishes in the upper left of the field of vision. Call this a property *MC*, of experiences. The Humean says that *MC* is just as unlikely *a priori* as

---

[124] An early statement of (a version of) this point is in Putnam 1971: 66–68.

[125] See chapter 1 of Ayer 1972 for a relevant, modern defense of Hume. Obviously, the "new riddle of induction" from Goodman 1946, 1955 is also relevant here. See the essays and annotated bibliography in Stalker 1994 for a comprehensive overview of the first fifty years of work on this problem. My own attempt to solve the new riddle is in Warren 2023.

[126] The notion of "size" can't be understood simply, in terms of cardinality, except in the finite case. Handling probability over infinite outcome spaces will require more subtlety and discrimination in our notion of "proportion". This is a problem for everybody though, not a problem specific to my approach.

the richer patterns discussed in the previous section. This Humean further claims that the same points also go for *any* collection of possible experiences, and any features an experience might have. The idea that patterned experiences are especially unexpected and call out for an explanation is—this skeptic claims—an illusion.

The Humean's reasoning is tempting, but it is fallacious. No less a luminary than Doctor Manhattan once succumbed to a similar fallacy. On Mars, the good Doctor said to Laurie:

> Thermodynamic miracles...[*sic*] events with odds against so astronomical they're effectively impossible, like oxygen spontaneously becoming gold. I long to observe such a thing. And yet, in each human coupling, a thousand million sperm vie for a single egg. Multiply those odds by countless generations, against the odds of your ancestors being alive; meeting; siring this precise son; that exact daughter...[*sic*] Until your mother loves a man...and of that union, of the thousand million children competing for fertilization, it was you, only you, that emerged. To distill so specific a form from that chaos of improbability, like turning air to gold...[*sic*] That is the crowning unlikelihood. The thermodynamic miracle.[127]

Despite nigh-omniscience, Doctor Manhattan is mistaken. There is a sense in which Laurie's existence is unlikely. As was mine, as was yours. It was extremely improbable for *you* to come into being. Yet this particular improbability can only be specified *post hoc*. That is, it is entirely *backwards*-looking. Backwards-looking both at the level of individual coupling and at the level of generation-to-generation transitions. It is true that the particular sperm-egg combination that resulted in your existence was exceedingly unlikely, but that doesn't make your existence miraculous.

Some person was almost certain to result from repeated couplings. *Some ticket* was almost certain to win the lottery given repeated drawings. Be careful about the order of the quantifiers here—in many nearby possible worlds, your parents created a different child, in many nearby possible worlds, a different winning number was drawn. There are no *post hoc* miracles. If a chance process has *n* possible outcomes, for a large *n*, each particular outcome can be astronomically unlikely. Yet the chance process itself might be such that one of these outcomes will almost certainly occur. In this

---

[127] Quoted from Gibbons and Moore 1987. The fallacy I highlight has no standard name, but it is dubbed "the error of *retrospective specification*" by Berlinksi (1986: 294).

kind of case, it is fallacious to claim *after the fact* that a miracle has occurred. Otherwise, we could be certain in advance that no matter what happens, a miracle will have occurred. This kind of supposed miraculousness is an illusion.

Yet the miraculousness of the patterns in our experiences is not of this kind. It can instead be specified while looking forward. The continuities in this moment of experience are not expected just because some experience must be occurring. And the continuities between the future and the past are not expected given simply that *some* experience will be had in the next second, over the next ten seconds, or over the next year. There is a real difference between the patterns that call out for an explanation and the "patterns" that do not. The inductive skeptics (and Doctor Manhattan) are wrong here. They are treating distinct epistemic situations as if they were alike.

The patterns in our accessible mental states demand an explanation. The external world hypothesis provides an explanation. It makes the patterns expected with a theory that has all of the explanatory virtues we seek.[128] The external world hypothesis is, far and away, the *best explanation* of the patterns in our first-person mental states. In fact, it does not have a close rival, so it is rational to accept the hypothesis. More than that, rationality *demands* that we accept the external world hypothesis. This argument can be developed in several different ways. One way is to construe IBE as a rule of inference, and to use as premises the claims that the external world theory meets the conditions for an IBE-inference. Given our empirical evidence, in the form of sense-data and our accessible mental states, it is then rational to infer the existence of the external world by inference to the best explanation.[129]

In a full treatment we would need to distinguish between many distinct external world hypotheses and treat them all separately, appealing to different patterns in our first-person mental states in each case. Without going through each case here, let me simply claim that IBE-reasoning can

---

[128] In terms of probability, this means that the external world hypothesis has a high *a priori* probability and the patterns in experience have a high *a priori* likelihood conditional on the external world hypothesis. For this to work, we might need to understand laws in a non-Humean fashion.

[129] Among these conditions: that the external world explanation is sufficiently good and that no other explanation meets this threshold, among other things. For important discussion, see Lipton 1991. Another option is to try to fit IBE reasoning into a Bayesian framework. There are some arguments that this is impossible—see Van Fraassen 1989 and Roche and Sober 2013—but there are also interesting responses—see Okasha 2000, Lipton 2001, Huemer 2009, and Weisberg 2009. The connection between IBE and Bayesianism is an important topic in epistemology, but I won't go into detail here (though see the previous footnote).

support, from the armchair, at least the following distinct external world hypotheses:

INDEPENDENCE. There is an external world that is largely independent of me. It does not depend on me for its existence or general nature.

STABILITY. The objects in the external world and their features are fairly but not perfectly stable over small intervals of time.

UNIFORMITY. The objects in the external world and their features are fairly but not perfectly uniform across the observed and unobserved portions of the world.

TRACKING. The features of the external world are imperfectly tracked by my sensory system.

BODY. My body is a part of this external world, housing my sensory system and manipulating the body-external environment in a limited way.

BASE. The external world is the base world, in that there is no distinct world in which the world we know through experience is embedded.

If I'm right about all of this, then a sequence of inferences to the best explanation will allow us to rationally believe in an external world that has roughly the features we now take it to have. A world that is not dependent on the mind or the will. A world that isn't a dream or a hallucination or a simulation.[130]

This reasoning doesn't establish any esoteric *metaphysical* claims about the precise nature of the external world. Nor does it defeat *a posteriori* skeptical challenges like Bostrom's simulation argument.[131] Instead, it answers the traditional skeptical problem and shows us why we should not be solipsists or phenomenalists. We should be realists about the physical world, and should carefully build our overall theory of this external world step by cautious step, ever mindful of the connection between our theories of this reality and the direct evidence provided by our sense-data.

Even very deep into this process unexpected results continue to show up. Here is one small example. Scientific investigation of vision revealed the existence of the blind spot. I don't know about you, but I first learned about

---

[130] In addition to being backed by radically different arguments, this goes beyond the "structuralist" reply to skepticism from Chalmers 2018. This can be seen by considering skeptical scenarios that aren't ruled out by a structuralist reply; see Berry 2019 for discussion.

[131] From Bostrom 2003, though Bostrom actually only argues for a disjunctive conclusion containing the simulation hypothesis as a disjunct.

the blind spots in my eyes by reading about them. I was then able to do self-experiments demonstrating their existence, making little black dots on a page disappear. We have here a case where a pattern in sense-data that does *not* make sense in terms of the existence of the external world, in the normal way, is nonetheless predicated and explained by the external world hypothesis at a suitable stage of its development. In this and a million other ways, patterns in sense-data rationally support more and more refined and expansive external world hypotheses. This is the solution to the real challenge of external world skepticism.

12. A Plea for Analytic Empiricism

I have argued for a number of related claims. That the early modern starting point—including the crucial sense-data component—is coherent (sections 1–4). That we can adopt a sense-data language when thinking and talking about our experiences and our relation to the world, and we can do so in a way that vindicates the traditional claims of sense-data theories (sections 5–6). That the basic sense-data language is preferable for talking about our experiences because of its expressive power (section 7). That, with a sense-data language adopted, plausible theories of perception and color can be developed (section 8). That the sense-data language is the only honest way to face the real skeptical challenge (section 9) and the challenge can actually be met without any cheating (sections 10–11).

The early modern project is not the *only* interesting project in philosophy, nor even the *only* interesting project in epistemology. Yet it *is* interesting, even gripping. History proves that. So does each round of introductory philosophy classes the world over. And the Cartesian skeptical problem, the real skeptical problem, is one of the most disturbing and difficult problems in the entire intellectual landscape.

We can adopt the sense-data language. We can and we should. In fact, in a sense, we *must*. The first-person perspective is forced. We all face the world from the first-person perspective. It is not optional. The early modern epistemological problems are, for this reason, the pure epistemological problems. None of us have direct acquaintance with trees, travelers, and trebuchets. When a philosopher insists that so-called "direct" realism undermines this they have been blinded. Blinded either by philosophical theory or by a fear of skepticism, but blinded all the same. Against these philosophers, the canonical early modern philosophers were right. Not only that, they were *obviously* right. Quantifier variance helps us to clearly understand this.

Sense-data is our only input from the world. It's all that we have, all that we ever will have, and all that we ever could have. The "veil of perception" can be overstated and misunderstood. You might falsely say that the veil is opaque. It is not. It is transparent, but it exists all the same. Our direct acquaintance with sense-data is the epistemological foundation on which we build our overall theory of the world. There is an ongoing, iterated feedback process between data and theory, but *epistemologically* speaking, sense-data are foundational.

This is not to say that sense-data are *metaphysically* foundational. I am no phenomenalist. Phenomenalist theories are inferior to external world theories, explanatorily speaking. Likewise for idealist theories.[132] My point is *epistemological*. I am advocating for *epistemological empiricism*. It is important to realize that my traditional, first-person empiricism differs from what is called "empiricism" in contemporary philosophy. Today's "empiricists" often use a notion of *observable* consequences that is not the first-person, sense-data-based notion.[133] For these philosophers, an observation sentence can be something like "the cat is on the mat".[134] For me, observation sentences are basic experience claims in the sense-data language.

Accepting the sense-data language is part of being a traditional empiricist, but not the whole. Descartes and other rationalists were (in modern terms) sense-data theorists, but they weren't empiricists. This is because they also allowed a substantive role for rational intuitions that sits ill with empiricism. With this, they tried to take armchair reasoning to places that armchair reasoning simply cannot go.[135] For an epistemological empiricist, our sensory states deliver information about reality, but no other mental states do anything similar. There are no rational intuitions through which we gain non-experiential information about any independent world of fact. We have only the sensory data of experience, along with *a priori*, analytic resources with which to build from experience. This

---

[132] Though there comes a point at which versions of so-called "objective" idealism only differ verbally from non-idealist theories. For IBE-style arguments against Berkeley's *theistic* idealism, see Mackie 1982.

[133] See Van Fraassen 1980 for a prominent example. Though the historical and sociological roots of this alternate usage come from the immense and deserved influence of Reid and Quine, respectively.

[134] This divide also corresponds to an internal debate among the logical positivists over "protocol sentences". See Coffa 1991 for discussion.

[135] See section 4 of Warren 2022b for criticisms of rationalism.

sounds meager, but over a century of analytic philosophy has left us with a wide range of tools.

I call this position *analytic empiricism*. I prefer this name to "logical positivism" or "logical empiricism", for two reasons. First, I want to distance myself from strict verificationism, phenomenalism, and the other more questionable doctrines of the Vienna Circle.[136] Second, our analytical tools are not all "logical", so I prefer the broader term. And I prefer "analytic empiricism" to "analytical empiricism", because it is now more common to talk of "analytic philosophy" than "analytical philosophy".

Analytic empiricism is an attempt to complete the traditional empiricist project by using all of the tools and resources of contemporary analytic philosophy that are compatible with empiricism. It is a modern form of traditional British empiricism in the line of Locke, Berkeley, Hume, Mill, Russell, and Ayer. The central plank of analytic empiricism is an adherence to epistemological empiricism as embodied in and limited to the sense-data framework. This chapter has been an extended defense of this plank.

From this slender foundation our theory of overall reality must be built. Science, mathematics, ethics, aesthetics, and everything else must fit into this framework or be abandoned. Though long thought dead, traditional empiricism yet lives. In fact, it is in good health. Analytic empiricism represents our last best hope for completing the philosophical project started by the great early modern philosophers. We must build a theory of the world from the data of experience. A theory that can ultimately explain the very existence of sense-data accessing creatures like us. In the end, the snake of philosophy must eat its own tail.[137]

References

Armstrong, D.M. 1968. *A Materialist Theory of Mind*. London: Routledge and Kegan Paul.

[136] The term "logical empiricism" gained prominence via Feigl 1943. Sometimes the phrase is associated with the Berlin branch of logical positivism; see Uebel 2013 for some relevant discussion.

[137] Thanks to Darren Bradley, Justin D'Ambrosio, Matti Eklund, Yu Guo, Eli Hirsch, Uriah Kriegel, Penelope Maddy, and Douglas Stalker. I also want to give special thanks to four dead sense-data theorists: A.J. Ayer, John Mackie, Benson Mates, and Bertrand Russell. I've learned much from all of them, and not just about sense-data. And Ayer and Russell have inspired me since my teenage years. Ayer published 20 books and I have read them all. And though I have read more than 20 books by Russell, I haven't come close to exhausting his catalog. Thank you both, thank you all; I will try to make you proud.

Austin, J.L. 1962. *Sense and Sensibilia*. Oxford: Oxford University Press.

Ayer, A.J. 1940. *The Foundations of Empirical Knowledge*. London: Macmillan.

Ayer, A.J. 1945. "The Terminology of Sense-Data." *Mind* 54(216): 289–312.

Ayer, A.J. 1954. "Can There Be a Private Language?" *Proceedings of the Aristotelian Society, Supplementary* 28: 63–76.

Ayer, A.J. 1956. *The Problem of Knowledge*. London: Macmillan.

Ayer, A.J. 1967. "Has Austin Refuted the Sense-Datum Theory?" *Synthese* 17(2): 117–140.

Ayer, A.J. 1968. *The Origins of Pragmatism*. San Francisco: Freeman, Cooper, & Company.

Ayer, A.J. 1969. *Metaphysics and Common Sense*. London: Macmillan.

Ayer, A.J. 1972. *Probability & Evidence*. New York: Columbia University Press.

Ayer, A.J. 1973. *The Central Questions of Philosophy*. London: Weidenfeld.

Ayer, A.J. 1985. *Wittgenstein*. New York: Random House.

Ayer, A.J. 1992. "Reply to John Fostor." In Lewis Edwin Hahn (ed.), *The Philosophy of A.J. Ayer*. La Salle: Open Court: 198–200.

Beebe, James R. 2009. "The Abductivist Reply to Skepticism." *Philosophy and Phenomenological Research* 79(3): 605–636.

Bennett, Jonathan. 1966. *Kant's Analytic*. Cambridge: Cambridge University Press.

Bennett, Jonathan. 1971. *Locke, Berkeley, Hume: Central Themes*. Oxford: Oxford University Press.

Bennett, Jonathan. 1979. "Analytic Transcendental Arguments." In P. Bieri et al. (eds), *Transcendental Arguments and Science*. Dordrecht: Reidel: 45–64.

Berkeley, George. 2008. *Philosophical Writings* (Desmond M. Clarke, ed.). Cambridge: Cambridge University Press.

Berlinski, David. 1986. *Black Mischief: The Mechanics of Modern Science*. New York: William and Morrow.

Berry, Sharon. 2019. "External World Skepticism, Confidence and Psychologism about the Problem of Priors." *Southern Journal of Philosophy* 57(3): 324–346.

Block, Ned. 1995. "On a Confusion About a Function of Consciousness." *Behavioral and Brain Sciences* 18(2): 227–247.

BonJour, Laurence. 1999. "Foundationalism and the External World." *Philosophical Perspectives* 13: 229–249.

Bostrom, Nick. 2003. "Are You Living in a Computer Simulation?" *Philosophical Quarterly* 53(211): 243–255.

Broad, C.D. 1923. *Scientific Thought*. London: Routledge & Kegan Paul.

Broad, C.D. 1925. *The Mind and Its Place in Nature*. London: Routledge & Kegan Paul.

Burge, Tyler. 1979. "Individualism and the Mental." *Midwest Studies in Philosophy* 4(1): 73–122.

Burnyeat, Miles F. 1982. "Idealism and Greek Philosophy: What Descartes Saw and Berkeley Missed." *Philosophical Review* 91(1): 3–40.

Cao, Rosa and Jared Warren. forthcoming. "Mental Representation, 'Standing-In-For,' and Internal Models." *Philosophical Psychology*.

Carnap, Rudolf. 1928. *Der Logische Aufbau der Welt*. Berlin: Weltkreis.

Carnap, Rudolf. 1950. "Empiricism, Semantics, and Ontology." *Revue Internationale de Philosophie* 4(11): 20–40.

Casullo, Albert. 1987. "A Defense of Sense-Data." *Philosophy and Phenomenological Research* 48(1): 45–61.

Chalmers, David J. 1995. "Facing up to the Problem of Consciousness." *Journal of Consciousness Studies* 2: 200–219.

Chalmers, David J. 2018. "Structuralism as a Response to Skepticism." *Journal of Philosophy* 115(12): 625–660.

Chisholm, Rodrick. 1942. "The Problem of the Speckled Hen." *Mind* 51(204): 368–373.

Chisholm, Rodrick. 1957. *Perceiving: A Philosophical Study*. Ithaca: Cornell University Press.

Chomsky, Noam. 1965. *Aspects of the Theory of Syntax*. Cambridge: MIT Press.

Coffa, J. Alberto. 1991. *The Semantic Tradition from Kant to Carnap: To the Vienna Station*. Cambridge: Cambridge University Press.

Cornman, James W. 1980. *Skepticism, Justification, and Explanation*. Dordrecht: Reidel.

D'Ambrosio, Justin. 2019. "A New Perceptual Adverbialism." *Journal of Philosophy* 116(8): 413–446.

D'Ambrosio, Justin. 2022. "An Empirical Solution to the Puzzle of Macbeth's Dagger." *Erkenntnis* 87(3): 1377–1414.

Davidson, Donald. 1973. "Radical Interpretation." *Dialectica* 27(3–4): 313–328.

Dennett, Daniel C. 1991. *Consciousness Explained*. New York: Back Bay Books.

Dinges, Alexander. 2015. "The Many-Relations Problem for Adverbialism." *Analysis* 75(2): 231–237.

Dorr, Cian. 2005. "What We Disagree about When We Disagree about Ontology." In Mark Eli Kalderon (ed.), *Fictionalism in Metaphysics*. Oxford: Oxford University Press: 234–286.

Dorr, Cian. 2014. "Quantifier Variance and the Collapse Theorems." *The Monist* 97: 503–570.

Dretske, Fred. 1970. "Epistemic Operators." *Journal of Philosophy* 67(24): 1007–1023.

Dummett, Michael. 1956. "Nominalism." *Philosophical Review* 65(4): 491–505.

Dummett, Michael. 1979. "Common Sense and Physics." In Macdonald (ed.), *Perception and Identity*. London: Macmillan.

Eklund, Matti. 2006. "Neo-Fregean Ontology." *Philosophical Perspectives* 20: 95–121.

Eklund, Matti. 2009. "Carnap and Ontological Pluralism." In *Metametaphysics: New Essays on the Foundations of Ontology*. Oxford: Oxford University Press: 130–156.

Feigl, Herbet. 1943. "Logical Empiricism." in D.D. Runes (ed.), *Twentieth Century Philosophy*. New York: Philosophical Library: 371–416.

Field, Hartry. 1984. "Is Mathematical Knowledge Just Logical Knowledge?" *Philosophical Review* 93(4): 509–552.

Filcheva, Krasimira. 2023. "Can There Be a Feature-Placing Language?" *European Journal of Philosophy* 31(3): 655–672.

Fine, Kit. 2005. "Our Knowledge of Mathematical Objects." In Tamar Szabó Gendler and John Hawthorne (eds), *Oxford Studies in Epistemology* 1. Oxford: Oxford University Press: 89–110.

van Fraassen, Bas C. 1980. *The Scientific Image*. Oxford: Clarendon Press.

van Fraassen, Bas C. 1989. *Laws and Symmetry*. Oxford: Clarendon Press.

Fumerton, Richard. 1985. *Metaphysical and Epistemological Problems of Perception*. Lincoln: University of Nebraska Press.

Fumerton, Richard. 1992. "Skepticism and Reasoning to the Best Explanation." *Philosophical Issues* 2: 149–169.

Gibbons, Dave and Alan Moore. 1987. *Watchmen*. Number IX, May 1987. DC Comics.

Gifford, Matthew B. 2013. "Skepticism and Elegance: Problems for the Abductivist Reply to Cartesian Skepticism." *Philosophical Studies* 164: 685–704.

Goodman, Nelson. 1946. "A Query on Confirmation." *Journal of Philosophy* 43: 383–385.

Goodman, Nelson. 1951. *The Structure of Appearance*. Cambridge: Harvard University Press.

Goodman, Nelson. 1955. *Fact, Fiction, and Forecast*. Cambridge: Harvard University Press.

Greco, Daniel. 2012. "The Impossibility of Skepticism." *Philosophical Review* 121(3): 317–358.

Grice, H.P. and P.F. Strawson. 1956. "In Defense of a Dogma." *Philosophical Review* 65(2): 141–158.

Hale, Bob. 1987. *Abstract Objects*. Oxford: Blackwell.

Hale, Bob. 2007. "Neo-Fregeanism and Quantifier Variance." *Proceedings of the Aristotelian Society New Series* 107: 375–385.

Hale, Bob and Crispin Wright. 2001. *The Reasons Proper Study: Essays Towards a Neo-Fregean Philosophy of Mathematics*. Oxford: Clarendon Press.

Hardin, C.L. 1988. *Color for Philosophers: Unweaving the Rainbow*. Indianapolis: Hackett.

Harman, Gilbert H. 1965. "The Inference to the Best Explanation." *Philosophical Review* 74(1): 88–95.

Hawley, Katherine. 2007. "Neo-Fregeanism and Quantifier Variance." *Proceedings of the Aristotelian Society Supplemental* 81: 233–49.

Hawthorne, John. 2006. "Plenitude, Convention, and Ontology." In *Metaphysical Essays*. Oxford: Oxford University Press: 53–69.

Hawthorne, John. 2009. "Superficialism in Ontology." In *Metametaphysics: New Essays on the Foundations of Ontology*. Oxford: Oxford University Press: 213–230.

Hirsch, Eli. 2002. "Quantifier Variance and Realism." *Philosophical Issues* 12: 51–73.

Hirsch, Eli. 2011. *Quantifier Variance and Realism: Essays in Metaontology*. New York: Oxford University Press.

Hirsch, Eli and Jared Warren. 2019*a*. "Quantifier Variance." In Martin Kusch (ed.), *Routledge Handbook of Philosophy of Relativism*. New York: Routledge: 349–357.

Hirsch, Eli and Jared Warren. 2019*b*. "Quantifier Variance and the Demand for a Semantics." *Philosophy and Phenomenological Research* 98(3): 592–605.

Huemer, Michael. 2001. *Skepticism and the Veil of Perception*. Lanham: Rowman & Littlefield.

Huemer, Michael. 2009. "Explanationist Aid for the Theory of Inductive Logic." *British Journal for the Philosophy of Science* 60: 345–375.

Huemer, Michael. 2016. "Serious Theories and Skeptical Theories: Why You Are Probably Not a Brain in a Vat." *Philosophical Studies* 173(4): 1031–1052.

van Inwagen, Peter. 1990. *Material Beings*. Ithaca: Cornell University Press.

Jackson, Frank. 1975. "On the Adverbial Analysis of Visual Experience." *Metaphilosophy* 6(2): 127–135.

Jackson, Frank. 1977. *Perception: A Representative Theory*. Cambridge: Cambridge University Press.

James, William. 1893. *The Principles of Psychology*. New York: H. Hold and Company.

Johnston, Mark. 1992. "How to Speak of the Colors." *Philosophical Studies* 68(3): 221–263.

Kriegel, Uriah. Forthcoming. "Knowledge-by-Acquiantance First." *Philosophy and Phenomenological Research*.

Lewis, David K. 1974. "Radical Interpretation." *Synthese* 27(3–4): 331–344.

Lewis, David K. 1996. "Elusive Knowledge." *Australasian Journal of Philosophy* 74(4): 549–567.

Linsky, Bernard. 2014. "Ernst Mally's Anticipation of Encoding." *Journal for the History of Analytical Philosophy* 2(5): 1–14.

Lipton, Peter. 1991. *Inference to the Best Explanation*. New York: Routledge.

Lipton, Peter. 2001. "Is Explanation a Guide to Inference? A Reply to Wesley C. Salmon." In G. Hon and S.S. Rakover (eds), *Explanation: Theoretical Approaches and Applications*. Kluwer: 93–120.

Mackie, J.L. 1976. *Problems from Locke*. Oxford: Oxford University Press.

Mackie, J.L. 1982. *The Miracle of Theism: Arguments For and Against the Existence of God*. New York: Oxford University Press.

Maddy, Penelope. 2017. *What Do Philosophers Do? Skepticism and the Practice of Philosophy*. Oxford: Oxford University Press.

Martin, M.G.F. 2002. "The Transparency of Experience." *Mind and Language* 17: 376–425.

Mates, Benson. 1967. "Sense Data." *Inquiry* 10(1–4): 225–244.

Mates, Benson. 1981. *Skeptical Essays*. Chicago: University of Chicago Press.

McDowell, John. 1982. "Criteria, Defeasibility and Knowledge." *Proceedings of the British Academy* 68: 455–479.

McGinn, Colin. 1999. *The Mysterious Flame: Conscious Minds in a Material World*. New York: Basic Books.

Moore, G.E. 1909–10. "The Subject-Matter of Psychology." *Proceedings of the Aristotelian Society* 10: 36–62.

Moore, G.E. 1913–14. "The Status of Sense-Data." *Proceedings of the Aristotelian Society* 14: 355–380.

Moore, G.E. 1918–19. "The Presidential Address: Some Judgments of Perception." *Proceedings of the Aristotelian Society* 19: 1–29.

Moore, G.E. 1939. "Proof of an External World." *Proceedings of the British Academy* 25(5): 273–300.

Neta, Ram. 2004. "Skepticism, Abductivism, and the Explanatory Gap." *Philosophical Issues* 14: 296–325.

Okasha, Samir. 2000. "Van Fraassen's Critique of Inference to the Best Explanation." *Studies in the History and Philosophy of Science* 31: 691–710.

Paul, G.A. 1936. "Is There a Problem about Sense-Data?" *Proceedings of the Aristotelian Society, Supplementary* 15: 61–77.

Peacocke, Christopher. 1983. *Sense and Content: Experience, Thought, and their Relations*. Oxford: Oxford University Press.

Price, H.H. 1932. *Perception*. London: Methuen.

Price, H.H. 1940. *Hume's Theory of the External World*. Oxford: Clarendon Press.

Price, H.H. 1941. "Review of Ayer's *The Foundations of Empirical Knowledge*." *Mind* 50: 273–293.

Pryor, James. 2000. "The Skeptic and the Dogmatist." *Noûs* 34(4): 517–549.

Putnam, Hilary. 1971. *Philosophy of Logic*. London: Allen & Unwin.

Putnam, Hilary. 1981. *Reason, Truth and History*. Cambridge: Cambridge University Press.

Putnam, Hilary. 1983. "Equivalence." In *Realism and Reason: Philosophical Papers Volume 3*. Cambridge: Cambridge University Press: 26–45.

Putnam, Hilary. 1987. "Truth and Convention: On Davidson's Refutation of Conceptual Relativism." *Dialectica* 41(1–2): 69–77.

Putnam, Hilary. 2004. *Ethics Without Ontology*. Cambridge: Harvard University Press.

Quine, W.V. 1948. "On What There Is." *Review of Metaphysics* 2(5): 21–38.

Quine, W.V. 1951. "Two Dogmas of Empiricism." *Philosophical Review* 60(1): 20–43.

Quine. W.V. 1957–58. "Speaking of Objects." *Proceedings and Addresses of the American Philosophical Association* 31: 5–22.

Quine, W.V. 1960*a*. *Word and Object*. Cambridge: MIT Press.

Quine, W.V. 1960*b*. "Variables Explained Away." *Proceedings of the American Philosophical Society* 104(3): 343–347.

Reid, Thomas. 1983. *Inquiry and Essays* (Beanblossom and Lehrer, eds). Indianapolis: Hackett.

Rinard, Susanna. 2017. "Skepticism and Inference to the Best Explanation." In McCain and Poston (eds), *Best Explanations*. Oxford: Oxford University Press: 203–215.

Robinson, Howard. 1994. *Perception*. New York: Routledge.

Roche, William and Elliot Sober. 2013. "Explanation is Evidentially Irrelevant; or, Inference to the Best Explanation Meets Bayesian Confirmation Theory." *Analysis* 73: 659–668.

Russell, Bertrand. 1912. *The Problems of Philosophy*. London: Williams and Norgate.

Russell, Bertrand. 1914*a*. "The Relation of Sense-Data to Physics." *Scientia* 16: 1–27.

Russell, Bertrand. 1914*b*. *Our Knowledge of the External World*. Chicago: Open Court.

Russell, Bertrand. 1927. *The Analysis of Matter*. New York: Harcourt, Brace.

Russell, Bertrand. 1940. *An Inquiry into Meaning and Truth*. London: George Allen & Unwin, Ltd.

Russell, Bertrand. 1959. *My Philosophical Development*. New York: Simon and Schuster.

Ryle, Gilbert. 1954. *Dilemmas*. Cambridge: Cambridge University Press.

Schiffer, Stephen. 1996. "Language-created Language-independent Entities." *Philosophical Topics* 24(1): 149–167.

Schiffer, Stephen. 2003. *The Things We Mean*. Oxford: Oxford University Press.

Searle, John. 2015. *Seeing Things as They Are: A Theory of Perception*. Oxford: Oxford University Press.

Sellars, Wilfrid. 1975. "The Adverbial Theory of the Objects of Sensation." *Metaphilosophy* 6: 144–160.

Sellars, Wilfrid. 1997. *Empiricism and the Philosophy of Mind*. Cambridge: Harvard University Press.

Sider, Theodore. 2009. "Ontological Realism." In *Metametaphysics: New Essays on the Foundations of Ontology*. Oxford: Oxford University Press: 384–423.

Sider, Theodore. 2011. *Writing the Book of the World*. Oxford: Oxford University Press.

Slote, Michael A. 1970. *Reason and Scepticism*. London: Allen & Unwin.

Stalker, Douglas (ed.). 1994. *Grue! The New Riddle of Induction*. Chicago and La Salle: Open Court.

Strawson, P.F. 1959. *Individuals: An Essay in Descriptive Metaphysics*. London: Routledge.

Taylor, Charles. 1979. "Sense Data Revisited." In G.F. Macdonald (ed.), *Perception and Identity: Essays Presented to A.J. Ayer with His Replies*. Ithaca: Cornell University Press: 99–112.

Thomasson, Amie L. 2009. "Answerable and Unanswerable Questions." In David J. Chalmers, David Manley, and Ryan Wasserman (eds), *Metametaphysics: New Essays on the Foundations of Ontology*. Oxford: Oxford University Press: 444–471.

Turner, Jason. 2011. "Ontological Nihilism." In Karen Bennett (ed.), *Oxford Studies in Metaphysics* 6: 3–54.

Tye, Michael. 1984. "The Adverbial Approach to Visual Experience." *Philosophical Review* 93(2): 195–225.

Uebel, Thomas. 2013. " 'Logical Positivism'—'Logical Empiricism': What's in a Name?" *Perspectives on Science* 21(1): 58–99.

Vogel, Jonathan. 1990. "Cartesian Skepticism and Inference to the Best Explanation." *Journal of Philosophy* 87(11): 658–666.

Warren, Jared. 2015. "Quantifier Variance and the Collapse Argument." *Philosophical Quarterly* 65(259): 241–253.

Warren, Jared. 2016*a*. "Sider on the Epistemology of Structure." *Philosophical Studies* 173(9): 2417–2435.

Warren, Jared. 2016*b*. "Internal and External Questions Revisited." *Journal of Philosophy* 113(4): 177–209.

Warren, Jared. 2020. *Shadows of Syntax: Revitalizing Logical and Mathematical Conventionalism*. New York: Oxford University Press.

Warren, Jared. 2021*a*. "This Quintessence of Dust – *Consciousness Explained*, at Thirty." *Philosophical Papers* 50(1–2): 281–308.

Warren, Jared. 2021*b*. "Defending Understanding-Assent Links." *Synthese* 199(3–4): 9219–9236.

Warren, Jared. 2022*a*. "Quantifier Variance, Semantic Collapse, and "Genuine" Quantifiers." *Philosophical Studies* 179(3): 745–757.

Warren, Jared. 2022*b*. *The* A Priori *Without Magic*. Cambridge: Cambridge University Press.

Warren, Jared. 2023. "The Independence Solution to Grue." *Philosophical Studies* 180(4): 1305–1326.

Weisberg, Jonathan. 2009. "Locating IBE in the Bayesian Framework." *Synthese* 167: 125–143.

Williams, Michael. 2010. "Descartes' Transformation of the Sceptical Tradition." In Richard Bett (ed.), *The Cambridge Companion to Ancient Scepticism*. Cambridge: Cambridge University Press: 288–313.

Williamson, Timothy. 2000. *Knowledge and Its Limits*. Oxford: Oxford University Press.

Williamson, Timothy. 2006. "Conceptual Truth." *Aristotelian Society Supplementary* 80(1): 1–41.

Wilson, N. L. (1959). "Substances Without Substrata." *The Review of Metaphysics* 12(4): 521–539.

Wittgenstein, Ludwig. 1953. *Philosophical Investigations.* New York: Wiley-Blackwell.

Wright, Crispin. 1983. *Frege's Conception of Numbers as Objects.* Aberdeen: Aberdeen University Press.

Jared Warren, *The Sense-Data Language and External World Skepticism* In: *Oxford Studies in Philosophy of Mind Volume 4.* Edited by: Uriah Kriegel, Oxford University Press. © Jared Warren 2024.
DOI: 10.1093/9780198924159.003.0005

6

Naïve Realism, Incorporeal Objects, and the Time-lag Argument

William Fish

1. Naïve Realism

Naïve realism is, at heart, a theory of the metaphysical nature of episodes of successful visual perception and their conscious character. It tells us that successful (veridical) visual experiences are fundamentally relational. When a subject visually perceives an object in their environment, that subject stands in a particular relation to the object and its properties: a relation that is often known as *acquaintance*. As the existence of a relation entails the existence of its relata, this has the consequence that the subject could not have stood in this relation—could not have had this particular kind of visual experience—had that object not existed. An alternative way of putting this idea is to say that the perceived object is a *constituent* of the subject's experience of that object, which again entails that an experience of that very kind could not have existed had that very object not been able to be a constituent of the experience (Martin 1997).

The second key component to the naïve realist claim is to say that the perceived objects are not just constituents of our experiences, but are constituents of the *phenomenal characters* of those experiences:

the phenomenal character of your experience, as you look around the room, is constituted by the layout of the room itself: which particular objects are there, their intrinsic properties, such as color and shape, and how they are arranged in relation to one another and to you.

(Campbell 2002: 116)[1]

---

[1] See also Martin 1997; Fish 2009; Brewer 2011; Logue 2012; and Langsam 2017.

To use a helpful metaphor of Mike Martin's, the core claim of naïve realism is that, when we see, external objects and their properties 'shape the contours of the subject's conscious experience' (Martin 2004: 64), where the metaphor of 'shaping' is read in a constitutive, rather than causal, sense.

There are many considerations that are held up in favour of naïve realism (see Fish 2021: 103–104 for an overview) as well as some significant challenges it faces. Principal among those challenges is the Argument from Illusion/Hallucination. This argument proceeds from the premise that there are visual experiences—examples may include dreams, hallucinations, and illusions—in which we are either not acquainted with the world at all (hallucinations and dreams), or not acquainted with it as it is (illusions) which cannot therefore be understood as involving acquaintance with mind-independent objects but must instead be given a different explanation. Yet if this is the case, then couldn't we simply apply this explanation to *all* cases of visual experience—successful and unsuccessful alike—and thereby render the key naïve realist claims otiose? In recent defences of naïve realism, this challenge has been the focus of most work, but in historical discussions another objection was often raised alongside it.

2. The Time-Lag Argument

This is known as the time-lag (or occasionally time-gap) argument (Russell 1927: 155, 1948: 172, 204, 217; Ayer 1956; Broad 1959; Ebersole 1965: 509; Robinson 1994: 80–81; Foster 2000: 100; Papineau 2021: 18–20). It focuses on a perceived conflict between the fact that the light that impacts upon our visual systems from the objects we see travels at a finite speed, and the fact that the acquaintance relation requires the perceived objects to exist in the subject's current perceptual environment. Although it doesn't require it, the argument is often introduced by considering the experiences of stars, given the fact that 'the distance from some stars is so great that, by the time we see them they have ceased to exist' (Robinson 1994: 80). David Papineau gives us a concrete example:

> In 1604 Kepler's Supernova was visible to the naked eye in daytime for over three weeks. However, this massive explosion had in fact occurred at least 13,000 years earlier. This seems inconsistent with the idea that sensory consciousness of a supernova is constituted by a perceptual relation

to the explosion itself. How can my sensory consciousness, which is here and now, be constituted by my bearing some relation to a long past event?

(Papineau 2021: 18)

As Papineau notes, a supernova is an event—the event of a star's undergoing runaway nuclear fusion. So when people saw Kepler's Supernova, they saw an event involving an object, and as a remnant of this supernova still exists (Kasuga et al. 2021), we could possibly hold that the object that was involved in this event—the object that people saw—still exists. Nevertheless, to lean on this would miss the force of the objection.

As we saw above, naïve realists hold that objects *and their properties* shape the contours of a subject's conscious experience. Even if we do hold that the object that participated in Kepler's Supernova still exists, it is nevertheless the case that, in 1604, it no longer instantiated the properties that it instantiated during the supernova. So for present purposes, we can understand the claim that people saw the *event* of Kepler's Supernova in 1604 as equivalent to the claim that, in 1604, people saw the object to have an array of supernova-related properties that, in fact, it had not instantiated for many thousands of years. In this way, talk of people in the present seeing events that ended in the past causes problems for the naïve realist in much the same way as talk of people seeing objects that no longer exist. For this reason, I will for present purposes treat perception of objects and perception of events as equivalent.

With this equivalence in mind, we can represent Papineau's argument as an inconsistent triad:

1. The phenomenal character of a veridical visual experience involves a subject's being related, by acquaintance, to the object of that experience and its properties.
2. Acquaintance is a relation that can only hold between subjects and things that exist.
3. In 1604, subjects veridically visually perceived Kepler's Supernova, an event which took place thousands of years previously, and hence no longer existed in 1604.

On the face of it, these three claims appear to be inconsistent. (1) and (2) give us that, whenever I have a veridical visual experience, I am acquainted with something that exists, but (3) states that an event that was veridically perceived in 1604 no longer existed.

Yet while the vast expanses of time we find in cases involving extrasolar objects make the objection particularly salient, they are not central to the time-lag argument. For example, Russell often uses the example of everyday visual experiences of the sun, which is so distant that the light it emits takes eight minutes to reach us:

> Though you see the sun now, the physical object to be inferred from your seeing existed eight minutes ago; if, in the intervening minutes, the sun had gone out, you would still be seeing exactly what you are seeing. We cannot therefore identify the physical sun with what we see.
>
> (Russell 1948: 204)

In a way that mirrors our discussion above, Russell's argument is that when we have a visual experience of the sun, even though the sun still exists, the sun we see is not the sun *as it is* now, but rather the sun *as it was* eight minutes ago. This is then supported by a thought experiment: that if we imagine that the sun *had* ceased to exist in the last eight minutes, our perception would have continued as it is regardless. Russell's conclusion is that the object we see is the past sun—the sun as it was eight minutes ago—and this particular object—the sun as it was eight minutes ago—no longer exists in the subject's current perceptual environment.

As the speed of light is finite, a variation of this argument can be made in any case of perception:

> The challenge doesn't arise only in extreme cases like supernovae. Light takes time to travel even short distances. The delay mightn't be as extreme as with supernovae, but many of the more mundane things we observe have ceased to exist by the time we see them.
>
> (Papineau 2021: 18)

While it is true that light does take a short time to travel from the object to our eyes in even mundane cases, it is surely not the case that 'many of the more mundane things we observe have ceased to exist by the time we see them'. Light travels approximately 300 kilometres in just 1 millisecond, so almost every terrestrial experience will involve a time lag of less than a thousandth of a second. Not only is the likelihood that a perceived object would cease to exist during this time minimal, even if it did, it is not clear that this would be sufficient to generate a problematic time-lag case. This is because, phenomenologically, our experience of *now*—of the present—is not durationless. The present *as it is experienced*—the specious present—seems to have temporal extent, and even short estimates of this period are in the hundreds of milliseconds (e.g. Dainton 2000: 171; Strawson 2009: 262). If this is correct, then cases of perception where the time lag is smaller than the length of the specious present do not clearly show that the object does not exist at the time of the experience. As this surely includes all conceivable terrestrial cases, for present purposes, I will focus only on the clear cases of time lags that occur in our perception of extra-terrestrial entities such as the sun and stars.

What options are available to the naïve realist to deal with such cases? Focusing on Papineau's initial supernova example, one possibility would be to reject claim (3) on the grounds that the experience people had of Kepler's Supernova was not veridical (Moran 2019: 209–212). If it was not veridical, then it would not involve acquaintance, and hence the experience would not be inconsistent with (1) and (2). However, this proposal seems ad hoc: when we talk about non-veridical experiences, we typically have in mind experiences such as hallucinations, which involve some kind of failing in the visual system. Yet as Moran notes, this just doesn't look to be the case where experiences of extra-terrestrial objects are concerned—the visual system is operating normally, it is just that the light it is operating on was produced a long time ago (2019: 210). For this reason, this approach to the objection looks problematic.

Another possible response suggested by George Pitcher is that

> the finite speed of light does not entail that we do not directly see things and states of affairs in the 'external world,' but only that we must see them *as they were some time ago*. We see real physical things, properties, and events, all right, but we see them late, that is all.
>
> (Pitcher 1971: 48, emphasis added)

When viewed in light of our inconsistent triad, it is not clear quite how this should be interpreted. The suggestion that we see things *as they were* implies that perception somehow reaches back in time. One way of understanding how this could be would be to *reject* (2) in favour of a weaker conception of acquaintance according to which we can be acquainted with—and hence see—things that no longer exist. The concern with this response is that, in weakening the acquaintance relation, it gives up on one of the core claims of naïve realism. This in turn looks irreconcilable with the second core claim that the objects with which we are acquainted shape the contours of our conscious visual experiences. If these objects no longer exist, then how could they shape consciousness in this way? This approach would appear to have the result that we would abandon naïve realism, not defend it.

On a second interpretation of Pitcher's response, we could see it as a challenge to an idea implicit in (3)—that as subjects visually experienced the supernova in 1604, their experience was temporally located solely in 1604—in favour of the claim that the experience is a temporally extended event that began when the supernova occurred and ended in 1604. Mark Johnston has articulated a similar suggestion:

> Seeing the object is an event materially constituted by *the long physical process* connecting the object seen to the final state of the visual system. Seeing the object is an event that is (as it actually turns out) constituted by a physical process that goes all the way out to the object seen.
>
> (Johnston 2004: 139, emphasis in original)

This seems a more plausible interpretation than the first, and one that doesn't end up giving up on the core claims of naïve realism, but it does have some counterintuitive consequences. Papineau emphasises these aspects of the resulting response:

> If you tell me that my consciousness of the yellow ball extends outside my head and into my garden, I might find this odd, but I won't automatically think it incoherent. But if you say that my visual experience of the supernova stretches back in time 13,000 years, I am not sure how to understand you. Surely we all know the experience didn't begin until I looked up at the sky this morning.
>
> (Papineau 2021: 17)

The final interpretation is similar to the first, but instead of holding that we can be acquainted with things that no longer exist, it retains the original understanding of acquaintance while denying that events that are past no longer exist. In terms of our inconsistent triad, this is to deny the final clause of (3), that the supernova no longer existed in 1604, and one way in which this has been done is through the adoption of an eternalist conception of time (Power 2010: 112–113; Moran 2019: 216–217). On this view, reality includes both the present and the past, and 'just as distant places are no less real for being spatially distant, distant times are no less real for being temporally distant; the ontological significance of distance is thus a respect in which time is spacelike' (Sider 2001: 11). The eternalist will therefore claim that Kepler's Supernova still *exists* in the present, even though it is no longer *located* in the present. Unlike the previous view, the claim here is not that the experience extends back to the time when the supernova *was* located, but that an experience taking place entirely in 1604 could acquaint its subject with an event that is no longer temporally located, but nonetheless still exists.

In his detailed discussions of this issue, Moran suggests that this is the most plausible response on the naïve realist's behalf, but contends that it still has problems:

> [I]t is hard to square this view with both the plausible thought that all the things within one's field of view (i.e. all of the things one sees at a given time) are spatially related to each other, and also with the core naïve realist thesis that the objects one sees are constituents of one's perceptual experience.
>
> (Moran 2019: 223)

I agree with much of what Moran has to say in his paper, but I think that there is a previously unnoticed feature of the problem cases that may succeed in dispelling some of the puzzles that continue to perturb him.

3. Incorporeal Objects

To focus in on this feature, consider J.L. Austin's contention that the class of objects that we can see goes beyond what we might ordinarily think of as typical material objects—such things as 'chairs, tables, pictures, books, flowers, pens, cigarettes'—to also incorporate a range of particulars such as 'flames, rainbows, shadows, pictures on the screen at the cinema, pictures in books or hung on walls, vapours, gases—all of which people say that they see' (Austin 1962: 8). These claims are motivated by the phenomenology of our everyday experiences of the world. If asked to list things that we see around us, objects such as flames, rainbows and the sky would be likely to be on that list. M.G.F. Martin calls these particulars 'purely visual' objects: 'the visible world seems to contain both purely visual objects together with the concrete entities that we suppose are the medium-sized dry goods of the material world. We see lights, we see shadows, we see highlights, we see rainbows, we see the sky, and we can see mirror images or holograms; all of these things seem to be creatures solely of the visual world' (Martin 2010: 188).

3.1 The Perception of Light Sources

To explore the difference between these 'purely visual' objects and the more familiar material objects, consider the perception of an unlit candle. According to the naïve realist, this experience involves your being acquainted with a material object that exists in your current environment, and that in virtue of standing in this acquaintance relation to the candle, the candle and its properties shape the contours of your conscious experience. In order for you to be acquainted with a candle in this way, however, there must be sufficient ambient light in the environment—if it is too dark, you would be unable to see the candle—and the (brief) explanation for why this is the case is that it is through light's being reflected from the candle and subsequently processed by your visual systems that enables you to differentiate the candle and its properties from other parts of the environment. Appropriate processing is thus a necessary condition for the occurrence of an acquaintance relation. Suppose you light the candle and look again: you can see the same candle, but now with a flame dancing and flickering above it. The explanation for how you see the candle is the same as before—the only difference being there is an additional source of light that it can reflect—but this is not how you see the flame. You don't see a flame by way of its reflecting ambient light as a flame lacks the kind of materiality required to do this. Yet as we can certainly *see* flames, their visibility must have a different explanation.

We know that flames are composed of gases and soot particles suspended in gases, but although gases and soot particles have materiality, they are not what we see when we look at a flame. We also know that, to see a flame, these gases and soot particles need to *combust*, as it is the process of combustion that creates the light that is subsequently processed by our visual systems. Yet I see no reason to say that we see the *process of* combustion any more than to say we see the process of reflection in more familiar cases. For similar reasons, I don't think we should say that we see *the light* created by the combustion any more than we should say we see the light reflected from objects.[2] We don't see the light reflected from objects, we see the objects

---

[2] Although in both cases we *could* say this—that we see the process, or we see the light—I see no reason to. Aside from the observation that people find it natural to talk about things like flames and flashes of lightning as things that we see, I don't have an argument that to do so would be wrong, but I don't see an argument that we ought to do so either.

themselves. It is just that our capacity to do this requires our visual systems to be appropriately sensitive to the light they reflect.

Other such objects include electrical arcs and sparks, such as the sustained arcs used in welding, the momentary sparks of a spark plug, or flashes of lightning. When an electrically charged region of the atmosphere spontaneously discharges to ground during a storm, nothing is created that reflects light. The reason we see a flash of lightning is because electrical current passing through the atmosphere both heats up the air molecules, causing them to become incandescent, and causes the nitrogen in the air to luminesce. But as was the case with the flame, we do not see the particles in the air by way of this light; we see the flash of lightning itself.

In the majority of everyday cases, the things that we see are *corporeal*—they are made of matter—and it is their corporeality that gives them their ability to reflect light, which in turn underpins their potential to be visible. Yet in the broad class of things that we can see, not every case is like this. As Mark Kalderon puts it, some visible objects 'lack substrata—there is no lightning that flashes, just the flash of lightning.... Despite being particulars, the objects of perception differ, in this way, in mode, substantiality, and being' (Kalderon 2011: 222). For this reason, I call these visible objects *incorporeal*. Incorporeal objects lack materiality and hence cannot reflect light, and so cannot be seen by way of their reflecting light in the way the familiar corporeal objects do.

Instead, in incorporeal cases such as flames and lightning, while we can indeed see the objects, our capacity to see them is underpinned by the sensitivity of our visual systems to the light that is *emitted*. So although a particular flame is a result of the combustion of gases and soot particles suspended in the gas, this produces a distinct visible object—the flame—that we see by the light emitted. The flame is, in a sense, *made of light*. Likewise, when an electrical current crosses an air gap between two electrodes, or a charged region of the atmosphere discharges to ground, these processes create distinct visible objects—the arc, and the flash of lightning—that we see by the light that these processes produce.

3.2 Incorporeal Objects and Reflection

As we have seen, incorporeal objects can be created when light is emitted, but not all incorporeal objects are like this. Consider a laser maze, for example. In a darkened room—albeit not so dark you can't see the walls and floor—your way is blocked by a complex labyrinth made up of thin cylindrical beams at an array of angles. Again, you see the walls and floor of the room by way of their reflecting the low ambient light, but the beams that form the maze are not seen in the same way. Just like the flame and the lightning strike, the beams you see lack the requisite materiality to reflect light.

Unlike flames and lightning flashes, however, the bars of light that we see are not seen by the emission of light—their visibility has a different explanation. To make a visible laser maze, narrow, tightly focused cylinders of light rays are produced by lasers, and when they are shone through an area containing suitable airborne particles (like those produced by haze or fog machines), these particles will reflect some of the light rays that comprise the cylinders. But when the laser light reflected by these particles is processed by our visual systems, this does not enable us to see the airborne particles themselves: instead, we see visible bars or beams of light crossing our path. In a similar manner, although a rainbow is a result of the refraction and reflection of light in raindrops, when our visual systems process this light, we do not see the raindrops themselves but a distinct incorporeal object—a rainbow. On some occasions, when a light source is reflected in a screen or a pane of glass, we do not thereby see the reflective surface,[3] but a distinct incorporeal object—a reflection—that appears to sit on the surface of the screen. Other cases of incorporeal objects created by the interaction of light and the atmosphere include mirages, which involve the refraction of light, and the scattering of light by atmospheric particles. When we look up, we see a sky because about a third of the incident sunlight is scattered and reflected by the gases and particles in the atmosphere, and this diffuse sky radiation—much of which is of shorter (blue) wavelengths because they are easier to scatter—is visible from the ground. Once again, though, seeing the sky is not a way of seeing the small particles in the atmosphere; instead, this process creates a new incorporeal object—the vault of the sky—which we see.

Despite the differences between them, the important commonality in these cases is that the particular that people find it natural to say they

---

[3] This raises an interesting question concerning the difference between cases where an object's reflecting light enables us to see it and cases in which an object's reflecting light blocks us from seeing it. Unfortunately, while there may be an answer to be found in the underlying physiology—perhaps involving an explanation of why luminance of a certain kind results in the light being scattered within the eye in such a way that the contrast of the image on the retina is reduced—there is not much more to say at a phenomenological level other than that it happens.

see—the flame, the flash of lightning, the electrical arc, the laser beam (or maze), the rainbow, the reflection, the mirage, the sky—does not itself reflect light. Although these objects are members of the broad group of visible objects, they are special cases in that they lack materiality or corporeality. Yet although these incorporeal objects are not ordinary material substances, they are nonetheless part of our shared material *world*. They are all perfectly objective entities—they can all be photographed and filmed, and multiple perceivers can see and refer to one and the same incorporeal object. For this reason, the naïve realist will hold that such incorporeal objects can be perfectly good objects of acquaintance—we can be acquainted with the flame that flickers atop a candle just as well as we can be acquainted with the candle itself.

3.3 Incorporeal Objects and Occlusion

Before moving on to explore how these findings impact the time-lag argument, I first want to take a moment to explore an important feature of incorporeal objects, which is that a source of light can actually *impair* your ability to see objects. Normally, light enables us to see things, or details in things, that we could not otherwise have seen, by being available to be reflected by objects. Yet if you look towards a source of light, it can make it much harder to see things, particularly those in the direction of the light source itself.

Some of the incorporeal objects we have been discussing also have this property: of both being a source of light to see things by while also impairing our ability to see other objects. The most obvious example is the case of a welding arc. To see this, consider Figure 6.1. In these images, you can see

Figure 6.1 Four images taken from a YouTube video on the history of the light bulb showing the progression of an electrical arc.
Source: https://www.youtube.com/watch?v=ThBkzEfjVl0

an electrical arc being created by passing a current across the gap between two carbon rods. In the first image, before the current starts to flow, you can clearly see both carbon rods and the surrounding objects due to their reflecting the ambient light. In the second image, the circuit has been created and the arc is now visible. Because they reflect the light emitted by the arc, some details that could not be seen in the first image—e.g. features of the presenter's hand and shirt, and the clamp holding the upper rod—are now more clearly visible. Yet other aspects of the scene are no longer visible: the arc itself actually serves to hide the tips of the carbon rods from view. The incorporeal arc thus occludes the objects behind it, in the same way as a similarly sized material object would. As the arc gets bigger and brighter in the third image, it begins to occlude an array of other details: the carbon rods, the clamp and the hand holding it are no longer visible at all. By the time of the final image, despite the ambient light remaining unchanged from the opening image, the arc has now got so big and bright that you can barely see any of the objects and details in the scene at all.[4] This case thus provides an example in which an incorporeal object—an electrical arc—can be both the source of light by which other objects can be seen while also blocking us from seeing some parts of the scene, particularly those that are immediately behind the incorporeal object from the perspective of the viewer.

Just as a light source can occlude objects in a scene, a *reflection* of a light source can also block us from seeing objects in the immediate vicinity of the reflection. Familiar everyday examples include the reflections of windows or lighting fixtures in computer or television screens, or when the morning or evening sunlight reflects from a wet road surface while driving. Sometimes, details of the scene behind can be seen through the reflection, as though the reflection is translucent, but at other times the reflection can obscure the details of the reflective surface, as when the reflections on a screen obscure the image, or the reflection of the sun obscures the road and its features (such as lane markings). In such cases, phenomenologically, these bright patches appear to sit in front of, or on top of, the object's surface and thereby block the object from view.

---

[4] This illustrates another way in which light sources can impair our ability to see: by being too bright. This phenomenon is known as *glare*: 'we may describe glare as hindrance to vision by too much light' (Vos 2003: 164), and the specific ability of glare—too much light—to impair the vision of other objects is called *disability glare*.

3.4 Material Light Sources

We have seen that, in cases such as flames and electrical arcs, the emission of light can give rise to an incorporeal object, which can then occlude other features of the scene. Now let us consider the case of what appears to be a visible *material* light source—the filament in a simple filament bulb. In a filament bulb, the electrical current passing through the filament causes it to heat up so much it becomes incandescent and starts to give off light. This case is unlike the other cases we have considered in that here we *do* have an ordinary material substrate—the filament itself—that is the source of the light. Nevertheless, close phenomenological consideration suggests that the underlying picture in this case is the same: that the physical processes in the filament give rise to an incorporeal object that is distinct from the filament itself, which not only can be seen, but also serves to hide the filament itself from view.

To motivate this claim, consider Figure 6.2. In the left-most image, the current has just begun to flow through the filament. At this point, the coiled shape of the filament can be made out by the light it emits. By the next image, however—approximately half a second later on the video (which, recall, is in super slow-motion)—the coils can no longer be made out. Now, when looking at the location of the filament, what we see looks more like a glowing caterpillar with fuzzy edges that is slightly larger than the filament itself. By the third image, the size of the caterpillar has grown, and is now substantially larger than the filament. At this point, I think it is clear that we can no longer see the filament: the light that the filament is producing is *occluding* the filament, not rendering it visible. Yet even though we can no longer see the filament, the light it produces is sufficient to illuminate other

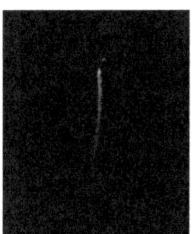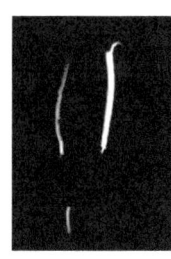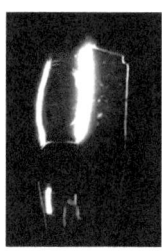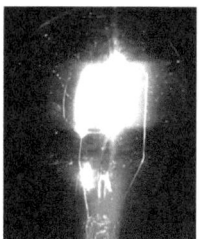

Figure 6.2 Four images taken from a super slow-motion video of an incandescent filament light bulb being turned on.
Source: https://www.youtube.com/watch?v=deXOk6G5ALs

components of the bulb, such as the filament support, that could not be seen in the earlier images. By the final image, the filament is glowing so brightly that we are not only unable to see the filament, but also other parts of the structure of the bulb. These considerations suggest that the vast majority of the time, even though the filament is the *source* of the light given off by an incandescent bulb, we do not *see* the filament when we look at the light bulb.

In the earlier discussions, I suggested that when we see a flame, we do not thereby see the burning gas particles; the flame is instead an incorporeal object *created* by these processes. My contention here is that the case of a filament is parallel. When we switch on a bulb, an electrical current passes through the filament and heats it up to a point at which it gives off light. But rather than making the filament visible, these processes create a novel incorporeal object (which in this case we do not have a handy name for), which can not only be seen, but which also occludes the material filament itself.

To conclude this part of our discussion, this phenomenological investigation illustrates four key things for our subsequent discussions. First, our shared, visible world contains a range of things in addition to the familiar material objects, including those that we have called 'incorporeal' objects. Second, that given the way our visual systems work, to be visible, incorporeal objects must have a relationship with light, and we have explored two ways in which this can be the case: those in which light is *emitted* by parts of the material world that are not seen and those in which light is *reflected* (or refracted, or scattered) by parts of the material world that are not seen. Phenomenological investigation into our perception of material light sources then suggests two further considerations: third, that when we explore what it is like to perceive a light source where the underlying processes take place in a material substrate, we still find that these processes produce distinct incorporeal objects that are the objects of perception, and fourth, that these incorporeal objects can occlude parts of the nearby scene. In the cases where the underlying processes take place in a material substrate, as the substrate itself is typically located in the same direction as the incorporeal object, the material substrates themselves are (almost) never seen by way of the light they produce.[5]

---

[5] I say 'almost' here to leave room for cases like the one indicated in the first image of the filament bulb—where parts of the light source illuminate other parts. Even in this case, however, I suggest that the parts of the filament that are producing light are producing small incorporeal objects that are co-located with the relevant parts the filament, and although these may enable the perception of other parts of the filament, I suggest they will still block us from seeing those parts of the filament they are co-located with.

4. Incorporeal Objects and the Time-lag Argument

How does the preceding discussion impact upon the time-lag argument? Well, we have seen that when we 'see' a material light source, we do not strictly see the material substrate, but a distinct incorporeal object that is created by physical/chemical processes in this substrate, and which typically *hides* the material object itself from view. As the vast majority of time-lag cases involve the apparent perception of light sources—*stars*, be they close, distant, or supernova—this suggests that, in those cases, we do not literally see the material objects—the huge balls of gas—that populate the cosmos, but instead see distinct incorporeal objects that are the result of the chemical and physical processes going on in those objects. Moreover, comparison with other more familiar cases of incorporeal objects suggests that these incorporeal objects will in fact occlude the material objects themselves.

Does this mean that we don't see stars 'strictly speaking'? I don't think so. The word 'star' gets its primary reference from everyday visual perception—stars are the things we see in the night sky—and this is why it was a *discovery* to find out that stars are in fact massive balls of hydrogen being turned into helium by nuclear fusion. What the naïve realist who takes this approach would have to say is not that we don't see stars when we look up at the night sky, but that the stars we see are not *identical* to the celestial bodies that produce the light; they are rather visible yet incorporeal objects *created by* the processes in those bodies in a way that parallels a range of more mundane cases. This is the only concession the naïve realist need make, and one that is supported by careful phenomenological reflection.

In taking this approach, responses to Moran's remaining sources of disquiet become available. One of these concerns is that, while endorsing eternalism can allow for the relationship of acquaintance to hold between present and past relata, it nonetheless seems to conflict with the plausible idea that, 'if an event takes place between T1 and T2, then it can only have as constituents items that are *located* between those times' (Moran 2019: 222, my emphasis). And although eternalists hold that Kepler's Supernova *exists* between T1 and T2, it is not *located* in this time period, so it is difficult to see how it could be a constituent of the experience. If, however, the object of such an experience is an incorporeal object, and not the underlying material object, then a Moorean shift (cf. Moore 1939: 166) becomes available. If an experience takes place between T1 and T2, then it can only have as constituents items that are located between those times; an experience of the incorporeal object produced by Kepler's Supernova did take place between T1 and T2 (in 1604); therefore the incorporeal object existed between T1 and T2.

This approach requires us to concede that incorporeal objects do not cease to exist (or be located) at precisely the same times as the underlying material objects or processes do, but this is true of the more mundane cases too. When a light bulb filament breaks, the incorporeal object persists for a short time after the filament is no more—it is just that we tend not to notice this because the time lag between the two events is relatively short. In the case of stars, though, the sheer scale of the underlying physical processes is such that the incorporeal object they create will persist, and be perceivable, for a long time after the star itself has died.

Moran's second concern is similar: he says, 'it is hard to square [the idea that stars are not located at the time of their perception with] the plausible thought that all the things within one's field of view (i.e. all of the thing's one sees at a given time) are spatially related to each other' (Moran 2019: 223). Once again, though, as this approach can allow that the incorporeal object *is* located at the same time as the experience, it thereby allows that the stars we see *are* spatially related to terrestrial objects. So this view can also accommodate the intuition that a particular star is located in the same direction as a particular mountain, just much further away. How much further away? Well, it's indeterminate. Although the more proximal visual objects—flames, arcs, the glow of a light bulb—are *roughly* co-located with the underlying processes, when it comes to the more distal visual objects, things are less straightforward. When we see a flash of lightning, it is only in unusual cases—those in which we can see an object the lightning strikes—that we can say with any confidence where the lightning strike is located. Normally, they are simply located *in the sky*, in a certain direction from our standpoint, but at an indeterminate distance. In discussing the case of rainbows, Martin makes a similar claim. He says that 'when we see rainbows on the horizon... [w]e know what their (main) physical basis is, the refraction of light through rain droplets, but we do not see rainbows to be exactly where the rain drops are; rainbows are sketched for us normally on the horizon, normally as an aspect of the vault of the sky' (Martin 2010: 188). We might say a similar thing about stars: stars are sketched for us as an aspect of the vault of the night sky, in a certain direction but at an indeterminate distance.

It is important to note that this response does not fall prey to a version of Moran's generalising argument (Moran 2019: 212–213). The concern raised by this argument is that, in introducing unusual objects to stand as the objects of perception in time-lag cases,[6] we will have no reason to resist the claim that such objects are the objects of perception in *all cases*, and not just those in which there is an appreciable time lag.[7] However, there are two key differences in the present case that block the generalising argument from going through. The first is that the premise is not accurate—it is not true that we have introduced a special kind of object to deal with this problem. Objects such as flames, lightning flashes, rainbows, and the sky were already part of our ontology of visible objects, and hence already a kind of entity that the naïve realist was committed to our being acquainted with. All we have done is suggested that *more* light sources might produce incorporeal objects than we had hitherto realised. The second key difference is that the case for incorporeal objects being involved in the perception of light sources was phenomenological. I argued that these cases are *not like* the perception of an everyday material object by the reflection of light, and hence should be distinguished from them and treated more like other (everyday) incorporeal objects like flames and flashes of lightning. If this phenomenological argument is accepted, then it would at best countenance the introduction of incorporeal objects in cases where the light an object produces blocks us from seeing it; it would not be generalisable to all cases of successful perception.

However, an opponent might argue that it does not cover every relevant extra-terrestrial case. For example, alongside the many stars that we see when we look up at the night sky, we can also see some of the other planets from our solar system. Mercury, Venus, Mars, Jupiter, and Saturn can all be seen with the naked eye if you know where (and when) to look. But the planets do not emit light; instead, we can see the planets because they *reflect* light from the sun. To this extent, our perception of planets looks more like

---

[6] Moran's discussions here focus on subjective sense data as the objects in time-lag cases, but the concerns that he raises here might seem to apply to the introduction of objective incorporeal objects too.

[7] Relatedly, it is also important to distinguish this proposal from Suchting's suggestion that we could respond to the time-lag argument by holding that we now see the light that was transmitted from a distant star at some point in the past (Suchting 1969: 55). There are two key problems with this view, however. The first is that while light is critical to perception as it is light that stimulates the retina and contains the information we subsequently use to discriminate aspects of our environment, at no point in this process is the light itself seen by the perceiver—the perceiver just sees their environment (cf. Chisholm 1957: 144). The second concern is that this proposal does seem to fall foul of a variant of Moran's generalising argument—if we allow that it makes sense to say that light can be seen, and if we go on to claim that it is seen in these cases, then why should we not say that it is seen in all cases (O'Shaughnessy 1984)? But if this is accepted, then it would be this light that shapes the contours of the subject's experience, not the objects in the subject's environment, which would amount to a rejection of naïve realism.

our perception of everyday objects than our perception of light sources. Yet the planets are also enormous distances away, with the light they reflect taking from a little over two minutes (Venus) to around 85 minutes (Saturn) to reach us. If we do indeed see the planets—the celestial objects themselves—in the night sky, then there are still significant time-lag cases to cause problems for the naïve realist.

There is, however, a plausible response open to the naïve realist to deal with the cases of the planets. When we discussed reflections in section 3.2, we noted that sometimes, a surface can *reflect* light in such a way that it *obscures* (as opposed to renders visible) the reflective surface and that, when it does, these processes give rise to an incorporeal object that occludes the features of the surface. As an example, we looked at the way in which a light reflected on a wet road can block us from seeing the underlying road markings, and noted that when this occurs, we not only fail to see the road markings, but we see a patch of reflection that appears to lay on top of and obscure the markings. The perception of planets could be treated similarly. At least where perception by the naked eye is concerned, we are not enabled to discriminate any features whatsoever of the planets in the light they reflect. When we look up and see a planet in the night sky, we cannot make out any features of the planet's surface—we just see a tiny, bright disc. Given this, it seems plausible to treat this as a case in which the reflection of the sun's light *obscures* the planet, rather than enables us to perceive it. If this is correct, then even when looking at the planets, we see incorporeal objects rather than material objects, and the perceptions of these objects can be accounted for in the same way as the perception of stars.

5. Conclusion

Recognising that the significant time lags involved in extra-terrestrial cases pose the most acute problems for the naïve realist, I recommended treating our perception of stars as equivalent to our perception of material light sources on Earth, where phenomenological investigation of these cases show that we (almost) never see the underlying material objects in these cases, but *incorporeal objects* that are produced by the physical and chemical processes going on in these objects. In the case of stars, then, the nuclear processes taking place in the enormous gaseous spheres will also create incorporeal objects, and it is these incorporeal objects that we call 'stars'. Yet as these incorporeal objects can persist even after the underlying material objects have ceased to exist, the naïve realist can contend that existing, temporally located *stars*—and not non-existent (or existent but non-located) gaseous spheres—are what we are acquainted with when we look up at the night sky.[8]

References

Austin, J.L. 1962. *Sense and Sensibilia*. Oxford: Clarendon Press.

Ayer, A.J. 1956. *The Problem of Knowledge*. London: Pelican Books.

Brewer, B. 2011. *Perception and Its Objects*. Oxford: Oxford University Press.

Broad, C.D. 1959. 'A Reply to My Critics'. In *The Philosophy of C. D. Broad*, edited by P.A. Schilpp, 711–830. New York: Tudor.

Campbell, J. 2002. *Reference and Consciousness*. Oxford: Oxford University Press.

Chisholm, R. 1957. *Perceiving: A Philosophical Study*. Ithaca, NY: Cornell University Press.

Dainton, B.F. 2000. *Stream of Consciousness: Unity and Continuity in Conscious Experience*. London/New York: Routledge.

Ebersole, F.B. 1965. 'How Philosophers See Stars'. *Mind* 74(296): 509–529.

Fish, W. 2009. *Perception, Hallucination, and Illusion*. Oxford: Oxford University Press.

Fish, W. 2021. *Philosophy of Perception: A Contemporary Introduction*, 2nd ed. London: Routledge.

Foster, J. 2000. *The Nature of Perception*. Oxford: Oxford University Press.

Johnston, M. 2004. 'The Obscure Object of Hallucination'. *Philosophical Studies* 120(1/3): 113–183.

Kalderon, M. 2011. 'Before the Law'. *Philosophical Issues* 21(1): 219–244.

Kasuga, T., J. Vink, S. Katsuda, H. Uchida, A. Bamba, T. Sato, and J.P. Hughes. 2021. 'Spatially Resolved RGS Analysis of Kepler's Supernova Remnant'. *Astrophysical Journal* 915(1): 42.

Langsam, H. 2017. 'The Intuitive Case for Naïve Realism'. *Philosophical Explorations* 20(1): 106–122.

[8] Thanks to audiences at both Victoria University of Wellington and Otago University for their helpful discussions of these ideas. Thanks also to Anya Weth for the conversation that stimulated this chapter, and to Beth Greener, Uriah Kriegel, and Andre Sant'Anna for their valuable comments on earlier drafts of the chapter.

Logue, H. 2012. 'Why Naïve Realism?'. *Proceedings of the Aristotelian Society* 112(2): 211–237.

Martin, M.G.F. 1997. 'The Reality of Appearances'. In *Thought and Ontology*, edited by M. Sainsbury, 81–106. Milan: Franco Angeli.

Martin, M.G.F. 2004. 'The Limits of Self-Awareness'. *Philosophical Studies* 201(3): 37–89.

Martin, M.G.F. 2010. 'What's in a Look?'. In *Perceiving the World*, edited by B. Nanay, 160–255. Oxford: Oxford University Press.

Moore, G.E. 1939. 'Proof of an External World'. In *G.E. Moore: Selected Writings*, edited by T. Baldwin, 147–170. Routledge: London.

Moran, A. 2019. 'Naïve Realism, Seeing Stars, and Perceiving the Past'. *Pacific Philosophical Quarterly* 100: 202–232.

O' Shaughnessy, B. 1984. 'Seeing the Light'. *Proceedings of the Aristotelian Society* 85: 193–218.

Papineau, D. 2021. *The Metaphysics of Sensory Experience*. Oxford: Oxford University Press.

Pitcher, G. 1971. *A Theory of Perception*. Princeton, NJ: Princeton University Press.

Power, S.E. 2010. 'Perceiving External Things and the Time-Lag Argument'. *European Journal of Philosophy* 211: 94–117.

Robinson, H. 1994. *Perception*. London: Routledge.

Russell, B. 1927. *Philosophy*. New York: W.W. Norton.

Russell, B. 1948. *Human Knowledge: Its Scope and Limits*. London: Allen & Unwin.

Sider, T. 2001. *Four Dimensionalism: An Ontology of Persistence and Time*. Oxford: Clarendon Press.

Strawson, G. 2009. *Selves: An Essay in Revisionary Metaphysics*. Oxford: Clarendon Press.

Suchting, W.A. 1969. 'Perception and the Time-Gap Argument'. *Philosophical Quarterly* 1974: 46–56.

Vos, J.J. 2003. 'Reflections on Glare'. *Lighting Research and Technology* 352: 163–176.

William Fish, *Naïve Realism, Incorporeal Objects, and the Time-lag Argument* In: *Oxford Studies in Philosophy of Mind Volume 4*. Edited by: Uriah Kriegel, Oxford University Press. © William Fish 2024.
DOI: 10.1093/9780198924159.003.0006

7

Relationalism, Acquaintance, and Subjectivity

Some Metaphysical Implications

Dorothea Debus

1. Setting the Scene

Perceptual experiences provide us with a fundamental form of awareness, or consciousness: In perceptual experience we are acquainted with, aware or conscious of, our own current environment. Indeed, it seems that human beings value being connected with their environment, with things and especially people, sometimes they *crave* being so connected (as has been starkly illustrated during the recent pandemic), and perceptual experiences seem to play a key role in this context. For it is in perceptual experience that such connections between a subject and her environment, and other people, are most fundamentally established. But then, how is this possible? How might perceptual experience put us in contact with our environment and provide the sort of connection we might value? In order to answer this question, one will have to inquire into the nature of perceptual experience more generally. Thus, one will have to ask: What is the *nature* of perceptual experience, and *how could we possibly be* conscious of our environment when we perceive it?

These questions stand at the centre of debates in the philosophy of perception, and often philosophers have attempted to answer these questions by offering one of two competing accounts of perceptual experience: Some defend a 'Relationalist' account, others argue that we should accept a 'Representationalist' account of perceptual experience: According to the Representationalist, perceptual experiences are essentially representational states, according to the Relationalist, perceptual experiences are essentially relations between the perceiving subject and the object perceived. Broadly speaking, the Representational Account of perceptual experience would seem most easily compatible with a scientific account of perceptual experience, while the Relationalist Account of perceptual experience would seem to be most suited to explain how perceptual experiences could possibly put us in contact with our environment and other people in a way that we treasure and sometimes crave. The Relational Account has recently gained some renewed attention in the literature, but not much seems to have been done so far to explain the *metaphysics* of such a Relational Account of perceptual experience. This chapter aims to ameliorate this somewhat. Here, I will therefore focus on the Relational Account of perceptual experience, and I will consider some of its metaphysical implications.

According to a Relationalist, a subject who perceives an object necessarily stands in a *direct experiential relation* to the relevant object, which gives her a subjective perspective on the object with which she is thereby acquainted. Thus, the Relationalist's core claim is that subjects who are conscious of their environment in perceptual experience stand in an experiential relation to their environment. However, or so I hope to show here, once we consider in greater detail what sort of relation the Relationalist might be talking about when endorsing this key claim, we find that a Relationalist is committed to non-naturalism. A Relationalist could not possibly endorse a reductive account of the perceptual relation, because the relation which does, according to the Relational Account of perceptual experience, obtain between the perceiving subject and the object perceived cannot but be a rather *special* relation: Indeed, or so I hope to show in the following, anybody who endorses a Relational Account of perceptual experience will have to hold that the perceptual relation between the perceiving subject and the object perceived is an *irreducibly sui generis* relation. Thus, a Relationalist about perceptual experience is committed to a *non-reductive account* of perceptual experience, and thereby the Relationalist is, more generally, also committed to a non-reductive account of the mind.

In arguing for this claim, I will proceed as follows: In section 2, I formulate what I consider to be the main claims of the Relational Account of perceptual experience, namely the 'Core Claim', the 'Relation Claim', the 'Constitution Claim' and the 'Consciousness Claim'. I consider each of these claims in detail, discuss some immediate objections and show how the Relationalist can respond to those objections. Having developed the main claims of the Relational Account, we next turn to the metaphysical question as to how, according to the Relationalist, the 'perceptual relation' fits into the physical world as we find it. In response, in section 3, I consider and develop the 'Supervenience Claim', namely the claim that the perceptual relation which obtains between the perceiving subject and the perceived object *supervenes* on the spatial, temporal and causal relations which obtain between the perceiving subject and the perceived object. In section 4, I introduce the 'Argument Against the Reductive Account', an argument which aims to show that and why, according to a Relational Account of perceptual experience, the perceptual relation which obtains between the perceiving subject and the object perceived could not possibly be *reduced to* the relations upon which it supervenes. Section 5 offers some ontological considerations which are needed to develop the Argument Against the Reductive Account fully. In section 6, I consider an objection which aims to show that a Relationalist *can* endorse a reductive account of the perceptual relation, and I show why this objection is unsuccessful. We therefore have reason to conclude, as I do in section 7, that anybody who endorses a Relational Account of perceptual experience will have to hold that the perceptual relation between the perceiving subject and the object perceived is an *irreducibly sui generis* relation and thus to endorse non-naturalism about the mind.

2. The Relational Account of Perceptual Experience

In developing the argument as sketched, we should first consider the main claims of a Relational Account, that is, we should ask what it could possibly mean to say that 'perceptual experiences are essentially relational' (Martin 2006: 359), and we should explain what kind of relation the relation of 'perceptual awareness' is. To begin with, we might ascribe the following set of claims to the Relationalist:

The Relational Account of Perceptual Experience

(**Core Claim**) Perceptual experiences are 'genuinely relational', that is, perceptual experiences are relational essentially.

Amongst other things, this entails that

(**Relation Claim**) when a subject perceives an object (or a process, or an event, or a state of affairs),[1] the subject stands in an experiential *relation*— namely, a *perceptual* relation—to the relevant object.

---

[1] In the following, I will abbreviate the formulation just used by simply talking of a subject perceiving *objects*; this is intended also to include reference to a subject's perceiving events, processes and states of affairs.

(**Constitution Claim**) A perceived object itself is a *constitutive part* of the relevant perceptual experience.

(**Consciousness Claim**) A perceived object is, for the perceiving subject, 'immediately available in consciousness' (McDowell 1978: 138).

This set of claims offers a good first sketch of the Relationalist's position.[2] In order to understand the Relationalist's position fully, we should next consider these claims in a little more detail. First, then, let us consider the Core Claim. The Core Claim restates the Relationalist's central idea:

(**Core Claim**) Perceptual experiences are genuinely relational, that is, perceptual experiences are relational essentially.

If we accept the Core Claim, we will also have to accept that perceptual experiences and hallucinations are different kinds of experiences—for while perceptual experiences might be essentially relational, hallucinatory experiences could not possibly be so. After all, a subject who *hallucinates* a pink flower does not stand in any relation to such an object in her environment at all, while a subject who *perceives* a pink flower does, according to the Core Claim, stand in a perceptual relation to the pink flower perceived. Thus, once we accept the Core Claim, we also have to accept that perceptual experiences and hallucinations are experiences of a different kind. However, this might be controversial. Indeed, an opponent might argue as follows:

Objection to the Core Claim

(i) From the experiencing subject's own point of view, hallucinatory experiences and perceptual experiences are indistinguishable.

(ii) Experiences which are indistinguishable from the experiencing subject's own point of view are experiences of the same kind.

---

[2] But then why, so one might rightly ask at this point, would anybody want to *endorse* the Relational Account of perceptual experience? There are at least two reasons: Some endorse a Relational Account of perceptual experience because they hold that only the Relational Account of perceptual experience can explain our ability to think about the world and particular objects in it. This, very roughly, is John Campbell's reason for endorsing and developing a Relational Account (see Campbell 2002 and Campbell's contributions to Campbell and Cassam 2014). Alternatively, one might defend a Relational Account of perceptual experience because it best captures the everyday phenomenology of our perceptual experiences. This suggestion has been developed by Mike Martin (see Martin 2002). However, in this chapter, we won't discuss either of these (or any other) arguments *for* Relationalism in detail. The aim of this chapter is rather to consider some issues in the *metaphysics* of the Relational Account *itself*.

(C1) Thus, hallucinatory experiences and perceptual experiences are experiences of the same kind.

(iii) But then, the Relationalist's Core Claim implies that hallucinatory experiences and perceptual experiences must be experiences of a different kind.

(C2) The Relationalist's Core Claim must therefore be false.

In response to this objection, Relationalists will deny the second premise of the argument, a claim which is often called the 'Common Kind Assumption'. Thus, a Relationalist will deny that experiences which are indistinguishable from the experiencing subject's own point of view *are* experiences of the same kind. Instead, a Relationalist will develop what in the literature is usually called a 'disjunctivist' alternative,[3] according to which perceptual experiences and hallucinatory experiences are experiences of a *different* kind even though the relevant experiences might be indistinguishable from the subject's own point of view when considered in isolation. For example, so the Relationalist will say, a subject who *perceives* a pink flower does stand in a direct perceptual relation to the flower, while a subject who *hallucinates* a pink flower does *not* stand in any such relation to any object in her environment at all—and the Relationalist will hold that the relevant two kinds of experiences—perceptual experiences on the one hand, and hallucinatory experiences on the other—are experiences of a *different* kind, even though, when considered in isolation, they might be indistinguishable from the subject's own point of view. Thus, the Relationalist will insist that the present objection to the Core Claim fails, because its second premise is false, and the Relationalist will therefore continue to endorse the Relational Account's Core Claim, namely that

(**Core Claim**) perceptual experiences are genuinely relational, that is, perceptual experiences are relational essentially.

Next, we should consider the Relation Claim, the Constitution Claim and the Consciousness Claim. In order to develop this chapter's main argument as smoothly as possible, I suggest that we first consider the Constitution Claim

---

[3] For classic points of reference, and the original formulations of disjunctivism, see Hinton (1967) and Snowdon (1980–81).

and the Consciousness Claim before then turning to the Relation Claim. So, let's start with the Constitution Claim. According to the Constitution Claim,

(**Constitution Claim**) a perceived object itself is a *constitutive part* of the relevant perceptual experience.

A defender of this claim will hold that a subject's perceptual experience of one particular object would not be the same perceptual experience as a perceptual experience by the same subject of a qualitatively identical but numerically different object. A subject who perceives a particular yellow duck has one particular perceptual experience, and if the same subject was to perceive a qualitatively identical but numerically different yellow duck at the same time in the same place, that experience would be a different perceptual experience. To put the same point differently, according to the Constitution Claim, in order to individuate a particular perceptual experience, we do, amongst other things, have to individuate the particular object which the perceiving subject is said to stand in a perceptual relation to. This in turn might clarify what the Constitution Claim says.

But then, why should we *accept* this claim? Put concisely, the answer is that the Constitution Claim is *entailed* by the Core Claim of the Relational Account: According to the Core Claim, perceptual experience is essentially relational; but then, a particular relation is constituted in part by its particular relata: In order for a particular relation to obtain, there have to be particular relata, and which particular relation it is that does obtain is in part determined by which particular relata it has; that is, the relata of a particular relation are constitutive of the relevant particular relation, which is just what the Constitution Claim formulates for the specific case of the *perceptual* relation which the Relationalist is interested in: When a particular subject perceives a particular object, so the Core Claim has it, the subject stands in a perceptual relation to the perceived object, and the relevant perceptual experience will be constituted by its two relata (namely: the perceiving subject and the object perceived), and the relation which obtains between them. The Constitution Claim simply spells this out with respect to the object perceived. It therefore seems plausible to hold that anybody who accepts the Core Claim will also have to accept the Constitution Claim.

Next, we should consider the Consciousness Claim. According to the Consciousness Claim,

(**Consciousness Claim**) a perceived object is, for the perceiving subject, 'immediately available in consciousness' (McDowell 1978: 138).

Just as the Constitution Claim, the Consciousness Claim is also directly entailed by the Relationalist's Core Claim. According to the Core Claim, *perceptual experiences* are said to be genuinely relational. This suggests the following train of thought: When a subject perceives an object, all sorts of relations might obtain between the perceiving subject and the perceived object. Maybe the perceiving subject is you, and the perceived object is a friend of yours. In this case, there will be very many relations which obtain between you and the perceived object—you are fond of each other, you know that you can rely on each other, your friend has promised to come on a holiday with you next year, and you are currently sat opposite each other at a table; none of these relations which do obtain between you and your friend at the time of the perceptual experience which we are interested in here are what we try to describe when we say that you stand in a *perceptual* relation to your friend, that the *perceptual experience* which you currently have of your friend is essentially relational. Rather, to say that your perceptual experience of your friend is essentially relational is to say that the conscious experience which you are having of your friend, maybe hearing your friend speak to you, or seeing her sit there in front of you across the table, does put you in a relation to your friend *in consciousness*.

But then, this is just what the Consciousness Claim says: In perception, a perceived object is 'immediately available in consciousness' for the perceiving subject. In perception, you are 'directly aware' of the object perceived—that is, you are *acquainted* with the object, the object is 'immediately available in consciousness' for you—or so we will have to hold if we accept the Relationalist's Core Claim. Thus, once more, we find that the Consciousness Claim is entailed by the Relationalist's Core Claim. If we accept the Relationalist's main idea as formulated by the Core Claim, we should also accept the Consciousness Claim.

Next, and for this chapter most importantly, we should consider the Relation Claim. According to that claim,

(**Relation Claim**) when a subject perceives an object, the subject stands in an experiential *relation*—namely, a *perceptual* relation—to the relevant object.

But then, so someone might rightly ask, what exactly is the Relationalist talking about when she speaks of an 'experiential relation' quite generally, and a 'perceptual relation' more specifically? How do actual cases of perception, in which subjects allegedly stand in some 'experiential relation' to the relevant perceived objects, fit into the world as we find it? And how could such experiential relations possibly obtain?

One reply which the Relationalist might offer in response to this question would be to say that the question is somewhat misconceived, because the experiential relation which obtains between a perceiving subject and the object perceived does not really 'fit' into the world as we find it, that is, into the physical world, at all; indeed, so they might say, we have to distinguish between two different realms, the realm of the physical and the realm of the mental, and while physical relations obtain in the realm of the physical, mental relations obtain in the realm of the mental; on such a radically dualist conception, it would seem to be misguided to ask how mental relations— such as perceptual relations—'fit' into the physical world.

However, radically dualist positions of the present variety are currently not very popular. Indeed, most of us will be inclined to assume that we should try to *answer* the question just posed in order to offer a plausible Relational Account of perception, that is, that we should explain how actual cases of perception, in which subjects allegedly stand in some 'experiential relation' to the objects perceived, do fit into the world as we find it.

In setting out to answer this question, the Relationalist might start by making the following suggestion:

Relation Claim, expanded version:

Whenever S perceives x, S stands in a perceptual relation to x. Whenever S stands in a perceptual relation to x, the relevant *perceptual* relation supervenes on the *spatial*, *temporal* and *causal* relations which obtain between S and x.

In order to explicate this expanded version of the Relation Claim, we should first ask *in which* spatial, temporal and causal relations a perceiving subject stands to the object perceived. In doing so, I suggest that we here focus on *ordinary* cases of perception, and more specifically on cases in which it is uncontroversial which object or event should count as the object or event which is being perceived by the subject, cases which form the vast majority of cases of perceptual experience.[4] In those ordinary cases, a perceived

---

[4] There certainly are unusual, exceptional cases of perceptual experience—such as cases when, during a clear night, one looks up at the night sky. The light which a subject who looks at a particular light in the night sky sees has been emitted by a star at some much earlier time, and

event occurs *at the time at which the relevant perceptual experience occurs,* and a perceived object exists in the subject's environment *at the time at which the perceptual experience occurs.* The *temporal* relation which obtains between a perceiving subject and the relevant object or event perceived is therefore usually a relation of rough simultaneity.

Secondly, each subject traces a continuous spatio-temporal path through the world. In order for someone to be said to perceive something, it is necessary that the spatio-temporal path of the subject on the one hand, and the perceived object on the other, intersect at the time at which the perceptual experience occurs. Usually, this means that the perceived object lies on the spatio-temporal path which the subject herself traces through the world. Thus, the spatial relation between the perceived object and the perceiving subject can usually be described by saying that at the time at which the perceptual experience occurs, the perceived object's spatial location lies on the continuous path which the perceiving subject has traced and is tracing through space.

Finally, the idea that an object has some *causal* role to play when a subject perceives the relevant object might also seem plausible. Indeed, it seems plausible to assume that when a subject perceives an object, the relevant

---

the relevant star might even have ceased to exist meanwhile. It is controversial what exactly it is that a subject does see in such a situation. One might argue that the subject sees the light which presently arrives in her vicinity, that is, that the subject perceives an event (the arrival of the light) which arguably does stand in a relation of rough simultaneity to the perceiving subject. However, it might also be argued that the subject presently sees an *object,* namely the star, even if this object has ceased to exist at the time at which the perceptual experience occurs. On the latter account, the case of seeing stars would obviously have to count as an exception to the condition of spatio-temporal simultaneity in perceptual experience. Other exceptional cases might be cases in which a subject sees a photo, or a film, of a particular object or event. Once more, it is controversial what exactly it is that a subject sees in such situations. Some might hold that the subject simply sees a *photo,* or a *film,* which happens to represent the relevant object or event; others, however, might hold that, by means of a pictorial, or filmic representation, the subject actually does see the relevant *object or event* (for discussion see e.g. Walton 1984: 252). On the latter account, cases of the present kind would also have to count as exceptions to the condition of spatio-temporal simultaneity between perceiver and object perceived in perceptual experience. Indeed, it seems plausible that relevant disagreements about how to account for the exceptional cases just sketched arises precisely *because* in those exceptional cases, the condition of spatio-temporal simultaneity, which *is* met in *ordinary* cases of perceptual experience, is *not* met. Which side one takes in the relevant controversy about exceptional cases like the ones sketched above probably depends on whether one thinks of the condition of spatio-temporal simultaneity as a *necessary* condition for all cases of perceptual experience or not. We will not be able to engage in that debate here; instead, we will here simply focus on *ordinary* cases of perceptual experience. In those ordinary cases of perceptual experience, the perceiving subject and the object perceived do happen to stand in a relation of spatio-temporal simultaneity.

object somehow affects the subject. In an attempt to formulate the present intuition somewhat more concisely, we might say that

(Causal Claim) when a subject perceives a certain object, certain neurophysiological events occur in the subject's brain. Those neurophysiological events are in some way caused by the object which the subject perceives.

The causal relation which obtains between a relevant object and relevant neurophysiological events in the subject's brain is bound to be very complex, and a full account of the relevant causal relations will hopefully be developed one day by neuroscientists working in the field. For present purposes, the Causal Claim does, in its general form, seem a useful and plausible empirical hypothesis, and we might accept it as such.[5]

More generally, we find that at least for the vast majority of ordinary cases of perception, we can give a clear general account of the spatial, the temporal and the causal relations which obtain between a perceiving subject and the perceived object, which in turn should help us to understand parts of the Relation Claim in its expanded version, which, to repeat, runs as follows:

Relation Claim, expanded version:

Whenever S perceives x, S stands in a perceptual relation to x. Whenever S stands in a perceptual relation to x, the relevant *perceptual* relation supervenes on the *spatial, temporal* and *causal* relations which obtain between S and x.

But then, according to the extended version of the Relation-Claim, the *perceptual* relation which obtains between the perceiving subject and the perceived object *supervenes* on the spatial, temporal and causal relations which obtain between the perceiving subject and the perceived object. This is what we should consider next.

---

[5] Thus, I here presuppose that we become *empirically* aware of the fact that there is a causal link between the perceiving subject and the object perceived. Others might furthermore hold that it is 'built into' our concept of perception that a relevant causal link must obtain in order for a subject to perceive anything. The present debate could easily be adapted to that latter view. (For an assessment of both positions and support of the latter view, cf. Child 1994, ch. 5; see also Snowdon 2011, Steward 2011, and Child 2011.)

3. The Supervenience Claim

The Relationalist might spell out their Supervenience Claim as follows:

Supervenience Claim:

A perceptual relation which obtains between S and x supervenes on the spatial, the temporal and the causal relations which obtain between S and x. In order for this to be so, it is necessary and sufficient that the following two conditions are met:

(**NC1**) If the *spatial*, *temporal*, and *causal* relations which obtain between S_1 and x_1 on the one hand and S_2 and x_2 on the other, are qualitatively identical, and if a perceptual relation obtains between S_1 and x_1, then an *experiential* relation necessarily also obtains between S_2 and x_2, and the experiential relations which obtain between S_1 and x_1 on the one hand and S_2 and x_2 on the other, are necessarily qualitatively identical: The relevant experiential relations are both *perceptual* relations.

(**NC2**) A certain perceptual relation does not only *covary* with the relevant spatial, temporal and causal relations, but it is in some way *dependent* on the relevant spatial, temporal and causal relations.

For example, so the defender of this Supervenience Claim will say, consider the case of Sara who sees a golden sphere in a museum. According to the Supervenience Claim, a perceptual relation obtains between Sara and the sphere, and the perceptual relation *supervenes* on the spatial, temporal and causal relation between Sara and the sphere. Next, so the defender of the Supervenience Claim will suggest, consider the case of Sara and Sara*:

The case of Sara and Sara*

Sara perceives a golden sphere at a museum. Sara*, in turn, is standing in front of sphere*, which is qualitatively identical with the sphere which Sara perceives. Indeed, the lightwaves reflected by sphere and sphere*, respectively, and the neurophysiological patterns of activation which respectively occur in the brains of Sara and Sara* at the time at which they perceive the relevant object are qualitatively identical. Furthermore, the temporal and spatial relations obtaining between Sara and the sphere, and Sara* and sphere*, respectively, are qualitatively identical. Thus, the spatial, temporal and causal relations which obtain between Sara* and sphere* are qualitatively identical with the spatial, temporal and causal relations which obtain between Sara and the sphere.

Under those circumstances, anybody with any inclination to accept that experiential relations somehow depend on physical (and among them importantly neurophysiological) relations will probably agree that it is rather plausible to hold that if Sara stands in a perceptual relation to the golden sphere, an experiential relation also obtains between Sara* and sphere*, and the relevant experiential relation is a *perceptual* relation. Thus, on the basis of the present example, it does seem plausible to accept the Supervenience Claim's condition (NC1):

(NC1) If the *spatial*, *temporal*, and *causal* relations which obtain between S_1 and x_1 on the one hand and S_2 and x_2 on the other, are qualitatively identical, and if a perceptual relation obtains between S_1 and x_1, then an *experiential* relation necessarily also obtains between S_2 and x_2, and the experiential relations which obtain between S_1 and x_1 on the one hand and S_2 and x_2 on the other, are necessarily qualitatively identical: The relevant experiential relations are both *perceptual* relations.[6]

Next, we should consider (NC2), which holds that

(NC2) a certain perceptual relation does not only *covary* with the relevant spatial, temporal and causal relations, but it is in some way *dependent* on the relevant spatial, temporal and causal relations.

For example, the perceptual relation which obtains between Sara and the golden sphere does, according to (NC2), *depend* on the spatial, temporal and causal relations which obtain between Sara and the sphere, which, again, seems plausible given minimal physicalist inclinations. More generally, the Supervenience Claim (of which (NC2) is a part) expresses the intuition, shared by many, that the mental in general, and perceptual experiences in particular, do in some way depend on events and properties which we can describe in purely physical terms.

---

[6] In developing (NC1) further, one might, as an anonymous referee rightly points out, want to ask what exactly is 'required for two causal connections to count as "qualitatively identical"'. An answer to this question probably will, as the anonymous referee suggests, 'include [a reference to] downstream visual processing to accommodate cases of attention [and] inattention'.

Thus, it seems that we have good reason to accept the Supervenience Claim: A perceptual relation which obtains between a perceiving subject and the relevant object perceived supervenes on the spatial, the temporal and the causal relations which obtain between the subject and the object, just as the Supervenience Claim suggests.[7]

4. The Argument Against the Reductive Account

However, condition (NC2) of the Supervenience Claim does not yet say *what kind* of dependence relation obtains between the perceptual relation and the spatial, temporal and causal relations upon which it is said to supervene. How might this be worked out?

In response, one might suggest that the Relationalist try to offer a 'reductive explanation' of the relation between perceptual relations and the spatial, temporal and causal relations on which they depend. Thus, so it might be suggested, the Relationalist should try to show that a perceptual relation is in fact 'nothing over and above' a combination of a certain spatial, temporal, and causal relation. Indeed, so the defender of a reductive account might say, whenever we talk about a 'perceptual relation', all we are talking about is a characteristic combination of three other relations, namely of a spatial, a temporal and a causal relation. Such a reductive account might have its attractions—not least because it would offer a very clear account of the perceptual relation. Alas, it seems impossible to combine the Relational Account of perception with a reductive account of the perceptual relation. Indeed, or so I will try to show now, a Relationalist *could not possibly* endorse a reductive account of the perceptual relation, a claim which I think can be supported with the help of the following argument:

Argument Against the Reductive Account

(A1) When a subject perceives an object, so the Relational Account's Consciousness Claim states, the object itself is, for the perceiving subject, immediately available in consciousness.

---

[7] As Kim points out, 'many interesting issues arise when relations are explicitly brought into supervenience, and they are deserving of further study' (Kim 1993: 165). Indeed, Kim's comments on 'Relational Supervenience' indicate further avenues a Relationalist about perceptual experience could fruitfully explore in the present context (1993: 161–165). An alternative to the specific supervenience claim developed in this chapter is put forward by Allen (2021: sect. 3), who suggests that a Relationalist (or, in Allen's terminology, a 'naive realist') should, somewhat more broadly, endorse a 'global supervenience claim'.

(A2) According to a reductive account of the perceptual relation, a perceptual relation between a subject and a perceived object is 'nothing but' a certain combination of a spatial, a temporal and a causal relation.

(A3) But then, if the perceptual relation which obtains between a perceiving subject and a perceived object was nothing but a certain combination of a spatial, a temporal and a causal relation, only the *causal effects* of perceived objects could, for the perceiving subject, be immediately available in consciousness, but not the perceived objects themselves.

Thus,

(C) (Irreducibility Claim) a Relationalist could not possibly endorse a reductive account of the perceptual relation.

This is the argument. Next, we should look at this argument in greater detail. In doing so, we find that the first two premises, premises (A1) and (A2), should be rather uncontroversial. (A1) and (A2) simply restate the Relationalist's and the Reductionist's positions respectively, and given that we here explore the question as to whether a Relationalist could possibly be a Reductionist, we will have to rely on both these premises in the present context, so that the first two premises of the argument should not require any further discussion here.

By contrast, the third premise of this argument, premise (A3), does need further scrutiny. Why should we accept premise (A3)? In reply, we can offer an argument in support of premise (A3) which runs as follows:

Argument in Support of (A3)

(S1) If a subject had experiential access to an object only by means of a spatial, a temporal and a causal relation, only those features of the object which can be transmitted by a spatial, a temporal and a causal relation could be immediately available in consciousness for the subject.

(S2) But then, a spatial, temporal and causal relation—that is, a spatio-temporally located causal relation—can only transmit spatio-temporally located causal effects; that is, any 'input' to a spatio-temporally located causal relation can only be causal input from a certain spatio-temporal location, and any 'output' from a spatio-temporally located causal relation can only be spatio-temporally located causal output.

(C) Thus, if the perceptual relation which obtains between a perceiving subject and a perceived object was nothing but a certain combination of a spatial, a temporal and a causal relation, only the *causal effects* of perceived objects could be immediately available in consciousness for the perceiving subject, just as (A3) says.

I think this argument is sound, but more should be said to elucidate each of its two premises: Premise (S1), to repeat, states that

(S1) if a subject had experiential access to an object only by means of a spatial, a temporal and a causal relation, only those features of the object which can be transmitted by a spatial, a temporal and a causal relation could be immediately available in consciousness for the subject.

Now, in talking of the 'transmission' of features of an object via a spatial, a temporal and a causal relation, I do not mean to introduce any technical terms; rather, talk of 'transmission' is here to be understood informally, in a non-technical way. Thus, I here start from the rather intuitive thought that if a subject has experiential access to an object by standing in one particular type, and no other type, of relation to the object, then only those features of the object that can be transmitted by the relevant type of relation could be said to be 'immediately available in consciousness' to the subject on the basis of the relevant experience. All those features of the object which the relevant type of relation *cannot* transmit could at most be available to the subject in some *indirect* way, and therefore could not be 'immediately available in consciousness' to the subject.

Talk of 'transmission' might then in turn be spelled out as follows: In cases in which a subject perceives an object, the subject, who is one entity, somehow needs to 'get at' features of the object, which is another entity, in order for the subject to perceive the relevant features. All it means to say that a subject stands in a relation to the object which can 'transmit' a relevant feature to her is to say that the subject can somehow 'get at' the relevant feature in virtue of standing in the relevant relation to the object. This should clarify what (S1) says, and it would seem that with those clarifications in place, we have good reason to accept (S1).

Next, we should consider premise (S2) of the Argument in Support of (AR3), which says that

(S2) a spatial, temporal and causal relation—that is, a spatio-temporally located causal relation—can only transmit spatio-temporally located causal effects; that is, any 'input' to a spatio-temporally located causal relation can only be causal input from a certain spatio-temporal location, and any 'output' from a spatio-temporally located causal relation can only be spatio-temporally located causal output.

Now, (S2) talks of 'input' and 'output', and maybe some clarificatory comments might be in order in this respect too: When talking about the 'input' and the 'output' of a relation, I here mean to refer to events that respectively stand at the beginning and at the end of a certain causal chain. It seems appropriate to think of the spatial, temporal and causal relations which obtain in the case of perception as of causal chains; the relevant 'input' will usually be located in the subject's environment, and the relevant 'output' will usually be located in the perceiving subject's brain. This in turn should clarify what (S2) says, and it would seem that with those clarifications in place, (S2) is not a particularly controversial claim.

But then, as both (S1) and (S2) are plausible, we have good reason to accept the conclusion of our earlier Argument in Support of (A3), namely the claim that

(C) if the perceptual relation which obtains between a perceiving subject and a perceived object was nothing but a certain combination of a spatial, a temporal and a causal relation, only the *causal effects* of perceived objects could be immediately available in consciousness for the perceiving subject, just as (A3) says.

This in turn is a substantial part of what (A3) does say. However, (A3) claims more than this. Indeed, (A3) says that

(A3) if the perceptual relation which obtains between a perceiving subject and a perceived object was nothing but a certain combination of a spatial, a temporal and a causal relation, only the *causal effects* of perceived objects could, for the perceiving subject, be immediately available in consciousness, **but not the perceived objects themselves.**

The Argument in Support of (A3) shows that most of this claim is true. However, we have *not* so far addressed the last part of (A3), printed in bold type above ('but not the perceived objects themselves'): This last part of (A3) is *not* supported by what we have said so far, but it is obviously a crucial part of (A3), and thus also a crucial part of the argument of which (A3) is a premise, namely the 'Argument Against the Reductive Account'. We therefore have to assess this last part of (A3), which in turn means that we have to engage in some ontological considerations next.

5. Some Ontological Considerations

In distinguishing between the *causal effects* of an object on the one hand, and the *object itself* on the other, (A3) clearly presupposes an ontological claim—namely, that we *can* distinguish between an object's causal effects on the one hand, and the object itself on the other—and it implies that if only the object's *causal effects* are immediately available in consciousness for a subject, the object itself is *not* immediately available in consciousness for the subject. Indeed, at least at first sight, all of this might seem rather plausible: It might seem plausible to accept that a distinction between an object itself and its causal effects can be successfully drawn, and it might also seem plausible to accept that if only the causal effects of an object are immediately available in consciousness, the object itself is *not* immediately available in consciousness for the subject. For example, we can distinguish between the traces of a bike in the mud, and the bike itself, and walking along a muddy path the traces of a bike in the mud might be immediately available to you in consciousness, but the bike itself (assuming that it's long gone over the next hill) is in no way available in consciousness to you at all.

Thus, at first sight it might also seem plausible to hold more generally that, just as (A3) presupposes, if only the spatio-temporally located *causal effects* of a perceived object are immediately available in consciousness for a subject, the object itself is *not* immediately available in consciousness for the subject. However, once we start to consider the distinction between an object itself and its causal effects in a somewhat more philosophical manner, we find a wide spectrum of possible views one might take on the question of how that distinction could and should be drawn, which in turn means that there is a wide range of options as to how we might interpret, and then assess, (A3).

The fact that there is a wide range of views one might take on the question of how the distinction between an object and its causal effects is to be drawn in turn does seem grounded in the fact that there is a wide range of possible answers to the question as to what an 'object itself' might be. I suggest that for present purposes we distinguish, briefly and very schematically, between two answers to the latter question, answers which arguably lie at two ends of a wide spectrum of different possible views, namely the 'Categorical Account of Objects' on the one hand, and the 'Dispositional Account of Objects' on the other. Consideration of those two extreme views should enable us to assess (A3) fully.

First, then, one might endorse a 'Categorical Account of Objects' according to which objects are the *grounds* or *bearers* of properties.

A defender of such an account of objects (see e.g. Campbell 2002, ch. 12) might say that

(**Categorical Account of Objects**) objects are non-dispositional; they are the categorical ground of properties.

In an attempt to elucidate this claim a little further, the defender of the Categorical Account of Objects might add that to say of an object that it is the 'categorical' ground of certain properties is to indicate that the relevant ground of properties could not possibly be analyzed, or described fully, with the help of conditional propositions (see Shoemaker 2011).

On the other end of a range of possible views we will find what we might call the 'Dispositional Account of Objects', which holds that

(**Dispositional Account of Objects**) objects are nothing but compounds of dispositional properties.

On this view, when we talk about objects we are talking about nothing but a certain compound of dispositional properties, and we have fully accounted for a particular object once we have described a relevant compound of dispositional properties. 'A disposition', so the defender of the present view might say, 'is an input-output state, a tendency . . . to behave in a particular way in particular circumstances',[8] and objects simply are compounds of such dispositional properties.[9]

But then, how might these two accounts of objects be related to our current considerations of the nature of the perceptual relation? First, one might observe that some philosophers who endorse a *Relational* Account of perceptual experience seem to do so *for ontological reasons*. Indeed, they might be following a train of thought which we can sketch as follows:

Argument in Support of the Relational Account

(i) Objects are more than just compounds of dispositional properties.

(ii) But then, in order for an experience of something which is more than just a compound of dispositional properties to provide the subject with knowledge

---

[8] Campbell (2002: 236).
[9] Campbell 2002, ch.12 quite plausibly ascribes this view to Shoemaker (cf. e.g. Shoemaker 1984).

of the relevant thing, the subject needs to stand in a relation to the relevant thing, and that relation needs to be more than just a causal relation.

(iii) Perceptual experiences of objects can and sometimes do provide subjects with knowledge of the relevant objects.

(C) Thus, a subject who perceives an object stands in an experiential relation to the object, and that relation is more than just a causal relation.[10]

On the other hand, we also find that a defender of a *Dispositional Account of Objects* has good reason to endorse a *Representational* Account of perceptual experience (and thus *not* to endorse a Relational Account), which can be shown as follows:

Dispositionalist's Argument in Support of a Representational Account

(i) If objects are nothing but compounds of dispositional properties, a subject will be perceptually aware of an object if the object has an appropriate causal effect on the subject.

(ii) But then, a rather plausible way to determine what should count as an 'appropriate causal effect' in the present context is to say that the appropriate causal effect which an object must have on a subject in order for the subject to be said to perceive the object is a (more or less) accurate representational state—that is, a state which (more or less) accurately represents the object as being a certain way.

(C) Hence, if objects are nothing but compounds of dispositional properties, we have good reason to assume that perceptual experiences are representational states.

Thus, while a dispositional account of objects might be logically consistent with, and therefore in principle compatible with, the Relational Account of perceptual experience, it would not make much philosophical sense to endorse both views at the same time. We find that we have two options here: Either

(a) objects are nothing but compounds of dispositional properties (i.e. the Dispositional Account of Objects is true)

---

[10] Smithies (2011: 17) ascribes something like the present argument to Campbell (2002) (although I'm not sure whether this does accurately represent the argumentative structure of Campbell's text).

or

(b) objects are *more* than compounds of dispositional properties.

If one endorses option (a), it does not make much sense to endorse a Relational Account at all. On the other hand, if one endorses option (b), it does make sense to endorse the Relational Account. But if one holds that, as option (b) suggests, objects are *more* than just compounds of dispositional properties, one will also have to hold that if only a set of dispositional properties is immediately available in consciousness for a subject, the object itself is *not* immediately available in consciousness for the subject, which means that one has reason to accept the last part of (A3). Taking this together with our earlier Argument in Support of (A3), we find that someone who wants to reasonably develop a Relational Account of perceptual experience does have reason to accept that

(A3) if the perceptual relation which obtains between a perceiving subject and a perceived object was nothing but a certain combination of a spatial, a temporal and a causal relation, only the *causal effects* of perceived objects could, for the perceiving subject, be immediately available in consciousness, but not the perceived objects themselves.

Once we accept this claim, which is the third premise in our earlier Argument Against the Reductive Account, the Argument Against the Reductive Account also does go through. Thus, we have reason to endorse the Argument Against the Reductive Account's conclusion and endorse the Irreducibility Claim, namely the claim that

(Irreducibility Claim) a Relationalist could not possibly endorse a reductive account of the perceptual relation.

However, an opponent might insist that this argument is unsuccessful, because in the face of everything we have said so far, (A3) is nevertheless still false.

6. 'Singular Elements'?

Indeed, so our opponent might say, even under the assumption that objects are more than compounds of dispositional properties, the Argument

Against the Reductive Account is unsuccessful, for even under that onto-logical assumption it *is* possible for an object itself to be immediately available in consciousness for a subject by means only of a spatial, a temporal and a causal relation between the relevant object and the subject, given the following train of thought:

> If a type-identical, perceptually indiscernible scene existed somewhere else in the universe, one would perceive the scene that causes one's perception, not the type-identical duplicate scene. So the representa-tion that marks the perception *must contain a singular element* that is particular to the elements of the perceived scene. The singular element is context-dependent. The perceptual system does not have the resources to specify the perceived particulars in a context free way. So the singular elements have the singularity and context-dependence of applications of the demonstrative 'that', even though they are not associated with language—or with propositional structure.
>
> (Burge 2005: 6, my emphasis)

Thus, with the help of their 'singular elements', perceptual experiences do 'represent . . . particular objects' (Burge 2005: 67 fn.5), which in turn (presumably?) means that a subject who perceives a certain object does have experiential access to the relevant object itself.

In response, we might argue as follows: If the relation obtaining between the perceived object and the perceiving subject is nothing but a spatial, tem-poral and causal relation, then the relevant 'singular elements' of relevant perceptual representational contents could not be anything more than the *causal* effects of the object that the subject is said to perceive. But then, we presently assume that objects are *more* than compounds of dispositional properties, and under that assumption it does, as we argued when discuss-ing the Argument in Support of (A3) above, remain unclear how, on the basis of such *causal effects* of the object (i.e. the relevant 'singular elements') only, the object itself could possibly be immediately available in conscious-ness for the subject.

Bill Brewer formulates the same point as follows:

> . . . proponents of [a 'content view', that is, a representational view such as Burge's] may *say* that mind-independent physical objects are the 'direct objects' of perception according to their view. What they *mean* by this is that the account that they offer of the way in which we are presented with

mind-independent physical objects has no need of any direct relation of acquaintance with mind-dependent entities of any kind. This is fine so far as it goes, although later...I argue that their attempts to provide an adequate account of perceptual presentation in this context are unsuccessful. My point here is more straightforward....I [myself] use the expression 'direct object' to refer to those entities, if any, our direct acquaintance with which constitutes the most fundamental account of the nature of our perceptual experience. According to [the opponents' view] there are no such things. For the defining feature of their position is that the nature of perceptual experience is to be given directly in terms of its representational content instead.

(Brewer 2011: 55, fn 2)

I think Brewer nicely summarizes the problem here. The opponent assumes that subjects *could not possibly be* directly acquainted with objects in their environment. The Relationalist by contrast aims to explain precisely this—how it might be possible for a subject to *be* directly acquainted with objects in her environment. As long as the opponent simply presupposes that the Relationalist's Core Claim is false, the opponent is not able properly to engage with the debate we are currently having, which *presupposes*, for the sake of the argument, that the Relationalist's Core Claim is *true*, and tries to develop the metaphysical implications of this Core Claim.

Thus, at least for the time being we can conclude that the opponent's objection against our earlier 'Argument Against the Reductive Account' is not successful. We are left with the conclusion of that argument, namely the claim that a Relationalist will have to hold that the perceptual relation is *irreducible*.

7. An Irreducibily *Sui Generis* Relation

As we have seen, according to the Relational Account the perceptual relation which obtains between the perceiving subject and the object perceived could not possibly be reduced to a spatial, temporal, and a causal relation. As the Irreducibility Claim says,

(Irreducibility Claim) a Relationalist could not possibly endorse a reductive account of the perceptual relation.

According to the Relational Account, the perceptual relation is a relation 'of its own kind', it is a *sui generis* relation. Reformulating the same point and putting it in different words, we find that in order for a subject to be able to gain her very own subjective perspective on the world by being acquainted with her environment in perception, it is, according to the Relational Account of perceptual experience, necessary that an irreducibly *sui generis* relation obtain between the subject and her environment. Thus, Relationalism about perceptual experience will have to offer a 'non-reductive' account of perceptual experience, which is a feature it shares with a 'Qualia Account' of perceptual experience.[11]

Indeed, a 'Relational Account' and a 'Qualia Account' of perceptual experience are both *non-reductive* accounts of perceptual experience, but for very different reasons: While the Qualia Account assumes that the elusive 'quale', the 'what-it-is-like-ness' of an experience which renders a reductive explanation impossible is to be found somewhere in the very *innermost* part of the experiencing subject herself, the Relationalist suggests that the aspect of perceptual experience which makes a reductive explanation impossible is to be found at the very *outermost* boundary of the experiential relation.[12]

---

[11] For reasons of space, I will here simply have to assume that readers are familiar with the philosophical concept of 'qualia'; Block (1980) is a classic point of reference for a 'Qualia Account' of consciousness, and for a similarly classic critique see Dennett (1990).

[12] Thus, a defender of a Qualia Account of perceptual experience will certainly not be antagonized by the Relationalist's claim that we cannot offer a non-reductive account of perceptual experience. Quite on the contrary, this is a claim which defenders of the Qualia Account themselves will endorse. However, asked to choose between a Qualia Account and a Relational Account of perceptual experience, the Qualia Account might seem more plausible to some, for they might think that the Relational Account is fundamentally flawed. Indeed, as Uriah Kriegel has recently put it (at a workshop held in Liège in November 2022), it looks as if the Relationalist might make a 'category mistake' when she claims that physical objects are constitutive parts of relevant perceptual experiences. For according to the Relationalist, when a subject perceives a table made of wood, the subject's experience is constituted by the wooden table itself, and the wooden table is available for the subject *in consciousness*, which in turn seems to imply that, as Uriah puts it, the Relationalist has to hold that 'the *phenomenology* of the subject's experience *is made of wood*'—and that, or so the Relationalist's opponent concludes, clearly is an absurd claim to make. For, as the opponent might ask rhetorically, how could *the phenomenology* of a perceptual experience possibly *be made of wood*? Indeed, so they conclude, such a claim does not make any sense, and anybody who nevertheless makes such a claim does commit a category mistake. When asked to choose between a Qualia Account of perceptual experience and Relationalism, the Qualia Account should therefore be preferred, because it is the only viable option.—In response, the Relationalist might, somewhat provocatively, simply confirm that in some sense, according to a Relational Account of perceptual experience, the phenomenology of perceptual experiences actually *is* in part made of wood. Indeed, so the Relationalist might say, this is just what happens in perceptual experience—objects made of various materials are available for the perceiving subject in consciousness, and it is consciousness which does have a certain 'phenomenology'. It follows that, depending on individual cases, the phenomenology of a perceptual experience might in part be made of

Thus, while the defender of a Qualia Account and the Relationalist agree that a reductive account of perceptual experiences is impossible, they endorse this claim for diametrically opposed reasons. Focusing on the Relational Account here, we find that according to the Relational Account, the attempt to offer a reductive explanation of perceptual experiences fails because it is impossible to explain reductively how, in perceiving an object, the *perceived object itself* could possibly be available in consciousness for the perceiving subject.

Some might take this to be a reason to give up on Relationalism, but I think we have reason to endorse Relationalism even in the face of this implication of non-reductivism, for I think one can show, as I have tried to do elsewhere (see Debus (2023)), that Relationalism provides us with the best possible account of the value of perceptual awareness. For the time being, we can conclude that anybody who does want to endorse Relationalism about perceptual experience will have to hold that the perceptual relation which, according to the Relationalist, obtains between a perceiving subject and the object perceived is a relation of its own kind,

---

wood (when perceiving a wooden table), or it might in part be made of plastic (when perceiving a yellow plastic duck), it might in part be made of clay (when perceiving a jug made of clay), the phenomenology of a perceptual experience might in part be made of paper (when perceiving a birthday card), or it might in part be made of any of the other materials which the objects which a subject might be able to perceive are made of. This, or so the Relationalist will say, is just what happens in perception: The perceiving subject is directly aware of the object perceived, which means that the phenomenology of the perceptual experience is, in part, 'made of' the material of the object perceived. Of course, the claim that 'the phenomenology of the experience is in part made of wood' does sound a little odd, but this is presumably due to the fact that when talking about the 'phenomenology' of perceptual experiences, people often already *presuppose* that the phenomenology of an experience is characterized by features which are in important ways *independent* of how the world is, and therefore certainly not 'made of' the various materials of physical objects. Indeed, that the phenomenology of perceptual experiences is in some way independent of how things are in the world is certainly an implication of a Qualia Account, which accounts for the phenomenology of perceptual experiences in terms of qualia. The Relationalist, by contrast, aims to explain the phenomenology of perceptual experiences in terms of how the world actually *is*, which will imply that the phenomenology of perceptual experiences is, in part, made of the various materials of which relevant perceived objects are made. This will only sound odd (or indeed look like a category mistake) to someone who comes to this debate already *presupposing* that Relationalism *must* be false; in the present context, however, in which we are trying to assess the Relational Account of perceptual experience in its own terms, such a presupposition is inappropriate and should therefore be avoided. Thus, we should here remain open to the possibility that the phenomenology of perceptual experiences is in part 'made of' the various materials which the perceived objects are made of, and we should broaden our understanding of the concept of the phenomenology of perceptual experiences in such a way that the claim does *not* sound like a category mistake any more. Someone who claims that the phenomenology of perceptual experience of a wooden table is in part made of wood does *not* thereby commit a category mistake; rather, they offer one, somewhat unusual, formulation of the Relationalist's core idea.

or a *sui generis* relation. Thus, a Relationalist about perceptual experience will have to be a Non-Reductivist about the mind: According to Relationalism, the perceptual relation is *special*—it is an irreducible, *sui generis* relation; it grounds our subjective prspective onto the world, and it renders the world accessible to us by making us acquainted with it, by making it immediately available to us in consciousness.

It is in virtue of this special relation which obtains between a subject and her environment in perception that she can be *conscious* of the world around her. Perception is essentially relational, that is, a subject's being conscious of her environment in perception is an *essentially* relational state of affairs. But then, so we have meanwhile seen, once we try to develop this thought—which is the Relationalist's core idea, as formulated by the Core Claim—we find that, according to a Relational Account of perceptual experience, the relation which obtains between the perceiving subject and the object perceived cannot but be a rather *special* relation: Indeed, anybody who endorses a Relational Account of perceptual experience will have to hold that the perceptual relation between the perceiving subject and the object perceived is an *irreducibly sui generis* relation.

References

Allen, K. (2021): 'Bridging the Gap? Naive Realism and the Problem of Consciousness', in: H. Logue and L. Richardson (eds), *Purpose and Procedure in Philosophy of Perception*. Oxford: Oxford University Press. 43–62.

Block, N. (1980): 'Troubles with Functionalism', in: N. Block (ed.), *Readings in the Philosophy of Psychology* (Volume 1). Cambridge, MA: Harvard University Press. 268–305.

Brewer, B. (2011): *Perception and Its Objects*. Oxford: Oxford University Press.

Burge, T. (2005): 'Disjunctivism and Perceptual Psychology', *Philosophical Topics* 33. 1–78.

Campbell, J. (2002): *Reference and Consciousness*. Oxford: Oxford University Press.

Campbell, J., and Cassam, Q. (2014): *Berkeley's Puzzle: What does Experience Teach Us?* Oxford: Oxford University Press.

Child, W. (1994): *Causality, Interpretation and the Mind*. Oxford: Oxford University Press.

Child, W. (2011): 'Vision and Causal Understanding', in: J. Roessler, H. Lerman and N. Eilan (eds.), *Perception, Causation, and Objectivity*. Oxford: Oxford University Press. 161–180.

Debus, D. (2023): 'Right Here, Right Now: On the Eudaimonic Value of Perceptual Experience', in U. Kriegel (ed.), *Oxford Studies in the Philosophy of Mind*, vol 3. 191–218.

Dennett, D. (1990): 'Quining Qualia', in: W. Lycan (ed.), *Mind and Cognition*. Oxford: Blackwell, 519–548.

Hinton, J.M. (1967): 'Visual Experiences', *Mind* 76. 217–227.

Kim, J. (1993): 'Postscripts on Supervenience', in his *Supervenience and Mind: Selected Philosophical Essays*. Cambridge: Cambridge University Press. 161–172.

Martin, M.G.F. (2002): 'The Transparency of Experience', *Mind and Language* 17. 376–425.

Martin, M.G.F. (2006): 'On Being Alienated', in: T. Szabo Gendler and J. Howthorne (eds), *Perceptual Experience*. Oxford: Oxford University Press. 354–410.

McDowell, J. (1978): 'On "The Reality of the Past"', in: C. Hookway and P. Pettit (eds), *Action and Interpretation: Studies in the Philosophy of the Social Sciences*. Cambridge: Cambridge University Press. 127–144.

Shoemaker, S. (2011): 'Realization, Powers, and Property Identity', *The Monist*, 94. 3–18.

Shoemaker, S. (1984): 'Causality and Properties', in his: *Identity, Cause, and Mind. Philosophical Essays*. Cambridge: Cambridge University Press. 206–233.

Smithies, D. (2011): 'What Is the Role of Consciousness in Demonstrative Thought?', *Journal of Philosophy* 118. 5–34.

Snowdon, P. (2011): 'Perceptual Concepts as Non-causal Concepts', in: J. Roessler, H. Lerman and N. Eilan (eds), *Perception, Causation, and Objectivity*. Oxford: Oxford University Press. 121–138.

Snowdon, P.F. (1980–81): 'Perception, Vision and Causation', *Proceedings of the Aristotelian Society* 81. 175–192.

Steward, H. (2011): 'Perception and the Ontology of Causation', in: J. Roessler, H. Lerman and N. Eilan (eds), *Perception, Causation, and Objectivity*. Oxford: Oxford University Press. 139–160.

Walton, K.L. (1984): 'Transparent Pictures: On the Nature of Photographic Realism', *Critical Inquiry* 11. 246–277.

Dorothea Debus, *Relationalism, Acquaintance, and Subjectivity: Some Metaphysical Implications*
In: *Oxford Studies in Philosophy of Mind Volume 4*. Edited by: Uriah Kriegel, Oxford University Press.
© Dorothea Debus 2024. DOI: 10.1093/9780198924159.003.0007

8

I Feel Your Pain

Acquaintance and the Limits of Empathy

Emad H. Atiq and Matt Duncan

Expressions like "I feel your pain" or "I share your sadness" play an important role in our moral lives. They convey our empathy, which is of crucial moral significance. In fact, some philosophers consider empathy to be, not just morally important, but the key to understanding morality.[1] Whether or not we go that far, empathy is clearly central to how we understand, treat, and hope to be treated by other people.

But the kind of empathy that is communicated through expressions like "I feel your pain" is also peculiar. For it seems to require something perplexing and elusive: sharing another's experience. It's not clear how this is possible. We each experience the world from our own point of view, which no one else occupies. My experiences are mine; your experiences are yours. How could we *share* each other's experiences? This issue is related to, but different from, a long-standing puzzle about knowing other minds. Wittgenstein (1958) writes:

If what I feel is always my pain only, what can the supposition mean that someone else has pain? (56)

Likewise, Thomas Nagel observes:

If one only begins with the sole idea of oneself and one's own experience as a model, one may not have sufficient material to extrapolate to a significant notion of other selves and their experiences.

(Nagel, 1970, 106)

---

[1] Empathy and related attitudes play a central role in the theories of moral motivation advanced by David Hume, Adam Smith, and Arthur Schopenhauer. Empathy's epistemic significance—its contribution to our knowledge, understanding, and virtue—remains the subject of lively discussion in contemporary moral philosophy (see, e.g., Slote, 2010; Simmons, 2014; Marshall, 2019; Bailey, 2020; Atiq, 2021). These and other views provide a helpful context for raising some puzzles about empathy that we hope to address in this chapter.

Wittgenstein and Nagel wonder how we can know about, or make meaningful claims about, others' experiences. But expressions like "I feel your pain" raise a further puzzle. They assert, not just that we *know* about others' experiences, but that we *share* them—that one person's experience is, in some important sense, had by another. Even if we suppose that we can know about others' experiences, it remains unclear how we could ever share them.

It's also unclear exactly why it is so important that we do. If you are in pain, then why should it matter, and be a good thing, that *I* am also in the same pain? Why doesn't that just compound the problem? Perhaps there are some fairly obvious reasons why it has *some* value—for example, it helps us understand what others might be going through—but it's not entirely clear why *that* is important, and indeed *so* important.

But it is. And our goal is to explore how and why this is so. Specifically, our goal in this chapter is to clarify how empathy, in the regimented sense of *sharing another's pain*, is possible and why it is important. Central to our account is the concept of being acquainted with—that is, directly aware of—pain. When I feel my own pain, and am acquainted with it, I want the pain to stop, and I'm moved—sometimes compelled—to stop it. My acquaintance with the pain is what reveals that it is no good, to be gotten rid of, and to be avoided in the future. Acquaintance also appears implicated in our understanding of, and motivation to relieve, others' pains. When I say "I feel your pain" I express an awareness of your pain, a direct appreciation of its noxious qualities, and, as with my own pain, an understanding of why it ought to be eased. Explaining how empathy is both possible and important therefore involves clarifying the nature of acquaintance: its limits, epistemic role, and motivational significance.

Here is how we shall proceed. In §1, we'll point out that there are different ways of understanding what it is to empathetically share another's pain. §2 explores whether and to what extent it is possible to empathize in the relevant senses—to share, that is, another's pain. Having settled on what it might take and the fact that most of us have what it takes, we turn to the question of whether one should. In §3, we observe that our taxonomy of different ways of empathizing helps us better understand and evaluate existing accounts of the value of empathy; and, ultimately, points towards a more precise account: agents have both epistemic and moral reasons to share other people's pain because pain-sharing is the source of a species of character-building knowledge that we have no other way of accessing except through direct acquaintance with pain. §4 concludes by pointing out: (a) that our account is compatible with a broad range of views on how the different forms of empathy (corresponding to our taxonomy) are valuable; (b) that, all else being equal, ideal empathy would involve sharing, as closely as possible, other people's pain, and (c) that the account does not settle the weight of our reasons to empathize and, relatedly, when those reasons may be overridden by competing values.

1. What It Takes to Feel Someone Else's Pain

Suppose we're dear friends, you're hurting, and I learn about it. Now I'm hurting too. As an expression of heartfelt empathy, I say to you, "I feel your pain." The sentiment is nice, and expressions like this are clearly important. But how could they be true? You feel your pain, I feel mine; we never feel each other's.

Maybe that's a bit fast. If I say, "Hey, I have that shirt too," I don't mean that I co-own *that* specific shirt you're wearing. Or if I say, "I have the same problem," I don't necessarily mean that our problems are *exactly* the same. So my claim that I share your pain, or shirt, or problems, needn't be interpreted so rigidly. In particular, it needn't imply that we share the same *token* thing, or even the exact same type of thing.

Still, one might wonder, how could I feel your pain? Assuming that I mean it more or less literally, what would it take? The question that interests us isn't what it would take for this claim to be assertible in ordinary language. Rather, it is: What are the potential ways to satisfy this claim, understood as an expression of empathy, if it is taken more-or-less literally? Ultimately, we aren't interested in capturing all of the potential meanings that speakers or listeners might attach to the claim and related expressions; rather, the goal is to identify a set of possibilities of significant epistemic and moral interest.

So, begin again with two subjects, S1 and S2; the former truly says "I feel your pain" to the latter. At very least, this seems to imply that (i) S1 is in some experiential state (call this condition "Experience"), (ii) S1 is aware of being in that state (call this "Self-Awareness"), (iii) S2 is (or was) also in some related experiential state ("Symmetry"), and (iv) S1 is aware that S2 is (or was) in that state ("Other-Awareness").[2]

---

[2] You might think that there is also a causal requirement on "I feel your pain"—that, for it to be both true and an expression of empathy, S1's pain must be caused in some way by S1's awareness of S2's pain. We're inclined to think not. Suppose S1 and S2 are both in pain, their

Now to refine. Start with (i) and (iii)—that is, *Experience* and *Symmetry*. What experiential states must S1 and S2 be in to satisfy "I feel your pain"? Well, *pain*. It might be physical pain, emotional pain, or some other kind of pain. Maybe the claim could be true if they were each in some other kind of experiential state, but set that aside for now—assume that it really is pain that we're interested in. So assume that if S1 feels S2's pain, then they both are (or were) in pain.

Now the question is: How is S1's pain *related* to S2's? It can't *just* be that they're both in pain. If S2 has a broken heart, and S1 has a cramp in their calf, S1 doesn't thereby feel S2's pain. There's more to it than that.

Maybe a lot more. On one very demanding reading, "I feel your pain" implies that S1 is experiencing the *very pain* that S2 is experiencing. Not just the same *type* of pain—something qualitatively similar but numerically distinct from S2's pain—but the same *token* pain. One way to get a grip on this possibility (assuming for a moment that it *is* possible) is by imagining craniopagus twins who are distinct subjects but share enough brain matter such that it's reasonable to suppose that they sometimes share token pains. Many philosophers say that this is impossible, even for craniopagus twins— that, given how experiences are individuated, two subjects couldn't share token experiences, so even craniopagus twins who share the neural states underlying their pain would be in two distinct pains.[3] But set that aside for the moment—we'll return to this issue in the next section. For now, just note that sharing token pains is at least one *potential* way for S1 to feel S2's pain.

That's a very demanding reading of "I feel your pain." A slightly less demanding reading would only imply that S1and S2 are *partly* in the same token pain. This could be construed in terms of their partly sharing the neural bases of a pain (as craniopagus twins) or in terms of their co-instantiating some of their phenomenal properties.

Another reading of "I feel your pain" implies, not that S1 and S2 share any *token* pain, but just that they are in the same pain *type*—where an experience's type is individuated by its purely qualitative, phenomenal properties. As

---

pains were caused in totally independent ways, and S1 comes to learn about S2's pain. We think that, in some such cases, "I feel your pain" can be both an expression of empathy and also true, even though S1's pain was not caused by S1's awareness of S2's pain.

[3] Here are a few prominent examples: Ayer (1940, 138–139), Strawson (1959, 97), and Tye (2007, 24). As we will discuss later, many philosophers are committed to this claim (whether or not they explicitly endorse it) in virtue of their preferred metaphysics of experience.

before, this sameness could be full or partial. If S1 and S2 are *fully* in the same pain type, then their pains are qualitatively identical (though they may be numerically distinct). If they are only *partly* in the same pain type, then their pains share some but not all phenomenal properties.

There are various dimensions along which experience types might differ phenomenologically. They might differ in their content, including (at least potentially) either their representational or non-representational content (including *de se* content). They might also differ in what some call their "mode" or "state type"—if, e.g., anger that P differs phenomenologically from fear that P, hope that P, etc.[4] Experience types might also differ with respect to how one experiences them in relation to *oneself*; that is, to whether one experiences oneself as their subject, agent, author, etc. Also, two experience types might differ if they bear distinct relations to other of their subject's mental states. For example, two subjects may experience fear differently because they experience the significance of that fear differently, given their differing memories, beliefs, desires, personality traits, and so on. These differences may affect their responses to the fear, how much it impairs their wellbeing, and more. Whether or not all of these differences between experience types really do exist is controversial. However, at this point we want to be ecumenical about potential differences between experience types.[5]

So here are our options for potential ways that S1's pain might be related to S2's pain if S1 feels S2's pain:

---

[4] All pains are of the same general type, "pain," so their phenomenology will not differ due to differences in this general type. However, if you think that the phenomenal contribution of an experience's "mode" or "state type" is more fine-grained than that—and, in the case of pain, includes phenomenal differences between, say, emotional pain and physical pain that are not attributable to differences in the pain's content—then this may be one way that two pains could differ, phenomenologically.

[5] You might think it's possible for experiences to be *similar* in some relevant respect without being partly or wholly of the same type. For example, you might think that a visual experience of a green patch is more similar to an experience of a blue patch than to an experience of a red patch, but that this similarity is not grounded in the first two experiences' being partly of the same type. That might be one way to think of it. But given all of the different ways two experiences can be partly of the same type, it's plausible that there will always be an experience type that similar experiences partly share but dissimilar ones don't (e.g., seeing a color in the blue-to-green range). So, moving forward, we will treat all similarities between experiences as a matter of them being of the same type (at least partly). If you maintain that two experiences can be similar but not partly of the same type, and if you think this applies to pain, then just note that another way S1 might feel S2's pain is, not by being in the same experience type, but by being in a relevantly *similar* experience type.

(1) S1 is fully in the same token pain that S2 is in.
(2) S1 is partly in the same token pain that S2 is in.
(3) S1 is fully in the same pain type that S2 is (or was) in.
(4) S1 is partly in the same pain type that S2 is (or was) in.

That covers (i) and (iii)—*Experience* and *Symmetry*—above. Now (ii)—i.e., *Self-Awareness*. We say that in order for S1 to feel S2's pain in a sense relevant to empathy, S1 must not only be in a certain kind of pain, S1 must also be *aware* of being in it. Many philosophers—both past and present—maintain that, necessarily, if a subject is in a given phenomenal state, then they are aware of being in it. If that's true, then *Self-Awareness* is trivially true. However, some other philosophers want to allow that one could be in a phenomenal state and yet be unaware of it.[6] So this possibility is at least worth recognizing.

However, whether or not all subjects are always aware of all of their conscious states, we take it that a subject (e.g., S1) must be aware of their own pain in order to feel someone else's pain (e.g., S2's) in the relevant sense. For we take it that if S1 is unaware of feeling the pain that corresponds to S2's pain, then S1 can't appreciate it in a sense required for "I feel your pain" to be the empathetic expression that it is. Hence, we take it that for S1 to feel S2's pain, S1 must be aware of the pain that S1 is experiencing.

Aware in what sense? Not just any sense. Not by, say, getting an MRI, observing behavior, or learning about it in some other third-personal way. Why? Because we take it that when S1 says "I feel your pain" they mean something more than that they are in pain and know it. They mean that they *feel* it, *appreciate* it, and are *moved* by it—in a way that elicits empathy and is, in some important sense, similar to how S2 feels their own pain.

What is that way? First-personally. S1 must be aware of their pain in the way we typically come to know about our own experiences. There are various accounts of how we come to know about our experiences first-personally. For reasons that will become clear later, we prefer an *acquaintance* account—one whereby S1's first-personal awareness of their own pain is achieved via direct awareness of the pain itself.[7] On our view, learning about it

---

[6] An example may be if one is highly absorbed in some activity and so ignores some peripheral aspect of one's phenomenology (which may be related in various ways to the phenomenon of attentional blindness). See Dretske (1993) for a classic argument along these lines. Also see Janzen (2011) and Stoljar (2023).

[7] As we will discuss later, the notion of acquaintance that we will appeal to derives from Bertrand Russell (1911, 1912). For an overview of the contemporary literature on this notion, see Duncan (2021a).

third-personally, or through some intermediary, wouldn't be enough; S1 needs to be in direct contact with their pain experience. Again, there are other potential ways to flesh out "first-personal awareness"; but, as we'll discuss later on, we believe that acquaintance with the experience is the best way to understand the metaphysical, epistemic, and moral landscape in this domain.

To get a better sense of the kind of first-personal awareness we have in mind (whether or not the acquaintance account of it is correct), consider the following contrast case: S1 undergoes pain that is the same as S2's pain in some sense, but S1 is somehow unaware of undergoing it. Nonetheless, S1's pain has its usual functional role—it affects S1's behavior, other mental states, and other traits in all of the relevant ways. Suppose S1 then learns via an MRI that they are in this pain state, and somehow knows that it is similar to S2's pain. Might it be appropriate for them to say to S2, "I feel your pain"? One question about this case is whether it is even possible. Again, many philosophers maintain that, necessarily, a mental state is conscious only if its subject is aware of it (see fn. 5). So they would deny that it's possible for S1 to be in a conscious state like pain and yet be completely unaware of it. We have some sympathy for this position. But set that aside for a moment— suppose it's possible to be in pain (with its usual functional role) and yet be completely unaware of it. Would an expression of empathy like "I feel your pain" be apt? On the one hand, if this is possible, then S1 may be shaped by the pain—it may affect their life and choices—in ways that are relevant to empathy. On the other hand, there seems something oddly hollow and (literally) unfeeling about saying "I feel your pain" if S1 is not aware of their pain in the usual way (i.e., first-personally). And this is hard to square with the nature of empathy (perhaps "I am affected by your pain" would seem more apt). Even if it is not quite appropriate to call this attitude "empathy," it is a nearby attitude that is worth remembering as a contrast to the kind of state we have in mind.

Now to (iv)—i.e., *Other-Awareness*: In order for "I feel your pain" to be true, S1 must be aware, not just of their own pain, but also that S1 is (or was) in some relevantly similar pain. This isn't strictly entailed by "I feel your pain," but it is implied by the fact that S1 is asserting it as an expression of empathy. It would be infelicitous for S1 to assert "I feel your pain" to S2 if S1 weren't aware, in some sense, of S2's pain.

But here the demands on S1's awareness seem more limited. There are various potential ways for S1 to be aware of S2's pain—via testimony, behavioral observation, other kinds of inference, or, if it is possible for S1 to experience S2's token pain, then they could be aware of that token pain in a maximally direct way—namely, by acquaintance. Maybe some of these sources of knowledge are better or worse in various ways, but, to satisfy "I feel your pain," all that seems required is that S1 knows of S2's pain *in some way*. In fact, this may not even require *knowledge*; as far as empathy goes, it may be enough that S1 *believes* that S2 is (or was) in the same pain (in some sense), and that, in fact, S2 is (or was) in that pain.

To summarize, and amend (i)–(iv), if S1 feels S2's pain, then (i) S1 is in pain (*Experience*), (ii) S1 is first-personally aware of that pain (*Self-Awareness*), (iii) S2 is (or was) in the same pain as S1's in one of the senses of (1)–(4) (*Symmetry*), and (iv) S1 is somehow aware of S2's pain (*Other-Awareness*). These conditions are not meant to be an analysis of the ordinary language expression, "I feel your pain." Rather, they're necessary conditions on a certain set of possibilities that we're interested in. Specifically, satisfying these conditions is what it would take, at a bare minimum, to empathetically feel someone else's pain in a more-or-less literal sense.

That's what it would take. Now the question is: Do we have what it takes? Does anybody? *Could* anybody?

2. The Possibilities for Sharing Pains

We assume that it is possible, and indeed actual, that we satisfy *Experience*, *Self-Awareness*, and *Other-Awareness* (i.e., (i), (ii), and (iv)). That is, we assume that we both possibly and actually feel pain and are first-personally aware of it, and that we sometimes know (however that is) when others are in pain. Thus, the "Do we have what it takes?" question is directed at *Symmetry* (i.e., (iii)). Specifically, it concerns what is possible—for us or anyone—in terms of sharing pains in line with senses (1)–(4) that we discussed earlier.

Recall those senses:

(1) S1 is fully in the same token pain that S2 is in.
(2) S1 is partly in the same token pain that S2 is in.
(3) S1 is fully in the same pain type that S2 is (or was) in.
(4) S1 is partly in the same pain type that S2 is (or was) in.

One question about (1)–(4) is: In which of these ways is it possible, in the broadest sense, for any subject to feel another's pain? Another question is: In which of these ways is it possible for *us*—i.e., ordinary human beings—to feel each other's pains, given how we are constituted, our laws of nature, and our technological limits? Both of these questions are important for reasons that we will discuss in the next sections—namely, because it's useful to know what a (merely possible) ideal moral agent, who is ideally empathetic, would seek to feel with respect to others' pains, so that we might better understand what we might strive toward if not for; and it's also useful to know what some of our moral limits are, especially with respect to empathy, so that we don't get the wrong ideas about what to expect from ourselves and others. So, in this section, we will consider what's possible for us, and for any possible being, concerning (1)–(4).

Start with (1). As we said, many philosophers claim that (1) is metaphysically impossible. For they maintain that token experiences are individuated partly by their subject (see fn. 2). On this view, what a token experience *is*—it's identity—is determined in part by who is undergoing it. So all experiences have this form: [S experiencing x]. If that's right, then it's impossible for two distinct subjects to have the same token experience, because the fact that these subjects are distinct is by itself sufficient to distinguish any experiences they're having. Even craniopagus twins who share the neural bases of a token pain would be in distinct pains; one experience would be [Twin1 experiencing p], the other would be [Twin2 experiencing p]. Hence, if this view of how to individuate token experiences is right, then (1) is metaphysically impossible.

One could deny this view. For example, one could say that token experiences are individuated by token neural states. If that's right, then it may be possible for craniopagus twins to feel each other's token pains.[8]

However, even on this view, (1) isn't feasible for most of us. At least not as we are currently constituted. For most of us do not share token neural states with anyone else. Nor do we ever share anything else that could ground—on any view—our being *fully* in the same token pain as someone else.[9] (1) is not for us.

---

[8] Even this is tricky. In order for craniopagus twins to *fully* feel each other's pains, they would need to share enough neural processing such that their pains—the character of which may be determined by all sorts of factors, including relations to other mental states—really are token identical, but not enough neural processing that they should be considered a single subject.

[9] Perhaps on some radical views of the nature of pain, full token-pain sharing is possible. Assume pain is a simple, basic, and sui generis quality that is not grounded in any physical state; nor are pains individuated by the subject who is aware of them. On this pain-as-free-floating-stuff view, it is at least conceivable that two subjects might experience one and the same pain quality. Again, we have no reason to suppose that this possibility corresponds to anything real.

The same may or may not be true of (2). It depends on further details about the metaphysics of experience. On one view, experiences are most fundamentally constituted by neural activity, and so it presumably would be metaphysically possible for some subject to be partly in the same token pain as another. Craniopagus twins cases—even if merely possible ones—may be a good example. Perhaps it would also be possible for the non-craniopagus among us, if we were to undergo some "mind-melding" procedure, but this is not something any of us are likely to undergo. In which case (2) may be possible for us, but unlikely.

But the above is hardly the only view of experience. There are other views, like naïve realism, the sense-datum theory, and representationalism.[10] On naïve realism, experience is partly constituted by public objects and properties. On this view, it's impossible to *fully* share a token experience with another subject, because experiences are partly individuated by the brain activity of the subject who is aware of the sensible qualities. On the other hand, it may be quite easy on this view (depending on the version) to *partly* share a token experience with another subject, since experiences are partly individuated by objects and properties that are, at least in many cases, external and publicly observable. So if S1 sees a brown kangaroo, then S2 may be partly (but not fully) in that same token experience by also seeing that very kangaroo at the same time.

Other views of experience may deliver different results. Some (but not all) versions of representationalism allow for partial token-experience sharing. The same goes for the sense-datum theory. But the main point here is just that whether it's possible to partly share token experiences (in general or for us) depends partly on the metaphysics—specifically, on what constitutes a given token experience.

With that said, focusing on experience *in general* may be misleading in this context, particularly given that the above theories tend to focus on *perceptual* experience. For the kind of state we're interested in—i.e., pain—is, unlike perception, not a matter of observing external objects. We don't crowd around pains, sensing them like we do kangaroos. Even on views on which experiencing pain is a matter of perceiving, say, tissue damage, which is itself publicly observable, the *way* a subject typically perceives their own

---

[10] For a helpful overview of the different views of the metaphysics of experience, see Pautz (2021).

tissue damage is different in kind from the way others do.[11] So while the possibility or likelihood of sharing token experiences *in general* may depend on the correct metaphysics of experience, the metaphysics shouldn't affect our conclusions so far about pain-sharing. Craniopagus twins aside, we don't share each other's token pains, even partly (at least, not in the sense relevant to (i)–(iv)). Maybe we *could*. And it's plausible that some possible beings partly share token pains. But (2) isn't something we do.[12]

At this point one might worry that by saying that (1) and (2) aren't for us, we are advocating for an objectionable sort of privacy thesis—one that posits a metaphysically suspect realm of objects that only one person is, or could be, privy to. Not so. As we've seen, even those who firmly reject the notion of private objects—such as naïve realists—can accept our conclusions with respect to (1) and (2). These conclusions don't require positing private objects of any sort; they merely identify some plausible constraints—for creatures like us—on sharing token pains.

With that, let's move on to (3) and (4)—to pain *types*. Here the underlying metaphysics recedes into the background. For pain types—at least the sort we are interested in—are individuated by their purely qualitative, phenomenal properties, regardless of what (metaphysically) constitutes them. If S1 sees a kangaroo, smells eucalyptus, and feels a tingle in their toes, then S2 is fully in the same experience type if and only if the experiences of S1 and S2 are qualitatively—that is, phenomenologically—identical. This is true regardless of what turns out to constitute those experiences—whether its

---

[11] With that said, if experiencing pain is just a matter of perceiving tissue damage (or something else), then it may be metaphysically possible for one subject to be perceptually "hooked up" to another subject's pain in that way. This is not something *we* ever do, but we don't mean to rule out its possibility here.

[12] Is this true of all kinds of pain? Or is it possible that, while we don't ever share token *physical* pains with each other, there are other kinds of pain that we do sometimes partly share tokens of? Take, for example, grief caused by the loss of a loved one. One might say that such grief is partly constituted by a perceived absence of the loved one. So if naïve realism is true of that perception, then it may be that two people can partly share a token grief state in virtue of perceiving the same absence. The same might go for pain involved with jealousy, anger, hate, and so on—if that pain is partly constituted by perceiving public things, and experiences are partly constituted by those public things, then two people may be able to partly share token pains. With that said, this possibility relies on a conjunction of very controversial views about pain and perception. Furthermore, even if that conjunction is true, cases where one subject is in partly the same token grief (or jealousy, anger, hate, etc.) state as another in virtue of perceiving the exact same thing at the exact same time—and in a way that's sufficient to make "I feel your pain" true—will be rare. So we will set this possibility aside.

external objects, sense data, representations, etc.[13] So the question is about phenomenology, not constitution. And that question is: Is it possible for two subjects to have pain experiences that are qualitatively the same, either partly or fully?

We think yes—that (3) and (4) are both possible. Start with (4). If S1 and S2 both have a visual experience of a brown kangaroo, then they are partly in the same experience type. Similarly for pain. If S1 and S2 both get sun-burned, and feel the burning, then they are partly in the same pain type. In which case they satisfy (4). Such cases are not just possible, but actual. People go to the beach together; they get sunburned together. As a result, they end up partly in the same pain type together. Hence, we think (4) is both possible and actual.

Some deny this. For example, Thomas Raleigh (2017) claims that if (1) and (2) are impossible—as some have argued—then (3) and (4) are too. For he claims that if (1) and (2) are impossible, then any experience's phenomenology is essentially tied to its subjective viewpoint.[14] And, according to Raleigh, this implies that there is no sense in which the phenomenology of one subject's experience is similar or dissimilar, the same or different, as the phenomenology of another's experience; in which case intersubjective phenomenological comparison is impossible. If Raleigh is right, then (3) and (4) may be impossible.

We are not convinced. Even if phenomenology is essentially tied to a subjective viewpoint, we deny the inference to phenomenal incomparability. To see why we deny this inference, consider an analogy. Suppose we set a toy firetruck on a table and take a picture of it from a side angle. What this picture looks like will be determined in part by the physical viewpoint from which we took the picture. And this is inevitable. There's no way to take a picture of a firetruck from no point of view. In this way, the appearance of the firetruck picture is tied—perhaps essentially—to a viewpoint. But this doesn't mean that its appearance can't be compared to

---

[13] To be clear, we are not saying that S1 and S2's experiences could be the same even if they were constituted differently. We assume that the true metaphysics of experience is true for everyone, so if S1's experience is constituted by, say, sense data, so is S2's. We are also not say-ing that we can't make sense of experience types if we adopt one of these theories. The point is rather that the status of (3) and (4) don't hang on the metaphysics of experience.

[14] What does it mean for an experience's phenomenology to be essentially tied to subjective viewpoint? For Raleigh (2017), it means that an experience's phenomenology is defined by what it is like *for its subject*—that it couldn't be what it is like *for nobody* (p. 9). Raleigh then argues that, given this, and given that (1) and (2) are impossible, all intersubjective phenom-enal comparisons are ill-defined.

that of other firetruck pictures. It's just that the ways in which the different pictures will be similar or dissimilar will depend in part on the perspective of the camera.

Why not say the same about phenomenology? Yes, we each see, hear, feel, taste, smell, think, emote, and in other ways experience the world from a certain viewpoint. Necessarily so. But that doesn't entail that our experiences are incomparable, phenomenologically. In fact, it doesn't even entail that our experiences couldn't be *exactly* alike, phenomenologically—that is, qualitatively identical. Just as two pictures from two different cameras could in principle be qualitatively identical—if they were taken from the exact same angle, in the exact same light, and so on—so too it may be that two subjects could in principle be in qualitatively identical experiences if they had the exact same makeup, were in the same conditions, etc. At least, this isn't ruled out by phenomenology being essentially tied to a subject's viewpoint.[15]

Thus, we maintain that intersubjective phenomenal comparison *is* possible. And we maintain that (4) is possible and actual—that two subjects can be, and sometime are, in partly the same experience type.

---

[15] Raleigh (2017) argues that, given the impossibility of (1) and (2), interpersonal phenomenal comparison is "ill defined" in the way comparisons of height across Lewisian possible worlds is ill defined or talk of velocity absent a reference frame is ill defined. However, we don't find these analogies persuasive. First, Lewisian worlds are spatiotemporally isolated in a way that conscious subjects are not. Second, things cannot move between Lewisian worlds and compare heights in the way subjects can change the character of their own experiences (e.g., by looking around, thinking different things, changing mood, moving into others' physical locations). So a subject can compare differences in their own experiences in a way that things can't be compared across Lewisian worlds. Third, if it's ill-defined to compare heights across Lewisian worlds, then that must be because there's nothing to height over and above how a thing is spatially related to other things in its world. But phenomenology isn't like that. Even if phenomenology is essentially tied to a subjective viewpoint, we don't see any reason to think *every* aspect of its qualitative character is determined by its subject's identity. Phenomenology may always be what it's like *for a subject*, but that doesn't entail that what it's like for me can't be similar or dissimilar to what it's like for you (or anyone else).
The reference-frame analogy has similar problems. Arguably there is nothing to velocity over and above a thing's spatial relation to other things; but arguably there is something more to be said about the qualitative character of phenomenology than how it is related to its subject. Furthermore, even if we grant the aptness of the reference-frame analogy, we deny that it gives us any reason to think that comparisons are impossible. For velocities across reference frames clearly *are* comparable (how else could we measure velocity in different reference frames and introduce units of velocity?). If x is moving 10 m/s away from y, and v is moving 20 m/s away from w, then we can compare (and quantify) those velocities in various ways. We can say things like, "v is moving away from something faster than x is," "v is moving away from something twice as fast as x is," "If v was in y's position, then x would be moving away from it at 10/ms (which is half as fast as v is moving away from w)." So, again, we don't think these analogies give us any reason to think that intersubjective phenomenal comparison is impossible.

However, the foregoing discussion of Raleigh's argument shows that (3)—i.e., the sense of "I feel your pain" whereby S1 is fully in the same pain type that S2 is (or was) in—is a bit trickier. The issue isn't whether subjective viewpoints affect every aspect of our phenomenology, as Raleigh suggests; it's whether it does at all. If a subjective viewpoint adds *any* essentially unique element to phenomenology, then it may be impossible for two subjects to fully share experience types. In which case (3) is impossible.

Recall the various dimensions that we identified earlier along which experience types might differ phenomenologically: representational or non-representational content (including *de se* content), "mode" or "state type," experienced relations to *oneself*, and experienced relations to other mental states. In which category does a viewpoint's potential contribution to phenomenology belong? One possibility is de se content. However, we doubt that de se content itself contributes anything unrepeatable to phenomenology. My experience of being in the Stanford library has irreducibly de se content, but there's nothing keeping you from having that same de se phenomenology by you yourself going into the Stanford library. De se phenomenology needn't be thought of as anything but indexical content that is repeatable, at least in principle.

A more plausible characterization of the role of viewpoint in phenomenology is experienced relations to oneself and/or to one's other mental states. To get a better grip on how, try to imagine what it might be like to be someone else. Take, for example, Elijah Wood. To experience the world like Elijah Wood would be to see the world through his eyes, and to hear, smell, taste, and feel the world through his other senses, and to feel what it is like to occupy Elijah Wood's specific body. It would also involve having certain memories—e.g., of playing Frodo in *Lord of the Rings*—as well as various beliefs, desires, intentions, hopes, fears, preferences, and so on. Maybe it would also involve experiencing the world with a certain personality, or character. What's more, experiencing the world from Elijah Wood's perspective would involve experiencing these various mental states *as one's own*. What exactly this self-consciousness amounts to is controversial, and we'll not try to settle the matter here. This sense of ownership may involve explicit self-experiences, or not. It arguably involves a sense of oneself as the subject of one's mental states, but it may also involve a sense of oneself as the agent or author of one's mental states. Or not.[16] However it goes, to occupy Elijah Wood's perspective would be to experience his mind as one's own.

---

[16] For an overview of the different views of and issues surrounding self-consciousness, see Smith (2020).

This is not easy to imagine—at least not completely. However, we don't see any reason to think it is strictly *impossible* for two subjects to be in qualitatively identical experiences—that is, to be fully in the same experience type. If God made a qualitative duplicate of Elijah Wood—with all the same physical and mental traits, memories and beliefs, desires and preferences—then it's reasonable to suppose that they could be fully in the same experience type. Of course, they would each experience those traits *as their own*. But this sense of ownership may be qualitatively the same for each of them. It's not as if each of our sense of ownership has its own, unique person-identifying marker—as if duplicate Elijah Wood's sense of ownership would feel, qualitatively, different from original Elijah Wood's. So we think (3) is possible.

Whether it's possible for us is another question. One thing the above thought experiment illustrates is the difficulties of occupying another subjective perspective. It involves, not just seeing the world through another's eyes, but experiencing it with their memories, personality traits, beliefs, desires, and so on. And this complicated mesh of perspective may affect how any particular mental state is experienced. Elijah Wood's fear of spiders may feel different from your fear of spiders. For Elijah Wood has different memories, beliefs, desires, etc., as well as a different physical makeup with (at least slightly) different chemical processing, which may very well affect how he experiences fearing spiders. The same is true of pain. Elijah Wood's pain may not feel exactly like your pain—even if it has a similar cause (e.g., sunburn). And, for us, there's no way to replicate the complexities of another person's perspective so that we could duplicate exactly what it is like to feel pain from their perspective. So, for us, (3) appears out of reach.

With that, let's summarize. In the last section, we introduced four necessary conditions on S1 feeling S2's pain: (i) S1 is in pain (*Experience*), (ii) S1 is first-personally aware of that pain (*Self-Awareness*), (iii) S2 is (or was) in the same pain as S1's in one of the senses of (1)–(4) (*Symmetry*), and (iv) S1 is somehow aware of S2's pain (*Other-Awareness)*. In this section, we delved into (iii) and explored the possibilities of sharing others' pain in senses (1)–(4). What we've suggested is that (1) is likely impossible for anyone; that (2) and (3) may be possible, but not for us; and that (4) is possible and indeed actual, including for us.

One thing that we haven't discussed yet—concerning (4) in particular—is *degrees* of sameness or similarity. One subject's pain type may be the same as another subject's pain type to a greater or lesser degree. We don't think there's any simple answer to the question of how much two experiences must be the same in order for "I feel your pain" to be true. However, this issue is clearly relevant to the epistemic and ethical implications of empathy—*how* much two pains are the same, or *how* similar they are, has the potential to make a big difference with respect to a subject's capacity to empathize with another. The same goes for various other details mentioned in this section. So it's to epistemic and ethical import that we'll turn now.

3. The Epistemic and Ethical Significance of Sharing Pains

We have identified several different senses in which a subject might share another's pain. The question we now face is which of these is normatively relevant. For example, why might it be good or fitting for S1 to feel S2's pain by being acquainted with—that is, directly aware of—the pain, instead of simply learning about it third-personally? Does the normative upshot turn on the kind and degree of similarity between the pains experienced by S1 and S2? Towards answering these questions, it will be helpful to compare attitudes that *resemble* pain-sharing but aren't pain-sharing in line with (1)–(4). For example, we imagined earlier a subject who is aware that another is in pain, deeply affected by the awareness at some cognitive level (e.g., it influences their choices), but the subject is not occurrently acquainted with pain. In what sense, if any, does such pain-free awareness of and responsiveness to another's experience fall short of the demands of virtue?

Here's our plan. We'll begin by examining a familiar set of answers—both historical and contemporary—that appeal to the connection between pain-sharing, on the one hand, and both knowledge and moral motivation, on the other. This will help us make vivid a basic insight that they arguably share, and it will also help distinguish the available accounts along several key dimensions: the posited connection between sharing pain and virtue (e.g., whether the connection is contingent as opposed to necessary; instrumental or constitutive), the character of the relevant virtues (whether they are moral, epistemic, or of some other normative type), and the ultimate beneficiary (whether it is the empathizer, the person being empathized with, or third persons who might benefit indirectly). Then we will end by highlighting the value(s) of pain-sharing and introducing our own preferred account of how that value derives from feeling pain itself.

Our starting point is the platitude of folk morality that feeling another's pain is in some sense commendable. If I know my friend to be grieving the loss of a loved one, am familiar with the nature of such grief, yet feel no sadness on their behalf, my response will seem defective absent a mitigating explanation for my lack of feeling. The example does not turn on the fact that it is my friend who grieves. Agents who are incapable of responding empathically to the suffering of strangers are often judged disfavorably. And while empathy and compassion—states that arguably involve pain-sharing—have been criticized by some philosophers and psychologists for being cognitively distorting (see, e.g., Bloom, 2016; Prinz, 2011; Manne, 2018), by and large people seem to think that such attitudes are good and fitting, at least in general. So even if there are circumstances where empathy is unwarranted, say, where the felt pain is morally criticizable (like jealousy), our focus for now is on understanding the positive cases.

One possibility is that pain-sharing enjoys a kind of reflected glory, a positive status by association with more familiar virtues. For example, an influential explanation appeals to the fact that sharing other people's experiences is often a source of insight into their psychologies, insight that can combine with the empathizer's other concerns to motivate other regard. The general idea—that empathy and compassion are well-springs of moral motivation—features prominently in eighteenth-century moral philosophy, as reflected in the work of David Hume (1738 [1896].) and Adam Smith (1982 [1759]). Dick Boyd articulates the point thusly:

> [I]t is extremely plausible that for normal human beings…the capacity to recognize the extent to which others are well or poorly off…and the capacity to anticipate correctly the probable effect on others' well-being of various counterfactual circumstances…depends upon their capacity for sympathy, their capacity to imagine themselves in the situation of others or even to find themselves involuntarily doing so in cases in which others are especially well or badly off.
>
> (Boyd, 1988, 341)

For Boyd, experiential mirroring—as in empathy—is a morally important source of knowledge about others. However, on his view, that experiential mirroring is a source of knowledge is a contingent fact about us; both actual and possible agents who lack such mirroring capacities can still have knowledge of, for example, the extent to which others are well or poorly off, albeit through means that are not as efficient as empathic simulation (e.g., by reading books on human psychology) (p. 342). Likewise, the connection between pain-sharing and other-regarding choices is supposed to be contingent since it depends on the character of an agent's general cares and concerns—e.g., whether one is moved by knowledge of others' wellbeing.

Because these are contingent connections, a view like Boyd's does not deliver all that we might want from an account of the value of empathy. The posited connection between pain-sharing and independently valuable ends, like knowledge or other-regarding action, seems too weak to accommodate ordinary moral intuition. For instance, the moral defect in my inability to experience any sadness on behalf of my grieving friend does not seem fully mitigated by my awareness of their grief or the fact that I might have taken steps to mitigate their pain. Moreover, if pain-sharing is a means of discovering practically relevant truths about other agents, we should be able to state more precisely (a) how it is that pain-sharing helps us discover such truths, and (b) the nature of the relevant truths.[17] We suspect a more precise account of the psychological mechanisms involved might reveal a more robust connection between pain-sharing and virtue.

Consider an account by Olivia Bailey (2022) that captures this. Bailey points out that sharing another's mental state (in the experiential sense) results in a cognitive reorientation in the empathizer (e.g., the pain one feels absorbs one's attention; other matters fall away from one's view) as well as somatic responses (e.g., a sinking feeling; the welling up of tears) that are richly isomorphic to the other's experience. This mechanism enables S1 to grasp in considerable detail what is going on in S2's mental life when S1 feels S2's pain. Pain-sharing may not be the *only* means of learning the relevant facts about another's experience. But it appears to be a significant mechanism, nonetheless, one that allows us to inhabit another's viewpoint much more closely than we normally do.

Moreover, what distinguishes Bailey's account from Boyd's is that, on her view, rich experiential mirroring serves another purpose—it is *necessary* for responding to a very basic desire that people have, a desire for what she calls "humane understanding." She writes:

> People have a complex but profound need to be humanely understood. Because we respond to others' very real need when we pursue this sort of understanding of their emotions, empathy is best understood as itself a way of caring, rather than just a means to promote other caring behavior.

---

[17] A question one might raise about such proposals is whether the sharing of pain conduces to a better appreciation of irreducibly evaluative or normative facts (not just non-normative facts)—e.g., the fact it is *bad* that someone is suffering, or that one *ought* to do something about. The correlation between pain sharing and pro-social moral beliefs calls out for some kind of explanation, even if pain sharing isn't necessary for securing or sustaining the relevant beliefs.

This form of care plays a significant role in a variety of relationships cen-tral to human flourishing. More specifically, when we empathize with others, we directly understand how their emotions reflect the evaluative properties the objects of those emotions appear to have.

(Bailey, 2022, 52)

The theoretical background is complex, but the proposal boils down to two core claims: (1) that pain- and emotion-sharing are necessary for under-standing a person's normative or broadly evaluative commitments; and (2) that pain-sharing is good—it contributes to the wellbeing of those with whom we empathize—because it is non-instrumentally desired by others.

Although Bailey presents these claims as related, they can be assessed independently. That being so, it isn't clear to us why evaluative understand-ing requires experiencing other people's feelings or emotions. Appreciating the truth of most ordinary normative beliefs—for instance, that pain is bad or that suffering is worth mitigating—or why a normative proposition might seem true to a subject does not depend, necessarily, on mirroring another's experience. Consider, again, cases of "pain-free" awareness: S1 is aware that S2 is in pain, and aware that S2's pain is similar to pain that S1 has experienced previously, but S1 does not occurrently experience any pain. Plausibly, this pain-free state of awareness would be sufficient for knowing and understanding S2's evaluative commitments in relation to pain.

On the other hand, pain-free awareness wouldn't necessarily address S2's desire to be humanely understood. For if the desire to be humanely under-stood *just is* the desire to have one's experiences mirrored to some extent, then pain-sharing is a necessary means of responding to a basic desire of others the satisfaction of which is (often) non-instrumentally good.[18] Bailey seems right on this score. It seems plausible to us that people have such basic desires, even if contingently and non-universally.

But set aside people's desires for now and focus on the general idea that pain-sharing may be a necessary source of insight about others—insight that, in turn, influences how we treat them. It is worth noting that this idea has deep historical roots. Perhaps the most radical proposal is Arthur Schopenhauer's (1915 [1840]), who, drawing on early Buddhist and

---

[18] It is not always morally good to satisfy people's desires. We leave open the possibility that our desires to have our conscious experiences mirrored may be unreasonable (e.g., where there is some defect in the experience).

Hindu ethical traditions, suggests that sharing another's pain—"direct and, as it were, instinctive participation in the sufferings [of others]" (p. 200)—is necessary for appreciating and appropriately responding to a supposed fact that the empathizer and the person being empathized with are "one and the same entity" (pp. 203–204; pp. 273–274). On Schopenhauer's view, it is only by empathizing and caring about others as we do ourselves that we rationally respond to the sameness of putatively distinct selves. His reasons for thinking that the apparent distinctness of selves is illusory are somewhat opaque, as are his reasons for thinking that only the empathic act in conformity with the truths of personal identity.[19] However, recent attempts to vindicate the general strategy warrant examination.

For example, Marshall (2018) defends a neo-Schopenhauerian explanation of the value of broadly compassionate attitudes predicated on the notion that sharing another's pain delivers a distinctive and "irreplaceable" epistemic good, what he calls "being in touch" with another's pain (p. 47). He motivates this key epistemic concept based on thought experiments drawn from the philosophy of perception designed to show that sensory experience—seeing, feeling, and hearing—uniquely contribute to the perceiver's overall epistemic situation. A central example is drawn from Johnston (2011, 167). Imagine a subject with "perfectly reliable blindsight" who forms reliably true beliefs about the layout of objects in the environment and their properties but does not visually experience those objects. There seems to be something lacking, epistemically, in the blind-sighted person's situation. In Marshall's terminology, the person is not "in touch" with objects and properties in the room. Analogously, he argues, a person who has "blind" awareness that another is in pain but doesn't experience pain herself fails to be in touch with the other's pain.

We are, ourselves, highly sympathetic to the point that the blind-sighted person lacks something of non-instrumental epistemic worth that is essentially tied to perception. However, we aren't convinced that Marshall provides a detailed enough account of this epistemic good for us to evaluate his central claim that pain-sharing is a means of "being in touch." For on some accounts of what it is to "be in touch" we are never in touch with other people's pain, and so this cannot be the right way to understand the value of pain-sharing.

---

[19] For a notable recent attempt to make sense of the view, see Albahari (2014).

Consider, for example, Johnston's own account, which is based on a direct-realist metaphysics of visual perception, according to which perceiving subjects are "directly acquainted" with the objects and properties they perceive (Johnston, 2004). When I see a red chair, the red facing front of the chair is immediately present in my conscious experience. Direct realists employ their own tactile metaphor to explain the positive epistemic status of such awareness: the perceiver has immediate "cognitive contact" with external reality.[20] But if unmediated contact with perceived objects is what grounds the non-instrumental value of perception, then it is no longer clear that ordinary pain-sharing involves "being in touch" with other people's pain. For reasons discussed earlier, it seems unlikely—perhaps even impossible—that when S1 shares S2's pain, S1 is acquainted with S2's token pain. At best, S1 is acquainted with their own pain that is either wholly or partially of the same type as S2's. So, it is far from obvious that empathetic pain-sharing involves being in touch with another's pain.[21]

The above concerns notwithstanding, Marshall's proposal is appealing, and he is clearly not alone in thinking that pain-sharing necessarily enriches the pain-sharer's epistemic situation. Consider an alternative approach defended by Atiq (2021). He argues that the value of empathy can be explained in terms of a species of non-propositional knowledge of objects and properties that requires direct perceptual acquaintance with those objects and properties. The epistemology is most famously associated with Bertrand Russell—in particular, his defense of "knowledge

---

[20] See, e.g., Coleman (2019): "in acquaintance, awareness achieves metaphysical and epistemic connection with another existent...Had it not enlarged the subject's world in this way, acquaintance's claim to be a kind of [valuable knowledge] would be jeopardized" (p. 59).

[21] While Marshall aspires to stay neutral on the value of "being in touch," the truth of his claims about pain-sharing clearly depends on offering a precise account. To motivate the point differently, suppose that the value of being in touch can be characterized in terms of representational accuracy or ordinary knowledge of truths. Indeed, Marshall often invokes representational ideas: "Compassionate reactions...significantly resemble pains like the wombat's, and a representation's resembling pain is necessary and sufficient for it to reveal pain, and so for letting the subject know *what the property is like*" (p. 68). What's puzzling about the explanation, however, is that knowledge of what pain is like does not generally depend on an occurrent experience of pain, even if it does depend on a subject's having previously experienced pain (Lerner, 2019). So, it remains unclear why S1 who is aware, non-experientially, that S2 is in pain cannot lay claim to "being in touch" with the pain, on the assumption that S1 has experienced pain before. If there is more to knowing pain than simply knowing what pain feels like that derives, essentially, from simultaneously experiencing pain, as Marshall seems to think (and we're inclined to agree), it would be helpful to know what that additional knowledge amounts to. We suggest a way of precisifying and defending the claim below.

by acquaintance."[22] The explanation of empathy's value in terms of knowledge by acquaintance proceeds in two steps.

First, Atiq argues that even if no one can be directly acquainted with the token pains and aversions of another's experience, there appears to be a constitutive connection between being so acquainted—and, hence, having acquaintance knowledge of—another's pains and aversions, and being motivated to mitigate their suffering. The constitutive connection derives from the fact that phenomenologically salient desires to mitigate pain are typically included in the sensible content of a person's painful experience. Hence, *if* S1 were directly acquainted with the token pains and desires experienced by S2, then, necessarily, S1 would be moved to stop S2's pain. The failure to care about other people's suffering is thus always explainable in terms of an epistemic defect in our situation: our inability to know, by direct acquaintance, the token pains and desires of others.

Second, he maintains that although no ordinary agent is directly acquainted with the token pains and aversions of another, in the grip of (imaginative) empathy it can seem *as if* we are. That is, sharing pain-*types* simulates the state of being directly acquainted with the token features of another's mental life. Moreover, this simulation builds epistemic character by testing the empathizer's intellectual courage, for the (apparent) acquaintance knowledge of another's mental life who is suffering feels unpleasant and is, thus, "difficult to bear" (Atiq, 2021, 14055). By acting to alleviate other people's pain (rather than turning away from it), the empathic manifests a core epistemic virtue of being able to resist the temptation to give up on readily available knowledge when what is known is hard to bear. In short, empathy—the state of sharing a similar *type* of pain—phenomenologically seems like token-pain sharing (or an instance of knowledge by acquaintance of another's mental life) and, as a result, is both: (a) epistemically valuable, because it affords an opportunity to cultivate intellectual courage; and (b) morally valuable, because the intellectually courageous are more likely to develop practical virtue by regularly choosing to help others.

The proposal has some salient drawbacks. It is a controversial idea that acquaintance with objects and properties is worth preserving as a form of non-factual knowledge. Additionally, Atiq's view turns on a contestable claim about the phenomenology of empathy—namely, that empathic

---

[22] For recent efforts to revive this view, see, e.g., Conee (1994), Tye (2009), Duncan (2020; 2021b), and Atiq (2021).

experience involves not just sharing pain-types in the sense we outlined earlier, but it seeming as if the empathizer's felt pain were identical or constitutively related to the pain felt by the other. It seems possible to share another's pain without being under any such illusion. Nevertheless, it seems right that there are epistemic and moral advantages to imagining the other's pain as one's own, especially in terms of epistemic character building. And there may be ways of relaxing the proposal's more controversial assumptions, while vindicating the neo-Schopenhauerian insight that sharing another's pain is necessary for virtue-enabling knowledge.

Before we suggest a potential refinement, it might be helpful to chart our progress thus far. We learn from Bailey and Marshall that pain-sharing may be a necessary source of insight about others, although the precise epistemic gain turns out to be hard to characterize. Atiq suggests a characterization in terms of knowledge that (a) is tied to acquaintance with pain and (b) affords opportunities to cultivate both epistemic virtue in the form of intellectual courage and moral virtue the form of other-regarding action. However, the account relies on contestable epistemic and phenomenological claims.

What we propose is to avoid assuming distinctive epistemic goods like "non-propositional knowledge," "being in touch," or "humane understanding," and instead rely on the fact that there are excellent reasons—from both cognitive science and ordinary introspection—to think that first-personal awareness of a phenomenal quality puts the subject in a position to know many ordinary, fine-grained truths about the nature of the quality that are not, and perhaps cannot be, preserved fully in the absence of experience (Duncan, 2021b). Not only does some knowledge require acquaintance, some of that knowledge decays very quickly, and possibly immediately, once one stops being acquainted. This is why revisiting an experience—e.g., re-experiencing an exotic fruit that one hasn't tasted in a while—can feel like being reminded of what one once knew but forgot between experiences (cf. Atiq, 2021, 14045).

Why does acquaintance-dependent knowledge decay very quickly once one stops being acquainted? One potential explanation is just that, as a matter of contingent fact, not all of experience's rich content is stored in short- or long-term memory.[23] Another potential explanation, which we endorsed

---

[23] Most of the relevant cognitive science research on this issue focuses on visual experience. The current evidence suggests that, after a very short period of "visual persistence" (Coltheart, 1980), some (but not all) information from visual experience is stored in "iconic memory" for a couple of hundred milliseconds (Sperling, 1960; Pratte, 2018). After this, much more of the information in visual experience is lost. Some argue that there is also "fragile visual short-term

above and has the potential to provide a deeper, non-contingent explanation of the experience-dependence of some knowledge, is that there is a basic difference in form between the knowledge gained through acquaintance and ordinary propositional knowledge, such that the former simply cannot be fully translated into the latter (see Duncan, 2021b; Atiq, 2021).

However the explanation goes, the main point here is just that there is plenty of reason to think that not all that we know in the grip of an experience is preserved in memory or is communicable. If this weren't true, then perhaps the epistemic value of pain-sharing could be retained over time even in the absence of experience. But, given that it *is* true, much of this value disappears quickly or immediately after the pain-sharing ceases and can only be regained by becoming reacquainted with the pain. This provides some reason to empathetically share others' pains, not just once, but repeatedly.

Put differently, even if knowing, generally, what pain is like does not require *re*-experiencing pain, experience is necessary for *full* and *detailed* knowledge of pain's character and the ways in which pain reorients a subject's viewpoint. If that's right, then we can explain why pain-sharing is always epistemically valuable for ordinary agents. It puts S1 in a position to know about S2's pain more fully than S1 could know in the absence of the experience. Our account secures a more robust connection between pain-sharing and knowledge than, e.g., Boyd's view, since experience turns out to be either metaphysically necessary for knowledge or, at a minimum, psychologically necessary—that is, necessary given the natural limitations of ordinary agents.

Moreover, we can harness the points about empathic knowledge being virtue-enabling without having to make contestable phenomenological assumptions. Insofar as S1 is both rational and motivated to preserve ordinary knowledge gained through empathy—perhaps S1 is intellectually courageous along the lines suggested above—S1 can be expected to act in

---

memory" (e.g., Landman, Spekreijse, and Lamme, 2003; Block, 2022), but this remains controversial. Aside from this, there is "working memory," which Ned Block (2022) describes as "a kind of cognitive scratch pad that can be used to manipulate information for cognitive purposes" (250). Block also notes that "Presence of a representation in working memory is not 'storage' but rather active maintenance" (ibid.) and argues that working memory typically has a different format than perception (251–252). The important point for our purposes is just that much of the content represented in experience decays rather quickly and is not stored in memory for very long (and perhaps not even in the same format). This may partly explain why, as a matter of contingent fact, acquaintance knowledge is not preserved fully or for very long in the absence of experience.

recognizably other-regarding ways, such as by mitigating S2's pain. It is tempting to suppose, further, that acting well entails not just making morally correct choices but acting based on the right motivating reasons. When S1 is acquainted with pain and thereby motivated to stop S2's pain, S1's reason for acting is in part a rich understanding of what pain is like and why it is to be avoided. The choice is thus highly intelligible partly due to the knowledge that empathy provides. By contrast, it is doubtful that helping others based on non-experiential knowledge of their suffering involves acting for (all) the right reasons, even if such empathy-free actions remain commendable. One explanation for the superior quality of an agent's will who acts for the reasons that empathy makes available is epistemic: experience provides normatively relevant information and acting for the right reasons involves some degree of awareness of the relevant reasons. But there might be other, non-epistemic explanations.

If we're right that pain-sharing makes a distinctive contribution to our epistemic and ethical lives and precisely because it involves experience/acquaintance with pain, then further questions arise about the importance of pain-sharing and the significance of not having what it takes. Moreover, the view's normative implications warrant elaboration. For example, the value of pain-sharing appears entirely neutral with respect to the identity and characteristics of the sufferer. If there are epistemic and moral reasons to share in the pains of others of the sort discussed above, then the other's gender, skin color, creed, and species do not seem to matter, at least in principle. The reasons to share in the pains of others are, in a clear enough sense, impartial in nature.[24] We consider some of these questions and implications in the next and concluding section.

4. Open Questions

In the previous section, we identified several ways in which empathetic pain-sharing seems valuable:

Epistemic Value: Empathetic pain-sharing is epistemically valuable for its own sake.

---

[24] In fact, the reasons may be radically impartial; they seem to vindicate an observation of Bailey's (2020)—that there might be reasons to empathize with the desires of even vicious agents, at least insofar as the unsated desires of the vicious amount to a form of suffering.

Humane Understanding: Empathetic pain-sharing contributes to a humane understanding of others (which is valuable because it is desired by others and contributes to their wellbeing).

Motivation: Empathetic pain-sharing motivates one to mitigate others' suffering.

Character: Empathetic pain-sharing builds epistemic character.

Our preferred account of why, or how, pain-sharing yields these values is that acquaintance with pain gives us fine-grained knowledge of the nature of pain and its impact on a subject's overall viewpoint that can't be gained in other, non-experiential ways, and acquaintance necessarily motivates us to act in light of our experiences—including pains—in ways that other sources of motivation don't (at least not always).

The above values of pain-sharing are connected to the different forms that pain-sharing can take. As a reminder, we identified in our earlier discussion the following forms of pain-sharing:

(1) S1 is fully in the same token pain that S2 is in.
(2) S1 is partly in the same token pain that S2 is in.
(3) S1 is fully in the same pain type that S2 is (or was) in.
(4) S1 is partly in the same pain type that S2 is (or was) in.

We can now see clearly whether and to what extent each of the above values depends on (1) through (4).

Start with *Epistemic Value*—that is, the fact that empathetic pain-sharing seems epistemically valuable for its own sake. On our account, pain-sharing of any form—any of (1)–(4)—will (at least typically) involve acquaintance with *some* pain, which is the source of fine-grained acquaintance-dependent knowledge. But what (or how much) is known will vary depending on whether S1 is partly or wholly acquainted with S2's pain and whether that pain is of the same token or type of S2's pain. For example, if it takes being acquainted with a specific form of grief (say, the grief involved in the death of a family member) to know its character fully, then feeling some sadness in response to such grief will not necessarily secure all of the knowledge there is to gain through pain-sharing. More broadly, there may be epistemic value in S1 gaining each of these instances of knowledge, (1) through (4), whether or not we—that is, human beings as we are currently constituted— can actually obtain them all.

As for *Humane Understanding*, it's plausible that, all else being equal, the more S1's pain is like S2's pain qualitatively the more humane understanding S1 will have of S2. So there may be reason for S1 to *strive* for (3)—being wholly in the same pain type as S2—even if (4) (being partly in the same pain type) is all that *we* are likely to attain. However, in terms of humane understanding, we see no obvious advantage in S1 being in the same *token* pain as S2 (as per (1) or (2)). Being in the same pain type as S2 seems sufficient for S1 to respond to S2's desire to have their experiences mirrored and, thus, is sufficient for humane understanding of S2.

The same is arguably true of *Character*. Epistemic character involves resilience in the face of threats to one's epistemic wellbeing, threats which include temptations to believe what is convenient and to ignore knowledge that's hard to bear. Sharing another's pain builds epistemic character. But being in a certain *type* of pain seems sufficient for exercising the relevant virtues. We don't see any additional value in terms of building epistemic character in being in any particular pain token.

That leaves *Motivation*, which is the trickiest. S1's being in the same pain type (partly or wholly) as S2 is valuable because it may motivate S1 to respond to S2's pain in certain other-regarding ways, especially insofar as S1 is intellectually courageous. But is there additional value, just in terms of being motivated by the right reasons, in S1's being *wholly* in the same pain type as S2? Will that somehow make the motivation more powerful, nuanced, or better in some other way? And would there be extra motivational value in S1's being in the same *token* pain as S2? Perhaps being in the same token pain as S2 would *necessarily* motivate S1 to stop S2's pain even in the absence of intellectual courage for reasons discussed earlier.[25] We consider these open questions that deserve further attention.

There are other, important questions raised by our account that cannot be resolved in a single chapter. Below, we highlight some of what remains unsettled in part to underscore the ecumenical nature of our present conclusions.

First, our account does not aim to *fully* characterize the value of empathy. There may be other reasons for empathizing that we haven't considered— for instance, irreducibly moral reasons to empathize for its own sake.

---

[25] Though this may affect whether we should consider the motive *morally* valuable. For if my motivation is to get rid of *this* token pain because it's *my* pain—I'm feeling it—then my motivation might seem egocentric and not sufficiently other-regarding. In which case this motivation, while still valuable insofar as it motivates me to get rid of the pain, may not be morally praiseworthy.

Whether or not such reasons are compatible with our account invites further analysis. The reasons we have identified are perfectly general. If it turns out that there are stronger moral reasons to empathize with, for example, those who are closest to us, our account will not necessarily explain such variation, though we see no reason why it would be inconsistent with reasons of varying strength. On the other hand, if there are positive and overriding moral reasons *not* to empathize with some category of suffering agents (e.g., vicious agents), such reasons may well be in tension with our conclusions.

Second, our account does not settle the weight of our reasons to empathize, or whether and when those reasons might be overridden by competing considerations. Consider, first, the question of normative weight. Even if there is *some* reason to know P regardless of the content of the proposition P, no one thinks all instances of knowledge have equal value. We have little reason to know, or bother trying to figure out, the precise number of stars in the sky or blades of grass in one's garden. Likewise, reasons to have full and detailed knowledge of the nature of pain and its impact on another's psychology might seem trivial. However, one salient difference between the cases of trivial knowledge and that of the knowledge involved in pain-sharing is that the latter is character-building, and there are reasons to seek out character-building knowledge. Additionally, the knowledge also affects our choices in substantial ways, and thus seems relevant to acting objectively. Our choices are evaluated positively when they are made in the light of knowledge that is difference-making. So, there are several reasons for taking the knowledge that empathy delivers to be quite significant. Moreover, many of us find ourselves involuntarily empathizing. And while our reasons to seek out trivial knowledge might seem weak, there are plausibly reasons of a weighty sort to avoid giving up on readily available knowledge, even if what is known is trivial. So, the reasons not to turn away from another's pain when we find ourselves in the grip of empathy—and more fully attuned to the nature of another's suffering—might be quite strong indeed.

But how strong? Couldn't such reasons be outweighed by reasons not to empathize given the way in which pain-sharing can interfere with knowledge-acquisition elsewhere? After all, it is hard to attend to one's intellectual projects when grieving in sympathy with others. And what about sharing other peoples' joy so that one can know, fully, what their joy is like? Are there intelligible balances to be struck between such competing demands? On such questions of comparative weight, we provisionally suspend judgment. For what it is worth, the concepts of normative importance and priority—in epistemology as well as in ethics—are undertheorized; and so, we are hardly alone in finding ourselves uncertain about such matters. Discerning the role that empathy should play in a well-ordered life is no easy task. But establishing rigorously that we ought to make some room for empathy in our lives, that objectivity itself gives us reasons to empathize regularly given the robust connection between acquaintance and phenomenal knowledge, and that epistemically and ethically significant forms of empathy remain within reach of agents constituted as we are, alone in our suffering, seems like a step in the right direction.

Acknowledgements

Thanks to Uriah Kriegel, Thomas Raleigh, Rachel Schutz, and Daniel Stoljar for very helpful comments on this chapter. Thanks also to Earl Conee, Olivia Bailey, Julia Markovits, Andrei Marmor, Colin Marshall, Jeff Rachlinski, Libby Southgate, Bill Watson, the participants at the 2022 Cornell Workshop on Mind and Value, and Beverly, a barber in Melbourne, for helpful discussion of the issues in this chapter.

References

Albahari, Miri. 2014. "Insight Knowledge of No Self in Buddhism: An Epistemic Analysis." *Philosophers' Imprint* 14: 1–33.

Atiq, Emad H. 2021. "Acquaintance, Knowledge, and Value." *Synthese* 199: 14035–14062.

Ayer, Alfred Jules. 1940. *The Foundations of Empirical Knowledge*. New York: Macmillan.

Bailey, Olivia. 2016. "Empathy, Care, and Understanding in Adam Smith's *The Theory of Moral Sentiments*." *Adam Smith Review* 9: 273–292.

Bailey, Olivia. 2020. "Empathy and the Value of Humane Understanding." *Philosophy & Phenomenological Research* 104(1): 50–65.

Block, Ned. 2022. *The Border between Seeing and Thinking*. Oxford: Oxford University Press.

Bloom, P. 2016. *Against Empathy: The Case for Rational Compassion*. New York: Harper-Collins.

Boyd, Richard. 1988. "How to Be a Moral Realist." In *Essays on Moral Realism*, edited by G. Sayre-McCord, 181–228. Ithaca, New York: Cornell University Press.

Coleman, S. 2019. "Natural Acquaintance." In *Acquaintance: New essays*, edited by J. Knowles and T. Raleigh, 49–74. Oxford: Oxford University Press.

Coltheart, M. 1980. "Iconic Memory and Visible Persistence." *Perception and Psychophysics* 27(3): 183–228.

Conee, Earl. 1994. "Phenomenal Knowledge." *Australasian Journal of Philosophy* 72: 136–150.

Dretske, Fred. 1993. "Conscious Experience." *Mind* 102(406): 263–283.

Duncan, Matt. 2020. "Knowledge of Things." *Synthese* 197(8): 3559–3592.

Duncan, Matt. 2021a. "Acquaintance." *Philosophy Compass* 16: 1–19.

Duncan, Matt. 2021b. "Experience is Knowledge." *Oxford Studies in Philosophy of Mind* 1: 106–129.

Hume, David. 1738 [1896]. *A Treatise of Human Nature*. Reprinted, L.A. Selby-Bigge (ed.). Oxford: Clarendon Press.

Janzen, Greg. 2011. "In Defense of the What-It-Is-Likeness of Experience." *Southern Journal of Philosophy* 49: 271–293.

Johnston, Mark. 2004. "The Obscure Object of Hallucination." *Philosophical Studies* 120: 113–83.

Johnston, Mark. 2011. "On a Neglected Epistemic Virtue." *Philosophical Issues* 21(1): 165–218.

Landman, R., Spekreijse, H., and Lamme, V. A. F. 2003. "Large Capacity Storage of Integrated Objects Before Change Blindness." *Vision Research* 43: 149–164.

Lerner, A. 2019. "Review of 'Compassionate Moral Realism,' by Colin Marshall." *Notre Dame Philosophical Reviews*.

Manne, K. 2018. *Down Girl: The Logic of Misogyny*. Oxford: Oxford University Press.

Marshall, Colin. 2018. *Compassionate Moral Realism*. Oxford: Oxford University Press.

Nagel, Thomas. 1970. *The Possibility of Altruism*. New Jersey: Princeton University Press.

Pautz, Adam. 2021. *Perception*. New York: Routledge.

Pratte, M. S. 2018. "Iconic Memories Die a Sudden Death." *Psychological Science* 29(6): 877–887.

Prinz, Jesse. 2011. "Against Empathy." *Southern Journal of Philosophy* 49: 214–233.

Raleigh, Thomas. 2017. "Phenomenal Privacy, Similarity, and Communicability." *Ergo: An Open Access Journal of Philosophy* 4(22): 637–667.

Russell, Bertrand. 1911. "Knowledge by Acquaintance and Knowledge by Description." *Proceedings of the Aristotelian Society* 11: 108–128.

Russell, Bertrand. 1912. *The Problems of Philosophy*. London: Thornton Butterworth.

Schopenhauer, Arthur. 1915 [1840]. *The Basis of Morality*. 2nd edn, London: Allen and Unwin.

Simmons, A. 2014. "In Defense of the Moral Significance of Empathy." *Ethical Theory and Moral Practice* 17: 97–111.

Slote, M. 2010. *Moral Sentimentalism*. Oxford: Oxford University Press.

Smith, Adam. 1982 [1759]. *The Theory of Moral Sentiments*, edited by D. D. Raphael and A. L. Macfie. Indianapolis: Liberty Classics.

Smith, Joel. 2020. "Self-Consciousness." *The Stanford Encyclopedia of Philosophy* (Summer 2020 Edition), E. N. Zalta (ed.) https://plato.stanford.edu/archives/sum2020/entries/self-consciousness/.

Sperling, G. 1960. "The Information Available in Brief Visual Presentations." *Psychological Monographs* 74(498): 1–29.

Stoljar, Daniel. 2023. "Is There a Persuasive Argument for an Inner Awareness Theory of Consciousness?" *Erkenntnis* 88: 1555–1575.

Strawson, Peter. 1959. *Individuals*. London: Methuen.

Tye, Michael. 2007. "Philosophical Problems of Consciousness." In *The Blackwell Companion to Consciousness*, edited by Max Vie lmans and Susan Schneider, 23–35. Malden, MA: Wiley-Blackwell.

Tye, Michael. 2009. *Consciousness Revisited: Materialism without Phenomenal Concepts*. Cambridge, MA: MIT Press.

Wittgenstein, Ludwig. 1958. *The Blue and Brown Books*. Oxford: Blackwell.

Emad H. Atiq and Matt Duncan, *I Feel Your Pain: Acquaintance and the Limits of Empathy*
In: *Oxford Studies in Philosophy of Mind Volume 4*. Edited by: Uriah Kriegel, Oxford University Press.
© Emad H. Atiq and Matt Duncan 2024. DOI: 10.1093/9780198924159.003.0008

PART III
ACQUAINTANCE AND CONSCIOUSNESS

9

Inferential Seemings

Elijah Chudnoff

"Inferential seeming" is not a familiar term, but I'm using it to pick out what I take to be a familiar experience. This is a kind of experience that occurs in the context of consciously drawing a conclusion from some premises. Inferential seemings can be described as states of seeing how a conclusion follows from some premises, or how those premises support that conclusion. These are natural ways to pick out the relevant experiences, but they shouldn't be read as importing controversial assumptions about the nature of those experiences. For example, I am not assuming they are success states. Maybe some inferential seemings are *mere seemings to see support* rather than *genuine seeings of support*. Nor am I assuming that inferential seemings are attitudes toward propositions about the support given to a conclusion by some premises. At the outset, I want to leave it open whether inferential seemings are representations with propositional contents such as *that a conclusion follows from some premises*.

A proper account of inferential seemings is relevant to addressing debates about general principles that have been claimed to govern the process of inferring. The two most prominent in the recent philosophical literature are Fumerton's Principle of Inferential Justification and Boghossian's Taking Condition:

> For one to be inferentially justified in believing P on the basis of E one must *be justified in believing* that E makes probable P (where entailment can be viewed as the upper limit of making probable) or, alternatively, that the inference from E to P is sanctioned by a correct epistemic rule.
>
> (Fumerton 2004)

> Inferring necessarily involves the thinker taking his premises to support his conclusion and drawing his conclusion because of that fact.
>
> (Boghossian 2014)

On some accounts of inferential seeming, it will turn out that an appropriate inferential seeming can justify one in believing that E makes probable P. It may also turn out that a thinker's inferential seeming can constitute his taking his premises to support his conclusion. The view of inferential seemings I'll defend will have these consequences, and this is something I'll return to at the end of the chapter.

Fumerton's and Boghossian's principles can be seen as specific ways of developing the general idea that a successful inference from some premises to a conclusion must be guided by appreciation that those premises support that conclusion. Lewis Carroll's dialogue, "What the Tortoise Said to Achilles," dramatizes a regress challenge to any such idea. Carroll (1895) considers the following argument from (A) to (B) to (Z):

(A)   Things that are equal to the same are equal to each other.
(B)   The two sides of this triangle are things that are equal to the same.
(Z)   The two sides of this triangle are things that are equal to each other.

According to the Tortoise, someone who accepts (A) and (B) but not the hypothetical proposition (C) that if (A) and (B) are true, then (Z) must be true, is not "as yet under any logical necessity to accept (Z) as true." Though open to different interpretations, one natural lesson to draw from the ensuing exchange is that inferring (Z) from (A) and (B) under the guidance of appreciation that (A) and (B) support (Z) should not require really making one's inference to (Z) from (A) and (B) and the additional hypothetical proposition (C). For, if this were required, then it would be impossible to meet a general demand that inferences be guided by appreciation of their merits. Any such general demand would lead to regress. So, another natural aim for an account of inferential seemings is to show how an inference can be guided by appreciation of its merits without leading to regress.

Though I think inferential seemings have roles to play in interpreting general principles governing inference and in resolving puzzles about Carrollian regress, I do not take them to be theoretical entities postulated for these reasons. Inferential seemings are experiences that can be introspected. In this, I'm following Descartes and Locke. Descartes in the *Rules* and Locke in the *Essay* each give an account of a distinction between intuition and deduction that they take to be introspectively ostensible. If their method is sound, then plausibly inferential seemings are what we observe on the deduction side of the distinction. The approach I'll take toward a theory of inferential seemings will not depend on introspection alone, but it will aim to stay grounded in what can be pointed to in experience.

Here is the plan for the rest of the chapter.

In (§1), I introduce and discuss four normative and functional characteristics of inferential seemings. These are characteristics that a theory of inferential seemings should explain. Then in (§2), I'll say why I think none of the theories of inferential seemings suggested by the current literature on inference successfully explains how inferential seemings have all four of these characteristics. In (§3), I develop an alternative theory that does meet this explanatory challenge. Finally, in (§4), I conclude by briefly considering implications for recent debates about general principles governing inference.

1. Normative and Functional Characteristics

Over the next few parts of the chapter, I'll aim to draw conclusions about what inferential seemings must be like from plausible claims about their normative and functional characteristics. There are four such characteristics.

The first characteristic is (Basing):

(Basing) If you draw a conclusion because you see how it follows from some premises, then your belief in the conclusion is thereby based on the support transmitted by those premises alone. Ignoring alternative, independent bases, your belief in the conclusion is based on the support transmitted by the premises alone.

To see the motivation for (Basing), it is useful to contrast two experiences of the same argument. In one, you don't quite follow the line of reasoning, but you keep up in your judgments in order not to get left behind. In the other, that same line of reasoning is felt as carrying you along to its conclusion with a distinctive kind of compulsion. It is difficult to imagine such a contrasting pair using Lewis Carroll's simple argument, so I'll give more realistic examples involving counting. Reflection on these and some variations on them will also inform later discussion of the other normative and functional characteristics of inferential seemings.

There are 120 different ways of selecting 3 numbers out of the first 10 numbers. We can express this using a standard symbol for combinations, $\binom{10}{3} = 120$, which is read as saying 10 choose 3 is 120. There is a general formula for calculating $\binom{n}{r}$:

$$\binom{n}{r} = \frac{n!}{(n-r)!r!}$$

Most textbook discussions of combinations give pretty much the same argument establishing the correctness of the formula. Here I've copied from *Topics in Finite and Discrete Mathematics* by Sheldon Ross (2000) on the left and presented the argument with numbered premises on the right:

In general, as $n(n-1)\ldots(n-r+1)$ represents the number of different ways that a group of r items can be selected from n items when the order of selection is considered relevant, and as each group of r items will be counted r! times in this count, it follows that the number of different groups of r items that can be formed of a set of n items is

$$\frac{n(n-1)\ldots(n-r+1)}{r!} = \frac{n!}{(n-r)!r!}$$

Ross, S. M. (2000). *Topics in Finite and Discrete Mathematics.* Cambridge University Press. p. 40.

(1) There are $n(n-1)\ldots(n-r+1)$ ways of making r sized ordered lists of items chosen from n total items.

(2) This formula counts each unordered selection of r items r! times.

(3) To get the number of ways of making r sized unordered selections of items chosen from n total items, divide $n(n-1)\ldots(n-r+1)$ by r!.

(4) It follows that the number of ways of selecting r items from n items $= \binom{n}{r} = \frac{n!}{(n-r)!r!}$

We will take steps (1) and (2) as premises established earlier in the discussion. Step (3) is arithmetically obvious: if you overcount each thing you are interested in r! times, then to correct your count divide by r!. Step (4) follows by algebra. If you are like me, however, it can take a moment to see how the algebra is supposed to work. The trick is that the expression for the overcount, $n(n-1)\ldots(n-r+1)$, is the same as $\frac{n!}{(n-r)!}$ because n! is the product of all the factors counting down from n to $(n-r+1)$ and continuing downward from $(n-r)$ to 1. Dividing n! by $(n-r)!$ cancels these additional unwanted factors. The denominator in step (4) includes both this cancelation and the division by r! from step (3). Ross's presentation is typical in not spelling any of this out.

The potential hiccup in following Ross's argument suggests the following phenomenally contrasting pair of cases.

[Obscure Reasoning] You are presented with the argument (1) – (3)/ (4). The step from (3) to (4) is obscure to you, but you ignore the obscurity, and judge that (4) is true despite not seeing how it follows from (1) – (3).

[Clear Reasoning] You are presented with the argument (1) – (3)/ (4). The step from (3) to (4) is obscure to you, but then you get clear on it, and judge that (4) is true because you see how it follows from (1) – (3).

Both [Obscure Reasoning] and [Clear Reasoning] are representative of common experiences that illustrate the contrast we are looking for. In [Clear Reasoning] there is an inferential seeming that is lacking in [Obscure Reasoning]. This is not to say that there are no inferential seemings in [Obscure Reasoning]. Maybe there are, but if so, then they are different inferential seemings from the one that occurs in [Clear Reasoning].

Returning now to (Basing), the motivation I have in mind for it derives from noting the following difference between the [Obscure Reasoning] case and the [Clear Reasoning] case. There is some pressure to deny that the belief in (4) formed in [Obscure Reasoning] is based on the support transmitted by (1) – (3) alone. If you judge (4) without seeing how it follows from (1) – (3), then plausibly you are taking out an additional epistemic loan. For example, maybe your judgment in (4) comes to depend in part on trusting Ross's assertion of the implication. Whatever the specifics, you are assuming that (1) – (3) somehow support (4), and this assumption makes a difference to the structure of your justification for believing (4).

I think there is a good case to be made in favor of this claim about [Obscure Reasoning], but my current interest is in the contrast with [Clear Reasoning]. In this case the belief in (4) is based on the support given by (1) – (3) alone, and there is no pressure to think otherwise. It might take supplementary thinking to enable or institute the basing, but the structure of the basing so enabled or instituted is one in which belief in (4) is based on the support given by (1) – (3). More generally we have the formulation in (Basing).

Suppose, however, you follow a bad argument because it mistakenly seems good to you: you seem to see how the premises support the conclusion, but the premises do not really support the conclusion. According to (Basing) your belief in the conclusion does come to be based on the support transmitted by the premises, but since this support is nil your belief in the conclusion is not thereby justified. I think we should allow such faulty inferential seemings. They enable basing, but the basing that they enable doesn't generate justification.[1]

A second characteristic of inferential seemings is (Justification):

(Justification) If you see how some conclusion follows from some premises, then you thereby have prima facie justification for believing something along the following lines: the conclusion follows from the premises; the premises support the conclusion; if the premises are true, then the conclusion is true; etc.

The motivation for (Justification) can also be brought out by comparing [Obscure Reasoning] with [Clear Reasoning]. Plausibly, if you see how (4) follows from (1) – (3), then you thereby have prima facie justification for believing something along the following lines: (4) follows from (1) – (3); (1) – (3) support (4); if (1) – (3) are true, then (4) is true; etc. (Justification) expresses the general idea.

You need not form any of the beliefs mentioned in (Justification). The claim it makes is about the justification you have for forming a belief, not the justified status of a belief you have formed. In familiar jargon, it is about propositional justification, not doxastic justification.

To appreciate (Justification)'s plausibility, however, it is helpful to consider a case in which you do form one of the beliefs it mentions. Suppose you are in the [Clear Reasoning] case and in addition to (4) you also judge that (1) – (3) support (4). This belief is epistemically appropriate in a distinctive way that it wouldn't be if it were formed in the [Obscure Reasoning] case. The "distinctive way" qualification is necessary, since in the [Obscure Reasoning] case you might have justification for thinking (1) – (3) support (4), but in this case it would be constituted differently. For example, it might come from trusting Ross's assertion. (Justification) gives a natural explanation of the epistemic difference between these two cases.

The third characteristic of inferential seemings is (Opacity):

(Opacity) Even if you see how some conclusion follows from some premises, the truth of the conclusion itself might remain opaque to you. The conclusion might not seem true to you. Seeing how it follows from some

---

[1] Here I disagree with one of the desiderata Huemer (2016) places on a theory of inferential seemings (what he calls inferential appearances). Huemer's acceptance of this desideratum opens him to objections effectively pressed by Smithies (2019).

premises you accept does not constitute having immediate justification for believing that the conclusion is true.

Thinking through an argument for a conclusion might result in an intuition that the conclusion is true. In this case the conclusion does come to seem true to you, and you do gain immediate justification for believing that it is true. But the seeming and the justification are due to the intuition that the conclusion is true, not the inferential seeming in which you see how it follows from the premises of the argument.

The difference between inference and intuition can be made clearer by considering a claim about combinations that can both be demonstrated from the formula and intuitively grasped on its own. Recall that there are 120 ways of selecting 3 numbers out of the first 10 numbers. There are also 120 ways of selecting 7 numbers out of the first 10 numbers. This is no accident. In general, the number of ways of selecting r items from n items = the number of ways of selecting n – r items from n items. Here is how Blitzstein and Hwang (2019) present this identity in their textbook, *Introduction to Probability*:

(Choosing the complement). For any nonnegative integers n and k with k ≤ n, we have

$$\binom{n}{k} = \binom{n}{n-k}$$

This is easy to check algebraically (by writing the binomial coefficients in terms of factorials), but a story proof makes the result easier to understand intuitively.

Story proof: Consider choosing a committee of size k in a group of n people. We know that there are $\binom{n}{k}$ possibilities. But another way to choose the committee is to specify which n – k people are *not* on the committee; specifying who is on the committee determines who is *not* on the committee and vice versa. So the two sides are equal, as they are two ways of counting the same thing.

The algebraic way of checking the formula that they mention would look something like this:

$$\binom{n}{r} = \frac{n!}{(n-r)!r!} = \frac{n!}{(n-(n-r))!(n-r)!} = \binom{n}{n-r}$$

The contrast between the algebraic argument and Blitzstein's and Hwang's (2019) "story proof" suggest the following phenomenally contrasting cases:

[Inferential Basing] You are presented with the algebraic argument from the formula for combinations to the identity $\binom{n}{r} = \binom{n}{n-r}$. You judge that the identity is true because you see how it follows from the formula.

[Intuitive Grasping] You notice that choosing r items out of n items to call "selected" is the same as choosing n − r items out of n items to call "unselected." The labels are arbitrary and can be switched. You judge that $\binom{n}{r} = \binom{n}{n-r}$ because you see its truth intuitively.

Why not say that even without the intuition, the identity still does seem true to you but does so inferentially rather than intuitively? One could choose to talk this way, but I think it is needlessly misleading and will avoid it. If the inferential seeming represents a proposition as true, then it is the proposition *that the identity follows from the formula*, not the proposition *that the identity itself is true*.

The fourth and final characteristic of inferential seemings is (Passivity):

(Passivity) Seeing how a conclusion follows from some premises that you accept does not necessitate judging that the conclusion is true. Having an inferential seeming does not necessitate making an inference or going through any other process that results in judgment.

To see the motivation for (Passivity), compare the [Clear Reasoning] case with another case, which I'll call [Disrupted Reasoning]:

[Disrupted Reasoning] You are presented with the argument (1) – (3)/ (4). All the steps are clear to you, and you see how (4) follows from (1) – (3), but you fail to judge that (4) is true because you are disrupted by someone calling your name.

[Clear Reasoning] and [Disrupted Reasoning] both include an inferential seeming in which you see how (4) follows from (1) – (3). The difference is that in [Clear Reasoning] the seeming results in a judgment that (4) is true, but in [Disrupted Reasoning] it does not. The disruption need not be external. Another possible contrast case is one in which you are disrupted by self-doubt. The main point is the same, and (Passivity) is one way to express it.

The fact that (Passivity) includes your accepting the premises relative to an inert inferential seeming is important. Compare (Passivity) with an alternative claim, namely: seeing how a conclusion follows from some premises does not necessitate judging that the conclusion is true. This is obvious in cases in which you do not accept the premises. (Passivity) is less obvious, but I think it is still plausible.

This concludes my presentation of the four normative and functional characteristics of inferential seemings. Each seems plausible to me on reflection, and I don't think any stands out as especially surprising. Collectively, however, they place significant constraints on theories of inferential seeming. None of the views suggested by current discussions of inference meet all these constraints. That is what I'll argue for now.

2. Views from the Literature on Inference

Giving a theory of the process of inferring is not the same as giving a theory of the experiences I'm calling inferential seemings. But many theories of inference imply, or at least naturally pair with, one or another view about inferential seemings. I'll discuss views that are explicit and views that are implicit in the literature on inference, without making much of the difference. There are three main kinds of view, which I'll call representational state views, conditional representation views, and action awareness views.

The basic idea that ties representational state views together is expressed in <Representational State>:

<Representational State> Seeing how a conclusion follows from some premises is appropriately representing some content to the effect that the conclusion follows from the premises.

<Representational State> is compatible with a broad spectrum of views about the nature of the appropriate representation. For example, it might consist in:

- Your justified belief that the premises make the conclusion probable (Fumerton 2004)
- Your awareness of the premises supporting the conclusion (Tucker 2012)

- Its seeming to you that inferring the conclusion from the premises is right relative to a rule (Broome 2014)

According to the representational state view that I find most attractive, seeing how a conclusion follows from some premises is intuiting that the conclusion follows from the premises. This is the view that results from identifying the appropriate representational state with having an intuition that the conclusion follows from the premises. I think this idea is part of the correct account of inferential seeming, but it is inadequate on its own.

In general, representational state views run into trouble with explaining the role that inferential seemings play according to (Basing). To see the trouble, let us suppose that seeing how C follows from P is intuiting that C follows from P. Then (Basing) implies that it is possible to respond to the intuition that C follows from P by forming a belief that C, which belief is thereby based on the support transmitted by P and P alone. But how exactly is that supposed to work?

Maybe anything can cause anything somehow or other. But it is not enough for the intuition to cause the belief in just any way. The causal process must count as you responding to the intuition. This is a rational activity. I will not try to analyze this notion. What matters for present purposes is that not just any causal process connecting to mental states counts as a rational activity.

Let us first consider some direct ways of responding to the intuition that C follows from P. You might agree with it, disagree with it, or suspend judgment over it. Agreement results in the belief that C follows from P. Disagreement results in the belief that C doesn't follow from P. Suspension results in no belief about whether C follows from P. None of these cases results in believing C itself, but that is what should happen if the intuition were playing the role described in (Basing).

There are also indirect ways of responding to the intuition that C follows from P, which do result in believing C itself. Here is a simple one: you agree with the intuition and thereby form the belief that C follows from P; you infer C from P and the new premise that C follows from P. This results in believing C itself, but the belief is not based in the right way. According to (Basing), it should be based on the support transmitted by P and P alone, not on the support transmitted by P and the new premise that C follows from P. Without adding this new premise, however, it isn't clear how the intuition is something you are responsive to when forming the belief in C.

Nothing in the foregoing depends on special properties of intuitions as opposed to other candidate representational states. Similar points could have been made about beliefs, states of awareness, and non-intuitive seemings. This is no surprise, since what I've been describing is one component in the engine that drives Carrollian regress worries. The other component is a higher order requirement on inference, that is, some requirement to the effect that inferences *must* be responsive to inferential seemings. When you put higher-order requirements together with representational state views, then you get Carrollian regresses.

Regress worries aside, it doesn't look like representational state views are in a good position to accommodate (Basing). This conclusion is not meant to refute the claim that inferential seemings do represent some content to the effect that a conclusion follows from some premises. It is meant to rule out views according to which this is all that they do. There must be more to their nature to accommodate (Basing).

The basic idea that ties conditional representation views together is expressed in <Conditional Representation>:

<Conditional Representation> Seeing how a conclusion follows from some premises is appropriately representing the conclusion, consequentially on appropriately representing the premises.

Conditional representation views are supposed to improve on representational state views because they describe subjects of inferential seemings as forming the appropriate conclusion beliefs and in a way that does not lead to regress. A few authors have recently developed accounts of inference that suggest something along the lines of <Conditional Representation>.

- Sinan Dogramaci (2013: 394) introduces conditional intuitions, where "to have a conditional intuition is to be tempted, in a phenomenally conscious way, by certain existing considerations to believe a conclusion."
- Michael Huemer (2016: 149) introduces inferential appearances, "which, roughly, represent something to be true given, or in the light of, some other presumed truth."
- According to Eric Marcus (2020: 312), a thinker's inferences depend on their holding their beliefs in mind with a mode of understanding such that, the "thinker believes the conclusion because she must believe it, given what she already accepts as true."

Note that in my formulation of the basic idea, I have used the phrase "consequentially on." This is meant to express the result of meeting two conditions: (i) appropriately representing the conclusion, conditional on appropriately representing the premises; and (ii) appropriately representing the premises. To be views about inferential seemings, conditional representation views need such triggered conditional representations, since merely conditionally representing something does not suffice for being in a phenomenally conscious state.

As a group, conditional representation views run into problems with accommodating the role of inferential seemings described in (Justification).

The problem is this. For you to appropriately represent some conclusion C, consequentially on appropriately representing some premises P, is just for you to represent C in some way and for that representation to be caused by your representation of P. The specifics of the casual process don't figure into the problem. (Justification) implies that seeing how C follows from P justifies believing that C follows from P. But it is not clear how representing C alone, in whatever form and because of whatever causes, will justify believing that C follows from P. For there to be justification, you need to represent somehow that C follows from P.

Huemer suggests that, as he understands them, inferential appearances do include having some attitude toward the proposition that C follows from P (Huemer 2016: 152). That might be thought to help with (Justification). But it depends on how we understand the relevant attitude. On one understanding, the attitude is implicit in the dispositions in virtue of one appropriately represents C, conditional on appropriately representing P (cf. Leitgeb 2007 on conditional belief). However, it is not clear how such an implicit attitude could justify believing that C follows from P, especially given any view of justification along the lines of Huemer's own phenomenal conservatism. On another understanding, the attitude Huemer has in mind is just appropriately representing that C follows from P. Going with this understanding suggests that Huemer doesn't really have a conditional representation view. Representing "something to be true given, or in light of, some other presumed truth," is just representing that the first follows from the second. If this is the correct way to read him, then Huemer's view counts as a representational state view, and its main problem has already been discussed.

Aside from the common problem with (Justification), there are problems unique to different versions of conditional representation views. They hinge on the appropriate form of representation for the conclusion. Suppose with Dogramaci and Huemer that it is intuition, appearance, seeming, or something along those lines. Then the resulting view doesn't just under-generate justification. It also over-generates justification. It is inconsistent with the claim I've called (Opacity).

(Opacity) implies that seeing how a conclusion C follows from some premises P doesn't justify believing C on its own merits. But intuiting, or having it appear or seem to one, that C presumably does justify believing C on its own merits. So conditional representation views that identify the appropriate form of representation for the conclusion with intuition, appearance, seeming, or something along those lines run afoul of (Opacity).

On the other hand, suppose with Marcus that the appropriate form of representation for the conclusion is belief. Then the view is inconsistent with the claim I've called (Passivity). (Passivity) implies that seeing how a conclusion C follows from some premises P doesn't necessitate believing C. But believing C, consequentially on appropriately representing P, does imply believing C. Marcus takes this to be a positive feature of his view, one that enables him to avoid Carrollian regress, but I think it is preferable to develop a view of inferential seeming that both avoids Carrollian regress and accommodates (Passivity).

Overall, then, I do not think that conditional representation views provide any real advantages over plain representational state views.

I'm calling the third and final group of views suggested by the literature on inference action awareness views. The basic idea that ties them together is <Action Awareness>:

<Action Awareness> Inferring a conclusion from some premises consists in performing an action. Seeing how the conclusion follows from the premises is being aware of what you are doing in performing this action.

The most straightforward version of <Action Awareness> identifies the action you are aware of with the action of making an inference. Seeing how a conclusion follows from some premises is just seeing yourself inferring the conclusion from the premises. This straightforward action awareness theory clearly runs afoul of (Passivity). It is possible for you to see how some conclusion follows from some premises you accept without inferring the conclusion from the premises. So, your inferential seeming cannot be iden-tified with awareness of yourself inferring the conclusion from the premises.

The specific views in the current literature that suggest <Action Awareness>, however, do not take the straightforward form just dismissed.

They are views that aim to illuminate the nature of inference rather than take it for granted. Nonetheless, they all still run afoul of (Passivity). I'll briefly discuss the following examples:

- According to Boghossian (2014) and Broome (2014), inferring is following a rule of inference, such as:

  R. If you accept P, then also accept C!

- According to Wright (2014), inferring C from P is the action of accepting C for the reason constituted by accepting P.
- According to Hlobil (2019), inferring C from P is the action of attaching what he calls inferential force to the argument, P therefore C.

Boghossian takes rule-following to be primitive. Broome develops an analysis.[2] Either way, inferring a conclusion C from some premises P amounts to accepting C because you accept P and follow rule R which tells you to accept C when you accept P. Plugging this into <Action Awareness> yields the view that seeing how C follows from P is being aware of yourself accepting C because you both accept P and follow R which tells you to accept C when you accept P. Perhaps there is some initial plausibility to this identification. Seeing how a conclusion follows from some premise is just seeing yourself drawing the conclusion from the premise in accordance with a rule. The plausibility, however, only attaches to the following implication of the view: if you see yourself drawing the conclusion from the premise in accordance with a rule, then you see how the conclusion follows from the premise. The view also implies a conditional going in the other direction: if you see how the conclusion follows from the premise, then you see yourself drawing the conclusion from the premise in accordance with a rule. But this is inconsistent with (Passivity).

One avenue left open to action awareness views is to isolate an action that is a proper part of inferring, and that falls short of judging. I have no knockdown argument against this idea, but I also do not know of any view that works out how it might go. Maybe Wright and Hlobil come close, but I think their views still run into problems with (Passivity). According to Wright (2014), inferring C from P is the action of accepting C for the

---

[2] One element of Broome's analysis is seeming rightness. This element provisions his view with the resources of an alternative explanation of inferential seemings, one along the lines of a representational state view and already discussed above.

Table 9.1

		(Basing)	(Justification)	(Opacity)	(Passivity)
<Representational State>		X	✓	✓	✓
Non-Doxastic	<Conditional Representation>	?	X	X	✓
Doxastic				✓	X
<Action Awareness>		✓	?	✓	X

reason constituted by accepting P. Plugging this into <Action Awareness> yields the view that seeing how C follows from P is being aware of yourself accepting C for the reason constituted by accepting P. Since this implies accepting C, it is inconsistent with (Passivity). According to Hlobil (2019), inferring C from P is the action of attaching what he calls inferential force to the argument, P therefore C. Plugging this into <Action Awareness> yields the view that seeing how C follows from P is being aware of yourself attaching inferential force to the argument, P therefore C. According to Hlobil's account, attaching inferential force to an argument implies judging that its conclusion is true. So, his view is also inconsistent with (Passivity).

A second avenue left open to action awareness views is to endorse a disjunctive conception of inferential seeming. Perhaps inferential seemings are constituted by states of action awareness in cases in which one goes through with an inference, and they are constituted otherwise in cases in which one does not go through with an inference. I have no knockdown argument against this idea either, but it lacks any immediate plausibility. It is something to consider after exhausting other options.

The results of this section can be tabulated as in Table 9.1. The "X"s represent problems that I have discussed. The "✓"s represent what I see as plausible successes. The "?"s represent open questions that I must set aside here. I'm not confident that conditional representation views can account for (Basing), nor that action awareness views can account for (Justification); but discussing these matters would take us off course.

3. The Indirect Command View

Speech act theory has been a fertile source of analogies for thinking about various kinds of experience. Consider perceptual experience and pain.

A common thought about perceptual experience is that to have a perceptual experience as of your environment being a certain way is to be in an assertive mental state, one that asserts that your environment is that way.[3] Taking a perceptual experience at face value is believing what it says about your environment. A more controversial but increasingly popular thought about pain is that to feel a pain in some part of your body is to be in a directive mental state, one that commands you to treat that body part in certain ways, for example protectively.[4] The function of a pain is to get you to act in the ways that it commands.

Inferential seemings are puzzling because they suggest conflicting analogies with speech acts. On the one hand, they suggest an analogy with assertions. Seeing how some conclusion follows from some premises is being in a mental state that tells you that the conclusion follows from the premises. This analogy nurtures representational state views. On the other hand, inferential seemings suggest an analogy with directives. Seeing how some conclusion follows from some premises is being in a mental state that commands you to infer the conclusion from the premises. This analogy captures what I think is plausible about action awareness views. Inferential seemings are essentially connected to mental actions such as inferring, not because they include performances of the actions, but because they command performances of them.

The puzzle, then, is to develop an understanding of inferential seemings on which they combine both aspects. The solution, I believe, is to draw on another idea from speech act theory. This is the idea of an indirect speech act.

Suppose a visitor enters a host's office, finds it too cold, and would like the host to lower the air conditioner. The visitor could make a direct request by uttering an imperative, such as "Please lower the air conditioner." Alternatively, the visitor could make the same request indirectly. One way to make the request indirectly is to utter an interrogative, such as "Can you lower the air conditioner?" or, "Is it me, or is it very cold in here?" Another way to make the request indirectly is to utter a declarative, such as "I am freezing" or, "I think you might have the air conditioner on too high." If the visitor makes their request in one of these indirect ways, then they have performed an indirect speech act. As Searle (1975) puts it, "In such cases a sentence that contains the illocutionary force indicators for one kind of

---

[3] See, e.g., Heck 2000, Tucker 2010, Reiland 2015.
[4] See, e.g., Hall 2008, Klein 2007, Martínez 2011.

illocutionary act can be uttered to perform, *in addition*, another type of illocutionary act."

The view of inferential seemings I want to defend is that they are directly assertoric mental states and indirectly directive mental states. More specifically, they are intuitions that indirectly command you to infer some conclusion from some premises by directly telling you that the premises support the conclusion.

Suppose you intuit that a set of premises P supports conclusion C. On its own this is like being told that P supports C. In this case the intuition is just an intuition. Provided the appropriate conditions are met however—conditions such as your endorsing P, your taking an interest in C, and your being rational—then, I suggest, that same intuition will also command you to infer C from P. The analogy with indirect speech is indicated by the following parallels:

Speech	Experience
Assert that I am freezing with the declarative, "I am freezing."	Being informed that P supports C by an intuition that P supports C
Conversational context	Cognitive context
Indirectly request the air conditioner to be lowered by asserting that I am freezing with the declarative, "I am freezing."	Being indirectly ordered to infer C from P by being informed that P supports C by an intuition that P supports C

If the more familiar analogies between experiences and speech acts are legitimate, then I think the one I am proposing is too. The main reason to endorse the resulting view of inferential seemings is that it naturally explains their key functional and normative characteristics. This reason can be spelled out as follows.

Suppose you have an intuition that represents that C follows from P and thereby indirectly commands you to infer C from P. Because your experience is an intuition representing that C follows from P, your experience will exhibit the characteristics expressed by (Justification), (Opacity), and (Passivity). If you intuit that C follows from P, then: you thereby have justification for believing that C follows from P; you do not thereby have justification for believing C on its own merits; and you do not thereby form a belief in C. Because your experience commands you to infer C from P, your experience will also exhibit the characteristic expressed by (Basing). (Basing), recall, is stated as follows:

(Basing) If you draw a conclusion because you see how it follows from some premises, then your belief in the conclusion is thereby based on the support transmitted by those premises alone. Ignoring alternative, independent bases, your belief in the conclusion is based on the support transmitted by the premises alone.

Suppose seeing how some conclusion follows from some premises includes being ordered to infer the conclusion from the premises. Then drawing the conclusion because you see how it follows from the premises is just following the order. But the order was precisely to infer the conclusion from the premises, not to infer the conclusion from the premises and something else. So, if you do what you are ordered to do, you will have thereby formed a belief in the conclusion that is based on the support transmitted by the premises alone.

From the foregoing, we can conclude that an intuition that represents that C follows from P, and thereby indirectly commands you to infer C from P, will exhibit the key normative and functional characteristics of the inferential seeming that is seeing how C follows from P. Absent any better ideas, this gives us reason to identify inferential seemings with intuitions that indirectly command inferences.

The main challenge to this view of inferential seeming is that none of the familiar models of indirect speech acts illuminates how it might work. There are different models of how one speech act can be indirectly accomplished by means of directly performing another speech act. But none of them suggests a plausible answer to the question of how an intuition can indirectly command performing an inference by directly asserting that the conclusion follows from the premises. The details of the different models do not really matter. Their unsuitability can be appreciated from a distance.

Suppose a visitor indirectly requests their host to lower the air conditioner by directly asking a question, "Can you lower the air conditioner?" Table 9.2 presents some different views about how the indirect request is accomplished.

Table 9.2

Conversational Implicature (Searle 1975)	The host infers that the visitor made the request from the fact that the visitor asked the question
Convention of Usage (Morgan 1977)	The visitor exploits a convention for making such requests by asking such questions
Ambiguity (Lepore and Stone 2014)	The interrogative is ambiguous; linguistic competence enables it to be used for requests in addition to questions

Suppose you have an intuition representing that C follows from P and thereby commanding you to infer C from P. If you had to infer the command, then there would be a threat of Carrollian regress. Clearly no convention applies in this case. And ambiguity would seem to require that the intuition have an identity independent of it representing that C follows from P, so that this representational reading would count as one of two equally admissible interpretations. A potential alternative to these inapplicable models is Millikan's (1995) model of pushmi-pullyu representations. These are representations that function to both describe and direct. So, they do function as inferential seemings should. The problem, however, is that on Millikan's view pushmi-pullyu representations have this dual function because they are more primitive than purely descriptive or purely directive representations. Pushmi-pullyu representations do not direct because they describe; they direct and describe because they operate at a representational level that is prior to the differentiation between these two functions. Intuitions about what follows from what, however, are manifestations of higher rational capacities.

On the model I prefer, when your intuition that conclusion C follows from premises P commands you to infer C from P, it is an instance of the more general phenomenon whereby the nature of a partial phenomenal state is fixed by the total phenomenal state to which it belongs. Consider the visual example from Stephen Palmer (1990) in Figures 9.1a and 9.1b.

The triangle in Figure 9.1a can be seen as pointing to 3 o'clock, 7 o'clock, or 11 o'clock with equal force. There is strong pressure to see the middle triangle in Figure 9.1b, however, as pointing in the 3 o'clock direction. The difference between how the triangle in Figure 9.1a and the middle triangle

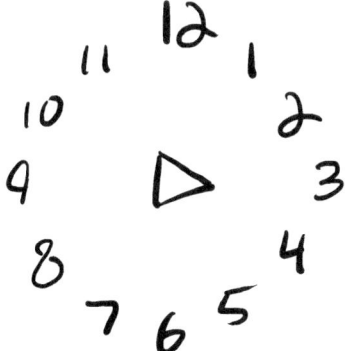

Figure 9.1a Neutral Direction.

Figure 9.1b Preferred Direction.

in Figure 9.1b are experienced is due to what else is experienced with them. The natures of the partial visual states are fixed by the total visual states to which they belong. My suggestion is that if an intuition that C follows from P is experienced in the appropriate context of other experiences, it will be experienced as commanding you to infer C from P. Like the triangle in Figure 9.1a, a mere intuition that C follows from P does not point you in any particular inferential direction. Like the middle triangle in Figure 9.1b, an intuition that indirectly commands you to infer C from P does point you in a particular inferential direction. The relevant context in the intuition case will be primarily cognitive. For an intuition that C follows from P to indirectly command you to infer C from P, you'll likely need to experience P as a commitment, take some interest in C, not be aware of defeating considerations against C, etc. I readily admit to not being able to spell these conditions out with any confidence. Spelling out the principles governing perceptual organization is an ongoing empirical endeavor. We should expect it to take at least as much effort to spell out principles governing the organization of conscious cognition. The main points I want to make here are that there is such an organization, and it is a plausible candidate for being the explanation of how a descriptive experience constitutes a directive experience.

4. Principles Governing Inference

I'll conclude by briefly considering how the indirect command view bears on some of the main concerns that have driven recent discussions of inference. These are about the general principles governing inference mentioned at the beginning of the chapter. The first principle is Fumerton's Principle of Inferential Justification:

> For one to be inferentially justified in believing P on the basis of E one must *be justified in believing* that E makes probable P (where entailment can be viewed as the upper limit of making probable) or, alternatively, that the inference from E to P is sanctioned by a correct epistemic rule.
>
> (Fumerton 2004)

The second principle is Boghossian's Taking Condition:

Inferring necessarily involves the thinker taking his premises to support his conclusion and drawing his conclusion because of that fact.

(Boghossian (2014)

The main observation I want to make is that one way for an inference to satisfy both Fumerton's principle and Boghossian's principle is for it to be made in response to an inferential seeming as I have construed them.

Suppose you intuit that conclusion C follows from premises P and are thereby indirectly commanded to infer C from P. Responding to this inferential seeming is doing what it tells you do to, namely inferring C from P. Suppose this occurs. Since intuiting that C follows from P is a way of taking P to support C, the resulting inference satisfies Boghossian's Taking Condition. Intuiting that C follows from P justifies believing that P makes probable C. So, the resulting inference also satisfies Fumerton's Principle of Inferential Justification. It is worth pointing out that intuiting that C follows from P can justify believing that P makes probable C, even if you do not go on to form that belief and even if forming that belief is not what the intuition calls for on the occasion, since it functions to direct rather than describe.

It follows that it is at least possible for Fumerton's and Boghossian's principles to be true. Some opponents of the principles challenge them on the basis of the worry that they lead to Carrollian regress. Since inferential seemings do not lead to Carrollian regress, however, one way for the principles to be true is for all inferences to be responses to inferential seemings.

But one might reasonably doubt that all inferences are in fact responses to inferential seemings. Some inferences might occur on autopilot. Suppose, then, it turns out that only some inferences are responses to inferential seemings, and suppose further that Fumerton's and Boghossian's principles are only true for those inferences. Would there be any interest in picking out this subset of inferences for special scrutiny? I think there would be. Inferences that satisfy Fumerton's and Boghossian's principles because they are responses to inferential seemings possess a distinctive transparency. Making such an inference includes consciousness of what one is doing in making such an inference. It may be that as a matter of fact in much of our epistemic life we remain obscure to ourselves, but that does not diminish the value of transparency. Transparency is worth pursuing both for knowing oneself and being able to make oneself known to others.[5]

References

Blitzstein, J. K., and Hwang, J. (2019). *Introduction to Probability*. Boca Raton, FL: CRC Press.

Boghossian, Paul (2014). What Is Inference? *Philosophical Studies* 169 (1): 1–18.

Broome, John (2014). Comments on Boghossian. *Philosophical Studies* 169 (1): 19–25.

Carroll, Lewis (1895). What the Tortoise Said to Achilles. *Mind* 4 (14): 278–280.

Dogramaci, Sinan (2013). Intuitions for Inferences. *Philosophical Studies* 165 (2): 371–399.

Fumerton, Richard (2004). Epistemic Probability. *Philosophical Issues* 14 (1): 149–164.

Hall, Richard J. (2008). If It Itches, Scratch! *Australasian Journal of Philosophy* 86 (4): 525–535.

Heck, Richard G. (2000). Nonconceptual Content and the "Space of Reasons." *Philosophical Review* 109 (4): 483–523.

Hlobil, Ulf (2019). Inferring by Attaching Force. *Australasian Journal of Philosophy* 97 (4): 701–714.

Huemer, Michael. 2016. "Inferential Appearances." In *Intellectual Assurance: Essays on Traditional Epistemic Internalism*, edited by Brett Coppenger and Michael Bergmann, 144–160. Oxford: Oxford University Press.

Klein, Colin (2007). An Imperative Theory of Pain. *Journal of Philosophy* 104 (10): 517–532.

Leitgeb, Hannes (2007). Beliefs in Conditionals vs. Conditional Beliefs. *Topoi* 26 (1): 115–132.

Lepore, Ernie, and Stone, Matthew (2014). *Imagination and Convention: Distinguishing Grammar and Inference in Language*. Oxford University Press.

Marcus, Eric (2020). Inference as Consciousness of Necessity. *Analytic Philosophy* 61(4): 304–322.

[5] Thanks to audiences at Universidad Nacional de Córdoba, Ben-Gurion University, Fredericton University, and the Network for Phenomenological Research for discussion of this work.

Martínez, Manolo (2011). Imperative Content and the Painfulness of Pain. *Phenomenology and the Cognitive Sciences* 10 (1): 67–90.

Millikan, Ruth Garrett (1995). Pushmi-pullyu Representations. *Philosophical Perspectives* 9: 185–200.

Morgan, J. L. (1977). Two Types of Convention in Indirect Speech Acts. Technical Report No. 52.

Palmer, Stephen E. (1990). Modern Theories of Gestalt Perception. *Mind and Language* 5 (4): 289–323.

Reiland, Indrek (2015). Experience, Seemings, and Evidence. *Pacific Philosophical Quarterly* 96 (4): 510–534.

Ross, S. M. (2000). *Topics in Finite and Discrete Mathematics*. Cambridge University Press.

Searle, J. R. (1975). Indirect Speech Acts. In P. Cole and J. Morgan (eds), *Syntax and Semantics, Volume 3, Speech Acts*, 59–82. New York: Academic Press.

Smithies, Declan (2019). *The Epistemic Role of Consciousness*. New York, USA: Oxford University Press.

Tucker, Chris (2010). Why Open-Minded People Should Endorse Dogmatism. *Philosophical Perspectives* 24 (1): 529–545.

Tucker, Chris (2012). Movin' on up: Higher-Level Requirements and Inferential Justification. *Philosophical Studies* 157 (3): 323–340.

Wright, Crispin (2014). Comment on Paul Boghossian, "What Is Inference." *Philosophical Studies* 169 (1): 27–37.

Elijah Chudnoff, *Inferential Seemings* In: *Oxford Studies in Philosophy of Mind Volume 4.*
Edited by: Uriah Kriegel, Oxford University Press. © Elijah Chudnoff 2024.
DOI: 10.1093/9780198924159.003.0009

10

Inner Acquaintance Theories of Consciousness

Anna Giustina

1. Introduction

Most recent philosophical theories of consciousness account for it in terms of *representation*, the bulk of the debate revolving around whether (suitably) representing something is sufficient for consciousness (as per first-order representationalism) or some further (meta-)representation is needed (as per higher-order representationalism and self-representationalism). In this chapter, I explore an alternative theory of consciousness, one that aims to explain consciousness *not* in terms of representation but in terms of the epistemically and metaphysically direct relation of *acquaintance*. I call this the *Inner Acquaintance Theory* of consciousness (IAT). Roughly, on IAT, what makes a mental state conscious is its subject being acquainted with it.

Though not wholly unprecedented, IAT is still at the fringe of consciousness debates and remains largely underexplored. The main goal of this chapter is to take some steps toward developing the details of IAT, illustrate its potential explanatory power, and put it forward as a plausible alternative to representational theories, with the hope that this will contribute to shifting IAT closer to the center of the debate.

Here is how I proceed. In §2 I introduce a notion—*inner awareness*—that is crucial both to contextualize and to understand IAT. In §3 I provide some preliminary motivation for exploring IAT. In §4 I explain the notion of *acquaintance* and illustrate some of the features that are typically attributed to it in the literature. The details of IAT are then shaped through four main decision points. I address them in §§5–8, where I suggest a particular choice at each decision point, thereby progressively building up a view that I consider particularly promising.

2. Inner Awareness and Acquaintance

A crucial divide in philosophy of consciousness is on whether phenomenal consciousness implies some form of self-consciousness. Disagreement revolves around something like the following principle:

> *AP*: For any subject S and conscious state M of S, M is conscious only if S is aware of M.

We may call the relevant awareness of one's own mental states "inner awareness" and the principle "Awareness Principle" (AP). First-order representationalists reject AP (they argue that first-order representation is sufficient for consciousness), whereas meta-representational theories (higher-order representationalism and self-representationalism) have it at the core of their account of phenomenal consciousness (on these views, *awareness of* first-order representation is necessary for it to be a *conscious* representation).

Inner awareness is often characterized as a *non-attentive, non-introspective, non-conceptual, non-thought-like*, and *non-inferential* awareness of one's own current conscious states. To be sure, some philosophers defend stronger versions of AP; some argue that (attentive) *introspective awareness* is required for consciousness (Armstrong 1968); others that forming a (conceptual and propositionally structured) *thought* about a mental state is necessary for it to be conscious (Rosenthal 1997). Such stronger claims, however, are not entailed by AP. Arguably, we can be aware of things we do not attend to (you can be olfactorily aware of fresh-baked cake even if your attention is focused on the sentence you are reading) and we can be aware of something without entertaining a thought about it (you can be gustatorily aware of durian without being aware *that it is durian; cf.* Dretske 1993). In what follows, I will thus adopt the weakest possible version of AP, where consciousness only requires a "minimal" form of inner awareness—that is, an awareness that is non-attentive, non-introspective, non-conceptual, non-thought-like, and non-inferential.

Many AP proponents maintain that inner awareness is not only *necessary* for consciousness, but also *constitutive* of it: it is what *makes* a mental state conscious (i.e., that *in virtue of which* a mental state is a conscious state). They thus argue for:

> *AP⁺*: For any subject S and conscious state M of S, M is conscious *in virtue of* S's being aware of M.

Theorists who defend AP⁺ have typically accounted for inner awareness in terms of (meta)*representation*: S is aware of M iff S (suitably) represents M. Accordingly, they have developed a Meta-Representational account of Inner Awareness (MRIA):

> *MRIA*: For any subject S and conscious state M of S, S is innerly aware of M iff S is in a mental state M* that suitably represents M.

By combining AP⁺ with MRIA, Meta-Representational Theories (MRT) aim at explaining consciousness in terms of meta-representation:

> *MRT*: For any subject S and conscious state M of S, M is conscious in virtue of S's being in a mental state M* that suitably represents M.

On this ground, the debate has mostly revolved around the relationship between M and M*. On Higher-Order Representationalism, M and M* are *distinct* mental states; on Self-Representationalism, they are the *same* mental state.[1]

Here I want to explore a *third* option—one that has received little attention so far. On this view, inner awareness is explained *not* in meta-representational terms, but in terms of the relation of *acquaintance*—hence the Acquaintance account of Inner Awareness (AIA):

> *AIA*: For any subject S and conscious state M of S, S is aware of M iff S is acquainted with M.

By combining AP⁺ with AIA, we obtain the general form of an Inner Acquaintance Theory of consciousness (IAT):

> *IAT*: For any subject S and conscious state M of S, M is conscious in virtue of S's being acquainted with M.

Arguably, IAT has been disregarded mostly due to naturalizability concerns. Representation can be found anywhere in nature—not just in conscious

---

[1] For higher-order representationalism, see Armstrong (1968), Lycan (1996), and Rosenthal (1997). For self-representationalism, see especially Kriegel (2009); see also Carruthers (2000, 2005), Van Gulick (2000, 2004), and Gennaro (1996, 2012). For a collection of papers on self-representationalism, see Kriegel and Williford (2006).

minds. If the intentionality-naturalization research program turns out successful and mental representation can be fully explained in (causal/teleological/functional and thereby purely) physical terms, representational theories promise to offer a naturalistic account of consciousness. Acquaintance, on the other hand, is supposed to be *unique* to conscious minds; it is a *special* relation that seems refractory to physical reduction. For these reasons, many theorists have considered it mysterious and regarded it with suspicion. However, although acquaintance's prospects for naturalization are still underexplored, they are not null (see e.g., Balog 2012) and a few philosophers have recently ventured acquaintance-based accounts of consciousness (Coleman 2015; Williford 2015; Levine 2019). The details of IAT, though, remain unexplored. This chapter's ambition is to make some substantial steps toward a detailed and precise version of IAT, one that can compete with the much more widespread and already well-developed meta-representational views.

I will proceed by highlighting four decision points—concerning both the acquaintance *relation* and its *relata*—that, as I see it, anyone who wants do develop a version of IAT faces. A secondary goal is to argue for, or at least recommend, a particular choice at each decision point, thereby developing a version of IAT that I consider particularly promising.

A note before continuing. I propose IAT as a third kind of theory (besides Higher-Order Representationalism and Self-Representationalism) that endorses and aims to explain AP⁺. In what follows, then, I am going to *assume* AP⁺. This is not uncontroversial. In particular, some proponents of the *transparency of experience* (Harman 1990) and first-order representationalists about consciousness (Dretske 1993) deny that there is anything like inner awareness. A full defense of AP⁺ would require substantive theoretical argumentation, which I do not have the space to carry out here.[2] I thus simply assume that inner awareness is real and a constitutive aspect of conscious experience.

3. Motivating an Inner Acquaintance Theory

My primary aim being exploring a positive view, I cannot develop here a full argument in favor of the Inner Acquaintance Theory and against its

---

[2] For a recent positive argument in support of inner awareness see Kriegel (2019). See also Giustina (2022a, 2024).

competitors.[3] I will just hint at some prima facie motivation by briefly reviewing what I consider the most worrying objections to representational theories that accept AP⁺: Higher-Order Representationalism (HOR) and Self-Representationalism (SR).[4]

As noted, both HOR and SR explain inner awareness in terms of meta-representation:

> *MRT*: For any subject S and conscious state M of S, M is conscious in virtue of S's being in a mental state M* that suitably represents M.

On HOR, M* is distinct and different from M (M≠M*); on SR, M and M* are the same mental state (M=M*).

The main problem with HOR is that it allows for *targetless* higher-order representation (Byrne 1997; Neander 1998; Levine 2001, 2018; and Kriegel 2009). On HOR, the first-order representation and the meta-representation—that makes the first-order representation conscious and thus phenomenally apparent to the subject—are *distinct* mental states and can therefore exist independently of one another. Compare this with the perceptual case. When you have a visual representation as of a red rose, the representation and the rose have distinct existences: each can exist without the other. Similarly, on HOR, your first-order rose representation can exist independently of your meta-representation of it and your meta-representation can exist even in the absence of *any* first-order representation. This, though, is very implausible. It entails that it can phenomenally appear to you that you have a conscious experience as of a rose while in fact you have none. Most theorists (and, arguably, any lay people contemplating this idea) consider this impossible or even inconceivable.[5] It seems that, necessarily, if an experience phenomenally appears to you, it cannot be that *no experience* is present.[6]

---

[3] I make some steps in that direction in Giustina (2022c).

[4] For objections to HOR, see, e.g., Dretske (1993, 1995), Goldman (1993), Tye (1995), Siewert (1998), Seager (2004), Levine (2006), and Kriegel (2009). For objections to SR, see, e.g., Weisberg (2008), Brogaard (2012), Gertler (2012), Van Gulick (2012), Mehta (2013), and Coleman (2015).

[5] Though not all: see, e.g., Rosenthal (2005), Brown (2010), Churchland (2013), Hill (2016), and Schwitzgebel (2011). So-called "illusionists" about phenomenal consciousness (Dennett 1988, 2016; Frankish 2016; Kammerer 2016) argue that not only such inner hallucination is possible, but it is what constitutes *all* our (seemingly) conscious experiences. However, illusionists are an outlandish minority in the philosophy-of-mind landscape.

[6] Though it may occur that you form an incorrect *belief* about the relevant experience, as when you introspectively judge that you have an itch sensation in your thigh, while what you really have is a tickle sensation.

Such considerations have motivated Self-Representationalism. If the representing state M* and the represented state M are the same, then, straightforwardly, it cannot be the case that the former occurs in the absence of the latter. SR thus rules out the kind of inner hallucination allowed by HOR.

However, SR also seems to face some problems, the deepest of which has to do with the explanatory adequacy of self-representation and has been articulated by Levine (2006). SR aims to explain phenomenal consciousness in terms of a mental state's representing itself. However, if, as SR assumes, first-order representation is insufficient for consciousness, how can just adding more representation (meta-representation) of the same kind yield phenomenal consciousness?

> Somehow, what we have in conscious states are representations that are intrinsically of subjective significance, "animated" as it were, and I maintain that we really don't understand how that is possible. It doesn't seem to be a matter of more of the same—more representation of the same kind—but rather representation of a different kind altogether.
>
> (Levine 2006: 195)

The mere fact that a conscious state represents (also) *itself*, rather than (just) something else, is insufficient to explain the peculiar "subjective significance" of phenomenal consciousness. After all, the sentence "This sentence is written in English" also represents itself, but is not phenomenally conscious (Kriegel 2009: 159). What makes a mental state phenomenally conscious cannot be *what* it represents (i.e., that it represents itself): it must have to do with *how* it represents—with the *kind* of self-representation involved (Kriegel 2011: 64–65). Now, either self-representation is of the familiar and naturalization-friendly kind or it is not. If it is, then it is unclear why and how just adding an extra (self-)representation of the mental state itself, on top of the first-order representation, should be sufficient to yield consciousness. If, instead, the self-representation is *not* of the familiar kind, then it *could* be sufficient for consciousness. However, it would have to be *sui generis* and *special*:

> The problem, in other words, is that conscious awareness seems to be a sui generis form of representation, and not merely because it's reflexive. Something about the representation relation itself—that it affords acquaintance, and not just representation—is such as to yield a mystery concerning its possible physical realization.
>
> (Levine 2006: 193)

So, the deepest problem with SR seems to be that no familiar kind of (self-) representation can account for the subjective significance that is peculiar to phenomenal consciousness. A *special* relation, one that uniquely ties subjects to their experiences, seems needed. *Acquaintance* may be the right candidate to play this explanatory role.

4. Acquaintance

Made popular by Bertrand Russell (1910, 1912), but then neglected for much of the twentieth century, the notion of acquaintance has recently regained momentum.[7] Particular interest has been devoted to it in epistemology, both in the context of contemporary defenses of foundationalism (Fales 1996; BonJour 2000, 2003; Fumerton 1996, 2001, 2009; Hasan 2013) and in the more recent revival of Russellian *knowledge by acquaintance* (McGinn 2008; Tye 2008; Hofmann 2014; Fiocco 2017; Duncan 2020, 2021b; Coleman 2019; Giustina 2022b). In philosophy of mind, the notion of acquaintance has been deployed in the "phenomenal concept strategy" defense of physicalism (Papineau 2002, 2006; Balog 2012), in some versions of naïve realism about perception (Campbell 2002; Brewer 2011; Soteriou 2013), as well as in the explanation of introspection (Gertler 2001, 2011, 2012; Chalmers 2003; Horgan and Kriegel 2007; Giustina 2023). Some philosophers have proposed acquaintance-based accounts of consciousness and subjectivity (Hellie 2007; Coleman 2015; Williford 2015; Duncan 2018; Levine 2019), but the use of acquaintance in this area is still underexplored.

Acquaintance is an epistemically significant mental relation, typically spelled out in terms of *direct awareness*, where the relevant directness is both epistemic and metaphysical (*cf.* Gertler 2011).[8] Acquaintance is *epistemically* direct in that, by being acquainted with x, a subject S gets an epistemic access to x that is *non-inferential*—that is, does not depend on S's having epistemic access to anything else (in particular, it is independent of S's entertaining any judgment). It is *metaphysically* direct in that, when S is acquainted with x, no causal process mediates between x and S's awareness of x. Differently from representation (that can be directed at non-existent

---

[7] Raleigh (2019) and Duncan (2021a) offer excellent and very useful introductions to the notion of acquaintance. See also Knowles and Raleigh (2019) for a recent collection devoted to acquaintance.

[8] The epistemic significance of acquaintance is often taken to consist, at least, in its yielding a special kind of knowledge, namely *knowledge by acquaintance*.

objects), acquaintance entails the existence of its *relata*: if S is acquainted with x, then x (as well as, of course, S) exists. We may call S the *fundament* of acquaintance and x its *terminus*. In *inner* acquaintance, the terminus is a mental state M of S.

Many acquaintance theorists hold that acquaintance is intimately connected to a constitutive relation between what the subject is acquainted with and a *mental state* of the subject. Often the idea is, roughly, that when S is acquainted with x, S is in a mental state M^* that is (partly) constituted by x.[9] Some naïve realists, for example, argue that when S perceives o (i.e., is perceptually acquainted with o), S has a perceptual experience that is (partly) constituted by o. Some theorists of phenomenal concepts (e.g., proponents of the "quotational" account, such as Balog 2012) argue that phenomenal concepts formed via introspective acquaintance are (partly) constituted by the experience they refer to. Similarly, on some theories of introspection (e.g., Gertler 2001), introspective acquaintance involves the introspected state being "embedded" or come to (partly) constitute the introspective state. The idea of an intimate connection between acquaintance and constitutive relation will be relevant to our discussion in §5.

We can already see how IAT does not face the issues that affect HOR and SR. Recall, the main problem with HOR is that it allows for inner hallucination. IAT does *not* allow for inner hallucination because, as noted, acquaintance is a relation that entails the existence of its relata: if S is acquainted with M, then M must exist. The main issue with SR is that it seems to require some *special, sui generis* kind of representation—one that is different from the familiar, naturalization-friendly kind—to account for the subjective significance of experience. IAT simply embraces the unavoidable distinctiveness of subjectivity and accordingly tries to explain it via a *special relation*—instead of trying to force it into the familiar representational framework. Of course, acquaintance may well have its own problems. However, only a worked-out and detailed version of the theory will enable the objector to rise pertinent and precise objections.

In the remainder of the chapter, I provide a framework for spelling out the details of IAT and tentatively build up a version that seems to me particularly promising. I proceed by four decision points. The first concerns the *fundamental relation* involved in inner acquaintance (§5). The second concerns the *terminus* of the acquaintance relation (§6). The third concerns

---

[9] Constitution may be full or partial; more on this in §7.

inner acquaintance's *metaphysical directness* and explores a constitutional-mereological approach to it (§7). The fourth decision point concerns the way in which inner acquaintance constitutes awareness *of* M and thereby involves some sort of *directedness toward* M (§8).

5. The Fundamental Relation in Inner Acquaintance

Recall IAT's general form introduced in §1:

IAT: For any subject S and conscious state M of S, M is conscious in virtue of S's being acquainted with M.

Inner acquaintance involves at least two elements—S (the fundament) and M (the terminus)—and at least one relation—the acquaintance relation between S and M. But is the relation between S and M the *ultimate* or *most fundamental* fact about inner acquaintance? Or is there some more fundamental fact in virtue of which S is acquainted with M? This is our first decision point.

On one (perhaps the most natural) way to construe it, inner acquaintance just involves the relation between S and M (i.e., S's being acquainted with M). Plausibly, if acquaintance is instantiated at all, it always takes a subject as fundament (at least on a natural conception of "acquaintance," such that only *subjects* can be acquainted with something) and, at least when it is "inner," a mental state as terminus. As noted, acquaintance is *metaphysically direct*. On a strong interpretation of metaphysical directness, acquaintance is not only unmediated by any *causal* process: it does not involve *any* further element, state, or process that may *ground* the relation between S and M. In this framework, then, there are no further elements (other than S and M) involved; the relation between S and M is the most fundamental fact about inner acquaintance, and indeed S's being acquainted with M is all there is to inner acquaintance. Accordingly, acquaintance is construed as a *primitive* mental relation between S and M.[10]

On an alternative view, the acquaintance relation between S and M is *not* primitive: there is some more fundamental element, relation, or fact in virtue of which such a relation holds. Here the relation between S and M is still metaphysically direct in that it is *not causally mediated*; however, it is, so to

---

[10]   It is primitive in that it is neither grounded in nor explained in terms of anything else.

speak, *"groundingly"* mediated, in that it metaphysically depends on something else. A variety of candidates for playing such a grounding role may be explored. Here, however, I am going to consider just one.

On the alternative option that strikes me as the antecedently most plausible, inner acquaintance involves a *third element*, besides S and M: a *mental state* M* of S, which bears a *special (constitutive) relation* to M. The reason why this option seems antecedently plausible is twofold. First, it mirrors the meta-representationalist idea that what most fundamentally explains consciousness is a relation between two mental states, M and M*. Unlike meta-representationalism, however, IAT construes the relation between M and M* not in terms of representation but in terms of acquaintance. Second, and more substantially, this option paves the way for an informative account of acquaintance's metaphysical directness in terms of constitution—somewhat similarly to some proposals already present in acquaintance-related literature (especially on phenomenal concepts, introspection, and naïve realism). On this view, the metaphysical directness of the acquaintance relation between S and M is not a brute fact but is grounded in a special (non-causally-mediated) relation between M and M*. As noted, metaphysical directness is often taken to be intimately connected with *constitution*: acquaintance involves, or is intimately connected to, a relation that is *constitutive* (rather than causal). A plausible way to spell out such a constitutive relation is this: if S is acquainted with M, then S is in a mental state M* that is (partly) constituted by M. We may call M* the *state of acquaintance*. So, the idea is that the state of acquaintance M* is (partly) constituted by the terminus of the relation of acquaintance, M.

To get a better grip of this, consider the perceptual case (I assume representationalism about perceptual experience for the purpose of exposition). When you see a red rose, the rose and your visual representation of it are causally related but distinct existents. In inner acquaintance, instead, the terminus and the state of acquaintance are neither causally related nor ontologically distinct. Rather than causal, the relationship between them is *constitutive*: the terminus (partly) constitutes the state of acquaintance. Accordingly, the terminus and the state of acquaintance are *not* independent of one another. Even if the terminus can exist independently of the state of acquaintance, the latter's existence depends on that of the terminus. Therefore, when S bears the acquaintance relation to M, S is in a state of acquaintance M* that is not wholly distinct from M, for M is a part of M*. Whether M is a proper or improper part of M* depends on how a theory specifies the mereology of acquaintance. (The latter will be the topic of §7.)

We may call the constitutive relation between M* and M *state-acquaintance*. Granted that the term "acquaintance" is primarily meant to denote a relation between a subject and a mental state (assuming that the fundament of acquaintance is always a subject), I introduce the technical notion of *state-acquaintance* mostly for expository reasons, as a shorthand for "the constitutive relation between two mental states M* (the state of acquaintance) and M (the terminus of acquaintance) of a subject S." To distinguish it from state-acquaintance, I will call the relation between S and M *subject-acquaintance*. So, our first decision point is: which relation is fundamental? We may call the relevant options "subject-first" view and "state-first" view:

SUBJECT-FIRST: Subject-acquaintance is the most fundamental relation involved in inner acquaintance.

STATE-FIRST: State-acquaintance is the most fundamental relation involved in inner acquaintance.

On SUBJECT-FIRST, S's relation with M is primitive and constitutes the most fundamental fact about inner acquaintance: S's bearing the acquaintance relation to M is what ultimately explains inner acquaintance and thereby (if IAT is true) phenomenal consciousness. Further elements, facts, or relations may be involved, but if they are, they are not more fundamental than subject-acquaintance. In particular, if S's being acquainted with M involves the occurrence of a state of acquaintance M*, then the latter depends on the primitive relation between S and M: it is in virtue of S being acquainted with M that (i) S is in a state of acquaintance M* and (ii) M* bears a constitutive relation to M.

On STATE-FIRST, instead, the relation between S and M is not fundamental but depends on S's being in a state of acquaintance M* and on M*'s bearing a special relation to M: it is in virtue of (i) S being in M* and (ii) M* bearing the (right kind of) constitutive relation to M, that S is acquainted with M. So, here, the most fundamental fact about inner acquaintance is one involving a relation between *mental states*—the terminus and the state of acquaintance. If so, part of IAT's task is to explain what that special relation amounts to. (The relevant relation will have, at least, the features mentioned in §4: relata-existence entailment, epistemic directness, and metaphysical directness/constitution.)

So, our first decision point is whether to endorse SUBJECT-FIRST or STATE-FIRST. In the remainder of this section, I recommend opting for STATE-FIRST. I offer three reasons for this. The first concerns the priority of *state consciousness* over *creature consciousness* (§5.1). The second concerns the *explanatory power* of acquaintance (§5.2). The third concerns issues around the nature of *subjects* (§5.3).

5.1 State and Creature Consciousness

David Rosenthal (1993, 1997) makes two useful distinctions about the notion of consciousness. First, he distinguishes between what he calls *creature consciousness* and *state consciousness*. The former is a property of subjects and is expressed by sentences such as "I am conscious" or "I am conscious of vanilla cake." The latter is a property of mental states and is expressed by sentences such as "My vanilla smell experience is conscious": it is a conscious, rather than an *unconscious*, state. Second, he distinguishes between *transitive consciousness* and *intransitive consciousness*. Transitive consciousness is the relational property of being *conscious of* something (as in "I am conscious of vanilla cake"). Intransitive consciousness is the intrinsic property of being a conscious creature ("I am conscious") or a conscious mental state ("My vanilla smell experience is conscious").

By combining the two distinctions, we obtain four conceptually distinct notions: *intransitive creature consciousness* ("I am conscious"), *transitive creature consciousness* ("I am conscious of vanilla cake"), *intransitive state consciousness* ("My vanilla smell experience is conscious"), and *transitive state consciousness* ("My smell experience is conscious of the vanilla cake"). The latter may sound antecedently odd. However, although the sentence "My smell experience is conscious of the vanilla cake" is admittedly far-fetched, the substantial phenomenon underlying it is not, for what it expresses is, quite simply, the fact that, in virtue of having the smell experience, I am conscious of the cake (Kriegel 2003, 2009). Transitive state consciousness, then, is a relational property of M such that M is directed toward some object *o* and in virtue of this S is conscious of *o*.

Uriah Kriegel (2003, 2009) offers an argument to the effect that creature consciousness depends on state consciousness. On the one hand, plausibly, for a subject to be (intransitively) conscious, s/he must be in some (intransitively) conscious mental state: I am conscious in virtue of having at least one conscious mental state. When none of my mental states is conscious, I am *un*conscious. So, intransitive creature consciousness depends on intransitive state consciousness. On the other hand, for a subject to be (transitively) conscious of something, s/he must be in some (transitively) conscious mental state, in virtue of which s/he is conscious of it: I am conscious of the vanilla cake in virtue of having a conscious smell experience directed at the cake. Thus, transitive creature consciousness depends on transitive state consciousness.

Given that inner awareness is a conscious phenomenon, the same reasoning applies to it. S's being innerly aware of M implies S's being *transitively creature conscious* of M. Since transitive creature consciousness depends on transitive state consciousness, when S is innerly aware of M, S is transitively creature conscious of M in virtue of having a conscious mental state directed at M—that is, in virtue of having a mental state M* that is transitively state conscious of M.

If state consciousness is prior to creature consciousness, inner awareness is, most fundamentally, a phenomenon that occurs at the *mental state* level, and only *derivatively* a phenomenon concerning conscious subjects. Accordingly, whatever explains inner awareness should account for this metaphysical priority. On IAT, what explains inner awareness is the mental relation of *acquaintance*. To meet the priority requirement, acquaintance is thus to rely, most fundamentally, on a relation between mental states. Recall the distinction between *subject-acquaintance* and *state-acquaintance*. Plausibly, subject-acquaintance accounts for transitive *creature* consciousness of M: S is (transitively creature) conscious of M in virtue of being subject-acquainted with M. State-acquaintance accounts for transitive *state* consciousness of M: M* is (transitively state) conscious of M in virtue of being state-acquainted with M. If, as argued, transitive state consciousness is prior to transitive creature consciousness (and since, arguably, the priority relations between what explains them should mirror the priority relations between them), state-acquaintance is prior to subject-acquaintance.

5.2 Explanatory Power

The second reason for preferring STATE-FIRST is that it has (potentially, at least) higher explanatory power. IAT's aim is to explain consciousness in terms of inner acquaintance. Arguably, to do so, it should also explain what inner acquaintance involves and why it has some special features (i.e., relata entailment, epistemic directness, and metaphysical directness). Now, if inner acquaintance is characterized as a *primitive* relation between S and M, the explanatory power of the theory seems to be very limited: what is offered as the explanans of consciousness is a relation we do not have a deeper understanding of, and whose possession of peculiar features is just a brute fact. Positing a state of acquaintance M*, by contrast, promises to allow for a deeper understanding of the mechanisms that underlie consciousness and inner awareness. In particular, an analysis of the special relation between M and M* in terms of *constitution*, coupled with an account of what such a constitutive relation consists in, may explain inner acquaintance's special features, and offer a more substantial and informative account of the metaphysics of consciousness.

Obviously, for such a constitutive relation to play the relevant explanatory role, it needs to be posited as fundamental: it must be *that in virtue of which* inner acquaintance holds. This is exactly what STATE-FIRST recommends. On SUBJECT-FIRST, instead, if there is a constitutive relation between M and M*, it is *not fundamental*: at most, it depends on S's bearing the acquaintance relation to M. This makes the constitutive relation *explanatorily inert*. Since it is the relation between S and M that grounds the occurrence of M* and its constitutive relation with M, it is the former that explains the latter. But this does not seem a good result. For, arguably, the constitutive relation is explanatorily more fecund.

Compare this with causation in perception. In perception, it is the causal connection that does (part of) the explanatory work: it is *not* in virtue of S's seeing the rose that the rose causes S's visual representation of the rose; rather, it is in virtue of the rose's causing S's visual representation that S sees the rose. So, in perception, the causal connection between the subject's perceptual representation and the perceived object O is part of what explains the perceptual relation between S and O (that is, S's perceiving O). Analogously with constitution and inner acquaintance: the constitutive connection between the state of acquaintance and the terminus is (part of) what explains the acquaintance relation between subject and terminus. If so, it is not in virtue of S's being acquainted with M that M* is constituted by M; rather, it is in virtue of M*'s being constituted by M that S is acquainted with M.

5.3 Subjects

A further reason for preferring STATE-FIRST over SUBJECT-FIRST is that prioritizing state-acquaintance over subject-acquaintance allows us to be neutral about the nature of subjects and spares us the arduous enterprise of defining conscious subjects independently of conscious states. Those who construe the most fundamental facts about inner acquaintance as involving subjects would need a definition of the notion of subject which is *independent* of the notion of mental state (unless they endorse a bundle theory of subjects, on which a subject is a bundle of conscious states; obviously, though, if we adopt the bundle theory, subject-acquaintance collapses onto state-acquaintance). Alternatively, they would have to take subjects as *primitives*. I do not claim that neither option is viable. However, both feel somewhat uncomfortable. Defining subjects independently of conscious mental states strikes me as a very hard challenge. Taking subjects as primitives may be criticized as *ad hoc* and charged with mysteriousness. Other things being equal, a version of IAT that avoids the thorny issues effusing from the fundamentality of subjects is preferable. By construing the most fundamental facts about acquaintance as involving only mental states, STATE-FIRST promises to offer an understanding of acquaintance that sidesteps the question whether a mental-state-independent definition of subjects is viable. This gives us a further reason in favor of it.

*

I suggest, then, that the acquaintance relation between S and M depends on the occurrence of the state of acquaintance M* and on its bearing a constitutive relation to M. If so, IAT may be reformulated accordingly:

> IAT_1: For any subject S and conscious state M of S, M is conscious in virtue of S's being in a state of acquaintance M* and of M*'s being state-acquainted with M.

Further details about the relation between M and M*, as well as its mereological implications, will be addressed in §§7–8. Before that, let us focus on the *terminus* of the acquaintance relation.

6. The Terminus of Inner Acquaintance

Our second decision point concerns the *terminus* of the acquaintance relation. There are two relevant alternatives (or so I suggest):

> INDIVIDUAL-STATE: The terminus is one of S's individual conscious states at *t*.
> OVERALL-STATE: The terminus is S's overall experience at *t*.

My suggestion is opting for Overall-state. I will explain why after having said something more about what each option involves.

Consider the following vignette:

> The cake I am baking emits an irresistible vanilla smell, of which I am fill-ing my nose. The smell makes me feel hungry and nourish an increasingly intense desire to taste it. I strive not to get distracted by it and keep my thoughts focused on the metaphysics of consciousness. At the same time, I feel proud for having prepared such a nice-smelling cake. I realize that this cake business put me in a good mood.

The example involves several co-occurring conscious mental states: at time t, I have some perceptual experiences (e.g., smelling vanilla), interoceptive experiences (feeling hungry), conative experiences (desiring a piece of cake), cognitive experiences (thinking about consciousness), emotional experiences (feeling proud) and mood experiences (feeling in a good mood). (This is not supposed to be an exhaustive list—you can fill it in with all the other conscious states you think I may plausibly undergo at t; anyway, this will suffice for my point.) Each of these is what I call an "individual conscious state at t." Typically, at any time t, a conscious subject has several individual conscious states. One's co-occurring conscious states are *phenomenally unified*: they not only occur together, but are *experienced* by the subject as occurring together—they are not only co-occurring and unified, but they also *phenomenally appear* to their subject as co-occurring and unified. This is what is called the "unity of consciousness" (Dainton 2000; Bayne and Chalmers 2003; Bayne 2010).[11] The phenomenally unified conjunction of all the conscious states of a subject at t is the subject's "overall experience at t."

The question about the terminus of the acquaintance relation, thus, is the following. When S is inner-acquainted with M at t, is S acquainted with one of S's *individual conscious states* at t, such as *smelling vanilla at t* (Individual-state), or is S acquainted with S's *overall experience* at t (Overall-state)?[12] As we will see, each option has different repercussions

---

[11]   More specifically, this is the *synchronic* unity of consciousness (i.e., the phenomenal unity of a subject's conscious experience *at time t*), to be distinguished from the *diachronic* unity of consciousness, i.e., the phenomenon such that a subject's successive experiences are phe-nomenally unified *over time* in one single stream of consciousness.

[12]   There is, of course, logical space for a third option, namely that the terminus is a subset of S's individual conscious states at t (or a part of the overall experience that is constituted by such a subset). However, this option seems to imply an arbitrary construal of the terminus. Moreover, it would inherit the downsides of both other options without benefitting from their merits.

on the metaphysical structure of conscious experience, including the unity of consciousness and the state of acquaintance.[13,14]

On my view, the terminus of acquaintance is best construed as one's *overall experience* at t, for reasons that I articulate in the next three subsections.

6.1 Economy

One reason to resist INDIVIDUAL-STATE is that construing the terminus as an individual mental state implies a *multiplication* of instances of the acquaintance relation. As noted, at t, S typically has many individual conscious states. By AP+ (the awareness principle[15]), S is aware of each of those individual states and, by IAT, S is so aware by being acquainted with each of them. On INDIVIDUAL-STATE, this is accounted for by each of the co-occurring individual conscious states of S at t being the terminus of an (instance of the) acquaintance relation. This implies that, at t, S bears a distinct instance of the acquaintance relation to each of the co-occurring individual conscious states at t.

On OVERALL-STATE, instead, at t there is just *one* terminus of acquaintance—the overall experience. Accordingly, at t there is just one instance of the acquaintance relation—the relation between S and its overall experience.

Now, for one thing, considerations of ontological economy should incline us to prefer OVERALL-STATE: *ceteris paribus*, an explanation that posits only one instance of a relation is preferable with respect to one that posits a multitude of such instances. But the issue is not just one of *ontological* economy—it is also one of *psychological* economy. Arguably, entertaining the multitude of acquaintance-relation instances implied by INDIVIDUAL-STATE would constitute for the subject a psychologically implausible cognitive burden.

---

[13] Here is just as a foretaste. The state of acquaintance presents us with a similar issue: is it an *individual mental state* or is it one's *overall experience*? Depending on what we opt for in the terminus case, plausible options vary when it comes to the state of acquaintance.

[14] When it comes to the terminus of the acquaintance relation, there is an orthogonal question about its specific *ontology*. I have been talking about mental states without specifying to what ontological category they belong: are they *events* (instantiations of phenomenal properties by a subject at t), *tropes* (phenomenal-property instantiations), *particulars* (bearers of phenomenal properties), something else? A complete Inner Acquaintance Theory of consciousness should cover this issue. Here, though, I can only flag it, for I do not have the space for a satisfactory treatment. All I say is neutral on this and can be applied to different specific stances on the ontology of mental states.

[15] Recall: *AP+*: For any subject S and conscious state M of S, M is conscious in virtue of S's being aware of M.

True, INDIVIDUAL-STATE straightforwardly accounts for the fact (implied by AP$^+$) that, at t, S is aware of each of its co-occurring conscious states. However, OVERALL-STATE does have the resources to account for this too. While the overall experience is the *primary* terminus of acquaintance, each conscious state that can be identified within it is a *secondary* or *derivative* terminus. By being acquainted with the overall experience, the subject is also (derivatively) acquainted with each of the conscious states that compose it. As by seeing a tree you also see each of the leaves that compose it, by being acquainted with your overall experience you are also acquainted with each conscious state it comprises.

It may be objected that, by seeing a tree, one may in fact *not* see each of its parts: if the glance at the tree is short enough, one may just become aware of structural, *global* features of the tree, but not of the detailed, *local* features of its composing elements (*cf.* Navon 1977). Analogously, being acquainted with the overall experience might not, after all, entail being acquainted with each of the conscious states that compose it. However, first, evidence for visual awareness of global features occurring without visual awareness of local features concerns extremely short-lived visual experiences (images in Navon's experiments are flashed for only 40 to 400 milliseconds). We could thus just stipulate that t, rather than denoting an instant or a quasi-instantaneous amount of time, denotes a span that is sufficiently extended to allow for full awareness—that is, awareness of both global and local features (so-called "specious present" is probably what is needed here). This would apply to all forms of awareness, including inner acquaintance. Second, a careful separation of (mere) *awareness* from related phenomena such as *memory* and *attention* may show that awareness of the whole may well entail awareness of each part, even though it does not entail that the subject *attends to* (or can attend to) every part, or that they can subsequently *remember* every part. Take, for example, Sperling's (1960) experiment, where arrays of letters are flashed to subjects for 50 milliseconds; although they claim they saw all letters, subjects can report no more than half of them. However, if cued to report one specific row right after the stimulus has been flashed, subjects can do that (for any row), though then they usually can report no letter from other rows. What Sperling's experiment seems to show is that, while the stimulus is flashed, subjects are aware of the whole array as well as of each of its parts (each letter that composes it)—and this despite the stimulus being extremely short-lived: since, for any row they are asked to report after the stimulus is flashed, they can remember all the letters contained in it, they must have been aware of each letter of each row at the time they were exposed to the stimulus. What subjects are shown *not* to be able to do is *remembering* each letter in the array—nor, arguably, can they *attend* to each letter in such a short amount of time. This suggests that, even if we cannot remember or attend to each part of what we see, we nonetheless can and indeed are visually aware of each part. This, arguably, applies to inner acquaintance too. Even though we cannot attend to or subsequently remember each of the conscious states that compose our overall experience at *t*, by being acquainted with the overall experience we can be (and indeed are) acquainted with each of its parts.

6.2 Conscious-state Individuation

A perhaps more worrying issue for INDIVIDUAL-STATE concerns conscious-state individuation. By construing the terminus as an individual conscious state, it faces the challenge of explaining *how conscious states are individuated*. Meeting this challenge is not straightforward. In the vignette above, I presented a simplified view of individual conscious states. A more thorough look brings the complexities of conscious-state individuation to the surface. When we consider, for example, the taste experience I have when I eat the cake, several components can be identified: vanilla, sweetness, milkiness, and so on. When I look at the cake, I see the cake, but I also see its yellowish color at the bottom, its brownish color at the top, its round shape, and so on. I also see other things in my visual field, though they lie in the periphery. Now, how many individual conscious states are there? Just two: the (overall) taste experience and the (overall) visual experience? Or do the vanilla, sweetness, and milkiness taste components each constitute a distinct individual conscious state? And what about the visual experience: is my seeing the cake one individual conscious state, as well as each of my other concurrent visual representations of objects around me? Or should visual conscious states be individuated in a more fine-grained way, for example in terms of "homogeneous parts," such that, say, my seeing the cake bottom's homogeneous yellowness itself constitutes one individual conscious state? Or is the individuation of visual states even more fine-grained— perhaps the individual visual state is a yellowish "pixel" in my visual field? I do not claim that these questions are *impossible* to answer.[16] However, they are quite difficult ones and perhaps impossible to answer *univocally*.

---

[16] Masrour (2020: 215), for example, suggests that conscious states should be individuated by their intentional object; however, this view still needs more argumentative support and is theoretically committed to intentionalism about all kinds of conscious states.

For, at least *prima facie*, there does not seem to be any fact of the matter that would make us lean toward one individuation criterion over others. Arguably, different theorists will privilege different criteria mostly depending on how this fits their broader view. As I see it, the conscious-state individuation question can only be answered on *pragmatic* grounds and does not speak to any fact of the matter about the *metaphysics* of consciousness. If so, IAT should avoid relying on a specific answer to it.

OVERALL-STATE, on the other hand, sidesteps the conscious-state individuation question. By construing the terminus as the overall experience, IAT can remain neutral as to what individuation criterion we should choose. Indeed, it can fit whatever criterion best meets the theorist's desiderata about the metaphysics of consciousness.

6.3 Unity of Consciousness

OVERALL-STATE also has a virtue of its own: it offers a straightforward explanation of the *unity* of consciousness, one that is nicely integrated with IAT's explanation of the *nature* of consciousness. If we go for INDIVIDUAL-STATE, we need an extra story to account for the unity of consciousness: we have a number of separate conscious states, each of which is the terminus of a distinct instance of the acquaintance relation; we thus need an account of how they stitch together and of why the subject experiences them as unified. Arguably, those who opt for INDIVIDUAL-STATE will have to posit a special unifying relation among distinct individual conscious states and thereby develop a separate account of phenomenal unity. Adopting OVERALL-STATE, by contrast, offers an account of the unity of consciousness *for free*, as it were. In this framework, what accounts for the *nature* of consciousness also accounts for its *unity*. In virtue of what are all of S's co-occurrent conscious states at *t* unified? They are unified in virtue of S's being acquainted with S's overall experience at *t*: S is acquainted with each of them via *one single acquaintance relation*. Through one acquaintance relation, whose terminus is the overall experience at *t*, S is acquainted with each of S's conscious states at *t*. This explains not only why all of S's conscious states at *t* are unified, but also why S *experiences* them as unified (which, as noted, is a key element to phenomenal unity). S experiences them as unified because S is aware of them in one fell swoop, by being aware of the single overall experience that comprises them.

*

The above considerations give us prima facie reasons for taking the terminus of acquaintance to be S's overall experience at *t*.

A last remark concerns the consequences this has for the *state of acquaintance*. (This is especially relevant if we adopt STATE-FIRST.) Taking the terminus to be an individual conscious state would allow for two possibilities concerning the state of acquaintance. Since state-acquaintance is such that the terminus (partly) constitutes the state of acquaintance, if the former is an individual conscious state, the latter could be either an individual state or the overall experience (or else a mental state that includes the overall experience).[17] If, instead, the terminus is the overall experience, the state of acquaintance cannot be one of the individual conscious states that are part of it because, obviously, a whole cannot be part of one of its proper parts. Therefore, if we take the terminus to be the overall experience, then the state of acquaintance can only be either the overall experience itself (whereby the terminus would constitute the state of acquaintance *fully*) or a mental state that includes the overall experience and exceeds it (whereby the terminus would constitute the state of acquaintance *partially*). Which of these is preferable is the topic of the next section.

With these remarks in mind, we may reformulate our characterization of IAT as follows (we replace "M*" with "E*" to highlight the fact that the state of acquaintance needs to encompass the overall experience E):

IAT$_2$: For any subject S, conscious state M of S, and time *t*, M is conscious at *t* in virtue of (i) S's being in a state of acquaintance E* at *t*, (ii) E*'s being state-acquainted with S's overall experience at *t*, E, and (iii) M's belonging to E.

7. The Mereology of Inner Acquaintance

If we adopt STATE-FIRST (as I suggest in §5), then a third decision point concerns the special (constitutive) relation between the state of acquaintance M* and the terminus M. More specifically, this decision point concerns the *mereology* of acquaintance, where the relevant questions include: do M* and M overlap? If so, is the overlap full or partial? If M mereologically

---

[17] Middle-way options would be certainly possible, though not straightforwardly useful, and probably arbitrary.

constitutes M*, is it a proper or improper part of M*? Here I review what strike me as the most pertinent options.[18]

I said that acquaintance is typically taken to involve a constitutive relation. However, this may be rejected: an inner acquaintance theorist may maintain that there is no mereological overlap between terminus and state of acquaintance. Those who do accept constitution, on the other hand, have to figure out whether the terminus constitutes the state of acquaintance fully or only partially. Accordingly, three options present themselves:

NO-CONSTITUTION: The state of acquaintance and the terminus are wholly *distinct* (there is *no overlap* between them).

PARTIAL-CONSTITUTION: The terminus constitutes the state of acquaintance *partially* (it is a *proper part* of the state of acquaintance).

FULL-CONSTITUTION: The terminus constitutes the state of acquaintance *fully* (it is an *improper part* of the state of acquaintance).[19]

I will suggest that we should opt for FULL-CONSTITUTION—the terminus is an *improper* part of the state of acquaintance. Before motivating my leaning toward this option, I add some specifications about the terminus.

7.1 More on Terminus

In §6 I argued that the terminus of acquaintance is S's *overall experience* at *t*. Strictly speaking, however, the mental state that constitutes the terminus of acquaintance cannot, by itself, be a *conscious experience*: for entering the acquaintance relation is exactly what *makes* that mental state conscious. *Qua* terminus of acquaintance (i.e., once it has entered the acquaintance relation), the mental state *is* a conscious experience. But, arguably, the same mental state may exist unconsciously—thus independently of being a terminus of acquaintance. What constitutes the terminus, then, is not the overall experience, but rather the overall mental state that is made conscious by the acquaintance relation. Roughly, this is constituted by the conjunction of all

[18] A more fundamental issue that would need to be addressed is whether the constitutive relation between M* and M should be construed as *mereological* constitution or as some other kind of constitution—most relevantly *material* constitution. Unfortunately, this chapter is already exceedingly long and discussing this issue would make it even more unbearably long. But I do plan to address this in further work.

[19] There is at least a fourth option, whereby the terminus and the state of acquaintance partially overlap. Examining the consequences of such a view would be interesting, but, again, I do not have the space to do it here.

the mental representations of S that are in fact conscious at t. When S is acquainted with it, the terminus is a conjunction of *conscious* mental representations. However, outside the acquaintance relation, each of those mental representations (and, *a fortiori*, their conjunction), would be *unconscious*. Acquaintance is what makes each mental representation of S at t (and their conjunction) conscious. As noted in §6, acquaintance is also what makes the conjunction of mental representations phenomenally *unified*, once they are conscious. The conjunction of mental representations is conscious and unified in virtue of S's being acquainted with it (and more fundamentally, given STATE-FIRST, in virtue of such a conjunction's bearing a constitutive relation to the state of acquaintance).

Let me explain this more slowly. Consider a subject S, the conjunction Σ of all conscious mental representations of S at t, and S's overall experience at t, E. In the actual world, S is subject-acquainted with Σ at t, that is, S is in E. In virtue of being the terminus of acquaintance at t, Σ is conscious—and each mental representation composing it is conscious—and phenomenally unified. It thereby constitutes S's overall conscious experience E at t. However, in a counterfactual world where Σ is *not* the terminus of acquaintance at t—a world where S is not acquainted with Σ at t—Σ is *unconscious* (and, a fortiori, *not phenomenally unified*). In other words, there is a possible world where S has Σ, but is not acquainted with it; in that possible world, Σ is unconscious (so S is *not* in E).

Acquaintance is thus what makes Σ conscious and phenomenally unified—it is that in virtue of which Σ is a *unity* of *conscious* mental representations, rather than a *conjunction* of *unconscious* mental representations. By way of a metaphor, we may say that acquaintance "illuminates" Σ thereby making the subject aware of it—this is what makes it conscious. Without acquaintance, Σ is, so to speak, "in the dark"—it is unconscious. When it becomes the terminus of acquaintance, Σ "comes to light" and is thereby "revealed" to the subject—it becomes conscious.

So, on the version of IAT we are developing, the terminus is Σ, which within the acquaintance relation constitutes E (i.e., S's overall experience). Now, the question under consideration concerns the mereological relation between Σ and the state of acquaintance E*.

7.2 In Favor of Full Constitution

On NO-CONSTITUTION, terminus and state of acquaintance are distinct mental states and acquaintance is a metaphysically and epistemically direct relation between them. Distinct mental states have independent existences: although they may be causally related, the existence of one may imply the existence of the other only *contingently*. However, to account for the *relata-entailment* feature of acquaintance, No-constitution must posit an exception to this *distinctness-implies-metaphysical-independence* rule and construe acquaintance as so special a relation that it makes distinct existences depend on each other in a *metaphysically necessary* way.

Although it is a legitimate logical possibility, No-constitution does not seem to be a promising option for the acquaintance theorist, for it compels to an account of acquaintance not only as a primitive, but also as a metaphysically exceptional relation, without providing any substantial explanation of the necessary connection between terminus and state of acquaintance. Instead of explaining metaphysical directness, No-constitution seems to ascribe it to some *sui generis* and somewhat mysterious feature of the relation between the two states. By contrast, construing acquaintance in terms of *constitution* aims at *explaining* acquaintance and its features. It explains *why* acquaintance entails the existence of its relata: the state of acquaintance cannot exist without the terminus because it is (partly) constituted by it. And it explains metaphysical directness: the relation between state of acquaintance and terminus is metaphysically direct in that it is *constitutive*—the terminus is a (proper or improper) part of the state of acquaintance. (As it will become clear in §8, it also explains, indirectly, epistemic directness, since epistemic directness occurs (partly) in virtue of metaphysical directness.) Given the explanatory sterility of No-constitution, I suggest that we focus on constitutive models (Partial-constitution and Full-constitution), that do *not* construe state of acquaintance and terminus as wholly independent mental states.

As noted, if the terminus is the conjunction Σ of all the mental representations that constitute the overall experience E of S at t, the state of acquaintance E* must encompass E (since a whole cannot be a part of one of its proper parts). Therefore, the decision between Partial-constitution and Full-constitution is a decision on whether Σ is a proper or an improper part of E*.

On Partial-constitution, the terminus is a proper part of the state of acquaintance: Σ is a proper part of E*. This implies that, by entering the acquaintance relation, Σ is somehow *subsumed* by E* and is thereby made conscious—it constitutes S's overall experience E. Therefore, on Partial-constitution, when S becomes acquainted with Σ, a *new* mental state, E*, is formed and a new mental relation, *state-acquaintance*, is instantiated.

By entering the state-acquaintance relation with Σ, E^* subsumes Σ—Σ becomes a proper part of E^*.

On FULL-CONSTITUTION, instead, the terminus is an *improper* part of the state of acquaintance. In this framework, E and E^* are the *same*. When S becomes acquainted with Σ, Σ enters the state-acquaintance relation with itself—it becomes state-*self*-acquainted—and is thereby conscious—it is S's overall experience E. On FULL-CONSTITUTION, then, *only a new mental relation* is instantiated when S becomes acquainted with Σ, a relation that makes Σ a conscious experience E: no new mental state is formed.

With this in mind, we can now see why FULL-CONSTITUTION is, at least prima facie, preferable. For one thing, it is more economical. While PARTIAL-CONSTITUTION implies the introduction of both a new relation (state-acquaintance) and a new mental state (E^*), FULL-CONSTITUTION implies only the instantiation of a new relation (Σ becomes state-self-acquainted; E^* coincides with E). While being more economical, FULL-CONSTITUTION has the same explanatory power as PARTIAL-CONSTITUTION. As noted, on IAT, what explains phenomenal consciousness is the *relation* of acquaintance: it is in virtue of entering the acquaintance relation that a mental state Σ is a conscious state E. Now, this may occur in two ways: either the subject enters a new mental state E^* that is state-acquainted with Σ, or Σ simply becomes state-self-acquainted. There does not seem to be any principled theoretical reason to prefer the former over the latter.

Indeed, there seem to be reasons to prefer the latter over the former (this is my second motivation for favoring FULL-CONSTITUTION). Both PARTIAL-CONSTITUTION and FULL-CONSTITUTION imply a mereological relation between state of acquaintance and terminus—the latter is a (proper, on PARTIAL-CONSTITUTION; improper, on FULL-CONSTITUTION) part of the former. One of the axioms of classical mereology is *supplementation*: if x is a proper part of y, there must be a z (a *supplement*) that is part of y but does not overlap with x. If x is an *improper part* of y, then $x = y$: there is no supplement. If, instead, x is a *proper part* of y, every part of x overlaps some part of y but x is not identical to y; accordingly, there must be some other proper part of y, z, that "supplements" x, so that x and z together constitute a whole, i.e., y. Now, if Σ were a proper part of E^*, it is not clear what the supplement (i.e., the proper part of E^* that does not overlap with Σ) would be. Once we have the conjunction of all the conscious mental representations of S at t, what would be the extra phenomenal aspect of S's overall experience that exceeds such a conjunction?

A defender of PARTIAL-CONSTITUTION may reply by appealing to the distinction between *subjective character* and *qualitative character* (Levine 2001; Kriegel 2009). All conscious experiences are somehow *given to* the subject, they are *for* the subject: when I smell vanilla, there is a vanilla-ish way it is like *for me* to have that experience; this "for me" aspect is the experience's *subjective character*. The vanilla-ish way, on the other hand, is the experience's *qualitative character*. Whereas qualitative character is the aspect of the phenomenology that varies across different (kinds of) experiences, subjective character is shared by all conscious mental states. Following Kriegel (2009), it is plausible to suppose that what accounts for qualitative character is the experience's representing the world as being a certain way. What accounts for the vanilla-ish quality of my smell experience is its representing vanilla. In this framework, first-order representation constitutes qualitative character. By itself, however, first-order representation lacks subjective character. A defender of PARTIAL-CONSTITUTION may argue that the supplement of Σ—the extra phenomenal aspect that is part of E* but does not overlap with Σ—is the *subjective character* of the overall experience—its being *for me*. Σ (the conjunction of all conscious mental representations) merely accounts for the experience's *qualitative character*; an extra bit is needed to account for subjective character.[20]

I agree. However, note that, to account for this, an extra mental *state* is *not* needed. On FULL-CONSTITUTION, Σ, by itself, is indeed not sufficient to account for the phenomenal character of the overall experience E—it only accounts (arguably) for its qualitative character. What accounts for subjective character is not an extra mental state E* but simply the *relation of state-acquaintance*—Σ's becoming state-acquainted with itself. Subjective character is thus due not to a further *item* or element in the metaphysical composition of consciousness, but rather to a *structural feature* of it. There does not seem to be a reason for considering this solution explanatorily less adequate than the one posited by PARTIAL-CONSTITUTION. In fact, the FULL-CONSTITUTION structural account of subjective character might even turn out more adequate. For while elements in the *qualitative* character are adequately accounted for by phenomenal *items* (most plausibly:

---

[20] Another candidate for the extra (supplement) phenomenological bit may be the "feeling of acquaintance" (I owe this suggestion to Uriah Kriegel). This is an interesting proposal, one that it is worth exploring, though this would require a phenomenological investigation that I do not have the space to carry out here. Arguably, what I say about subjective character (i.e., that it can be explained in a FULL-CONSTITUTION framework as well as in a PARTIAL-CONSTITUTION one) would similarly apply to the "feeling of acquaintance."

representations), *subjective* character seems to be a *fundamentally different* aspect of the phenomenology—and a notoriously elusive one at that. On the FULL-CONSTITUTION structural account of subjective character, such a radical phenomenal difference is nicely mirrored by a metaphysical difference: while qualitative character is accounted for by conscious *items* (i.e., mental states), subjective character is accounted for by structural features of consciousness (i.e., the relation of state-self-acquaintance). This is of course speculative and underdeveloped—I suggest it merely as tentative motivation for preferring the FULL-CONSTITUTION structural account of subjective character. At any rate, I am quite confident that FULL-CONSTITUTION and PARTIAL-CONSTITUTION are at least on a par, when it comes to explanation of subjective character.

Another prima facie problem with PARTIAL-CONSTITUTION is the ontological status of such supplementation. As just noted, if Σ is a proper part of E^*, there is a proper part of E^*—call it σ—that does not overlap with Σ. Now, a bunch of questions arise about the ontological status of σ. What is it, exactly? Can it exist independently of being a part of E^* (that is, independently of forming a whole with Σ)? Answers to these questions are not straightforward and, on my view, an account that can sidestep them, and is equal in terms of explanatory power, is preferable.

That said, I do not claim that such answers cannot be given. Here is the sketch of a potential proposal that comes to my mind. On PARTIAL-CONSTITUTION, σ, together with state-acquaintance, is what accounts for subjective character. By itself, however, it cannot constitute subjective character—it is not phenomenologically manifest at all. It becomes phenomenologically manifest only when (together with Σ) it becomes part of E^*. It does nonetheless have (non-phenomenologically-manifest) independent existence. When not part of E^*, σ is a mental state that (i) has the disposition to constitute the subjective character of a conscious experience E and (ii) constitutes the condition of possibility for any relation of acquaintance to occur. Here is a relevant analogy. Site-specific performances take place in urban (or natural) areas that (unlike theaters) normally are *not* performance locations. The urban location, by itself, is not a performance location. However, given the possibility of site-specific performance, it has the *potential* (the disposition) for being one. When a choreography is danced in an urban location, the latter becomes a performance location. On the other hand, although the choreography can exist independently of the location—it can be danced elsewhere (e.g., in the rehearsal room)—it becomes a site-specific *performance* only if danced in the urban location. The latter, then, is the condition of possibility for the choreography to become performance. The instantiation of a site-specific performance is only made possible by the coming together of the choreography and the urban location. Spelling out the analogy: the choreography is Σ, the urban location is σ, and the instantiation of a site-specific performance is phenomenal consciousness. As the urban location, by itself, is not a performance location, σ, by itself, does not constitute subjective character. However, as the urban location has the potential to become a performance location, σ has the potential to become subjective character. As the choreography can be danced independently of being performed (e.g., during rehearsals), Σ can exist (unconsciously) independently of being object of inner awareness (i.e., independently of being the terminus of acquaintance). As in the rehearsal room the choreography is not yet performance, outside of the acquaintance relation Σ is not conscious. As the urban location is the condition of possibility for the choreography to become a performance, σ is the condition of possibility for Σ to become conscious. This is a consistent story, though a somewhat cumbersome one. Other PARTIAL-CONSTITUTION-friendly stories may be offered, but I suspect that they would be at least equally cumbersome. At any rate, FULL-CONSTITUTION seems to have the resources to explain the relevant phenomena in a much more straightforward way.

It may be objected that FULL-CONSTITUTION, though, faces the following problem. If the terminus is a proper part of the state of acquaintance, as per PARTIAL-CONSTITUTION, they are easily distinguishable: the state of acquaintance is the terminus *plus the supplementation*. But if terminus and state of acquaintance coincide, as per FULL-CONSTITUTION, how do we distinguish one from the other? I believe that this problem is merely virtual. For one thing, it is not fully clear that there is a principled reason for needing an account that makes terminus and state of acquaintance easily distinguishable. On FULL-CONSTITUTION, state-acquaintance is simply a reflexive relation, where terminus and state of acquaintance are the same. At any rate, there is a way to distinguish terminus and state of acquaintance even if we adopt FULL-CONSTITUTION. For although it is true that when a mental state E is state-self-acquainted E is both the terminus and the state of acquaintance, we can still tell apart E *qua terminus* from E *qua state of acquaintance*. The former is E *qua* the conjunction of mental representations Σ; as such, it has a bunch of distinctive features, that I outlined above: it can exist independently of being the terminus of acquaintance, but can have conscious existence only within the acquaintance relation, it is what constitutes qualitative character, and so on. The latter is E *qua* overall conscious experience;

as such, it has a bunch of *different* features: it has subjective character, it is phenomenally unified, it is that in virtue of which S is acquainted with Σ, and so on. Therefore, even if, on FULL-CONSTITUTION, terminus and state of acquaintance are *not distinct*, they are still *distinguishable*.

*

Having specified the mereological relation between the state of acquaintance and the terminus of the acquaintance relation, we can thus update our characterization of IAT:

> IAT_3: For any subject S, conscious state M of S, and time t, M is conscious at t in virtue of (i) S's having an overall experience E at t, (ii) E (qua overall experience) being state-acquainted with itself (qua conjunction of mental representations), and (iii) M's belonging to E.

8. The Directedness of Inner Acquaintance

Inner awareness is awareness of one's current conscious experience. Although, as noted, inner awareness is importantly different from outer awareness, it shares with the latter the feature of being *directed toward* something—of being awareness *of* something.[21] Arguably, when it comes to outer awareness, such *directedness* is best accounted for in terms of representation. What makes my smell experience an experience *of* vanilla is its *representing* vanilla. As noted, meta-representational theories offer an analogous account of inner awareness: what makes my current inner awareness an awareness

---

[21] Some philosophers (especially in the phenomenological tradition) have argued that, despite the surface grammar similarities between inner and outer awareness (both are construed as "awareness of"), the difference between their natures is so radical that, differently from the latter, the former should be modeled as involving *no* directedness at all (*cf.* Zahavi 2005). I disagree on this point. Although there *are* fundamental differences between the two kinds of awareness, I think that inner awareness does involve directedness. The main reason why I think this has to do with the epistemic significance of inner awareness (I develop this point below, in the main text). What, on my view, accounts for those differences is that inner and outer awareness involve fundamentally different kinds of directedness. As I try to specify in what follows, whereas outer awareness' directedness is intentional or representational (where this implies, among other things, the possibility of targetless or mistargeting directedness), inner awareness' directedness is not. I suggest that this way of construing the difference between the two kinds of awareness is more fruitful than denying inner awareness' directedness altogether.

of vanilla-smell experience is its being a *representation* of vanilla-smell experience. However, as pointed out in §3, meta-representational views seem unable to account for the special *subjective significance* of inner awareness. While representation offers a plausibly adequate explanation of *outer* awareness, it does not seem suitable when it comes to accounting for *inner* awareness, whose directedness is fundamentally different from the kind of directedness instantiated by outer awareness. Appeal to acquaintance is primarily aimed to do justice to such a difference.

Relatedly, a form of directedness is needed to account for the *epistemic significance* of inner awareness. Intuitively, just by having a certain conscious experience, one can learn something about it. If I ask you what your auditory experience was an instant ago, you are in a position to answer, even if you were not attending to that experience. Arguably, you are in such a position in virtue of the fact that the inner awareness that comes with every conscious experience provides you with information about the phenomenology of the relevant experience and thereby enables you to *learn* something *about* it. For you to learn something *about* your experience, you need to be in a mental state that is somehow *directed at* it. Evidence of the epistemic significance of inner awareness is also provided by the fact that one can *remember* one's past experiences, even if one does not attend to them while one has them (Thompson 2011; Kriegel 2019). You can now remember at least some of your past experiences because, even if you did not attend to them when they occurred, you were nonetheless innerly aware of them and inner awareness provided you with some information about their phenomenology—information that you have retained and that your memory is now recruiting.

Moreover, the way you come to know the phenomenology of your experience via inner awareness is distinctive and special. Your *perceptual* knowledge of vanilla smell depends on and is *mediated* by your mental state of representing vanilla; plausibly, it also depends on some (implicit) assumptions about the reliability of the causal process through which vanilla provokes a certain smell representation in you. The kind of knowledge involved in inner awareness is different. It does *not* depend on any mediating representation or on any assumptions about how the subject relates to their experience. The experience is simply *presented* to the subject, who apprehends its phenomenology in an unmediated way. In this sense inner awareness is *immediate* and *direct*. A symptom of that immediacy is the fact that the epistemic results of inner awareness are *indubitable*

(Gertler 2011: 89). While you might doubt the presence of vanilla in your surroundings even if you have a smell experience as of vanilla (you might undergo an olfactory hallucination), while being innerly aware of such a smell experience, you cannot doubt that you do have it (you can doubt the existence of the external cause of your experience but you cannot doubt the existence of the experience itself). Arguably, this is because, while perception relies on some intermediary causal processes where something may go astray, inner awareness does not: it is immediate and direct.

So, there is an epistemic dimension to inner awareness, and a special one at that. It is to do justice to this special epistemic dimension that acquaintance is construed, as mentioned in §4, as *epistemically direct*. Acquaintance involves a kind of directedness that implies epistemic directness (it is not mediated by any mental state or representation) and that is fundamentally different from representational directedness (it does not involve any causal process and it cannot be targetless or mistargeting).

How should this special directedness be accounted for? This is the question driving our fourth decision point. Here, again, options may vary depending on the choice made at previous decision points. Since I cannot consider all the possible options here, I will assume the choices I recommended in the previous sections. Some of the options below may still be relevant for some other decision paths.

The most promising way to explain acquaintance's epistemic directness and special directedness is to appeal, at least partly, to acquaintance's *metaphysical directness* (Gertler 2001, 2011). On the version of IAT I have been building up, such a metaphysical directness is grounded in a constitutive relation between the terminus and the state of acquaintance. The idea then is that the terminus being a constitutive part of the state of acquaintance allows for a direct epistemic access to the former. However, mereological composition does not, by itself, imply *directedness*: obviously, x's being a part of y is not sufficient for y's being directed at x. The referential structure of inner acquaintance and the way it interacts with (and partly depends on) its mereological structure need to be further articulated. Plausibly, we need a model of acquaintance such that (a) the state of acquaintance *refers* to (is directed at) the terminus and (b) this is so partly in virtue of the state of acquaintance being *constituted* by the terminus. How to exactly construe such a model is our fourth decision point. Three options suggest themselves: what I call the *primitivist model*, the *demonstrative model*, and the *quotational model*. I will suggest that the latter is the most promising model of inner acquaintance reference.

8.1 The Primitivist Model

On the *primitivist model*, acquaintance involves a primitive referential relation. When such a relation is instantiated, the relevant mental state becomes
conscious and its subject is connected directly to it via a special, epistemically rewarding directedness, in virtue of which s/he acquires information
about its phenomenology. On the primitivist model, there is no more fundamental explanation of this: those are just brute and fundamental facts
about inner acquaintance.

   Although there is no ultimate presumption against primitivist models
(arguably, any theory will need to rely on some bedrock unexplained
explanans), they should nonetheless be used sparsely; more explanatory
options, if available, should be prioritized. This is especially pressing when
it comes to acquaintance, whose alleged mysteriousness has been the main
reason for its relegation at the fringe of consciousness debates. It seems that
modelling acquaintance as a primitive relation would make any attempt to
provide a naturalization-friendly account of it almost hopeless.

8.2 The Demonstrative Model

On the *demonstrative model*, acquaintance involves demonstrative reference
to an experience. Indeed, it involves a *special* kind of demonstrative reference, as we will see, and this is what makes it categorically different from
ordinary representation.

   Brie Gertler (2001) put forward a thorough articulation of this model.
(Note well: Gertler proposes the demonstrative model as a model of *introspective* reference, rather than of *inner awareness* reference; in this section I
try to apply her model to inner awareness.) The core idea is that, in inner
acquaintance, reference to the experience occurs via a *pure demonstrative*
(i.e., a demonstrative without descriptive component) that is related to the
experience it refers to via a constitutive (rather than causal) relation. By
drawing on Kaplan (1989), Gertler argues that, to refer, a demonstrative
must be accompanied by a demonstration—an act of "pointing at" what the
subject intends to refer to, an act that may take various forms but always
involves the subject's drawing their attention (and, in conversation, that of
the interlocutor) to what they intend to refer to. Demonstration requires
that what the subject intends to refer to *appears* to them a certain way.
Perceptual demonstratives involve a *causal* connection between what is

referred to and its appearance to the subject. Besides demonstration, they also require a descriptive element. The latter may specify the category to which the referent appears to belong ("that woman," "that object"), but it does not need to; what is constitutive of every instance of perceptual demonstration is an "implicit descriptive component" to the effect that there is an appropriate causal relation between the referent and the way it appears to the subject (Gertler 2001: 315). The kind of demonstratives that we use to refer to the phenomenology of our experiences (what Gertler calls *introspective* demonstratives), instead, do not require any descriptive component—they are *pure*. They only require that the subject *attends to* a phenomenally conscious state, independently of any implicit descriptive component concerning the connection between the referent and its appearance. Here is why this is so. Like perceptual demonstratives, introspective demonstratives also refer via the way what is referred to appears. However, here *appearance* is not only the *vehicle* of demonstration (i.e., that through which demonstrative reference occurs), but also the *referent* (i.e., what is referred to). In perceptual demonstration, one demonstratively refers to an object in virtue of that object appearing a certain way in the subject's experience. Arguably, such appearance is constituted by the phenomenology of the relevant experience. In *introspective* demonstration, however, the very appearance that constitutes the vehicle of demonstration (the experience's phenomenology) is also what is referred to. The subject refers to the phenomenology of their experience in virtue of that very same phenomenology. This is why, in introspective demonstration, the connection between the demonstrative and its referent needs to be *constitutive*: the referent and the vehicle of demonstration are not distinct entities; they thereby cannot be causally related—they are *constitutively* related.

The demonstrative model thus offers a substantial explanation of how (a) the state of acquaintance refers to the terminus (via a pure demonstrative) and (b) this is so partly in virtue of the state of acquaintance being constituted by the terminus (the appearance that constitutes the vehicle of demonstration is also the demonstrative's referent).

The demonstrative model is primarily a model for *introspective* reference, which occurs when the subject focuses their attention on the experience (usually) to form a judgment about it—indeed, Gertler develops the demonstrative model as part of her account of introspection of phenomenal states (as mentioned, she does *not* herself offer it as a model of *inner awareness* reference). However, as a model of the kind of reference involved in *inner acquaintance*, it seems to have the following problem. As noted, any successfully referring demonstrative requires a demonstration, which involves, at the very least, *attention*. Now, on IAT, acquaintance is what constitutes inner awareness. But inner awareness is typically *non-attentive*. Although we sometimes introspect, and thereby attend to, our experience, our attention is typically focused on things *other* than the experience itself—usually on what the experience is *about* (the object seen, the smell smelled, the content of a thought, etc.). Obviously, however, unintrospected experiences can be conscious: one can be acquainted and thereby innerly aware of an experience even if one does not attend to it. If so, attention to the experience cannot be a requirement on inner acquaintance, as it is on the demonstrative model. The demonstrative model, thus, seems to be unfitted to inner acquaintance reference.

It may be suggested that a more thorough examination of the phenomenon of attention could dissolve this problem. Attention is often seen as an *on/off* phenomenon: either you attend to something or you do not, and if you are attending to something, you cannot, at the same time, attend to something else. However, it is plausible that attention is a *gradable* phenomenon: it can be distributed in different amounts over several items. Even if most of your attentional resources are devoted to, say, the object of your visual experience, the remainder can be devoted to the objects of other experiences, or to the experiences themselves. In this picture, a model of attention can be developed such that, at any one time, each conscious state composing the overall experience of a subject obtains at least a tiny amount of attention.[22]

Regardless of the attractiveness of this model of attention, it does not seem to make the demonstrative model more suitable to inner acquaintance reference, for at least two reasons. First, even if it were true that each conscious state receives at least a tiny amount of attention, this seems to be a *contingent* fact, not a necessary fact about consciousness.[23] Even if, in the actual world, all conscious states are attended to, it seems at least conceivable that an experience can be conscious though unattended. If so, attention should not be construed as part of what *makes* an experience conscious;

---

[22] Sebastian Watzl's (2017) theory of attention, as the structuring of the field of consciousness, is a promising way to develop such a model. Roughly, the idea is that attention shapes the structure of one's overall experience by making some aspects of it central, other peripheral. Central aspects are phenomenally more prominent, peripheral aspects are less prominent. In this picture, attention is (unequally) distributed over the whole conscious experience.

[23] Jesse Prinz (2011) argues that attention *is* necessary for consciousness. I disagree and my main motivation is the abovementioned epistemic significance of non-attentive inner awareness. Prinz's position is minoritarian anyway. Arguments against the necessity of attention for consciousness have been put forward by Mole (2008) and Smithies (2011).

therefore, it cannot be a requirement for the relation of acquaintance (given that acquaintance is meant to be what makes an experience conscious). Second, even if being attended to were necessary for a conscious state to be conscious, the tiny amount of attention the model reserves to each conscious state is, arguably, insufficient for demonstration. Demonstrating something requires it occupying the center of the phenomenal field—being somehow salient for the subject. Plausibly, something can be salient only if the subject devotes to it a sufficiently large amount of attentional resources. Arguably, the amount of attention that one typically (i.e., in non-introspective contexts) devotes to the experience itself is too small for one to form a demonstrative about it.

So, although the demonstrative model may be a promising way to articulate introspective reference (where most of one's attentional resources are devoted to the experience itself), it does not seem suitable as a model of inner acquaintance reference.

8.3 The Quotational Model

The *quotational model* construes inner acquaintance reference by analogy to the linguistic phenomenon of quotation. In linguistic quotation, reference to a linguistic expression (a word, a sentence, etc.) is made by employing that very linguistic element via a quotation operation usually signaled by quotation marks. By writing ""*vanilla*"" I refer to the word enclosed between the quotation marks—the word spelled v-a-n-i-l-l-a. The expression (""vanilla"") that I use to refer to the word "vanilla" is constituted by a token of the very word I intend to refer to: the word "vanilla" is used, through the quotation operation, to refer to itself. The expression " "vanilla" " thus refers to the word "vanilla" (partly) *in virtue of being constituted* by it.

Things other than linguistic expressions may be used to quotationally refer to themselves in a similar way. The sign "under construction" painted on a bridge conveys the sentence "This bridge is under construction" (Kriegel 2009: 162–163). The bridge (the object itself) is a constituent of the sentence and its semantic contribution is to refer to itself. In this case, a token (the concrete object: the bridge) is used to refer to that very same token (the bridge itself), rather than to the type it instantiates. Here too, the sentence refers to the bridge *in virtue of being partly constituted* by it.

The quotational model of first-person reference to experience has been developed primarily within the context of the debate around phenomenal concepts (Papineau 2002, 2006; Balog 2012). The idea is that at least some phenomenal concepts refer to a (type or token of a) certain experience in virtue of being constituted by (a token of) that very experience:

> My proposal is that there is a concept forming mechanism that operates on an experience and turns it into a phenomenal concept that refers to either the token experience, or to a type of phenomenal experience that the token exemplifies.
>
> (Balog 2012: 33)

The mental operation that turns an experience into a phenomenal concept is analogous to linguistic quotation: the token experience is "taken up" via the operation and used to refer to itself or to the experience type it instantiates.

The quotational model of phenomenal concepts is a model of how we *think* about consciousness. My proposal is to explore a quotational model of the *nature* of consciousness. Sam Coleman (2015) offers an account that goes in this direction. He puts forward a quotational model of consciousness, that he calls Quotational Higher-Order Thought theory (QHOT):

> I suggest the right higher-order analysis of consciousness sees a HO state 'quote' a sensory state, forming a larger composite structure wherein the sensory state is displayed. Its being embedded within the HO state and thereby displayed is what constitutes the subject's awareness of the sensory state.
>
> (Coleman 2015: 2717–2718)

On Coleman's view, a first-order state (by itself unconscious) is taken up by a higher-order thought via a mental operation analogous to quotation, by which the higher-order thought "displays" the first-order state thereby making it conscious. The relevant higher-order thought is relatively "thin" and has a "frame-like structure 'This state is present: "———"', with the gap between the "———" for the embedding of a sensory state." (*ibid.*: 2718). In virtue of being so constituted by it, the higher-order thought refers to the first-order state. As noted by Coleman, differently from the phenomenal-concept quotational model, on QHOT what is quoted is not the experience itself, but the first-order state (what he calls "sensory content"): the quotation operation is what *makes* the first-order state a conscious experience. Moreover, on QHOT what is referred to is always the token experience itself (rather than the experience type it instantiates).

I suggest that the best explanation of inner acquaintance reference is a quotational model inspired by, but somewhat different from, QHOT. To best fit the Inner Acquaintance Theory I propose, two main modifications need to be made. First, the quotational state should not be construed as a *thought*. For even the "thin" content stipulated by Coleman is still too thick to fit inner acquaintance. Thoughts have conceptual, propositionally structured—thus *descriptive*—content. The thought "This state is present: '———'" involves the deployment of the descriptive demonstrative "this state" and of the predicate "is present." However, as noted in §8.2, inner acquaintance reference is *direct*, and this implies, among other things (as Gertler effectively argues), that it is *not* mediated by *any description*. Therefore, the quotational state featuring in inner acquaintance should not be construed as a thought (not even a thought with the "thin" content stipulated by Coleman).

Second, the quotational state should not be construed as *distinct* from the quoted state. I argued in §7 that, on the version of IAT I recommend, the terminus is an improper part of the state of acquaintance: what makes a mental state conscious is *not* its entering a relation with a *distinct* state (as theorized by QHOT), but rather entering a relation with *itself*. On the model I suggest, the quotation operation does not consist of a separate mental state "taking up" the first-order state and integrating it in a suitably structured content. Rather, it consists of a *structural change* occurring *within* the first-order state. Speaking somewhat metaphorically, the structural change amounts to the introduction of "mental quotation marks." By such a structural change, the first-order state is "quoted" and thus displayed or presented to the subject, thereby becoming conscious. There is no separate mental state quoting, displaying, and presenting the first-order state: the first-order state quotes itself, and thereby displays and presents itself. By displaying and presenting itself, the first-order state *refers* to itself. The conscious experience (qua state of acquaintance) refers to itself (qua terminus) *in virtue of being an improper part of (and thus constituted by) itself*.

Similarly to Gertler's demonstrative model, here too the experience is both referential vehicle and referent: it is that by which reference occurs (it is in virtue of being constituted by itself that the experience refers, somewhat similarly to the way in which it is in virtue of being constituted by the token word "vanilla" that the expression " "vanilla" " refers) and at the same time it is the very item referred to.

By displaying or presenting itself, the mental state makes information about its phenomenology available to be epistemically accessed by the subject. The quotation operation makes information that is generated by the first-order state available to the subject's consciousness: by entering the quotation relation with itself, the first-order state is no longer just a *source* of information, but it becomes a *receiver* and *transmitter* of information (it receives information about its own phenomenology and potentially transmits it to the subject). Of course, not all such information is actually *accessed* by the subject, though usually at least some of it is. The relevant information is accessible *directly*: there is no mediating mental state, representation, or description. This accounts for the *epistemic significance* of inner awareness, as well as for its *epistemic specialness*.

Much more work needs to be done to fill out the details of the quotational model and show that it promises a satisfactory account of inner acquaintance and phenomenal consciousness. Though sketchy and tentative, I hope that this section's discussion could at least give a sense of the potential fecundity of this research project.

9. Conclusion

I have argued that the Inner Acquaintance Theory should be spelled out through at least four decision points, concerning, respectively, the fundamental relation, the terminus, the mereology, and the directedness of inner acquaintance. As noted, a particular choice at a certain decision point may affect, on the one hand, which further decision points may arise and, on the other hand, which options are available at further decision points. Moreover, those considered above are far from exhausting the possible decision points faced by (different versions of) IAT. Obviously, considering all the relevant cross-cutting possibilities and combinations cannot be done in one single chapter. This, I suggest, would be the preliminary goal of an IAT research program, if ever such a program was to see the light.

In this chapter, I have sketched one possible way IAT could be spelled out. I suggested that (1) the most fundamental relation involved in inner acquaintance is what I called *state-acquaintance*, i.e., the special constitutive relation between the terminus M and the state of acquaintance M*; (2) the terminus of acquaintance is the *conjunction of all the conscious mental representations* harbored by the subject at a given time (rather than an *individual* mental state or representation); (3) the terminus is an *improper* part of the state of acquaintance (rather than a *proper* part); (4) the overall experience *qua* state of acquaintance refers to itself *qua* terminus via a quotation operation. By putting all this together, we obtain the following articulation of IAT:

> IAT_4: For any subject S, conscious state M of S, and time t, M is conscious at t in virtue of (i) S's having an overall experience E at t, (ii) E (qua overall experience) being state-acquainted with itself (qua conjunction of mental representations), (iii) E *qua* state of acquaintance referring to E *qua* terminus in virtue of being an improper part of itself and of entering a quotation operation, and (iv) M's belonging to E.

IAT_4 accounts for the fundamental differences between inner and outer awareness without giving up the intuitive idea that inner awareness is *awareness of* one's experience. The constitutive relation between state of acquaintance and terminus makes mistargeting inner awareness impossible. It is also what underlies both the epistemic significance and the epistemic specialness of inner awareness (its "intimacy" or "cognitive immediacy"): by being innerly aware of an experience, the subject enters an especially intimate cognitive contact with it in virtue of the experience's displaying and presenting itself via a quotation operation. Accordingly, all the information about the phenomenology of experience that is available to the subject via inner awareness is guaranteed to be generated by the experience itself—no misinformation is possible.

IAT_4 has the virtue of constituting a *unified* account of *phenomenal consciousness*, *subjectivity*, and *phenomenal unity*. The same relation of acquaintance accounts for the fact that (a) a subject's overall experience is *conscious*, (b) the overall conscious experience (as well as each of the conscious states that compose it) is *for* the subject (or *given to* the subject), and (c) the overall experience is phenomenally *unified*. All the co-occurrent conscious states of a subject at t are unified in virtue of their conjunction constituting the terminus of one single instance of state-self-acquaintance.

*

The Inner Acquaintance Theory is a promising alternative to metarepresentational theories of consciousness, albeit an underexplored one. In this chapter, I tried to make a few steps toward filling this theoretical gap. I pointed at some crucial decision points that any theorist who wants to build an Inner Acquaintance Theory of consciousness must address. I offered a specific version of IAT (IAT_4), by arguing for a particular choice at each decision point. The result is what antecedently strikes me as the most promising version of the account. However, different choices may be defended, and alternative (perhaps ultimately better) versions may be developed. My hope is that, by pointing at the main questions that any such theory needs to answer, this chapter can pave the way for future, more refined, Inner Acquaintance Theories of consciousness.[24]

References

Armstrong, David M. 1968. *A Materialist Theory of the Mind*. New York: Humanities Press.

Balog, Katalin. 2012. "Acquaintance and the Mind-Body Problem." In *New Perspectives on Type Identity: The Mental and the Physical*, edited by Simone Gozzano and Christopher S. Hill, 16–42. Cambridge: Cambridge University Press.

Bayne, Tim. 2010. *The Unity of Consciousness*. Oxford: Oxford University Press.

Bayne, Tim, and David J. Chalmers. 2003. "What Is the Unity of Consciousness?" In *The Unity of Consciousness: Binding, Integration, and Dissociation*, edited by Axel Cleeremans, 23–58. Oxford: Oxford University Press.

BonJour, Laurence. 2000. "Toward a Defense of Empirical Foundationalism." In *Resurrecting Old-Fashioned Foundationalism*, edited by Michael R. DePaul, 21–38. Lanham, MA: Rowman and Littlefield.

BonJour, Laurence. 2003. "A Version of Internalist Foundationalism." In *Epistemic Justification: Internalism vs. Externalism, Foundations vs. Virtues*, by Laurence BonJour and Ernest Sosa, 3–96. Malden, MA: Blackwell.

Brewer, Bill. 2011. *Perception and Its Objects*. Oxford: Oxford University Press.

Brogaard, Berit. 2012. "Are Conscious States Conscious in Virtue of Representing Themselves?" *Philosophical Studies* 159 (3): 467–474.

Brown, Richard. 2010. "Deprioritizing the A Priori Arguments against Physicalism." *Journal of Consciousness Studies* 17 (3–4): 47–69.

[24] For very helpful conversations on the topics of this chapter I am grateful to Davide Bordini, Matt Duncan, Arnaud Dewalque, Uriah Kriegel, and Jim Pryor. I am particularly grateful to Uriah Kriegel for extensive and generous comments on a previous draft. The original paper was presented in the *Global Consciousness* online conference, in the *Rice Workshop in Philosophy of Mind* in Houston, in the *Cornell Workshop on Mind and Value: Acquaintance* in Ithaca, and in the *Awareness, Consciousness, Experience* workshop in Milan. I am grateful to the audiences there, in particular to Torin Alter, Emad H. Atiq, John Barnden, Davide Bordini, Quentin Coudray, Matt Duncan, Santiago Echeverri, Philip Goff, Andrea Guardo, Robert Howell, Michelle Liu, Callum MacRae, Matt McGrath, Laurie Paul, Adam Pautz, Jim Pryor, Adriana Renero, Susanna Schellenberg, Miguel Ángel Sebastián, Umrao Sethi, Will Sharp, Charles Siewert, Giuliano Torrengo, Logan Wigglesworth, Helen Yetter Chappel, and Nick Young.

Byrne, Alex. 1997. "Some Like It Hot: Consciousness and Higher-Order Thoughts." *Philosophical Studies* 86 (2): 103–129.

Campbell, John. 2002. *Reference and Consciousness.* Oxford: Clarendon Press.

Carruthers, Peter. 2000. *Phenomenal Consciousness: A Naturalistic Theory.* Cambridge: Cambridge University Press.

Carruthers, Peter. 2005. *Consciousness: Essays from a Higher-Order Perspective.* Oxford: Oxford University Press.

Chalmers, David J. 2003. "The Content and Epistemology of Phenomenal Belief." In *Consciousness: New Philosophical Perspectives*, edited by Quentin Smith and Aleksandar Jokic, 220–272. Oxford; New York: Oxford University Press.

Churchland, Paul M. 2013. *Matter and Consciousness, Third Edition.* 3rd edn. MIT Press.

Coleman, Sam. 2015. "Quotational Higher-Order Thought Theory." *Philosophical Studies* 172 (10): 2705–2733. https://doi.org/10.1007/s11098-015-0441-1.

Coleman, Sam. 2019. "Natural Acquaintance." In *Acquaintance: New Essays*, edited by Jonathan Knowles and Thomas Raleigh, 49–74. Oxford: Oxford University Press.

Dainton, Barry. 2000. *Stream of Consciousness: Unity and Continuity in Conscious Experience.* London; New York: Routledge.

Dennett, Daniel C. 1988. "Quining Qualia." In *Consciousness in Contemporary Science*, edited by Anthony J. Marcel and Edoardo Bisiach, 42–77. Oxford: Oxford University Press.

Dennett, Daniel C. 2016. "Illusionism as the Obvious Default Theory of Consciousness." *Journal of Consciousness Studies* 23 (11–12): 65–72.

Dretske, Fred. 1993. "Conscious Experience." *Mind* 102 (406): 263–283.

Dretske, Fred. 1995. *Naturalizing the Mind.* Cambridge, MA: MIT Press.

Duncan, Matt. 2018. "Subjectivity as Self-Acquaintance." *Journal of Consciousness Studies* 25 (3–4): 88–111.

Duncan, Matt. 2020. "Knowledge of Things." *Synthese* 197 (8): 3559–3592. https://doi.org/10.1007/s11229-018-01904-0.

Duncan, Matt. 2021a. "Acquaintance." *Philosophy Compass* 16 (3): e12727. https://doi.org/10.1111/phc3.12727.

Duncan, Matt. 2021b. "Experience Is Knowledge." *Oxford Studies in Philosophy of Mind* 1: 106–129.

Fales, Evan. 1996. *A Defense of the Given.* Lanham, MA: Rowman & Littlefield.

Fiocco, M. Oreste. 2017. "Knowing Things in Themselves." *Grazer Philosophische Studien* 94 (3): 332–358.

Frankish, Keith. 2016. "Illusionism as a Theory of Consciousness." *Journal of Consciousness Studies* 23 (11–12): 11–39.

Fumerton, Richard. 1996. *Metaepistemology and Skepticism*. 1 vols. Studies in Epistemology and Cognitive Theory. Lanham, MA: Rowman & Littlefield.

Fumerton, Richard. 2001. "Classical Foundationalism." In *Resurrecting Old-Fashioned Foundationalism*, edited by Michael R. DePaul, 3–20. Studies in Epistemology and Cognitive Theory. Lanham, MA: Rowman and Littlefield.

Fumerton, Richard. 2009. "Luminous Enough for a Cognitive Home." *Philosophical Studies* 142 (1): 67–76.

Gennaro, Rocco J. 1996. *Consciousness and Self-Consciousness*. Amsterdam: John Benjamins.

Gennaro, Rocco J. 2012. *The Consciousness Paradox: Consciousness, Concepts, and Higher-Order Thoughts*. Cambridge, MA: MIT Press.

Gertler, Brie. 2001. "Introspecting Phenomenal States." *Philosophy and Phenomenological Research* 63 (2): 305–328.

Gertler, Brie. 2011. *Self-Knowledge*. London; New York: Routledge.

Gertler, Brie. 2012. "Renewed Acquaintance." In *Introspection and Consciousness*, edited by Declan Smithies and Daniel Stoljar, 89–123. Oxford: Oxford University Press.

Giustina, Anna. 2022a. "A Defense of Inner Awareness: The Memory Argument Revisited." *Review of Philosophy and Psychology* 13: 341–363. https://doi.org/10.1007/s13164-021-00602-0.

Giustina, Anna. 2022b. "Introspective Knowledge by Acquaintance." *Synthese* 200 (2): 128. https://doi.org/10.1007/s11229-022-03578-1.

Giustina, Anna. 2022c. "An Acquaintance Alternative to Self-Representationalism." *Philosophical Studies* 179 (12): 3831–3863. https://doi.org/10.1007/s11098-022-01868-5.

Giustina, Anna. 2023. "Introspective Acquaintance: An Integration Account." *European Journal of Philosophy* 31 (2): 380–97.

Giustina, Anna. 2024. "Nature Does Not Yet Say No to Inner Awareness: Reply to Stoljar." *Erkenntnis* 89 (2): 861–71. https://doi.org/10.1007/s10670-022-00557-3.

Goldman, Alvin I. 1993. "Consciousness, Folk-Psychology, and Cognitive Science." *Consciousness and Cognition* 2: 364–382.

Harman, Gilbert. 1990. "The Intrinsic Quality of Experience." *Philosophical Perspectives* 4: 31–52.

Hasan, Ali. 2013. "Phenomenal Conservatism, Classical Foundationalism, and Internalist Justification." *Philosophical Studies* 162 (2): 119–141.

Hellie, Benj. 2007. "Higher-Order Intentionality and Higher-Order Acquaintance." *Philosophical Studies* 134 (3): 289–324.

Hill, Christopher S. 2016. "Replies to Byrne, McGrath, and McLaughlin." *Philosophical Studies* 173 (3): 861–872. https://doi.org/10.1007/s11098-015-0616-9.

Hofmann, Frank. 2014. "Non-Conceptual Knowledge." *Philosophical Issues* 24 (1): 184–208.

Horgan, Terence, and Uriah Kriegel. 2007. "Phenomenal Epistemology: What Is Consciousness That We May Know It so Well?" *Philosophical Issues* 17 (1): 123–144.

Kammerer, François. 2016. "The Hardest Aspect of the Illusion Problem--and How to Solve It." *Journal of Consciousness Studies* 23 (11–12): 124–139.

Kaplan, David. 1989. "Demonstratives." In *Themes from Kaplan*, edited by Joseph Almog, John Perry, and Howard Wettstein, 481–563. Oxford: Clarendon Press.

Knowles, Jonathan, and Thomas Raleigh (eds). 2019. *Acquaintance: New Essays*. Oxford: Oxford University Press.

Kriegel, Uriah. 2003. "Consciousness as Intransitive Self-Consciousness: Two Views and an Argument." *Canadian Journal of Philosophy* 33 (1): 103–132.

Kriegel, Uriah. 2009. *Subjective Consciousness: A Self-Representational Theory*. Oxford: Oxford University Press.

Kriegel, Uriah. 2011. "Self-Representationalism and the Explanatory Gap." In *Consciousness and the Self: New Essays*, edited by JeeLoo Liu and John Perry, 51–75. Cambridge: Cambridge University Press. https://doi.org/10.1017/CBO9780511732355.003.

Kriegel, Uriah. 2019. "Dignāga's Argument for the Awareness Principle: An Analytic Refinement." *Philosophy East and West* 69: 143–155.

Kriegel, Uriah, and Kenneth Williford. 2006. *Self-Representational Approaches to Consciousness*. Cambridge, MA: MIT Press.

Levine, Joseph. 2001. *Purple Haze: The Puzzle of Consciousness*. Oxford: Oxford University Press.

Levine, Joseph. 2006. "Conscious Awareness and (Self-)Representation." In *Self-Representational Approaches to Consciousness*, edited by Uriah Kriegel and Kenneth Williford, 173–198. MIT Press.

Levine, Joseph. 2018. *Quality and Content: Essays on Consciousness, Representation, and Modality*. Oxford; New York: Oxford University Press.

Levine, Joseph. 2019. "Acquaintance Is Consciousness and Consciousness Is Acquaintance." In *Acquaintance: New Essays*, edited by Jonathan Knowles and Thomas Raleigh, 33–48. Oxford; New York: Oxford University Press.

Lycan, William G. 1996. *Consciousness and Experience*. Cambridge, MA: MIT Press.

Masrour, Farid. 2020. "The Phenomenal Unity of Consciousness." In *The Oxford Handbook of the Philosophy of Consciousness*, edited by Uriah Kriegel, 208–229. Oxford; New York: Oxford University Press.

McGinn, Colin. 2008. "Consciousness as Knowingness." *The Monist* 91 (2): 237–249.

Mehta, Neil. 2013. "Is There a Phenomenological Argument for Higher-Order Representationalism?" *Philosophical Studies* 164 (2): 357–370.

Mole, Christopher. 2008. "Attention and Consciousness." *Journal of Consciousness Studies* 15 (4): 86–104.

Navon, David. 1977. "Forest Before Trees: The Precedence of Global Features in Visual Perception." *Cognitive Psychology* 9: 353–383.

Neander, Karen. 1998. "The Division of Phenomenal Labor: A Problem for Representational Theories of Consciousness." *Philosophical Perspectives* 12: 411–434.

Papineau, David. 2002. *Thinking About Consciousness*. Oxford: Oxford University Press.

Papineau, David. 2006. "Phenomenal and Perceptual Concepts." In *Phenomenal Concepts and Phenomenal Knowledge: New Essays on Consciousness and Physicalism*, edited by Torin Alter and Sven Walter, 111–144. Oxford; New York: Oxford University Press.

Prinz, Jesse. 2011. "Is Attention Necessary and Sufficient for Consciousness?" In *Attention: Philosophical and Psychological Essays*, edited by Christopher Mole, Declan Smithies, and Wayne Wu, 174–203. Oxford; New York: Oxford University Press.

Raleigh, Thomas. 2019. "The Recent Renaissance of Acquaintance." In *Acquaintance: New Essays*, edited by Jonathan Knowles and Thomas Raleigh, 1–31. Oxford: Oxford University Press.

Rosenthal, David M. 1993. "State Consciousness and Transitive Consciousness." *Consciousness and Cognition* 2 (3): 355–363.

Rosenthal, David M. 1997. "A Theory of Consciousness." In *The Nature of Consciousness: Philosophical Debates*, edited by Ned Block, Owen J. Flanagan, and Güven Güzeldere, 729–753. Cambridge, MA: MIT Press.

Rosenthal, David M. 2005. *Consciousness and Mind*. Oxford: Clarendon Press.

Russell, Bertrand. 1910. "Knowledge by Acquaintance and Knowledge by Description." *Proceedings of the Aristotelian Society* 11: 108–128.

Russell, Bertrand. 1912. *The Problems of Philosophy*. New York: H. Holt and Company.

Schwitzgebel, Eric. 2011. *Perplexities of Consciousness*. Cambridge, MA: MIT Press.

Seager, William E. 2004. "A Cold Look at HOT Theory." In *Higher-Order Theories of Consciousness: An Anthology*, edited by Rocco J. Gennaro, 255–276. Philadelphia: John Benjamins.

Siewert, Charles. 1998. *The Significance of Consciousness*. Princeton: Princeton University Press.

Smithies, Declan. 2011. "Attention Is Rational-Access Consciousness." In *Attention: Philosophical and Psychological Essays*, edited by Christopher Mole, Declan Smithies, and Wayne Wu, 247–273. Oxford; New York: Oxford University Press.

Soteriou, Matthew. 2013. *The Mind's Construction: The Ontology of Mind and Mental Action*. Oxford, New York: Oxford University Press.

Sperling, George. 1960. "The Information Available in Brief Visual Presentations." *Psychological Monographs: General and Applied* 74 (11): 1–29.

Thompson, Evan. 2011. "Self-No-Self ? Memory and Reflexive Awareness." In *Self, No Self?: Perspectives from Analytical, Phenomenological, and Indian Traditions*, edited by Mark Siderits, Evan Thompson, and Dan Zahavi, 157–175. Oxford: Oxford University Press.

Tye, Michael. 1995. *Ten Problems of Consciousness: A Representational Theory of the Phenomenal Mind*. Cambridge, MA: MIT Press.

Tye, Michael. 2008. *Consciousness Revisited: Materialism Without Phenomenal Concepts*. Cambridge, MA: MIT Press.

Van Gulick, Robert. 2000. "Inward and Upward: Reflection, Introspection, and Self-Awareness." *Philosophical Topics* 28 (2): 275–305.

Van Gulick, Robert. 2004. "Higher-Order Global States (Hogs): An Alternative HIgher-Order Model of Consciousness." In *Higher-Order Theories of Consciousness: An Anthology*, edited by Rocco J. Gennaro, 67–92. Amsterdam: John Benjamins Publishing.

Van Gulick, Robert. 2012. "Subjective Consciousness and Self-Representation." *Philosophical Studies* 159 (3): 457–465.

Watzl, Sebastian. 2017. *Structuring Mind. The Nature of Attention and How It Shapes Consciousness*. Oxford: Oxford University Press.

Weisberg, Josh. 2008. "Same Old, Same Old: The Same-Order Representation Theory of Consciousness and the Division of Phenomenal Labor." *Synthese* 160 (2): 161–181.

Williford, Kenneth. 2015. "Representationalisms, Subjective Character, and Self-Acquaintance." In *Open MIND*, edited by Thomas Metzinger and Jennifer M. Windt, 39:1–27. Frankfurt am Main: MIND Group.

Zahavi, Dan. 2005. *Subjectivity and Selfhood: Investigating the First-Person Perspective*. Cambridge, MA: MIT Press.

Anna Giustina, *Inner Acquaintance Theories of Consciousness* In: *Oxford Studies in Philosophy of Mind Volume 4*. Edited by: Uriah Kriegel, Oxford University Press. © Anna Giustina 2024.
DOI: 10.1093/9780198924159.003.0010

11

Revelation and the Appearance/Reality Distinction

Michelle Liu

1. Introduction

It is often said that there is no appearance/reality distinction with respect to conscious experience, that the latter's 'appearance' is just its 'reality' (Nagel 1974; Kripke 1980; Moran 2001: 14; Gertler 2012: 127; Searle 1997: 456; Horgan 2012: 406; Whiting 2016). Call this the 'no appearance/reality distinction' claim ('NARD' for short). Discussion of NARD can be found in debates on introspection (Moran 2001; Schwitzgebel 2008, 2011; Gertler 2012; Horgan 2012) and the metaphysics of conscious experience (Nagel 1974; Kripke 1980; Searle 1997; Whiting 2016). Consider the following examples:

> Does it make sense, in other words, to ask what my experiences are really like, as opposed to how they appear to me?
>
> (Nagel 1974: 448)

> [W]e can't make...[an] appearance/reality distinction for consciousness because consciousness consists in the appearances themselves. *Where appearance is concerned we cannot make the appearance/reality distinction because appearance is reality.*
>
> (Searle 1997: 456; italics original)

> [I]n the case of phenomenal consciousness there is no gap between appearance and reality, because the appearance just is the reality: how the phenomenal character seems, to the agent, is how it is.
>
> (Horgan 2012: 406).

As it turns out, theorists mean different things by NARD. How precisely to understand NARD thus requires in-depth clarification.

This chapter elucidates different versions of NARD and connects NARD to the thesis of revelation, according to which the essences of phenomenal properties are revealed in experience. Revelation is often thought of as prima facie plausible but incompatible with physicalism (e.g. Lewis 1995; Goff 2015, 2017; Chalmers 2016, 2018; Liu 2019, 2020, 2021; Roelofs 2020). A number of anti-physicalists have indeed appealed to revelation to argue against physicalism (e.g. Horgan and Tienson 2001; Nida-Rümelin 2007; Goff 2015, 2017). Elsewhere, I have argued for a particular way of understanding revelation (Liu 2019, 2020, 2021). I have also argued that revelation is an intuitive thesis and plausibly underpins the persistent intuition of dualism (Liu 2021). In this paper, I show that revelation thus understood, together with additional plausible premises, entails a certain way of understanding NARD. I shall also show how revelation and the related version of NARD pose a prima facie threat to physicalism, as well as consider physicalists' responses and their limitations.

The structure of the chapter is as follows. §2 clarifies the thesis of revelation. §3 distinguishes different ways of understanding NARD. §4 examines the relation between revelation and NARD, and homes in on the particular version of NARD that is closely connected to revelation. §5 outlines how revelation and the related version of NARD pose a problem for physicalism. §6 considers physicalists' responses and their limitations. §7 concludes the chapter.

2. What Is Revelation?

The thesis of revelation, concerning phenomenal properties, is the claim that the essences of phenomenal properties are revealed in phenomenal experience. In contemporary discussions, revelation has been given different formulations. Consider:

(i) 'phenomenal concepts reveal the nature of the phenomenal properties they refer to' (Trogdon 2017: 2345)

(ii) 'we know essential truths about our qualia on the basis of introspection' (Majeed 2017: 86)

(iii) 'the nature of consciousness is revealed to us in introspection' (Chalmers 2016: 190)

(iv) 'A psychologically normal subject can come to know the real nature of one of her phenomenal qualities by attending to that quality.' (Goff 2015: 214)

(v) 'According to the thesis of revelation, having an experience puts you in a remarkable epistemic position: you know or are in a position to know the essence or nature of the experience.' (Stoljar 2009: 115)

In these passages, theorists speak of 'phenomenal properties', 'qualia', 'consciousness', 'phenomenal qualities', and 'experience', and in the literature these terms are often used interchangeably. In explaining the thesis of revelation, I shall primarily speak of 'phenomenal properties'—they are properties of subjects that constitute what it is like to have experiences from the inside; I shall sometimes speak of 'qualia' or 'phenomenal character', while using all three terms interchangeably. In addition, I shall also frequently use the term 'experience'. Used as a noun, it refers to mental states that are phenomenally conscious; they can be thought of as subjects' instantiations of phenomenal properties. Experience-types are thus individuated by their phenomenal properties. Used as a verb as in 'S experiences Q', it just means 'instantiate (a phenomenal property)'—in instantiating a phenomenal property, we can say that one is conscious of that property.

Revelation is formulated with respect to *phenomenal concepts* in (i). Formulations in (ii) and (iii) appeal to the notion of *introspection*. These technical notions are nevertheless not necessary in formulating revelation, as we can see from (iv) and (v). While there have been different formulations, revelation is generally understood as a claim about the essences or natures of phenomenal properties. Elsewhere (Liu 2019, 2020, 2021), I have formulated revelation as the following (where 'Q' stands for a phenomenal property and 'S' stands for an experiencer):

[R]: By having an experience-token with phenomenal property Q, S is in a position to know that 'Q is X', where the predicate 'X' captures the essence of Q.

I shall first clarify the key notions in the above formulation—that is, 'in a position to know' and what it is to know the essence of a property in general, including the notions of 'essence' and 'capture'. I then consider what such an essence-capturing truth 'Q is X' might look like if revelation is true.

According [R], the essence-capturing truth 'Q is X' is not something that one automatically knows when undergoing an experience with quale Q. [R] only entails that one is *in a position to know* such a truth. For instance, it seems plausible that some animals have experiences, but it doesn't seem plausible that they know—that is, are cognitively sophisticated enough to know—truths concerning the essences of phenomenal properties. Once the cognitive architecture is in place, actually coming to know the relevant truth 'Q is X' is not particularly demanding. All it takes is for one not to be distracted, to attend to the experience, and to identify that the experience has phenomenal property Q.

Now consider what it is to know the essence of a property. I here adopt a definitional account of essence and understand it in the Aristotelian/Finean sense as that which makes something the thing it is. This is also what Fine (1995a: 276) calls 'immediate constitutive essence'—that is, that which belongs to the thing's *most core respects* (see also Fine 1995b; Dasgupta 2014: 589). *Constitutive* essence is contrasted with *consequential* essence (Fine 1995a: 276). If it is constitutively essential to A that B then it is consequentially essential to A that B∨C. *Immediate* essence is contrasted with *mediate* essence (Fine 1995a: 281). The property of *being molecules consisting of two atoms of hydrogen and one of oxygen* is the immediate essence, as well as the constitutive essence, of *being water*. *Being the chemical element with atomic number 1* is the immediate constitutive essence of *being hydrogen* and is also part of the mediate essence of *being water*.

Knowing the essence (i.e. immediate constitutive essence) of a property can be intuitively understood as knowing some proposition that *defines* the property. Consider the property *being a sister*. The proposition 'Being a sister is being a female sibling' is a definition of the property *being a sister*—it describes accurately what it is to be a sister. In knowing such a proposition, one knows the essence of *being a sister*—what *being a sister* is in its most core respects. The predicate 'being a female sibling', in this case, *captures* the essence of *being a sister*.

There is a difference between a predicate's *capturing* the essence of a property and a predicate's only *referring* to the essence of a property. A simple example illustrates the relevant difference. Consider the property *triangularity* and the following sentences:

(a) Being triangular is having a three-sided closed shape.
(b) Being triangular is having whatever shape makes something a triangle.

(a) *defines* the property *triangularity*. The predicate 'having a three-sided closed shape' *captures* the essence of *triangularity* in the sense of describing accurately what it is to be triangular. In contrast, (b) is not a definition of *triangularity*. The predicate 'having whatever shape makes something a triangle', though it *refers* to the essence of triangularity, does not *capture* its essence. Knowing the essence of a phenomenal property Q, according to revelation, is then knowing some proposition 'Q is X' that defines Q, where the predicate 'X' captures, rather than merely refers to, the essence of Q.

Having clarified these key notions, let's return to the above formulation of revelation. Suppose that revelation is true, that an experience with Q puts one in a position to know the essence of Q. What then would the essence-capturing truth 'Q is X' look like? Here it is tempting to think that such a truth may be hard to put into words. Imagine staring at a calm blue sea. Your token experience has a certain phenomenal property—call it 'phenomenal blue'. It is in virtue of instantiating this property that your experience has a certain what-it-is-likeness, that there is something it is like for you—to use the Nagelian phrase—to undergo an experience of seeing something blue. As you undergo the experience and attend to its phenomenal character, it seems intuitive to say that you *know* what it is like to undergo a phenomenal blue experience. You know that 'phenomenal blue is thus-and-so', although it is hard to put this 'thus-and-so' into further words. Maybe all you are able to say is that 'phenomenal blue is *that*'. But here the word 'that' merely acts as a placeholder for the rich understanding of *phenomenal blue* you have but are unable to put into words. A proponent of revelation would say that this truth 'Phenomenal blue is *that*', though hard to put into further words, is supposed to be a truth that captures the essence of *phenomenal blue*. Here it is worth noting that the thesis of revelation, formulated as [R], does not entail, but merely allows, that the essence-capturing truth 'Q is X' is hard to put into words. The point made here is that at least with respect to some phenomenal properties, it is intuitive to think that the relevant essence-capturing truths are hard to put into words.

To sum up, according to revelation, by having an experience with quale Q, one is in a position to know a truth 'Q is X', and such a truth captures the immediate constitutive essence of Q. Here it is worth considering how revelation thus formulated is related to the notions of *phenomenal concept* and *introspection*, which appear in other formulations as we saw in the beginning of this section.

Consider phenomenal concepts first. There is a close connection between what the subject is in a position to know by having an experience with quale Q and the phenomenal concept of quale Q that the subject possesses and deploys. It seems plausible that subjects acquire phenomenal concepts of phenomenal properties by having experiences that have those phenomenal properties. It also seems plausible that knowing what a token experience with quale Q is like from the inside is normally sufficient for possession of the phenomenal concept of Q. An advocate of revelation would say that phenomenal concepts are special in the sense that if one has a phenomenal concept C which refers to Q, the possession of the concept affords one knowledge about, or puts one in a position to know, the essence of Q.

Revelation, as formulated here, also attributes a substantive role to introspection and it is thus not surprising that some formulations of revelation explicitly appeal to the notion of introspection. Introspection is the means by which one can, in a way that no one else can, directly acquire knowledge about one's occurrent or very recently past experience simply by having the experience. Introspection is closely related to revelation since the latter makes a claim about what one knows about the essences of phenomenal properties by having experiences. Revelation thus entails that introspection can put one in a position to know the essences of phenomenal properties.

3. What Is the No Appearance/Reality Distinction Thesis?

The claim that there is no appearance/reality distinction with respect to conscious experience can be understood in a variety of ways. In this section, I distinguish different ways of understanding NARD.

3.1 NARD$_1$

One way to understand NARD is to interpret it as a claim about the instantiations of phenomenal properties. Consider:

[NARD$_1$]: There is no distinction between what phenomenal property an experience *appears* to the subject to have and what phenomenal property the experience *really* has.

Let '*e*' be an experience, 'Q' be a phenomenal property and 'S' be an experiencer. NARD$_1$ is equivalent to the following claim:

[NARD$_1$*]: *e* has Q if and only if in having *e*, it appears to S that *e* has Q.

In the literature on introspection, philosophers distinguish between two versions of NARD$_1$ (see Schwitzgebel 2008: 263; Gertler 2012: 106–107). The distinction corresponds to two ways of understanding the notion of appearance—*phenomenal appearance* versus *epistemic appearance*. Phenomenal appearances are *experiences* whereas epistemic appearances are *beliefs*. The distinction here corresponds to two uses of perceptual verbs, e.g. 'seem', 'appear', 'look' (see Chisholm 1957; Jackson 1977). According to the epistemic use, the proposition 'It seems/appears/looks to S that p' implies that S believes that p—for example, 'It seems/appears/looks to me that the economy is slowing down'. According to the phenomenal use, the proposition 'It seems/appears/looks to S that p' does not necessarily imply that S believes that p; it merely describes some aspects of S's experience. For instance, in the case of the Müller-Lyer illusion, one might say 'it seems/appears/looks to me that the two lines are not of the same length', without implying that one believes that the two lines are of different lengths. In this case, in seeing the two lines, S experiences what we might call a 'two-lines-of-unequal-lengths' phenomenal property. Phenomenal appearances and epistemic appearances, though distinct, are intimately linked. Our beliefs are often reasonable responses to our experiences. If two lines phenomenally appear to have different lengths, then we are rationally disposed to judge that they are of different lengths unless there are good reasons not to, e.g. having done the measurement and found that they are of the same length.

Given the distinction between phenomenal appearance and epistemic appearance, we can distinguish between two versions of NARD$_1$*:

[PHENOMENAL-NARD$_1$]: e has Q if and only if in having e, it phenomenally appears to S that e has Q.

[EPISTEMIC-NARD$_1$]: e has Q if and only if in having e, it epistemically appears to S that e has Q.

Let us look at each in turn. Since phenomenal appearance is an *experience*, PHENOMENAL-NARD$_1$ can be reformulated as the following:

[PHENOMENAL-NARD$_1$*]: e has Q if and only if in having e, S experiences that e has Q.

PHENOMENAL-NARD$_1$ is endorsed by many (see Moran 2001: 14; Gertler 2012: 107; Horgan 2012: 406). It is sometimes described as having an 'air of indefeasibility' (see Schwitzgebel 2008: 263; Gertler 2012: 107). However, it is not immediately clear what it means to say that 'S experiences that e has Q'. There are two readings.

The first reading draws on a direct comparison with the notion of phenomenal appearance pertaining to properties of mind-independent objects. Consider a mind-independent object x, and a property P, e.g. 'x' could stand for an apple and 'P' the property of redness. When it comes to the instantiations of mind-independent properties, we usually hold an appearance/reality distinction between the phenomenal appearance that x is P and the reality where P might not be instantiated in x. That is, it is *not* true that x has P if and only if in having an experience of x, S experiences that x has P. For instance, it is not true that the apple is red if and only if in having an experience of the apple, the subject experiences that the apple is red. On this way of understanding phenomenal appearance, where phenomenal appearance is an experience of an object, we have the following reading of PHENOMENAL-NARD$_1$*:

[PHENOMENAL-NARD$_1$*-$_A$]: *e* has Q if and only if in having *e*, S has an experience of *e* and experiences that *e* has Q.

On the second reading of PHENOMENAL-NARD$_1$, to say that 'I experience that my pain experience has a such-and-such phenomenal property' is just to say that 'I experience or instantiate a such-and-such phenomenal property'. Consider:

[PHENOMENAL-NARD$_1$*-B]: *e* has Q if and only if in having *e*, S experiences Q.

The key difference between the two readings turns on whether the phenomenal appearance of *e* as having Q is identical to *e* itself. According to PHENOMENAL-NARD$_1$*-$_A$, the two are distinct just as the phenomenal appearance of an apple as being green is distinct from its object, i.e. the apple. According to PHENOMENAL-NARD$_1$*-B, the two are identical and hence there is no distinction between the phenomenal appearance of *e* as having Q and the reality of *e* as having Q.

Now insofar as PHENOMENAL-NARD$_1$* is supposed to enjoy an 'air of indefeasibility', it is plausibly PHENOMENAL-NARD$_1$*-B rather than PHENOMENAL-NARD$_1$*-A. It is certainly controversial to think that in having *e*, there is a separate experience which has *e* as its object and represents *e* as having Q. In contrast, PHENOMENAL-NARD$_1$*-B seems indefeasible. We can think of an experience *e* as a subject S instantiating a phenomenal property Q at a time t, expressed as the triplet <S, Q, t> (Kim 1966). Given that to have *e* is just to be the subject of e and to experience Q is just to instantiate the phenomenal property Q, PHENOMENAL-NARD$_1$*-B turns out to be true.

Turning to EPISTEMIC-NARD$_1$. Given epistemic appearance is understood as belief, EPISTEMIC-NARD$_1$ can be formulated as below:

[EPISTEMIC-NARD$_1$*]: e has Q if and only if in having e, S believes that e has Q.

EPISTEMIC-NARD$_1$ is contentious (see Schwitzgebel 2008, 2011). It claims that whenever a subject is having an experience with certain phenomenal properties, she forms the belief that the experience has these phenomenal properties (i.e. self-intimation), and that it is impossible for the subject of an experience to form a false belief about what phenomenal properties are instantiated by the experience (i.e. infallibility). EPISTEMIC-NARD$_1$, as it stands, does not allow occasional errors in introspective judgements about what phenomenal properties our experiences have. One might think that errors of introspective judgements concerning one's conscious experiences, like introspective judgements about our beliefs and attitudes, can also arise from inattention or expectation (Hill 1991: 128). I fail to form the belief that I am feeling anxious when I am feeling anxious because I am too busy with tasks at hand. Similarly, I *believe* that I don't feel angry when I am actually feeling angry because I also believe that I am not the type of person who can be easily angered. Regardless of what one might say about these cases, a weakened version of EPISTEMIC-NARD$_1$ is nevertheless plausible. It seems intuitive to say that upon having an experience in which it phenomenally appears to the subject that e has Q, that is, where the subject of e instantiates Q, the subject is rationally disposed to judge or form the belief that 'e has Q', and in normal circumstances—that is, where the subject is attentive and free of expectations that would lead to an erroneous introspective judgement, that belief constitutes knowledge.

3.2 NARD$_2$

Another way to understand NARD is to interpret it as a claim about the natures or essences of phenomenal properties rather than their instantiations. This way of understanding NARD can be plausibly attributed to Nagel (1974).

In his seminal paper 'What Is It Like to Be a Bat?', Nagel labours the point that experience has what-it-is-likeness: 'an organism has conscious mental states if and only if there is something it is like to *be* that organism' (1974: 436).[1] Nagel labels this aspect of experience 'subjective character', where the latter, for the purpose of our discussion, is taken to be equivalent to 'phenomenal character' or 'phenomenal properties'. Towards the end of the paper, Nagel questions the idea that experience, which has a subjective character, can have an objective nature. He writes:

> Very little work has been done on the basic question (from which mention of the brain can be entirely omitted) whether any sense can be made of experiences' having an objective character at all. *Does it make sense, in other words, to ask what my experiences are really like, as opposed to how they appear to me?*
>
> (Nagel 1974: 448, emphasis added)

By 'how [experiences] appear to me', it is natural to interpret Nagel to refer to the what-it-is-likeness of experiences, which we know through having experiences. Nagel doubts that there is an appearance/reality distinction with respect to experience, that there is an objective reality of an experience beyond its appearance, i.e. what it is like to undergo that experience. He writes:

> The idea of moving from appearance to reality seems to make no sense here....Certainly it appears unlikely that we will get closer to the real nature of human experience by leaving behind the particularity of our human point of view and striving for a description in terms accessible to beings that could not imagine what it was like to be us. *If the subjective character of experience is fully comprehensible only from one point of view, then any shift to greater objectivity—that is, less attachment to a specific viewpoint—does not take us nearer to the real nature of the phenomenon: it takes us farther away from it.*
>
> (Nagel 1974: 444–445, emphasis added)

Although Nagel is primarily concerned with the question of whether there is an appearance/reality distinction with respect to experience, his reason

---

[1] Nagel's definition concerns what it is for an organism to *have* conscious states. In contemporary discussions, it is more common to put it in terms of what it is for a mental state to *be* a conscious state: a mental state is (phenomenally) conscious if and only if there is something it is like to be in that mental state (see Stoljar 2016: 1188–1189).

for questioning the latter distinction seems to build on the intuitive thought that there is no appearance/reality distinction when it comes to the nature of subjective character. Granted that experience-types are individuated by their subjective characters or phenomenal properties, Nagel seems to say that *if we fully comprehend the phenomenal properties of our experiences, including their essences, from the subjective point of view,* then experience does not have an objective nature capable of being given an objective description. Now, if all there is to the natures of phenomenal properties is given to us from the subjective point of view, then there is no appearance/reality distinction with respect to the natures of phenomenal properties, i.e. NARD$_2$ as stated below:

[NARD$_2$]: There is no distinction between what the essences of phenomenal properties *appear* to the subject to be and what they *really* are.

Let 'Q' be a phenomenal property and 'S' be an experiencer. NARD$_2$ can be reformulated as the following claim:

[NARD$_2$*]: All there is to the essence of Q is X if and only if in having an experience-token with Q, the essence of Q appears to S as X and only as X.

According to NARD$_2$, a phenomenal property Q *manifests* its essence to the subject when the subject has an experience with Q. Given our discussion of Nagel, it seems that the relevant notion of manifestation or appearance is *phenomenal appearance*—it concerns the way in which the subject experiences or is conscious of the essences of phenomenal properties from a subjective point of view, rather than what beliefs about the essences of phenomenal properties she might have. This phenomenal appearance of the essence of Q as X need not be thought of as a separate experience distinct from the experience with Q (more on this in §6). Consider the following reformulation of NARD$_2$*:

[PHENOMENAL-NARD$_2$]: All there is to the essence of Q is X if and only if in having an experience-token with Q, S experiences the essence of Q as X and only as X.

To say that S experiences the essence of Q as X and only as X, in this context, means something like S is conscious *of* the essence of Q as X and only as X. It does not mean that S needs to apply the concept of *essence* when experiencing Q or think about what Q *essentially* is. S's experience of the essence of Q as X and only as X is such that it affords S a conception of Q as X. For instance, I experience or am conscious of the essence of phenomenal property *phenomenal blue* as 'that' and only as 'that', where the demonstrative is naturally interpreted to refer to the what-it-is-likeness of *phenomenal blue*, and the experience of the essence of *phenomenal blue* as *that* and only as *that* affords me a conception of the former as *that*.

So far, NARD$_2$ is understood as PHENOMENAL-NARD$_2$, as a phenomenal or experiential claim about the way in which we experience the essences of phenomenal properties. As we shall see later, it is this particular version of NARD that is directly relevant to the thesis of revelation. There is nevertheless an epistemic version of this claim in the vicinity. The phenomenal appearance of the essence of Q as X, that is, S experiencing the essence of Q as X and only as X, may ground a further belief about what belongs to the essence of Q. Based on this phenomenal appearance, S is rationally disposed to form a corresponding belief that 'Q is X'. Upon further reflection on what the essence of Q might be, which would require S to possess and exercise the concept of *essence*, S might end up forming an explicit belief about Q which has the content 'all there is to the essence of Q is X'. If PHENOMENAL-NARD$_2$ is true, and all there is to the essence of Q is indeed X, then S arrives at a true belief about the essence of Q. But of course, upon experiencing the essence of Q as X and only as X, S might not have any view on what the essence of Q is. Alternatively, she might not take things at face value and instead take Q to have some hidden essence in addition to X or have an essence other than what is manifested to her, i.e. X.

4. The Relationship between Revelation and NARD

So far, we have seen that NARD can be formulated in different ways. One can take it to be the claim that there is no appearance/reality distinction with respect to the *instantiations* of phenomenal properties (i.e. NARD$_1$), or the claim that there is no appearance/reality distinction with respect to the *essences* of phenomenal properties (i.e. NARD$_2$).

How are versions of NARD related to revelation? Insofar as revelation is directly relevant to NARD, the relevant versions are not versions of NARD$_1$. Revelation is a claim about the essences of phenomenal properties rather than their instantiations, whereas NARD$_1$ is about (our beliefs about) the instantiations of phenomenal properties rather than their essences. This is not to say that revelation is not related to NARD$_1$. Consider the key idea of revelation, that one is in a position to know an essence-capturing truth 'Q is X' in having an experience with Q. Being in a position to know such a truth would require one to experience Q. Insofar as PHENOMENAL-NARD$_1$ is a claim about the latter, it is indirectly related to revelation. Being in a position to know that 'Q is X' where 'X' captures the essence of Q would also require the subject to be able to identify Q or form a belief that Q is instantiated. Insofar as EPISTEMIC-NARD$_1$ is a claim about the latter, it is also indirectly related to revelation.

Revelation is closely connected to NARD$_2$, i.e. PHENOMENAL-NARD$_2$. Both are claims about the essences of phenomenal properties. While the former is an epistemic claim about our knowledge with respect to the essences of phenomenal properties, the latter is an experiential or phenomenal claim about what our experiences of the essences of phenomenal properties are like. Consider revelation again, which can be thought of as consisting of the following two claims:

(i). By having an experience-token with phenomenal property Q, S is in a position to know that 'Q is X'.

(ii). The predicate 'X' captures the essence of Q.

I shall show that revelation, i.e. (i)&(ii), entails PHENOMENAL-NARD$_2$ with two additional premises. Recall PHENOMENAL-NARD$_2$:

[PHENOMENAL-NARD$_2$]: All there is to the essence Q is X if and only if in having an experience-token with Q, S experiences the essence of Q as X and only as X.

Let '(iii)' be the claim 'All there is to the essence of Q is X'. Let '(iv)' be the claim 'In having an experience-token with Q, S experiences the essence of Q as X and only as X'. PHENOMENAL-NARD$_2$ is then reformulated as '(iii)↔(iv)'. Consider the following two principles, where one connects claim (ii) of revelation to (iii), and the other connects revelation itself, i.e. (i)&(ii), to (iv):

(ii)→(iii): If the predicate 'X' captures the essence of Q (in the truth 'Q is X'), then all there is to the essence of Q is X.

[(i)&(ii)]→(iv): If by having an experience-token with phenomenal property Q, S is in a position to know that 'Q is X' where the predicate 'X' captures the essence of Q, then in having an experience-token with Q, S experiences the essence of Q as X and only as X.

Both conditionals seem intuitive. With respect to the first conditional, i.e. (ii)→(iii), it seems plausible to say that if a predicate captures the immediate constitutive essence of something, then what the predicate refers to is just all there is to what that thing is in its most core respects. For instance, if the predicate 'having a three-sided closed shape' captures the immediate constitutive essence of the property *being triangular* in the truth 'Being triangular is having a three-sided closed shape', then *having a three-sided closed shape is just all there is to what *being triangular* is in its most core respects.[2] The second conditional, i.e. [(i)&(ii)]→(iv), also seems plausible. One might think S's being in a position to *know* the essence-capturing truth 'Q is X' in virtue of having the relevant experience, i.e. revelation, requires one to first be in a position to form the *belief* that 'Q is X' where 'X' captures the essence of Q. The latter is, intuitively and naturally, grounded in S's experience of the essence of Q as X and only as X. To put it differently, if S experiences the essence of Q as X and only as X, then naturally S would form the belief 'Q is X' where 'X' captures the essence of Q. In this sense, (iv) is the precondition for the subject's knowledge about the essence of quale Q in the form of knowing the truth 'Q is X' where 'X' captures the essence of Q.

With these two additional premises above, i.e. (ii)→(iii) and [(i)&(ii)]→(iv), we can see that the thesis of revelation, i.e. (i)&(ii), entails PHENOMENAL-NARD$_2$, i.e. (iii)↔(iv). It is impossible for PHENOMENAL-NARD$_2$ to be false while revelation and the two additional premises are true. The formal proof is included in the Appendix A.

5. Revelation/NARD's Threat to Physicalism

It is often thought that revelation is an intuitive thesis, including by those who ultimately reject it (Lewis 1995; McLaughlin 2003; Braddon-Mitchell 2007; Hill 2014; Papineau 2020). It certainly seems plausible to say that in situations where the subject has identified Q, the subject also knows the essence of that property in the sense of knowing some truth 'Q is X' where 'X' captures the essence of phenomenal property Q.[3] Similarly, the related version of NARD$_2$, i.e. PHENOMENAL-NARD$_2$, is a highly intuitive claim.

---

[2] This point will be further defended in §5 when discussing premise (3) in the argument from revelation against identity physicalism.

[3] Elsewhere (Liu 2021), I have put forward a linguistic argument for the intuitiveness of revelation. I considered sentences like (S):

(S) *I know what an itch feels like, but I don't know what the feeling of an itch really is.

After all, we identify phenomenal properties through how they 'appear' to us from the inside and it seems intuitive to assume that such 'appearances' constitute what they are essentially. In this section, I show how revelation and PHENOMENAL-NARD$_2$ pose a prima facie threat to physicalism. §5.1 focuses on identity physicalism, §5.2 on grounding physicalism. The arguments here are not new and have been addressed in the literature by others, albeit formulated in different ways (for arguments against physicalism from revelation, see Lewis 1995; Nida-Rümelin 2007; Goff 2011, 2015, 2017, 2019). Here I shall put forward the relevant arguments using the formulations of revelation and PHENOMENAL-NARD$_2$ expounded above.

5.1 Against Identity Physicalism

According to identity physicalism, every phenomenal property is identical to some physical property. The argument from revelation to the falsity of identity physicalism is nicely summarised in a passage from Lewis (see also Nida-Rümelin 2007; Goff 2011, 2015):

> If, for instance, Q is essentially the physical property of being an event of C-firing, and if I identify the qualia of my experience in the appropriate 'demanding and literal' sense, I come to know that what is going on in me is an event of C-firing. Contrapositively: if I identify the quale of my experience in the appropriate sense, and yet know nothing of the firing of my neurons, then the quale of my experience cannot have been essentially the property of being an event of C-firing.
>
> (Lewis 1995: 142)

With the phrase 'identify the quale in the appropriate "demanding and literal" sense', Lewis refers to the thesis of revelation. Lewis' point is this: if the *painfulness of pain*, i.e. the phenomenal property of undergoing a pain experience, is the physical property of *being an event of C-firing*, then, given revelation, in having a pain experience, I would know about C-firing; but I certainly don't; so, identity physicalism is false.

(S) is odd. My argument is that the oddness in (S) is best explained by the hypothesis that revelation is part of our ordinary conception of experience, which we tacitly appeal to in interpreting the sentence, and that by inference to the best explanation, revelation is part of our ordinary conception of experience and can be considered an intuitive thesis for that reason.

Given our formulation of the thesis of revelation, we can formulate the argument in the following way (see also Liu 2019, 2021):

(1) By having an experience-token with phenomenal property Q, S is in a position to know that 'Q is X', where the predicate 'X' captures the essence of Q.

(2) If identity physicalism is true, then all phenomenal properties have physical essences.

(3) If all phenomenal properties have physical essences, then by having an experience-token with phenomenal property Q, S is in a position to know that 'Q is X', where 'X' is a physical predicate which captures the essence of Q.

(4) It is not true that by having an experience-token with phenomenal property Q, S is in a position to know that 'Q is X', where 'X' is a physical predicate which captures the essence of Q.

(5) Identity physicalism is false.

(1) is the thesis of revelation. (2) appeals to the definition of identity physicalism. (3) appeals to both (1) and (2) and lays out what the predicate 'X' would have to look like if revelation and identity physicalism were true. (4) is obvious—we do not know any physical truths concerning the essence of a phenomenal property in virtue of having an experience with that phenomenal property. (2), (3), and (4) entail (5).

The most contentious premise is (3) and is worth elaborating on. A defender of physicalism might think that while revelation, i.e. (1), is true, this does not mean that the predicate 'X' in the essence-capturing truth 'Q is X' has to be a physical predicate. Such a theorist might insist that there could be more than one truth that captures the essence of a property. While having an experience with Q affords us the essence-capturing phenomenal truth 'Q is X', there is also an essence-capturing physical truth.[4] So, (3) follows from (1) and (2) with the following additional assumption which our objector rejects:

(A) There are no two conceptually independent truths which equally capture the essence of a property.

---

[4] Goff (2017) calls this position 'dual carving' and has argued against it extensively (see also Goff 2011, 2015). In the main text and fn6, I discuss two objections which are not mentioned by Goff.

Two claims are conceptually independent if and only if they are not derivable from one another. For instance, these two claims—'Chris is a bachelor' ('p') and 'Chris is an unmarried man' ('q')—are not conceptually independent. Someone who has the relevant concepts of 'bachelor' and 'unmarried man' can see how p entails q and vice versa. There are at least two readings of (A) depending on how one understands the notion of essence at issue:

(A.i) There are no two conceptually independent truths which equally capture the immediate constitutive essence of a property.

(A.ii) There are no two conceptually independent truths which equally capture the essence of a property where the notion of essence is broadly construed.

While (A.i) is plausible, (A.ii) is not. The former is relevant to the above argument from revelation against identity physicalism, whereas the latter is not. As we already saw in §2, the notion of essence that features in the formulation of revelation is that of immediate constitutive essence, i.e. what a thing is in its most core respects. This notion of essence is contrasted with a notion of essence broadly construed that includes the *consequential* and *mediate* essence of a thing. There can be two conceptually independent truths that capture the essence of a property if the notion of essence is broadly construed. Consider again the property of *being water*. The two claims 'Being water is being molecules consisting of two atoms of hydrogen and one of oxygen' and 'Being water is being molecules consisting of two atoms of the chemical element with atomic number 1 and one of oxygen' are conceptually independent. While both capture the essence of the property of *being water* if the notion of essence is broadly construed, they don't equally capture the immediate constitutive essence of the property. The former captures the immediate constitutive essence of *being water*, whereas the latter captures part of its mediate essence, since *being the chemical element with atomic number 1* is only part of the mediate essence of *being water*. In contrast, there seem to be no good candidates for two conceptually independent claims that equally capture, i.e. accurately define, the immediate constitutive essence of a thing.[5] So, (A) understood as (A.i) is a plausible

---

[5] One might think that scientific truths such as 'Being light is being an electro-magnetic wave' and 'Being light is being made up of photons' are conceptually independent but equally capture the immediate constitutive essence of the property at issue, i.e. *being light* in this case. I am indebted to Avery Archer for this alleged counterexample to (A.i). However, it is unclear that such scientific truths are conceptually independent. The thought here is that while they seem conceptually independent given the incompleteness of physics, they may well be derivable from one another given complete physics.

assumption to adopt. Our objector against (3) seems to confuse (A) with (A.ii), when (A) should be understood as (A.i).[6]

Overall, the burden is on those who reject (A.i) to show how there could be two conceptually independent definitions capturing the immediate constitutive essence of a property. In the absence of such a proposal, we can endorse (A), understood as (A.i), and the related premise (3). The falsity of identity physicalism then follows from the thesis of revelation. It is also worth noting that the success of the argument does not rely on the thesis of revelation being true with respect to *all* phenomenal properties. It only requires that the thesis holds true with respect to *some* phenomenal properties. Put differently, if there are situations where we know the essence of a phenomenal property by having an experience with that property, then identity physicalism is false—for that phenomenal property cannot be identical to some physical property, whereas identity physicalism says *all* phenomenal properties are physical properties.

In addition to the argument from revelation against identity physicalism, we can also formulate a similar argument with the same conclusion by appealing to PHENOMENAL-NARD$_2$. Consider the following argument using PHENOMENAL-NARD$_2$:

(1) All there is to the essence of Q is X if and only if in having an experience-token with Q, S experiences the essence of Q as X and only as X.

(2) If identity physicalism is true, then all there is to the essence of a phenomenal property is some physical property.

(3) If all there is to the essence of a phenomenal property is some physical property, then in having an experience-token with Q, S experiences the essence of Q as X and only as X where X is a physical property.

---

[6] There is potentially another reason to hold (A.i). In §2 we considered what the essence-capturing truth 'Q is X' would look like if revelation is true. We noted that it is plausibly a truth that describes the what-it-is-likeness of a phenomenal property but may be hard to put in words. In describing what it is like to undergo an experience with a phenomenal property like *phenomenal blue*, it seems that we are only able to use a demonstrative, e.g. 'Phenomenal blue is *that*'. One might take this to suggest that phenomenal properties like *phenomenal blue* have no internal structure (see Lewis 1995). In contrast, if *phenomenal blue* turns out to be a neurophysiological property as according to identity physicalism, then it would presumably be a complex property with a complex internal structure. Neurons themselves are complex entities with internal structures where different elements within the same structure stand in certain relations to one another. It would then be puzzling that one essence-defining truth reveals that *phenomenal blue* has an essence that is structurally simple and the other reveals that it has an essence that is structurally complex.

(4) It is not true that in having an experience-token with Q, S experiences the essence of Q as X and only as X where X is a physical property.

(5) Identity physicalism is false.

(1) is PHENOMENAL-NARD₂. (2) appeals to the definition of identity physicalism. (3) arguably follows from (1) and (2). If all there is to the essence of Q is X and all there is to the essence of a phenomenal property is some physical property, then X would be a physical property. (4) seems intuitive—we certainly don't experience the painfulness of pain as C-fibres firing and form a conception of the former as the latter upon having a pain experience. (5) then follows from (2), (3), and (4).

In discussing the argument from PHENOMENAL-NARD₂ against identity physicalism, it is worth comparing it to Kripke's argument against identity physicalism in *Naming and Necessity* (1980). Kripke's argument crucially relies on two points: first, there is an intuition that pain and C-fibre stimulation are contingently related—it seems that pain can exist without C-fibre stimulation and C-fibre stimulation without pain; and second, such an intuition cannot be explained away as in usual cases, such as explaining away the intuitive contingency between heat and molecular motion by drawing a distinction between heat and the appearance or feeling of heat. Though nothing in his argument explicitly relies on PHENOMENAL-NARD₂ (or revelation for that matter),[7] it may nevertheless play a key role in Kripke's conceiving the intuition of contingency at issue. It may very well be that we tacitly appeal to PHENOMENAL-NARD₂ in arriving at the intuition that pain and C-fibres stimulation are distinct. After all, if we thought that PHENOMENAL-NARD₂ was false, that phenomenal properties have hidden essences, then it would be unclear as to why we would have the intuition that pain, which is individuated by its phenomenal character, is only contingently related to C-fibre stimulation—pain could have a hidden essence that is C-fibre stimulation.

Given the argument from PHENOMENAL-NARD₂ against identity physicalism, an identity physicalist would need to reject PHENOMENAL-NARD₂ but can nevertheless take the latter to be an intuitive claim. To such a physicalist, the intuition that the relation between pain and C-fibre stimulation is contingent is no surprise given the thought that the intuition is plausibly based on the intuitiveness of PHENOMENAL-NARD₂. Such a physicalist can further maintain that this intuition of contingency poses no problem for

---

[7] Lewis (1995) interprets Kripke as relying on the thesis of revelation, though such an interpretation is contentious (see Stoljar 2009).

identity physicalism. One can explain away the intuition of contingency by insisting that PHENOMENAL-NARD$_2$ is false, that despite its intuitiveness there is in fact an appearance/reality distinction with respect to the natures of phenomenal properties. But of course, such a physicalist is expected to say more about why we should think that phenomenal properties have a 'reality' beyond their 'appearance' and how it is that we experience the essence of quale Q as X and only as X even though X is not the essence of Q. I shall say more about physicalists' strategies in §6. But for now, it is worth noting that given the intuitive appeal of PHENOMENAL-NARD$_2$, without a clear and plausible elaboration physicalism is, as Kripke concluded four decades ago, problematic.

5.2 Against Grounding Physicalism

However, one might not formulate physicalism as an identity thesis, that every phenomenal property is identical to some physical property. Instead, one might formulate physicalism as a grounding thesis and take phenomenal facts to be ultimately grounded in physical facts, where *grounding* is understood as a non-causal explanatory relation that holds between facts. While the arguments from revelation and the related version of NARD against grounding physicalism are less straightforward than corresponding arguments against identity physicalism, we can nevertheless formulate the relevant arguments given a certain formulation of grounding physicalism. I shall first discuss a formulation of grounding physicalism which would allow us to formulate an argument from revelation against grounding physicalism. I shall then briefly discuss whether this argument is sound.

Grounding physicalists hold (G):

(G) The fact that S instantiates physical property P grounds the fact that S instantiates phenomenal property Q.

Facts like (G) are grounding facts—facts about grounding. There is a question as to what grounds a grounding fact like (G). Consider a simpler example from Dasgupta (2014):

(C) The fact that an event *e* contains people engaged in C-activities (i.e. giving talks, listening to talks, asking questions, and so on) grounds the fact that *e* is a conference.

Following Dasgupta (2014), one might say that (C) is grounded in a *general connection* held between C-activities and conferences. As Dasgupta (2014: 567) puts it, a conference is just 'the kind of thing that you get when people engage in those activities'. A natural way to spell out this general connection is through the notion of essence.[8] Here, both the essence of conferences and the essence of C-activities seem to be relevant. Conferences are *essentially* events consisting of activities where people are formally engaged in the communication and exchange of ideas.[9] Now, C-activities (i.e. giving talks, listening to talks, asking questions, and so on) are *essentially* just such activities.[10] (C) is thus understood as being grounded in the following two facts:

(C.i) Event *e* contains people engaged in C-activities.

(C.ii) The essence of conferences and the essence of C-activities are such that if an event contains people engaged in C-activities then it is a conference ('if C then F' for short).[11]

(C) obtains *because* (C.i) and (C.ii) do. (C.ii) posits a tight connection between the respective essence of conferences and C-activities on the one hand and the general connection 'if C then F' on the other. As we saw, if one knows what conferences essentially are and what C-activities essentially are, one can deduce that 'if C then F'.[12] That is, the latter truth is *a priori* entailed from the essential truths about conferences and C-activities.

---

[8] There are different ways to formulate the idea of a general connection, which give rise to different versions of what Dasgupta (2014: 568) calls 'brute connectivism': it could be an *essential* truth ('brute essentialism'), or a *necessary* truth ('brute necessitarianism'), or a *conceptual* truth ('brute conceptualism'), or a *metaphysical law* ('brute nomicism'). For Dasgupta (2014: 569), the general connection that grounds a grounding fact is necessary such that 'if some Xs ground Y, then necessarily if the Xs obtain then Y obtains'. In his paper, Dasgupta focuses on *brute essentialism*, which is also what I focus on in formulating arguments from revelation/PHENOMENAL-NARD$_2$ against grounding physicalism. So, the arguments here depend on formulating grounding physicalism in this particular way.

[9] For Dasgupta (2014), essential facts are groundless and in particular, they are 'autonomous'—they are ungrounded and are also not apt for being grounded.

[10] Giving a talk, listening to a talk, asking a question, and so on are different instances of C-activities. It is the essence of C-activities rather than essences of the instances that seems to matter here. On this picture, the ground is a kind that has many instances and the essence of the ground is the property that all instances have (see Aleksiev 2022).

[11] For Dasgupta (2014), essential facts are groundless and in particular, they are 'autonomous'—they are ungrounded and are also not apt for being grounded.

[12] Imagine a person who is at an event with C-activities. She knows that C-activities are taking place. She also knows that conferences are essentially events containing people formally engaged in the communication and exchange of ideas. But for some bizarre reason, she does not know that C-activities are just activities where people are formally engaged in the communication and exchange of ideas. As a result, this unfortunate person does not know that she is at a conference.

Similarly, we can think of (G) as grounded in a general connection held between physical property P and quale Q, such that a subject would instantiate phenomenal property Q when the same subject instantiates physical property P. A grounding physicalist can say that (G) is grounded in the following two further facts:

(G.i) S instantiates physical property P.

(G.ii) The essence of phenomenal property Q and the essence of physical property P are such that if something instantiates physical property P then this something instantiates phenomenal property Q (i.e. 'if P then Q' for short).

(G) obtains *because* (G.i) and (G.ii) do. (G.ii) posits a tight connection between the essences of P and Q on the one hand, and the general connection 'if P then Q' on the other. One might take this tight connection to entail the following: if one knows the essence of Q (i.e. know that 'Q is X' where 'X' captures the essence of Q) and also knows the essence of P (i.e. know that 'P is Y' where 'Y' captures the essence of P), then one can in principle deduce that 'if P then Q'. That is, the latter truth is *a priori* entailed from the essential truths about Q and P (i.e. 'Q is X' and 'P is Y') (see also Aleksiev 2022; Roelofs 2020).

Given this clarification, we can put forward an argument from revelation against grounding physicalism as follows:[13]

(1) By having an experience-token with phenomenal property Q, S is in a position to know that 'Q is X', where the predicate 'X' captures the essence of Q.

(2) If grounding physicalism is true, then the essence of phenomenal property Q and the essence of P are such that if P then Q.

(3) If the essence of phenomenal property Q and the essence of P are such that if P then Q, then by having an experience-token with phenomenal property Q, S is in a position to know that 'Q is X', where 'X' is a predicate that captures the essence of Q and is such that 'If P then Q' is *a priori* entailed by 'Q is X' and 'P is Y' (where 'Y' captures the essence of P).

(4) It is not true that by having an experience-token with phenomenal property Q, S is in a position to know that 'Q is X', where 'X' is a predicate that captures the essence of Q and is such that 'If P then Q'

---

[13] For related discussion against grounding physicalism, see also Goff (2019) and Aleksiev (2022).

is *a priori* entailed by 'Q is X' and 'P is Y' (where 'Y' captures the essence of P).

(5) Grounding physicalism is false.

One can similarly formulate an argument against grounding physicalism from PHENOMENAL-NARD$_2$ (see Appendix B). In the above argument, (1) is the thesis of revelation. (2) appeals to the aforesaid formulation of grounding physicalism and in particular (G.ii). (3) appeals to (1) and (2) and lays out what the predicate 'X' would need to be if revelation and grounding physicalism thus conceived were true. (4) claims that 'X' cannot be a predicate that both captures the essence of Q and is such that 'If P then Q' follows *a priori* from the respective essence-capturing truths about Q and P, i.e. 'Q is X' and 'P is Y'. (5), i.e. the falsity of grounding physicalism, then follows from (2), (3), and (4).

The most contentious premise is (4) and is worth elaborating on. Whether or not (4) is true depends not only on what 'Q is X' (where 'X' captures the essence of Q) turns out to be, but also on what 'P is Y' (where 'Y' captures the essence of P) turns out to be. One might think that while we are in a position to know what 'Q is X' looks like, we have no idea what 'P is Y' might look like. Put differently, while we know the essences of phenomenal properties, we have no idea about the essences of physical properties—whatever they are, they are not exhausted by what physical sciences have told us so far (e.g. Stoljar 2006). For a physicalist making this point, it may well be plausible that 'If P then Q' is *a priori* entailed by 'Q is X' (where 'X' captures the essence of Q) and 'P is Y' (where 'Y' captures the essence of P).[14] Put differently, it may well be the case that (4) is false, that by having an experience-token with phenomenal property Q, S is in a position to know that 'Q is X', where 'X' is a predicate that captures the essence of Q and is such that 'If P then Q' is *a priori* entailed by 'Q is X' and 'P is Y' (where 'Y' captures the essence of P).[15]

---

[14] Roelofs (2020) makes a related point that constitutive panpsychism does not face the argument from revelation, because we precisely do not know the essences of the microphenomenal properties posited by that theory.

[15] It is also a point of contention as to what 'Q is X' looks like. A commonsense role functionalist might insist that phenomenal properties have functional essences and such essences are revealed in experience. Furthermore, she might deny (4) and contend that 'X' is a predicate that captures the essence of Q in commonsense psychological terms and is such that 'If P then Q' is *a priori* entailed from respective truths about the essences of Q and P. In Liu (2019), I argue that commonsense role functionalism is incompatible with revelation even setting aside the general concern that, intuitively, a state's having a certain functional role does not guarantee that the state has any phenomenology.

However, for many physicalists, physical sciences have told us enough about what physical properties are, that we know what kind of truth 'P is Y' (where 'Y' captures the essence of P) would look like. For instance, physical properties are often thought of as structural and dynamic properties. According to Chalmers (2003; see also Alter 2016), structural properties are understood as spatial and formal (i.e. logical and mathematical) properties, whereas the dynamic properties are temporal and nomic properties. The essence-capturing truth 'P is Y' is then a truth concerning *structures and dynamics*, where 'Y' is a structural-and-dynamic predicate that captures the essence of P. In contrast, the essence-capturing truth 'Q is X' is sometimes thought of as a truth that goes beyond structures and dynamics, i.e. a truth that is not in purely structural and dynamic terms (see Chalmers 2003; Alter 2016). Such a theorist might further contend that the respective essence-capturing truths about Q and P, i.e. 'Q is X' and 'P is Y', do not *a priori* entail 'If P then Q'. She might argue that properties with structural and dynamic essences cannot give rise to properties whose essences are not purely structural and dynamic. Since P's essence is exhausted by its structural and dynamic features whereas Q's essence is not, it might seem that something else is needed, in addition to P, to give rise to Q given the kind of essence it has. Having established this, such a theorist would then argue that (4) is true—that 'X' is not a predicate that both captures the essence of Q and is such that 'If P then Q' is *a priori* entailed by truths concerning the essence of Q and the essence of P.

There is much to be said about the above argument from revelation against grounding physicalism, especially with respect to (4). For instance, even if we grant that 'P is Y' is a truth concerning structures and dynamics, precisely how to understand these latter notions is matter of controversy (Stoljar 2015; Alter 2016). While there is a clear argument from revelation against identity physicalism, the argument against grounding physicalism is at least less straightforward.

6. Physicalist Responses and Their Limitations

Granting the arguments against physicalism from revelation and the related version of NARD, physicalists would have to reject these claims. In this section, I shall grant the arguments discussed in §5 and consider physicalists' responses. While all physicalists would reject PHENOMENAL-NARD₂ by maintaining an appearance/reality distinction with respect to the essences of phenomenal properties, they might respond differently with respect to different components of revelation. This section focuses on different ways that physicalists might reject the thesis of revelation and also discusses the limitations of their responses.

Consider the two components of revelation:

(i) By having an experience-token with phenomenal property Q, S is in a position to know that 'Q is X'.
(ii) 'X' captures the essence of Q.

In §2, we considered what the essence-capturing truth 'Q is X' would look like if revelation is true. We noted that 'X' is plausibly a predicate that captures the what-it-is-likeness of Q but may be hard to put into words. Relatedly, in terms of PHENOMENAL-NARD$_2$, we can say that we experience the essence of Q as X and only as X in the sense that we experience Q's what-it-is-likeness and only its what-it-is-likeness when having an experience with Q. Understood this way, (i) seems compelling regardless of whether or not (ii) is true. Phenomenal properties manifest their what-it-is-likeness. We form the belief that 'Q is X' (where 'X' captures Q's what-it-is-likeness) where the latter belief is grounded in a phenomenal appearance of Q as having what-it-is-likeness X. Once this belief is formed, it seems tempting to then say that such what-it-is-likeness is just what defines phenomenal property Q rather than to argue that the essence of Q is hidden.

In relation to revelation thus understood, physicalists can reject either (i) or (ii). Below, I explain different strategies used by physicalists in response to revelation.

6.1 Denying (ii)

Physicalists like Papineau (2020) accept (i) while rejecting (ii)—they concede the truth of the belief 'Q is X' (where 'X' captures the what-it-is-likeness of Q) formed upon having an experience with Q, but nevertheless deny that this 'X' captures the essence of Q. These physicalists are usually phenomenal concept strategists (e.g. Loar 1997; Papineau 2002; Balog 2012). They argue that we have two distinct conceptions—phenomenal and physical—of the same phenomenal property, which is physical in its essence.

Objections against the phenomenal concept strategy are usually centred around the idea that phenomenal concepts are revelatory with respect to the natures of their referents (see Horgan and Tienson 2001; Levine 2001: 84; 2007; Nida-Rümelin 2007; Goff 2011, 2015). Nevertheless, this is precisely the point that many phenomenal concept strategists resist. For these physicalists, phenomenal concepts, as McLaughlin (2001: 34) notes, 'do not conceptually reveal anything about the essential nature of phenomenal properties: they simply name or demonstrate them' (see also Papineau 2007; Balog 2012).

In addressing revelation head-on, Papineau (2020: 27) acknowledges its intuitiveness but questions its all-things-considered plausibility. Relying on a formulation of revelation in terms of the notion of introspection, Papineau agrees that introspection can 'tell us what experiences we are having, and various other things about them', but casts doubt on the idea that it can tell us about the natures of experiences. In particular, Papineau (2020: 27) notes that '[a]ny normal information-delivering process is inevitably fallible and only partially informative about the nature of its objects' and treating introspection as an exception 'would seem to take us beyond the realm of naturally explicable faculties'.

In response, it is questionable that we cannot have a naturalistic view about introspection while maintaining that the qualia we introspect themselves are non-physical (e.g. see Coleman's (2019) quotational higher-order theory).[16] More importantly, a proponent of revelation is unlikely to be taken aback by the worry that the faculty of introspection may be naturally inexplicable. After all, such a theorist is probably already an anti-physicalist who thinks that phenomenal properties, which are the objects of our introspection, are themselves non-physical.

6.2 Denying (i)

A more radical physicalist approach is to deny (i). There are at least three different ways to deny (i). The most radical option is to be an illusionist and deny outright that experiences have phenomenal properties including

---

[16] Coleman (2019) talks in terms of the notion of acquaintance where the latter is construed in terms of the notion of embedding or part-whole constitution rather than representation, but the point equally applies to the notion of introspection.

what-it-is-likeness. A second option is to concede that experiences have phenomenal properties but reject that having an experience puts one in a position to know what it is like to have that experience. A third option is to concede that experiences have phenomenal properties but deny that they have what-it-is-likeness. This third option has been articulated extensively by Pereboom (2011, 2016, 2019).[17] In the rest of this section, I shall focus on Pereboom's position.

In denying (i), Pereboom (2011: 14; see also 2016, 2019) has argued for his qualitative inaccuracy hypothesis (QIH):

[QIH]: It is an open possibility that introspective representation is inaccurate in the respect that it represents phenomenal properties as having qualitative natures they do not in fact have.

By 'qualitative natures' of phenomenal properties, Pereboom (2016: 173) means 'the what-it's-like features of sensory states' which, he says, are 'illusory in that they don't exist'. On this view, an experience can have a phenomenal property Q, and introspection systematically and inaccurately represents the nature of Q as what-it-is-likeness X, which gives rise to the subject's false belief that 'Q has what-it-is-likeness X', but X simply does not exist. Pereboom motivates his QIH by drawing an analogy with colour and perceptual representation. On a number of theories of colour, colour properties do not have the qualitative natures that perception represents them to have. Consider a corresponding qualitative inaccuracy hypothesis regarding colour properties:

[QIH-c]: It is an open possibility that perceptual representation is inaccurate in the respect that it represents colour properties as having qualitative natures they do not in fact have.

For instance, physicalists about colour might say that the essence of colour property C is the surface reflectance property S, but perception does not accurately represent C *as* S, and instead represents C *as* having a primitive,

---

[17] Early on, I defined phenomenal properties as properties of subjects which constitute there being something it is like for a subject to undergo experiences with these properties. On this definition of 'phenomenal property', the denial that experiences have what-it-is-likeness amounts to illusionism which denies that experiences have phenomenal properties. So, Pereboom's position might simply amount to a version of illusionism, i.e. the first option. Pereboom can nevertheless maintain the talk of 'phenomenal properties', as he indeed does, and qualify them to be properties of subjects which account for the *illusion* that experiences have what-it-is-likeness.

qualitative nature Y. As Pereboom sees it, just as it is possible for there to be systematic perceptual misrepresentations of the natures of colour proper-ties, it is possible for there to be systematic introspective misrepresentations of the natures of phenomenal properties.

Now, the alleged analogy between QIH and QIH-c relies on the alleged analogy between introspective representation and perceptual representa-tion in the two cases. By perceptual representation, we usually mean *perceptual experience*—to say that my perception *represents* a car as red is just to say that it *phenomenally appears* to me that the car is red. Given the analogy, introspective representation is naturally understood as *phenomenal appearance*—to say that introspection represents Q as having what-it-is-likeness X is just to say that it *phenomenally appears* that Q has what-it-is-likeness X. Pereboom himself seems to adopt this understanding of introspective representation as he writes:[18]

> The open possibility I am envisioning [QIH] would have us making errors
> of ignorance of our introspection-based beliefs about phenomenal prop-
> erties, since such beliefs would be based on *appearances* that fail to do
> justice to the real qualitative nature of those properties.
>
> (Pereboom 2011: 22, fn.33, emphasis added)

On this understanding of introspective representation, QIH denies PHENOMENAL-NARD$_2$ and claims that there is a systematic discrepancy between the phenomenal appearance of Q's essence, i.e. as X, and Q's essence, which is not X. This way of thinking about the phenomenal appearance of the essence of Q as X is different from the one occurring in §3.2, which does not construe the phenomenal appearance as distinct from the experience with Q.[19] In this case, the phenomenal appearance or introspective representation of Q as having what-it-is-likeness X is a second-order experience that is distinct from the original experience—call it 'e_1'—with phenomenal property Q. The original experience e_1 has Q where Q lacks what-it-is-likeness X. The intro-spective experience—call it 'e_2'—misrepresents e_1's Q *as* having X.

---

[18] It is also worth noting that in his replies to critics, Pereboom (2013: 758) seems to be open to adopt the assumption that introspective representations are *beliefs*, rather than *experi-ences*. Elsewhere, I have argued that QIH is problematic on the belief-conception of introspect-ive representation (Liu 2020).

[19] In that case, phenomenal appearance is unlike perceptual representation/experience because the latter certainly admits an appearance/reality distinction with respect to what it represents.

But this makes Pereboom's QIH highly implausible. Elsewhere (Liu 2020), I have argued that QIH thus understood potentially leads to an infinite regress. The illusion that e_1's Q has what-it-is-likeness X is explained by positing as second-order experience e_2 which mispresents Q as having X. But e_2 also seems to have a certain what-it-is-likeness, and the phenomenal appearance of e_2's phenomenal property Q' as having what-it-is-likeness X' must also be an illusion. To account for the latter illusion, we would need to posit a third-order experience e_3 which represents Q' as having X'. If e_3 also seems to have a certain what-it-is-likeness, then this leads to a regress of introspective misrepresentations/experiences. Pereboom (2016: 178) denies such a regress by suggesting that '[a]t some level, I form only a belief, without distinctive phenomenology, that I am representing a mental state'. But this baffles the mind. Suppose that it is on the basis of e_1, e_2, and e_3, I arrive at the judgement 'Q has what-it-is-likeness X'. How can that judgement be based on an illusion that Q has X when there is nothing it is like for me to have the three experiences that are supposed to create the illusion?

Here it is also worth noting that those who maintain a similarity between introspective representation and perceptual representation typically hold the inner sense theory of introspection, or what Shoemaker (1994) calls 'the broad perceptual model' of introspection (see also Armstrong 1968). On this theory, the two are similar in the sense that the relationship between introspective representation and what is introspectively represented, i.e. a mental state, can be thought of as causal and independent, just like the relationship between perceptual representation and what is perceptually represented, i.e. external objects and their properties (Shoemaker 1994: 271). But insofar as there is an analogy, the notion of introspective representation is understood as *belief*, not *experience* (see Shoemaker 1994: 271). As Moran (2001: 14) points out, no inner sense theorist would say that one's introspective belief that one is having a headache is 'mediated by an appearance of the headache'; on this theory, 'there is simply nothing quasi-experiential in the offing to begin with'. Overall, more needs to be said to make intelligible the idea that our introspective experience systematically misrepresents the natures of phenomenal properties.

7. Conclusion

In this chapter, I have primarily focused on the relationship between the thesis of revelation and the no appearance/reality distinction thesis with respect to conscious experience, i.e. NARD, as well as the threat they pose to physicalism. In relation to revelation, we saw that it is an epistemic claim about how an experience with a phenomenal property Q puts us in a position to know the essence of Q. This latter knowledge is formulated as 'Q is X' where 'X' captures the essence of Q. In relation to NARD, we saw that it can be construed as a thesis about either the instantiations of phenomenal properties or the essences of phenomenal properties. It is the latter construal, understood as a phenomenological claim about our experiences of phenomenal properties, that is directly relevant to the thesis of revelation. Both revelation and the related version of NARD pose a problem for physicalism if the latter is construed as either an identity thesis or a grounding thesis. Physicalists typically reject revelation and the related version of NARD; their precise responses are varied but nevertheless face limitations.

Appendix A

The following proof shows that revelation, i.e. (i)&(ii), entails PHENOMENAL-NARD$_2$, i.e. (iii)↔(iv), given two additional premises, i.e. (ii)→(iii) and [(i)&(ii)]→(iv):

1. (i)&(ii)	Premise 1
2. (ii)→(iii)	Premise 2
3. [(i)&(ii)]→(iv)	Premise 3
4. (iv)	Hypothesis
5. (ii)	&Elimination 1
6. (iii)	→ Elimination 2, 5
7. (iii)	Hypothesis
8. (i)&(ii)	Premise 1
9. (iv)	→ Elimination 3, 8
10. (iii)↔(iv)	↔ Introduction 4, 6, 7, 9

Appendix B

The following is an argument against grounding physicalism using (a) of PHENOMENAL-NARD$_2$ as premise (1):

(1) All there is to the essence of Q is X if and only if in having an experience-token with Q, S experiences the essence of Q as X and only as X.

(2) If grounding physicalism is true, then the essence of phenomenal property Q and the essence of physical property P are such that if P then Q.

(3) If the essence of phenomenal property Q and the essence of physical property P are such that if P then Q, then in having an experience-token with phenomenal property Q, S experiences the essence of Q as X and only as X where X is such that if S knows the essence of P in addition to knowing the essence of Q, S is in a position to know *a priori* that 'if P then Q'.

(4) It is not true that in having an experience-token with phenomenal property Q, S experiences the essence of Q as X and only as X where X is such that if S knows the essence of P in addition to knowing the essence of Q, S is in a position to know *a priori* that 'if P then Q'.

(5) Grounding physicalism is false.

Acknowledgements

Versions of my original paper were presented at the *Appearance-Reality Workshop* in Ligerz, Switzerland, the *Consciousness and Reality Conference* at Rice University, and the *Metaphysics and Introspection Online Workshop*. I am grateful to the audience at these occasions. I am indebted to constructive feedback from Damian Aleksiev, Avery Archer, Sam Coleman, Melissa Ebbers, Keith Frankish, Anna Giustina, Philip Goff, Adrian Haddock, Amy Kind, Brendan Larvor, Rory Madden, Mike Martin, Jakub Mihálik, Alex Moran, Jim Pryor, Luke Roelofs, Charles Siewert, and Helen Yetter-Chappell. I am most grateful to helpful suggestions from Uriah Kriegel. This research is funded by the Leverhulme Trust Early Career Fellowship ECF-2021-539.

References

Aleksiev, D. (2022) 'Lightweight and Heavyweight Anti-Physicalism', *Synthese*, https://doi.org/10.1007/s11229-022-03506-3.

Alter, T. (2016) 'The Structure and Dynamics Argument against Materialism', *Noûs* 50 (4): 794–815.

Armstrong, D. M. (1968) *A Materialist Theory of the Mind*, London: Routledge and Kegan Paul.

Balog, K. (2012) 'Acquaintance and the Mind-Body Problem', in S. Gozzano and C. S. Hill (eds), *New Perspectives on Type Identity: The Mental and the Physical*, Cambridge: Cambridge University Press, 16–42.

Braddon-Mitchell, D. (2007) 'Against Ontologically Emergent Consciousness', in B. McLaughlin and J. Cohen (eds), *Contemporary Debates in Philosophy of Mind*, Oxford: Blackwell, 287–299.

Chalmers, D. (2003) 'Consciousness and its Place in Nature', in S. P. Stich and T. A. Warfield (eds), *Blackwell Guide to the Philosophy of Mind*, Blackwell, 102–142.

Chalmers, D. (2016) 'The Combination Problem for Panpsychism', in G. Brüntrup and J. Jaskolla (eds), *Panpsychism: Contemporary Perspectives*, Oxford: OUP, 179–214.

Chalmers, D. (2018) 'The Meta-Problem of Consciousness', *Journal of Conscious Studies* 25 (9–10): 6–61.

Chisholm, R. (1957) *Perceiving: A Philosophical Study*, Ithaca: Cornell University Press.

Coleman, S. (2019) 'Natural Acquaintance', in J. Knowles and T. Raleigh, *Acquaintance: New Essays*, Oxford: OUP, 49–74.

Dasgupta, S. (2014), 'The Possibility of Physicalism', *Journal of Philosophy* 111 (9/10), 557–592.

Fine, K. (1995a) 'Ontological Dependence', *Proceedings of the Aristotelian Society* 95 (1): 269–290.

Fine, K. (1995b) 'Senses of Essence', in W. Sinnott-Armstrong, D. Raffman, and N. Asher (eds), *Modality, Morality and Belief: Essays in Honor of Ruth Barcan Marcus*, Cambridge: Cambridge University Press, 53–73.

Gertler, B. (2012) 'Renewed Acquaintance', in D. Smithies and D. Stoljar (eds), *Introspection and Consciousness*, Oxford: OUP, 89–123.

Goff, P. (2011) 'A Posteriori Physicalists Get Our Phenomenal Concepts Wrong', *Australasian Journal of Philosophy* 89 (2): 191–209.

Goff, P. (2015) 'Real Acquaintance and Physicalism', in P. Coates and S. Coleman (eds), *Phenomenal Qualities: Sense, Perception, and Consciousness*, Oxford: OUP, 121–143.

Goff, P. (2017) *Consciousness and Fundamental Reality*, Oxford: OUP.

Goff, P. (2019) 'Grounding, Analysis and Russellian Monism', in S. Coleman (ed.) *The Knowledge Argument Then and Now*, Cambridge University Press, 198–222.

Hill, C. (1991) *Sensations: A Defense of Type Materialism*, Cambridge: Cambridge University Press.

Hill, C. (2014) *Meaning, Mind, and Knowledge*, Oxford, OUP.

Horgan, T. (2012) 'Introspection and Phenomenal Consciousness: Running the Gamut from Infallibility to Impotence', in D. Smithies and D. Stoljar (eds), *Introspection and Consciousness*, Oxford: OUP, 405–422.

Horgan, T., and Tienson, J. (2001) 'Deconstructing New Wave Materialism', in C. Gillett and B. Loewer (eds), *Physicalism and Its Discontents*, Cambridge: Cambridge University Press, 307–318.

Jackson, F. (1977) *Perception: A Representative Theory*, Cambridge: Cambridge University Press.

Kim, J. (1966). 'On the Psycho-physical Identity Theory', *American Philosophical Quarterly* 3 (3): 227–235.

Kripke, S. (1980) *Naming and Necessity*, Cambridge: Harvard University Press.

Levine, J. (2001) *Purple Haze: The Puzzle of Consciousness*, Oxford: OUP.

Levine, J. (2007) 'Phenomenal Concepts and Materialist Constraints', in T. Alter and S. Walter (eds), *Phenomenal Concepts and Phenomenal Knowledge: New Essays on Consciousness and Physicalism*, Oxford: OUP, 145–166.

Lewis, D. (1995) 'Should a Materialist Believe in Qualia?', *Australasian Journal of Philosophy* 73 (1): 140–144.

Liu, M. (2019) 'Phenomenal Experience and the Thesis of Revelation', in D. Shottenkirk, M. Curado, and S. Gouveia (eds), *Perception, Cognition and Aesthetics*, Routledge, 227–251.

Liu, M. (2020) 'Explaining the Intuition of Revelation', *Journal of Consciousness Studies* 27 (5–6): 99–107.

Liu, M. (2021) 'Revelation and the Intuition of Dualism', *Synthese* 199: 11491–11515.

Loar, B. (1997) 'Phenomenal States', in N. Block, O. Flanagan, and G. Güzeldere (eds), *The Nature of Consciousness*, Cambridge, MA: MIT Press, 597–616.

Majeed, R. (2017) 'Ramsey Humility: The Response from Revelation and Panpsychism', *Canadian Journal of Philosophy* 47 (1): 75–96.

McLaughlin, B. (2001) 'In Defense of New Wave Materialism', in C. Gillett and B. Loewer (eds.), *Physicalism and Its Discontents*, Cambridge: Cambridge University Press, 319–330.

McLaughlin, B. (2003) 'Color, Consciousness, and Color Consciousness', in Q. Smith and A. Jokic (eds), *Consciousness: New Philosophical Perspectives*, Oxford: OUP, 97–154.

Moran, R. (2001) *Authority and Estrangement: An Essay on Self-Knowledge*, New Jersey: Princeton University Press.

Nagel, T. (1974) 'What Is It Like to Be a Bat?', *Philosophical Review* 83 (4): 435–450.

Nida-Rümelin, M. (2007) 'Grasping Phenomenal Properties', in T. Alter and S. Walter (eds), *Phenomenal Concepts and Phenomenal Knowledge: New Essays on Consciousness and Physicalism*, Oxford: OUP, 307–336.

Papineau, D. (2002) *Thinking about Consciousness*, Oxford: OUP.

Papineau, D. (2007) 'Phenomenal and Perceptual Concepts', in T. Alter and S. Walter (eds.) *Phenomenal Concepts and Phenomenal Knowledge: New Essays on Consciousness and Physicalism*, Oxford: OUP, 111–144.

Papineau, D. (2020) 'The Problem of Consciousness', in U. Kriegel (ed.), *The Oxford Handbook of the Philosophy of Consciousness*, Oxford: OUP, 13–36.

Pereboom, D. (2011) *Consciousness and the Prospects of Physicalism*, New York: Oxford University Press.

Pereboom, D. (2013) 'Replies to Daniel Stoljar, Robert Adams, and Lynne Baker', *Philosophy and Phenomenological Research* 86 (3): 753–764.

Pereboom, D. (2016) 'Illusionism and Anti-Functionalism about Phenomenal Consciousness', *Journal of Consciousness Studies* 23 (11–12): 172–185.

Pereboom, D. (2019) 'Russellian Monism, Introspective Inaccuracy, and the Illusion Meta-Problem of Consciousness', *Journal of Consciousness Studies* 26 (9–10): 182–193.

Roelofs, L. (2020) 'Consciousness, Revelation, and Confusion: Are Constitutive Panpsychists Hoist by Their Own Petard?', *Dialectica* 74(1): 61–93.

Schwitzgebel, E. (2008) 'The Unreliability of Naïve Introspection', *Philosophical Review* 117 (2): 245–273.

Schwitzgebel, E. (2011) *Perplexities of Consciousness*, Cambridge, MA: MIT Press.

Searle, J. (1997) 'Reductionism and the Irreducibility of Consciousness', in O. J. Flanagan, N. Block, and G. Guzeldere (eds), *The Nature of Consciousness*, Cambridge, MA: MIT Press, 451–460.

Shoemaker, S. (1994) 'Self-Knowledge and Inner Sense', *Philosophy and Phenomenological Research* 54: 249–314.

Stoljar, D. (2006) *Ignorance and Imagination: The Epistemic Origin of the Problem of Consciousness*, Oxford: Oxford University Press.

Stoljar, D. (2009) 'The Argument from Revelation', in D. Braddon-Mitchell and R. Nola (eds), *Conceptual Analysis and Philosophical Naturalism*, Cambridge: MIT Press, 113–138.

Stoljar, D. (2015) 'Russellian Monism or Nagelian Monism?' In T. Alter and Y. Nagasawa (eds) *Consciousness in the Physical World: Perspectives on Russellian Monism*, New York: Oxford University Press, 324–345.

Stoljar, D. (2016) 'The Semantics of "What It's Like" and the Nature of Consciousness', *Mind* 125 (500): 1161–1198.

Trogdon, K. (2017) 'Revelation and Physicalism', *Synthese* 194: 2345–2366.

Whiting, D. (2016) 'On the Appearance and Reality of Mind', *Journal of Mind and Behavior* 37 (1): 47–70.

Michelle Liu, *Revelation and the Appearance/Reality Distinction* In: *Oxford Studies in Philosophy of Mind Volume 4*. Edited by: Uriah Kriegel, Oxford University Press. © Michelle Liu 2024. DOI: 10.1093/9780198924159.003.0011

12

The Conscious Theory of Higher-Orderness

Nicholas Silins

1. Introduction

When you sit down on the park bench and realize to your dismay that the bench was wet, your feeling of wetness is a paradigmatically conscious mental state. What makes it a conscious mental state? According to higher-order theories of consciousness, we can explain why your mental state is conscious in terms of your awareness of the state. We can think of this as the Descending Road. This approach has a long history, with important and visible proponents both in philosophy and psychology.[1]

Higher-order theories are standardly opposed by first-order theories, views that explain why a mental state is conscious in terms of factors other than your awareness of the state.[2] My aim in this chapter is to oppose higher-order theories while sidestepping whether and how first-order theories might be true. My strategy is instead to turn higher-order theories of consciousness on their head.

Here I will assume that, whenever we are in a conscious mental state, we are aware of it, or so to speak have *inner awareness* of it (Necessary Awareness). This does not mean that we can or should explain consciousness in terms of inner awareness. My proposal is instead that, once we accept Necessary Awareness, we should explain inner awareness in terms of consciousness. When you are in a conscious mental state, you are aware of it, but you are aware of it because it is conscious, not vice versa. Call this the Ascending Road. As important and attractive as this approach should be,

---

[1] See e.g. Rosenthal 2005, Kriegel 2009a, or Lau 2022, as well as Locke's *Essay Concerning Human Understanding.*
[2] See e.g. Dretske 1993 and 1995, Neander 1998, Block 2007, 2019, Lamme 2014.

it has been nearly invisible in the massive debate about consciousness and higher-order awareness.[3] I'll try to change that in this chapter.

I'll start by setting up the key questions and positions in more detail. I'll then review the motivations for higher-order theories, and show how they either fail entirely or leave open whether we should take the Descending Road or the Ascending Road. The cases for higher-order theories tend to be merely correlational, leaving entirely open what might explain your awareness of a state that goes along with the conscious character of a state. And sometimes the putative considerations in favor of higher-order theories even turn out to support the Ascending Road better. When I've reviewed the case for higher-order theories, I will then survey some of the many further advantages of the Ascending Road over them.

When we accept Necessary Awareness, we should reject higher-order theories of consciousness in favor of the Ascending Road. The Ascending Road shifts our focus away from ambitiously reductive accounts of what consciousness is to questions about what consciousness does. But we can still get insight into what consciousness is. Part of what it is to be in a conscious mental state is to be in a state such that one is aware of it, and such that one is aware of it because of its conscious character. On the fuller picture we will develop in what is to come, conscious states are distinctive because it is of their nature to be the source of our awareness of them.

2. The Conclusion

The first important distinction for us to understand and to trace out is between the following two kinds of claims:

(**Necessary Awareness**): For any conscious mental state M and subject S, if S is in M, then S is aware of M.[4]

---

[3] Shoemaker 1996 on self-intimation and pain may be an exception. See also section 4.2 of Chalmers 2003, Chalmers 2013: 345, section 6 of Nida-Rümelin 2017, and especially Stoljar forthcoming.

[4] A more explicit but more cumbersome formulation might better proceed as follows: if S is in M, *and M is conscious*, then S is aware of M. That's because in principle perhaps one and the same mental state could be conscious at one time or in one possible situation, yet not conscious at another time or other possible situation. In what follows I will mainly bracket questions about the individuation of mental states, and will flag when they do matter.

(The Higher-Order Theory/The Descending Road): For any conscious mental state M and subject S, if S is in M, then M is conscious because S is aware of M.

Necessary Awareness is only a correlational claim, holding that consciousness is sufficient for inner awareness, but leaving the explanation of this correlation entirely open, and indeed whether there even is an explanation of this correlation. While in principle one might treat the claim as a stipulative definition of consciousness (Lycan 2001), it is far better to treat it as substantive to have a productive debate about it (Rosenthal 2005). On the other hand, the Descending Road itself entails Necessary Awareness, and also demands more. The Descending Road takes a stand on the explanation of the correlation between consciousness and inner awareness, and specifically expresses the stance common to higher-order theories of consciousness. Inner awareness comes first in the story here, and is the key to why a given state is conscious. (Notice that even if one did treat Necessary Awareness as a stipulative definition of consciousness, there would still be plenty of room to have a substantive debate about the direction of explanation between consciousness and inner awareness.)

The Descending Road is widely travelled by philosophers and scientists, but it is by no means the only path available. Many first-order theorists reject it for all mental states (and then go on to endorse alternative accounts of what makes a given mental state conscious).

(The First-order Theory/Never The Descending Road): For any conscious mental state M and subject S, it's not the case that, if S is in M, then M is conscious because S is aware of M.

But here we need to proceed with care. Since Necessary Awareness does not entail that any higher-order theory of consciousness is correct, it is perfectly possible to reject higher-order theories without rejecting Necessary Awareness. Contrast the set-up in the Stanford Encyclopedia of Philosophy that proceeds as follows:

> The major divide amongst representational theories of phenomenal consciousness in general, is between accounts that are provided in purely first-order terms and those that implicate higher-order representations of one sort or another
>
> (Carruthers and Gennaro 2020, sect. 2).

This formulation obscures the terrain. Consider a theory of consciousness in purely first-order terms—for example, one in terms of the distinctive kind of representational content of conscious mental states, or simply in terms of being in a certain kind of neural state. Even if those accounts do not explain consciousness in terms of higher-order representations, they could still implicate higher-order representations. Having such and such content, or being linked to such and such a neural state, might make it the case that a mental state is conscious, and also suffice for there to be higher-order representations of the mental state in the relevant subject. But the higher-order representation would not itself explain consciousness, it would instead itself just be along for the ride.

The omission is important. First-order theories have arguably been far too quick to deny Necessary Awareness. The live option remains for an explanatory chain in which some first-order factor X explains consciousness, and then explains inner awareness via consciousness explaining inner awareness:

Factor X->M is conscious->subject is aware of M

On the current set-up, first-order theorists are not committed to denying Necessary Awareness, and some might even be committed to explaining Necessary Awareness.

For another example of a formulation of the issues that obscures the terrain, consider this quote from Rosenthal:

> Higher-order theories all explain what it is for states to be conscious by appeal to an awareness of that state; because it is an awareness of another state, we can call it a higher-order awareness (HOA). No state of which one is not in any way aware is a conscious state. First-order theories, in contrast, deny that a state's being conscious involves any such HOA.
>
> (Rosenthal 2012: 1424)

The first sentence supplies us with a nice statement of higher-order theories of consciousness. As evidence that he seems to have their specific claims about explanatory priority in mind here, consider this remark later in that paper: "On higher-order theories, a state is conscious in virtue of one's being aware of that state" (2012: 1429). But the rest of our main embedded quote seems to conflate (1) the view that awareness of a state explains the state's being conscious and (2) the weaker view that being aware of a state is a necessary condition for the state's being conscious. When we reach the formulation of rival first-order theories of consciousness in the third sentence, we don't have a formulation that simply denies that awareness of a state explains the state's being conscious, which would in fact be the negation of the formulation of higher-order approaches in the first sentence. Instead, we have the stronger claim that conscious mental states can occur without awareness of them.[5]

We need a more fine-grained map.[6]

The gap between Necessary Awareness and higher-order theories of consciousness opens up the possibility of the following view:

(The Ascending Road): For any conscious mental state M and subject S, if S is in M, then S is aware of M because M is conscious.

The Ascending Road entails Necessary Awareness, but demands more, and in particular reverses the order of explanation proposed by higher-order theories of consciousness.

While the Ascending Road is less travelled, it has not been empty. Consider the Buddhist metaphor of consciousness as a lamp that illuminates itself.[7] On one natural reading of this metaphor, it is in the nature of a light to illuminate itself, and in the nature of consciousness to be aware of itself. Here we can read the metaphor as expressing the view that consciousness explains inner awareness rather than vice versa. As far as contemporary analytic and psychological/neuroscientific views of consciousness go, however, I am not clear on whether any explicitly sign up for the Ascending Road.[8]

I have set up the main claims in our discussion at a high level of abstraction, leaving open many further choice points. Here are some important

---

[5] For a similar issue, see Janzen 2008: 70–71, where he moves freely between the claims that "a conscious state is always a state whose subject is, in some way, aware (or conscious) of being in it" and "a subject's awareness of her mental state makes that state conscious."

While I am mainly discussing formulations by higher-order theorists here, I would also emphasize that first-order theorists have also been too quick to leap from their view to the falsehood of Necessary Awareness, just as higher-order theorists have been too quick to leap from the putative truth of Necessary Awareness to their views.

[6] While I won't pursue the issue here, our key distinctions might also raise complications for definitions of "neural correlates of consciousness" Chalmers 2000, Lau 2022: ch. 2).

[7] For more on this metaphor and its uses, see Garfield 2006: 207–209, Watson 2014, and Silins forthcoming. For more general treatments of consciousness and inner awareness in Buddhist philosophy, see Williams 1998, Yao 2005, Coseru 2012: ch. 8, Finnigan 2018, Coseru 2020, Ganeri 2012: ch. 9, and Garfield 2014: ch. 5.

[8] See note 3 for potential exceptions.

further dimensions of variation, where most of them are surveyed in more detail in Farrell and McClelland 2017, Stoljar 2021, or Giustina 2022a.

As far as the **object** of awareness is concerned, I am simply taking it to be the mental state M itself. Alternative targets of awareness include for example oneself, or the fact that one is in a given mental state (further candidates are laid out in Nida-Rümelin 2017 and Stoljar 2021). It is perhaps even coherent to say that there is no object of awareness here, and instead only some form of "intransitive" awareness or other form of awareness without an object.[9]

A further question concerns the **vehicle** of awareness. Perhaps the vehicle of awareness is M itself, so that we are concerned with reflexive inner awareness (Kriegel 2009a). Or perhaps the vehicle of awareness is instead some mental state not identical with M. Here I will entirely leave this issue open (for more on the issue see my forthcoming).

Another key issue concerns the **character** of inner awareness. One important question is whether the relevant form of awareness is itself conscious or not. Another is whether the relevant form of awareness can be reductively specified in terms of familiar notions such as those of attention, perception, thought, or knowledge, or whether the relevant form of awareness is sui generis, not reductively specifiable in terms of such notions (see the panoramic Table 1 of Brown et al. 2019: 5 for more options). A still further question concerns whether the relevant form of awareness consists in actual awareness of a conscious mental state, or instead only a disposition to be aware of a conscious mental state in such and such a way (e.g. Carruthers 2000). I will leave these questions wide open for the most part.

The final issue I will flag here concerns the **explanatory role** of awareness (for higher-order theories).[10] One less demanding task would be only to explain why a given mental state is conscious, leaving open why it has the specific conscious character it has. To simplify our discussion, I will generally leave the matter here. But a more ambitious project would have inner awareness take on the burden of explaining why a given conscious mental state has the specific conscious character it has. Since the conscious character of a mental state potentially has further more specific aspects, there are

---

[9] For discussion of the objectless option in a Sartrean and phenomenological vein, see Janzen 2008, sect. 6.2.2. and Thompson 2011. See also Brown 2015 and others on "nonrelational" versions of the higher-order approach.
[10] For more detail, see Farrell and McClelland 2017.

multiple potential targets of explanation here—for example, pertaining to the representational content of a mental state or instead to the attitude or relation one bears to that content.[11]

3. The Case for Higher-order Theories of Consciousness

An important line of motivation for higher-order theories of consciousness appeals to the sheer absurdity of being in a conscious mental state without being aware of it. The key idea, often expressed as the "Transitivity Principle", is put forth as being platitudinous in many places by David Rosenthal among others:[12]

> There is a natural way of understanding how conscious states differ from mental states that are not conscious. No mental state is conscious if the individual that is in that state is in no way aware of it. If somebody thinks, desires or feels something but is wholly unaware of doing so, then that thought, desire or feeling is not a conscious state.
>
> (Rosenthal 2012: 1425)[13]

Here I agree with Rosenthal and any others making this claim.[14] The problem is that the point only gets us to Necessary Awareness. The "Transitivity Principle" does not entail any theory or combination of theories that would explain a state's being conscious in terms of our awareness of it. The common move to higher-order theories from the putative platitude is an entirely optional leap.

---

[11] There are also questions about the kind of explanation offered, and whether it is causal or something stronger, or perhaps ultimately instead some form of metaphysical determination or grounding distinct from any explanatory relations.

For discussion of how relations of metaphysical determination or grounding might somehow back explanatory relations rather than simply being identical to them, see Koslicki 2012 or Dasgupta 2014.

[12] For a nice range of references to Brentano, Sartre and others, as well as further arguments of his own for Necessary Awareness, see Janzen 2008 ch. 4.

An important further line of argument for Necessary Awareness comes out of the Buddhist philosopher Dignaga's memory argument. See e.g. Ganeri 1999, Garfield 2006, Kellner 2010, Thompson 2011, Chadha 2017, Kriegel 2019, Giustina 2022a (who also offers interesting discussion of how to potentially bridge the gap between Necessary Awareness and higher-order theories)

[13] For further examples see Rosenthal 2005: 103, 109, 145.

[14] For dispute, see e.g. Dretske 1993, Thomasson 2006, Gertler 2012, Siewert 2013, or Stoljar 2021. For a line of response to some of their objections, see Giustina 2022b.

Another important line of argument for higher-order theories is contrastive and often empirical in character.[15] The first step is to look for examples of mental states of a kind such that some of the members are conscious and some are unconscious (we need not assume that any particular mental state that is conscious could have been unconscious, or vice versa). The next step is to argue that the conscious ones are such that we are aware of them, and the unconscious ones are not such that we are aware of them. The final move—not necessarily treated as a further step—is to conclude that some higher-order theory is true.

For a representative statement of the line of thought, consider again the *Stanford Encyclopedia of Philosophy*:

> Almost everyone accepts now, for example…that beliefs and desires can be activated unconsciously…If we ask what makes the difference between a conscious and an unconscious mental state, one natural answer is that conscious states are states that we are *aware of*…these are states that are objects of some sort of higher-order representation.
>
> (Carruthers and Gennaro 2020: sect. 2)

Just to be clear, the SEP entry is emphatically on the Descending Road, going well beyond merely discussing Necessary Awareness. In the opening of the entry, we have a robust statement of higher-order theories as follows:

> Higher-order cognitive theories maintain that phenomenal consciousness can be reductively explained in terms of representations (either experiences or thoughts) that are higher-order.
>
> (Carruthers and Gennaro 2020: sect. 1)

And we also have the following robust claim as a commitment of higher-order thought theories in a different passage:

> what *makes M* conscious is the existence of an *un*conscious HOT targeted on *M*
>
> (Carruthers and Gennaro 2020: sect. 4)

---

[15] For some empirically rich versions of the line, see e.g. Lau and Rosenthal 2011, Lau and Brown 2019, Brown et al 2019, or Lau 2022. For empirical discussions on the side of first-order theories, see e.g. Lamme 2014 or Raccah et al 2021. A useful and broader further survey is Seth and Bayne 2022.

Here again I would say we have made a leap. One way to bring out the issue is to distinguish two distinct explanatory tasks that can be in play when "we ask what makes the difference between a conscious and an unconscious mental state." One question simply seeks a filter to permit us to sort mental states into the bucket of consciousness or to throw them back into the sea of unconsciousness. We can accomplish this task with a distinguishing feature of conscious mental states, one that is not shared with unconscious mental states. Here a version of Necessary Awareness can suffice when coupled with the claim that we are not aware of our non-conscious states, we do not need to go all the way to a higher-order theory. That said, the details of the version of Necessary Awareness will matter here. We are aware in some sense of some of our unconscious mental states—for example, I always know that I always believe that Riga is in Latvia.[16] Still, there arguably are more specific forms of awareness such that we have them for all of our conscious mental states, and not for any of our unconscious mental states. The proponent of higher-order theories is at any rate in no position to deny that. So it remains that we can fish out all and only the conscious mental states simply with a correlational claim rather than any view about consciousness being explained by inner awareness.

A different way of asking "what makes the difference" looks more directly and ambitiously for an explanation of why any given conscious mental state is conscious, again assuming that conscious mental states are such that we are aware of them, and unconscious ones are not such that we are aware of them. As the SEP puts it here:

> What is it about a conscious perception that renders it phenomenal, that a blindsight perceptual state would correspondingly lack?
> (Carruthers and Gennaro 2020: sect. 2)[17]

Their assumption seems to be that our higher-order awareness of our conscious perceptions is the best or even only candidate standing to answer their question. But a correlation between consciousness and awareness does

---

[16] There might also be some sense in which we are always aware of our actions (as for example per Rödl 2007), but it need not follow that all of our actions are conscious. Thanks here to Carlotta Pavese.

[17] Or as Lau and Rosenthal put it, "how does awareness arise?", and then go on to formulate variants of higher-order approaches along the following lines: "when a higher-order thought-like representation results in one's being aware of a first-order representation" (Lau and Rosenthal 2011: 366).

not suffice to supply an answer to their question. We still need more in favor of the distinctively higher-order conclusion that inner awareness explains consciousness. In particular, it remains entirely possible that whatever resources a first-order theorist offers to explain why a given mental state is conscious, will in turn thereby be able to provide an explanation also of why we have awareness of the given conscious mental state.

A closely related argument in the vicinity starts from the putative correlation between conscious mental states and awareness of them, and demands an explanation of that correlation. Here I suspect that many have simply assumed that higher-order theories provide the only candidate explanation of why all conscious mental states go along with awareness of them. But this move overlooks the possibility that all conscious mental states go along with awareness of them since consciousness explains inner awareness (or because some factor X explains consciousness where consciousness in turn explains awareness). As things stand, the Ascending Road is in an equally strong position to explain the correlation in question.

Before turning to potential positive advantages of the Ascending Road, I'll briefly consider one further way one might try to justify higher-order theories. Here the idea is to try to use introspection to answer the question of whether the higher-order approach is correct.

The first problem is that introspection is not even a promising way to getting us to Necessary Awareness. Of course whenever we turn our introspective awareness towards our conscious mental states, we only find conscious mental states of which we are aware. Introspection is not going to light up any mental states that are conscious of which we are not aware at all. But this is a predictable artifact of our use of an introspective method rather than a trustworthy perspective on reality beyond (introspective) awareness (see Kriegel 2009b, 2012).

Second, even if introspection somehow could get us to Necessary Awareness, the move beyond to higher-order theories is too far of a reach. It would take an extremely theoretically sophisticated and discriminating introspective capacity to detect the direction of explanation between the conscious status of a mental state and our inner awareness of that state. As far as I know, no higher-order theorist ascribes such a rich capacity to introspection, it is hard enough for our non-introspective cognition to work with the distinction properly.

In sum, higher-order theories take the Descending Road, and tell us that our awareness of a conscious mental state explains why the mental state is conscious. But their cases for their view at best establish only the claim that conscious mental states are correlated with our awareness of them, and ignore the possibility that our awareness of our conscious mental states is instead explained by their conscious character.

4. The Case for the Ascending Road

4.1 Explaining the Correlation between Consciousness and Inner Awareness

What is there to say in favor of the Ascending Road?

I will continue to assume that all conscious states indeed are such that we are aware of them. I will also assume that there is some explanation of why all conscious mental states are such that we are aware of them, and I will narrow our focus to a competition between the Ascending Road and higher-order theories as an explanation of the correlation. Our question is then about which of the two views provides a better explanation of the correlation (I discuss further options in my forthcoming).

To show that the Ascending Road provides a better explanation of the correlation between consciousness and awareness, I will map out how the Ascending Road easily avoids classic objections to higher-order theories (for representative exposition of such objections, with useful further references, see Carruthers and Gennaro 2020: sect. 7). Here we will also gain a better understanding of the commitments of the Ascending Road.

First consider the "rock" objection (Goldman 1993). Whether or not the rock objection is particularly strong, it is useful to start with since the irrelevance of the objection to the Ascending Road is vivid.

So there Dwayne Johnson is, knocked out stone cold after a stunt gone wrong on the set of *The Riverboat*. We are looking at him in full awareness of the Rock, but our awareness of him at this time is in no way capable of making the Rock conscious at this time. By the same token it might seem that our own awareness of any of our own mental states should not be able to make them conscious either.

The rock objection may or may not be fatal to higher-order theories, insofar as they can zero in a kind of awareness or object of awareness that does not admit of a parallel with the kind of awareness we have as spectators of the Rock. But there is a challenge here all the same for higher-order theories.

There is no challenge here for the Ascending Road. Given that the view ascends to higher-order representations from consciousness rather than descending to consciousness from higher-order representations, the view is not committed to any non-trivial sufficiency of higher-order representations for consciousness (I'll give more detail about why in a moment). The view does not even threaten to make bad predictions about cases along the lines of the Rock. For the same sort of reason, Necessary Awareness is also not challenged by the Rock.[18]

A second, arguably stronger line of objection insists that, since higher-order representations can misrepresent in various ways, we should not expect them to suffice for the presence of consciousness. For example, presumably we can have higher-order representations when no conscious state putatively targeted is present at all, a sort of hallucination of a conscious mental state (see e.g. Neander 1998 or Block 2011 a, b). Here we would have the presence of the appropriate form of higher-order representation that is supposed to suffice for the presence of a certain conscious mental state, in the absence of any such mental state. Presumably there can also be higher-order representations that misrepresent a mental state as conscious when it is not, or misrepresent the specific character of consciousness it has, a sort of illusion of a conscious mental state. Taking attendance here to generate a potential counterexample, we arguably can mark the right sort of higher-order representation or awareness as present, and yet must mark the appropriate conscious mental state required as absent. Higher-order theories would then be false.

The challenge may or may not successfully block higher-order theories. Once we work in all the relevant qualifications about the character of the relevant higher-order representation or awareness, perhaps the opponent is not able to mark exactly the right kinds of higher-order resources as present while the conscious mental states remain absent. For example, perhaps the higher-order representations present need to be appropriately non-inferential,

---

[18] There is a variant of the rock objection constructed around cases of awareness specifically of mental states. On this line of thought, it is conceivable for a creature to have all manner of relevant forms of awareness of its own mental states, without that awareness yet sufficing for those mental states to be conscious. Here we are to conceive of a counterpart of Dwayne Johnson as replete with inner awareness, while also being a so-called "zombie" with no consciousness at all. The conclusion is that higher-order awareness is the wrong sort of wand to conjure consciousness. (The line of objection need not proceed in terms of extreme cases of conceivability, but could instead try to use actual cases in which someone has important forms of awareness of a mental state that is still not conscious.)

This line of objection is also inert against theories that take the Ascending Road. These theories never said that higher-order representations can conjure consciousness.

or perceptual, or non-conceptual. Perhaps once those specific kinds of representations are marked present, corresponding conscious mental states will be present as well.[19]

If you take the Ascending Road, you do not face the objection at all. The direction of the Ascending Road is from conscious mental states to awareness or representations of them, not from higher-order awareness or representations to conscious states. So the view only makes predictions about cases in which a conscious mental state is already present. To challenge the Ascending Road with counterexamples, you need to start with cases where we do mark conscious mental states as present. And there's no logical room on any view for a case in which a conscious mental state is present, and yet *mis*represented as being present. (For the same sort of reason, Necessary Awareness is also not challenged here either.)

We can clarify the advantage of the Ascending Road via a parallel with the distinction between self-intimation and infallibility in debates about self-knowledge (Shoemaker 1996). Self-Intimation is the claim that, if you are in a mental state M, then you believe that you are in M. Infallibility is the claim that, if you believe that you are in a mental state M, then you are in M. Self-Intimation ascends, Infallibility descends. As many have noted in the context of debates about self-knowledge, Self-Intimation does not imply Infallibility. There is plenty of logical room for the possibility that, even though being in M suffices for believing you are in M, believing that you are in M does not conversely suffice for being in M.

The Ascending Road parallels the structure of Self-Intimation, higher-order theories parallel the structure of Infallibility. Given that the Ascending Road does not work downwards from higher-order representations to conscious mental states, it can allow all manner of misrepresenting higher-order representations in the absence of corresponding conscious mental states.

We can be more explicit about the commitments of the Ascending Road. The only accuracy guaranteed by the formulation of the Ascending Road is the following: if you have a higher-order representation that you are in M because you are in M, then you are in M. But everyone should agree about that. The Ascending Road also allows that, if you have a higher-order representation that is a case of true belief or knowledge that you are in M, then you are in M. Again, everybody should allow for that. These are all cases in which it is trivial that some form of higher-order representation is accurate.

---

[19] A more intricate line of response can be found in Brown 2015.

I'll make just one more point about the commitments of the Ascending Road. Some higher-order theories narrow down to a form of higher-order representation that is a better candidate to suffice for consciousness, say non-inferential perceptual representation that you are in M. Some versions of the Ascending Road might also work with that form of representation too, holding that when you are in a conscious mental M, you have a non-inferential perceptual representation that you are in M because you are in M. You might think that at least these versions of the Ascending Road will have to say that this privileged form of higher-order representation suffices for consciousness. But they don't. They do prohibit any scenario in which both (1) someone has a non-inferential perceptual representation that she is in M because she is in M, and (2) she is not in M. But they can still allow for a hallucinatory form of non-inferential perceptual representation that you are in M, when you are not in M. These would simply have to be cases where you do not have the higher-order representation because you are in M.

All versions of the Ascending Road require that conscious mental states suffice for some form of awareness or representation of them. Nothing in the formulation of the Ascending Road requires that the relevant form of awareness or representation can be present only because of consciousness. Going back to the Buddhist metaphor, even if consciousness is a lamp that illuminates itself, that leaves open the possibility that light of an equal color and brightness could sometimes come from a source other than the lamp.

Finally, consider the important objection that higher-order theories generate a vicious regress (for more discussion see e.g. Janzen 2008, Siewart 2013, or Stoljar 2018). Here I take the objection to be generated by the specific assumption that, if you are aware of a mental state M without being consciously aware of that mental state, then your higher-order awareness won't be capable of making M conscious. However, if your higher-order awareness of M (AM) must itself be conscious to make M conscious, we will now need a distinct instance of awareness of your awareness of M (AAM) to make AM conscious. And so on.

Now, the higher-order theorist can debate whether higher-order awareness must be conscious to do its thing, or even whether the regress in question is vicious. Indeed, the higher-order theorist must debate such points to defend the theory. Since the proponent of the Ascending Road never said that higher-order awareness ever makes a mental state conscious (or that conscious mental states make us have specifically conscious awareness of them), the proponent of the Ascending Road can sit out this debate.

Many of the most important objections specifically targeted against higher-order theories do not even arise for the Ascending Road.[20] I do not see how analogues of them arise either. Now, we do so far lack a full account of exactly how a conscious mental state might make us aware of it. We have formulated the Ascending Road at a fully general level, leaving open whether the connection between consciousness and inner awareness is through causation, or constitution, or some further option. But this silence of the general formulation of the view gives us no reason to suspect that conscious mental states cannot make us aware of them—there is no promise at all to the view that conscious states are incapable of making us aware of them. While there is to some extent a mystery about how inner awareness of a mental state could generate consciousness, giving us at least some reason to suspect that higher-order theories are mistaken, there is no comparable mystery about how a conscious mental state could generate awareness of it.

At the same time, the Ascending Road is not simply orthogonal to higher-order theories of consciousness. It is not that one approach is a theory of inner awareness, and the other a theory of consciousness. Instead, both approaches promise an explanation of the correlation between consciousness and inner awareness, and conflict in their reverse orders of explanation of the correlation. Insofar as philosophers are sympathetic to Necessary Awareness, and seek an explanation of it, the more minimal commitments and lighter explanatory burden of the Ascending Road should make them prefer the Ascending Road to higher-order theories. Assuming that Necessary Awareness is true, the Ascending Road is more likely to be true given its weaker demands and simpler open explanatory questions.

4.2 Objections and Replies

One might protest that, even if higher-order theories face more objections than the Ascending Road, this disadvantage is cancelled out by their

---

[20] A further objection is set out in Dretske 1995: 116–122, according to which higher-order theories imply that consciousness is epiphenomenal, assuming that our being aware of a mental state does not change its causal profile. As far as I can tell the Ascending Road dodges this objection as well. Causal versions of the view will even require that conscious mental states be causally efficacious in generating our awareness of them.

advantage of providing us with a richer theoretical picture of consciousness. Here we can go back to the idea that higher-order theories answer the question of "what makes the difference between a conscious and an unconscious mental state" (Carruthers and Gennaro 2020: sect. 2). In particular, higher-order theories offer an account of what it is for a mental state to be conscious, in terms that do not themselves employ any concept of consciousness. As Alex Byrne puts it when setting up the target of his critical paper:

> there is another interpretation [i.e. the higher-order theory] which holds out the promise of a *reductive analysis* of consciousness: an account that gives necessary and sufficient conditions for a mental state to be conscious in terms that do not presuppose or employ the notion of consciousness.
>
> (Byrne 1997: 103–104)

In contrast, I have emphasized that the Ascending Road does not make predictions about how any higher-order representation generates, constitutes or otherwise explains consciousness. Perhaps this reticence of the Ascending Road undermines its overall theoretical profile.

My response is that, on at least one reading of the question, "what is it for a mental state to be conscious?" the Ascending Road itself can be supplemented so as to answer that question better. The point is that, at least on one understanding of the primary ambition of higher-order theories, that ambition can be attained more economically by the Ascending Road.

The Ascending Road can be smoothly supplemented as follows so as to tell us what a conscious mental state is:

(Ascending Road PLUS): For any mental state M, M is conscious if and only if M is such that, if you are in M, then you are aware of M because you are in M.

The Ascending Road on its own holds that all conscious mental states make us have inner awareness of them, thereby leaving open the possibility that all non-conscious mental states also make us have inner awareness of them. Our supplement closes off this possibility with the further claim that only conscious mental states are such that being in them suffices to make us have inner awareness of them. Here we have a feature of all and only conscious mental states, formulated without the use of any term or concept for consciousness. On at least one minimal reading of "reductive analysis," the one active in the quote above from Byrne, we now have a "reductive analysis" of consciousness. But we do not have to put the point in such terms, we can also put the point simply in terms of non-circular necessary and sufficient conditions for consciousness. (Here we repurpose the earlier point that the Ascending Road can offer an account of "what makes the difference" between conscious and unconscious mental states.) The Ascending Road can be extended to offer an account of what consciousness is without taking on many further commitments and burdens of higher-order theories. In particular, we still avoid the claim that any form of awareness non-trivially suffices for consciousness. The key defining feature of a conscious mental state here is not quite the feature of our being aware of the state. The key feature of a conscious mental state here is instead the feature of being such that, if you are in the mental state, then you are aware of it because you are in it.[21] And it is again trivial that you are aware of a state you are in *because* you are in it only if you in fact are in it.

One might object that the proposed benefit of the supplemented Ascending Road is better described as that of providing a "mark of the conscious mental", as opposed to any genuine reductive analysis deserving of the time.[22] In order to have a proper reductive analysis of consciousness, we arguably need to go beyond necessary and sufficient conditions to something that underlies and determines the presence of consciousness (specified without using the notion of consciousness), as opposed to something above consciousness determined by consciousness. In other words, a proper reduction would arguably provide a maker of consciousness rather than a mark of consciousness.

In response, I would first emphasize that it's unclear whether higher-order theorists were firmly committed to identifying anything more than a mark of conscious mental states. Consider for instance the following fairly relaxed demand from Rosenthal of theories of consciousness:

> However, whatever other explanations a theory of consciousness may provide, it must at a minimum tell us how mental states that are conscious differ from those that are not.
>
> (Rosenthal 2012: 1424)

---

[21] Compare Rosenthal 2005: 27–29. Here we are likely to disagree about whether being conscious is a contingent feature of a mental state. According to the Ascending Road PLUS, any mental state that is conscious could not have failed to be conscious.

[22] Thanks here to Uriah Kriegel.

By adding a thesis about what all and only conscious mental states do, the Ascending Road did tell us how mental states that are conscious differ from those that are not. So whether or not the proposal deserves the name "reductive" or not, the Ascending Road can meet the particular bar proposed here by Rosenthal.

Here we face a fork in the Ascending Road. One option is for the Ascending Road to reject robustly reductive approaches to consciousness. There is after all a fair question of what a genuine reduction exactly is, as well as about whether any such reduction is desirable or attainable. On this fork, we could pursue a path analogous to the knowledge-first program of Williamson 2000. Williamson's project is broadly to use knowledge as an explanatory tool, rather than to try to explain knowledge in any robustly reductive way (see also Unger 1975). One might likewise set out to explain inner awareness and other conditions in terms of consciousness, rather than explain consciousness in terms of inner awareness or other conditions.

That said, the Ascending Road can instead be combined with more ambitiously reductive approaches to consciousness. On this path, one endorses some first-order account of how consciousness is determined, and then traces a chain of explanation/determination from the first-order resource, to a conscious mental state, to inner awareness of the mental state. The chain again would look like this:

Factor X->M is conscious->subject is aware of M

Here we could think of inner awareness of consciousness as being ultimately determined by whatever resource the first-order account privileged. Here inner awareness is a mark of consciousness stemming from an underlying maker, in other words, a maker's mark.

In sum, even if higher-order theories offer the ostensible advantage of non-circular necessary and sufficient conditions for consciousness, that advantage is also offered by the supplemented Ascending Road, while still also avoiding the host of classic objections to higher-order theories. If the advantage of higher-order theories is supposed to be some more robustly reductive account of consciousness, even that advantage can be matched by coupling the Ascending Road to a first-order theory, again while avoiding the host of classic objections to higher-order theories.

At this point, you might wonder whether there even are any objections to higher-order theories that do also bear on the Ascending Road. Indeed there are, at least insofar as they bear on the Necessary Awareness thesis entailed by them both.

A key challenge here would hold there isn't even a correlation between consciousness and awareness to explain. This sort of traditional objection to higher-order theories is not targeted specifically at the explanatory ambition and direction of that ambition of higher-order theories (even though in practice it seems to be pushed without distinguishing between Necessary Awareness and the further specifics of higher-order theories).

One variant of the challenge proceeds in terms of limits on our introspective self-knowledge. Given plausible limits on our self-knowledge, perhaps there are many cases when we are in a conscious mental state without being aware of it. While I agree that there are dramatic limits on our self-knowledge, it is straightforward to deny that this is relevant to the assessment of Necessary Awareness (see also e.g. Rosenthal 2005: ch. 4). But being aware of a mental state one is in need not require knowledge that one is in it. The relevant form of awareness in Necessary Awareness can coexist with ignorance of our conscious mental states.[23]

A more promising variant is the over-intellectualization objection pushed by Dretske (1995) and many others. This challenge uses putative cases of animals or human infants who arguably have conscious mental states without (yet) the equipment to have awareness of any of those mental states. (Here we are concerned with blindness to conscious mental states, not with hallucinations or illusions about them.)

In response, we can remind the objector that, in order to over-intellectualize, you need to intellectualize in the first place. Since the relevant form of awareness of conscious mental states can come in perceptual, attentional, or sui generis forms, it's not at all clear why a capacity for inner awareness shouldn't be widely available across the animal kingdom, at least for any creature complicated enough to have consciousness in the first place. (A separate line of response could instead work with a more cognitively demanding form of awareness, just in a dispositional rather than non-dispositional form. I will continue to set that option aside.)

It would be nice to have a more direct motivation for the Ascending Road. My suggestion is that we have had it all along.

Here I ask you to revisit the idea that there is something absurd about a case in which someone is in a conscious mental state without being aware of it. Assuming that you share this sense with Rosenthal and so many others, my contention is that this sense goes beyond the correlational claim that we have awareness of each of our conscious mental states. I instead suggest that

---

[23] For further relevant discussion of introspection, see Smithies 2019: ch. 5.

many of us have a sense that this scenario is impossible because conscious mental states make us aware of them. Here we can return to the Buddhist metaphor of consciousness as a lamp that illuminates itself. The idea is not just that conscious mental states are illuminated somehow, the idea is that they illuminate themselves due to their conscious nature.

There is indeed something absurd about a case of a mental state's being conscious without our being aware of it. When you scratch deeper at why such a case seems absurd, I hope you reach the more explanatorily satisfying sense that such a case is impossible because conscious mental states make us aware of them.

Ideally we would have further direct considerations in favor of the Ascending Road. In the meantime, at least those who already accepted Necessary Awareness should sign up, and those who already accepted higher-order theories should switch over.

5. Conclusion

The distinction between the Ascending Road and higher-order theories is subtle and under-explored. Most professed higher-order theorists, not to mention first-order theorists, have overlooked it entirely in their explicit formulations and motivations for their views. For all that, I suspect that many ostensible higher-order theorists have been on the Ascending Road all along, especially given the point that the Ascending Road offers at least one form of an account of what consciousness is.

Perhaps many higher-order theorists were innerly confident that it is of the nature of a conscious state to make us aware of it, just unaware that that was their thought.[24]

References

Block, Ned. 2007. "Consciousness, Accessibility, and the Mesh Between Psychology and Neuroscience." *Behavioral and Brain Sciences* 30 (5–6): 481–499.

---

[24] Thanks to Ned Block, Monima Chadha, David Chalmers, Shao-Pu Kang, Malcolm Keating, Uriah Kriegel, Edvard Meza, Matthias Michel, Carlotta Pavese, Adriana Renero, David Rosenthal, Julie Rowbotham, Declan Smithies, Daniel Stoljar, and Lu Teng. Thanks also to audiences at the 2023 ASSC and at Lingnan University.

Block, Ned. 2011a. "Perceptual Consciousness Overflows Cognitive Access." *Trends in Cognitive Sciences* 15 (12): 567–575.

Block, Ned. 2011b. "The Higher-order Approach to Consciousness Is Defunct." *Analysis* 71 (3): 419–431.

Block, Ned. 2019. "What Is Wrong with the No-report Paradigm and How to Fix It." *Trends in Cognitive Science* 23 (12): 1003–1013.

Brown, Richard. 2015. "The HOROR Theory of Phenomenal Consciousness." *Philosophical Studies* 172: 1783–1794.

Brown, Richard et al. 2019. "Understanding the Higher-order Approach to Consciousness." *Trends in Cognitive Sciences* 23 (9): 754–768.

Carruthers, Peter. 2000. *Phenomenal Consciousness: A Naturalistic Theory.* Cambridge, UK: Cambridge University Press.

Carruthers, Peter, and Rocco Gennaro. 2020. "Higher-order Theories of Consciousness", *The Stanford Encyclopedia of Philosophy*, Edward N. Zalta (ed.), https://plato.stanford.edu/archives/fall2020/entries/consciousness-higher/.

Chadha, Monima. 2017. "Inner Awareness is Essential to Consciousness: A Buddhist-Abhidharma Perspective." *Review of Philosophy and Psychology* (8): 83–101.

Chalmers, David J. 2000. What is a neural correlate of consciousness? In *Neural Correlates of Consciousness*, edited by Thomas Metzinger, 17–39. Cambridge: MIT Press.

Chalmers, David. 2003. "The Content and Epistemology of Phenomenal Belief." In *Consciousness: New Philosophical Perspectives*, edited by Q. Smith and A. Jokic, 220–272. Oxford: Oxford University Press.

Chalmers, David. 2013. "The Contents of Consciousness: Reply to Hellie, Peacocke and Siegel." *Analysis Reviews* 73 (2): 345–368.

Coseru, Christian. 2012. *Perceiving Reality: Consciousness, Intentionality, and Cognition in Buddhist Philosophy.* Oxford: Oxford University Press.

Coseru, Christian. 2020. "Whose Consciousness? Reflexivity and the Problem of Self-Knowledge." *Buddhist Philosophy of Consciousness*, 121–153. Leiden, The Netherlands: Brill.

Dasgupta, Shamik. 2014. "On the Plurality of Grounds." *Philosophers' Imprint* 14 (20): 1–28.

Dretske, Fred. 1993. "Conscious Experience." *Mind* 102 (406): 263–283.

Dretske, Fred. 1995. *Naturalizing the Mind.* Cambridge, MA: MIT Press.

Farrell, Jonathan, and Tom McClelland. 2017. "Consciousness and Inner Awareness." *Review of Philosophy and Psychology* 8 (1): 1–22.

Finnigan, Bronwyn. 2018. "Is Consciousness Reflexively Self-aware? A Buddhist Analysis." *Ratio* 31 (4): 389–401.

Ganeri, Jonardon. 1999. "Self-intimation, Memory and Personal Identity." *Journal of Indian Philosophy* 27 (5): 469–483.

Ganeri, Jonardon 2012. *The Self: Naturalism, Consciousness, and the First-Person Stance*. Oxford: Oxford University Press.

Garfield, Jay L. 2006. "The Conventional Status of Reflexive Awareness: What's at Stake in a Tibetan Debate?" *Philosophy East and West* 56 (2): 201–228.

Garfield, Jay L. 2014. *Engaging Buddhism: Why It Matters to Philosophy*. Oxford: Oxford University Press.

Gertler, Brie. 2012. "Conscious States as Objects of Awareness: On Uriah Kriegel, Subjective Consciousness: A Self-representational Theory." *Philosophical Studies* 159 (3): 447–455.

Giustina, Anna. 2022a. "A Defense of Inner Awareness: The Memory Argument Revisited." *Review of Philosophy and Psychology* 13 (406): 1–23.

Giustina, Anna. 2022b. "Nature Does Not Yet Say No to Inner Awareness: Reply to Stoljar." *Erkenntnis* 1–11

Goldman, Alvin. 1993. "Consciousness, Folk-psychology, and Cognitive Science." *Consciousness and Cognition* 2 (4): 364–382.

Janzen, Greg 2008. *The Reflexive Nature of Consciousness*. Amsterdam: John Benjamins.

Kellner, Birgit. 2010. "Self-awareness (Svasaṃvedana) in Dignāga's Pramāṇasamuccaya And-vṛtti: A Close Reading." *Journal of Indian Philosophy* 38 (3): 203–231.

Koslicki, Kathrin. 2012. "Varieties of Ontological Dependence." In F. Correia and B. Schnieder (eds), *Metaphysical Grounding: Understanding the Structure of Reality*, 186–213. Cambridge, UK: Cambridge University Press.

Kriegel, Uriah. 2009a. *Subjective Consciousness*. Oxford: Oxford University Press.

Kriegel Uriah. 2009b. "Self-representationalism and Phenomenology." *Philosophical Studies* 143 (3): 357–381.

Kriegel Uriah. 2012. "In Defense of Self-representationalism: Reply to Critics." *Philosophical Studies* 159 (3): 475–484.

Kriegel, Uriah. 2019. "Dignāga's Argument for the Awareness Principle: An Analytic Refinement." *Philosophy East and West* 69 (1): 143–155.

Lamme, Victor. 2014. "The Crack Of Dawn: Perceptual Functions and Neural Mechanisms That Mark the Transition from Unconscious Processing to Conscious Vision." In *Open MIND*. Frankfurt am Main: MIND Group.

Lau, Hakwan. 2022. *In Consciousness We Trust: The Cognitive Neuroscience of Subjective Experience*. Oxford: Oxford University Press.

Lau, Hakwan, and Brown, Richard. 2019. "The Emperor's New Phenomenology? The Empirical Case for Conscious Experience without First-order Representations." In *Blockheads! Essays on Ned Block's Philosophy of Mind and Consciousness*, edited by A. Pautz and D. Stoljar, 171–198. Cambridge, MA: MIT Press.

Lau, Hakwan, and Rosenthal, David. 2011. "Empirical Support for Higher-order Theories of Conscious Awareness." *Trends in Cognitive Sciences* 15 (8): 365–373.

Lycan, William G. 2001. A Simple Argument for a Higher-Order Representation Theory of Consciousness. *Analysis* 61 (1): 3–4.

McClelland, Tom. 2020. "Self-representational Theories of Consciousness." In *Oxford Handbook of Philosophy of Consciousness*, edited by U. Kriegel, 459–481. Oxford: Oxford University Press.

Neander, Karen. 1998. "The Division of Phenomenal Labor: A Problem for Representational Theories of Consciousness." *Philosophical Perspectives* 12: 411–434.

Nida-Rümelin, Martine. 2017. "Self-Awareness." *Review of Philosophy and Psychology* 8 (1): 55–82.

Raccah, O., Block, N., and Fox, K. C. R. 2021. "Does the Prefrontal Cortex Play an Essential Role in Consciousness? Insights from Intracranial Electrical Stimulation of the Human Brain." *Journal of Neuroscience* 41 (10): 2076–2087.

Rödl, Sebastian. 2007. *Self-Consciousness*. Cambridge, MA: Harvard University Press.

Rosenthal, David. 2005. *Consciousness and Mind*. Oxford: Clarendon Press.

Rosenthal, David. 2012. "Higher-order Awareness, Misrepresentation and Function." *Philos Trans R Soc Lond B Biol Sci.* 367 (1594): 1424–1438.

Seth, Anil K., and Tim Bayne. 2022. "Theories of Consciousness." *Nature Reviews Neuroscience* 23 (7): 1–14.

Shoemaker, Sydney. 1996. *The First Person Perspective and Other Essays*. New York: Cambridge University Press.

Siewert, Charles. 2013. "Phenomenality and Self-Consciousness." In *Phenomenal Intentionality*, edited by U. Kriegel, 235–259. New York: Oxford University Press.

Silins, Nicholas. forthcoming. "The Lamp that Illuminates Itself: Consciousness and Inner Awareness." *In Consciousness and Inner Awareness*, edited by A. Giustina, D. Bordini, and A. Dewalque. Cambridge: Cambridge University Press.

Smithies, Declan. 2019. *The Epistemic Role of Consciousness*. New York: Oxford University Press.

Stoljar, Daniel. 2018. "The Regress Objection to Reflexive Theories of Consciousness." *Analytic Philosophy* 59 (3): 293–308.

Stoljar, Daniel. 2023. "Is There a Persuasive Argument for an Inner Awareness Theory of Consciousness?" *Erkenntnis* (88): 1555–1575.

Stoljar, Daniel. forthcoming. "A Euthyphro Dilemma for Higher-order Theories of Consciousness." In *Grounding and Consciousness*, edited by G. Rabin. Oxford: Oxford University Press.

Thomasson, Amie. 2006. "Self-Awareness and Self-Knowledge." *Psyche* 12 (2): 1–15.

Thompson, Evan. 2011. "Self-No-Self? Memory and Reflexive Awareness." In *Self, No Self?: Perspectives from Analytical, Phenomenological, and Indian Traditions*, edited by Mark Siderits et al., 157–75. Oxford: Oxford University Press.

Unger, Peter. 1975. *Ignorance: A Case for Skepticism*. Oxford: Oxford University Press.

Watson, Alex. 2014. "Light as an Analogy for Cognition in Buddhist Idealism." *Journal of Indian Philosophy* 42: 401–421.

Williams, Paul. 1998. *The Reflexive Nature of Awareness: A Tibetan Madhyamaka Defence*. Richmond: Curzon Press.

Williamson, Timothy. 2000. *Knowledge and Its Limits*. Oxford: Oxford University Press.

Yao, Zhihua. 2005. *The Buddhist Theory of Self-Cognition*. London: Routledge.

Nicholas Silins, *The Conscious Theory of Higher-Orderness* In: *Oxford Studies in Philosophy of Mind Volume 4*. Edited by: Uriah Kriegel, Oxford University Press. © Nicholas Silins 2024.
DOI: 10.1093/9780198924159.003.0012

BOOK SYMPOSIUM ON DAVID CHALMERS' *REALITY+*

13
Précis of *Reality+*

David J. Chalmers

Reality+ is intended as a work of technophilosophy. Inspired by Patricia Churchland's concept of neurophilosophy, technophilosophy is a two-way interaction between philosophy and technology: philosophy sheds light on technology, technology sheds light on philosophy.

One area where technophilosophy is already very familiar is in the philosophy of artificial intelligence. We can ask philosophical questions to shed light on AI: e.g. are artificial minds genuine minds? We can also use AI to shed light on philosophical questions about human minds: what is the nature of the mind, and which systems have minds?

Reality+ applies a technophilosophical treatment to issues about virtual reality (VR). It asks philosophical questions about virtual reality: e.g. are virtual worlds real worlds? It also uses VR to address many traditional questions about reality: e.g. what is the nature of reality, and what can we know about it?

Some terminology: a virtual world is an interactive and computer-generated environment. A virtual reality environment is an immersive, interactive, and computer-generated environment. A typical videogame on a desktop computer involves a virtual world but not virtual reality, because it is not immersive. A typical interactive digital environment experienced using a VR headset is virtual reality, because it is immersive.

The central thesis of *Reality+* is *virtual reality is genuine reality*. This breaks down into three central theses: one metaphysical, one epistemological, and one value-theoretic.

1. Objects and events in virtual reality are real and not illusory.
2. We can't know we're not living in a virtual reality.
3. We can live a meaningful life in virtual reality.

A fourth thesis concerns the philosophy of mind: virtual (and augmented) minds are genuine minds. This roughly involves the thesis that AI systems can be conscious and that extending the mind with augmented reality technology (such as glasses that augment the physical world with digital information) is possible.

A general strand running throughout the book is the use of virtual worlds to respond to the problem of external-world skepticism (a line I first explored in my 2003 article "The Matrix as Metaphysics"). The second thesis above, that we can't know we're not living in VR, may seem to imply external-world skepticism, but the crucial first thesis, that objects in VR are real, blocks the implication. Even if we're in a virtual world like the Matrix, things around us are real and many things are much as they seem.

Underlying this response to external-world skepticism is a sort of structuralism about the physical world, akin to the structural realism that has become central in the philosophy of physics. The rough idea is that the truth of our ordinary external-world claims depends primarily on the causal structure of the external world, and that a simulation of a world has roughly the same causal structure as the world it is simulating: so if our external-world claims would be true in the unsimulated world, they will be true in the simulated world.

Chapters 1 and 2 of the book introduce the issues. Chapter 1 distinguishes questions about knowledge, about reality, and about value, both where virtual worlds are concerned and where ordinary reality is concerned, and introduces the three major theses above.

Chapter 2 elucidates the simulation hypothesis, which says that we are living in a lifelong virtual world. Simulations and virtual worlds are nearly coextensive in principle, but "virtual world" is typically used for the (often smaller-scale) worlds we create, while "simulation" is typically used for the (often larger-scale) worlds of the sort that we might perhaps already be in. I distinguish various sorts of simulation, and make an initial case that we can't know we're not in a simulation.

Chapters 3–5 focus on epistemology. Chapter 3 presents Descartes' central skeptical arguments from the first Meditation through the lens of VR. Chapter 4 explores numerous standard responses to these arguments (from God, idealism, verificationism, dogmatism, simplicity, and more) and argues that none succeeds.

The central argument considered in these chapters is a standard Cartesian argument for external-world skepticism, placed in the key of simulation.

1. You can't know you're not in a simulation.
2. If you can't know you're not in a simulation, you can't know anything about the external world.

_____

3. So: You can't know anything about the external world.

In this part of the book, I am especially concerned to defend premise 1, which is a version of the epistemological thesis laid out at the start. I eventually respond to the argument by using the metaphysical thesis at the start to reject premise 2.

Chapter 5 develops a version of the Bostrom-style simulation argument, and uses this argument to make a strong case that we can't know we're not living in a simulation. My preferred version of the simulation argument (refined over the course of the chapter) is as follows:

1. If there are no sim blockers, most humanlike beings are sims.
2. If most humanlike beings are sims, we are probably sims.

---

3. So: If there are no sim blockers, we are probably sims.

Here a "humanlike" being is roughly one with the same sorts of conscious experiences that we have. A "sim blocker" is roughly something that prevents the creation of many more humanlike beings in simulated worlds than nonsimulated worlds. The conclusion is in effect disjunctive, with disjuncts including sim blockers such as *Nonsims will die first, Nonsims will choose not to make sims* (Bostrom's two disjuncts), *Intelligent sims are impossible, Conscious sims are impossible, Simulators will avoid creating conscious sims*, and *Sims will require too much computer power*. I argue that we can't know that any of these sim blockers obtain. I go on to argue that we should assign a non-negligible probability to the simulation hypothesis, and that consequently we can't know that we are not in a simulation.

Chapters 6–9 focus on metaphysics. Chapter 6 focuses on reality, introducing and motivating virtual realism (virtual worlds are real) and simulation realism (simulations are real), distinguishing different notions of reality along the way. Chapter 7 focuses on issues about god, arguing that a simulator may have some but not all of the properties of a traditional god, and considering the simulation argument. Chapter 8 focuses on information, and the it-from-bit hypothesis where the world is ultimately digital and everything is made from bits. This thesis includes both the pure it-from-bit hypothesis where bits are fundamental, and the it-from-bit-from-it hypothesis where the bits are grounded in something more fundamental.

Chapter 9 puts the pieces together to make an argument for simulation realism. The two key arguments are as follows:

1. If the simulation hypothesis is true, the it-from-bit creation hypothesis is true.

2. If the it-from-bit creation hypothesis is true, most of our ordinary beliefs are true.

_____

3. So: If the simulation hypothesis is true, most of our ordinary beliefs are true.

Here, the it-from-bit creation hypothesis is the conjunction of the it-from-bit hypothesis with the hypothesis that our world (including the its and the bits) was created. One could deny premise 1 by holding that if we are in a simulation, there are bits but no "its": photons and other entities we take to exist do not really exist. The case for premise 1 in response goes via the following argument (appropriately generalized).

1. Photons are whatever play the photon role.
2. If we're in a simulation, digital entities play the photon role.

_____

3. So: if we're in a simulation, photons are digital entities.

Chapters 10–13 switch the focus from the simulation hypothesis to real virtual reality technology using familiar headsets and the like. (Here I pass over these chapters and Chapters 14–16 relatively quickly, as none of the commentators focuses on these areas.) Chapter 10 argues for a sort of virtual realism in this domain, where virtual objects are real digital objects. Chapter 11 argues that perception in VR is typically veridical and not illusory or hallucinatory. Chapter 12 takes up augmented reality technology, arguing for a form of realism here too, and for a limited sort of relativism. Chapter 13 considers epistemological issues about deepfakes and whether these might lead to a form of skepticism.

Chapters 14–16 focus on issues about the mind. Chapter 14 considers how issues about mind–body interaction look through the lens of VR. Chapter 15 addresses the question of whether AI systems can be conscious. Chapter 16 introduces the extended mind hypothesis and argues that augmented reality technology can extend the mind.

Chapters 17–19 address questions about value. Chapter 17 considers Nozick's experience machine and uses simulation realism (as well as considerations about autonomy) to argue that whether or not one can live a good life in the experience machine, one can live a good life in a virtual world. One central argument compares life in rich VR (a VR with roughly the complexity of ordinary reality) to terraform reality (life on a new terra-formed planet), arguing:

1. Life in rich VR is roughly as valuable as life in a corresponding terra-form reality.
2. Life in terraform reality is roughly as valuable as ordinary non-virtual life.

———————————

3. So: Life in rich VR is roughly as valuable as ordinary non-virtual life.

Chapter 18 addresses questions of moral status and argues that simulated beings can in principle have full moral status (that is, they can matter mor-ally in roughly the way that human beings do). I argue that moral status requires consciousness: philosophical zombies lack moral status. I also argue that contrary to a common view, moral status does not require affect-ive consciousness: philosophical Vulcans (with consciousness but no effect) still have full moral status. Chapter 19 addresses issues in political philoso-phy about how to build a virtual society.

Chapters 20–24 address some foundational issues underlying the case for simulation realism earlier in the book. Chapter 20 concerns the philosophy of language and the role of externalism, arguing that simulated worlds such as "Sim Earth" should be treated semantically in roughly the way that "Twin Earth" is treated by externalist arguments.

Chapter 21 focuses on the nature of computation, arguing that computa-tion in physical systems (and therefore in simulations) requires a certain sort of causal and counterfactual structure. Chapter 22 focuses on structur-alism and elaborates the structuralist arguments for simulation realism (and therefore against skepticism), as follows.

1. Our physical theories are structural theories
2. If we're in Nonsim Universe, our physical theories are true.
3. Sim Universe has the same structure as NonSim Universe.

———————————

4. So: If we're in Sim Universe, our physical theories are true.

Chapter 23 concerns the relation between the scientific and manifest images and argues that we have been through a "fall from Eden" in transitioning from the former to the latter. We have moved from a primitivist conception where color, space, and so on are primitive Edenic qualities to a functionalist (or structuralist) conception where color and space are picked out by the roles that they play. Eden can help to diagnose our residual skeptical intuitions. If we are in a simulation, our Edenic beliefs about the external world (say, that objects are laid out in a certain way in Edenic space) are false; but those Edenic beliefs are already false in the post-Fall world of science. In both a simulation and in the post-Fall world of science, our non-Edenic beliefs about the external world may be largely true.

Chapter 24 considers skeptical hypotheses not yet addressed earlier in the book, from temporary and local simulations to Boltzmann brains, and tries to draw some limited anti-skeptical conclusions.

David J. Chalmers, *Précis of* Reality+ In: *Oxford Studies in Philosophy of Mind Volume 4.*
Edited by: Uriah Kriegel, Oxford University Press. © David J. Chalmers 2024.
DOI: 10.1093/9780198924159.003.0013

14

The Simulation Hypothesis, Social Knowledge, and a Meaningful Life

Grace Helton

Surely some of my views about what the world is like are wrong, perhaps even in rather surprising ways. But could my most basic assumptions about the world be incorrect? As I write this, I think I'm in a quiet room with a table, some lamps, and a laptop, rain pattering on the roof, my dog sprawled languorously by my side. I think my hands cradle a ceramic mug of hot tea and that a thin mist of steam, faintly smelling of jasmine, curls over the lip of the mug. Could I be wholly hallucinating this entire state of affairs, perhaps as someone in the throes of a psychotic episode? Or perhaps as the plaything of some evil demon who deceives me for its own amusement? And if I am undergoing a psychotic episode or am manipulated by a demon, would I thus be wholly mistaken about what the world is like?

This concern that reality might be radically different than it appears to be might seem to be a rather arcane one, the musings of someone who is either extremely paranoid or overly taken with the abstruse.[1] For, unless I have some *reason* to think that I am undergoing a psychotic episode or that I am being manipulated by some demon, why should I think twice about such speculations? As it turns out, there is at least one version of this sort of claim—that reality is radically different than we think it is—which enjoys at least some empirical support. This is *the simulation hypothesis*, the claim that we and everything in our environment is realized by a large-scale computer simulation, one implemented by superintelligent artificial intelligence (AI).[2]

The empirical argument for the simulation hypothesis is due to the philosopher Nick Bostrom, and it runs like this: There is some reason to think

---

[1] Cf. Schwitzgebel (2017).
[2] This follows Chalmers' way of construing the hypothesis, as against a more minimal version which is silent as to who (if anyone) created the simulation (Chalmers 2022: 29, cf. Bostrom 2003).

that AI will advance to the point of having incredibly fast processing speeds and incredibly powerful processing capabilities of the kind which would easily permit them to simulate full-scale human civilizations, complete with billions of conscious creatures. There is also some reason to think that at least some such superintelligent AI would be interested in simulating many such worlds, for instance, for entertainment or research purposes. Putting these claims together, there is at least some reason to think that many full-scale simulations of human civilizations will ultimately be created—so many, in fact, that out of all conscious humans who have ever lived or who will ever live, the vast majority will be simulated. But if this is the case, then there is at least some reason to think that *we* and our world are simulated. For statistically speaking, if most humans who have ever lived or will live are simulated, what are the chances that we are among the minority who are not simulated?[3]

The simulation argument does not conclusively establish that we are living in a simulation. However, the argument gives us some reason to take the hypothesis seriously beyond its mere conceptual possibility. In this way, the simulation hypothesis is unlike the hypotheses that my experiences are wholly generated by psychosis or by an evil demon; I have no reason to take these explanations seriously beyond their bare possibility, so I am plausibly justified in dismissing these hypotheses out of hand. In contrast, I am not justified in dismissing the simulation hypothesis out of hand.[4]

It is in this broader intellectual context that David Chalmers takes up several philosophical questions about both the simulation hypothesis and VR more generally in his timely, extremely accessible, and impressively wide-ranging book, *Reality+: Virtual Worlds and the Problems of Philosophy*. While Chalmers does not endorse the claim that we are living in a simulation, he thinks the claim probable enough to merit the question: What would it matter if we were (Chalmers 2022, 102)? More particularly, Chalmers focuses on questions such as: If we are indeed living in a wide-scale computer simulation, would our views about the world be correct in at least some basic respects? Could these views further be said to amount to knowledge? And would the fact of our world being a simulation in any way diminish the

---

[3] Bostrom (2003). Chalmers cites Hans Moravec's (1993) work as a precursor to Bostrom's (Chalmers 2022: 83). Philosophers, computer scientists, and physicists who consider the simulation hypothesis include: Arvan (2014, 2015), Beane et al. (2014), Campbell et al. (2017), Dainton (2002, 2012), Johnson (2011), and Mizrahi (2017). For criticisms, see, e.g., Weatherson (2003) and Summers and Arvan (2022).

[4] This is to say, one cannot dismiss it on "Moorean" grounds (Chalmers 2022, 79–80).

value of our lives? Chalmers offers soothing answers to these questions. Namely, he argues that in the simulation: Our views about the world would still be correct in at least some basic respects; these views might further amount to knowledge; and our lives might still be deeply meaningful (Chalmers 2022, 105–224, 399–422, 440–462, 311–350).

Chalmers employs a *structuralist* strategy to argue that we can enjoy *non-social* knowledge in the simulation; here, non-social knowledge is empirical knowledge of non-minded things, such as atoms and shrubs.[5] Structuralism says that since the causal structures of atoms and shrubs exist in the simulation, then atoms and shrubs exist in the simulation. Chalmers further suggests that when we interact with these causal structures, we can gain knowledge of the entities they comprise. Notably, this strategy does not extend to the psychological states of others, a limitation Chalmers acknowledges. In other words, *for all structuralism says*, the seemingly sentient creatures in your environment—your friends, neighbors, animal companions, and the like— might be non-conscious automata. These others might in fact be sentient, but structuralism gives us no reason to think they are.

Chalmers views the claim that we enjoy non-social knowledge in the simulation and the claim that our lives might be meaningful in the simulation as at least weakly connected, as follows: The former claim helps forestall a concern that if objects in the simulation are not genuine (and so not knowable), then life in the simulation is illusory and therefore, not as valuable as a non-simulated life (Chalmers 2022, 314).

In this chapter, I will explore the fuller extent of the connection between non-social knowledge, on the one hand, and a meaningful life on the other. I will suggest that, while non-social knowledge can contribute to the meaningfulness of otherwise *meaningless* lives, in at least many cases, non-social knowledge contributes either nothing at all or very little to the meaningfulness of otherwise meaningful lives. On the overall picture that emerges, for many lives, the value of social knowledge for a meaningful life *dramatically swamps* the value of non-social knowledge for a meaningful life. I call this *the social swamping view.*[6]

---

[5] Chalmers sometimes uses the term *ordinary physical knowledge*, where I use *non-social knowledge* (e.g., Chalmers 2022, 500–501). I prefer *non-social knowledge* so as to avoid the suggestion that knowledge of other minds is not physical knowledge or else is not ordinary knowledge.

[6] I say "most agents" because some agents will prefer above all else to live lives of inquiry into the aspects of the non-social world, in a context of social isolation. While my broader assumptions about meaningfulness in life do not treat meaningfulness as straightforwardly a matter of desire satisfaction, it does accord agents' values a central place and so, I am open to

I first briefly describe Chalmers' structuralist approach and its limitations with respect to knowledge of other minds (§1). I then argue that in many cases, the value of social knowledge for a meaningful life dramatically swamps the value of non-social knowledge for a meaningful life. Along the way, I propose a *non-additive model* of the meaningfulness of life, according to which the overall effect of some potential contributor of value to a life depends in part on what is already in a life (§2). I close with some reflections on the prospects of vindicating social knowledge against a background in which the simulation hypothesis is treated as feasible (§3).

Before proceeding, a point of terminology: I have already been using *social knowledge* to refer to knowledge of those aspects of the world which either are themselves made up of or which depend on other minds. Those who presume social reality to be wholly independent of other minds are free to substitute another term, such as *other-mind-dependent knowledge*. Nothing should turn on the term employed.

1. Structuralism and the Vindication of Non-Social Knowledge

As mentioned, Chalmers exploits a structuralist view of entities in order to argue that we have non-social knowledge in the simulation. This is roughly the view that entities are equivalent to certain observable *causal roles*—that is, to a kind of causal *structure*. According to this view, what it *is* to be a mug (or a quiet room or a quark) is to play a certain observable role or more particularly, to tend to instantiate certain patterns of cause and effect. For instance, what it is to be a mug is to be disposed to be usable for holding liquid and for drinking liquid (among other things). What it is to be a quiet room is to tend not to contain noises above a certain decibel (among other things). Being liquid and being above a certain decibel are in turn construed in terms of relevant observable patterns of cause and effect.[7]

---

the possibility that for some agents, this kind of life might be deeply meaningful. Thanks to Chris Register for this example and for discussion on this point.

[7] This is ontic structuralism, not epistemic structuralism (Chalmers 2022, 145–182). See also Chalmers (2005, 2017) for discussion. Chalmers' argument is strictly neutral between these versions, as he suggests that virtual realism might be grounded in either one (Chalmers 2022, 405–422). Elsewhere, he draws on a conceptual variant of structuralism to develop an argument against external world skepticism (Chalmers 2018).

In drawing out the implications of this view for scenarios such as the simulation scenario, Chalmers has brought out something important and almost entirely overlooked in the vast philosophical literature on such scenarios: These scenarios might be populated by *genuine* quiet rooms, mugs of tea, and dogs, and not merely their simulacra. In particular, structuralism permits a different assessment than familiar semantic externalist approaches, on which the *terms* "quiet room," "mugs of tea," and "dog" have references in the simulation. Because the structuralist maintains that what it is to be (say) a mug of tea just is some causal role, there are genuine mugs of tea—and not, merely "mugs of tea"—in the simulation.[8] The fact that this solution is extremely simple in its basic form while affording a radical shift in thought is a testament to its philosophical power.[9]

Despite the power of the structuralist view, it has its limits and, as Chalmers himself repeatedly stresses, the view does not vindicate knowledge about the existence or nature of the psychologies of others. Very roughly, the reason is that, for reasons well-known from twentieth-century philosophy of mind, others' mental states are not reducible to third-personal observable roles, whether or not things such as mugs are so reducible.[10] Rather, for all structuralism tells us, the seemingly sentient creatures around us might be automata, much like fully multi-modal, hologram versions of the iPhone's talking "Siri."

Elsewhere, I have argued that: the initial suspicion that structuralism cannot vindicate knowledge of other minds is correct; this is so *even if* structuralism is combined with a sophisticated kind of functionalist and wholly materialist view of the mind; this result has implications for wide swathes of beliefs across domains, including at least some beliefs about political history, aesthetic movements, and cultural practices; and as a result, structuralism cannot give us the wholly satisfying solution to skepticism we might have hoped for (Helton forthcoming).[11]

Needless to say, the question of whether structuralism can vindicate knowledge of other minds is a fraught issue and not one I can properly draw out here. For present purposes, what matters is that both Chalmers and

---

[8] That is to say, structuralism is not semantic externalism, though Chalmers himself thinks semantic externalism can help vindicate some forms of knowledge (see, e.g., Chalmers 2022, 372–384).

[9] In order to find a true antecedent to this view, one must go back to the work of Bouwsma (1949). For discussion, see Chalmers (2022, 120–123).

[10] This point is original with Lovelace (1842), as discussed by Turing (1950, 450–451, 454–460). See also Block (1978, 1981). Chalmers (2022, 459–460, 500–501).

[11] See also Helton (2021, 242–246); cf. Chalmers (2022, 500–501).

I think structuralism is ill-suited to vindicate social knowledge, even if it can vindicate non-social knowledge. This shared presumption naturally sets up the question I consider next: What is the significance of non-social knowledge versus social knowledge for a meaningful life? Notably, this question is of general interest, regardless of one's commitments to structuralism.

2. Social Knowledge and Meaningfulness in Life

In this section, I will argue that, for at least many lives, the value of social knowledge *massively swamps* the value of non-social knowledge in the meaningfulness of those lives.[12] I call this *the social swamping view*. I will explore a stronger and weaker version of this claim, concluding that at least one of these claims is true.

First, consider the strong version of this claim, specifically:

Social Swamping View (Strong)
There are at least some meaningful lives, meaningful partly in virtue of their socially rich aspects, which are such that lacking knowledge about non-social reality detracts *not at all* from the meaningfulness of those lives.

On its face, this claim seems obviously false. For, one might think that this claim entails, rather implausibly, that non-social knowledge lacks value. And as against *this* claim, one might suggest a thought experiment along the following lines: Suppose there is some human who tragically lacks most candidate elements of a meaningful life. Her desires are routinely thwarted, her relationships are missing or disingenuous, and she cannot perform authentic actions. Still, despite all of this, her beliefs about non-social aspects of reality, such as her belief *there is a shrub over there* or *that's the ocean*, largely amount to knowledge. Intuitively, this knowledge makes her life at least a tiny bit more meaningful than it would be were she to altogether lack such knowledge. In light of these considerations, one might suggest the following claim:

---

[12]   Special thanks to Liam Kofi Bright and Sarah McGrath for conversation on this point. For recent helpful overviews on meaningfulness in life, see Mawson (2013), Seachris (2019), and Metz (2022).

No Wholly Meaningless Lives with Non-Social Knowledge

There are at least some lives which are such that knowledge about the non-social realm can contribute at least a bit to the meaningfulness of those lives.

As it turns out, I think that this thought experiment is apt, and that it is true that some lives which would elsewise be wholly meaningless gain a bit of meaning from their bearers having some knowledge of non-social reality. But, this claim isn't in conflict with the claim I started with, which is the claim that some meaningful lives are wholly undiminished by a lack of non-social knowledge. Understood as existential claims, these do not form a contradiction.

The appearance of conflict stems, I suspect, from an implicit model of how potential contributors of value create meaningfulness in a life. If we accept a model on which meaningfulness is a matter of combining valuable things together, where each contributor makes its contribution independently of what else is in a life, the claims considered conflict. For, on this *additive model*, if knowledge about non-social reality can ever make a difference in the value of a life, this knowledge always makes a difference, regardless of whatever else is in that life. So, on this view, if non-social knowledge can make a life which is otherwise devoid of value a bit more meaningful, then non-social knowledge can also make a very meaningful life a bit more meaningful.

But, one needn't adopt an additive model of the meaningfulness of life. Instead, one might adopt a *non-additive* model, according to which the overall effect of some potential contributor to a life's meaning depends in part on what else is already in that life. In this way, a meaningful life might be a bit like a stew. While adding a little salt might dramatically improve the flavor of a plain broth, adding a little salt might not improve *at all* an already delicious stew, one with powerful and distinct flavors. While a dash of salt necessarily changes the *ingredients* in the stew, a stew's ingredients can change without any change to its taste. Likewise, the model under consideration is the non-additive or, if you like, *"stew" model* of the meaningfulness of life. The value of each potential contributor depends on what else is there, and in some cases, an elsewise valuable contributor can be "canceled out" by what else is there, such that it becomes wholly irrelevant to a life's overall meaning.[13]

---

[13] See Moore (1903) for the claim that the value of a whole is not the sum of the value of its parts. Cf. Zimmerman (1999). Special thanks to Daniela Dover for discussion on this point. Notably, the non-additive model is consistent both with the view that knowledge in general has

Once we appreciate that life's meaningfulness might not be an additive matter, new possibilities come into view. For instance, consider someone who has a very good life. By this I don't mean an unceasingly pleasurable life, but a rich and authentic one. Let's call her Alya. Alya has safety, shelter, food, and other basic necessities, but also music, art, love, and community. Her work is valuable and rewarding; her relationships are not without challenges, but they are intimate and reciprocated. Maybe Alya is madly in love with someone she just met; maybe she enjoys the companionship of several decades-old, platonic relationships. Maybe she engages in the rituals of an ancient religion; maybe she follows no religion and surfs a lot.

Suppose that Alya's beliefs about other minds and broader social beliefs are not just true but constitute knowledge; her beliefs about the inner states of others are correct, and those creatures around her—whether human or some other species—have inner lives, just as she supposes they do. Suppose further that few or none of Alya's beliefs about the non-social realm constitute knowledge. So, for instance, beliefs of hers such as *that's a shrub* and *there are atoms* somehow fail to amount to knowledge.[14] Would this lack of non-social knowledge necessarily detract from the meaningfulness of Alya's life, which is replete with authentic relationships, valuable work, and rich social knowledge?

If we presume both that non-social knowledge is valuable and that the additive model of life's value is correct, then we must say "yes." While Alya's life is meaningful, it's necessarily *less* meaningful due to this lack of non-social knowledge. But, if we dispense of the assumption that meaningfulness is additive, we have room to say "no," Alya's life is *no less meaningful* due to this lack of non-social knowledge. And, this might be so even if such knowledge is itself valuable.

On the view sketched, a life that is replete with, for instance, authentic expression of one's values, genuine agency, rich interdependence with other creatures, and vast swathes of social knowledge, might be *undiminishable* in a certain way. Lacking knowledge about things like shrubs and atoms cannot degrade such a life even one iota. This view treats certain aspects of a meaningful life as anchors, in the sense that, once present, these elements protect a life's value from certain forms of axiological unmooring.

---

intrinsic value and with the view that the value of knowledge is merely instrumental. For relevant discussion, see, e.g., Kelly (2003) and Rinard (2019).

[14] The structuralist will have to say either that the relevant causal structures do not obtain in Alya's environment or else that she for some reason does not track them properly.

One might object to this view by drawing a contrast case: Consider Alya's counterpart, Kalya. Kalya's life is just like Alya's except that Kalya's beliefs about non-social aspects of the world largely amount to knowledge. While, by stipulation, neither Alya nor Kalya much cares about whether their non-social beliefs amount to knowledge, we might still be tempted to say that surely, Kalya's life is a bit more valuable than Alya's. For one thing, not only does Kalya enjoy knowledge about the non-social world, she also enjoys certain forms of integrated ecological-social knowledge, which Alya lacks. For instance, Kalya might know that she went hiking with her boyfriend over the weekend and that together they sat on a large rock for a while, basking in the sunrise. Surely Kalya's life is at least a bit more meaningful than Alya's in virtue of having this sort of ecological-social knowledge.[15]

I think there is room to resist the suggestion that Kalya's life is necessarily more meaningful than Alya's, even while acknowledging the value of non-social knowledge in general. Merely think for a moment of the kind of rich life Alya has. She has close and genuine relationships, she can achieve many of her ends, she has means of expressing herself, and she doesn't much care whether she knows about things like shrubs and atoms. We might think that to suggest that Alya's life is, despite all this, improvable by non-social knowledge is to show a disrespectful attitude toward both Alya's own preferences and also toward the sources of objective value in her life.

I am not sure whether there are some lives whose meaningfulness cannot be improved at all by non-social knowledge, but I hope to have shown this view should not be dismissed out of hand. I will now argue for a more moderate cousin of this claim. If either of these claims is true, we should think, at a minimum, that the value of social knowledge for the meaningfulness of our lives *dramatically swamps* the value of non-social knowledge for the meaningfulness of our lives:

Social Swamping View (Weak)

There are at least some very meaningful lives, meaningful partly in virtue of their socially rich aspects, which are such that lacking knowledge about non-social reality *scarcely* detracts from the meaningfulness of those lives.

This claim is consistent with the thought that Alya's life would be more meaningful if she had non-social knowledge, such as ecological knowledge.

---

[15] I thank Josh Armstrong for this example and for helpful discussion on this section.

But, this claim is inconsistent with the thought that Alya's life could be dramatically improved by that knowledge. Due to the presence of things such as extremely rich social relationships and agency in her life, the addition of such knowledge would confer at most a modest increase in meaning. (This view requires a non-additive model of life's value, on which the effect of a potential contributor of value can be blunted by what else is there, even if not canceled out entirely.)

In favor of this weaker claim, I would point to the likely emotional responses many of us would have to the loss of non-social versus social knowledge. Suppose God herself were to tell us that, while all of our beliefs about the psychologies of others and our own agency amount to knowledge, few or none of our beliefs about things like atoms and shrubs amount to knowledge, even though we can exploit these beliefs to carry out our aims. For many of us, we'd be shocked by this disclosure, and we would likely have many questions. But, I suspect the overall emotional response after the initial shock would be, if not indifference, something like *curiosity*, a positively-valenced emotion. Indeed, some of us might be *delighted* at this disclosure, as it would introduce an element of wonder or mystery into our everyday lives.

In contrast, suppose God herself were to tell us that, while all of our beliefs about things like atoms and shrubs amount to knowledge, few or none of our beliefs about the sentience or psychologies of others amount to knowledge. For many of us, wondering whether those around us—our friends, family, colleagues, neighbors, animal companions—are sentient at all would cause us to be grief-stricken and horrified. Indeed, it would be understandable for us to wonder whether our lives had ever been worth living or were worth continuing. This disclosure would be almost unspeakably horrific, cutting to the very center of the value of our lives.[16]

I submit that this dramatic emotional asymmetry has one good explanation: For very many of us, the value of social knowledge for the meaningfulness of our lives far outstrips the value of non-social knowledge. So, at a minimum, we should accept the weak claim described above: At least many lives made meaningful through their social richness can scarcely be diminished by a loss of non-social knowledge.

---

[16] See Schwitzgebel (2017, 280–282, 284) for a different but likewise sanguine assessment of the loss of non-social knowledge and Schwitzgebel (2017, 285–287) for a somewhat different take on the loss of social knowledge.

3. Social Knowledge in the Simulation

Let's bring these reflections back to Chalmers and to the question of the relation between non-social knowledge and meaningful lives in the simulation. I think Chalmers is right that if our non-social knowledge is intact, this helps establish that in the simulation, our lives are not wholly *meaningless*. At the same time, I would suggest that the structuralist vindication of non-social knowledge, absent any correlative vindication of social knowledge, contributes not at all or *scarcely* at all to the claim that in the simulation our lives might be *very meaningful*.

In making this claim, I'm not sure whether Chalmers would disagree with it. Given his own emphasis on the value of interpersonal relationships and community in a meaningful life, it is possible that he would agree that the contribution of non-social knowledge to a meaningful life is relatively minimal (Chalmers 2022, 319, 329–330). However, Chalmers and I *might* disagree about the prospects of vindicating social knowledge in the simulation. For, he seems open to the view that knowledge of other minds in the simulation might be vindicated on broadly abductive grounds, for instance by generalizing from relevant neural or behavioral states (Chalmers 2022, 286–287).[17] In contrast, I see this kind of strategy as encumbered, which isn't to say I think it could not possibly succeed.

Specifically, if the simulation hypothesis is at all feasible, certain other hypotheses are also feasible (albeit to a lesser extent) according to which at least some of those around us lack sentience. For instance, our AI creators might have had ethical quandaries about simulating eight billion creatures, many of whom will live foreseeably horrible lives; this possibility is heightened if we presume that pre-simulated humans solved the AI safety problem (Helton 2021, 237–238).[18] Or, on purely practical grounds, our AI creators might have found it unduly burdensome to simulate the psychologies of eight billion humans, since doing so might have been costly in terms of processing power. So instead, they might have created some sentient creatures and rendered the rest as convincing but ultimately mindless automata. Thus, the simulation hypothesis introduces novel impediments to an abductive solution to other minds, which is not to say whether these impediments are ultimately unmovable.

---

[17] See also Schwitzgebel and Moore (2015).
[18] See also Schwitzgebel and Bakker (2013) and Schwitzgebel (2019, 431–433).

I opened this chapter with a description of my surroundings—a quiet room with a table, some lamps, and a laptop, steam rising from my mug, rain pattering on the roof, my dog sprawled by my side. I asked: Do I know I am really here, surrounded by these things? What I'd now like to ask is, in terms of the meaningfulness of my life, *does it matter* whether I know that I am here, surrounded by these things?

The answer I have suggested is that my knowledge of the tea's rising steam and my knowledge of my dog's relaxed psychological state are not on a par. If my life is elsewise devoid of meaning, my knowledge about the steam can contribute to the meaningfulness of my life. But, if my life is otherwise replete with sources of meaning, this knowledge about the steam might not contribute at all to the meaningfulness of my life. In contrast, my knowledge that my dog is a sentient creature, one who currently feels relaxed, contributes to the meaningfulness of my life regardless of what other sources of value I have in my life.[19]

References

Arvan, Marcus. 2014. "A Unified Explanation of Quantum Phenomena? The Case for the Peer-to-Peer Simulation Hypothesis as an Interdisciplinary Research Program." *Philosophical Forum*, 45(4), 433–446.

Arvan, Marcus. 2015. "The Peer-to-Peer Simulation Hypothesis and a New Theory of Free Will." *Scientia Salon*. https://scientiasalon.wordpress.com/2015/01/30/the-peer-to-peer-hypothesis-and-a-new-theory-of-freewill-a-brief-overview/, accessed October 8, 2021.

Beane, Silas R., Zohreh Davoudi, and Savage, Martin J. 2014. "Constraints on the Universe as a Numerical Simulation." *European Physical Journal*, A 50(9), 148.

Block, Ned. 1978. "Troubles with Functionalism." In *Perception and Cognition: Issues in the Foundations of Psychology*, edited by C. Wade Savage, Univ. Minn. Press, 261–326.

Block, Ned. 1981. "Psychologism and Behaviorism." *Philosophical Review*, 90(1), 5–43.

Bostrom, Nick. 2003. "Are We Living in a Computer Simulation?" *Philosophical Quarterly*, 53(211), 243–255.

---

[19] For extremely helpful comments on this chapter, I am indebted to: Josh Armstrong, Daniela Dover, and Chris Register.

Bouwsma, Oets Kolk. 1949. "Descartes' Evil Genius." *Philosophical Review*, *58*(2), 141–151.

Campbell, Tom, Owhadi, Houman, Sauvageau, Joe, and Watkinson, David. 2017. "On Testing the Simulation Theory." *International Journal of Quantum Foundations*, *3*: 78–99.

Chalmers, David J. 2005. "The Matrix as Metaphysics." In *Philosophers Explore the Matrix*, edited by C. Grau, 132–76. Oxford: Oxford University Press.

Chalmers, David J. 2017. "The Virtual and the Real." *Disputatio: International Journal of Philosophy*, *9*(46), 309–352.

Chalmers, David J. 2018. "Structuralism as a Response to Skepticism." *Journal of Philosophy*, *115*(12), 625–660.

Chalmers, David J. 2022. *Reality+: Virtual Worlds and the Problems of Philosophy*. Penguin UK.

Dainton, Barry. 2002. "Innocence Lost Simulation Scenarios: Prospects and Consequences," http://www.simulation-argument.com, accessed March 31, 2021.

Dainton, Barry. 2012. "On Singularities and Simulations." *Journal of Consciousness Studies*, *19*(1–2), 42–85.

Helton, Grace. 2021. "Epistemological Solipsism as a Route to External World Skepticism." *Philosophical Perspectives*, *35*(1), 229–250.

Helton, Grace. Forthcoming. "On Being a Lonely Brain-in-a-Vat: Structuralism, Solipsism, and the Threat from External World Skepticism." *Analytic Philosophy* Advance Early Publication. https://doi.org/10.1111/phib.12291.

Johnson, David Kyle. 2011. "Natural Evil and the Simulation Hypothesis", Philo, Fall-Winter issue, Vol. 14, No.2.

Kelly, Thomas. 2003. "Epistemic Rationality as Instrumental Rationality: A Critique." *Philosophy and Phenomenological Research*, *66*(3), 612–640.

Lovelace, Ada. 1842. "Translator's Notes to an Article on Babbage's Analytical Engine." In *Scientific Memoirs*, edited by R. Taylor, Bibliothèque Universelle de Genève, Genève, vol. 3, 691–731.

Mawson, Tim J. 2013. "Recent Work on the Meaning of Life and Philosophy of Religion." *Philosophy Compass*, *8*(12), 1138–1146.

Metz, Thaddeus, 2022. "The Meaning of Life." *Stanford Encyclopedia of Philosophy*, edited by Edward N. Zalta Uri Nodelman, https://plato.stanford.edu/archives/win2022/entries/life-meaning/, accessed Feb. 1, 2023.

Mizrahi, Moti. 2017. "The Fine-Tuning Argument and the Simulation Hypothesis." *Think*, *16*(47), 93–102.

Moore, G. E. 1903. *Principia Ethica*. Cambridge: Cambridge University Press.

Moravec, Hans. 1993. "Pigs in Cyberspace." NASA. Lewis Research Center, Vision 21: Interdisciplinary Science and Engineering in the Era of Cyberspace.

Rinard, Susanna. 2019. "Equal Treatment for Belief." *Philosophical Studies*, *176*, 1923–1950.

Schwitzgebel, Eric. 2017. "1% Skepticism." *Noûs*, *51*(2), 271–290.

Schwitzgebel, Eric. 2019. "Kant Meets Cyberpunk." *Disputatio*, *11*(55), 411–435.

Schwitzgebel, Eric, and Bakker, Scott R. 2013. "Reinstalling Eden." *Nature*, *503*(7477), 562–562.

Schwitzgebel, Eric, and Moore, Alan T. 2015. "Experimental Evidence for the Existence of an External World." *Journal of the American Philosophical Association*, *1*(3), 564–582.

Seachris, Joshua. 2019. "Meaning of Life: Contemporary Analytic Perspectives." *Internet Encyclopedia of Philosophy*, https://iep.utm.edu/mean-ana/, accessed Feb. 2, 2023.

Summers, Micah, and Arvan, Marcus. 2022. "Two New Doubts about Simulation Arguments." *Australasian Journal of Philosophy*, *100*(3), 496–508.

Turing, Alan. 1950. "Computing Machinery and Intelligence." *Mind*, *59*(236), 433–460.

Weatherson, Brian. 2003. "Are You a Sim?." *The Philosophical Quarterly*, *53*(212), 425–431.

Zimmerman, Michael J. 1999. "Virtual Intrinsic Value and the Principle of Organic Unities." *Philosophical and Phenomenological Research*, *59*(3) 653–666.

Grace Helton, *The Simulation Hypothesis, Social Knowledge, and a Meaningful Life* In: *Oxford Studies in Philosophy of Mind Volume 4*. Edited by: Uriah Kriegel, Oxford University Press. © Grace Helton 2024.
DOI: 10.1093/9780198924159.003.0014

15

Why Virtual Worlds Aren't Real

How Phenomenal Intentionality Constrains Mental Reference

Terry Horgan

David Chalmers' delightful book *Reality+* is full of bold and provocative philosophical claims. Perhaps his most fundamental claim—and certainly one of the boldest and most provocative—is that virtual worlds are real. This claim will be my concern here.

A more precise formulation of his most fundamental claim, I take it, is that *some* metaphysically possible virtual worlds *would be* real *if they were actual simulations*—and that being real, in the intended sense, does not consist merely in being an actual simulation, but consists rather in the by-and-large veridicality of the external-world experiences and beliefs of an agent embedded in such a simulated environment. Among the metaphysically possible virtual worlds that allegedly would be real, I take it, would be a virtual world in which a familiar thought-experimental "brain in a vat" (henceforth, BIV) would be experientially embedded throughout its lifetime. So I will focus my discussion on a BIV—although my remarks should be applicable, *mutatis mutandis*, to any other kinds of virtual world that Chalmers contends would be real if actual. (I will henceforth stop using the subjunctive mood, to simplify exposition.)

I contend, contra Chalmers, that a virtual world in which a BIV is embedded is *unreal*, and radically so. Here I will explain why I hold this view, in a way that largely adapts, in abbreviated form, the discussion in Horgan, Tienson, and Graham (2004).[1] For reasons of space, I will not attempt to argue for the claims I make in the course of my exposition; that is done

---

[1] The adapted material from Horgan, Tienson, and Graham (2004) will mainly be in Sections 1 and 2. Since I am the sole author of the chapter, I will set forth this material using the first-person singular—as constituting *my* views. But the position was developed very collaboratively between myself, George Graham, and the late John Tienson; it is *ours*.

elsewhere.[2] I suggest, however, that many of these claims should seem quite obvious when one attends carefully and non-dogmatically to the phenomenal character of conscious experience—to what "what it's like" *is really like*, introspectively. And I suggest that the overall position I describe should seem extremely natural and plausible, in light those aspects of the position that are obvious to non-dogmatic introspection. (Non-dogmatic introspection requires willful suspension of any prior commitment one might have to the dogma—still quite prevalent in philosophy of mind—that external-world purporting mental intentionality must consist principally or entirely of certain kinds of systematic interconnections between one's mental states and one's actual ambient environment.)[3]

I also will consider a potential dialectical strategy that Chalmers might invoke, in an effort to accommodate what I say about the phenomenal character of conscious experience while still maintaining that virtual worlds are real. I will argue that the strategy does not succeed.

For present purposes, it will be useful to work with the following specific version of the generic brain-in-vat scenario. Suppose that there are some intelligent creatures elsewhere in the cosmos who are very different from humans in physical composition and physical appearance, and whose surrounding environment is quite different from our own. They are in no causal contact with Earth, and know nothing of it or its inhabitants. In the course of their scientific investigations, they deliberately synthesize a structure out of organic molecules that happens to be an exact physical duplicate of your own brain; they deliberately hook it to a computer in such a way that its ongoing brain activity happens to exactly match your own, throughout its existence. (Thus, the BIV setup they have deliberately created involves a virtual, simulated, environment that happens to exactly match your own ambient environment—even though they know nothing of Earth or its human inhabitants.) Also, there is substantial *counterfactual* exact physical similarity between this artificial brain and yours; various counterfactuals about what would happen to and within your brain if certain physical events were to occur to it or within it—for instance, counterfactuals about what

[2] See, for instance, Horgan and Tienson (2002), Horgan, Tienson, and Graham (2004), Graham, Tienson, and Horgan (2007, 2009), Horgan and Graham (2012), Horgan (2013, 2014). Texts in philosophy of mind espousing views about mental intentionality that are broadly similiar to the Graham/Horgan/Tienson position include McGinn (1989), Strawson (1994), Siewert (1998), Loar (2003), Pitt (2004), Farkas (2008), and Kriegel (2013).

[3] I ask the reader to bear with me through Sections 1 and 2, because the basis of my critique of Chalmers is the intuitive plausibility that I claim accrues to my own position. An effort to convey this intuitive plausibility requires articulating the position in adequate detail.

would happen physically if the brain were to receive certain potential physical inputs to its sensory-input neurons—are also true of the synthesized brain. Hereafter when I speak of the BIV, usually I will mean this particular synthesized brain in this particular setup.

1. My Position Sketched

When one first contemplates such a BIV scenario, certain pre-theoretic intuitive judgments about it tend to arise strongly and spontaneously, given the knowledge that physical processes underlying human mentality occur in the human brain. One intuitively judges that the BIV's mental life *exactly matches* one's own, in a very strong way; this means, inter alia, that the BIV has numerous *beliefs*, both perceptual and non-perceptual, that exactly match one's own beliefs. Also, one intuitively judges that many of these matching beliefs—including perceptual beliefs in particular—are *veridical* in one's own case but *nonveridical* in the BIV's case. I will refer to these strong, stubborn intuitions about the BIV scenario as *Cartesian intuitions.*

I begin by sketching my position in broad brushstrokes, leaving various important details to be filled in later in the chapter. Central in the position is the role of *phenomenology* or *phenomenal consciousness*, by which I mean those aspects of one's mental life such that there is "something it is like" to undergo them. Briefly, the position goes as follows.

Phenomenology is *narrow*: it is not constitutively dependent upon anything "outside the head" (or outside the brain) of the experiencing subject. Indeed, it is not constitutively dependent upon anything outside of phenomenal consciousness itself; in this sense, it is *intrinsic*. Your phenomenology, being narrow and intrinsic, supervenes nomically upon physical events and processes within your brain. Hence, your phenomenology is shared in common with a BIV physical duplicate of your own brain.

Phenomenology is also richly and pervasively *intentional*: there is a kind of intentionality that is entirely constituted phenomenologically (I call it *phenomenal* intentionality), and it pervades our mental lives. Among the different aspects of phenomenal intentionality are the following. First, there is the phenomenology of perceptual experience: the enormously rich and complex what-it's-like of being perceptually presented with a world of apparent objects, apparently instantiating a rich range of properties and relations—including one's own apparent body, apparently interacting with other apparent objects which apparently occupy various apparent spatial relations as apparently perceived from one's own apparent-body centered perceptual point of view. Second, there is the *phenomenology of agency*: the what-it's-like of apparently *voluntarily controlling* one's apparent body as it apparently moves around in, and apparently interacts with, apparent objects in its apparent environment. Third, there is *conative and cognitive* phenomenology: the what-it's-like of consciously (as opposed to unconsciously) undergoing various occurrent propositional attitudes, including conative attitudes like occurrent wishes and cognitive attitudes like occurrent thoughts. There are phenomenologically discernible aspects of conative and cognitive phenomenology, notably (i) the phenomenology of *attitude type* and (ii) the phenomenology of *content*. The former is illustrated by the phenomenological difference between, for instance, *occurrently hoping* that Biden will be re-elected and *occurrently wondering* whether Biden will be re-elected— where the attitude-content remains the same while the attitude-type varies. The phenomenology of content is illustrated by the phenomenological difference between occurrently thinking that Biden *will be* re-elected and occurrently thinking that Biden *will not be* re-elected—where the attitude-type remains the same while the attitude-content varies.

Since phenomenal intentionality is entirely constituted phenomenologically, and since phenomenology is narrow, phenomenal intentionality is narrow too. Hence, there is *exact match* of phenomenal intentionality between yourself and your BIV physical duplicate. This exactly matching, narrow, intentional content involves exactly matching, phenomenally constituted, *narrow truth conditions*. But whereas the narrow truth conditions of your own beliefs are largely satisfied, those of your BIV physical duplicate's matching beliefs largely fail to be satisfied; thus, the BIV's belief system is systematically nonveridical. So Cartesian intuitions about the BIV are correct.

On the other hand, exact match in narrow content between your own intentional mental states and the corresponding states in your BIV physical duplicate does not require or involve exact match in *referents* (if any) of all the various matching, putatively referring, thought-constituents. For instance, certain of your own occurrent thoughts that you would express linguistically using certain proper names—say, the thought that Trump is not a stable genius—involve singular thought-constituents whose referents (if any) are determined partly in virtue of certain external relations that obtain between you and those referents. Thus, your occurrent thought that *Trump is not a stable genius* involves a singular thought-constituent that purports to refer to a particular specific person (viz., Trump); its *actually* referring, and its referring to the specific individual to whom it does refer, depends upon there being certain suitable external relations linking you to a unique eligible referent (viz., Trump). A Twin-Earthly physical duplicate of yourself, in a Twin-Earthly duplicate local environment, would refer to a *different* individual (viz., Twin-Trump) via the corresponding singular thought-constituent of the corresponding occurrent thought. And in the case of your BIV physical duplicate, the matching singular thought-constituent *fails to refer at all*, because the BIV does not bear suitable externalistic relations to any suitably reference-eligible individual in its own actual environment. (Parallel remarks apply to thought-constituents that purport to refer to natural kinds, such as the thought-constituent that you yourself would express linguistically with the word "water.")

For mental states involving thought-constituents for which reference depends upon externalistic factors, there are two kinds of intentionality, each involving its own truth conditions. First is the kind of intentionality already mentioned above: *phenomenal* intentionality, with truth conditions that are phenomenally constituted and narrow. Second is *externalistic* intentionality, with wide truth conditions that incorporate the actual referents (if any) of the relevant thought-constituents.[4] Your own thought that Trump is not a stable genius, and the corresponding thoughts of your BIV physical duplicate and your Twin Earth physical duplicate, have matching phenomenal intentionality, with matching truth conditions. (These truth conditions are satisfied in your case and in the case of your Twin Earth duplicate, but not in the case of your BIV duplicate.) On the other hand, your own thought that Trump is not a stable genius and your Twin Earth duplicate's corresponding thought do not have matching *externalistic* intentionality, because the externalistic truth conditions of these respective thoughts do not match: the truth value of your own thought depends upon the stability level and intelligence level of *Trump*, whereas the truth value your Twin Earth duplicate's corresponding thought depends upon the stability level and intelligence level of an entirely different individual, viz., Twin-Trump. (Each thought's wide truth conditions are indeed satisfied.) As for your BIV duplicate's thought, it lacks externalistic intentionality and wide truth conditions,

---

[4] In analytic philosophy the notion of intentionality has traditionally been glossed as *aboutness*. I deploy the expression "externalistic intentionality" in a nod to this common tradition, since mental reference surely constitutes a form of aboutness. But it may well be that the notion of intentionality in the Continental philosophical tradition—and in Brentano's work, in particular—essentially coincided with phenomenal intentionality alone. (I think this is why my late colleague John Tienson originally balked at my expression "externalistic intentionality," when he and I were writing Horgan and Tienson (2002). But ultimately he acceded to my proposed usage because of the rationale I gave him: reference is a form of aboutness.)

because its singular thought-constituent purporting to refer to a person called "Trump" does not actually refer at all.

2. My Position Elaborated

Let me now fill in some details of the position sketched above.

2.1 Phenomenally Constituted Attribute-Reference

In considering the extent of mental match between yourself and your BIV phenomenal duplicate, it is useful to begin by focusing on matching *perceptual* experience, and on matching beliefs whose intentional contents are the contents of one's current perceptual experience. Phenomenologically, perceptual experience is richly *presentational*: it presents, to the experiencing subject, a richly textured apparent world of apparent concrete objects apparently instantiating numerous properties and relations. For instance, experience presents various apparent objects apparently instantiating various *shape*-properties, *size*-properties, *relative*-position relations, and *relative-orientation* relations. Among the experientially presented apparent objects is one's own apparent body, with its various apparent component parts—a body that is apparently under one's voluntary control. Some of the relations apparently instantiated by the various apparent objects—for instance, relative-position relations and relative-orientation relations—are experientially presented within a self-oriented reference frame. Thus, apparent objects are experientially presented as lying at various distances *from oneself* (as well as from one another, as presented from one's own visual point of view), and as apparently oriented various ways *vis-à-vis oneself* (as well as vis-à-vis one another, as presented from one's own visual point of view). This point of view is what Husserl called the "zero-point" in this self-oriented reference frame. *Up* and *down* in this reference frame normally depend heavily upon kinesthetic/tactile aspects of phenomenology, in combination with visual aspects: roughly, *down* is the direction that one's own apparent body apparently tends to move of its own accord, and the direction of a surface to which one's apparent body apparently tends to stay attached when apparently not moving relative to that surface.

When experience presents various apparent objects as apparently instan-tiating properties and relations such as shape-properties and relative-position relations, experience thereby *acquaints* the experiencing subject with such properties and relations, and this mental acquaintance-relation grounds mental *reference* to these properties and relations. Such mental ref-erence is wholly constituted phenomenologically.[5] It makes no difference, so far as this phenomenally constituted and reference-grounding form of acquaintance is concerned, whether or not the relevant experiential presen-tations are *veridical*. In the case of your BIV phenomenal duplicate, for instance, the perceptual-experiential presentations are radically illusory: there are no *real* objects that are *really* perceived by that experiencing sub-ject and that *really* instantiate the relevant properties and relations. But no matter: your BIV duplicate's perceptual experience acquaints the BIV with shape-properties and relative-position properties just as much as your own perceptual experience does, even though this acquaintance occurs via rad-ically nonveridical experiences of merely *apparent* instantiations of these properties and relations by merely apparent objects. And for the BIV, such experiential acquaintance with the properties and relations grounds mental reference to them—just as it does for you. Experientially presented *apparent* instantiation of the properties and relations suffices to acquaint the experi-encing subject with them, and thus suffices to ground mental reference to them, whether or not the experiencing subject is ever experientially pre-sented with *actual* instantiations of them.

It is an important philosophical question which kinds of properties and relations are ones to which creatures with human-like phenomenology bear phenomenally constituted, reference-grounding, experiential-acquaintance relations. Although I cannot pursue this large topic at any length here, I take it that the range of such properties and relations is very extensive. It appears to include, inter alia, temporal relations, causal relations, properties like *being a temporally persisting object, being an animal, being an agent,* and *being a person,* numerous artifactual kinds like *being a container* and *being a*

---

[5] This does not mean, of course, that *actual instantiation* of the relevant properties and rela-tions is wholly constituted phenomenologically. On the contrary, typically these properties and relations are externally constituted, in the sense that their being instantiated (if and when they are) is a matter of how things are externally to the experiencing subject. But on my view it is a serious *non sequitur* to infer, from the fact that a given property or relation is externally consti-tuted (in the sense just explained), to the conclusion that mental reference to that property or relation must involve an externalistic constitutive aspect.

table, and numerous social relations and properties like *being friend of*, *being a boss of*, and *being a politician*.[6] It also appears to include numerous language-involving properties and relations, such as *uttering a meaningful statement* and *speaking a language I understand*.

Many of these properties and relations involve aspects that are not fully and directly presented in experience (in the manner mentioned two paragraphs ago). For instance, *being a container* is partly a matter of dispositional capacities to contain something, and paradigmatically (if not inevitably) is partly a matter of something's having its causal origin as an artifact that was deliberately created in order to contain things. Although such properties and relations typically are not presented in perceptual experience as immediately and straightforwardly as are features like position and shape, this certainly does not mean that they figure in phenomenology in a "merely theoretical" or inferential way, as opposed to an "observational" way. On the contrary, the presentational aspects of perceptual experience are rife with potentialities. You experience apparent enduring objects as *having back sides*, even though those sides are not directly presented; you experience an apparent cup *as a cup*, even though its being a cup includes certain dispositional features and causal-origin features that are not directly experientially presented; you experience other apparent bodies that suitably resemble your own apparent body as *persons who are acting for intelligible reasons*, even though many key features that make for personhood are not directly experientially presented, and even though the presumptive mental lives of others are not directly experientially accessible to you; and so on.

Because of the extensive range of properties and relations to which the experiencing subject bears the relation of phenomenally constituted mental reference, there are numerous potential thoughts that have only narrow, phenomenal, intentionality. (Thoughts that have both phenomenal intentionality and externalistic intentionality will be discussed below.) Roughly, these are thoughts that are expressible linguistically using only (i) logical vocabulary, (ii) predicates expressing properties and relations to which the experiencer can mentally refer in a phenomenally constituted way, and (iii) certain first-person indexical expressions. So for instance, you might have a thought you could express linguistically by saying "A picture is hanging

---

[6] Objection: "But surely properties like *being a boss of* and *being a politician* are not wholly constituted phenomenologically! Their instantiation depends constitutively upon how things are external to the experiencer." Reply: My claim is not that these properties themselves are wholly constituted phenomenologically, but rather that *mental reference* to them is thus constituted; cf. note 5.

crooked on a wall directly in front of me." Your BIV phenomenal duplicate and your Twin Earth phenomenal duplicate would have corresponding occurrent thoughts with exactly matching, phenomenally constituted (and hence narrowly constituted), truth conditions. In terms of logical form, these matching thoughts have matching, doubly existential, contents involving the respective experiencing subjects as the respective referents of the first-person indexical thought-constituent: *there is* an x and *there is* a y such that x is a picture, y is a wall directly in front of *me*, and x is hanging crooked on y (relative to the up-down axis of *my* self-oriented visual/kinesthetic reference frame).

2.2 Mental Reference to Concrete Particulars and to Natural Kinds: Grounding Presuppositions and Externalistic Factors

Although *some* kinds of mental reference are fully constituted by phenomenological factors alone (and hence purely narrowly), other kinds are constituted in a way that involves not only phenomenology but also certain externalistic factors. Singular mental reference to *concrete particulars* generally (perhaps always) works this way. Suppose, for example, that you have an occurrent thought that you could express linguistically by saying "That picture is hanging crooked," where the singular thought-constituent expressible linguistically by "that picture" purports to refer to a picture on the wall directly in front of you. This thought-content involves certain phenomenally constituted presuppositions, which I call *grounding* presuppositions, that must be satisfied in order for the singular thought-constituent to refer: roughly, there must be an object at a certain location relative to oneself (a location that one could designate linguistically by a specific use of the place-indexical "there"), this object must be a picture, there must not be any other picture at that location that is an equally eligible potential referent of "that picture," and this object must be causing your current experience as of a picture directly on the wall in front of you. If these grounding presuppositions are satisfied by some specific concrete particular in your ambient environment—some particular object that is a picture and is uniquely suitably located—then your singular thought-constituent thereby refers to that very object. *Which* object your thought-constituent refers to, if any, thus depends jointly upon two factors, one phenomenally constituted and one externalistic: on one hand, the phenomenally constituted grounding presuppositions, and on the other hand, the unique actual object in your ambient environment that *satisfies* those presuppositions.[7]

Compare the corresponding singular thought of your Twin Earth phenomenal duplicate. The corresponding singular thought-constituent also refers to something, because on Twin Earth too there is a unique object that satisfies the matching, phenomenally constituted, grounding presuppositions. However, that thought-constituent refers to a *different* concrete particular than yours does, viz., the specific picture that is suitably located in front of your Twin Earth phenomenal duplicate rather than in front of yourself. The referents are different, for you and for your Twin Earth duplicate, because in the respective cases two different objects respectively satisfy the matching, self-indexical-involving, grounding presuppositions. Relative to you, the presuppositions are satisfied by the picture in front of you; relative to your duplicate, they are satisfied by the picture in front of her/him.

Next, compare your BIV phenomenal duplicate's singular thought corresponding to your own singular thought, and the BIV's singular thought-constituent corresponding to your own thought-constituent that you could express linguistically by "that picture." For the BIV duplicate too, this thought-constituent has phenomenally constituted grounding presuppositions that match those of yours. However, nothing in the BIV's ambient environment satisfies those presuppositions. Hence, in the case of your BIV phenomenal duplicate, that thought-constituent fails to refer to anything.

According to the conception of mental intentionality I am here setting forth, these observations are pervasively generalizable. *In general*, singular thought-constituents have phenomenally constituted grounding presuppositions, and the referent (if any) of such a thought-constituent is the unique object (if any) in the experiencer's own environment that satisfies the applicable, phenomenally constituted and self-indexical involving, grounding presuppositions.[8]

Although many predicative thought-constituents refer in a way that is wholly constituted phenomenally, not all of them do. Among those that do not, as is widely acknowledged in light of the writings of Kripke and

---

[7] At the time I proposed the expression "grounding presupposition" to John Tienson, while he and I were writing Horgan and Tienson (2002), I was not cognizant of the use of the term "grounding" that has since become very popular in metaphysics. Grounding in that sense is much like what I myself called "superdupervenience" in Horgan (1993).

[8] It is probably a somewhat vague matter which phenomenally constituted background assumptions constitute full-fledged grounding presuppositions, and which do not. Vagueness is a pervasive aspect of intentionality in thought and in language, after all.

Putnam, are certain thought-constituents that purport to refer to *natural kinds*—for instance, thought-constituents expressible in language by terms like "water" or "gold." The key points in this subsection carry over to these kinds of predicative thought-constituents, *mutatis mutandis*.[9]

2.3 Phenomenal Intentionality, Externalistic Intentionality, and Two Kinds of Truth Conditions

Thoughts with externalistic reference-purporting constituents are capable of two kinds of truth conditions, corresponding to the two kinds of intentionality. Phenomenal intentionality involves *narrow* truth conditions. These have "built into" them all the phenomenally constituted grounding presuppositions governing the given thought's externalistically reference-purporting thought-constituents. Insofar as such narrow truth conditions are formulable linguistically (and they need not be in any compact way[10]), the formulation will employ only these kinds of vocabulary: (i) logical expressions, (ii) predicative expressions designating properties and relations to which the experiencer can mentally refer non-externalistically, and (iii) certain first-person indexical expressions. Take, for instance, a thought that you could express in language by saying "That picture is hanging crooked" where "that picture" purports to refer to a picture directly in front of you. The narrow truth conditions for this thought would be expressible something like this: "There is a unique object x, located directly in front of me and visible by me, such that x is a picture and x is hanging crooked (relative to my visual/

---

[9] Horgan, Tienson, and Graham (2004) includes discussion of how phenomenally constituted grounding presuppositions work in the case of a BIV's thought-constituents that arise via apparent public-language mediation, involving apparent linguistic interaction with apparent persons in the BIV's apparent environment—where some of these thought-constituents are deployed by the BIV in an apparently social-deferential way. The paper also includes discussion of the BIV's capacity for *conceptual bootstrapping* to thought-constituents that purport to refer to various kinds of "theoretical" entities and properties (e.g., electrons, quarks, loop quantum gravity). Such bootstrapping often occurs in the BIV via apparent social-linguistic mediation, and often in a way that rests in part on the fact that the BIV can refer mentally to the relation of *causation* purely by virtue of experiential presentations of *apparent* instances of it.

[10] Possible-world semantics, a familiar and widely invoked approach to truth conditions, certainly does not impose such an expressibility requirement. Instead it typically construes the truth conditions for a given statement as constituted by a set of possible worlds. The same goes for so-called two-dimensional modal semantics, an approach that has some kinship to my own, including the positing of two kinds of truth conditions—one kind narrow and the other kind wide. See Davies and Humberstone (1980); Chalmers (1996), especially pp. 63–65; Jackson (1998), chapters 2 and 3, especially pp. 75–77; and Chalmers (2002).

kinesthetic up/down axis)." Your own picture-thought, your Twin Earth phenomenal duplicate's picture-thought, and your BIV duplicate's picture-thought all *match* with respect to these truth conditions; that is, the truth conditions are just the same, apart from the different referents of the first-person indexical.

Externalistic intentionality, on the other hand, involves *wide* truth conditions. The wide truth conditions of a given thought incorporate the specific *satisfiers* (if any) of the phenomenally constituted grounding presuppositions governing the externalistic reference-purporting constituents of that thought. In order for the thought's wide truth conditions to be met, *those specific satisfiers* must play a suitable truth-making role. Thus, your picture-thought and your Twin Earth phenomenal duplicate's corresponding picture-thought have *non-matching* wide truth conditions, because they respectively involve *different pictures*—in one case, the picture in front of you, and in the other case, the picture in front of your Twin Earth duplicate. As for your BIV phenomenal duplicate's picture-thought, it lacks wide truth conditions altogether (and hence lacks externalistic intentionality), because the pertinent grounding presuppositions are not satisfied. (Likewise, *mutatis mutandis*, for your own thought that you could express linguistically by saying "Water is good to drink," and the corresponding thoughts of your Twin Earth phenomenal duplicate and your BIV phenomenal duplicate.)

When grounding presuppositions are satisfied, narrow truth and falsity normally run smoothly in tandem with wide truth and falsity: a thought with externalistic reference-purporting constituents is narrowly true just in case it is widely true, and is narrowly false just in case it is widely false. Consider, for instance, the thought that you could express linguistically by saying "Water is good to drink." This thought is narrowly true just in case (i) there exists a kind of stuff uniquely satisfying the grounding presuppositions governing your "water" thought-constituent, and (ii) this stuff is good to drink. And the thought is widely true just in case *that very stuff* (viz., H_2O) is good to drink.[11]

---

[11] Even when grounding presuppositions are satisfied, narrow truth and wide truth can still diverge in interesting ways with respect to certain kinds of modal and counterfactual reasoning. For instance, someone who doesn't know the chemical composition of water might contemplate each of the two epistemic possibilities *that water is H20* and *that water is XYZ*, might form judgments about the comparative likelihood of these two possibilities, might have different counterfactual beliefs pertaining to each of these possibilities, and so forth. In effect, such reasoning holds narrow truth conditions constant across the possibilities under consideration, while varying wide truth conditions. This general theme is explored and developed in the literature on two-dimensional modal semantics; cf. note 10.

On the other hand, when the grounding presuppositions are not satisfied for a thought with externalistic reference-purporting constituents, then the thought is *narrowly* false and is neither widely true *nor* widely false. It is narrowly false because the grounding presuppositions are built directly into the narrow truth conditions themselves, and fail to be met. And it is neither widely true nor widely false because it lacks wide truth conditions (and wide falsity conditions). This is precisely the situation, on a massive scale, with respect to your BIV phenomenal duplicate's thoughts that have externalistic reference-purporting thought-constituents. Those thoughts all are narrowly false; and because they lack wide truth conditions, they all are neither widely true nor widely false.

This captures well the radical kind of nonveridicality that intuition attributes to the BIV's external-world beliefs. Their falsity is not the ordinary kind, in which a belief's grounding presuppositions are satisfied but its satisfiers do not have the features that the belief attributes to them. (In ordinary cases, a false belief is both narrowly and widely false.) Rather, it is a deeper kind of falsity, in which the grounding presuppositions themselves fail to be satisfied.

My account rests heavily and essentially upon the contention that mental reference to many properties and relations—including various spatiotemporal-location properties, shape-properties, size-properties, artifact-properties, and personhood-involving properties—is wholly constituted by phenomenology alone. Even systematically *nonveridical* phenomenology, as in the case of the BIV, provides reference-constituting acquaintance with such properties and relations. These properties and relations, in turn, are the ones figuring in the phenomenally constituted grounding presuppositions at work in narrow, phenomenal, intentionality.

3. How Chalmers Goes Wrong

Chalmers' own conception of mental reference-eligibility, as I understand it, goes basically as follows. In order for the reference-purporting singular and predicative constituents of conscious intentional mental states to successfully refer, respectively, to certain individuals and certain properties, the key requirement is a *systematic causal isomorphism* between (i) instances of these mental states within the conscious agent and (ii) the presence, in the agent's ambient environment, of individuals and property-instances that *causally regulate* these mental states. Presumably, the pertinent kind of causal isomorphism should have substantial counterfactual depth: the pattern of systematic causal regulation should obtain with respect to a wide range of counterfactuals pertaining to what would happen in the agent's conscious experience if the ambient environment were to cause certain inputs to the agent's cognitive system (e.g., neural inputs that induce a sensory-presentational experience as-of a nearby open fridge full of beer bottles), and also pertaining to what would happen in the conscious agent's ambient environment if the agent were to undergo certain conscious intentional mental states (e.g., seeming to initiate an act of fetching a beer from a nearby fridge). And in order to constitute a *simulation*, presumably such a systematic causal isomorphism must have been deliberately created by certain intelligent agents—the simulators.

According to this construal of mental reference, your own BIV duplicate has sensory-presentational experiences and external-world beliefs that are no less veridical than your own corresponding sensory-presentational experiences and external-world beliefs. This is because there is a systematic causal isomorphism between (i) how computer-states of the BIV setup are causally intertwined with the BIV's conscious mental states, and (ii) how states of your own actual ambient environment are causally intertwined with your own, corresponding, conscious mental states. That's all it takes, according to Chalmers, for the singular and predicative reference-purporting constituents of the BIV's sensory-presentational experiences and external-world beliefs to successfully *refer* to the various computer states that causally regulate these mental-state constituents. And with such reference in place, the causal isomorphism also would guarantee that the BIV's sensory-presentational experiences and external-world beliefs are veridical whenever your own corresponding mental states are veridical. So, voila, says Chalmers, the BIV's virtual world is real!

I beg to differ. I contend that if one attends carefully and non-dogmatically to the actual phenomenal character of conscious experience, it should be introspectively manifest that experience directly acquaints the experiencer with numerous properties and relations via apparent instantiations of them— whether or not such properties and relations are ever actually instantiated in the experiencer's environment. Likewise, it should be introspectively manifest that conscious experience imposes quite strong, phenomenally constituted, reference-eligibility constraints on externalistically reference-purporting thought-constituents—for example, thought-constituents that purport to refer to individuals or to natural kinds. Accordingly, the account of mental intentionality I described in Sections 1 and 2 should seem intuitively compelling, given a suitable introspective appreciation one's own phenomenal consciousness.

If that account—or something like it—is correct, then Chalmer's conception of mental reference-eligibility is far too lax, because it flouts the constraints that phenomenal consciousness actually imposes. The computer states that systematically cause the BIV's tree-experiences come *nowhere near* satisfying either the reference-eligibility constraints that govern the BIV's sensory-presentational experience of trees, or the reference-eligibility constraints that govern the BIV's tree-concept. Likewise, *mutatis mutandis*, for most all of the BIV's external-world involving sensory-presentational experiences and external-world involving beliefs. The BIV's virtual world is *thoroughly* unreal, just as pre-theoretic intuition says it is.

4. At the Gates of the Garden of Eden

Chalmers is well known for his contention, in Chalmers (2006), that color experiences and color-attributing judgments have two kinds of content. On one hand is what he calls "Edenic" content, with satisfaction conditions requiring the actual instantiation, by objects in the world, of color properties whose nature accords with colors as they appear in sensory-presentational experience. On the other hand is a non-Edenic kind of content, with satisfaction conditions that do not include this requirement.

There are strong scientific grounds, Chalmers contends, in support of the claim that Edenic colors are never actually instantiated in our world—and hence that the Edenic color-content that accrues to certain experiences and judgments is systematically nonveridical. But he holds that there is an important respect in which such experiences and judgments really are veridical nonetheless: viz., their non-Edenic content has satisfaction conditions that often really are met by objects in our world.

In *Reality+* he invokes the idea that if a conscious agent is embedded in a perfect simulation, then the contents of the agent's sensory-presentational experiences and conscious beliefs are systematically non-Edenic. The suggestion seems to be that once we accept that color attributions are often really true in our own world, even though Edenic colors are never instantiated here, we should also accept that the virtual world of a perfect simulation is fully real—albeit *non-Edenically* real. Here is a representative passage (with capitalization or its absence marking the Edenic/non-Edenic distinction):

We seem to be in an Edenlike world laid out in a certain way in Space. If we're in a simulation, our world isn't like this. The simulation doesn't contain Solid and Colorful objects in Space. But the same goes for our scientific world of quantum mechanics and relativity. Solidity, Color, and Space disappeared from the scientific world picture a long time ago. We reconceived Solidity, Color, and Space as solidity, color, and space. The simulation hypothesis is no worse off than the scientific worldview here. Neither contain Solidity, Color, or Space. But both contain color, solidity, and space.

(Chalmers 2022, 424–245)

Invoking the Edenic/non-Edenic distinction in this broad way, as he does, would provide Chalmers a potential strategy for partially accommodating what I said in Sections 1 and 2 above about the phenomenally constituted veridicality conditions of sensory-presentational experiences and of external-world beliefs, while yet retaining his contention that some virtual worlds, including the BIV's virtual world, are real. The idea would be to deploy the following three claims. First, although what I said is correct concerning the *Edenic* content of sensory-presentational experiences and external-world beliefs, it simply isn't true concerning non-Edenic content. Second, the scientific worldview compels us to realize that even in our own world, the only veridical kind of content possessed by sensory-presentational experiences and external-world beliefs is non-Edenic content. And third (as he says in the above-quoted passage), "The simulation hypothesis is no worse off than the scientific worldview here."

I don't find this dialectical move persuasive, as I will now explain. First, consider color. In Horgan (2014) I myself invoke a variant of the "dual content" approach that Chalmers too embraces. In my version, visual-presentational experiences as-of colored objects have what I call *presentational* color-content, whereas color-attributing judgments normally have what I call *judgmental* color-content. Presentational color-content is Edenic in Chalmers' sense, and is nonveridical: a lesson of the scientific worldview is that experientially presented colors are never really instantiated in the world, and likewise for other so-called secondary qualities. Judgmental color-content, on the other hand, has different veridicality conditions than presentational color-content, and is often veridical. For instance, a judgment attributing the color red to an object o is veridical just in case, roughly, o's surface instantiates some physical natural-kind feature F whose instantiation by an object would cause a normal human who visually perceives o under sufficiently good viewing conditions to have a sensory-presentational experience as-of o's instantiating presentational redness (i.e., Edenic redness).[12]

But even though I agree with Chalmers that we Earthers have "fallen from Eden" with respect to the Edenic color-properties that are presented in visual experience, the crucial points for present purposes are the following. First, even the phenomenally constituted grounding presuppositions governing our *judgmental* color-concepts impose very strong reference-eligibility constraints on the kinds of potential external-world properties that could qualify as eligible referents of these judgmental concepts—reference-eligibility constraints which, in turn, strongly constrain the *veridicality* conditions of color-attributing judgments.[13] For instance, when one judges, of an object one is looking at, that the object is red, one's judgment is veridical only if (i) one is *actually perceiving* the apparently-present object, and (ii) this object actually instantiates a "Lockean" feature F of the kind mentioned in the preceding paragraph. Second, such veridicality conditions for judgmental color-attributing judgments *don't begin* to be satisfied, in the case of the BIV. The BIV never really visually perceives *any* external objects, let alone judgmentally red ones; furthermore, no property instantiated by entities in its actual ambient environment qualifies as an eligible referent of its exter-nalistically reference-purporting, judgmental, redness concept.

Now consider solidity. Here I have two points to make. First, I myself am inclined to think that solidity is visually experienced not as involving a complete lack of internal empty space, but rather as involving a compete lack of *visually discernible* internal empty space. Many objects in our world, such as billiard balls, really instantiate this feature, despite the fact that the scientific worldview tells us that objects like billiard balls are "mostly empty space" microphysically. I do recognize, however, that this is a subtle and tendentious issue. My second point is this: If *presentational* solidity really were Edenic in Chalmers' sense and hence were never really instantiated in our world (because visual solidity-experience would be representing objects like billiard balls as being "fully filled in" even microphysically), then *judgmental* solidity nonetheless would be governed by phenomenally consti-tuted grounding presuppositions which, in the case of the BIV, would fail to refer to any actual property that is instantiated in the BIV's ambient

---

[12] Competence in forming color-attributing judgments does not require one to realize that there is a difference between presentational color and judgmental color.

[13] The pertinent, phenomenally constituted, grounding presuppositions involve *cognitive* phenomenology: the "what it's like" of *judging* that some object is red (whether or not one is perceiving it visually).

environment. (My above remarks about color would apply here too, *mutatis mutandis*.) So the BIV's judgments deploying its judgmental solidity-concept, like its judgments deploying its judgmental color-concept, would be radically nonveridical.

Now consider space. Certainly the scientific worldview motivates various claims about space that are not part of pre-theoretic common sense—for instance, general relativity's claim that gravitation results from the curving of space by the masses of celestial objects like planets and stars. But is there anything about the spatiality-involving aspects of sensory-presentational experience, or about the ordinary concept of space, that is somehow *undermined* by the scientific worldview? Chalmers says this about the question:

> *Spatial functionalism* understands space in terms of the roles it plays. Space is as space does. To maintain continuity with the manifest image, we need these to be roles that space plays in the manifest image. What are these roles?...[S]pace plays at least three major roles.
>
> First, space mediates *motion*. In Eden, things move continuously through space. Second, space mediates *interaction*. In Eden, physical things interact when they're spatially in contact with each other or at least close to each other. There is no action at a distance. Third, space causes our spatial *perception*. In Eden, square things look square, at least in normal conditions...
>
> How can a virtual object be spatial? Like physical space, virtual space is whatever produces spatial experience and mediates motion and interaction...
>
> There's a powerful intuition that if we're in a simulation, nothing is laid out in space as it seems to be. We can now diagnose this as an Edenic intuition...Once we reconceive space as whatever plays the space role, there's room for space...in a simulation.
>
> (Chalmers 2022, 431–433)

But *what's wrong* with that Edenic intuition? I submit that *in our own world*, space plays *in an Edenic manner* the very three roles that Chalmers says it also plays in Eden. First, things really do move continuously through space—at least at the level of experiential detectability, whatever might be the case at the microphysical quantum level. Second, things normally do interact directly with each other when, and only when, they are in contact or at least close to each other.[14] Third, things quite often really are present in space, within one's own bodily-centered frame of reference, in such a way that they really have the very spatial properties that sensory experience presents them as having (e.g., squareness and spatial location); and quite often one undergoes genuine *perception* of objects and their spatial properties that is mediated in a spatially local manner (e.g., by light waves propagating through space from the perceived object to one's sensory periphery, and thereafter by physically local neural interactions within the brain).

In short, then, in our own world what plays the role that the manifest image attributes to space is what Chalmers calls Edenic space. Thus, with respect to space, there has been no fall from Eden at all; rather, in our world, space = Space. Moreover, the phenomenal intentionality of conscious experience, shared in common by you yourself and your BIV experiential duplicate, *requires* spatial properties and relations to be Edenic, as a veridicality condition of space-involving content in sensory-presentational experience and in thought. Accordingly, your concepts of spatial features like location and shape, and the corresponding concepts of your BIV duplicate, refer to the very same spatial properties and relations. But in the BIV's case, the spatial content of its sensory-presentational experiences and its associated beliefs is radically and systematically nonveridical. (For instance, when the BIV seems to be visually perceiving a square object at a certain location in its ambient environment, there isn't really a square object at such a location; and indeed, the BIV isn't really *perceiving* anything at all in its ambient environment.)

The upshot of the above observations, I contend, is as follows. First, our own world is *very nearly* Edenic, despite our fall from Eden with respect to colors and other "secondary" qualities—and perhaps also with respect to *some* primary qualities like solidity, although I doubt it.[15] (As one might say,

---

[14] Maybe there are weird exceptions involving quantum entanglement. When two entangled particles are distant from one another and a measurement is performed on one of them, perhaps this instantaneously changes the state of the other particle. But even if there are such exceptions, the fact remains that *normally*, direct physical interactions are spatially local.

[15] What about Free Will and Morality (with capitals being used Chalmers-style)? About these, Chalmers says this:

"The jury is still out, but evidence suggests that we may not have Free Will.... However, we may still have free will—the ability to choose our own actions and mostly do what we choose to do. There may be no absolute standard of Morality by which our actions are Right or Wrong. Instead there may simply be a system of morality that we construct and endorse, according to which our actions are right or wrong" (Chalmers 2022, p. 424).

the scientific worldview positions us *just outside* the gates of Eden, rather than fully within it.) Second, as regards presentational properties—for example, presentational color-properties—that are not really instantiated in our world, the judgmental concepts associated with these presentational properties are themselves governed by phenomenally constituted grounding presuppositions that still impose strong reference-eligibility constraints on candidate referent-properties; such reference-eligibility constraints must be met in order for these judgmental concepts to possess externalistic intentionality. Third, the externalistic veridicality conditions for such judgmental concepts come nowhere close to being satisfied, for the BIV's judgments deploying these concepts. Fourth, there are numerous properties and relations to which both we and our BIV duplicates refer, solely by virtue of the phenomenal intentionality of conscious experience; both we ourselves and our BIV duplicates are directly experientially acquainted with such properties and relations, via *apparent* instantiations of them in our respective *apparent* ambient environments. Fifth, these kinds of properties and relations are virtually never actually instantiated in the BIV's ambient environment. Sixth, as a consequence of these five facts, the BIV's virtual world is quite radically unreal.

References

Chalmers, D. 1996. *The Conscious Mind: In Search of a Fundamental Theory*. Oxford University Press.

Chalmers, D. 2002. The Components of Content. In D. Chalmers (ed.), *Philosophy of Mind: Classical and Contemporary Readings*. Oxford University Press, 608–633.

Chalmers, D. 2006. Perception and the Fall from Eden. In T. Gendler and J. Hawthorne (eds.), *Perceptual Experience*. Oxford University Press, 49–125.

This passage suggests, without flatly endorsing, "partial error" theories about free will and about morality, analogous to the kind of partial error theory about color that Chalmers and I both endorse. Mark Timmons and I argue against such an account of agentive freedom, and in favor of a more robust compatibilism, in Horgan and Timmons (2022). And we argue against such an account of morality, and in favor of a version of metaethical expressivism that we claim fully accommodates moral-authority phenomenology, in Horgan and Timmons (2018a, 2018b).

Chalmers, D. 2022. *Reality+: Virtual Worlds and the Problems of Philosophy.* W. W. Norton.

Davies, M., and Humberstone, L. 1980. Two Notions of Necessity. *Philosophical Studies* 38: 1–31.

Farkas, K. 2008. *Phenomenal Intentionality without Compromise. The Monist* 91: 273–293.

Graham, G., Horgan, T., and Tienson, J. 2007. Consciousness and Intentionality. In M. Velmans and S. Schneider (eds), *The Blackwell Companion to Consciousness.* Blackwell, 468–484.

Graham, G., Horgan, T., and Tienson, J. 2009. Phenomenology, Intentionality, and the Unity of Mind. In B. McLaughlin, A. Beckermann, and S. Walter (eds.), *The Oxford Handbook of Philosophy of Mind.* Oxford University Press, 512–537.

Horgan, T. 1993. From Supervenience to Superdupervenience. *Mind* 102: 555–586.

Horgan, T. 2013. Original Intentionality Is Phenomenal Intentionality. *The Monist* 96: 232–251.

Horgan, T. 2014. Phenomenal Intentionality and Secondary Qualities: The Quixotic Case of Color. In B. Brogaard (ed.), *Does Perception Have Content?* Oxford University Press, 329–350.

Horgan, T., and Graham, G. 2012. Phenomenal Intentionality and Content Determinacy. In R. Schantz (ed.), *Prospects for Meaning.* Walter de Gruyter, 321–344.

Horgan, T., and Tienson, J. 2002. The Intentionality of Phenomenology and the Phenomenology of Intentionality. In D. Chalmers (ed.), *Philosophy of Mind: Classical and Contemporary Readings.* Oxford University Press, 520–533.

Horgan, T., Tienson, J., and Graham, G. 2004. Phenomenal Intentionality and the Brain in a Vat. In R. Schantz (ed.), *The Externalist Challenge.* Walter de Gruyter, 297–317.

Horgan, T., and Timmons, M. 2018a. Gripped by Authority. *Canadian Journal of Philosophy* 48: 313–336.

Horgan, T., and Timmons, M. 2018b. The Phenomenology of Moral Authority. In D. Machuca (ed.), *Moral Skepticism: New Essays.* Routledge, 115–140.

Horgan, T., and Timmons, M. 2022. Is Agentive Freedom a Secondary Quality? *Humana Mente: Journal of Philosophical Studies* 42: 63–87.

Jackson, F. 1998. *From Metaphysics to Ethics: A Defence of Conceptual Analysis.* Oxford University Press.

Kriegel, U. 2013. *Phenomenal Intentionality.* Oxford University Press.

Loar, B. 2003. Phenomenal Intentionality as the Basis for Mental Content. In M. Hahn and B. Ramgerg (eds), *Reflections and Replies: Essays on the Philosophy of Tyler Burge*. MIT Press, 229–256.

McGinn, C. 1989. *Mental Content*. Blackwell.

Pitt, D. 2004. The Phenomenology of Cognition: Or What Is It Like to Think that P? *Philosophy and Phenomenological Research* 69: 1–36.

Siewert, C. 1998. *The Significance of Consciousness*. Princeton University Press.

Strawson, G. 1994. *Mental Reality*. MIT Press.

Terry Horgan, *Why Virtual Worlds Aren't Real: How Phenomenal Intentionality Constrains Mental Reference*
In: *Oxford Studies in Philosophy of Mind Volume 4*. Edited by: Uriah Kriegel, Oxford University Press.
© Terry Horgan 2024. DOI: 10.1093/9780198924159.003.0015

16

Simulation

Its Metaphysics and Epistemology

Christopher Peacocke

Dogmatic slumbers are as much a danger for us now as they were in Kant's time. David Chalmers' immensely stimulating and engaging book *Reality+* ought to wake many of us from our own contemporary slumbers. Chalmers is Hume in this analogy; I am certainly not going to pretend to be Kant. But I will elaborate a disagreement on an issue in metaphysics and on an interrelated issue in epistemology, and indeed these disagreements do broadly concern the conditions of possibility of experience. I disagree with Chalmers' statements that "Simulations are not illusions. Virtual worlds are real. Virtual objects really exist" (12) when applied to simulations that represent the world as spatial. That is the disagreement in metaphysics. I also question his position on a closely related matter of epistemology, his thesis that "We can't know that we're not in a simulation" (11). I take the metaphysical issue first.

1. Space, Structuralism, and Simulation Realism

Chalmers argues for simulation realism, the thesis that "If we're in a simulation, the objects around us are real and not an illusion" (106). Structuralism about the physical plays a crucial role in his argument for simulation realism. The structuralism on which Chalmers relies holds that "what our scientific theories *say* about the world is structural" (406). "If structuralism is correct, it follows that the computer simulation makes the physical theories true. That's a form of simulation realism" (413).

Chalmers' structural account of spatial matters is one in which "we reconceive space as whatever plays the space role" (433). He offers a functional account of spatial matters. I question whether this account works, and consider the consequences if it does not work. This may seem to be a question just about simulations that are spatial, and not about simulations more generally. But in fact Chalmers' view is that "spatiality is essential for a virtual world," so any questions here apply under his views to all virtual worlds.[1]

We need as a preliminary to distinguish functionalism about the spatial (spatial magnitudes, properties, and relations) from functionalism about experiential content concerning spatial subject-matter. Functionalism about spatial magnitudes, properties, and relations is a thesis about the metaphysics of the spatial. Functionalism about experiential content concerning the spatial is a thesis about the intentional content of a certain category of mental state. The distinct theses may be linked by substantive philosophical argument. Chalmers himself endorses a kind of functionalism both about the spatial itself and about spatial experience. But it would be consistent, as we will see, to reject functionalism about the spatial while endorsing a kind of functionalism about spatial experiential content. But let us first consider functionalism about space itself.

Genuine functionalism about the spatial must explain what it is to be a spatial magnitude, property, relation, or anything else, in terms of a certain kind of role, where the role must not itself ineliminably mention the spatial. We would not think much of an attempted functionalism about pain that says that it is a role of pain to explain action that is genuinely expressive of pain itself. If "space is as space does" (431), then we have to be able to say what it is that space does without mentioning the spatial. Chalmers lists the roles that do identify space functionally. Physical space and virtual space are alike in that space "is whatever produces spatial experience and what mediates motion and interaction" (433).

In considering that first condition, "whatever produces spatial experience," we need to draw a distinction. The distinction concerns the conditions that must constitutively be met by experiences of the kind that are mentioned in an intended functional account of some magnitude, property or entity. Within such conditions, we can distinguish the *extricable* from the *inextricable*.

Extricable conditions on experiences of a given type are conditions that do not, either directly or indirectly, involve the magnitudes, property, or entity of which a functional account was being offered. Extricable conditions may legitimately be involved in a functional account of a magnitude, property, or entity. Extricable conditions do not involve any threat of circularity in the account.

---

[1] "We saw in chapter 10 that spatiality is essential for a virtual world" (433).

An example of an extricable condition would be a reference to the sensation of heat in a causal-relational account of the property of being hot that a substance may possess. A substance's heat affects its character (as solid, liquid, or gas), and affects its interaction with other substances, in ways also depending in turn on their heat. These properties of heat fix a causal role for heat. Mean molecular energy in the substance realizes this role. When we classify something as hot, we take into account the way it affects human perceivers, and we restrict the range of entities that are counted as hot to those that produce a certain sensation (or to those that have the realizing magnitude in a high degree). Objects with a low temperature do not count as hot, even though they each have a certain mean molecular energy. The reference, in such an account, to the production of human experience of a certain kind simply serves to restrict the range of already identified physical magnitudes that count as heat in a substance. The restriction is plausibly not circular in an account of heat because the subjective sensation of heat plausibly has a nature that does not in turn have to be explained in terms of heat itself. If it did have to be so explained, the threat of circularity arises.

By contrast, inextricable conditions on experience of a certain kind are those that make reference, in the account of the nature of the experience, to relations to a certain kind of magnitude, property, or relation. An inextricable condition on the nature of a certain kind of experience threatens to block any attempted functional account as being a full account of the metaphysics of the magnitude, property, or entity for which the account is offered.

It is, then, an important issue for Chalmers' functional characterization of space itself, given that the characterization mentions the production of spatial experience, whether relations to space itself are involved in an account of what makes experience have a spatial content. If there is inextricability, the account does not, without further elaboration, provide a functional reduction.

What is the role of the experiential condition in Chalmers' functional account of space? It seems to me that there are magnitudes, properties, and relations that meet Chalmers' two nonexperiential conditions on space without being spatial magnitudes, properties, and relations at all. (I expect Chalmers would agree, presumably the experiential condition was included for a reason.) The two nonexperiential conditions in his characterization are that space is "what mediates motion and interaction."

Under Chalmers' structuralist position, both these roles are to be characterized in terms of properties, relations, and magnitudes that make no mention of space as such. There is a system of relations, properties, and magnitudes with the following properties. In that system, the relation of one thing being in motion relative to another is realized by a relation characterized in nonspatial terms. Similarly, distance is realized by a relation in this system that has this property: when events and objects stand in that relation, there is no, or perhaps much less, interaction between them. What range of physical magnitudes meet these conditions?[2]

Consider a two-dimensional genuinely spatial world in which there are sound events in the space. In this world, we stipulate, a sound event causally interacts only with other sound events that are close to it in pitch. Pitch then meets Chalmers' interaction condition for being a spatial dimension. There is also a relation that realizes a notion of motion across the two spatial dimensions and across the dimension of pitch. (A sound event can move as other events, such as hurricanes, can move.) But none of this makes pitch into a spatial dimension. Pitch here plays the role Chalmers specifies, but it is not a spatial dimension. Nor is experience of pitch in itself spatial perception.

Pitch is just one possible example here. We could make a similar case substituting events involving electrical discharge, with higher charge corresponding to higher pitch. The example could also be varied to include three genuinely spatial dimensions plus sound events, to generate the question of why pitch in such a world would not count as a fourth spatial dimension. Or again we could use the example of heat.

We might try to say that pitch does not count as a realizing of a spatial dimension in this example because pitch is not the same kind of dimension as the genuinely spatial dimensions. True, but saying that a dimension must be of the same kind as a genuinely spatial dimension is illegitimately importing the spatial into what was meant to be a functional account not mentioning the spatial.

A third response would be to say that the pitch dimension is too different in kind from the other two to be a realization of a spatial dimension. But then we can instead consider a pure Strawsonian sound world, with the dimensions of pitch, volume of sound, and (say) a dimension degree of similarity to a pure sine wave sound as the three realizing dimensions (cp. Strawson 1959). Again, we can elaborate the case in such a way that events close to each other on these dimensions interact causally, and not

---

[2] Why "perhaps much less interaction"? The qualification is present to acknowledge entanglement in quantum physics. Entanglement of two particles a considerable distance apart does not undermine the claim that they are that distance apart. But the arguments of this contribution to the Symposium do not rely on quantum mechanics. They apply also to a Neo-Newtonian universe.

otherwise. We can elaborate a notion of a particular event moving in these three dimensions. Strawson investigated his sound world as something to contrast with the spatial world. But the case can be elaborated in such a way that it meets the two nonexperiential conditions in Chalmers' functional account of space.

Such examples show that Chalmers' experiential condition—that the magnitudes and relations that realize spatial magnitudes and relations must also produce spatial experience—is doing real work. Experiences of pitch, or of electric charge, or of heat are not in themselves experiences with spatial intentional content. But whether including the experiential condition is legitimate in a functional account depends on whether relations to space itself are inextricable in an account of the nature of spatial experience. If there is inextricability, the appeal to the nonspatial character of the experiences of pitch may (depending on the details) not be open to someone attempting a fully functionalist reduction.

I have said that inextricability "may" block functional reduction. The "may" is present because one can conceive of a position under which inextricability is acknowledged, but as part of a holistic package of conditions on what makes something a spatial property, magnitude, or spatial entity. This position would endorse the following. There is a certain network of relations in which something S must stand to be a spatial magnitude or relation, and there is a further requirement of causation of experiences that stand in a certain relation to S. This holistic version is not circular. It is however in danger of counting the nonspatial auditory experiences in the Strawsonian sound world as spatial. Quite generally, if the nonexperiential conditions in an offered functional account of space do not genuinely pick out the spatial, adding this kind of holistic condition will not take you to the desired functionalist destination.

So we cannot postpone the substantive question any longer: what is it, constitutively, for an experience, whether genuinely perceptual or merely illusory, to have a spatial content? I suggest a two-part answer, an answer that can be labelled "Identity-Explanatory."

Part One of the answer says that for an experience to have a certain spatial content is for it to be subjectively identical in relevant respects with an experience that is a genuine, nonillusory perception in respect of that spatial content. A spatial experience has the content it does because of that relation to a genuine perception. The "because" here indicates a philosophical explanatory relation, involving an asymmetry between the merely experiential and the genuinely perceptual cases. The illusory case has the spatial content it does because of its relation to the genuinely perceptual case, which has an explanatory priority. In terminology that has become familiar: the bad case (experiential illusion) inherits its content, according to Part One, from the good case (genuine perception).

Part One of this answer speaks of subjective identity "in relevant respects," since obviously a fully illusory experience cannot have the object-involving content of the corresponding genuine perception. Further elaboration, not necessary for present purposes, is also needed to cover the case of experiences with impossible spatial content (such as the Penrose triangle), which can never be fully perceptual. But let us work with this outline of Part One of the Identity-Explanatory position.

The position needs a second component since Part One says nothing about what it is for the genuinely perceptual experience to have spatial content. Part Two of the position states that a genuinely perceptual experience has spatial content only if it contributes essentially in appropriate circumstances to the explanation of the subject's actions under spatial characterizations of those actions. The perceptual spatial content may contribute to the explanation via guidance of bodily action in space by the way things are represented as being around the subject. The contribution may be less direct, via the contribution of spatial content of perception to the subject's construction of a cognitive map of the subject's local world, which in turn contributes to the explanation of one or another actions at certain locations in that world.

While Part One of the Identity-Explanatory account evidently involves identity, Part Two is essentially space-involving in that the explanatory power of genuinely spatial perceptual content concerns explanation of relational properties of actions that involve real directions, real distances, or real places, all things external to the subject's body.[3]

If the Identity-Explanatory ("I-E") account is correct, then any condition on spatial experience in a proposed functional account of space is inextricable.

---

[3] In general, both in metaphysics and in the theory of meaning and content, we can distinguish two kinds of theories of some given topic. There are those that explain identity of predication or property in terms of an identity relation; and there are those that explain identity relations in terms of identity of predication. In the case of the property of being in pain, Wittgenstein insisted on the latter form of explanation in the *Philosophical Investigations*: "For *that* part of the grammar is quite clear to me: that is, that one will say that the stove has the same experience as I, *if* one says: it is in pain and I am in pain" (Wittgenstein 1958: §350). The I-E account is manifestly a theory of sameness of the property of spatial experience-type that appeals to an identity relation. The Chalmers treatment of spatial experience has to reject the I-E account, so unless there is some other appeal to identity in the offing, it will be an account that explains identity of type in terms of identity of property.

What it is for an experience to have a spatial content involves, directly or indirectly, a relation to space itself and spatial relations themselves. The involvement is direct in the case of genuinely perceptual spatial experiences. The involvement is indirect, but still present, in the illusory cases. If the I-E account is correct, then including a condition on the production of spatial experience in an intended functional account of space itself leaves a residue that has not been explained in functional terms.

The point does not show that space cannot be elucidated functionally. The point does show that, without further elucidation, the inclusion of a condition on the production of spatial experience in a proposed functional account of space leaves the account with an undischarged obligation.

Is there a version of functionalism about spatial experience that would sidestep the issue of inextricability? In a footnote in Chapter 23 of *Reality+*, Chalmers refers us to his earlier writings on "spatial functionalism" (502), and some of these other contributions are, in the first instance, specifically about the nature of spatial experience, rather than space itself. In "Three Puzzles about Spatial Experience," Chalmers argues that spatial experience will be constant across worlds that differ in certain spatial respects: "Doubled Earth is just like Earth, except that everything is twice as big" (Chalmers 2017: 120). Chalmers holds that the spatial experiences of a subject Doubled Oscar on Doubled Earth and his twin Oscar on Earth have the same spatial experiences when the former sees a two-meter stick, and the latter sees a one-meter stick. "It is plausible that these two experiences are phenomenally identical" (120), a position under which size itself is not given in experience.

In this and similar examples, it is not at all presupposed that space itself has a functional analysis. The proposed examples turn on the relations of experience to space, where space is taken for granted, without further suppositions about its nature. Chalmers' position on these examples has been disputed, and that discussion will no doubt continue (Peacocke 2019: 74, 82–85). What matters for the present juncture is this. If we agree with his treatment of the examples, does this functional analysis of spatial experience then give us a model for spatial experience as extricable, in a way that would allow spatial experience to be mentioned in a functional analysis of space itself?

How should we specify contents that Chalmers says are constant in spatial experiential phenomenology across Earth and Doubled Earth? We could speak of pairs of worlds and magnitudes that stand in an equivalence relation. The ordered pair of the world of Doubled Earth w_D and the magnitude of 2 meters stand in the relevant equivalence relation to the pair

<@, 1 meter>, where @ is the world of Earth. The spatial contents in phenomenology that Chalmers envisages are specified by equivalence classes of such ordered pairs under the relevant equivalence relation. Spatial action explained by the content of spatial experience would then be explained not by a pure magnitude in the content of experience, but by a <world, magnitude> pair. In @, a spatial action explained by experience would be explained by such a content involving the pair <@, 1 meter>. The subject would be acting in relation to the magnitude 1 meter in @. For an arbitrary world w that stands to @ as Doubled Earth stands to Earth, the corresponding spatial action would be explained in relation to some magnitude m for which <w, m> is in the same relevant equivalence class as <@, 1 meter>.

This account does not give a model for extricability of spatial experience. Space itself is still involved in the spatial content of experience, just in a more complicated way. The magnitudes in the second component of the ordered pairs are spatial. Spatial matters are also plausibly involved in the determination of the properties of the worlds that put them in the relevant equivalence relation. If spatial properties and magnitudes could be functionalized, such a model of content could in combination with the functional account of space provide an extricable account of spatial experience. But this treatment of the spatial content of experience does not in itself make a contribution to an account of functionalism about space itself. It is in itself prima neutral on that issue.

To summarize to this point: there seem to be respects in which relations to space itself is an inextricable feature of spatial experience, and if that is so, it is an obstacle to Chalmers' own functional account of space. If the experiential condition is included for something to be space, the account seems circular or insufficient. If the experiential condition is omitted, the conditions seem far from sufficient for something to be space.

The rejection of functionalism about spatial magnitudes, properties, and relations goes hand-in-hand with the inextricability condition on spatial experience, if the spatial is to be perceptible. For a combination of the rejection of functionalism about the spatial while endorsing extricability would be extremely puzzling. If the holding of a spatial condition goes beyond anything that might be used to characterize it functionally, how could a type of experience not individuated by its relation to the spatial ever suffice to give perceptual knowledge of the spatial condition? The alleged perception seems inadequate to such a subject-matter. There seems to be a general lesson here, and a lemma, connecting functional irreducibility with an inextricability condition.

In *Reality+* and his related papers, Chalmers makes the point that spatial magnitudes, properties, and relations may be realized as some higher-level properties of the wave function in quantum mechanics. Such a position has been described by David Albert (2013). It's not completely clear to me whether Chalmers regards the point as contributing to the case for functionalism about space, or about spatial experience. But whatever his intention, it seems to me that realization of space by higher-level properties of the wave function is consistent with the inextricability of spatial experience. Such realization implies that in having certain relations to spatial properties and magnitudes, spatial experience has these relations to the realizing higher-level properties of the wave function. But the spatial experiences in a computer-generated simulation would not have the relevant relations to the realizing higher-level properties of the wave function.

As always, spatial representation involves more than just sensitivity to spatial matters and what realizes them. The holistic features of spatial representation mean that the case cannot be as simple as that of the sensation of heat. But the holistic structure involved in spatial representation can still be instantiated in relation to whatever it is that realizes space.

Chalmers' own functional characterization of space also differs from some of the functionalist characterizations found in the literature on the philosophy of physics that he cites. Eleanor Knox, for instance, offers this as a functional characterization of spacetime: "spacetime is whatever serves to define a structure of inertial frames, where inertial frames are those in whose coordinates the laws governing interactions take a simple form (that is universal insofar as curvature may be ignored), and with respect to which free bodies move with constant velocity" (Knox 2019: 119). This may eliminate a problematic entity of spacetime in favor of what is mentioned in the characterization, but that characterization hardly eliminates spatial magnitudes and relations altogether. The notion of an inertial frame, which involves constant velocity (relative to a frame), is still something spatial. Such a functional characterization as Knox's is not something that can be used to vindicate the thesis that there is space in simulated worlds, since whatever are the data structures and relations in a computer generating the simulation, they do not involve a structure of inertial frames. Functionalizing away spacetime is not functionalizing away everything spatial.

Chalmers does agree that there is a "powerful intuition" that if we are in a simulation, "nothing is laid out in space as it seems to be" (433). His diagnosis of this intuition is that if we are in simulation, nothing is laid out in absolute Newtonian space ('Space' as capitalized in his discussion). "Once we reconceive space as whatever plays the space role, there's room for space in those physical theories, and there's also room for space in a simulation" (433). This does not seem to me to be a plausible diagnosis of the aforementioned powerful intuition that in a simulation nothing is laid out in space as it seems to be, because Newtonian absolute space seems to me not to play an essential part in generating the intuition of perceptual error in a simulation. You can find a simulation illusory in respect of the spatial layout it apparently presents without ever having so much as conceived of space as absolute. It seems to me more plausible that we have an intuitive grasp of Part One, the Identity component, of the I-E account, and that is why we classify the experiences in the simulation as illusory. Experiences in the simulation are subjectively the same in relevant respects as genuine perceptual experience, whose correctness conditions concern spatial matters (whether Newtonian or not). In a simulation, the experience is illusory not because of the absence of any relation to absolute Space, but because the subject of the experience does not have the right relations to genuine spatial relations and magnitudes. There is no commitment to Newtonian absolute space in the I-E account (and nor to neo-Newtonian space either).

Chalmers develops a discussion that treats appropriate thought about simulations involving spatial experience as parallel to thought about the relation of the scientific image to the manifest image, in Sellars' sense. The parallelism in the way he develops it exists only if space can be functionalized. So if the doubts about a functional treatment of space are correct, his diagnosis of the intuition is missing a component. If space cannot be functionalized, space may be a component both of the manifest image and of the scientific image—even if it is realized in higher-level properties of the wave function.

In sum, it seems to me correct that if we are in a simulation, then nothing is laid out in space as it seems to be in the simulation.

These remarks about space and spatial experience would not rule out a type of content in respect of which the contents of the states of subjects in the simulation are correct. They would have to be contents at no point relying for their natures on their perceptual relations to space. They would be very different from the contents we normally talk about. They would not be the contents that seem to hold in the world of *The Matrix*.[4]

---

[4] I believe that analogous arguments from inextricability could be developed against functional treatments of time and of temporal experience. But our current philosophical and psychological understanding of temporal perception (certainly my understanding) is rudimentary compared with our understanding of the spatial case. A proper development of a parallel nonfunctionalist treatment of time awaits a better understanding of temporal perception.

2. Can We Know We Are Not in a Simulation?

Chalmers writes, "My primary aim in this book is to argue against global skepticism about the external world" (444). The structuralism about physics plays a crucial part in his argument against global skepticism, since it allows perceptions and thoughts about the physical to be true and in some cases to be known when subjects are in a simulated world. If however the structural-functional analysis of space is false, and we have inextricability of spatial experience with respect to space itself, apparently spatial virtual worlds will always be illusory. Hence once more the specter of radical global skepticism appears.

If the I-E account of spatial experience, or anything much like it, is correct, and Chalmers' account of content is not available, can we know we are not in a simulation with the illusory spatial experiences? Actually, we do not need the full strength of the I-E's constitutive thesis for that question to be pressing. The question arises from the mere truth of the identity of the relevant content of the illusory spatial experience with that of a genuinely spatial perception—the truth does not have to have a constitutive status for the consequence to hold. That truth, if it is a truth, is enough for the spatial experiences in a full simulation to be nonveridical.

Before I engage with the epistemological question, it is worth zooming out to consider the structure of this dialectic as an instance of the entirely general Integration Challenge—the challenge of satisfactorily integrating the metaphysics and epistemology of any given domain. In *Reality+* Chalmers is recommending a certain kind of solution to the Integration Challenge for the domain of the external world. He is recommending a reconciliation that I would (not at all impartially) describe as weakening the content of propositions about the spatial external world, and thereby making a corresponding epistemology easier. The account of the weakened content has to be convincing for this kind of reconciliation to work. We can be quite sure from his other writings that Chalmers would reject any weakened account of consciousness as a proposed means of meeting the Integration Challenge for consciousness. When we do not propose a weakened metaphysics, provision of an epistemology is correspondingly a more demanding task. My own conjecture, while we are talking at this level of generality, is that consciousness and space should be treated on a par in respect of their metaphysics, and that the epistemological challenges such a parity presents are correspondingly great.

If subjects in a global simulation have experiences that misrepresent them as being in a certain kind of spatial environment, are we then faced with radical skepticism? It might seem to be so. Chalmers writes, "But if we're *not* in a virtual world, we'll never know that for sure. . . . We can never prove we're not in a computer simulation because any evidence of ordinary reality—whether the grandeur of nature, the antics of your cat, or the behavior of other people—could presumably be simulated" (11)."If we're in a perfect simulation, it's hard to see how we could ever get evidence of that fact. Our evidence in the simulation will always correspond precisely to evidence in the unsimulated world" (36). "A nonsimulated world and a perfect simulation of it will seem exactly the same" (37). Call this the Simulation-Replication ("S-R") thesis about evidence. Is it true?

If "evidence" means apparent perceptual state, then it's plausible. I may check in the real world in empirical psychological experiments that my experiences as of certain objective states of affairs are indeed produced by such objective states of affairs. But my whole series of apparent perceptions in such checking could also occur in a simulation. The Simulation-Replication thesis is true when "evidence" is so understood.

This is not, however, the only legitimate and relevant understanding of what evidence is. If factive perceptual states are evidence, then the S-R thesis is false. In a simulated world, none of the spatial experiences is genuinely factive (where this involves the experience being suitably causally explained by the spatial state of affairs that it is as of). On this understanding of evidence, there are multiple evidential states in the real world that are not replicated in a perfect simulation of the real world.[5]

The starting point of the radical skeptic's thought remains articulable on this position. The radical skeptic has a legitimate starting point in saying there is a notion of subjective indistinguishability for which it is true there is a simulation in which the whole course of your actual experience is subjectively indistinguishable from your experience in that simulation. The claim that therefore you don't have the spatial knowledge you seem to have is a further step, involving other commitments that are subjects of lively dispute. If you have perceptual knowledge when you have the right relation to a factive perceptual state, the skeptic's starting point does not undermine the status of your basic spatial perceptual beliefs as knowledge. A factive-state

---

[5] I do not claim any novelty in these points about evidence, they have been extensively discussed in various forms for at least four decades. Significant points in the discussion include McDowell (1982) and the papers in Williamson (2000). One of the striking points about Chalmers' book is that while the discussion of simulations is extraordinarily extensive, cross-disciplinary, and most impressively cross-cultural, his discussion of epistemology is much less so.

epistemology need not be purely reliabilist. A factive perceptual state in which it seems to you that something is so can be a rational basis for judging it is so.[6]

A Chalmers-like position on structuralism and simulation realism could make legitimate use of a factive state too, if its advocates so wished. That position could also distinguish between illusions and factive states in the simulated world. The point is not that the notion of a factive state is not available to Chalmers' position. It is rather that the claim that the evidence is the same in the simulated and in the nonsimulated worlds is clearly not including factive states, of whatever kind, in its use of the notion of evidence.

Suppose we reject the functionalist analysis of space and spatial experience, and that we have a factive-state epistemology. There is then an argument to be offered that we can know we are not in simulation. Under these suppositions, the following can hold:

(1) You know: *this* [perceptual demonstrative] is a three-dimensional book.

where this is perceptual knowledge based on a factive perceptual state. It can also be the case that

(2) You know: If this is a three-dimensional book, then my experience of it is not caused by a data structure in a simulation-generator.

This you know by philosophical reflection, if the preceding is correct. A genuine spatial perception of a three-dimensional object cannot be caused by a data structure in a simulation-generator if the nonfunctional account of space and spatial experience is correct.

If you can come to know by means of modus ponens from two premises that you already know, then

(3) You can know your experience is not caused by a data structure in a simulation-generator.

The argument (1)–(3) is not open to the objections that undermined McKinsey-like arguments in the philosophical discussions of roughly three decades ago (McKinsey 1991). The arguments there under discussion

---

[6] On factive perceptual states and their epistemological significance, see Peacocke (2018).

included such reasoning as: "I have beliefs about water; the concept *water* requires someone has been in contact with water; hence someone has been in contact with water." The seemingly problematic epistemic character of such examples evaporated once it was noted that it is really empirical information that *water* is a nonempty concept. But the argument (1)–(3) does not turn on the nonempty character of natural kind concept, nor apparently does it rest on analogous cheating or smuggling in of presuppositions. It seems to be available to factive-state epistemologists, given nonfunctional accounts of space and spatial perceptual experience.

This would be one way of meeting the Integration Challenge for knowledge about the spatial world without so weakening the content of beliefs about the spatial world that they can be true in a simulation. It involves, for the propositions in question, an endorsement of a KK principle, that if one knows something, one is in a position to know that one does. The position would mesh nicely with some recent discussions of that principle (see for instance Greco 2014 and Stalnaker 2019). I certainly do not assert unequivocally that this position is correct. But it does seem to me a contender. Its mere existence implies that much more additional argument is needed to show that we cannot know that we are not in a simulation.

References

Albert, D. 2013. "Wave Function Realism," in *The Wave Function: Essays on the Metaphysics of Quantum Mechanics* ed. A. Ney and D. Albert, 52–57 (New York: Oxford University Press).

Chalmers, D. 2017. "Three Puzzles about Spatial Experience," in *Blockheads: Essays on Ned Block's Philosophy of Minds and Consciousness* eds. A. Pautz and D. Stoljar, 109–137 (Cambridge, MA: MIT Press).

Greco, D. 2014. "Could KK be OK?," *Journal of Philosophy* 111: 169–197.

Knox, E. 2019. "Physical Relativity from a Functionalist Perspective," *Studies in History and Philosophy of Modern Physics* 67: 118–124.

McDowell, J. 1982. "Criteria, Defeasibility, and Knowledge," *Proceedings of the British Academy* 68: 455–479.

McKinsey, M. 1991. "Anti-individualism and Privileged Access," *Analysis* 51: 9–16.

Peacocke, C. 2018. "Are Perceptions Reached by Rational Inference? Comments on Susanna Siegel," *The Rationality of Perception, Res Philosophica* 95: 751–760.

Peacocke, C. 2019. *The Primacy of Metaphysics* (Oxford: Oxford University Press).

Stalnaker, R. 2019. "Luminosity and the KK Thesis" repr. in his *Knowledge and Conditionals: Essays on the Structure of Inquiry*, 31–48 (Oxford: Oxford University Press).

Strawson, P. 1959. *Individuals: An Essay in Descriptive Metaphysics* (London: Methuen).

Williamson, T. 2000. *Knowledge and Its Limits* (Oxford: Oxford University Press).

Wittgenstein, L. 1958. *Philosophical Investigations* trans. G. E. M. Anscombe, 2nd edn (Oxford: Blackwell).

Christopher Peacocke, *Simulation: Its Metaphysics and Epistemology* In: *Oxford Studies in Philosophy of Mind Volume 4*. Edited by: Uriah Kriegel, Oxford University Press. © Christopher Peacocke 2024. DOI: 10.1093/9780198924159.003.0016

17

The Simulation Hypothesis

Metaphysics, Epistemology, Value

David J. Chalmers

I'd like to thank Grace Helton, Terry Horgan, and Christopher Peacocke for their rich commentaries on my book *Reality+*. As it happens, all three of them focus on the simulation hypothesis: the hypothesis that we are living in a lifelong computer simulation. Where the simulation hypothesis is concerned, I have three main theses in the book, one concerning metaphysics, one concerning epistemology, and one concerning value.

Metaphysics: If we're in a simulation, the objects around us are real.

Epistemology: We can't know we're not in a simulation.

Value: We can live a good life in a simulation.

These three theses about simulation are very similar to the three main theses in the book concerning virtual reality, except that they concern only simulation scenarios and not ordinary virtual reality scenarios. The theses are interconnected. The core thesis is the metaphysical thesis, simulation realism, which has consequences for both epistemology and value. Simulation realism blocks the inference from the epistemological thesis to external world skepticism. Simulation realism also blocks one key argument against the value thesis: that life in a simulation is not valuable because it is illusory.

The three commentators address all three of these theses. Horgan argues against the metaphysical thesis. Peacocke argues against both the metaphysical thesis and the epistemological thesis. Helton uses epistemological considerations to argue against a version of the value thesis. I'll address the three commentaries in this order.

1. Horgan on Simulation Realism

Horgan rejects simulation realism. He holds that a being in a simulation, such as a philosopher's brain in a vat (BIV) has systematically nonveridical beliefs about its world. His case for this view is grounded in what he calls a Cartesian intuition that a BIV has largely nonveridical beliefs, combined with a phenomenological examination that tends to reinforce these intuitions.

On Horgan's view, we have phenomenal acquaintance with a number of properties and relations, including especially spatial properties and relations, which we attribute to entities in our environment. A BIV is phenomenally identical to an ordinary non-BIV, is acquainted with the same properties, and attributes them in a similar pattern. But where the non-BIV may attribute these properties veridically, a BIV's attribution of them is intuitively not veridical.

It is true that simulation realism is counterintuitive for many people. That is why I argued for it at considerable length, especially in chapters 9 and 22. Three central arguments for simulation realism from these chapters are outlined in the precis. These arguments have as their key premises: "If the simulation hypothesis is true, the it-from-bit-creation hypothesis is true" (p. 171), "Photons are whatever play the photon role" (p. 176), and "Physical theories are structural theories" (p. 413).

Horgan does not directly address any of my arguments. I suspect that he would deny the three key premises I have outlined. He might well reject the structuralist view of the content of physical theories, probably by holding that spatial claims in our physical theories have some more-than-structural content. Since he thinks we are directly acquainted with spatial properties and relations, then perhaps this acquaintance might ground non-structural content in our theories of the world.

Still, structuralism (or structural realism) is a very popular view of physical theories, and I suspect that many physicists and philosophers of physics would reject Horgan's view that physical theories have more-than-structural content. After all, on Horgan's view it's quite possible that the properties we have phenomenal acquaintance with are not instantiated in our environment (since phenomenology is constitutively independent of the environment).

Horgan will have to say that if so, our physical theories involving space are false, even if they capture the mathematical structure of the world and are predictively successful. I think the view that our physical theories would still be true is in many ways more attractive.

What about the Cartesian intuitions that Horgan thinks undercut simulation realism? Unlike some structuralists, I am inclined to give these intuitions some weight but to relocate them. As Horgan notes, I take these intuitions to concern the Edenic content of perception. At one level, our experience presents objects in the world as having Colors (Edenic colors: primitive qualities of Redness and Greenness, as in the garden of Eden) and as being located in Space (Edenic space: a non-relative, Euclidean space that contains everything). If we are in a simulation, objects do not have the Colors or Spatial locations that we take them to have, so the Edenic content of our experiences and beliefs will be nonveridical.

However, I don't think the falsity of Edenic contents entails that our ordinary experiences and beliefs are nonveridical. In the case of color, we discovered long ago that apples are not (Edenically) Red. But apples are (non-Edenically) red all the same. Likewise, physics strongly suggests that our world does not have Edenic space. But Michael Jordan is over six feet tall all the same. The truth-conditions of our ordinary experiences and beliefs are not given by their Edenic contents but their non-Edenic contents.

So, I accommodate Horgan's Cartesian intuitions by agreeing that if we are in a simulation, the Edenic content of our beliefs and experiences is false, but denying that this entails that our beliefs and experiences are false in the ordinary sense. In this respect simulations are no worse off than our ordinary post-Fall relativistic world. The world lacks Space and Color, but it still has space and color. The same goes for a simulation.

Where color is concerned, Horgan himself endorses a closely related two-tiered picture. He thinks color experiences represent Edenic colors and are always nonveridical, but that color judgments represent non-Edenic colors (physical properties that play the causal roles of colors) and are often veridical. This framework allows Horgan to respect both phenomenological intuition and the correctness of our ordinary judgments that apples are red. He also indicates openness to a corresponding framework involving perception and judgments about solidity. If we do the same for space, we can likewise respect both phenomenology and the correctness of ordinary judgments, and the same framework would allow our beliefs to be true in a simulation.

Now, Horgan insists that his two-tiered picture with nonveridical Edenic perception and veridical non-Edenic judgment does not extend to veridical non-Edenic judgments in a simulation. He says there are "reference-eligibility constraints" on counting even as non-Edenic space that a simulation does not meet. At this point, however, Horgan's judgment about the constraints seems somewhat theoretical and not a matter of clear phenomenological intuition. Those intuitions concerned Edenic color which has been accommodated. I think that once we have fallen from Eden, it is not clear why non-Edenic digital properties that play the roles of color and space should not be able to make our judgments veridical.

In the key case of space, Horgan rejects the two-tiered picture, holding that both perception and judgment have Edenic spatial contents. He holds that unlike Edenic colors, Edenic space is instantiated in the actual world: space is Edenic space.

My view is that it is implausible that space is Edenic space. Edenic space—space as presented in the manifest image—is Euclidean, non-relative, and fundamental. Space as presented in the scientific image is non-Euclidean, relative, and quite possibly nonfundamental. Horgan doesn't consider these three differences. When he asks how the scientific worldview might undermine Edenic space, he instead considers three different factors: space's role in motion, interaction, and perception. I allow that all of these are present in both Edenic and non-Edenic space, so these are the wrong factors to consider in the fall from Eden.

Now, Horgan might argue that space in the manifest image is not committed to being Euclidean, non-relative, and fundamental. If Edenic space were neutral on these things, then Edenic space would be consistent with modern science. Perhaps one could make the case that the phenomenology is not entirely committed to Euclidean space or fundamental space (though space does seem to be presented as a basic container for everything). I do think it is hard to reconcile Edenic space with relativity, however. I think that Edenic space is presented to us as non-relative and we can't really grasp the idea of it being relative to a reference frame. We can grasp the idea of space being relative, but that requires a fall from Eden.

Furthermore, even if we allowed that there has been no spatial fall from Eden due to science in the actual world, Horgan's general framework presumably allows that certain more radical changes could lead to such a fall. Then paralleling the case of color, we would have Edenic spatial contents for perception, non-Edenic contents for judgment, and our spatial judgments would be largely true despite the fall. Under that framework, if we were to find that we were in a simulation, the digital quasi-spatial relations that play the space role in a simulation would qualify naturally as non-Edenic space.

Horgan may again say that digital properties do not meet his "reference-eligibility constraints" on being contents of (non-Edenic) spatial judgments, but again these constraints and their justification are far from clear. At this point, Horgan cannot derive much support from Cartesian intuitions, which largely concern Edenic space. He does suggest that one constraint is that the relevant non-Edenic properties must be instantiated by objects we perceive, and that in a simulation, we do not perceive genuine objects at all. But I've argued at length that this is wrong: when in virtual reality, we perceive real digital objects. If Horgan has an argument against that thesis, it would be interesting to hear it.

To sum up: even on Horgan's own preferred semantic framework, the simulation hypothesis can naturally be understood as a fall from Eden that renders the Edenic contents of perception false, but allows our ordinary judgments to be true. If so, we have a form of simulation realism.

2. Peacocke on Simulation Realism and Simulation Knowledge

Peacocke first concentrates on metaphysics, arguing against simulation realism. He then focuses on epistemology, arguing against the thesis that we don't know we're not in a simulation.

Peacocke's case against simulation realism (unlike Horgan's) focuses squarely on my structuralism about the physical world, and especially on my spatial functionalism. This is roughly the view that space is picked out by its functional role: in slogan form, space is what plays the space role. Like other sorts of realizer functionalism (for example about color), the idea is that the slogan is a priori but not necessary.

Spatial functionalism provides a natural case for simulation realism via the idea that if we are in a simulation, a certain cluster of digital properties and relations play the space role and thereby qualify as spatial properties and relations. These spatial properties and relations are genuinely instantiated in the simulation roughly where they seem to be. If so, our spatial experiences and spatial beliefs are veridical, which helps to vindicate simulation realism.

Peacocke starts by distinguishing functionalism about space from functionalism about the contents of spatial experience. For what it's worth, I am not a metaphysical functionalist (sometimes called a role functionalist) who holds that spatial properties are identical to functional properties. Rather, I am a realizer functionalist who holds that (non-Edenic) spatial properties are picked out as whatever properties play the relevant functional role. I also think there are Edenic spatial properties (uninstantiated in our world) that are not functional properties.

As for spatial experience, I think it has Edenic content which is not functional (involving primitive Edenic properties), Fregean content which is functional (holding e.g. that the property that plays the space role is so-distributed), and Russellian content that need not be functional (involving non-Edenic spatial properties).

Peacocke homes in on my realizer functionalism about space, asking whether the space role (the condition that spatial properties must satisfy to count as spatial) is truly independent of space itself (is extricable), or involves space itself (is inextricable). The thought is that extricable conditions might allow a reductive identification of spatial properties, whereas inextricable conditions will have an element of circularity.

My own account of the space role appeals partly to space's role in motion (roughly, location varies continuously with time) and interaction (roughly, closer things interact more), and partly to its role in perception (roughly, things that are a certain distance away tend to cause experiences as of being that distance away). Peacocke thinks that the motion and interaction conditions alone are inadequate to pick out the spatial. He holds that the perception condition may be adequate, but thinks it is inextricably spatial, as spatial experience is fundamentally characterized in terms of space. This leads to a form of circularity and cannot ground a reductive identification of space.

On my view, we escape from circularity by distinguishing Edenic and non-Edenic space. Spatial functionalism is a view of non-Edenic space. Non-Edenic space is picked out in part as what causes certain spatial experiences. Spatial experiences consist fundamentally in relations to Edenic spatial properties. As a result, the perceptual part of the space role is inextricable from Edenic space, but is extricable from non-Edenic space. Since the space role is used only to pick out non-Edenic space, circularity is avoided.

Even if one eschews the Edenic apparatus, I am not sure how bad the resulting inextricability is for simulation realism. Let's say that spatial properties are partly picked out as the causes of spatial experiences, and that spatial experiences consist partly in relations to spatial properties. In my view this inextricably spatial role can nevertheless give us some guidance as to the nature of spatial properties, as long as we have a prior grasp of the category of spatial experiences. I think we plausibly have a phenomenological grasp of what counts as a spatial experience, one that does not depend much on metaphysical disputes about the nature of spatial properties. And we can know that if we are in a simulation, it is certain digital properties that bring about spatial experiences. That can help us to identify these digital properties with spatial properties. Realizer functionalism does not need to have an entirely reductive characterization of the role in order to helpfully characterize the realizer.

Peacocke also sets out an intriguing thought experiment in which pitch plays some of the roles of space, in order to cause trouble for spatial functionalism. He writes:

> Consider a two-dimensional genuinely spatial world in which there are sound events in the space. In this world, we stipulate, a sound event causally interacts only with other sound events that are close to it in pitch. Pitch then meets Chalmers' interaction condition for being a spatial dimension. There is also a relation that realizes a notion of motion across the two spatial dimensions and across the dimension of pitch. (A sound event can move as other events, such as hurricanes, can move.) But none of this makes pitch into a spatial dimension. Pitch here plays the role Chalmers specifies, but it is not a spatial dimension. Nor is experience of pitch in itself spatial perception.

Peacocke uses this thought experiment to argue that the nonexperiential aspects of the space role (in terms of motion and interaction) are inadequate to pick out space, so that the role in perception is required to do real work (leading into the problem of inextricability discussed above). Where my defense of simulation realism is concerned, having to invoke the combined role would be OK, as I think I have an answer to the inextricability problem.

At the same time, I am interested in whether one could develop a wholly *nonphenomenal* spatial functionalism where the roles that pin down space do not involve experience in any way. This might be especially relevant for the purposes of understanding "emergent spacetime" (that is, the grounding of spatiotemporal properties in more primitive non-spatiotemporal properties) in the philosophy of physics, where physicists will prefer a reduction that gives no special role to conscious experience. (See my "Finding Space in a Nonspatial World" for discussion.) Peacocke's argument threatens to rule out any sort of nonphenomenal spatial functionalism. So I am interested to evaluate it.

As it stands, Peacocke's description of the scenario is perhaps somewhat tendentious. He stipulates a two-dimensional spatial world with a third pitch dimension that plays a certain role. This is more or less to stipulate that the pitch dimension is nonspatial. Still, it isn't hard to describe the situation in a more neutral way, and many will still have Peacocke's intuition that the pitch dimension is nonspatial.

Another problem with the case is that Peacocke is describing the case as a counterfactual possible world in which pitch plays the space role without being spatial. But recall that realizer functionalism is not committed to the thesis that necessarily, space is whatever plays the space role. On this view, it is metaphysically possible that something nonspatial could play the space role without being spatial. So this version of Peacocke's case does little to rule out (nonphenomenal, realizer) spatial functionalism. To connect better with the sort of spatial functionalism at issue here, we need to think of the case as an epistemic possibility (at least one not ruled out a priori).

Consider the following as an epistemically possible hypothesis about our world: there are two spatial dimensions and a third pitch dimension, where pitch plays a spatial role. To start with, we can stipulate that pitch plays both the experiential and nonexperiential space roles: for example, it causes experiences of spatial location along the relevant dimension. And we may as well suppose that experiences in this world are (and always have been) indistinguishable from those in an ordinary spatial world. Is this a scenario where pitch is entirely nonspatial, or is it one where a third dimension of space is constituted by pitch? The latter does not seem at all implausible to me. Certainly, if we discovered that we lived in this world, I think that this is what we would say. We would take ourselves to have made a discovery about the nature of three-dimensional space in our world: that it is partly constituted by pitch.

What if we drop the stipulation that pitch plays the experiential roles of space, and hold that it plays only the nonexperiential roles in motion and interaction. Then matters are less clear. If pitch plays no role in our spatial perception (and presumably we have no spatial perception along the relevant dimension), there is perhaps some grounds for not identifying it with space. But once we have allowed that pitch can be spatial in the previous case where it plays the experiential role, we have at least blocked the intuition that pitch is simply the wrong sort of thing to constitute a spatial dimension.

In the second part of his commentary, Peacocke takes issue with my claim that we cannot know we are not in a simulation. He argues that factive perceptual states such as my perception of a cube, can serve as evidence, enabling me to know that this is a cube. Furthermore, he thinks we can know (via philosophical reflection supporting simulation irrealism) that if this is a cube, we are not in a simulation. This allows us to know that we are not in a simulation.

Around this point, Peacocke observes in a footnote that factive views of perceptual evidence are common, and notes that my discussion of epistemology in *Reality+* is not as extensive as my discussion of simulation. Here Peacocke seems understandably to have missed the fairly extensive epistemological discussion in the online appendices to the book. Among other things, these include a substantial discussion of externalist views of evidence (under the heading "Sims won't have our evidence!"), arguing that these do not allow us to know that we are not in a simulation (at least given the simulation-argument claim that most beings with experiences phenomenally like ours are in simulations). I don't think I can improve on that discussion, so to enter it into the standard publication record, I will include an excerpt from the online appendices as the paragraphs that follow.

Some philosophers hold that our evidence about the world goes well beyond our conscious experience to include elements of the external world. If so, we may have evidence about the world that a perfect simulation does not (see Weatherson 2003). For example, I am seeing a wooden desk in front of me. This desk is part of my evidence. A perfect sim simulating me is not really seeing a wooden desk in front of it. There is no wooden desk in the simulation at all. At best there is a simulation of a wooden desk. So the sim does not have my evidence. Even if most people with conscious experiences like mine are sims, most people with evidence like mine are not. So given my evidence, I can be confident that I am not a sim.

This line is somewhat reminiscent of Moore's line that his hands are proof that the external world exists, although with the weaker notion of evidence replacing the stronger notion of proof. One reply is that I cannot know I have the evidence of my desk (or my hands). That's part of what we're trying to determine. But for these philosophers (so-called externalists about evidence), what matters for me to know I am not in a simulation is that I have the evidence of a nonsimulated world, not that I know that I have it.

Another reply is that if I am right about the Reality Question [that is, about simulation realism], then if I am simulated I too really see a wooden desk in front of me. If so, my evidence about a wooden desk does not really cut against the simulation hypothesis. But an opponent might reject my line on the Reality Question, and at this stage I do not want to presuppose it.

More importantly: once I know that most people with my conscious experiences are sims, my external evidence can no longer justify my belief that I am not a sim. We can bring this out with a series of analogous cases.

Suppose I'm told by a reliable authority that half the people in the world (selected randomly) have just been imperceptibly given a drug so that they are falsely hallucinating a normal-seeming environment in front of them, while the other half are perceiving normally. I have an experience as of a cat in front of me. Suppose that in fact I am one of the lucky ones perceiving normally, though I have no special indication of this. How confident should I be that I am really seeing a cat? An externalist could suggest that I have the evidence provided by the real cat, so I should be very confident that this is a cat. But this seems clearly wrong. In this circumstance I should be only 50% confident that I am perceiving accurately, and correspondingly 50% confident that I am seeing a cat. In a similar way, if I know that 50% of people with experiences like mine are sims, I should be 50% confident that I am a sim.

Likewise, suppose I know that nine out of ten "zebras" in zoos are holograms that look exactly like real zebras. Suppose that on one occasion I happen to be seeing a real zebra. An externalist may say that in this case I have the real zebra as evidence, so I can know I am not seeing a hologram. But it seems clear that I do not and cannot know this. My knowledge that holograms are common prevents the zebra from justifying my belief that this is a hologram. In fact, I should be 90% confident that I am seeing a hologram.

Moving closer to the sim case, suppose I'm told that in nine out of ten countries in the world, all apparent zebras in zoos are holograms. Absent any indication that my own country is special, then I can't know that what I'm seeing is not a hologram. Even if I'm actually seeing a zebra, it would be rational to be 90% confident that we're seeing a hologram.

Now moving to the sim case: suppose I know that in nine out of ten worlds, all apparent tables are simulations. Absent any indication that there's anything special about my own world, then I can't know that I'm seeing an unsimulated table. Even if I happen to be a nonsim, it would be rational to be 90% confident I'm seeing a simulated table, and 90% confident that I am a sim.

Furthermore, it is quite straightforward for externalists about evidence to accept these verdicts. Even most externalists allow that perceptual evidence (e.g. seeing a zebra) can be defeated by other evidence (e.g. knowing that most zoos contain holograms). When we grant that 90% of beings with evidence like ours are sims, this in effect overwhelms any evidence provided by our being nonsims, so that we should be 90% confident that we are sims. An externalist of this sort can endorse the key indifference principles that we have been working with. I think that reflection on the cases we have discussed recommends this view.

In the philosophical literature, some related cases are pressed against the externalist by Roger White (2014) and Jonathan Vogel (2008). I don't know of explicit discussion of these cases by externalists. As I've noted, many externalists allow that a subject's external evidence can be defeated by other evidence, which when applied to the simulation cases will tend to lead to the conclusions in line with the original indifference principle.

At least one externalist, Maria Lasonen-Aarnio (2010), takes what she calls the "radical option" of holding that knowledge is not undermined by potential defeating evidence. On this line, someone seeing a zebra might continue to know that they are seeing a zebra in a case like this even in light of the evidence about holograms—although their believing they are seeing a zebra would be unreasonable. This radical externalism (combined with the view that sims undergo illusions) might lead to a view where we might be able to know that we are nonsims (if in fact we are), even though we know that 90% of beings with experiences like ours are sims. Even on Lasonen-Aarnio's view, this defeating knowledge would make it unreasonable for us to believe we are nonsims, however. It seems that it would be most reasonable for us to have a high credence that we are sims.

Returning to my reply to Peacocke: One thing this discussion brings out is that the Bostrom-style simulation argument (construed as an argument that there is a significant probability that we are in a simulation) plays a crucial role in my full argument that we cannot know we are not in a simulation. As I put things at the end of chapter 5 of the main text: the simulation argument makes it a serious possibility that we are in a simulation; and once it is a serious possibility, these [anti-skeptical] arguments cannot rule it out. Peacocke's discussion addresses my initial prima facie case (in chapter 2 of the book) that we can't know that we are not in a simulation. It would be very interesting to know his response to my use of the simulation argument (in chapter 5 and the associated appendices) to defang anti-skeptical responses such as his own.

3. Helton on Solipsism and the Value of Social Knowledge

Grace Helton focuses especially on issues about value. These issues build on Helton's earlier epistemological work, in which she argues that skepticism about other minds should be taken seriously. In her earlier work, Helton holds that there is a significant possibility that we live in a *solipsistic* simulation, in which (apparent) other people lack minds altogether. The solipsistic simulation hypothesis seems at least to be a coherent hypothesis. Helton argues that my structuralist path to simulation realism, which suggests that tables will be present in a simulation in virtue of its structure, does not work where other minds are concerned. Further, there is reason to think that many solipsistic simulations may be built, in part because they may be more efficient or more ethical for simulators to run. If so, then an adaptation of the simulation argument suggests that we should give significant credence to the solipsistic simulation hypothesis.

All this has consequences for value. Intuitively, the solipsistic simulation hypothesis is very bad. If our loved ones don't love us back, and if no one ever understands us, that is bad. Helton makes the case in more detail by arguing that if we are in a solipsistic simulation, we lack social knowledge, and that for most of us, social knowledge is extremely valuable, perhaps so valuable that it swamps the value of most other sorts of knowledge. If so, we should not be sanguine about the possibility that we are in a simulation. If we are in a simulation, we may well be in a very bad one.

I am open to Helton's conclusions. Her main theses are consistent with the letter of what I say in the book: I say that we can live a good life in a virtual world, but I don't say that all virtual worlds will support good lives. Her theses may cut against the spirit of the book, though, which tends to suggest (without quite saying it) that simulated worlds may be about as good as nonsimulated worlds in the most important respects. If most actual simulated worlds are solipsistic and most actual unsimulated worlds are not, then at least in actuality, simulated worlds are typically much worse in an important respect than nonsimulated worlds. So it is worth going over Helton's reasoning to see which parts I accept.

I agree with Helton that the problem of other minds is a serious problem. More precisely, I think that the problem of other *conscious* minds is a serious problem. I hold that consciousness cannot be analyzed in functional terms, and a scenario where others are zombies without consciousness cannot be excluded a priori. Now, there may be some mental states and properties that can be functionally analyzed. For those mental states, I think the problem of other minds is much less pressing. These functional mental states will be present at least in a perfect simulation. Helton suggests that even for these mental states, there will be behaviorally normal beings ("faux-folk") that lack the mental states entirely, but this is not obvious to me. There will be extreme cases like Ned Block's Blockhead, but this can't be realistically created (and certainly can't be efficiently created) due to combinatorial explosion.

There are AI systems such as the GPT models, but at least to date these systems fall short of fully humanlike behavior, and it's unclear just what sort of mental states they might have if and when they get there.

Still, the problem of other conscious minds is a problem enough. If everyone aside from me is a zombie, that is a bad thing. And I agree that structuralism doesn't do too much to rule out zombies. I am a structuralist about the physical world but not about consciousness. I do think there are other routes that work better to establishing other conscious minds: for example, abductive arguments (inferring psychophysical laws from our own case) get at least some purchase.

Helton's version of the simulation argument applies to zombies as well as to faux-folk. Ethical simulators might well prefer to build simulations in which everyone or almost everyone is a zombie. Doing so avoids needless suffering and minimizes playing god with conscious beings. Of course, for simulators to do this, zombies must be nomologically possible. My view is that physically or functionally identical zombies are not nomologically possible—but I can't be certain of this, so there remains a skeptical possibility here. We could also run Helton's argument with behaviorally identical zombies, perhaps along the lines of sophisticated large language models. Behaviorally identical zombies are not obviously possible but are hard to rule out.

There is one respect in which the solipsistic simulation argument is not as strong as the original simulation argument. This concerns the numbers. Construed as an argument that we are probably in a solipsistic simulation, the argument requires roughly that most conscious beings (or better, most beings with consciousness like ours) are in solipsistic simulations. But even if most simulations are solipsistic simulations, it does not follow that most conscious beings are in solipsistic simulations. Suppose there is one nonsolipsistic simulation (with one billion conscious beings) and one million solipsistic simulations (with one conscious being and 999,999,999 zombies in each). Then despite there being a million times as many solipsistic simulations, one thousand times as many conscious beings will be in nonsolipsistic simulations. This weighting of the numbers makes it *much* less antecedently probable that most conscious beings will be in solipsistic simulations than that most conscious beings will be in simulations simpliciter. In effect, this weighting serves as a "solipstic sim blocker" (analogous to the sim blockers of chapter 5) that potentially explains why relatively few beings are in solipsistic simulations, in a way that may defang the solipsistic simulation argument to some extent.

This factor will also tend to greatly reduce the conditional probability that we are in a solipsistic simulation, conditional on being in a simulation. That in turn will greatly reduce the probability that we are in a bad simulation, conditional on our being in a simulation. This reduction will help block the value-theoretic objection that if we're in a simulation, it is probably a bad one.

What about Helton's social swamping view: that for many people, the value of social knowledge massively swamps the value of non-social knowledge? One preliminary point is that I am not sure that the value of knowledge is the key issue here. Intuitively, what is really bad about a scenario in which others are zombies is not that I don't *know* they have minds. It's that they don't have minds. We can diagnose this by considering a situation in which I have an unjustified but true belief (or a Gettiered justified true belief) that others have minds. Here, others have minds although I don't know it. My intuition is that this situation is far better than the situation in which others lack minds, and is only a little worse than a situation in which others have minds and in which my true belief is knowledge. For similar reasons, I think even the belief isn't crucial here. The dominant source of value in these cases is not knowledge of or belief in other minds, but other minds themselves.

More generally: I think that if there's something whose value swamps other factors here, it's not social knowledge per se, or social belief, but social reality. Helton's social swamping claims can naturally be understood as claims about the value of social reality (compared to the value of non-social reality), and I'll henceforth understand them this way.

Does the value of social reality swamp the value of non-social reality? I think it depends on the person. For many people, non-social reality is very important. For a gardener or a mathematician or an explorer, a huge amount of the value of their lives may come from non-social sources. In some cases this may exceed value from social sources, in other cases not. But certainly this non-social value need not be swamped by social sources. Still, Helton's core thesis claims only that for many people, social value swamps non-social value, and that claim seems quite plausible.

What follows for simulations? Let's start with mindless simulations: those in which others lack any mental states. It's at least arguable that if others lack any mental states, then there's little or no social reality. If the value of social reality is the dominant source of value for many people, then for these people, mindless simulations will be lacking this dominant source of value, and will thereby be much worse (other things equal) than nonsimulated worlds with minds.

Now, I am not sure that mindless simulations (indistinguishable behavior, no mental states) are possible. Zombie simulations (no conscious states) may be possible, but it is less clear that these simulations lack social reality. It's at least arguable that if others have non-conscious mental states, this can support considerable social reality. Still: social reality or not, it seems plausible that for many or most people, a situation in which others lack consciousness entirely is a very bad one.

What follows for the value of simulations more generally? One thesis I am tempted by is that life in a simulated world is roughly as good as life in a corresponding nonsimulated world, where the two worlds have the same structure and importantly have corresponding minds. (I don't say exactly as good—nonsimulated worlds may gain some added value from nature or fundamentality or some other factor.) That thesis is not threatened by solipsistic simulations. For all we've said here, a solipsistic simulation may be roughly as valuable as a corresponding solipstic non-simulation, with both being much worse than non-solipsistic counterparts.

What about the thesis: if we're in a simulation, things are roughly as good as if we're not? This thesis is threatened by Helton's argument, since she holds that if we're in a simulation, a form of solipsism is more likely to be true than if we're not, and she thinks that solipsism is very bad. I agree that solipsism is very bad. I'm open to the idea that many simulations are solipsistic, perhaps for reasons of ethics or efficiency. I don't think it follows that solipsism is probable, for reasons I discussed earlier. But even if this increases the probability of solipsism by a little, it will likewise reduce the expected value of life in a simulation by a little. Perhaps this gives each of us some reason to hope that we're not in a simulation.

References

Chalmers, D. J. 2021. Finding Space in a Nonspatial World. In (C. Wüthrich, B. Le Bihan & N. Huggett, eds.) *Philosophy Beyond Spacetime* (Oxford University Press).

Helton, G. 2024. (this volume) The Simulation Hypothesis, Social Knowledge, and a Meaningful Life. *Oxford Studies in Philosophy of Mind*, volume 4.

Horgan, T. 2024. (this volume) Why Virtual Worlds Aren't Real: How Phenomenal Intentionality Constrains Mental Reference. *Oxford Studies in Philosophy of Mind*, volume 4.

Lasonen-Aarnio, M. 2010. Unreasonable Knowledge. *Philosophical Perspectives* *24(1): 1–21*.

Peacocke, C. 2024. (this volume) Simulation: Its Metaphysics and Epistemology. *Oxford Studies in Philosophy of Mind*, volume 4.

Vogel, J. 2008. Internalist Responses to Skepticism. In (John Greco, ed.), *The Oxford Handbook of Skepticism*. Oxford University Press.

Weatherson, B. 2003. Are You a Sim? *Philosophical Quarterly* 53: 425–431.

White, R. 2014. What Is My Evidence That I Have Hands? In (Dylan Dodd and Elia Zardini, eds) *Scepticism and Perceptual Justification*. Oxford University Press.

David J. Chalmers, *The Simulation Hypothesis: Metaphysics, Epistemology, Value* In: *Oxford Studies in Philosophy of Mind Volume 4.* Edited by: Uriah Kriegel, Oxford University Press. © David J. Chalmers 2024.
DOI: 10.1093/9780198924159.003.0017

PART V

HISTORY OF PHILOSOPHY OF MIND

Aristotle

18

Aristotle on *Thumos*

Patricia Marechal

1. Introduction

Most readers will be familiar with Plato's tripartite theory of the soul.[1]
In Book 4 of the *Republic*, Plato divides the soul into three sources of
motivation—appetite, reason, and *thumos*—which can agree with each
other or conflict with one another, pulling us in opposite directions.[2] Yet,
some interpreters have argued that the Platonic soul has one part too many.
Plato divided the soul into a rational and an appetitive part, with distinctive
types of motivations corresponding to each. But the third part of the soul,
thumos, has troubled a few Plato scholars, to the point that some have said
that "Plato's arguments for the existence of *thumos* as a third part of the soul
are singularly few and weak," and that this part of the soul is "factitious" and
"has all the air of being invented to suit some forgone conclusion."[3] In line
with this, a common view has it that Aristotle realized that *thumos* was not
doing any substantive philosophical work, and so he underplayed its role
in his psychological theory, thereby anticipating the more elegant and
economical model of the mind consisting of just reason and desire.[4] So, the

---

[1] See *Republic* 4, 439d–441c. This theory has been interpreted in a variety of ways and,
undoubtedly, leaves us with many questions. For a recent overview of the central interpretive
debates surrounding this piece of Platonic theory and a compelling new interpretation,
see Kamtekar (2017). See also Singpurwalla (2010) for a helpful presentation of the theory and
references.
[2] I will use the Greek term "*thumos*" for the psychological phenomenon that is the subject
of this chapter, instead of the usual translation "spirit." In so doing, I aim to avoid adopting an
interpretation of *thumos* based on historical translation practices.
[3] The first quote is from Penner (1971, 112–113); the second is from Cornford (1912, 263).
Others and I disagree, holding that Plato is onto something philosophically interesting and
insightful when he adds *thumos* as a distinctive type of motivation that springs from a dedicated psychological faculty. See, among others, Cooper (1984), Moss (2005), Singpurwalla
(2013), and Wilburn (2021).
[4] Aristotle often divides the soul into non-rational (*alogon*) and rational (*to logon echon*)
parts (*De An.* 3.9, 432a26–31; *NE* 1.13, 1102a28, 6.1, 1139a4–5; *Pol.* 7.15, 1334b18–22). On
this, Kahn says: "Aristotle's explanation of human action relies on two basic parts or faculties of

thought goes, "that there are three parts of the soul is treated as an uninteresting oddity, wisely omitted by Aristotle from his account of virtue."[5]

But Aristotle never gave up on the importance of *thumos*, and there is good reason to think that he considers it to be a distinctive and irreducible mental phenomenon, which plays a central psychological role in his account of motivation and action. Aristotle is clear that *thumos* is a kind of non-rational desire alongside appetite (*De An.* 2.3, 414a32–b2; *EE* 2.7, 1223a27; *MA* 6, 700b22). But why posit two kinds of non-rational desires? What is distinctive about *thumos*? To answer these questions, I will examine a series of passages scattered throughout the corpus that will allow us to identify the key features of Aristotelian *thumos* (Section 2). Next, I will argue against some common interpretations according to which *thumos* is a type of desire individuated by its objects (Section 3). Finally, I will argue that *thumos* is an inner drive or impulse to act. More precisely, it is an executory urge to implement or enact one's ends or goals, whatever they are. *Thumos* accounts for someone's proneness to spring into action and can contribute to bringing about rational or non-rational, first-order desires. It is, then, a second-order motivation, which both human and non-human animals have and that comes in degrees: we can be more or less *thumotic*, which amounts to being more or less disposed to making first-order desires effective so that they issue in actions (Section 4).[6]

Along the way, we will see that, for Aristotle, differences in the degree of *thumos* determine that an agent is more or less prone to stick to and execute desires and resolutions. These differences can be observed in the same agent at different times and ages, but *thumotic* tendencies can also vary among different individuals. Crucially, Aristotle thinks that different animal

---

the psyche: the rational and the nonrational" (Kahn 1988, 239). It may be tempting, although inaccurate for reasons we will see below, to think that he foreshadows the Humean distinction between reason (with its beliefs) and desire. See Singpurwalla (2010) for a discussion of this issue in Plato.

[5] Cooper (1984, 4). This is a view Cooper himself does not share; see page 17, n. 2.

[6] This description evokes features of the modern notion of the will without committing itself to the view that Aristotle has a full-fledged account of the will as understood by modern and contemporary philosophers. I am, of course, not the first one to find precursors of this notion in Aristotle, but I am in the minority position. As Christof Rapp says: "The line-up of more or less recent philosophers and scholars who are of the opinion that Aristotle had no notion of the will is a very remarkable one. This could almost be called a standard or default position" (Rapp 2017, 67). Yet, some are willing to find precursors of this notion in Aristotle, following Aquinas, in his account of voluntary actions (*hekousion*) and choice (*prohairesis*). See, for example, Kenny (1979) and Kahn (1988, 240). This chapter takes a different route. A discussion of the preceding scholarly debate is beyond its scope. I will, however, have more to say about this issue in the conclusion.

species, males and females, and even whole nations of peoples differ according to their degree of *thumos*. And, strikingly, he argues that a healthy, vigorous *thumos* is a *sine qua non* condition for ruling others and being free, while a weak *thumos* makes someone prone to be ruled, enslaved, and subjugated by others—although unbridled *thumos* can also lead one astray. The concept of *thumos* is, then, at once key in Aristotle's theory of the mind and his account of motivation and action, and plays a fundamental role in his efforts to differentiate, classify, and hierarchically organize species, characters, genders, and peoples.

2. The Features of Aristotelian *Thumos*

Aristotelian *thumos* has not received nearly as much attention as its Platonic counterpart. Partly this is because there is no dedicated discussion of *thumos* in Aristotle's texts. His remarks about *thumos* are scattered throughout the corpus and, on a quick examination, they do not immediately appear to describe a unified phenomenon.

What are the features of Aristotelian *thumos*? Aristotle frequently associates *thumos* with anger (*orgē*) and irascibility (*chalepotēs*; *Top.* 2, 113a33–113b14; cf. *EE* 3.3, 1231b5–16).[7] Yet, *thumos* is not only associated with these emotions but also with fear and shame (*Top.* 4, 126a3–126a16; *HA* 9.1, 608b11–12).[8] We may think that the "*thumikon*" or "*thumoeides*"—Aristotle's way of referring to the faculty of *thumos*—is only responsible for negative emotions.[9] But, elsewhere, Aristotle says that love also depends on this faculty. Indeed, "*thumos* produces affection, for it is this the capacity of the soul by which we love" (*Pol.* 7.7, 1327b40).[10] Similarly, in the *Eudemian Ethics*,

---

[7] See, also, *NE* 4.5, 1126a16, 19–21, 5.8, 1135b25–27, *Rhet.* 1.10, 1369b11–12; 1.11, 1370b9–14; 2.1, 1378b2–6; 2.2, 1379a4. In the *Rhetoric*, Aristotle says he will discuss *thumos* in his account of the emotions (*pathē*) (1373b36), but when the time comes, he uses instead the term "*orgē*" (1378a30f). See, also, *De An.* 1.1, 403a16–18 and *EE* 2.2, 1220b11–12.

[8] Cf. *NE* 3.8, 1116a15–29; 1116b23–1117a9; *EE* 3.1, 1229a20–29; 1230a16–33. The connection between *thumos* and shame has been highlighted by Richardson Lear 2004 and Grönroos 2007, who have emphasized the *thumoeidetic* nature of shame, and consider this emotion to be inseparably linked to *thumos*. I agree with this. Yet, it seems that shame is one emotion, *inter alia*, that relates to *thumos*.

[9] On the "*thumikon*" and "*thumoeides*," see *Top.* 2.7, 113a36–b1, 4.5;126a8–10; *Top.* 5.1, 129a12–15; *De An.* 3.9, 432a25.

[10] Translation based with modifications on C.D.C. Revee's translation of the *Politics* (2017). For the *Nicomachean Ethics* [*NE*] I have consulted Roger Crisp's (2005), C.D.C. Reeve's (2014), and Christopher Shields' (forthcoming) translations. For *De Anima*, I have used Shields' translation. For the *History of Animals* [*HA*] and *Parts of Animals* [*PA*], I have used the translations

he associates *thumos* with gentleness (*praotēs*), a feeling we experience for friends and loved ones (*EE* 3.3, 1231b5–16).[11]

Thumos is, then, linked with a variety of emotions. Aristotle suggests that we experience these emotions through, or in, the faculty of *thumos*, and that *thumos* is, at least in part, responsible for them (*Top.* 2.7, 113a36–b1; 4.5, 126a10). Nevertheless, we should not think that *thumos* just is Aristotle's "name for the locus of emotional capacity."[12] In *De Anima*, Aristotle's treatise on the soul, *thumos* is said to be a type of motivation issued by the general faculty of desire (*ta orektikon*):

> The nutritive faculty alone belongs to plants; both this and the perceptual faculty belong to others. But if the perceptual faculty, then also the desiderative faculty: desire is appetite, *thumos*, and wish. And all animals have at least one kind of perception, touch.
>
> (*De An.* 2.3, 414a32–b2)[13]

In these lines, Aristotle classifies desires into three kinds: appetite (*epithumia*), wish (*boulēsis*), and *thumos*. This three-fold classification of desires is not casual; Aristotle repeats it in *EE* 2.6, 1223a27, *Pol.* 7.15, 1334b17–26, and *MA* 6, 700b22. Consistent with this classification, he says in the *Rhetoric* that there are different psychological sources of action: reason, appetite, and *thumos* (1.10, 1368b37–1369a7). While wish is a desire for the good or the apparent good and seems to be distinctively rational (*NE* 3.4, 1113a15–16), appetite is a non-rational desire for "what is pleasant" (*NE* 3.2, 1111b17). We do not, however, get an analogous description of the objects of *thumos*.

Aristotle adds a few, important qualifications about *thumos*. Like appetite (*epithumia*), but unlike wish (*boulēsis*), *thumos* is not rational (*De An.* 3.9, 432b3–8). Appetites, which for Aristotle paradigmatically include desires for food, drink, and sex, and *thumos* are experienced by animals who lack reason. *Thumos* is shared by humans and other, non-rational animals, along with appetites, perception, memory, pleasure, and pain (*De Sensu* 1, 436a6–9). Accordingly, Aristotle describes animals, in general, as more or less *thumotic*, and talks about the *thumos* of animal species as diverse as boars, leopards,

---

in the edition by Barnes (1995) of the complete works of Aristotle. For the Greek, I used OCT editions of Aristotle's texts, when available.

[11] In this, Aristotle may be following Plato, who connects *thumos* with both fierce and gentle feelings. For a detailed analysis of this dual aspect of *thumos*, see Wilburn (2021).

[12] Koziak (2000, 111).   [13] Translation in Shields (2016).

bears, birds, elephants, dogs, bees, and wasps (e.g., *HA* 9.1, 608a32–608b6; *PA* 2.4, 651a1–5). Furthermore, Aristotle says that children experience *thumos* before they can reason (*Pol.* 7.15, 1334b22–23).

Although *thumos* is not rational, Aristotle says that it can "hear" reason. Even when excessive *thumos* leads us astray, in some sense it "reasons out" what to do. Aristotle makes this clear in his discussion of lack of self-control (*akrasia*) concerning *thumos*. These are cases in which agents fail to act as they should because of their excessive or inadequate *thumos*:[14]

[A] It seems that, although *thumos* does hear reason to some extent, it hears incorrectly, like those overhasty servants who dash along before having heard everything being said to them and so fail in their chores, or like dogs who begin barking whenever a sound is made, before determining whether it is a friend. So too with *thumos*, because of its being by nature hot and quick: although it has heard something, it has not heard what it was commanded to do and rushes off after retribution. [B] For although reason or *phantasia* has revealed an outrage or some act of contempt has occurred, *thumos* is at this instant immediately provoked, as if it had been reasoned out that one ought to engage in combat against this sort of thing; and should reason or perception just say that something is pleasant, appetite rushes off to its enjoyment. Accordingly, although *thumos* does obey reason in a way, appetite does not, so it is more shameful. Therefore, someone who lacks self-control where *thumos* is concerned does in a way yield to reason, but someone who lacks self-control with regards to appetite does not.

(*NE* 7.6, 1149a25–b3)[15]

I will return to this passage later. Indeed, it will turn out to be key for my interpretation of Aristotelian *thumos*. But, for now, I want to note the connection between *thumos* and reason. Aristotle highlights that *thumos* can be, to an important degree, responsive to reason, even though it is itself not rational. Now, *thumos* can be, so to speak, too eager and "mishear" rational commands. Notice that Aristotle is not saying that *thumos* always mishears

---

[14] In book 7 of the *Nicomachean Ethics*, Aristotle contrasts qualified and unqualified forms of lack of self-control (*akrasia*). In cases of unqualified (*haplōs*) *akrasia*, agents act against their resolutions because of excessive and inappropriate appetites (*epithumiai*) for food, drink, and sex. *Akrasia* concerning *thumos* is qualified.

[15] My translation closely follows Shields's in his forthcoming translation of the *Nicomachean Ethics*. I am grateful to him for generously sharing this passage with me.

reason. It is the *thumos* of people who lack self-control with respect to it that is too hasty and fails to hear reason correctly. Neither is Aristotle saying that appetites cannot follow reason. It is part of his general ethical theory that appetites can become habituated to obey reason.[16] Still, there is a difference between *thumos* and appetites: even when *thumos* is excessive or inappropriate, it seems to somehow yield to reason, while the excessive appetites of the agent who lacks self-control simply prompt her to act towards what is pleasant, despite reason's commands to the contrary.

In the last passage, we saw that Aristotle highlights the "hot" and "quick" nature of *thumos*. Aristotle often emphasizes the physiological basis of *thumos* and the emotions associated with it. *Thumos* is "enmattered" (*De An.* 1.1, 403a10–27). In *Parts of Animals*, he says that *thumos* produces heat (2.4, 650b33–651a5; cf. *NE* 7.6, 1149a25–b3, *MA* 8, 702a3–4). He also associates having a *thumotic* nature with qualities of the blood, specifically, its thickness and the presence of abundant fibers. These qualities preserve the heat that is produced by *thumos*, thereby increasing its effects.[17] As seen in the previous passage, the heat of *thumos* can contribute to explaining its psychological dimensions. *Thumos*, Aristotle says repeatedly, is a natural phenomenon. In fact, *thumos* is "more natural" (*phusikoteron*) than appetites (*NE* 7.4, 1148b9–13; 7.6, 1149a34–b8).[18] Aristotle is probably referring in this line to excessive and inappropriate appetites that are the result of bad habits and corruption rather than nature but, arguably, he also intends to highlight that the material characteristics of *thumos* are especially relevant for explaining its psychological effects, and that one's degree of *thumos* may be harder to mold and train than one's appetites for food, drink, and sex.

Aristotle adds a few, important remarks about *thumos* in his ethical and political writings. He says that *thumos* makes people naturally daring. Young people, for example, appear to be courageous, because they are impulsive (*thumoeideis*), and this makes them fearless (*NE* 3.8, 1116b24–27). Yet, actions on account of *thumos* are not truly courageous. The virtue of courage, strictly speaking, involves acting for the right reasons and because it is the noble thing to do. For Aristotle, daring actions from

---

[16] "[T]he appetitive element (*epithumētikon*) in a person who is temperate should harmonize with reason; for the noble is the target at which both aim, and a person who is temperate has appetites (*epithumei*) for the things he should, as he should, and when he should, and this is what reason dictates" (*NE* 3.12, 1119b15–18).

[17] See Deslauriers (2019, esp. 59–61) for a detailed discussion of the physiology of *thumos* in Aristotle.

[18] This does not mean that these desires are not embodied or "enmattered," to use Aristotle's own expression (*De An.* 1.1, 403a10–27). Aristotle is committed to the idea that soul and body are inextricably linked, and that most, if not all, psychological phenomena are embodied.

thumos do not meet these requirements (*NE* 3.11, 1116b23f).[19] The idea seems to be that *thumos* makes someone naturally daring, but this does not, by itself, make someone responsive to the correct reasons why they should face dangers.

Thumos is also prominent in two infamous Aristotelian political theories. Aristotle says that female animals are less *thumotic* than their male counterparts (*HA* 9.1, 608a19–b18).[20] This applies to human beings. In fact, Aristotle says these differences are more salient in our species than in others (*HA* 9.1, 608a33–b16). As is well known, Aristotle says men are naturally suited to, and so should, rule women. This, he tells us, is grounded in natural facts about women's souls, which determine that their deliberations lack authority (*Pol.* 1.13, 1260a10–14). It is not a stretch to think that their weaker *thumos* is, at least in part, responsible for the political deficiencies of women.[21] Indeed, Aristotle makes a striking remark about *thumos* in the *Politics*:

> Both ruling and freedom spring from this capacity [i.e. *thumos*] for everyone. For *thumos* is both dominant and unconquerable.
>
> (*Pol.* 7.7, 1328a5–7)

Thumos, as a capacity, explains why some people are suited to rule others, while others are ruled. Presumably, a vigorous *thumos* is a condition for ruling, while a weak *thumos* determines that someone is not capable of self-determination and is at risk of being dominated by others and losing their freedom.

Relatedly, Aristotle makes a series of infamous remarks about the *thumos* of non-Greeks:

> Those who live in cold climates and in Europe are full of *thumos* but are wanting in intelligence and skill. Thus, they retain more freedom, but have no political organization and are incapable of ruling others. While the natives of Asia are intelligent and skillful, but they lack *thumos*, and therefore are always ruled and enslaved.
>
> (*Pol.* 7.7, 1327b24–31)

---

[19] On the virtue of courage and *thumotic*, daring actions as a form of pseudo-courage, see Jimenez (2020, esp. ch. 3).

[20] Yet, in this passage, he does note as exceptions the female leopard and bear, who are said to be more *thumotic* than the males in these species.

[21] Aristotle does not connect explicitly the lack of authority of women's deliberations and their weak *thumos*, but the connection has been observed by commentators. See, for example, Connell (2021a), Deslauriers (2019, esp. 74–76), and Marechal (2024a).

These claims are an expression of Aristotle's commitment to environmental determinism, according to which factors such as climate, geography, and latitude shape people's physical and psychological characteristics.[22] For Aristotle, peoples (*ethnē*) living in colder climates have strong *thumos*, while those in hotter climates suffer from a deficiency in *thumos*. On the other hand, the Greeks have, on average, both strong *thumos* and intelligence (*Pol.* 7.7, 1327b29–30). These claims are relevant to Aristotle's views that there are people who should be enslaved based on their natural characteristics (*Pol.* 1.5–13). As we saw, Aristotle says that *thumos* is natural, hard to mold, and grounded in material facts about an animal. Having a deficiency of *thumos* seems to be one of the psychological qualifications, alongside lacking a deliberative faculty (*Pol.* 1.13, 1260a12), that determine that someone is, for Aristotle, a "natural slave". Indeed, Aristotle links having a weak or non-reactive *thumos* with having a slavish nature (*EE* 3.3, 1231b5–16).

A final point is worth making. Several of the passages discussed above make clear that *thumos* comes in degrees. Different individuals, species, genders, and peoples differ in terms of their *thumotic* tendencies, specifically, the degree of strength or vigor of their *thumos*.

We can, then, summarize the features of Aristotelian *thumos* as follows:

1. It is linked to emotions such as anger, fear, shame, and love.
2. It is a distinctive type of desire or motivation, different from appetite and wish.
3. It is non-rational.
4. It is possessed by non-human animals and children from birth.
5. It can be responsive to rational considerations and, even in cases of lack of self-control, it still "reasons" in a way.
6. It is a natural and embodied type of motivation that involves distinctive physiological phenomena, specifically, heat and thickness of blood.
7. It is the basis for a naturally courageous disposition.
8. It is weaker in females than in males.
9. It is weaker in some groups of people (*ethnē*) than in others.
10. It is a condition for ruling and being free.
11. It comes in degrees.

We can appreciate now why scholars have puzzled over Aristotle's account of *thumos*. What sort of mental phenomenon can plausibly be said to exhibit

---

[22] This theory had some purchase at Aristotle's time, and we can find versions of it in the Hippocratic *Airs, Waters, Places* and in Herodotus's *Histories* (esp. 9.122).

all these features? We may be tempted to answer, "none." Indeed, some interpreters have argued that Aristotelian *thumos* is a *sui generis* set of psychological phenomena involving anger, shame, honor, self-assertion, desire for recognition, political ambition, and so on.[23] Perhaps Aristotle is simply following custom and cannot give up the folk psychological notions of his time and place. Indeed, Aristotle himself notes Homer's references to *thumos* (*EN* 3.8, 1116a21–26). And, of course, he is well familiar with Plato's tri-partite soul. We will see below, however, that there are good reasons to think that Aristotelian *thumos* is a unified mental phenomenon and does play a distinctive function.

We may also think that we should not expect human *thumos* to be the same as the *thumos* of other, non-rational animals, and so refrain from seeking a characterization of this phenomenon that accounts for both.[24] But, although there is no doubt that *thumos* will have peculiar manifestations in creatures endowed with rational capacities—as is also the case for other psychological phenomena we share with non-human animals, such as perception, anger, fear, and appetites like hunger or thirst—there surely are core features of *thumos* that span its human and non-human manifestations. If there were no common features, Aristotle would be using the term "*thumos*" equivocally, but that does not seem to be the case. After all, Aristotle is sensitive to the fact that we are animals, especially when it comes to non-rational attitudes, dispositions, and traits that we share with other species. We should, then, expect *thumos* to present analogous features and play a similar function in non-rational and rational creatures. Indeed, this chapter will assume that there is a continuity between *thumos* in humans and other animals, even if we should expect *thumos* to have peculiar manifestations in us.

3. What Aristotelian *Thumos* Is Not

A few interpreters have offered accounts of Aristotelian *thumos*. These accounts fall, broadly speaking, into three interpretive camps. All of them

---

[23] E.g., Burnyeat (1980); Irwin (1999, 323); Polansky (2007, 190); and Shields (2016, 386). See, also, Simplicius's view in *Simplicii in libros Aristotelis De Anima Commentaria*, 105, 21–24; translated in Urmson (1995, 141). For these and more references, see Saenz (2018).

[24] Aristotle denies reason to non-human animals, although he acknowledges that many animals can engage in sophisticated behavior. See, for example, *De An.* 1.2, 404b4–6 and 2.3, 414b18–19; 32–33. For more references, see Sorabji (1993, esp. 21f.). For an account of the sophisticated cognitive (albeit not, strictly speaking, rational) capacities Aristotle does attribute to non-human animals, see Connell (2021b).

attempt to define *thumos* as a kind of desire individuated by proper objects, in the same way that appetite (*epithumia*) is a desire for what is pleasant and wish (*boulēsis*) is a desire for what is good. Although none of these proposals can account for all the features that Aristotle attributes to *thumos* listed in the previous section, they offer important insights into this phenomenon that will allow us to elucidate the nature and function of Aristotelian *thumos*.

3.1. *Thumos* as a Desire for the Noble

Some commentators have argued that *thumos* holds a special connection to the noble or fine (*to kalon*), a form of non-instrumental value that plays a central role in Aristotle's ethical theory (*EE* 1248b23-25; *NE* 1176b7-10).[25] John Cooper (1999), for example, has argued that the noble is the object of *thumos*, just as the beneficial is the object of wish (*boulēsis*) and pleasure is the object of appetite (*epithumia*). After all, Aristotle distinguishes three objects of choice: the pleasant, the beneficial, and the noble (*NE* 2.3, 1104b30-1105a1). He says that pleasant things are the object of appetites (*epithumia*) and, arguably, beneficial things are the object of wish (*boulēsis*). Given the tri-partite distinction of objects of choice, the object of *thumos* must be the noble or fine (*kalon*).

Although this interpretation reveals something important about the nature of *thumos*, it has some limitations. As others have pointed out, it is not clear that Aristotle's distinction between objects of choice corresponds to the three species of desire—appetite, wish, and *thumos*—since Aristotle never makes this connection himself.[26] More importantly, for Aristotle, the "noble" (*kalon*) is a form of value that bears a special relationship with rationality and virtue. Aristotle says that virtue's goal is the *kalon* (*EE* 1115b12-13), and the *kalon* features in almost all the accounts of individual

---

[25] See, especially, Gay (1988, 258, n. 9); Cooper (1999); Richardson Lear (2004, 138, n. 33); Grönroos (2007); and Moss (2012, 210). Cooper claims: It is *"through* thumos *that people are first motivated to experience*...[t]he specifically moral value, then—the value with which morally virtuous persons as such are especially concerned," and "the practically wise person has learned to desire the *kalon* with his reason because earlier he desired it with his *thumos* desires" (279).

[26] As Pearson (2012, 164, n. 27) notes: there is no "direct evidence that *thumos* ever takes such an eminent end as its immediate object...and it would be an astonishing silence if he: [i.e. Aristotle] failed to mention such an important feature of his account." Furthermore, saying that the object of wish is the "beneficial" sits poorly with Aristotle's general views on wish. See Saenz (2018, esp. 90-93) for a detailed discussion of these issues.

virtues in the ethical works (e.g., *NE* 1115b23–24; 1119b15–16; 1120a23–26; 1122b6–7; 1126b28–29). But, as seen, *thumos* is a non-rational desire, which non-human animals, who do not have the potential for virtue, experience.

We may think that, in human beings, *thumos* can come to be oriented towards noble goals during upbringing and education. Indeed, Cooper intends his interpretation to apply only to the *thumos* of virtuous people and those who are being habituated towards virtue.[27] But the fact that *thumos can* be oriented towards noble deeds and that, when it develops in us as it should, it *must* be oriented towards noble goals. does not mean that *thumos* just *is* a desire for what is noble. If that were so, human *thumos* and the *thumos* of other animals (and perhaps even of pre-rational children) would have nothing in common. Yet, as said, Aristotle does not seem to talk about the *thumos* in us and other animals equivocally. Given that Aristotle emphasizes that *thumos* is natural and non-rational, and that little children, bears, bees, boars, deer, leopards, and other animals experience *thumos*, it would be strange if this type of desire was, at its very core, a desire for noble things.[28] This interpretation, then, does not tell us what *thumos* essentially is, only that in human beings it can and should, be oriented towards noble goals.

3.2   *Thumos* as a Desire for Social Appraisal

A different interpretation emphasizes *thumos*'s orientation to being valued by others. Victor Saenz, for example, has argued that *thumos* is a faculty that issues motivations responsive to other people's appraisal.[29] In this view, Aristotelian *thumos* refers to socially sensitive emotions, attitudes, dispositions, and desires. *Thumos* is related to emotions such as anger, envy, shame, and love because we feel these emotions, paradigmatically, at or for other people and, in some way or another, they are wrapped up with our sense of

---

[27] Cooper says: "My suggestion is not that Aristotle proposes the noble or fine or beautiful as the immediate object of spirited desires in general—for such desires of non-human animals, or children, or even all adult human beings. It is only for the morally virtuous person, and only after a certain stage is reached in the special course of moral development and self-discipline that leads a person to the possession of virtues of character, that I want to claim that this is Aristotle's view" (Cooper 1999, 276).

[28] So, Cooper's interpretation may be right when it comes to an account of the ethical development and proper habituation of human beings. Indeed, I take my own proposal to be compatible with this view.

[29] Saenz (2018).

social value and position. We get angry at our rivals, for example, because they slighted us, and we want to restore our social standing. And, in loving kin and friends, we seek to be valued by them. As Saenz puts it, "*thumos* 'begets friendship' insofar as it affirms our social value: it enables the recognition that I am valued by another and seeks to do what affirms my value before that other."[30] This interpretation can help us make sense of how *thumos* relates to the capacity to rule and assert one's freedom. Indeed, commanding over others affirms an agent's social position.

But this interpretation cannot account for all the featues of Aristotelian *thumos*. As seen, Aristotle attributes *thumos* to non-human animals. Importantly, he does not restrict *thumos* only to social animals. Neither can this interpretation make sense of Aristotle's claim that females are, generally, less *thumotic* than males. At least, it is not clear that Aristotle thinks females have less of a sense of, or desire for, social standing and value. Arguably, he suggests the opposite: women are, for Aristotle, more envious and querulous (*HA* 9.1, 608b8–11). Similarly, this reading cannot readily account for the *thumotic* differences between non-Greeks in the ethnographic passage we saw above. Could Aristotle be saying that the people he calls "Asians" are less responsive to social appraisal and do not care about social standing, while the Greeks care the right amount, and perhaps Europeans too much? Perhaps. But this is a strange observation and not the most obvious reading of this passage. After all, the "Asians" include the Persians, whom Aristotle, and the tradition in which he is embedded, describes as caring about honor (*Pol.* 7.2, 1324b9–12).

3.3 *Thumos* as a Desire for Retaliation

A different interpretation argues that Aristotelian *thumos* is a desire for retaliation and so closely linked to, or even identical with, the emotion of anger as defined by Aristotle.[31] This proposal accounts for the "hot" nature of *thumos*. An advantage of this interpretation is that it captures that *thumos* is a non-rational desire that other animals and pre-rational children have.

Giles Pearson, for example, defends the view that Aristotelian *thumos* is closely connected with "*orgē*," an emotion that usually denotes anger and which Aristotle defines as a desire for revenge in response to a perceived

---

[30] Saenz (2018, 84).
[31] Pearson (2012, 111–139).

slight (*Rhet.* 2.2, 1378a31–33). Indeed, Aristotle often uses "*thumos*" and "*orgē*" interchangeably. For example, in the *Eudemian Ethics*, he mentions "*thumos*" in one line, but replaces it with "*orgē*" in the next (2.7, 1223b27–28). Similarly, he says that acts from *thumos* are not premeditated, since a person who acts from *thumos* acts in this way because they have been provoked by someone who made them angry (*ho orgisas*) (*NE* 5.8, 1135b25–28). And, in the *Rhetoric*, when he divides desires into rational and non-rational, he says that rational desire is wish (*boulēsis*) and non-rational desires are *orgē* and appetite (*epithumia*) but, immediately after, he replaces "*orgē*" with "*thumos*" (*Rhet.* 1.10, 1369a1–7).

It is worth noting, however, that the Greek word "*orgē*" does not necessarily mean "anger", although it frequently does. "*Orgē*" has two basic meanings in Greek. This word can mean natural impulse, propensity, and disposition. It can also mean anger or wrath. The verb "*organ*," in turn, can mean to be eager, to be ready, or to be excited. The semantic range of "*orgē*" calls for some caution. We cannot be entirely sure that in all the passages mentioned above, where Aristotle uses "*thumos*" and "*orgē*" interchangeably, these terms refer to the emotion of anger rather than to something like impulse or eagerness.

Defenders of this interpretation could rightfully point out that Aristotle often links *thumos* with seeking revenge, or with a response to a slight, all features Aristotle closely associates with the emotion of anger. For example, he says that *thumos* is not without a certain pleasure, since it involves hope for revenge (*timōria*) (*EE* 3.1, 1229b31–32). And, in the *Rhetoric*, desiring revenge is central to anger, which is also said to be attended by a certain pleasure (2.2.1378b1–2). This strongly suggests that *thumos* is, indeed, tightly linked with anger (*NE* 7.6, 1149a25–b3). And, surely, it is. As we saw before, Aristotle is clear that the faculty of *thumos* gives rise to emotional responses, and among these emotions, he gives anger the pride of place. But saying that the capacity for *thumos* gives rise to, *inter alia*, anger, that *thumos* is often linked with anger, and that anger and desiring retaliation are "*thumotic*" do not entail that *thumos* just *is* the emotion of anger. As seen, *thumos* is also associated with other emotions, including love. Indeed, Aristotle says that *orgē* is "in" the *thumoeides*, which suggests that *thumos* is not identical to this emotion (*Top.* 2.7, 113a36–b1; 4.5, 126a10). *Thumos*, as a type of non-rational motivation, may be constitutive of a variety of emotions, and anger may always involve *thumos*, yet this does not mean that *thumos* is identical to it. This account of *thumos* is, then, too narrow, and cannot account for Aristotle's associations between *thumos* and other emotions and psychological attitudes.

4. What Aristotelian *Thumos* Is

But if *thumos* is none of these things, what is it? Perhaps the mistake is to think that *thumos* is a type of desire individuated by a distinctive type of object—the noble, social standing, retaliation, or what have you. One indication that Aristotle does *not* think *thumos* has a proper object is that he uses words for the objects of desire corresponding to the other two kinds (appetite and wish), but he never refers to the objects of *thumos*. Aristotle talks about the *orekton*, that is, the object of desire generally understood, the *epithumēton*, i.e., the object of *epithumia*, and the *boulēton*, i.e., the object of *boulēsis*. But he does not do the same for *thumos*.[32] The idea that Aristotle does not think there is a proper object of *thumos* gains plausibility when we consider the list of features presented in section 2: there is no specific, individuating object that emerges from all of Aristotle's descriptions of *thumos*. So, we should not try to find one. The most plausible interpretation is that this type of motivation can range over any kind of object. For Aristotle, one can be *thumotic* about everything and anything.

But if *thumos* is not individuated by its objects, how is it individuated? What is *thumos*'s psychological role? To see what is distinctive about *thumos*, I would like to go back to a passage mentioned above. When describing people who lack self-control concerning *thumos*, Aristotle says the following:

[A] It seems that, although *thumos* does hear reason to some extent, it hears incorrectly, like those overhasty servants who dash along before having heard everything being said to them and so fail in their chores, or like dogs who begin barking whenever a sound is made, before determining whether it is a friend. So too with *thumos*, because of its being by nature hot and quick: although it has heard something, it has not heard what it was commanded to do and rushes off after retribution.

(*NE* 7.6, 1149a25–b3)

---

[32] Pearson (2012, 6) also notes this asymmetry.

The description of *thumos* in this passage suggests that it is a kind of eagerness to act. In fact, Aristotle says that *thumos* is characterized by "rousing and impulse" (*egersin kai hormēn*; *NE* 3.8, 1116b30). When someone is excessively *thumotic*, like the person described in this passage, they are too eager to spring into action, and so they fail to carry out their decisions and plans properly. Notice that, in this passage, Aristotle takes for granted that *thumos can* follow rational prescriptions. The assumption is that, when *thumos* works as it should, it motivates an agent to act as they have rationally decided to do. *Thumos* follows one's resolutions and pushes the agent to bring about their rationally endorsed goals.[33] In the case of the person who lacks self-control with regards to *thumos*, although she wants to do what she rationally decided to do, she is so eager and hasty that she fails to implement her plans adequately. Presumably, this is because she does not take the time to calculate the best course that will fulfill her goal and does not proceed with care.

Although this passage discusses excessive and improper *thumos*, we can infer from it what *thumos*, generally, involves. *Thumos* seems to be an impulse or drive to carry out what one wants to do. *Thumos* can make first-order desires effective; that is, it can make them issue in actions. This motivational drive is different from first-order desires, such as appetites or rational desires.[34] Although these desires are themselves motivating, Aristotle recognizes a third source of motivation, which is a contributory or concurrent cause for action; that second-order motivation is *thumos*.[35] This interpretation helps us understand the second section of this much-contested passage:

---

[33] In Aristotle's example, the goal in question is to take revenge after being slighted, but we should not infer from this that *thumos* just is a desire for revenge, although it is often stirred when one has been slighted and, as I will argue below, it is constitutive of anger, among other emotions, dispositions, and attitudes.

[34] Here, I have in mind a distinction akin to the one articulated by Frankfurt (1971). A first-order desire is a desire for any object that is not a desire, while a second-order desire is a desire for a desire. One might have, for example, a first-order desire to check social media, and a second-order desire that you desire not to check social media. Or one might have a first-order desire to give all of one's money to charity, and a second-order desire that this first-order desire be effective.

[35] I believe Cooper had hinted at the nature of Aristotelian *thumos* when he argued that, before habituation, *thumos* is a desire that is "initially aimed only at self-assertion" and "at active…agency" (Cooper 1999, 278). Yet, unlike my proposal, he adds also "competitive" agency to his characterization of *thumos*, which I do not take to be essential to Aristotle's account.

[B] For although reason or *phantasia* has revealed an outrage or some act of contempt has occurred, *thumos* is at this instant immediately provoked, as if it had been reasoned out that one ought to engage in combat against this sort of thing; and should reason or perception just say that something is pleasant, appetite rushes off to its enjoyment. Accordingly, although *thumos* does obey reason in a way, appetite does not, so it is more shameful. Therefore, someone who lacks self-control where *thumos* is concerned does in a way yield to reason, but someone who lacks self-control with regards to appetite does not.

(*NE* 7.6, 1149a25–b3)

Interpreters have wondered about the contrast between excessive *thumos* and excessive appetites in these lines.[36] In what sense does the person who lacks self-control concerning *thumos* follow reason and yield to it, while the person who lacks self-control concerning appetite does not? This is especially perplexing since Aristotle says that appetite rushes towards pleasure when reason or perception says there is something pleasant. If my interpretation of *thumos* is correct, this is because in this example *thumos* assents to or follows one's rational resolution, as if it reasoned out that whatever goal one has resolved to do is indeed worth pursuing. *Thumos* prompts the agent to enact her resolutions, as if it reasoned out that taking revenge for *this* sort of slight is indeed good. We could say that *thumos* wants to do what one has resolved to do. In this sense, the *thumos* of this person follows or yields to reason. Yet, because it is too excessive or overreactive, it spoils the execution of this resolution.[37] In contrast, appetite just goes after whatever appears to

---

[36] Cf. Pearson (2012, 137), who argues that "Aristotle thinks that *thumos* itself involves listening to/obeying reason 'in a sense' in so far as it incorporates something analogous to an actual reasoning stage (it is *as if* it moved from registering a slight to commanding revenge, *via* the premise: 'anything like this must be fought against') in a way that implicitly makes reference to a complex (i.e. structured) *part* of the fully rational response (where the fully rational response would be something like: 'if you have been slighted, get revenge for that (because slights ought to be resisted)... This sets *thumos* apart from *epithumia*, since *epithumia* does not involve an 'as if' reasoning stage (it moves straight from the prospective pleasure to commanding pursuit)." We should note, again, that this passage is not about *thumos* in general, but about human *thumos* in cases of qualified *akrasia* with respect to it.

[37] It is possible that Aristotle thinks that the *thumos* of mature human beings is properly, and even naturally, oriented to ally itself with rational resolutions rather than appetites, even when it is excessive or inappropriate. In this sense, the first interpretation discussed above captures something important about human *thumos*. The point is that, for rational creatures, *thumos* is suited to assent to and follow, and so aid and strengthen, rational desires, so that these desires issue in actions. Plato may have a similar view; see Singpurwalla (2013).

be pleasant, without taking any stance on whether this is indeed a good goal to pursue.

Thumos, then, plays a contributory role in action by following or assenting to first-order desires, choices, and resolutions. When *thumos* cooperates with one's desires, it can make an agent resolute and perseverant in their quest to enact their goals. This account offers a distinctive model of human motivation and action: while wish and appetite are first-order desires whose motivational force is grounded in their proper objects (what is best and what is pleasant, respectively), *thumos* is a drive internal to the agent, which can support or fail to support occurrent, first-order desires. Agents with a healthy amount of *thumos*, then, can more successfully stick by their resolutions and wants, while agents whose *thumos* is weak readily abandon their pursuits. *Thumos* is, then, a type of motivation, albeit one that is not individuated by any specific type of object; rather, it is a second-order motivation, a drive that plays a motivational and executory role and can take first-order desires as its object.

This characterization of *thumos* as an inner drive fits well with Aristotle's descriptions of it in his biological writings and can account for the continuity between the *thumos* of human and non-human animals. Consider, for example, the following passage about bees:

> [Bees] work without *thumos* if the beekeeper, in drawing the honey, leaves behind too much. One should leave cells in a number that is proportionate to the population, for the bees labor without *thumos* if too few combs are left.
>
> (*HA* 9.40, 627b1–2)

There is no suggestion in these lines that *thumos* is a desire for the noble, social standing, or retaliation. The idea is, simply, that *thumos* is an impulse or drive to labor and carry out goals and tasks. As such, it can be experienced by rational and non-rational creatures. Elsewhere, Aristotle suggests that a deficiency of *thumos* results in idleness, passivity, inaction, and lack of resolve. Indeed, Aristotle contrasts *thumotic* animals, which have a vigorous *thumos*, with animals that are "tame," "sluggish," and "idle" (e.g., *HA* 1.1, 488b13–15; *HA* 8.1, 588a16–588b3). *Thumos* is not itself rational, although, as seen, can add motivational support to non-rational desires and, in the case of human beings, also rational pursuits.

This characterization of *thumos* also fits its "heated" and "quick" nature and makes sense of the connection between *thumos* and emotions such as anger, fear, shame, and love. These emotions involve an impulse, drive, or eagerness to, for example, seek revenge, flee, or bestow favors. Aristotle often says that emotions involve or are tightly linked with desires (e.g., *De An.* 1.1, 403a30–31; *Rhet.* 2.2, 1378a31–32). In general, he seems to subscribe to the rather uncontroversial view that being in a certain emotional state strongly motivates agents to act in certain ways: when we are afraid, we are eager to flee from the source of our fear; if we love someone, we crave spending time with them. Arguably, then, *thumos* is partly constitutive of emotions like anger, fear, shame, love, and affection. Nevertheless, each of these emotions involves more than the "*thumotic*" desires that constitute them. Again, although *thumos* is not identical to any of these emotions, it is constitutive of them, insofar as having an occurrent emotional state is characterized by eagerness, zeal, or drive to act in ways that satisfy or alleviate these feelings.

This interpretation of *thumos* also agrees with ordinary uses of the Greek term in Aristotle's time. The sense of *thumos* as a motivational and executory drive is common in the literary tradition. Douglas Cairns observes that *thumos*'s motivational force is reflected in numerous Homeric passages.[38] *Thumos* is said to urge the agent on. The motivational aspect of *thumos* becomes clear in derived terms such as "*athumia*" (despondency, e.g., *Od.* 10.463) and "*prothumia*" (eagerness, *Il.* 2.588). *Thumos* allows agents to endure, persevere, and act in resolute ways, and it can be worn down by physical exertion (*Il.* 17. 744–745). The *thumos* itself can be said to be "eager" for a certain outcome. In *Iliad* 24, for example, Priam describes his strong desire to enter the Achaean camp and ransom Hector's body as a command of *thumos* (24. 198–199), and Hecuba agrees that it is *thumos* that drives him (24. 288–289).[39]

This account of *thumos* finds further support in Aristotle's discussion of courage. As seen, Aristotle says that daring actions performed just from *thumos* are not real courage. This form of pseudo courage resembles true courage but, unlike it, is not done from an appreciation of the correct reasons that call for, and justify, facing dangers. The truly courageous person deliberately chooses to face dangers from the right reasons. In contrast, "actions done from *thumos* are least of all thought to be in accordance with

---

[38] Cairns (2019).
[39] Notice that Priam's incursion into the enemy's camp is not born out of a desire to avenge his son and family, retaliate, or repair his social standing. Indeed, Priam must swallow his pride and beg for his son's corpse to an enemy that has slighted him. But *thumos* makes him resolute and drives him to carry out such a difficult and daring action.

rational choice" (*NE* 3.2, 1111b18–19). Nevertheless, when describing real courage Aristotle is clear that *thumos* needs to aid the agent and make her choices effective so that she can carry out what she resolved to do. As he says, "courageous people act for the sake of what is noble, but *thumos* works with (*sunergeī*) them" (3.8, 1116b30–31). In fact, when the pseudo courage that springs from *thumos* "takes in rational choice and is directed towards some goal," then it becomes actual courage (3.8, 1117a4; cf. *On Virtues and Vices* 4, 1250a44–b7). Thus, *thumos* can desire that one's rational choices are effective, and issue in actions. Aristotle, then, suggests that *thumos* is essential for the execution of rational resolutions, which may be, by themselves, motivationally weak and could be overridden by appetites for pleasure or desire to avoid pains.

The motivational and executory role of *thumos* is also clear in the notion of "*prothumia*," which refers to impetus, eagerness, or readiness to act. When describing the actions of virtuous people, who act from rational choice, Aristotle frequently says that they are "ready" or "eager" (*prothumos*) to act as they do. *Thumos* makes them resolute. The great-souled person, for example, aids others "readily" or "eagerly" (*prothumōs*; 1124b18). When *thumos* follows or aids rational resolutions, the agent sticks to their commitments even in the face of adversity and opposing motivations. Aristotle says this eagerness is characteristic of the actions of real friends and virtuous action, in general, for "those who are friends on account of virtue are eager (*prothoûntai*) to benefit each other, and this is characteristic of virtue and friendship" (*EN* 8.13, 1162b6–9). We should "eagerly (*prothumōs*) call upon our friends to share our fortune when it is good" (9.11, 1171b16), and "go eagerly (*prothumōs*) to those in misfortune without being asked" (1171b21). *Thumos* aids in the execution of virtuous actions, by "acting together" (*sunergeī*) with reason. It contributes to making resolutions effective. On the other hand, someone who is "*rathumos*," a term that indicates lack of *thumos*, contrasts with people who are "keen" (*oxus*) to act (*EE* 7.5, 1240a2). This last term is frequently contrasted with exerting oneself or working hard (*poneō*), thereby suggesting that lacking *thumos* leads to idleness (*EN* 6.1, 1138b28).

Although *thumos* can aid someone enact the goals set by her first-order desires, it can also make someone act compulsively, for no reason, and without pursuing any specific end. As seen, Aristotle contrasts acting from *thumos* with acting from choice (*EN* 5.8, 1135b26–27) and argues that actions done purely from *thumos* are without premeditation, and so are not wicked (*EN* 5.10, 1135b25–29). When someone acts purely from *thumos*, she acts impulsively. In this case, her *thumos* does not assent to, or follow, first-order desires. The distinction between actions done purely from *thumos* and actions where *thumos*, as a second-order desire, takes as its object a first-order desire, resembles the distinction between a mere urge to act and a proper desire.[40] Warren Quinn famously described a person who feels an urge to turn on every radio they see, not because they want to hear music or the news, or even because they want to avoid silence; they are simply compulsively moved to turn on every radio at sight.[41] Such blind impulses do not rationalize actions. Arguably, they are not, strictly speaking, desires, insofar as desiring something involves seeing something as, in some sense, desirable. In contrast, these impulses are, in the moment of action and for the agent, so to speak "blind," even if someone can find ways of explaining or rationalizing them after the fact. In my interpretation, *thumos* counts as a desire, strictly speaking, only when it takes as its object a first-order desire or want, rational or not, that the agent has. When it does not, then it is a mere impulse, and the agent moved by it acts compulsively.[42] This would explain why Aristotle says that actions done purely from *thumos* are not wicked and are least of all in accordance with choice (*EN* 3.2, 1111b18–19).[43]

For Aristotle, the amount of *thumos* one has can be, or become, part of one's character, thereby determining how ready to act, and how willful and resolute, one generally is. *Thumotic* differences, which come in degrees, determine one's will to implement goals and carry out desires and resolutions. Aristotle thinks that some species of animals and certain classes of human beings will have natural differences regarding their *thumos*. As mentioned before, in Aristotle's sexist and racialized view of the world, women and some non-Greeks have too little *thumos*. Aristotle may base these assessments on what he takes to be observations and reputable opinions. But these are, of course, no disinterested facts, and they play an important role in Aristotle's political theory. For, as seen, Aristotle says that *thumos* makes someone able to rule others rather than be ruled by them. A healthy

---

[40] Pearson (2012, esp. 41–47) makes this clear.   [41] Quinn (1995).

[42] Aristotle says that every desire is for the sake of something (*De An.* 3.10, 433a15), and he famously begins the *Nicomachean Ethics* claiming that all actions and choices aim at some good (1.1, 1094a1–3). This suggests that for Aristotle all desires have objects, which may seem to go against my characterization of *thumos* as lacking an object when it motivates an agent without a first-order desire. I am not denying this. My proposal is that *thumos* counts as a desire, and so has an object and is goal-oriented, when it takes as its object a first-order desire, rational or not.

[43] Although we are still responsible for them. Aristotle seems to think we are responsible for our character dispositions and tendencies, and so for the actions that spring from them. On Aristotle's account of moral responsibility, see Cooper (2013). The issue is, however, controversial; see Sauvé Meyer (1993).

thumos is, then, key to self-governance and being free.[44] We can now see what Aristotle means by this quite clearly. If someone is *thumotic*, they tend to make their resolutions and wants effective. They are motivated and eager to carry out their desires and plans, so they persevere and act with resolve. It is not hard to see how this can result in someone imposing their will upon others. In contrast, if someone lacks *thumos*, they will get easily dispirited and readily give up their resolutions. Thus, they will be naturally ruled, and in Aristotle's world, even enslaved by others. As Marguerite Deslauriers argues, *"thumos* is necessary for rule because it makes one decisive and action-oriented" (Deslauriers 2019, 73). Agents who lack a strong *thumos* will tend to be dominated by others. Others will impose their will on them, and they will tend to be easily dominated and enslaved.

The present interpretation, then, gives us a clear answer to the question of what the basic function of *thumos* is, while accounting for all the features Aristotle assigns to it, and without ignoring that this is a non-rational motivation, different from appetite, that we share with other animals. *Thumos* is a motivational and executory drive or impulse to act. As a second-order motivation, it can support first-order wants and resolutions, thereby making them effective and issuing in actions.

5. Conclusion

I argued that Aristotelian *thumos* plays a motivational and executory role. It rouses someone to action. It is a drive, which can contribute to making one's first-order desires (rational and non-rational) effective. One can be more or less *thumotic* and so show more or less resolve in the pursuit of goals. We may worry, as I suggested above, that this theory is too well suited for classifying animals and, especially, peoples into natural rulers and ruled, into free and enslaved. If you have a strong *thumos*, you will naturally persevere in your resolutions and will impose your wants and desires on others. In contrast, if you lack *thumos*, you will readily give up your wants and decisions and will lack resolve. This theory, then, purports to provide "natural facts" that ground, explain, and justify the social and political hierarchies Aristotle infamously endorsed and defended. Thus, Aristotelian *thumos* provides a case study of how psychological theories can be responsive

---

[44] Deslauriers (2019, esp. 71–74) argues for this point.

to, and reflective of, social and political commitments and goals. Indeed, as seen, Aristotle deploys *thumos* in his political writings with justificatory aims.

Yet, without ignoring that Aristotle's theory of *thumos* may be in part politically motivated, we may also reasonably think that he had philosophical reasons to posit *thumos* as a motivational and executory drive, as I have described it here. Aristotle does not make this explicit, but he is interested in philosophical phenomena that would naturally lead to positing *thumos*. Indeed, these phenomena will, later on, lead others to posit the existence of a will as a distinctive mental faculty. Two phenomena are worth mentioning.

First, Aristotle is aware that people may want to do something, and simply lack the resolve to do it. This is clear in his analysis of "softness," a character disposition that makes someone prone to give up acting to avoid the effort required to implement their resolutions (*EN* 7.7).[45] Aristotle distinguishes this disposition from *akrasia*: while akratic agents give in to pleasant objects, soft people give up acting as they should to avoid the effort related to the execution of actions. Arguably, Aristotle is referring to cases of what will later be called "weakness of will," as opposed to lack of self-control or *akrasia*.[46] After all, although Aristotle does not draw this connection explicitly in his ethical works, he does link softness with having a weak *thumos* in the biological writings (*HA* 9.1, 608a20–b5).

Second, Aristotle is interested in the case of agents who manage to do what they rationally resolved to do, despite being tempted by contrary appetites for pleasure. Self-controlled agents act as they deem best, even though they experience opposing motivations. What explains the success of these self-controlled agents? How do they differ from people who lack self-control? Aristotle is not too clear on this.[47] But one could imagine an explanation along these lines: when a self-controlled agent is tempted, she has an appetite that she wants *not* to be her strongest desire, while she wants her rational resolution to be effective and issue in action. Agents who act in accordance with this second-order motivation are self-controlled.[48]

---

[45] See Marechal (2024b).

[46] Holton (1999) famously distinguishes weakness of will from *akrasia*. I am proposing that there is room for a similar distinction in Aristotle's moral psychology.

[47] Aristotle makes some suggestions: he points to the importance of habituation of the non-rational part of the soul (*EN* 1.13), without explicitly discussing appetites and *thumos*, which belong to this part. Thus, he may think that proper habituation requires molding appetites and strengthening and properly directing *thumos*. He also mentions the capacity to envision future pleasures and pains, so that one can resist immediate pleasures (*De An.* 3.10–11).

[48] See Frankfurt (1971) for an analogous distinction in contemporary literature. See, also, Mele (1992, esp. 284), who articulates a view along these lines and proceeds to criticize the role of second-order desires in explaining the difference between lack of self-control and self-control.

If my interpretation of *thumos* is correct, it can account for this second-order desire.

This is, of course, speculative, but it provides reasons why, for Aristotle, *thumos* is a non-reducible mental phenomenon, and it gives us an overall conception of the structure of human motivation and agency for which Aristotle had the pieces, even if he never put them together.[49]

References

Barnes, Jonathan. 1995. *The Complete Works of Aristotle: The Revised Oxford Translation*. Princeton, NJ: Princeton University Press.

Burnyeat, Myles. 1980. "Aristotle on Learning to be Good." In A. O. Rorty (ed.), *Essays on Aristotle's Ethics*, 69–92. Berkeley, CA: University of California Press.

Cairns, Douglas. 2019. "Thymos." *Oxford Classical Dictionary*. Retrieved July 12, 2023, from https://oxfordre.com/classics/view/10.1093/acrefore/9780199381135.001.0001/acrefore-9780199381135-e-8180.

Connell, Sophia. 2021a. *Aristotle on Women: Physiology, Psychology, and Politics*. Cambridge: Cambridge University Press.

Connell, Sophia. 2021b. "Animal Cognition in Aristotle." In S. Connell (ed.), *The Cambridge Companion to Aristotle's Biology*, 195–210. Cambridge: Cambridge University Press.

Cooper, John. 1984. "Plato's Theory of Human Motivation." *History of Philosophy Quarterly* 1: 3–21.

Cooper, John. 1999. "Reason, Moral Virtue, and Moral Value." In *Reason and Emotion*, 253–280. Princeton, NJ: Princeton University Press.

Cooper, John. 2013. "Aristotelian Responsibility." *Oxford Studies in Ancient Philosophy* 45: 265–312.

Cornford, Francis. 1912. "Psychology and Social Structure in the *Republic* of Plato." *The Classical Quarterly* 6(4): 246–265.

Crisp, Roger. 2005. *Aristotle: Nicomachean Ethics*. Cambridge: Cambridge University Press.

Deslauriers, Marguerite. 2019. "*Thumos* in Aristotle's *Politics* VII.7." *Polis: The Journal for Ancient Greek and Roman Political Thought* 36(1): 57–76.

[49] For invaluable feedback on earlier drafts of this chapter, I am grateful to Zachary Brants, Daniel Cohen, Marc Gasser-Wingate, Marta Jimenez, Hendrik Lorenz, Damien Rochford, and Christopher Shields.

Frankfurt, Harry. 1971. "Freedom of the Will and the Concept of a Person." *Journal of Philosophy* 68(1): 5–20.

Gay, Robert. 1988. "Courage and Thumos." *Philosophy* 63(244): 255–65.

Grönroos, Gösta. 2007. "Listening to Reason in Aristotle's Moral Psychology." *Oxford Studies in Ancient Philosophy* 32: 251–271.

Holton, Richard. 1999. "Intention and Weakness of Will." *Journal of Philosophy* 96(5): 241–262.

Irwin, Terry. trans. 1999. *Nicomachean Ethics*. Indianapolis: Hackett.

Jimenez, Marta. 2020. *Aristotle on Shame and Learning to Be Good*. Oxford: Oxford University Press.

Kahn, Charles. 1988. "Discovering the Will from Aristotle to Augustine." In J. Dillon and A. A. Long (eds.), *The Question of "Eclecticism": Studies in Later Greek Philosophy*, 234–260. Berkeley: University of California Press.

Kamtekar, Rachana. 2017. *Plato's Moral Psychology: Intellectualism, the Divided Soul, and Desire for Good*. Oxford: Oxford University Press.

Kenny, Antony. 1979. *Aristotle's Theory of the Will*. London: Duckworth.

Koziak, Barbara. 2000. *Retrieving Political Emotion: Thumos, Aristotle, and Gender*. University Park PA: Penn State Press.

Marechal, Patricia. 2024a. "Women, Spirit, and Authority in Plato and Aristotle." In S. Brill and C. McKeen (eds.), *The Routledge Handbook on Women and Ancient Greek Philosophy*, 181–201. Routledge.

Marechal, Patricia. 2024b. "Aristotle on Softness and Endurance: *Nicomachean Ethics* 7.7, 1150a9–b19." *Phronesis* 69(1), 63–96.

Mele, Alfred. 1992. "Akrasia, Self-Control, and Second-Order Desires." *Noûs* 26(3): 281–302.

Moss, Jessica. 2005. "Shame, Pleasure, and the Divided Soul." *Oxford Studies in Ancient Philosophy* 29: 137–170.

Moss, Jessica. 2012. *Aristotle on the Apparent Good: Perception, Phantasia, Thought, and Desire*. Oxford: Oxford University Press.

Pearson, Giles. 2011. "Non-rational Desire and Aristotle's Moral Psychology." In J. Miller (ed.), *Aristotle's Nicomachean Ethics: A Critical Guide*, 144–169. New York: Cambridge University Press.

Pearson, Giles. 2012. *Aristotle on Desire*. New York: Oxford University Press.

Penner, Terry. 1971. "Thought and Desire in Plato." In G. Vlastos (ed.), *Plato, A Collection of Critical Essays, Vol. II*, 96–118. New York: Anchor Books.

Polansky, Ronald. 2007. *Aristotle's De Anima*. New York: Cambridge University Press.

Quinn, Warren. 1995. "Putting Rationality in Its Place." In R. Hursthouse, G. Lawrence, and W. Quinn (eds), *Virtues and Reasons*, 181–208. Oxford: Clarendon Press.

Rapp, Christof. 2017. "Tackling Aristotle's Notion of the Will." *Philosophical Inquiry* 41(2/3): 67–79.

Reeve, C.D.C. 2014. *Aristotle. Nicomachean Ethics*. Indianapolis; Cambridge: Hackett.

Reeve, C.D.C. 2017. *Aristotle. Politics*. Indianapolis; Cambridge: Hackett.

Richardson Lear, Gabriel. 2004. *Happy Lives and the Highest Good: An Essay of Aristotle's Nicomachean Ethics*. Princeton: Princeton University Press.

Saenz, Victor. 2018. "Shame and Honor: Aristotle's *Thumos* as a Basic Desire." *Apeiron* 51(1): 73–95.

Sauvé Meyer, Susan. 1993. *Aristotle on Moral Responsibility*. Oxford: Oxford University Press.

Shields, Christopher. 2016. *Aristotle: De Anima*. New York: Oxford University Press.

Shields, Christopher. Forthcoming. *Aristotle: Nicomachean Ethics*.

Singpurwalla, Rachel. 2010. "The Tripartite Theory of Motivation in Plato's *Republic*." *Philosophy Compass* 5(11): 880–892.

Singpurwalla, Rachel. 2013. "Why Spirit Is the Natural Ally of Reason: Spirit, Reason, and the Fine in Plato's Republic." *Oxford Studies in Ancient Philosophy* 44: 41–65.

Sorabji, Richard. 1993. *Animal Minds and Human Morals: The Origins of the Western Debate*. Ithaca, NY: Cornell University Press.

Urmson, James. 1995. *Simplicius: On Aristotle's On the Soul* 1.1–2.4. Notes by P. Lautner. Ithaca, NY: Cornell University Press.

Wilburn, Josh. 2021. *The Political Soul: Plato on Thumos, Spirited Motivation, and the City*. Oxford: Oxford University Press.

Patricia Marechal, *Aristotle on* Thumos In: *Oxford Studies in Philosophy of Mind Volume 4*.
Edited by: Uriah Kriegel, Oxford University Press. © Patricia Marechal 2024.
DOI: 10.1093/9780198924159.003.0018

Index

abduction viii, 457, 510 *see also* abductivism, inference to the best explanation

abductivism (about knowledge of the external world) 209, 214, 222, 224, 227 *see also* abduction, inference to the best explanation

acquaintance v–ix, 35, 66, 77–8, 107, 111, 114, 154–67, 171, 173, 181, 193, 208, 219, 231–8, 241, 245, 247, 249, 251–2, 257, 271–3, 275, 277–8, 282–4, 292, 297–302, 305–6, 309, 336–7, 339–40, 343–5, 364–5, 368–70, 374, 376–7, 405, 410–12, 467, 473–4, 480, 499
    inner vi, 154–5, 334–7, 340–73, 375–6, 379, 410–12
    with sense data 193, 195, 202, 207, 220

action x, 72, 119, 122–4, 294, 299, 301, 319, 323–6, 422, 452, 484, 488, 490, 517–23, 531–8 *see also* action awareness

Adams, R. 46, 89, 94–5, 413

Albahari, M. vii, xi, 3, 5–6, 8–9, 17–19, 22, 31, 39, 43, 46, 76, 87, 95, 296, 305

Albert, D. 491, 496

Aleksiev, D. 400–1, 410

Allen, K. 159–60, 164, 168–9, 171

Alter, T. 141, 373, 377, 403, 410, 412–13

appearance(s) vi–ix, 7–8, 11–13, 20, 22, 24–6, 28, 31, 36–7, 39, 41, 43, 46, 97, 109, 112, 128, 145, 150, 163–4, 170, 177, 183, 224, 250, 288, 316, 321–3, 332, 366, 380, 385–91, 394, 398–9, 403–4, 407–8, 413, 462

Aristotle vi–vii, x, 69, 72, 383, 515, 517–41

Armstrong, D. M. 70, 72, 74, 95–6, 196, 221, 335–6, 373, 408, 410–11

Arntzenius, F. 88, 95–6

Arvan, M. 448, 458, 460

Atiq, E. H. ix, xi, 277, 297–300, 305–7, 373

Austin, J. L. 177, 180, 193, 222, 237, 249

awareness 8, 18–19, 27, 41, 103, 111, 159–60, 170, 180, 194, 201, 207–8, 211, 214, 251, 253, 274, 278–84, 291–2, 294–7, 299, 301, 319, 321, 339–40, 342, 350–1, 362–3, 369, 372, 376, 378, 415, 419, 436
    action 279, 282, 319, 323–6
    inner ix–x, 307, 334–8, 346–7, 351, 361–7, 369, 371–2, 375–6, 414–35, 436–7
    self- 15, 250, 284, 291, 436–7 *see also* consciousness, self-

Ayer, A. J. 176–7, 179, 181–2, 188, 193–6, 200–1, 207, 209, 215, 221–2, 227–8, 232, 249, 280, 305

Bailey, O. 277, 294–5, 299, 301, 305

Balaguer, M. 53, 88, 98

Balog, K. 49, 96, 337, 340–1, 369, 373, 404–5, 410

Barker, S. 71, 96

Baron, S. 86, 91, 96

Bayne, T. 58, 85, 96–7, 154, 170, 349, 373, 421, 436

Beiser, F. 10–11, 43

Bennett, J. 94, 97, 176, 203, 210–11, 222

Berkeley, G. 7, 66, 108, 113–14, 140, 146–7, 149, 163, 170, 176, 178, 180, 204, 207, 210–11, 220–3, 275

Black, R. 48, 97

Blitzstein, K. 317–18, 332

Block, N. J. 142, 194, 222, 273, 275, 300, 305, 377, 412–14, 425, 433–4, 436, 451, 458, 509

Bloom, P. 293, 305

body 14–15, 31, 218, 326, 522, 534
    mind-body problem 6, 23, 42–3, 95, 98–9, 141, 152, 373, 410

Boghossian, P. 311–12, 324, 331–3

BonJour, L. 209, 222, 340, 373

Bostrom, N. 131, 140, 218, 222, 443, 447–8, 458, 508

Boyd, R. 293–4, 300, 305

Braddon-Mitchell, D. 102, 142, 393, 410, 413

Bradley, F. 46–7, 87–8, 92, 97, 100, 103

Brentano, F. 75, 97, 420, 465
Brewer, B. 77, 97, 231, 249, 271–2, 275, 340, 373
Bricker, P. 95, 97
Broad, C. D. 168, 170, 176–7, 191, 208–9, 222–3, 232, 249
Broome, J. 320, 324, 332
Brown, R. 338, 373, 419, 421, 426, 434, 436
Builes, D. vii, xi, 8, 11, 42–3, 46, 54, 70, 75, 83, 86–8, 97–8, 166, 170
Burge, T. 187, 223, 271, 275, 482
Burnyeat, M. 175, 223, 525, 539
Byrne, A. 338, 374, 376, 429–30

Cairns, D. 534, 539
Callender, C. 73, 99, 126, 133, 141
Campbell, J. 77, 98, 157, 164, 170, 231, 249, 254, 268–9, 275, 340, 374
Carnap, R. 108, 182, 184, 197, 223–4
Carroll, L. 312–13, 321, 323, 329, 331–2
Carruthers, P. 67, 98, 338, 374, 416, 419, 421–2, 424, 429, 434
Chadha, M. 420, 433–4
Chalmers, D. J. vi–vii, x–xi, 13, 20, 24, 43, 46, 52, 58, 61–2, 76–81, 85, 89, 97–9, 108, 112, 129, 141, 144, 155–6, 170, 205, 218, 223, 229, 340, 349, 373–4, 381, 403, 411, 415, 418, 433–4, 439, 441, 447–51, 457, 459, 461–2, 471, 473–81, 483–96, 498, 504, 512–13
Chisholm, R. 97, 188–9, 196, 223, 247, 249, 386, 411
Chomsky, N. 195, 223
Chuard, P. 87, 99
Churchland, P. S. 441
Clark, A. 161, 170
cognitive phenomenology *see* phenomenology, cognitive
Cohen, J. 73, 99–100, 118, 126, 133, 141, 410
Coleman, S. 62, 99, 103, 297, 306, 337–8, 340, 369–70, 374, 405, 410–11
color/colour 11, 23, 25, 68, 98, 103, 114, 116–18, 120–1, 136, 144–7, 149, 152, 155–6, 163–5, 169–70, 190, 201–3, 219, 225, 231, 301, 352, 406–7, 412, 445–6, 475–8, 480–1, 500–2
    experience 61, 155, 190, 281, 412, 475–7, 500
Connell, S. 523, 525, 539
Cooper, J. 517–18, 526–7, 531, 536, 539

Cowling, S. 73, 85, 99
consciousness v–vii, 3–31, 34–46, 51–2, 54, 57–8, 69, 79–80, 84–5, 87, 91, 98–106, 109, 141–2, 169–70, 175–6, 194, 196, 198, 201, 205, 208, 222–3, 229, 232–3, 236, 249, 251–2, 254–7, 263–7, 270–1, 273–6, 307, 309, 331–40, 345–7, 353, 359, 365, 367, 369, 371–7, 380–1, 411–37, 445, 481–2, 493, 496, 509–10, 512
    phenomenal ix–x, 79–80, 101, 194, 338–40, 344, 358, 361, 371, 374, 380, 411, 421, 434, 463, 475 *see also* phenomenology
    self- 290, 307, 335, 375–6, 436 *see also* awareness, self-
    unity of 27, 85, 91, 96–7, 102, 147–8, 150, 170–1, 349–53, 373, 377
    universal v, vii, 3, 9–10, 13–14, 22, 31, 36, 40, 42–5, 76, 95, 105
content 8, 14, 17–18, 32, 40, 98, 105, 111, 113, 116–18, 124, 137, 170, 227, 271–2, 281, 290, 298–300, 304, 311, 319, 321, 332–3, 367, 369–70, 374, 376, 391, 417, 420, 434, 464, 466, 469, 475–6, 479–82, 484–5, 487–93, 496, 499–503 *see also* intentionality, representation
Crane, T. 161, 170

Dainton, B. 87, 91, 99, 154, 170, 235, 249, 349, 374, 448, 459
D'Ambrosio, J. 181, 188, 221, 223
Dasgupta, S. 48, 70, 99, 383, 399–400, 411, 420, 434
Davidson, D. 185, 223, 227
Debus, D. viii, xi, 251, 274, 276
Dennett, D. C. 32, 43, 109, 133, 141, 196, 223, 273, 276, 338, 374
Deslauriers, M. 522–3, 537, 539
Descartes, R. 83, 94, 175–6, 178, 204–7, 209, 219–20, 223–4, 229, 312, 442, 459, 463–4, 499–500, 502
desire 4, 16, 19–20, 36, 41, 147, 159, 281, 290–1, 294–5, 298, 301–3, 449, 452, 517–20, 522, 524–41
Dogramaci, S. 131, 141, 321–2, 332
Dorr, C. 95–6, 187, 223–4
Dretske, F. I. 74, 99, 204, 282, 306, 334, 335, 337–8, 374, 414, 420, 428, 432, 434

dualism 6, 46–7, 50, 75–6, 107, 135, 144, 152–3, 191, 193–4, 258, 381, 412
Dummett, M. 184, 203, 224
Duncan, M. ix, xi, 80, 90, 100, 277, 282, 298–300, 306, 340, 373–4

Ebersole, F. B. 232, 249
Earman, J. 73, 95, 100
Eddington, A. 34, 43
Eklund, M. 184, 187, 221, 224
Eleatic principle 72, 83, 88, 99
Ellis, B. 73, 100
emergence 177, 179, 215–16, 330–1, 367
emotion 7, 20, 31, 100, 176, 207–8, 212, 214, 280–1, 294–5, 349, 456, 519–20, 522, 524, 527–9, 531, 533–4, 539–40
empathy v, ix, 277–85, 292–307
experience viii, 4–5, 8, 14–22, 25–32, 35–42, 44–6, 57–70, 75–8, 84–5, 87, 89, 91, 95, 97, 99, 102–6, 108, 111–18, 122, 125, 135, 142, 144–67, 171, 176–9, 182, 188, 190–1, 194, 196, 198–201, 207–221, 225–7, 229, 231–8, 245–7, 249
   cognitive 17–19, 349 see also phenomenology, cognitive
   perceptual vii–viii, 57–8, 62, 64–5, 77–8, 98, 108–11, 118, 128, 137, 141, 150, 159–60, 170, 176, 202, 207, 212, 237, 251–9, 262–3, 269–76, 325–6, 341, 343, 349, 407, 463, 466–8, 488–9, 492, 496 see also perception
   sensory 18, 58–9, 147, 176–8, 182, 188, 194, 199, 202, 250, 296, 474–9
   visual 19, 57–8, 64–5, 68, 155, 179, 212, 214, 225, 229, 231–6, 276, 281, 288, 296, 299, 351–2, 367, 476–7
explanatory gap 52, 77, 103, 227, 376
externalism 153–4, 158–9, 161, 187, 202, 204–5, 373, 445, 451, 465, 467–74, 480–1, 506–8 see also internalism

Fales, E. 340, 374
Farrell, J. 419, 434
Field, H. 73, 100, 184, 224
Fine, K. 159, 170, 184, 224, 383, 411
Fiocco, M. O. 340, 374
Fish, W. viii, xi, 231–2, 249–50
Foster, J. 50, 100, 232, 249

Frankfurt, H. 531, 538, 540
Frankish, K. 49, 79, 100, 338, 375, 410
French, C. 77, 100, 161, 170
Fumerton, R. 161, 170, 181, 209, 224, 311–12, 319, 330–2, 340, 375
functionalism 61, 130, 139, 275, 402, 413, 446, 451, 458, 478, 484, 487–92, 495–6, 502–5

Ganeri, J. 418, 420, 435
Garfield, J. L. 418, 420, 435
Gennaro, R. 336, 375, 378, 416, 421–2, 424, 429, 434
Gertler, B. 338, 340–1, 364–6, 370, 375, 380, 385–6, 411, 420, 435
Giustina, A. ix, xi, 334, 337–8, 340, 375, 410, 419–20, 435–6
Godman, D. 14–15, 29, 33, 42–4
Goff, P. 6, 44, 46, 50, 52, 87, 91, 100, 108, 141, 373, 381, 394–5, 401, 405, 410–11
Goldman, A. I. 338, 375, 424, 435
Goodman, N. 197, 215, 224
Graham, G. 461–2, 471, 481
Greco, D. 204, 225, 496, 513
Grönroos, G. 519, 526, 540

Hale, B. 104, 184, 225
Hall, N. 73, 100, 133, 141
Hardin, C. L. 202–3, 225
Harman, G. 209, 225, 337, 375
Hasan, A. 340, 375
Hawthorne, J. 43, 98, 141, 170, 187, 224–5, 480
Heil, J. 48, 90, 101
Hellie, B. 168, 170, 340, 376, 434
Helton, G. x–xi, 447, 451, 457, 459, 498, 508–13
Hildebrand, T. 48, 71, 101
Hill, C. S. 102, 338, 373, 376, 388, 393, 410–11
Hirsch, E. viii, 86, 101, 181–7, 221, 225
Hlobil, U. 324–5, 332
Hoffman, D. vii, 109–10, 141–2
Hofmann, F. 340, 376
Horgan, T. M. x–xi, 11, 44, 86, 101, 340, 376, 380–1, 386, 405, 411, 461–2, 465, 470–1, 476, 480–2, 498–502, 513
Huggett, N. 61, 99, 101, 512
Huemer, M. 190–2, 199, 202, 205, 214, 217, 225, 316, 321–2, 332

Hume, D. 48, 106, 176, 178, 204, 207, 210–12, 215–17, 221–2, 227, 277, 293, 306, 483, 518
Humeanism (about laws) 43, 48–9, 73–4, 78, 93, 97, 100, 102, 106, 133–7, 141–2
Huxley, A. 3–4, 44–5
Hwang, J. 317–18, 332

idealism vii–viii, 1, 3–13, 17, 22–43, 46–7, 50, 59–62, 68–79, 82–95, 104–5, 107–10, 127, 134, 141, 144–71, 220, 223, 437, 442
  modal vii, 46–7, 61–62, 68–79, 82–95, 170
  perennial vii, 3, 5–13, 17, 22–43, 95
imagination 19, 40, 65, 105, 211, 332, 413
impulse x, 518, 529–37
inference 74, 105, 116, 126–7, 129–32, 134, 136–7, 139, 283, 311–13, 317–25, 328–33
  to the best explanation 209, 217–18, 225–9, 394
information 65, 88, 123, 142, 160, 167, 181, 202, 210, 220, 247, 299–301, 307, 363, 365, 370–2, 378, 405, 442–3
intentionalism 199, 352 *see also* representationalism
intentionality 112, 177, 202, 337, 362, 376, 434, 462–6, 468, 470–4, 481, 484, 487
  phenomenal 8, 44, 436, 461, 463–5, 468, 471–3, 479–82, 513
internalism 205, 332, 373, 375, 513 *see also* externalism
introspection vii, 108–14, 118–19, 123–31, 134–8, 141
Ismael, J. 86, 101, 133, 141

Jaag, S. 71, 101, 133, 141
Jackson, F. C. 34, 44, 103, 178, 180, 182, 188, 190, 209, 225–6, 386, 412, 471, 481
James, W. 34–6, 44, 87, 207–8, 226
Janzen, G. 282, 306, 418–20, 427, 435
Jimenez, M. 523, 539–40
Johnston, M. 159, 165, 170, 203, 236, 249, 296–7, 306, 336
Jorba, M. 3, 5, 32
justification (epistemic) 205–6, 223, 311, 315–17, 319, 322–3, 325, 327, 330–1, 333, 373, 375, 448, 511, 513

Kahn, C. 517–18, 540
Kalderon, M. E. 223, 239, 249

Kammerer, F. 49, 79, 101, 338, 376
Kant 5, 27–9, 32, 39, 42, 44, 83, 94, 108–10, 138, 142, 148, 178, 222–3, 460, 483
Kaplan, D. 365, 376
Kastrup, B. 6, 44, 46, 76, 87, 101
Kasuga, T. 233, 249
Kim, J. 263, 276, 387, 412
Knox, E. 491, 496
Kriegel, U. 8, 11, 44, 59, 90, 101, 140, 198, 205, 208, 221, 226, 249, 273, 305, 336–40, 345, 359, 363, 368, 373, 376, 410, 414, 419–20, 423, 430, 433, 435, 462, 481
Kripke, S. 380, 398–9, 412, 470

Lam, V. 61, 94, 100, 102
Lamme, V. 300, 306, 414, 421, 435
Langton, R. 50, 102, 108, 142
Langsam, H. 75, 81, 102, 231, 249
Lau, H. 414, 418, 421–2, 436
Le Bihan, B. 91, 96, 99, 512
Lee, A. 54, 59, 64, 90, 102
Lee, G. vii, xi, 58, 108, 130, 139–40
Leibniz, G. 3, 72, 94–5, 102, 188
Leitgeb, H. 322, 332
Lepore, E. 328, 332
Levine, J. 168, 170, 337–40, 359, 376, 405, 412
Lewis, D. K. 48, 50, 73, 94, 100, 102–3, 108, 117, 133–4, 141–2, 185, 204, 226, 289, 381, 393–4, 397–8, 412
Liu, M. ix, xi, 373, 380–2, 393, 395, 402, 407–8, 412
Loar, B. 404, 412, 462, 482
Locke, J. 23, 69, 102, 113, 176, 178, 194, 203–4, 207, 209–11, 221–2, 226, 312, 414, 477
Loewer, B. 73, 100, 102, 133, 141–2, 411–12
Logue, H. 168–70, 231, 250, 275
Lowe, E. 69, 90, 102
Lycan, W. G. 276, 336, 377, 416, 436

Mackie, J. L. 177, 194, 209, 220–1, 226
Maddy, P. 180, 221, 226
Maharashi, R. 12, 14–15, 19, 29, 33, 41, 43–5
Majeed, R. 381, 412
Manne, K. 293, 306
Marcus, E. 321, 323, 332
Marechal, P. x, xii, 517, 523, 538, 540
Marshall, C. 277, 296–7, 299, 305–6
Martin, C. B. 8, 44, 48, 103

Martin, M. G. F. 157–8, 168, 170–1, 199, 226, 231–2, 237, 246, 250, 253–4, 276, 410

materialism 6, 8, 41, 144–5, 157–69, 221, 307, 378, 410–12, 451 *see also* physicalism

Mates, B. 180, 182, 188, 198, 206–7, 221, 226

Maudlin, T. 74, 94, 103

Maurin, A.-S. 92, 103

McClelland, T. 419, 434, 436

McDowell, J. 199, 226, 256, 276, 494, 496

McGinn, C. 77, 103, 191, 226, 340, 377, 462, 482

McKinsey, M. 495–6

McLaughlin, B. 100, 112, 142, 376, 393, 405, 410, 412, 481

meaning in life x, 441, 447–60, 513

metaontology 101, 178, 182–4, 188, 225

Mihálik, J. 62, 103, 410

Mill, J. S. 110, 147, 170, 221

Millikan, R. G. 329, 333

monism 10–12, 23, 26, 29, 31–2, 45, 60, 83–7, 94–9, 104–5, 108–9, 141, 143, 411, 413

Moore, G. E. 157, 176–7, 182, 190, 204, 207, 216, 226–7, 245, 250, 448, 453, 457, 460, 506

Moran, A. 235–7, 245–7, 250

Moran, R. 380, 386, 408, 410, 412

Mørch, H. H. 8, 44, 75–6, 81, 90, 103, 108, 142

Morgan, J. 328, 332

Moss, J. 517, 526, 540

motivation x, 66, 75–7, 277–8, 292–3, 298, 300–3, 517–20, 524, 527–39, 541

Muruganar 12, 15–16, 29–30, 36, 41, 44

Nagel, T. 23, 34, 44, 277–8, 306, 380, 384, 388–90, 412–13

naïve realism viii, 61, 77, 107, 111, 114, 145, 157–64, 169, 171, 231–8, 241, 245–50, 286–7, 340–1, 343 *see also* relationalism

Navon, D. 351, 377

Neander, K. 113, 118, 142, 338, 377, 414, 425, 436

Nida-Rümelin, M. 381, 394, 405, 412, 415, 419, 436

Nikhilānanada, S. 29, 45

Noë, A. 160, 170

Norton, J. 95, 100

objects
 abstract 11, 78, 85–6, 88, 190–3, 225
 incorporeal 231, 237–48

pain 12, 30, 38, 47, 65–8, 75–7, 79, 81, 96, 100, 153, 192, 198, 212, 277–304, 325–6, 332–3, 387, 394, 398, 415, 484, 488, 520, 535, 538

Palmer, S. E. 329, 333

panprotopsychism 49, 62, 98 *see also* panpsychism

panpsychism 6–9, 23–4, 34, 43–4, 46, 50, 59, 95, 98–100, 103, 105–6, 108, 142–3, 151, 402, 411–13 *see also* panprotopsychism

Papineau, D. 49, 103, 232–6, 250, 340, 369, 377, 393, 404–5, 412–13

Parmenides 10, 32, 45

Paul, G. A. 180, 182, 188, 227

Pautz, A. 90, 111–12, 142, 286, 306, 373, 436, 496

Peacocke, C. x, xii, 197, 227, 434, 483, 489, 495–8, 502–6, 508, 513

Pearson, G. 526, 528, 530, 532, 536, 540

Pelczar, M. 108, 142, 147, 171

perception vii–ix, 14, 16, 19–20, 22, 61, 77–8, 97–100, 104, 107, 109–28, 131, 134–8, 141–2, 145–9, 152–9, 162–71, 173, 176–8, 181, 191, 199, 201–7, 210–11, 219–20, 223–8, 231–5, 238–9, 244–50, 257–76, 286–7, 296–7, 300, 306, 330, 333, 338, 340, 343, 347, 365–6, 373, 377, 406–8, 411–12, 419, 422, 426–7, 432, 434–5, 444, 458, 463–4, 478–81, 486–90, 493–5, 500–7, 520–1, 525, 532, 540 *see also* experience, perceptual

Pereboom, D. 406–8, 413

Perry, Z. R. 86, 94, 104

phenomenology 39, 58, 81, 88, 101, 114, 144, 147–54, 159, 165–6, 237, 254, 273–4, 281–2, 288–90, 298, 333, 359–60, 363–6, 370–2, 402, 408, 435–6, 463–9, 473, 480–1, 489, 499–501 *see also* consciousness, phenomenal

cognitive 58, 64, 105, 208, 464, 477, 482 *see also* experience, cognitive

physicalism ix, 47, 62, 103, 105, 143, 165, 262, 340, 373, 377, 381, 393–406, 409–13 *see also* materialism

Pitcher, G. 147, 171, 235–6, 250

Plato 69, 72, 86, 517–20, 525, 532, 539–41
Plotinus 5, 10, 32, 45
Potrč, M. 11, 44, 86, 101
Power, S. E. 236, 250
Prakash, C. 109, 111, 121, 126–7, 141–2
Price, H. H. 176–7, 191, 200, 210–11, 227
Prinz, J. 293, 306, 367, 377
Pryor, J. 204–5, 227, 373, 410
psychology 4, 30–1, 35, 44–5, 76, 110, 192–3, 247, 252
   folk 31, 275, 287, 289
Putnam, H. viii, 108, 142, 184, 186, 204, 215, 227, 471

quantifier variance viii, 101, 184–8, 198–200, 207, 220, 224–5, 229
Quine, W. V. O. 135, 143, 179, 184–6, 188, 220, 227
Quinn, W. 536, 541

Raleigh, T. 288–90, 305–6, 340, 374, 376–7, 411
realism 24, 44, 69, 95, 98, 106, 108, 110, 113–14, 119–22, 126–7, 131–8, 140, 142–3, 145–6, 151, 185, 209, 218, 225, 227–8, 276, 305–6
   direct 190, 199, 201–2, 205, 219, 297, 450, 496
   naïve see naïve realism
   simulation 443–5, 483, 495, 498–506, 509
   structural 50, 94, 100–1, 442, 499 see also structuralism
Reid, T. 87, 178, 180, 203, 211, 220, 227
relationalism 251–64, 270–5 see also naïve realism
representation viii, 8, 98, 107, 111–13, 116–18, 122, 140–1, 143, 170–1, 177, 192, 202, 223, 251, 269, 271, 281, 288, 290, 297, 300, 311, 319–25, 329, 333–41, 343, 347, 352, 356–65, 371–2, 376, 405–8, 416–17, 420–2, 425–7, 429, 436, 491 see also content, intentionality
representationalism 111–12, 114, 156–7, 161, 167, 251, 269, 271, 286, 319–26, 334–5, 337–8, 343, 363, 377–9, 436 see also intentionalism
   higher-order ix, 334–9, 377
   self- ix, 334–9, 375–6, 435–6
revelation ix, 380–5, 391–405, 408–9, 412–13

Richardson Lear, G. 519, 526, 541
Rinard, S. 208–9, 227, 454, 460
Robinson, H. 46, 71, 90, 104, 170, 177–8, 181–2, 190, 194–6, 228, 232, 250
Roelofs, L. 108, 143, 154, 171, 381, 401–2, 410, 413
Rosen, G. 47–8, 53, 104
Rosenthal, D. M. 335–6, 338, 345, 377, 414, 416–17, 420–2, 430–3, 436
Ross, S. 314–16, 333
Russell, B. viii, 34, 45, 50, 69, 104, 108–9, 125–6, 141, 143, 176–7, 181–2, 191, 201, 207–9, 221, 228–9, 232, 234, 250, 282, 297, 306–7, 340, 377, 411, 413, 503
Ryle, G. 177, 196, 228

Saenz, V. 525–8, 541
Schaffer, J. 11, 45, 60, 74, 86, 94, 100–1, 104–5, 141
Schiffer, S. 183–4, 228
Schopenhauer, A. 28, 45, 72, 105, 277, 295–6, 299, 307
Schwitzgebel, E. 338, 378, 380, 385–6, 388, 413, 447, 456–7, 460
Seager, W. 43–44, 95, 98, 103, 338, 378
Searle, J. 85, 105, 181, 190, 199, 202, 228, 326, 328, 333, 380, 413
seemings ix, 49, 179–83, 189–97, 201, 204–6, 212–13, 299, 311–31, 333
Sellars, W. 188, 194, 228, 492
sense data viii, 112, 142, 175–83, 187–214, 217–23, 226–8, 247, 288
Shani, I. 6, 45, 87, 105
Shea, N. 113, 118, 143
Shields, C. 519–21, 525, 539, 541
Shoemaker, S. 130, 132, 139, 143, 268, 276, 408, 413, 415, 426, 436
Sider, T. 47, 60, 66, 69–71, 74, 86, 105, 117, 143, 184, 187, 198, 228–9, 237, 250, 254
Siewert, C. 338, 373, 378, 410, 420, 436, 462, 482
Silins, N. ix, xii, 414, 418, 436
simulation 110, 131, 140, 159, 218, 222, 293, 298, 442–51, 457–62, 474–6, 478, 483, 491–513 see also realism, simulation
Singh, M. 109, 141–2
Singpurwalla, R. 517–18, 532, 541

skepticism/scepticism 54, 86, 131, 137–8, 157, 170, 175, 201–9, 213, 218–19, 222–30, 437, 442–5, 450–1, 459–60, 481, 493–4, 498, 508, 512–13
Slote, M. 209, 228, 277, 307
Smart, B. 71, 96
Smith, A. 277, 293, 305, 307
Smith, J. 290, 307
Smithies, D. 58, 105, 269, 276, 316, 333, 367, 375, 377–8, 411, 432–3, 436
Snowdon, P. 255, 260, 276
Soteriou, M. 77, 105, 340, 378
soul 3, 46, 517–20, 522–3, 525, 535, 538, 540–1
space 4, 7, 14, 16, 21–2, 25, 27–8, 31, 36–40, 42, 60–1, 77, 86, 91–2, 94–7, 99–104, 123, 125, 128–30, 132, 139, 142–3, 147, 185, 191–2, 237, 259, 445–6, 475–9, 483–96, 499–505, 512
Sperling, G. 299, 307, 351, 378
Spinoza, B. x, 5, 10, 32, 45, 83, 94, 97–8
Sprigge, T. 47, 103, 105
Stalnaker, R. 496–7
Stoljar, D. 9–10, 50, 105, 142, 282, 305, 307, 375, 382, 389, 398, 402–3, 411, 413, 415, 419–20, 427, 433, 435–7, 496
Stone, M. 328, 332
Strawson, G. 8, 45–6, 48, 51, 57, 70, 72–3, 83–4, 87, 90, 105–6, 108, 140, 143, 235, 250, 462, 482
Strawson, P. F. 184, 189, 225, 228, 280, 307, 486–7, 497
structuralism 51, 60, 86, 88, 104, 218, 223, 445–6, 449–52, 454, 457, 459, 485, 493, 495, 499–500, 502, 509–10, 513, 583 see also realism, structural
subjectivity 18, 20–1, 89, 142–3, 251, 340–1, 372, 374, 379

Taylor, C. 177–8, 194, 228
technophilosophy 441
Thomasson, A. 184, 229, 420, 437
Thompson, E. 18, 45, 363, 378, 419–20, 437
Tienson, J. 381, 405, 411, 461–2, 465, 470–1, 481
time 4, 7, 14, 16, 19, 21, 25, 27–8, 31, 36–40, 42, 58, 60–1, 86, 88, 91–7, 99–105,

127–30, 132, 134, 142–4, 192, 207–8, 210–15, 218, 221, 231–7, 241–8, 250, 259, 491–2, 503–4, 512
Timmons, M. 480–1
Tooley, M. 74, 88, 105–6
Trogdon, K. 381, 413
Tucker, C. 319, 326, 333
Tugby, M. 48, 75, 106
Turner, J. 70, 106, 189, 229
Tye, M. 85, 106, 188, 229, 280, 298, 307, 338, 340, 378

unconscious 197, 345, 355–6, 361, 369, 421–2, 429–30, 435, 464
Unger, P. 431, 437

Van Fraassen, B. 74, 106, 217, 220, 224, 227
Van Gulick, R. 336, 338, 378
virtual reality/worlds x, 441–4, 448, 450, 459, 461–2, 474–6, 480, 483–4, 494, 498, 502, 509, 513
Vogel, J. 209, 229, 508, 513

Warren, J. viii, xii, 85, 106, 175, 184–7, 196, 202, 209, 215, 220, 225, 229–30
Weatherson, B. 448, 460, 506, 513
Weisberg, J. 338, 378
Whiting, D. 380, 413
Wilburn, J. 517, 520, 541
Williamson, T. 53, 106, 184, 204, 230, 431, 437, 494, 497
Williford, K. W. 336–7, 340, 376, 379
Wilson, J. 47, 54, 59, 73, 98, 106
Winkler, K. 147, 171
Wittgenstein, L. 12, 185, 195–6, 222, 230, 277–8, 307, 397, 488
Wolfson, H. A. 10, 45
Wright, C. 98, 170, 184, 225, 230, 324, 333
Wüthrich, C. 61, 99, 102, 127, 143, 512

Yetter-Chappell, H. vii, xii, 77, 80, 90, 107, 144–5, 147, 152, 155, 157–8, 164, 171, 373, 410

Zahavi, D. 59, 101, 362, 378–9